SECOND EDITION

CRIMINAL LAW

George M Dery III

Kendall Hunt
publishing company

This book is meant for teaching purposes only and is not meant to provide legal advice. Legal advice should be obtained from a licensed attorney.

Cover image courtesy of Jen Dery.

www.kendallhunt.com
Send all inquiries to:
4050 Westmark Drive
Dubuque, IA 52004-1840

Published in the United States of America

To My Family

Brief Contents

Contents

CHAPTER—II

"Actus Reus" or Criminal Act: The Mandatory Element for All Crime   *33*

CHAPTER—XV

Defenses: Justification   *465*

CHAPTER—XVI

Defenses: Excuse   *503*

APPENDICES

Preface

Throughout the lifetime of our species, humans have told stories. According to *Scientific American*, this love of storytelling is a basic part of the human condition.[1] This book aims to exploit this aspect of our minds to teach criminal law. Criminal law cases are essentially stories about people caught in extreme situations. Criminals commit acts so outrageous that society formally punishes them with the severest of sanctions, including loss of liberty or even life itself. Victims suffer harms that the community deems too awful to go without public redress. Our government is tested by the continual clash of values between pursuing the guilty and preserving our rights. To teach the lessons of criminal law—where the stakes for everyone involved is at their highest—I have looked for cases that not only provide clear and accurate statements of law, but which possess facts that oftentimes provide the telling detail that will stick in the reader's mind and therefore make learning an easier endeavor.

This book contains cases that explore a wide range of criminal behavior. Several cases offer appalling examples of people at their absolute worst, such as a daughter who allows her elderly father to slowly die on a rotting mattress and a gynecologist who violates his patients' trust by deceiving them into believing that the intercourse they are having is a medical procedure. Other cases are simply bizarre, such as the cannibal who interviewed his victim about the prospect of killing and eating him and an involuntarily intoxicated man who steals a vehicle in a hallucinatory effort to save the President of the United States. Each situation, however, provides a window on a crucial ingredient, concept, or doctrine of criminal law. These cases offer insight into the rules and definitions that legislators, attorneys, and courts have developed to grapple with the vast array of questions arising from myriad situations.

The creation and interpretation of legal rules in order to address criminal law issues is a never-ending task. The need to decide new cases each day, or to fashion an argument for a novel set of facts, or to craft a law for a new criminal threat means that law is a continually moving target. Every time an officer confronts a criminal, a lawyer listens to the travails of a criminal defendant, or a judge reaches a decision, the law inches forward.

This continual change requires that students not only learn the law of today, but also be able to learn skills and strategies that enable them to adapt to the law of the future. First, students must realize that, since law is not a static body of fossilized rules, all they can achieve by memorizing a particular rule is to capture a snapshot of a continually changing process. This book therefore offers the rationales underlying the rules and explanations for their changes over time. Further, to truly appreciate the dynamic nature of the law, students must explore the entire body of law in order to understand how

---

1. Jeremy Hsu, *The Secrets of Storytelling: Why We Love a Good Yarn*, *Scientific American*, http://www.scientificamerican.com/article/the-secrets-of-storytelling/.

and why rules evolve. This work exposes students to the origins of our rules by exploring England's common law, offers insight into various solutions to legal problems by viewing cases and statutes from many jurisdictions, and brings home the immediacy of these issues by considering cases in the news. Moreover, a complete understanding of the law necessitates mastering legal analysis, or learning how to "think like a lawyer." Legal analysis breaks down even the most complex legal arguments into their crucial component parts: Facts, Issue, Rule, Analysis, and Conclusion. Legal analysis will discipline and organize the student's thinking process, enabling them to persuade and convince others not only in law but also in all matters of dispute.

Finally, understanding law means comprehending context. Law is a social institution that is affected by time and place, despite the best efforts of some judges to keep legal rules somehow "pure" of infection from the larger society. Law therefore evolves with its times. Judges watch the news, lawyers use the Internet, and juries exchange ideas with families and neighbors. Law, however, is typically reactive rather than proactive. For example, no legislature passed a law prohibiting computer crimes before the invention of the computer. The student of law must therefore read the rules with an eye to this bigger context.

As laws are part of society, individual rules are part of the greater whole of law. Law is often called a "seamless web." Lawrence Solum, author of *Legal Theory Blog,* has noted: "F.W. Maitland, the famous legal historian wrote, 'Such is the unity of all history that anyone who endeavors to tell a piece of it must feel that his first sentence tears a seamless web.'"[2] Solum notes that law could be seen as having an "organic unity" which is characterized by "strong interconnections."[3] Therefore, a student must keep in mind that, when learning one law, that rule must somehow fit (perhaps uncomfortably) into the whole of the law. Over centuries, rules have grown and combined to create a kind of whole. The law touches everything, and each rule in the law affects each other.

---

2. Lawrence Solum, *Legal Theory Blog,* October 1, 2006, at http://lsolum.typepad.com/legaltheory/2006/10/legal_theory_ le.html.
3. *Id.*

Acknowledgments

I would like to thank those who have offered generous and caring guidance that helped me in writing this book:

Paul B. Carty
Director of Publishing Partnerships
Kendall Hunt Publishing Company

Angela Willenbring
Senior Developmental Coordinator
Kendall Hunt Publishing Company

Cynthia Bruns
Reference Services Coordinator and Reference & Instruction Librarian, Pollak Library
California State University Fullerton

Jaclyn Bedoya
Electronic Resources Librarian, Pollak Library
California State University Fullerton

Charlotte Goldberg
Professor Emeritus
Loyola Law School, Los Angeles

SaRita Stewart
Cedar Valley College

Cynthia D. Sora
Burlington County College

Michelle Watkins
El Paso Community College

Nancy Dempsey
Cape Cod Community College

About the Author

Max Dery is a professor at California State University Fullerton at the Division of Politics, Administration, and Justice. He was a Deputy District Attorney at the Los Angeles District Attorney's Office. He earned his Bachelor of Arts at the University of California Los Angeles and his Juris Doctorate at Loyola Law School in Los Angeles, California. He has been teaching courses in criminal law and criminal procedure since 1990.

CHAPTER
I

The Sources of and Limits on Criminal Law

A. INTRODUCTION

1. The Purpose of Criminal Law

What is criminal law and what is its purpose? Rather than something lofty and separate from people's experiences, **criminal law is part of our daily lives**. All law uses commonly shared rules to enable people to prevent or resolve conflict. **Criminal law, aims to prevent conflict by putting people on notice to avoid conduct that society deems especially wrongful or harmful. To warn us against doing forbidden acts or failing to do required acts**, legislators and judges publish society's rules in statutes and cases. Citizens are then supposed to conform their conduct to follow these rules. When anyone violates these accepted and public laws, society first checks to see if a criminal law was broken. If we decide that a person did violate the law, then the government punishes that individual for the harm caused to all society. **The laws defining the forbidden conduct, and much of the procedures used to bring violators of those rules to justice, make up the criminal law**.

a)   Morality and Blame

We blame criminals for committing crimes. In arresting, charging, convicting, and punishing a criminal, we as a society express moral outrage at the wrongdoer. It is the blameworthiness of crime that allows us to take criminals' property with fines, their liberty with incarceration, and their lives with executions. Centuries ago in England, the great legal commentator of the common law, William Blackstone, expressly linked morality and criminal law. As noted by Arthur Leavens in *Beyond Blame—Mens Rea and Regulatory Crime*, 46 U. Louisville L. Rev. 1, 8 n. 36 (2007), citing 4 William Blackstone, Commentaries on the laws of England 176–77 (1765):

"There isn't enough blame to go around, there's only enough for you."

> [Common law crimes] are of a much more extensive consequence [than purely private wrongs]; 1. Because it is impossible they can be committed without a violation of the laws of nature; of the moral as well as political rules of right: 2. Because they include in them almost always a breach of the public peace: 3. Because by their example and evil tendency they threaten and endanger the subversion of all civil society. Upon these accounts it is, . . . the government also calls upon the offender to submit to public punishment for the public crime.

Chief Judge Posner, in *Milner v. Apfel*, 148 F.3d 812, 814 (1998), declared that **there was an "important moral difference between criminals and noncriminals" which permitted our legislatures to make law "with regard to morality."** Otherwise, asked Posner, "How else to explain prohibitions against gambling, prostitution, public nudity, and masturbation, fornication, sodomy, the sale of pornography, sexual intercourse with animals, desecration of corpses, and a variety of other 'morals' offenses?" In fact, a **"traditional purpose of criminal punishment is to express moral condemnation of the criminal's acts."**

In *Beyond Blame—Mens Rea and Regulatory Crime*, Leavens noted:

> [In applying criminal law common law judges] saw themselves as doing nothing more than giving formal recognition to behavioral norms already operative as a matter of societal consensus. Those who acted contrary to those norms were behaving at once immorally and unlawfully; the common law made no distinction between these two concepts. One who breached such a norm was by definition morally blameworthy and thus merited the formal censure of criminal conviction and punishment.

If criminals are "immoral" and therefore "deserving" of punishment, what is the purpose of that punishment beyond simple vengeance?

Is Texting While Walking Blameworthy Enough to Make It a Crime?

Bill Chappell, in the October 25, 2017, NPR article, "Honolulu's 'Distracted Walking' Law Takes Effect, Targeting Phone Users," explained that Honolulu, in ticketing pedestrians for using cell phones in crosswalks, is the first major municipality to outlaw such behavior. The full article can be visited at:

https://www.npr.org/sections/thetwo-way/2017/10/25/559980080/honolulus-distracted-walking-law-takes-effect-targeting-phone-users

Biography—Criminal

Richard Ramirez—The Night Stalker

- Born on February 29, 1960 in El Paso, Texas.
- The Case, *People v. Ramirez*, 39 Cal. 4th 398 (2006), reported the following:
- On June 28, 1984, Ramirez slit the throat of Jennie Vincow "almost from ear to ear," and stabbed her "multiple times in her upper chest, neck, arm, and leg." The elderly victim's "dress was partially lifted and her girdle had been pulled down and torn."
- On March 17, 1985, Ramirez killed Dale Okazaki by shooting her in the head. He then shot Maria Hernandez through her raised hand, failing to kill her when the bullet from his gun was deflected off the victim's keys.
- On March 28, 1985, Ramirez killed Vincent and Maxine Zazzara. Maxine was found with her pajama top pulled up, "exposing her breasts, and her pajama bottoms had been pulled down around her ankles. She had been shot in the head and neck at close range, stabbed in her neck, cheek, chest, abdomen, and pubic area, and her eyes had been cut out."
- On May 31, 1985, Ramirez attacked "83–year–old Mabel Bell and her 79–year–old sister, Florence." Bell's skull was fractured, possibly by a hammer, and a "red circle with a star in it (a pentagram) had been drawn on her thigh." Her sister, Florence, had been bound and sexually assaulted. A pentagon was left on the wall of the home.
- On July 5, 1985, Whitney B., a 16–year–old, suffered what a physician would later testify was "'the most massive head injury I've ever seen. She had greater than forty inches of linear lacerations criss-crossing every direction on her head.' She had been strangled, which resulted in a fractured larynx, and had a black eye."
- On August 8, 1985, Ramirez shot Sakina A.'s husband in the head. He then handcuffed Sakina A., beat, raped, and sodomized her, **forcing her to "swear upon Satan" that she would not scream**. He then handcuffed Sakina A. to a doorknob, threatening to return and kill her.
- In this case, Richard Ramirez was sentenced to death upon convictions of twelve counts of first degree murder, along with counts of attempted murder, rape, and forcible sodomy.
- When police released Ramirez's photograph to the public, civilians captured him.
- "On the ride to the police station, defendant asked the officer to 'just shoot me,' saying he wanted to die. He said, 'all the killings are going to be blamed on me.'"
- Ramirez reacted to being sentenced to death by saying, "No big deal (or "Big Deal"). Death always comes with the territory. **I'll see you (or "See you") in Disneyland.**" Video of Ramirez's statement can be viewed on YouTube at https://www.youtube.com/watch?v=Ge_mWdMeucY
- Ramirez died from complications due to lymphoma, outliving Phil Halpin, the prosecutor who successfully secured his death sentence.

b) The Principle of Legality and the Rule of Law

When Guantanamo Bay detainees challenged their confinement before the United States Supreme Court in the case, *Rasul v. Bush*, members of England's Parliament, in *Brief of 175 Members of Both Houses of the Parliament of the United Kingdom of Great Britain and Northern Ireland as Amici Curiae in Support of Petitioners* 2003 U.S. Briefs 334 (2004), filed a brief in support of the detainees. The members of Parliament emphasized the need for governments to stick to **"the rule of law"** as the **"keystone of our existence as nations."** These members harkened back to April 1689, when England crowned

There can be no crime without first having a law defining it.

William and Mary king and queen only after they swore "obedience to the laws of Parliament" and read "the Bill of Rights as part of their oaths." This "English Bill of Rights," as a "precursor to the American Bill of Rights," created "strict limits on the Sovereign's legal prerogatives," and made the existence of any government power "a matter of law." The members of Parliament asked the court to "vindicate the rule of law under the Constitution and preserve the role of the courts in ensuring that the exercise of executive power over the detainees in Guantanamo will not be above the law."

The members of Parliament purposely focused on the rule of law, for the United States has prided itself, at least since John Adams in *The Novanglus Letters*, No. vii, at: http://learning.hccs.edu/faculty/robert.tierney/govt2302/substantive-course-materials/unit-ii/readings-handouts/john-adams-government-of-law-not-men, and http://www.john-adams-heritage.com/quotes/, on being "a government of laws and not of men."

Unlike France in the age of Louis XIV, who famously proclaimed, "I am the State," America is the nation where no one is above the law. **The rule of law, when applied to criminal law, has led to the "principle of legality."** This doctrine of criminal law, as explained in *State v. Robbins*, 986 So. 2d 828, 835 (2008), deems that **"conduct is not criminal unless forbidden by law which gives advance warning that such conduct is criminal."**

State v. Robbins declared that the principle of legality:

> is based on four interconnected rules or principles: (1) the ancient rule of *nullem crimen sine lege* (**"No crime without law"**); (2) **the prohibition of retroactivity criminalizing conduct** (e.g., *ex post facto* laws); (3) the ancient rule of *nullem poena sine lege* (**"no punishment without law"**) (This principle operates to prevent a heavier penalty than that authorized by statute); and (4) **the prohibition against imposition of more severe penalties than previously authorized.**

The principle of legality actually combines several concepts into one doctrine. The *ex post facto* prohibition mentioned by *Robbins* is fully discussed in the "Limits on Criminal Law" section below. *United States v. Lanier*, 520 U.S. 259, 265, n. 5 (1997) interpreted the principle of legality to mean, "conduct may not be treated as criminal unless it has been so defined by [a competent authority . . . before it has taken place.]" This in turn brings up *State v. Robbins'* concerns about fair notice and avoidance of vague laws, also discussed in the "Limits on Criminal Law" section below.

c)   Punishment

As noted in *United States v. Cole*, 622 F. Supp. 2d 632, 637 (2008), **punishment** has been understood to **serve four goals**: (1) **retribution**, (2) **deterrence**, (3) **incapacitation**, and (4) **rehabilitation**.

(1)   Retribution

Retribution is vengeance. According to *United States v. Cole*, this purpose of punishment:

Punishment can serve the goals of retribution, deterrence, incapacitation, or rehabilitation.

> involves the calculation of moral culpability, with society gauging the seriousness of the offense and [its appropriate response]. In general, retribution imposes punishment to reflect respect for the dignity of the victim. Stated otherwise, society stands with victims and exacts punishment in rough approximation to the detriment caused by the defendant. Retributive or "just deserts" theory considerations study the defendant's past actions and the effect of these actions on the victim or victims of the crime, not the defendant›s probable future conduct or the effect that his or her punishment might have on others in society.

(2)   Deterrence

Deterrence aims to protect society by stopping persons from committing crime. *United States v. Cole* notes there are two kinds of deterrence: specific deterrence and general deterrence.

> Deterrence has both a specific and a general function. Specific deterrence dissuades the particular defendant from engaging in criminal conduct. In contrast, general deterrence discourages others from engaging in similar criminal conduct.

(3)   Incapacitation

Incapacitation is essentially isolation; the criminal is warehoused in prison so that he or she cannot cause harm to society. The court in *United States v. Spiers*, 82 F.3d 1274, 1281 (1996) declared that the "purpose of incapacitation alone might warrant imposition of consecutive terms of imprisonment." Professor Gray Sweeten in an April 16, 2013, article on Arizona State University's website entitled "ASU News: Age and the Decline in Crime," https://asunow.asu.edu/content/age-and-decline-crime, explained that probation officers have seen that an offender will typically "commit fewer crimes as he or she ages." The inevitable result of incapacitation is the passage of time, allowing an offender to age and therefore mature.

(4)   Rehabilitation

The punishment of imprisonment is meant to rehabilitate the prisoner. Many prisons, after all, are managed by a "Department of Corrections," which aim to "correct" the behavior of inmates. Courts are sometimes cautious about the potential for rehabilitation. In particular, *State v. Pederson*, 857 P.2d 658, 660–61 (1993) noted:

The primary consideration is, and presumptively always will be, the good order and protection of society. All other factors are, and must be subservient to that end. Important as are the humanitarian considerations affecting the accused, his family and other relatives, and the importance to society of rehabilitation itself, such considerations cannot be allowed to control or defeat punishment, where other factors are ignored or subordinated to the detriment of society.

According to *State v. Douglas*, 798 P. 2d 467, 469 (1990), a sentencing judge should "balance the goals of retribution, protection of society (incapacitation), and deterrence against the defendant's potential for rehabilitation."

VIDEO: A Judge Hands Down Unusual Sentences in an Effort to Change Behavior

Judge Michael Cicconetti offers convicted defendants choices between traditional sentences and creative punishments at:

https://www.youtube.com/watch?v=pZSTu98-Cus

---

2. The Distinctions between Crimes and Torts

Criminal law is a small part of all law. All law that is not criminal is called civil law. In the long list of civil law are included such kinds as property law, contract law, and tort law. It is relatively easy to distinguish between criminal law and the civil law subjects of property law and contract law. Property law often involves a previously established relationship between the parties (such as buyer v. seller or landlord v. tenant) that provides a context in which to decide the disputants' rights. Contract law involves the contract—an agreement containing mutual promises between the parties, which provides guidance in the dispute. In contrast, it is not always so easy to distinguish between crimes (public wrongs) and torts (private or civil wrongs). A particular wrongful act might be addressed in the courts as both a crime and a tort. For example, when O.J. Simpson's wife, Nicole Simpson, and her acquaintance, Ronald Goldman, were killed, O.J. Simpson faced accusations in both criminal and civil court. The criminal case, which ended in acquittal, charged O.J. Simpson with the crime of murder of the two victims, while the civil case, which ended in a verdict finding Simpson liable, pursued him for money damages for the tort of "wrongful death."

While some overlap can occur, crimes and torts are two different kinds of wrong. Consider two hypothetical scenarios:

1. After visiting a bar where she drank heavily, Ann drives drunk on the wrong side of the freeway at speeds of 90 miles per hour. Her outrageous driving causes her to collide with Bud's car, killing him instantly. Ann is charged with the crime of murder.
2. Carl, driving in a parking lot, rear ends another driver's car because, in changing the radio station to which he was listening, he failed to pay adequate attention to his driving. Carl is sued civilly for the damage he caused to the other driver's car bumper. Carl has committed a tort.

Crimes involve such a serious tear in the social fabric that they are considered **a wrong not just against the individual victim, but also against all of society**. Therefore, **crimes are known as "public offenses"** and are vindicated by lawsuits brought by a prosecutor, who represents the "State" or the "People." In contrast, **torts are private wrongs in which an individual is harmed**. The stakes are so high with crimes that **criminal law often employs greater procedural safeguards than does civil law**. Thus, juries cannot reach a verdict in criminal trials unless they are convinced "beyond a reasonable doubt," the highest level of certainty which applies to human affairs relying on the frailties of individual perception and memory. With civil cases, juries can reach a verdict with the less demanding standard of "preponderance of evidence." (These differing levels of proof are fully discussed in the "Limits on Criminal Law" section below.) Likewise, the higher dangers facing the criminal defendant, who could in some cases be facing loss of liberty or even life, allow the accused the privilege against self-incrimination under the Fifth Amendment. With only money at stake, no such comparable right exists to protect civil defendants from civil liability. Finally, **criminal law focuses on the criminal defendant**, spending valuable resources determining what the defendant did and thought and weighing the purposes of his or her punishment (whether, as noted above, the penalty is meant to further retribution, deterrence, incapacitation, or rehabilitation). The **focus in torts is on the victim** because much time is spent determining the harm the victim has suffered and the various means to make him or her whole.

LEGAL SKILLS: How to Make a Filing Decision

When officers visit the filing deputy district attorney to have their case filed, the police and the prosecution are both on the side of fighting crime. This unity, however, is probably at its weakest at this stage of the case. Police seeking the filing of charges will be vindicated when the prosecution decides the case is indeed strong enough to be filed. The district attorney, however, is aware that his or her filing of charges will make any challenges presented by the case the prosecutor's own to solve.

Further, prosecutors are ethically bound to file only cases that satisfy both: (a) factual guilt, and (b) legal guilt. Factual guilt is established when the prosecutor him or herself truly believes that the person about to be charged committed the crime. Legal guilt is a more challenging standard because the prosecutor has to not only be personally convinced of guilt, but must also believe that, considering all available evidence, the District Attorney's Office can prove the case to an objectively reasonable fact finder, considering all reasonably foreseeable defenses. Therefore, even if you are certain that the person is guilty of the crime, you cannot risk the state's resources and reputation unless you believe that the case can be proven to a reasonable jury. One should never file to simply satisfy the officers' hopes, or in the belief that further evidence might turn up, or that the threat from filing charges will make the guilty person plead to some crime in any event.

---

3.   Law as Constant Change

Change in law is constant. Each day, with the legislature's passage of a new law, the prosecution's choice to file a case, and a court's handing down of a decision, law is created. Some changes can be dramatic, as when the Congress passes a new law, a state implements a new initiative approved by the voters, or a high court overturns a case. Yet, even on the slowest days and in the smallest cases, every time a court reaches a conclusion, law is created by increments. Because of this constant and inevitable change, students of law must be familiar with legal analysis, which allows adaption to any change in the law.

B.   LEGAL ANALYSIS

My favorite professor in law school told us that we were not in "law school," but in "thinking school." We were going to master the ability to think for ourselves, judge the merits of any argument, and effectively persuade others. The tool for accomplishing all of these tasks was legal analysis. Every student of law, lawyer, judge, and supreme court justice employs legal analysis. This thinking tool is vital to understanding law and its continuing evolution. Therefore, this book explains the law by using legal analysis.

Legal analysis employs "IRAC" or "FIRAC," or "**F**" for Facts, "**I**" for Issue, "**R**" for Rule, "**A**" for Analysis, and "**C**" for Conclusion. When a lawyer reads a case, explains a matter to a client, or argues to a jury, he or she applies FIRAC. Legal analysis' component parts can be explained more fully as follows:

1.   Facts

Facts are the relevant events that create the setting of the crime or dispute. For example, in the hypothetical case of *People v. Ann*, where Ann killed Bud, the facts could be that Ann, angry at Bud for being promoted before her at work, came to work the next day with the intent to kill Bud. To carry out her plan, Ann, while still at home, hid a gun, which she made sure was loaded, in her purse. Ann then drove to work carrying the gun in her purse, sought out Bud in his office, and shot and killed him, yelling, "You may have gotten an early promotion, but I am giving you an early retirement!"

2.   Issue

The issue is the legal question presented in the case. It is often said that the issue is the most important part of legal analysis because which question you ask determines which answer you get. Parties will frame issues so that courts will answer a case in their favor. With Ann, the issue is: "Is Ann guilty of committing murder of Bud?"

3.   Rule

The rule is the tool that judges and lawyers use to answer the issue or question presented in the case. Without a rule, there can be no answer. **Rules come from the following sources**: (1) **Statutes** passed by legislatures, (2) **Case law** written by judges, (3) **Administrative regulations** promulgated by administrative agencies, and (4) **Constitutions** of states and the federal government. For criminal law, although administrative regulations and constitutions are certainly important, much of the law comes from statutes and case law, which will be discussed in "sources of law" below. For the case of Ann killing Bud, a statute, such as California's Penal Code 187: Murder, could be used to see if Ann is guilty of murder for killing Bud. This statute defines "murder" as the "unlawful killing of a human being or fetus with malice aforethought." Moreover, previous cases that have interpreted this statute for earlier killings could shed light on its meaning in this case.

4.   Analysis

Analysis involves taking a rule of general application (such as Penal Code Section 187, which applies to all murders,) **and applying it to the facts of the individual case** (such as Ann's shooting of Bud). Comparing the facts in Ann's case against the definition of murder in Penal Code 187 and the various cases with similar facts will allow the courts to determine if Ann is guilty of murder.

5. Conclusion

The **conclusion** is nothing more than **the decision reached in the case**. Instead of "concluding" that Ann is guilty of murder, courts say that they "hold" that Ann is guilty of murder. Thus, **a court's conclusion is called its "holding."** For example, in Ann's case, an appellate court might hold that, "the evidence is sufficient to support the jury's conviction of Ann for murder."

Tips for Success for Future Law Enforcement

Make the Right Life Decisions in the First Place

Public safety employees, on any given day, might have to make life-and-death decisions and even use lethal force. As representatives of the government, they have great powers that are vulnerable to corruption. Police, sheriffs, and prosecutors must not only avoid wrongdoing, but even the appearance of wrongdoing. Government employers, therefore, seek persons who have avoided committing certain troubling or questionable behavior. Those who aspire to be officers and deputies should avoid the following disqualifying behavior:

a. **Academic Dishonesty**—If you will plagiarize, lie, or cheat about something with such relatively small stakes as a test or quiz, government employers figure you are all the more likely to violate moral and ethical norms when the stakes are great, such as when your job or winning a case is on the line. Employers check with universities about any irregularities in academic performance.

b. **Crimes**—Prior felonies, misdemeanors, and even infractions can disqualify or harm an applicant. While felonies are the largest concern, any crime showing dishonesty or "moral turpitude" (essentially defined as a readiness to do evil), are red flags. Even traffic infractions, if they reveal a pattern of impulsiveness, immaturity, or a lack of respect for the rule of law, are viewed unfavorably. Domestic violence records might show a tendency to abuse a position of power and a lack of self-control.

c. **Drugs**—Use of any intoxicating or impairing substance is a red flag. Agencies have denied employment to persons with a history of marijuana use, even if recreational use is legal in the jurisdiction. Employers fear an employee who might be impaired, even with legal substances, when involved in dangerous situations where judgment is key. Drugs can signal impulsiveness or dependence.

d. **Being Fired**—The government is an employer just like anyone else, and so does not wish to hire a problem employee. Dishonorable discharges from the military can cause concern here as well.

e. **Bad Credit**—Public safety employees swear an oath to properly perform their duties. Bad credit could signal a person who does not stand behind his or her word or purchases so impulsively that prior promises cannot be fulfilled.

C. THE GENERAL PRINCIPLES OF CRIMINAL LIABILITY— ELEMENTS OF CRIME

1. "Elements" as Necessary Ingredients to Crimes

Chances are that you have a favorite meal or dessert, which is based on a particular recipe. The recipe provides a specific list of ingredients and instructions for how to combine and prepare them. If there is any substitution of ingredients or any change in preparation, you no longer have the original meal or dessert. To have the particular dish, one needs to faithfully stick to the specific recipe.

A criminal committing a crime is under the same mandate; **to commit a specific crime, the criminal has to commit all the "elements"—the necessary ingredients—of that particular crime. If the criminal fails to commit even one of the required elements, he or she has failed in committing that particular crime**. Likewise, prosecutors presenting a case to a jury must prove, beyond a reasonable doubt, that the defendant committed every element of the charged crime in order to prove guilt.

Both parties, aware of criminal law's requirement that each element of a crime must be established, often plan their strategies accordingly. Prosecuting attorneys, often called district attorneys, build their cases element-by-element just as a mason builds a wall brick-by-brick. Prosecutors will plan their cases by creating a witness list to ensure that they have a witness or a piece of physical evidence (an item such as a gun or fingerprint) to prove each element of the crime. As each witness testifies, the prosecutor can check off the element or elements the witness's testimony helped prove. If a witness is weak on a particular element, the prosecutor can call an additional witness to help establish that element or ingredient of the crime. Defense counsel, whether public defenders or private attorneys, are keenly aware that prosecutors must prove each element of a crime in order to gain a conviction of their client. A defense lawyer, therefore, plans a case by looking for the weakest link in the prosecution's proof. The defense attorney then hones in on and exploits this weakness by testing the witnesses that are called to establish this element. Defense attorneys can also call witnesses to disprove or cast doubt on a particular element. Many successful defenses are built not on proving the defendant's innocence (which is not required under our Constitution), but on establishing reasonable doubt as to any element of the charged crime. Even if the prosecution establishes four out of five elements needed for a crime, the case will end in acquittal if he or she failed to prove the fifth and last element.

A crime's elements, along with proof of the defendant's identity as the person committing those elements, form the crucial battleground in criminal cases. To fully understand a particular crime, and the war waged in the courtroom regarding that crime, one must know the elements that make up the crime. Most of criminal law in trials, appellate courtrooms, and in this book amounts to an examination of the elements of crime and the defenses used to block them.

2. "Elements" as Fundamental Aspects of Crime

Crime is a unique behavior in society. All three branches of our federal and state governments treat crimes—the most extreme and blameworthy acts in our communities—as fundamentally different from all other wrongful acts. **The term, "element," is often used to identify those fundamental aspects of crime that together cause it to differ from all other activity**. The fundamental elements of crime in this general sense are the evil or **criminal act, known as "*actus reus*,"** the **evil or criminal intent, called "*mens rea*,"** and **causation**. Although not all crimes need each of these elements ("strict liability" crimes, for instance, do not have a *mens rea* element in their definitions), and other kinds of behavior besides crime have wrongful intent and actions and can cause harm, these basic elements are often seen as distinguishing crime from other actions. The fundamental elements of crime—*actus reus*, *mens rea*, and causation, will be fully explored in Chapters 2, 3, and 4.

> ## What should be criminal? A mother is arrested for speaking profanity in front of her children
>
> *New York Daily News* reporter Philip Caulfield explained in his August 15, 2014, article, "S.C. woman arrested for cursing in front of kids — and later receives apology," that Danielle Wolf was arrested for using the F-word in the presence of her children while shopping at Kroger's. The article can be visited at:
>
> http://www.nydailynews.com/news/national/s-woman-arrested-cursing-front-kids-recieves-apology-article-1.1904846

D. SOURCES OF CRIMINAL LAW

1. Common Law Origins

When English colonists came to the New World, they were too pragmatic to reinvent the wheel when it came to law. They therefore borrowed the "Common Law" they brought with them from England. Thus, **the common law that judges had created and gradually changed over centuries in England was the starting point for criminal law in the United States**.

This is a picture of the Royal Courts of Justice in London. Common law was created over the centuries in England.

Many of the wrongs that are considered criminal today were first defined as crimes centuries ago in England. English judges, hearing individual cases, would make decisions by applying the customs and norms of the realm. Judges would write down their decisions, and the reasons for them, to explain their conclusions and to guide future courts. These cases came to form the case law of common law.

People v. Williams 57 Cal.4th 776 (2013) explained the difference between the common law of England and the current law of statues as follows:

> Unlike statutory law, whose authority rests upon an express declaration by a legislative body, the common law "consists of those principles and forms which grow out of the customs and habits of a people," enshrined in law by virtue of judicial decisions. *** Much of the law developed in English courts was later applied in England's American colonies and then, after independence, in this nation's states. [The term "common law" means] a "body of judge-made law ... developed originally in England." [The term "common law crime" means a "crime that was punishable under the common law, rather than by force of statute."]

Common law is significant not only because it provided the original substantive rules of our nation's criminal law, but also because it has influenced our law's structure and evolution.

a) Common Law's Contribution to Our Law's Substance: "Common Law" Crimes

If you went up to someone and asked that person to name a crime, chances are he or she would name a crime that was created centuries ago at common law. Thus, when the person responded by saying, "Murder, rape, or robbery," he or she would be listing crimes that judges created in England. Although most of the crimes that leap to our mind when we hear "criminal law" are of ancient origin, **states have now specifically defined these offenses in statutes passed by legislatures and signed into law**. Still, if courts have questions about how to interpret these laws, the common law cases provide them a wealth of guidance. Further, many of the defenses to crime also have a common law origin, so that common law concepts are still important today.

b) Common Law's Contribution to Our Law's Structure: *Stare Decisis*

People v. Williams, (2013) 57 Cal. 4th 776, 790 (2013) noted that in the law, "as Justice Oliver Wendell Holmes, Jr., observed, 'a page of history is worth a volume of logic.'" While lawyers pride themselves on presenting reasoned arguments and judges exalt logic in deciding cases, many of the legal decisions that are made daily are arrived at not by some brilliant proof of reason but simply because a judge follows a rule that some earlier jurist already created. Due to a doctrine known as *stare decisis*, the best judges do not set out to "make law" but simply apply earlier rules to today's cases. (Of course, even the most straightforward application of a past rule to current facts results in a slight change in the law, and therefore "makes law.") While this promotes consistency, and therefore reliability, in the law, it also brings truth to William Faulkner's idea that, "The past is never dead. It's not even past." The doctrine of *stare decisis* is a legacy of the common law.

Stare decisis is defined in *Black's Law Dictionary* Ninth Edition (2009 edited by Bryan A. Garner), as Latin for:

> **To stand by things decided. The doctrine of precedent, under which a court must follow earlier judicial decisions when the same points arise again in litigation.**

Since the Common Law grew each day through the addition of ad hoc decisions in whatever cases happened to come before judges, it was not known for being systematic and organized. The common law received some clarification in the eighteenth century when William Blackstone published his treatise on the law, known as **Blackstone's *Commentaries***. This work **had an enormous influence not only in England, but also in the United States**. Future presidents John Adams and Thomas Jefferson read Blackstone when studying to become lawyers. To this day, the United States Supreme Court quotes from Blackstone as one of the definitive sources regarding historical questions of law. Of particular interest to criminal law is Blackstone's *Commentaries on the Laws of England,* Book the Fourth (Vol. IV), Oxford, 1769, entitled "Of Public Wrongs," meaning public offenses or crimes.

2. Statutes

Although our nation first relied on England's common law as its starting point for criminal law, eventually the states passed statutes defining their own crimes. These statutes were collected, organized, and thus "codified" into "codes" such as the penal code. **Each state, as well as the federal government, has passed its own criminal law code.** Statutes are the best tools for defining which behavior is "criminal." Statutes are passed by legislatures and signed into law by either a governor or the president. These officials, being voted into office for relatively short terms, are the most representative branches of government and are therefore best positioned to speak for "society" in determining what behavior is so blameworthy as to be criminal. In contrast, the judiciary, which is either appointed to office or voted in for long terms, is too insulated to speak with authority as to what conduct should be deemed criminal. The passage of a statute provides every citizen with notice about what behavior should be avoided as criminal. (This process promotes the "principle of legality" discussed above.) In contrast, judges, in writing judicial opinions, often have an audience limited only to the parties in the particular case.

One example of a statute that vests the power to define what is a crime is California's Penal Code Section 6:

California Penal Code § 6 Effect of code upon past offenses

> No act or omission, commenced after twelve o'clock noon of the day on which this code takes effect as a law, is criminal or punishable, except as prescribed or authorized by this code, or by some of the statutes, which it specifies as continuing in force and as not affected by its provisions, or by some ordinance, municipal, county, or township regulation, passed or adopted, under such statutes and in force when this code takes effect. Any act or omission commenced prior to that time may be inquired of, prosecuted, and punished in the same manner as if this code had not been passed.[4]

3.   Case Law

Statutes are notoriously hard to read. Legislators, in trying to predict the future, attempt to cover each and every outcome that could possibly occur. This effort clutters statutes with long clauses and technical language. Also, try as they might, legislators cannot predict everything that might be relevant about new laws. The job of interpreting the statutes in individual cases and of clarifying language falls to judges. Being in the judiciary, a branch of government separate from the legislature, judges do not know what the lawmakers were intending when they created the

law. So, they do their best to divine legislative intent by studying the language of the statutes, looking at them in the bigger context of other laws, and considering the facts of the particular case. In doing all of this, **judges, tasked only with interpreting law, cannot help but create law when deciding in cases**. This case law is then read, interpreted, and followed by future judges and litigants. Over time, a large body of useful case law is created.

Most of this case law comes from appellate courts. The federal government and nearly all states have a three-tiered system of courts with trial courts at the bottom and two levels of appellate courts (an intermediate "Court of Appeals" and the highest court, typically known as the "Supreme Court") above. The trial courts, over which presides a single judge, try the "facts" of a case. In criminal cases, facts are the circumstances relevant to guilt. Examples of facts that a prosecutor might need to prove are the identity of the defendant as the criminal (the defendant was the one who committed the crime), the defendant's actions (he or she killed someone or stole something), and the defendant's mental state (he or she did something on purpose or recklessly). A jury or a judge (if the parties have waived the right to a jury) listens to witnesses, observes the exhibits, and decides what really happened—in other words, "finds the

4. From *Deering's California Codes Annotated*. Copyright © 2014 by Matthew Bender & Company, Inc., a member of the LexisNexis Group. Reprinted with the permission of LexisNexis.

facts." Since the jury finds the facts, it is called the "fact finder." The jury is best placed to decide the facts because it sits nearest the witness stand, sees the trial as it unfolds, and physically handles the exhibits. Higher (appellate) courts "give deference to," or respect, a jury's factual determinations. It is not the appellate court's job to find facts. Instead of hearing witnesses, they hear only the arguments of lawyers.

If appellate courts do not determine the facts in a case, what is left for them to do? **Appellate courts decide the law, creating rules by writing "opinions."** Appellate courts are "collegial bodies" because they have more than one judge (or, as they are known at the appellate level, "justice"). Most intermediate courts of appeal decide a case as a three-justice panel, while the United States Supreme Court has nine justices. The number of justices is odd so that the members of an appellate court can reach an agreement even in the most contentious of cases. For example, the closest ruling on the United States Supreme Court would be a 5 to 4 decision. Those justices voting with the larger number are among the "majority" and write **the "majority opinion,"** which **has the force of law under *stare decisis*.** The justices voting with the fewer number are left to write a "dissenting," or disagreeing opinion, which does not have the force of law. A dissenting opinion can foreshadow a rule at some time in the future when the law evolves to recognize that its position was the right one all along. Since this book aims to teach the law, it is generally filled with appellate opinions, because it is the appellate court that gives the law instead of the facts.

4. Regulations

Laws limiting criminal behavior can also come from regulatory agencies, such as the Internal Revenue Service, the Environmental Protection Agency, and the Securities Exchange Commission. To empower these agencies with lawmaking authority, legislatures pass enabling legislation allowing agencies to fill in the many details needed to fulfill policy goals, such as effective collection of taxes (IRS), clean water, land, and air (EPA), and fair and honest trading of stocks (SEC). Although regulations are an important source of law, they tend to offer insight to narrow and technical issues. These rules are, therefore, not typically the focus of criminal law and will receive only brief treatment in this book.

5. Constitutions

The most powerful and fundamental laws of any nation or state are constitutions. Criminal laws must abide by the limits of constitutions and, therefore, constitutions affect the substance and scope of criminal laws. Constitutional law, however, is such a rich field in its own right that it is typically addressed in books focused exclusively on this subject. This book will consider constitutional issues only as they affect the criminal law.

6. The Model Penal Code

There is no single code of criminal law that applies to every state in the nation. As suggested by Paul H. Robinson and Markus Dirk Dubber in *An Introduction to the Model Penal Code*, at 1, 5, https://www.law.upenn.edu/fac/phrobins/intromodpencode.pdf, the closest the law has come to creating a universal code is the American Law Institute's (ALI) Model Penal Code (MPC), originally drafted in 1962.

The ALI describes itself on its website as follows:

> The American Law Institute is the leading independent organization in the United States producing scholarly work to clarify, modernize, and otherwise improve the law. The Institute (made up of 4000 lawyers, judges, and law professors of the highest qualifications) drafts, discusses, revises, and publishes Restatements of the Law, model statutes, and principles of

law that are enormously influential in the courts and legislatures, as well as in legal scholarship and education. ALI has long been influential internationally and, in recent years, more of its work has become international in scope.

To learn more about the ALI, visit its website at:

http://www.ali.org/index.cfm?fuseaction=about.overview

Robinson and Dubber explain that the ALI found the criminal law of all the states and federal government to be so "chaotic and irrational," that it required the major overhaul of an entirely new model code—the Model Penal Code. Robinson and Dubber note that **the MPC has influenced legislation in thirty-four states**. Some major jurisdictions, such as California and the federal system, have not accepted the MPC. Still, the MPC has made such a significant impact that this book will refer to it repeatedly.

Want to Join the ALI? Not Just Anyone Can

To become a member of the ALI, one must be an expert in his or her field, be ready to work in improving the law, and know someone in the institute. The ALI describes election to the ALI as follows:

> Election of an individual to the ALI begins with a confidential nomination by an ALI member that is supported by two additional ALI members. In sponsoring a candidate for membership, the ALI member affirms his or her personal assessment that the candidate has demonstrated excellence in the law, is of high character, will contribute to the work of the Institute, and is committed to its mission to clarify and improve the law.[5]

For more information on ALI members, visit:

http://www.ali.org/index.cfm?fuseaction=membership.membership

---

7. Legal Commentary

Legal commentators offer insight on legal issues in law review articles, treatises, or books. Although some judges or attorneys have been known to write law review articles or books while they are still in practice, many of these commentators often do not hold positions in the legislative, executive, or judicial branches of government. **Law review articles are not binding on courts or legislatures, but can offer persuasive authority to decision makers**. Moreover, their analysis can bring clarity, perspective, or insight on the law, and so commentators will be considered in this book.

8. Jury Instructions

Lawyers, judges, and legislators try so hard to be precise that their language frequently turns into gobbledygook

---

5. From ALI Overview and Membership Overview, American Law Institute website. Copyright © 2014 by the American Law Institute. Used by permission.

that is called "legalize." While this language might suit lawyers and judges, it could be dangerous if misunderstood by juries deciding the fate of their fellow citizens. Further, since juries focus on deciding the facts—what happened in a particular case—they leave the decisions about the law to the trial judge. However, **when jurors enter the deliberation room to decide guilt in a trial, they must apply the law to make sure they properly find the facts.** The **jurors obtain the law they will apply in the case from the trial judge, who "charges the jury" by reading the law to them in "jury instructions."** To ensure that jurors can properly apply the law, the jury instructions are stripped of all unintelligible legalize. **Jury instructions are written in "plain language" so that all laypeople can understand them.** These jury instructions are so informative that this book includes many of them in the web links at the end of chapters.

Do's And Don'ts For Hearings, Trials, and Appeals

As a D.A., Don't Punish a Defendant Because of Dislike for His or Her Lawyer

Some attorneys can be quite irritating. Some bend the truth, whine, wheedle, or continually peck at prosecutors. There is a temptation to send a signal to an attorney by lowering the boom on his or her client, such as by "over filing" with unmerited charges or refusing a reasonable plea offer. **Don't** succumb to this temptation. This is simply unethical and so should be avoided in all cases. It is also nonsensical. The client has no real control over the behavior of his or her lawyer, even if he hired the attorney. Any punishment should be based solely on the merits of the case itself.

E. LIMITS ON CRIMINAL LAW

1. Criminal Cases Must Be Proved Beyond a Reasonable Doubt

What if, as a juror, you thought it more likely than not that the defendant in a criminal case had committed a crime? However, you were not convinced "beyond a reasonable doubt" that he or she was guilty; you still had doubts as to his guilt that were reasonable, as opposed to imaginary or fanciful. What should you do? **The criminal law requires that the prosecutor prove every element of his or her case "beyond a reasonable doubt" for conviction**, and therefore you must vote to acquit. This is required even though you think that the defendant "probably" committed the crime. This result might seem contrary to common sense or efficiency—why allow a criminal to escape conviction and punishment even when you believe he or she likely is guilty?

The answer depends on the values involved in a criminal trial. The stakes in a criminal case are of the highest importance; the wrong to the victim is so egregious and awful that society demands justice, while the consequences facing the accused are so dire (loss of reputation, property, liberty, or even life) that the decision in the case must be checked by procedural safeguards. Therefore, the "more likely than not" level of certainty, which essentially amounts to the "preponderance of evidence" standard of proof where the side having to prove the case must convince the jury to a degree of certainty exceeding 50 percent, is simply not good enough for criminal cases. **While civil cases can be decided by the "preponderance of evidence" standard, criminal trials must be proven "beyond a reasonable doubt."**

The **United States Supreme Court, in the case, *In Re Winship*, 397 U.S. 358 (1970), held that the requirement that each element of a criminal case be proven beyond a reasonable doubt was a constitutional right**. The court explained:

The requirement that guilt of a criminal charge be established by proof beyond a reasonable doubt dates at least from our early years as a Nation. The "demand for a higher degree of persuasion in criminal cases was recurrently expressed from ancient times, [though] its crystallization into the formula 'beyond a reasonable doubt' seems to have occurred as late as 1798. It is now accepted in common law jurisdictions as the measure of persuasion by which the prosecution must convince the trier of all the essential elements of guilt." ***

Mr. Justice Frankfurter stated that "it is the duty of the Government to establish . . . guilt beyond a reasonable doubt. This notion—basic in our law and rightly one of the boasts of a free society—is a requirement and a safeguard of due process of law. [The reasonable doubt requirement] developed to safeguard men from dubious and unjust convictions, with resulting forfeitures of life, liberty and property." *** "No man should be deprived of his life *** unless the jurors who try him are able, upon their consciences, to say that the evidence before them . . . is sufficient to show beyond a reasonable doubt the existence of every fact necessary to constitute the crime charged." ***

The reasonable-doubt standard *** is a prime instrument for reducing the risk of convictions resting on factual error. The standard provides concrete substance for the presumption of innocence. [An accused would be at a disadvantage] amounting to a lack of fundamental fairness, if he could be adjudged guilty and imprisoned for years on the strength of the same evidence as would suffice in a civil case." ***

The accused during a criminal prosecution has at stake interests of immense importance, both because of the possibility that he may lose his liberty upon conviction and because of the certainty that he would be stigmatized by the conviction. [A] society that values the good name and freedom of every individual should not condemn a man for commission of a crime when there is reasonable doubt about his guilt. *** "There is always in litigation a margin of error, representing error in factfinding." *** Where one party has at stake an interest of transcending value—as a criminal defendant his liberty—this margin of error is reduced as to him [by placing on the other party the burden of persuading the factfinder of his guilt beyond a reasonable doubt. The reasonable-doubt standard is indispensable, for it "impresses on the trier of fact the necessity of reaching a subjective state of certitude of the facts in issue."]

[Use] of the reasonable-doubt standard is indispensable to command the respect and confidence of the community in applications of the criminal law. It is critical that the moral force of the criminal law not be diluted by a standard of proof that leaves people in doubt whether innocent men are being condemned. It is also important in our free society that every individual going about his ordinary affairs have confidence that his government cannot adjudge him guilty of a criminal offense without convincing a proper factfinder of his guilt with utmost certainty.

[We] explicitly hold that the Due Process Clause protects the accused against conviction except upon proof beyond a reasonable doubt of every fact necessary to constitute the crime with which he is charged.

Justice Harlan, who wrote a concurring opinion, declared, "There is always in litigation a margin of error, representing error in factfinding, which both parties must take into account." The two basic mistakes that can occur are "conviction of an innocent man" and "acquittal of a guilty man." Justice Harlan concluded that, "In this context, I view the requirement of proof beyond a reasonable doubt in a criminal case as bottomed on a fundamental value determination of our society that it is far worse to convict an innocent man than to let a guilty man go free."

VIDEO: Marion County Indianapolis Offers Information about Securing Evidence at a Crime Scene

Various tips for preserving crime scene evidence are available at:

https://www.youtube.com/watch?v=ur1GxXZGnNl

---

2. Vagueness

How can a person abide by a law if he or she cannot figure out what it prohibits? How can police enforce such a law? These questions arise when a statute is so poorly written that courts deem it "**void for vagueness**." As noted by LaFave, in his *Criminal Law*, Fifth Edition at 109 (2010), and *Lanzetta v. New Jersey*, 306 U.S. 451, 453 (1939), "No one may be required at peril of life, liberty or property to speculate as to the meaning of penal statutes. All are entitled to be informed as to what the State commands or forbids." The classic case on this issue is *Kolender v. Lawson*, which is so significant, it has been cited in law reviews over 850 times.

Unconstitutionally vague laws fail to give notice to citizens or limits on arbitrary police conduct.

© Rachata Teyparsit/Shutterstock.com

Look for the court's mention in its conclusion of a "**facial challenge**," which *Black's Law Dictionary*, Ninth Edition (2009) **defines as meaning that the statute is so poorly written that just reading the statute, or looking at its "face," reveals a constitutional flaw in the law.** Consider if the language, "credible and reliable" is so **vague that citizens cannot understand it** and so do not have **adequate notice** to conform their conduct to the law. Also think about whether **police might exploit such vagueness to arbitrarily apply** the law.[6]

LEGAL ANALYSIS

Kolender, Chief of Police of San Diego v. Lawson
461 U.S. 352 (1983).
Justice O'Connor delivered the opinion of the United States Supreme Court.

Facts

This appeal presents a facial challenge to a criminal statute that requires persons who loiter or wander on the streets to provide a "credible and reliable" identification and to account for their presence when requested by a peace officer.

---

6. From *Criminal Law* 5e (Hornbook Series) by Wayne R. LaFave. Copyright © 2010 by West Academic. Used by permission of West Academic.

[California Penal Code Ann. § 647(e) (West 1970) provides:

"Every person who commits any of the following acts is guilty of disorderly conduct, a misdemeanor: . . . (e) Who loiters or wanders upon the streets or from place to place without apparent reason or business and who refuses to identify himself and to account for his presence when requested by any peace officer so to do, if the surrounding circumstances are such as to indicate to a reasonable man that the public safety demands such identification."][7]

Edward Lawson was detained or arrested on approximately fifteen occasions between March 1975 and January 1977 pursuant to Cal. Penal Code Ann. § 647(e).

[The trial transcript contains numerous descriptions of the police stops of Lawson. One police officer stopped Lawson while walking on an otherwise vacant street because it was late at night, the area was isolated, and the area was located close to a high crime area. Another officer detained Lawson, when he was walking at a late hour in a business area and asked for identification because unknown persons in the general area had committed burglaries.]

Lawson then brought a civil action *** seeking a declaratory judgment that § 647(e) is unconstitutional, a mandatory injunction to restrain enforcement of the statute, and compensatory and punitive damages against the various officers who detained him. [The lower courts found that § 647(e) was unconstitutional because it contained a vague enforcement standard susceptible to arbitrary enforcement and failed to give fair and adequate notice of the type of conduct prohibited.]

Issue

Whether California's loitering statute, which requires a suspect provide "credible and reliable" identification to an officer to avoid arrest, is so vague that it violates Fourteenth Amendment Due Process.

Rule and Analysis

[The] void-for-vagueness doctrine requires that a penal statute define the criminal offense with sufficient definiteness that ordinary people can understand what conduct is prohibited and in a manner that does not encourage arbitrary and discriminatory enforcement. *** Although the doctrine focuses both on actual notice to citizens and arbitrary enforcement, we have recognized recently that **the more important aspect of the vagueness doctrine "is not actual notice, but *** the requirement that a legislature establish minimal guidelines to govern law enforcement."** *** Where the legislature fails to provide such minimal guidelines, a criminal statute may permit "a standardless sweep [that allows police, prosecutors, and juries to pursue their personal predilections"].

Section 647(e) *** contains no standard for determining what a suspect has to do in order to satisfy the requirement to provide a "credible and reliable" identification. [The] statute vests virtually complete discretion in the hands of the police to determine whether the suspect has satisfied the statute and must be permitted to go on his way in the absence of probable cause to arrest. An individual, whom police may think is suspicious but do not have probable cause to believe has committed a crime, is entitled to continue to walk the public streets "only at the whim of any police officer" who happens to stop that individual under § 647(e). Our concern here is based upon the "potential for arbitrarily suppressing First Amendment liberties. . . ." *** In addition, § 647(e) implicates consideration of the constitutional right to freedom of movement.***

---

7. From *Deering's California Codes Annotated.* Copyright © 2014 by Matthew Bender & Company, Inc., a member of the LexisNexis Group. Reprinted with the permission of LexisNexis.

Section 647(e) *** requires that the individual provide a "credible and reliable" identification that carries a "reasonable assurance" of its authenticity, and that provides "means for later getting in touch with the person who has identified himself." *** In addition, the suspect may also have to account for his presence "to the extent it assists in producing credible and reliable identification." ***

At oral argument, the appellants confirmed that a suspect violates § 647(e) unless "the officer [is] satisfied that the identification is reliable." *** In giving examples of how suspects would satisfy the requirement, appellants explained that a jogger, who was not carrying identification, could, depending on the particular officer, be required to answer a series of questions concerning the route that he followed to arrive at the place where the officers detained him, or could satisfy the identification requirement simply by reciting his name and address.***

[The] full discretion accorded to the police to determine whether the suspect has provided a "credible and reliable" identification necessarily "[entrusts] lawmaking 'to the moment-to-moment judgment of the policeman on his beat.'" *** Section 647(e) "furnishes a convenient tool for 'harsh and discriminatory enforcement by local prosecuting officials, against particular groups deemed to merit their displeasure,'" *** and "confers on police a virtually unrestrained power to arrest and charge persons with a violation." [The] State fails to establish standards by which the officers may determine whether the suspect has complied with the subsequent identification requirement.

Appellants stress the need for strengthened law enforcement tools to combat the epidemic of crime that plagues our Nation. The concern of our citizens with curbing criminal activity is certainly a matter requiring the attention of all branches of government. As weighty as this concern is, however, it cannot justify legislation that would otherwise fail to meet constitutional standards for definiteness and clarity. *** Section 647(e) *** requires that "suspicious" persons satisfy some undefined identification requirement, or face criminal punishment. Although due process does not require "impossible standards" of clarity, *** this is not a case where further precision in the statutory language is either impossible or impractical. ***

Conclusion

We conclude that the statute * is unconstitutionally vague within the meaning of the Due Process Clause of the Fourteenth Amendment by failing to clarify what is contemplated by the requirement that a suspect provide a "credible and reliable" identification. *** § 647(e) is unconstitutionally vague on its face because it encourages arbitrary enforcement by failing to describe with sufficient particularity what a suspect must do in order to satisfy the statute. *** Accordingly, we affirm the judgment of the court below.**

It is so ordered.

Note

Jeffrey Skilling of Enron infamy challenged his conviction relying in part on vagueness. The United States Supreme Court in *Skilling v. United States*, 561 U.S. 358 (2010) described the case as follows:

> Founded in 1985, Enron Corporation grew from its headquarters in Houston, Texas, into one of the world's leading energy companies. Skilling launched his career there in 1990 [and] steadily rose through the corporation's ranks, serving as president and chief operating officer, and then [as CEO]. Six months later, on August 14, 2001, Skilling resigned from Enron.

Less than four months after Skilling's departure, Enron spiraled into bankruptcy. The company's stock, which had traded at $90 per share in August 2000, plummeted to pennies per share in late 2001. Attempting to comprehend what caused the corporation's collapse, the U. S. Department of Justice formed an Enron Task Force, comprising prosecutors and FBI agents from around the Nation. The Government's investigation uncovered an elaborate conspiracy to prop up Enron's short-run stock prices by overstating the company's financial well-being. In the years following Enron's bankruptcy, the Government prosecuted dozens of Enron employees who participated in the scheme. In time, the Government worked its way up the corporation's chain of command: On July 7, 2004, a grand jury indicted Skilling, Lay, and Richard Causey, Enron's former chief accounting officer.

These three defendants, the indictment alleged,

> "engaged in a wide-ranging scheme to deceive the investing public, including Enron's shareholders, ... about the true performance of Enron's businesses by: (a) manipulating Enron's publicly reported financial results; and (b) making public statements and representations about Enron's financial performance and results that were false and misleading." ***

Skilling and his co-conspirators, the indictment continued, "enriched themselves as a result of the scheme through salary, bonuses, grants of stock and stock options, other profits, and prestige." ***

Upon conviction, Skilling appealed, arguing the law under which he was convicted was unconstitutionally vague. The Supreme Court disagreed, noting:

> Interpreted to encompass only bribery and kickback schemes, § 1346 is not unconstitutionally vague. [The] void-for-vagueness doctrine addresses concerns about (1) fair notice and (2) arbitrary and discriminatory prosecutions. *** A prohibition on fraudulently depriving another of one's honest services by accepting bribes or kickbacks does not present a problem on either score.

"Seamless Web" Connection

As noted in *United States v. Williams,* 15 F.3d 1356 (1994), Oliver Wendell Holmes famously declared that the "law is a seamless web." In the law's seamless web, each issue or concept is connected to everything else. Since all law is connected, similar issues arise in even quite different cases. In this way, different cases link together across time and place.

Here, *Kolender's* "vagueness" directly connects to this chapter's concept of "Morality and blame." If a statute is so vaguely written that no one can properly understand it, the law cannot find a person who violated the statute to be worthy of "blame," and so the person cannot be convicted of an unconstitutionally vague law.

Kolender's "vagueness" issue also links up with Chapter 3's "mens rea" or wrongful intent requirement for crimes. The law cannot blame a person for intentionally committing a wrong if the law is so vague that no one knows whether he or she is violating it.

Tips for Success for Future Law Students and Lawyers

Step Back and Consider If and Why You Truly Wish to Be a Lawyer

Law is a stressful and demanding profession. Lawyers suffer some of the worst rates of depression, anxiety, substance abuse, divorce, and suicide. So, you must ask yourself, before making a commitment to spend typically over $150,000 on tuition and three years of your life studying more intensely than you ever have, why you should pursue this narrow path. Lawyers—whether litigating in court or negotiating a contract—are gladiators in constant pursuit of their client's best interests

against all adversaries. I was one of the lucky few who spent most days in a courtroom; most attorneys grind through reading and writing in an office. As a third-generation lawyer, I can tell you that there are easier and faster ways to gain wealth. To become a happy lawyer, one must wish to delve deeply into the subject of the law, be in an ever-changing job demanding life-long learning and daily challenges, and enjoy working with all sorts of people. You must wish to use your immense power to promote daily good. You must enjoy reading, writing and reasoning; appreciate arguments on both sides; and be meticulous about details. As a quick and rough test of your interest in the law, consider whether there were any words in this paragraph that you did not know and yet did not bother to look up. If so, perhaps you should not spend your resources in becoming a lawyer.

3. *Ex Post Facto* Laws

Suppose you walk across the lawn in front of the courthouse. The next day, the government passes a law making it a felony to walk on the courthouse lawn and then police arrest you for violating the law before it was even passed. Such an unfair law is forbidden by the U.S. Constitution's *Ex Post Facto* prohibition.

The United States Supreme Court, in *Peugh v. United States*, 133 S. Ct. 2072 (2013), noted:

> **The Framers considered *ex post facto* laws to be "contrary to the first principles of the social compact and to every principle of sound legislation."** The Federalist No. 44, *** (J. Madison). **The Clause ensures that individuals have fair warning of applicable laws and guards against vindictive legislative action.**

The United States Supreme Court, in *Calder v. Bull*, 3 U.S. 386, 1 L. Ed. 648 (1798), discussed *ex post facto* laws. This case is particularly important because it was handed down in 1798, when most of the framers (who wrote the Constitution and therefore had a good idea of the "framer's intentions") were still alive. The Supreme Court explained *ex post facto* laws as follows:

> **The Constitution of the United States, article 1, section 9, prohibits the Legislature of the United States from passing any ex post facto law**; and, in **section 10**, lays several restrictions

on the authority of the Legislatures of the several states; and, among them, "**that no state shall pass any ex post facto law.**" ***

[State legislatures] shall not pass laws, after a fact done by a *** citizen, which shall have relation to such fact, and shall punish him for having done it. The prohibition [protects an individual's personal security by protecting] his person from punishment by legislative acts, having a retrospective operation. ***

[Ex post facto laws include: 1) **Laws that make an action done before the passing of the law, and which was innocent when done, criminal**; and punishes such action. 2) **Laws that aggravate a crime**, or makes it greater than it was, when committed. 3) **Laws that inflict a greater punishment, than the law annexed to the crime, when committed**. 4). **Laws that alter the legal rules of evidence**, and receive less, or different, testimony, than the law required at the time of the commission of the offence, in order to convict the offender. Laws that take away, or impair, vested rights are unjust, and should not apply retrospectively.] I do not consider any law ex post facto, within the prohibition, that [lessens the harshness] of the criminal law; but only those that create, or aggravate, the crime; or encrease the punishment, or change the rules of evidence, for the purpose of conviction. ***

In other words, **if a law acts retrospectively but also** *helps or favors* **a criminal defendant, such as pardoning him for a crime he has committed or reducing a sentence for a crime, it will not be forbidden as** *ex post facto***, because it does not** *take away rights or impose penalties* **for past behavior, as** *ex post facto* **laws do.**

4.   Bills of Attainder

Some conflicts are so painful and divisive that the victors find it difficult to forgive the vanquished. The victorious might seek to punish a person or group of people by passing a law that applies penalties against persons without the protection of a trial. In *United States v. Lovett,* 328 U.S. 303 (1946), during the 1940s, Congress, in the thrall of the red scare, passed legislation cutting the pay of named individuals "found guilty of disloyalty." The Supreme Court declared this law unconstitutional as a bill of attainder. *United States v. Lovett* provided the following facts:

In 1943 the respondents, Lovett, Watson, and Dodd, [were employees of government agencies which] were fully satisfied with the quality of their work and wished to keep them employed on their jobs. Over the protest of those employing agencies, Congress provided in § 304 of the Urgent Deficiency Appropriation Act of 1943, [that] no salary or compensation should be paid respondents *** unless they were prior to November 15, 1943 again appointed to jobs by the President with the advice and consent of the Senate. [Despite the lack of reappointment, the agencies kept all the respondents at work on their jobs] after November 15, 1943; but their compensation was discontinued after that date. To secure compensation for this post-November 15th work, respondents [sued, arguing that § 304 was unconstitutional and void as a bill of attainder.]

The *Lovett* Court then considered if Congress, in passing Section 304, had created an unconstitutional bill of attainder. *Lovett* noted:

Our inquiry is thus confined to whether *** § 304 is a bill of attainder against these respondents, involving a use of power which the Constitution unequivocally declares Congress can never exercise. ***

In the background of the statute here challenged lies the House of Representatives' feeling in the late thirties that many "subversives" were occupying influential positions in the Government *** and that their influence must not remain unchallenged. As part of its program against "subversive" activities the House in May 1938 created a Committee on Un-American Activities, which became known as the Dies Committee, after its Chairman, Congressman Martin Dies. *** This Committee conducted a series of investigations and made lists of people and organizations it thought "subversive." *** The creation of the Dies Committee was followed by provisions *** which forbade the holding of a federal job by anyone who was a member of a political party or organization that advocated the overthrow of our constitutional form of Government in the United States. It became the practice to include a similar prohibition in all appropriations acts, together with criminal penalties for its violation. Under these provisions, the [FBI began wholesale investigations of thousands of federal employees].

While all this was happening, Mr. Dies [in a House speech] attacked thirty-nine named government employees [including the three respondents] as "irresponsible, unrepresentative, crackpot, radical bureaucrats" and affiliates of "Communist front organizations." [Dies said all thirty-nine employees were] unfit to "hold a Government position" and urged Congress to refuse "to appropriate money for their salaries." [He] proposed that the Committee on Appropriations "take immediate and vigorous steps to eliminate these people from public office." [Congress then amended the Treasury-Post Office Appropriation Bill to provide] that "no part of any appropriation contained in this act shall be used to pay the compensation of" the thirty-nine individuals Dies had attacked. *** All of those participating agreed that the "charges" against the thirty-nine individuals were serious. Some wanted to accept Congressman Dies' statements as sufficient proof of "guilt," while others referred to such proposed action as "legislative lynching," *** smacking "of the procedure in the French Chamber of Deputies, during the Reign of Terror." *** The Dies charges were referred to as "indictments," and many claimed this made it necessary that the named federal employees be given a hearing and a chance to prove themselves innocent. *** Congressman Dies then suggested that the Appropriations Committee "weigh the evidence and . . . take immediate steps to dismiss these people from the Federal service." *** The resolution which [passed authorized the Appropriations Committee investigate the allegations that the named employees were] unfit to continue in such employment by reason of their present association or membership or past association or membership in or with organizations whose aims or purposes are or have been subversive to the Government of the United States." ***

[The] Appropriations Committee held hearings in secret executive session. Those charged with "subversive" beliefs and "subversive" associations were permitted to testify, but lawyers, including those representing the agencies by which the accused were employed, were not permitted to be present. At the hearings, committee members, the committee staff, and whatever witness was under examination were the only ones present. The evidence, aside from that given by the accused employees, appears to have been largely that of reports made by the Dies Committee, its investigators, and [FBI] reports, the latter being treated as too confidential to be made public.

[The committee found respondents Watson, Dodd, and Lovett] guilty of having engaged in "subversive activity within the definition adopted by the committee" [and therefore] unfit for the present to continue in Government employment." [The committee submitted its report and Section 304 to the House.]

We hold that § 304 falls precisely within the category of congressional actions which the Constitution barred by providing that "No Bill of Attainder or ex post facto Law shall be passed." In *Cummings*, this Court said, "A bill of attainder is a legislative act which inflicts punishment without a judicial trial. [*Ex parte Garland* 4 Wall. 333] held invalid on the same grounds an Act of Congress which required attorneys practicing before this Court to take a similar oath. Neither of these cases has ever been overruled. They stand for the proposition that **legislative acts, no matter what their form, that apply either to named individuals or to easily ascertainable members of a group in such a way as to inflict punishment on them without a judicial trial are bills of attainder prohibited by the Constitution**. Adherence to this principle requires invalidation of § 304. We do adhere to it.

Section 304 was designed to apply to particular individuals [because] it "operates as a legislative decree of perpetual exclusion" from a chosen vocation. [A permanent ban on serving in government is a severe punishment.] It is a type of punishment which Congress has only invoked for special types of odious and dangerous crimes, such as treason, *** acceptance of bribes by members of Congress, *** or by other government officials, *** and interference with elections by Army and Navy officers. ***

Section 304 [punishes] named individuals without a judicial trial. The fact that the punishment is inflicted [by] cutting off the pay of certain named individuals found guilty of disloyalty, makes it no less galling or effective than if it had been done by an Act which designated the conduct as criminal. No one would think that Congress could have passed a valid law, stating that after investigation it had found Lovett, Dodd, and Watson "guilty" of the crime of engaging in "subversive activities," defined that term for the first time, and sentenced them to perpetual exclusion from any government employment. Section 304, while it does not use that language, accomplishes that result. The effect was to inflict punishment without the safeguards of a judicial trial and "determined by no previous law or fixed rule." The Constitution declares that that cannot be done either by a State or by the United States. ***

Those who wrote our Constitution well knew the danger inherent in special legislative acts which take away the life, liberty, or property of particular named persons because the legislature thinks them guilty of conduct which deserves punishment. They intended to safeguard the people of this country from punishment without trial by duly constituted courts. *** And even the courts to which this important function was entrusted were commanded to stay their hands until and unless certain tested safeguards were observed. An accused in court must be tried by an impartial jury, has a right to be represented by counsel, he must be clearly informed of the charge against him, the law which he is charged with violating must have been passed before he committed the act charged, he must be confronted by the witnesses against him, he must not be compelled to incriminate himself, he cannot twice be put in jeopardy for the same offense, and even after conviction no cruel and unusual punishment can be inflicted upon him. *** When our Constitution and Bill of Rights were written, our ancestors had ample reason to know that legislative trials and punishments were too dangerous to liberty to exist in the nation of free men they envisioned. And so they proscribed bills of attainder. Section 304 is one. ***

Section 304 therefore does not stand as an obstacle to payment of compensation to Lovett, Watson, and Dodd. ***

Learn from My (and Others') Mistakes

Avoid Saying, "I am a D.A. and I can do whatever I want!"

Our training deputy explained to our recruitment class the reason new deputy D.A.'s had to wait a year before receiving their badges by telling a story about a deputy D.A. who abused the power of her position while still in her probationary year. The D.A. went out drinking one night at a local bar. Feeling the effects of alcohol, she accidentally dropped her engagement ring down the sink drain when washing her hands. She told the restaurant manager to immediately have the plumbing dug up to retrieve her ring. When the manager politely refused, suggesting a plumber could come out the next day, the D.A. flashed her badge and shouted, "I demand you get that ring back now! I am a D.A. and I can do whatever I want!" The next day she learned that she was no longer a D.A. and that she could not do whatever she wanted.

5.   Double Jeopardy

Is Charging a Defendant for Murder When the Victim Died after the Defendant Already Served a Prison Term for Assault for the Same Act a Violation of the Protection against Double Jeopardy?

Ian Urbina reported on September 19, 2007, in the *New York Times* article, "New Murder Charge in '66 Shooting," that new charges were filed forty-one years after the original incident.

According to his sister, the victim, as a result of being shot, lived a life of pure "agony." Besides double jeopardy, a host of issues also arise regarding whether Barnes' shooting actually caused the death of the officer, who had suffered two car accidents and a hepatitis infection after the shooting.

The full article can be viewed at:

http://www.nytimes.com/2007/09/19/us/19philadelphia.html?pagewanted=all&_r=0

In an article in "Philly Mag," on December 22, 2009, entitled, "William Barnes Profile: This Man Shot a Cop In a case that may change how we think of justice, the D.A. wants him to go to jail for it. Again," it was reported that double jeopardy did not apply.

The full article can be viewed at:

http://www.phillymag.com/articles/william-barnes-profile-this-man-shot-a-cop/10/

What if an arsonist, intending to burn only one apartment room, set a fire that actually burned down three apartment rooms? Would it be **double jeopardy** to convict him of and sentence him to three arsons? Did he suffer **multiple punishments for the same offense** in violation of the Double Jeopardy Clause to the Constitution?

The following case involves a double jeopardy issue about arson.

LEGAL ANALYSIS

Richmond v. State
604 A.2d 483 (1992).
Justice Karwacki delivered the opinion of the Court of Appeals of Maryland.

Facts

On February 5, 1987, a fire broke out in a two story apartment building [containing] ten units. The fire originated in the ground floor apartment of Martha Gobert and quickly spread to the apartment located across a common hallway, occupied by Wanda Pfeiffer, and to the apartment located above the Gobert unit, occupied by Evelyn Saunders. All three apartment units were substantially damaged [by the fire].

An official investigation of the fire disclosed that Guy L. Richmond, Jr., the appellant, had arranged for three of his confederates to set fire to Gobert's apartment. Richmond and Gobert worked for the same employer, and Richmond recently had been suspended from his job because of a work place grievance filed against him by Gobert.

On October 19, 1987, *** Richmond was convicted of three separate counts of an indictment, charging violation of Maryland Code ***Article 27, § 6 1 for procuring the burning of the "dwelling houses" of Gobert, Pfeiffer, and Saunders. [He] was sentenced to 15 years imprisonment on each count with the terms to run consecutively.

[Article 27, § 6 provides:

"Any person who willfully and maliciously sets fire to or burns or causes to be burned or who aids, counsels or procures the burning of any dwelling house, or any kitchen, shop, barn, stable or other outhouse that is parcel thereof, or belonging to or adjoining thereto, whether the property of himself, or of another, shall be guilty of arson, and upon conviction thereof, be sentenced to the penitentiary for not more than thirty years."]

[Richmond argued that his sentences for three separate arsons from one act violated the Double Jeopardy Clause because he had multiple sentences imposed upon him for what he asserts was a single offense.]

Issue

Whether charging a person who has burned three residences of an apartment building by setting one fire violates the protection against double jeopardy.

Rule and Analysis

Richmond contends that the burning of three apartments was the result of one criminal act, [and so is] one offense proscribed by Art. 27, § 6, and that the imposition of multiple sentences for this one offense violates double jeopardy principles. **The Double Jeopardy Clause of the Fifth Amendment protects against a second prosecution for the same offense after acquittal, a second prosecution for the same offense after conviction, and multiple punishments for the same offense.** [Richmond's argument] deals with the prohibition against multiple punishments for the same offense. Multiple punishment challenges generally arise in two different sets of circumstances: those involving two separate statutes embracing the same criminal conduct, and those involving a single statute creating multiple units of prosecution for conduct occurring as a part of the same criminal transaction. *** Richmond's contention in the instant case is of the second type. ***

Whether a particular course of conduct constitutes one or more violations of a single statutory offense depends upon the appropriate unit of prosecution of the offense and this is ordinarily determined by reference to legislative intent. ***

[In seeking] legislative intent, "we look first to the words of the statute. *** [The statute's language shows that the legislature] intended the unit of prosecution to be "any dwelling house" burned. The issue before us is not thereby resolved, however, because the term "dwelling house" is not defined in the statute; we must determine whether each individual apartment unit burned constitutes a separate dwelling house. ***

Maryland has retained the common law definition of arson [which defines arson as] an offense against the security of habitation or occupancy, rather than against ownership or property. *** Expounding on what constitutes a "dwelling house," Blackstone stated that "if a landlord...sets fire to his own house, of which another is in possession under a lease from himself or from those whose estate he hath, it shall be accounted arson; for, during the lease, the house is the property of the tenant." **[Since] each leased apartment is the property of a separate tenant, and a burning of that property, whether by the landlord or some other individual, constitutes arson, each separate apartment burned constitutes a separate unit of prosecution.** ***

[Each individual apartment burned constitutes a separate dwelling house and a separate arson offense because the statute states that "Any person who willfully and maliciously sets fire to or burns ... *any* dwelling house" shall be guilty of arson.] We have previously construed the use of the word "any" in a criminal statute to mean "every." [In the earlier case,] *Brown*, the issue was whether the defendant could be sentenced for multiple counts of use of a handgun in the commission of a crime of violence arising out of a single robbery involving several victims. The statute [in that case stated] that "[a]ny person who shall use a handgun . . . in the commission of *any* felony or *any* crime of violence" is guilty of a handgun use offense. We held that the use of the word "any" before crime of violence meant "every" and indicated that the unit of prosecution was the crime of violence, not the criminal transaction. *** Thus, **where there were two victims, there were two crimes** of violence and two separate crimes of using a handgun to commit a crime of violence. Similarly, in the instant case, the use of the word "any" before the phrase "dwelling house" indicates that the Legislature intended the unit of prosecution to be each dwelling house burned. ***

[When] a fire obviously creates an unreasonable fire hazard for other nearby dwellings, and any of these is actually burned, common-law arson has been committed even if the wrongdoer did not actually intend the consequence and may have hoped it would not happen. ["On the principle that a man is presumed to have intended the natural and probable consequences of his voluntary acts, if a man does an unlawful act, the natural tendency of which is to set fire to and burn a house, and such a consequence follows, the burning is to be regarded as intentional and malicious."]

Conclusion

Providing for multiple punishments when there are multiple victims also [fits] with the notion that the punishment for criminal conduct should be commensurate with responsibility. *** **It makes sense that the Legislature would provide for a greater penalty for setting fire to an apartment building, containing many separate residences, than for setting fire to a single home. The language of the statute clearly reflects the legislative intention that the unit of prosecution be each dwelling house burned. Each of the separate apartments in the building, occupied by separate tenants, constituted a separate dwelling house. Thus, each apartment burning was a separate offense of arson.** ***

Judgments affirmed.[8]

F.   THE GAMBLE OF A JURY TRIAL

The criminal justice system is only as good as those who participate in it, and such people are only human. This is true of some of the most powerful people in a trial, the jury. While lawyers will laud juries in court as holding the collective wisdom of centuries, behind jurors' backs, attorneys speak of taking a case to a jury trial as if they were taking their life savings to a casino. The sad fact is that jurors too often return verdicts that confuse not only lawyers, judges, and defendants, but also the jurors themselves. The following U.S. Supreme Court case considers what courts should do with **inconsistent jury verdicts in the context of double jeopardy**, the issue just discussed in Part E. above.

LEGAL ANALYSIS

Bravo-Fernandez v. United States
137 S.Ct. 352 (2016).
Justice Ginsburg delivered the opinion of the court.

Facts

[Juan Bravo–Fernandez (Bravo), an entrepreneur, allegedly bribed Hector Martínez–Maldonado (Martínez), a senator of Puerto Rico.] The alleged bribe took the form of an all-expenses-paid trip to Las Vegas, including a $1,000 seat at a professional boxing match featuring a popular Puerto Rican contender. [The Government argued that Bravo intended the bribe to secure Martínez' help with legislation in the Puerto Rico Senate that, if enacted, would give Bravo's business "financial benefits."

A grand jury indicted Bravo for bribery and conspiracy to commit bribery. A jury convicted Bravo and Martínez of the standalone bribery offense, but acquitted them of the related conspiracy charge.

The Court of Appeals vacated the bribery convictions for an instructional error unrelated to the issue in this case.]

---

8. Reprinted with the permission of LexisNexis.

Issue

Whether, on retrial after an appellate court has "vacated" (rendered void) a bribery conviction, Double Jeopardy's "issue-preclusion" rule prevents prosecution for bribery when a jury already acquitted the defendants of conspiracy to commit bribery.

Rule and Analysis

This case concerns the "issue-preclusion" component of the Double Jeopardy Clause. ["**Issue-preclusion" means that "when an issue has once been determined by a valid and final judgment, that issue cannot again be litigated between the same parties in any future lawsuit."**]

[Issue preclusion applies when a jury returns inconsistent verdicts, convicting on one count and acquitting on another count, where both counts turn on the very same issue. In such a case, both verdicts stand. Double Jeopardy prevents the Government from challenging the acquittal. But, because the verdicts are irreconcilable, the acquittal does not preclude, or prevent, a retrial on the vacated conviction.]

[Here, the jury returned irreconcilably inconsistent verdicts of conviction and acquittal.] There could be no retrial of charges that yielded acquittals but, in view of the inconsistent verdicts, the acquittals would have no issue-preclusive effect on charges that yielded convictions. [But,] the guilty verdicts were vacated on appeal because of error in the judge's instructions unrelated to the verdicts' inconsistency. [Bravo and Martinez argue that the acquittal should prevent retrying them on the count voided on appeal.]

We hold otherwise.

[The principle of issue preclusion was considered in *Ashe v. Swenson,* which involved a robbery of six poker players by a group of masked men.] Ashe was charged with robbing one of the players, but a jury acquitted him "due to insufficient evidence". *** The State then tried Ashe again, this time for robbing another of the poker players. Aided by "substantially stronger" testimony from "witnesses [who] were for the most part the same," the State secured a conviction. [*Ashe*] held that the second prosecution violated the Double Jeopardy Clause. Because the sole issue in dispute in the first trial was whether Ashe had been one of the robbers, the jury's acquittal verdict precluded the State from trying to convince a different jury of that very same fact in a second trial.

[The defendant carries the burden to show that the issue whose re-litigation he seeks to stop was actually decided by a prior jury's verdict of acquittal. *United States v. Powell* held that a defendant cannot meet this burden when the same jury returns irreconcilably inconsistent verdicts on the question she seeks to shield from reconsideration. A jury had acquitted Powell of some drug charges but convicted her of using a telephone in "causing and facilitating" those same offenses. *** She appealed, arguing that "the verdicts were inconsistent, and that she therefore was entitled to reversal of the telephone facilitation convictions" because issue preclusion barred "acceptance of the guilty verdicts" on these offenses because the same jury had acquitted her of the drug felonies.]

Rejecting Powell's argument, we noted that **issue preclusion is "predicated on the assumption that the jury acted rationally."** [When a jury returns irreconcilably inconsistent verdicts,] one can glean no more than that "**either in the acquittal or the conviction the jury did not speak their real conclusions.**" [When a jury hands down inconsistent verdicts,] it is just as likely that "the jury, convinced of guilt, properly reached its conclusion on [one count], and then through mistake, compromise, or lenity, arrived at an inconsistent conclusion on the [related] offense." Because a court would be at a loss to know which verdict the jury "really meant," [principles of issue preclusion are not useful. *Powell* held] that the acquittals had no preclusive effect on the counts of conviction, and so Powell's convictions and her acquittals, albeit inconsistent, remained undisturbed. ***

When a conviction is overturned on appeal, [the Double Jeopardy Clause generally does not bar re-prosecution." Bravo and Martínez ask us to deviate from this general rule. They argue that when a conviction is vacated on appeal, an acquittal simultaneously returned should stop the Government from retrying the defendant on the vacated conviction. Here, the jury convicted Bravo and Martínez of bribery but acquitted them of conspiring to commit bribery. These convictions and acquittals are irreconcilable.] It is unknowable "which of the inconsistent verdicts—the acquittal[s] or the conviction[s]—'the jury really meant.'

["The problem is that the same jury reached inconsistent results."] The convictions' later invalidation on an unrelated ground does not erase or reconcile that inconsistency: It does not bear on "the factual determinations actually and necessarily made by the jury." ***

Conclusion

[We hold that Double Jeopardy's issue preclusion rule does not prevent a retrial on the vacated conviction that was inconsistent with an acquittal on a separate count having the same issue.]

Affirmed.

DISCUSSION QUESTIONS

1. What is the purpose of criminal law?

2. How is blameworthiness relevant to criminal law?

3. What is so important about the Rule of Legality?

4. What are the four rationales for imposing punishment on a criminal? Are they fulfilled by our current forms of punishment?

5. What are the differences that distinguish crimes from torts?

6. What are the stages of legal analysis?

7. What is an element of a crime?

8. What is the common law and why is it important?

9. Does case law generally come from trial courts or appellate courts? Why?

10. What is the Model Penal Code and why is it important?

11. Why does the U.S. Constitution forbid vague laws?

12. What are *ex post facto* laws and bills of attainder?

13. What are the dangers of holding a person twice in jeopardy in violation of the double jeopardy prohibition?

WEB LINKS

1. To fully view *Blackstone's Commentaries on the Laws of England*, visit: http://avalon.law.yale.edu/subject_menus/blackstone.asp

2. To view Paul H. Robinson and Markus Dirk Dubber, *An Introduction to the Model Penal Code*," visit: https://www.law.upenn.edu/fac/phrobins/intromodpencode.pdf

3. For the *FindLaw* article, "The Differences between a Criminal Case and a Civil Case" visit: http://criminal.findlaw.com/criminal-law-basics/the-differences-between-a-criminal-case-and-a-civil-case.html#sthash.wpftsKWH.dpuf

4. Delaware's "Pattern Criminal Jury Instructions" for "2.6 Presumption of Innocence/Reasonable Doubt" can be seen at 2.6 on page 12 of: http://courts.delaware.gov/superior/pattern/pdfs/pattern_criminal_jury_rev4_2016.pdf

5. Delaware's "Pattern Criminal Jury Instructions" for "2.8 Defendant's Choice Not to Testify" can be seen at 2.8 on page 14 of: http://courts.delaware.gov/superior/pattern/pdfs/pattern_criminal_jury_rev4_2016.pdf

CHAPTER II

"Actus Reus" or Criminal Act: The Mandatory Element for All Crime

A. WHAT IS MEANT BY CRIMINAL ACT OR "ACTUS REUS"?

1. Definition of "Actus Reus"

You slap someone in the face. The person's eyes water as his or her face stings and flushes red. Have you committed a criminal act? You have willingly moved your arm muscles and aimed to hit another person. The victim suffers pain and emotional upset, and so your act has harmful results. What if, however, you slapped the person in order to kill a malaria-infected mosquito before it bit the victim, or you slapped someone to wake him or her from a potentially fatal carbon monoxide-induced stupor? What precisely is a **criminal act** and what must accompany an act for it to be considered an element of crime?

An "actus reus" is a criminal act. A criminal act is a person's outward, objective, physical movement (or lack of movement when there is a legal duty to do something). **In most crimes, actus reus must occur with mens rea**, or criminal intent—the inward, subjective, mental aspect of crime.

Criminal Acts must be wrongful. Is every face slap a wrongful act?

33

2.   A Required Element for All Crime

Do you ever have a less than noble thought? Does such an evil intent alone make a person a criminal? Wayne LaFave explained in *Criminal Law*, "To wish an enemy dead, to contemplate the forcible ravishment of a woman, to think about taking another's wallet—such thoughts constitute none of the existing crimes (not murder or rape or larceny) so long as the thoughts produce no action to bring about the wished-for results." **Thoughts alone, no matter how evil or heinous, are not a crime.**

Why is this so? Several reasons have been offered. First, there is the practical problem of proof. If we were to prosecute a person for simply having evil thoughts, how would we go about proving the offense? Remember, all guilt would stem from merely thinking guilty, so no guilty actions would need to occur. Many thinking crimes could happen without any outward signs of a violation of the law—no movement, words, or behavior whatsoever. A prosecutor would have a difficult time convincing a jury beyond a reasonable doubt of an evil thought's existence, particularly if the defendant took the stand to deny any evil thinking. Having a crime on the books that could not be proven and therefore not enforced would undermine the legitimacy of the law.

Second, such prosecutions could come with terrible public costs. We pride ourselves on being a society of free thought and therefore avoiding George Orwell's *1984*, where committing a "thought crime" allowed the State to send any offender for torture in "Room 101." In trying to remove all evil from each individual's mind, we would be creating evil in the greater society.

Third, there is a genuine question of whether evil thoughts, by themselves, are dangerous or even undesirable. Perhaps being allowed to silently fantasize about killing your boss as he or she is berating you is not only not bad, but actually a positive good. It could offer people a safety valve through which to blow off the steam that otherwise could fester into violence.

Actus reus—the criminal act, is an essential element for all crime; without it, crime simply does not—cannot—occur. So what, exactly is required to commit a criminal act?

First, one need not break a sweat. Such small movements as injecting a drug by pushing the syringe, moving one's lips, tongue, and mouth in forming an agreement, moving one's eyes in being a lookout, or pulling a trigger in a killing, all can suffice. In certain circumstances, even *failing* to act can be a criminal act. **Any act, however, big or small, must first be guided by the will.**

3.   Volitional Act Requirement

The Model Penal Code, in Section 1.13(2), defines an "act" or "action" as "a bodily movement whether voluntary or involuntary." While this simple definition might be enough to describe an "act," it is not enough to tell us what is a "criminal act" or actus reus. The crucial missing ingredient is the will.

Yesterday and Today

The Common Law recognized that involuntary acts are neither blameworthy nor praiseworthy. Blackstone, in his *Commentaries*, Vol. IV, required that every act must be voluntary in order to be deemed criminal. He stated:

> An involuntary act, as it has no claim to merit, so neither can it induce any guilt: the concurrence of the will, when it has its choice either to do or to avoid the fact in question, being the only thing that renders human actions either praiseworthy or culpable.

Centuries later, Section 2.01 of the Model Penal Code shows that voluntariness is still a necessary ingredient of a criminal act.

The Model Penal Code: Section 2.01. Requirement of Voluntary Act; Omission as a Basis of Liability:

1. A person is not guilty of an offense unless his liability is based on conduct which includes a voluntary act or the omission to perform an act of which he is physically capable.

2. The Following are not voluntary acts within the meaning of this section:

    (a) a reflex or convulsion;

    (b) a bodily movement during unconsciousness or sleep;

    (c) conduct during hypnosis or resulting from hypnotic suggestion;

    (d) a bodily movement that otherwise is not a product of the effort or determination of the actor, either conscious or habitual.

In Texas, Vernon's Texas Statutes and Codes Annotated (V.T.C.A.) Penal Code § 6.01 "Requirement of Voluntary Act or Omission" states:

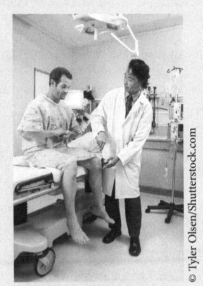

As noted below, the knee reflex is an example of a muscle contraction that is not an actus reus.

© Tyler Olsen/Shutterstock.com

    (a) A person commits an offense only if he voluntarily engages in conduct, including an act, an omission, or possession.

In California, Penal Code § 26: "Persons capable of committing crime; exceptions" provides:

All persons are capable of committing crimes except those belonging to the following classes:

Four—Persons who committed the act charged without being conscious thereof.

In criminal law, **an actus reus must be voluntary, "volitional," or guided by the will**. A stumble, spasm, or sneeze occurs without voluntary control, and therefore cannot be a "criminal act." Yet, what actually makes an act "voluntary"? Is it the existence of a *choice* to commit or refuse to do an act?

In *State v. Eaton*, 168 Wn.2d 476; 229 P.3d 704 (2010), police arrested Thomas Harry Eaton for driving under the influence. Once at the jail, police searched Eaton and found a small bag of methamphetamine taped to his sock. The State charged Eaton not only with DUI and possession of methamphetamine, but also included a *sentencing enhancement* for "possessing a controlled substance in a jail or prison." Did Eaton *voluntarily* possess an illegal drug within an "enhancement zone" when it was the police who forcibly moved him to this location? In purposely taping the meth into his sock, Eaton certainly committed a willful act. Further, once inside the jail, he tried to hide the meth, causing police to tackle him in order to recover the illicit substance. Eaton's presence in the prohibited area of the jail, however, was not by his own choice.

Eaton explained why an act, in order to be deemed criminal, must be voluntary:

Fundamental to our notion of an ordered society is that people are punished only for their own conduct. Where an individual has taken no volitional action, she is not generally subject to criminal liability as punishment would not serve to further any of the legitimate goals of the criminal law. We punish people for what they do, not for what others do to them. We do not punish those who do not have the capacity to choose. Where the individual has not voluntarily acted, punishment will not deter the consequences.

Eaton quoted Oliver Wendell Holmes in noting, "**Movements must be willed; a spasm is not an act.**" The Court continued,

[It is] and unjust to make a man answerable for harm, unless he might have chosen o therwise . . . [The choice to act] must be made with a chance of contemplating the consequence complained of, or else it has no bearing on responsibility for that consequence.

A person cannot be held responsible for a consequence unless she could have done something to avoid it. The law required that "a defendant took some voluntary act to be placed within the enhanced zone in order to subject the defendant to an enhanced sentence." Since here such a voluntary act was lacking, so was the justification for any enhancement.

The *Eaton* Court might have oversimplified the case. Eaton, after all, did have a choice that could have prevented his being in possession of contraband inside the jail. First, he could have refrained from possessing an illegal drug in his sock. Putting drugs in your clothing increases the risk that your person will be arrested and therefore ultimately placed in jail. Or, having chosen to possess the meth, Eaton could have simply warned the officers as they placed him in the police car that he held meth in his sock. While exposing himself to possession liability, he could have avoided the extra punishment stemming from the enhancement. Putting aside the *Miranda* rights issue, this last choice presented to Eaton returns us to the issue of the actual meaning of involuntariness.

Can a person be unconscious while at the same time seeming to be awake? The person in such a state is operating much as a robot or automaton, and therefore his or her condition has been called "automatism." **Generally, actions committed while suffering automatism are involuntary and thus automatism usually can be a complete defense**.

Can you relate to this person? Not all unconscious persons appear to be unconscious. Many of those who do appear unconscious are my readers.

Is a Reflex an Act? The Kick You Give Your Doctor after She Hits Your Knee with a Hammer

Ever wonder why a routine part of an annual physical involves a doctor striking the patient's knee? Esther Inglis-Arkell, in her article "Here's why doctors always whack you in the knee—no, it's not what you think," at: http://io9.com/5858178/heres-why-doctors-always-whack-you-in-the-knee-++-no-its-not-what-you-think, explains the mechanics of this test: "The hit to the knee causes the thigh muscle to stretch. This stretch sends a signal along a sensory neuron to the spinal cord where it interacts directly with a motor neuron which goes to the thigh muscle. The muscle contracts and the leg kicks." During the entire process of this reflex, "[t]he brain never gets involved." A YouTube video provides a demonstration of this medical exam at: http://www.youtube.com/watch?v=qpw31bvoLpg. So, what if your doctor unwisely stands in front of you when performing this test, causing your knee to "kick" your trusted physician? Have you assaulted your doctor? Have you even performed anything that could be called an "act"?

Tips for Success for Future Law Enforcement

You Need Not Be a Saint to Be Hired as a Police Officer

The facts that can disqualify persons from joining law enforcement might seem many and harsh, but no one has to be perfect to become an officer or deputy. Law enforcement agencies are aware that people make mistakes, particularly when they are young. Some agencies have "washout" periods of several years over which prior mistakes will lose their relevance to what a candidate can currently offer an employer. The key error to avoid is lying about your past. This not only usually fails to hide the bad act, but also makes whatever bad behavior occurred more troublesome because it is compounded by the dishonesty of the current lie and makes the old problem become a new one due to the recent falsehood.

Typically fewer factors exist to disqualify those considering law school, although state bars do run background checks to ensure the morality of those wishing to join the profession. Prison inmates, however, have been known to become lawyers, being inspired to do so from their experience in the system.

Even though, in certain circumstances, unconsciousness prevents conscious or voluntarily action, not all unconsciousness relieves a person of criminal liability. Whether unconsciousness will operate as a defense will turn on the *way in which a person became unconscious* in the first place. A person can become unconscious in two ways: voluntarily and involuntarily. **Voluntary unconsciousness is generally not a valid defense,** for the criminal defendant is at fault for knowingly placing him or herself either in a situation where he or she will likely become unconscious (such as purposely drinking alcohol until suffering a blackout) or where dangers can occur to others due to their being unconscious (such as driving for so long without sleep that when the driver falls asleep at the wheel, the essentially driverless car collides with others). In contrast, **involuntary unconsciousness is a valid defense**, for the defendant is not at fault for losing consciousness, and in fact is a victim of circumstances. Such unconsciousness can occur, for example, if a person unknowingly drinks a punch that has been secretly spiked with a narcotic. As will be seen below, unconsciousness can occur due to a variety of situations.

a) Involuntariness Due to Medical Condition

What if a person chooses to drive despite knowing he or she suffers from a medical condition that causes sudden loss of unconsciousness? Suppose further that, while driving, this person loses consciousness, causing the essentially driverless car to kill pedestrians. Would this **unconsciousness** be **voluntary** or **involuntary**? What would be the **legal consequences** of labeling the unconsciousness as "voluntary" or "involuntary"?

Voluntary unconsciousness is generally not a valid defense.

LEGAL ANALYSIS

People v. Decina
138 N.E. 2d 799 (1956).
Judge Froessel, of the New York Court of Appeals (the highest court in the state),
wrote the majority opinion.

Facts

[On a bright and sunny afternoon on March 14, 1955, the defendant was driving his car when suddenly it swerved to the left, across the centerline in the street, so that it was completely in the south lane, traveling 35 to 40 miles per hour. The car then veered sharply to the right, mounting the curb and moving at about 50 or 60 miles per hour.

Defendant's car struck a group of six schoolgirls as they walked on the sidewalk, propelling some of the bodies of the children onto the street and a lawn.] Three of the children, 6 to 12 years old, were found dead on arrival by the medical examiner, and a fourth child, 7 years old, died in a hospital two days later as a result of injuries sustained in the accident.

After striking the children, defendant's car continued on . . . striking and breaking a metal lamppost. With its horn blowing steadily—apparently because defendant was "stooped over" the steering wheel—the car proceeded on the sidewalk until it finally crashed through a 7 1/4-inch brick wall of a grocery store, injuring at least one customer and causing considerable property damage.

When the car came to a halt in the store, with its horn still blowing, several fires had been ignited. Defendant was stooped over in the car and was "bobbing a little." To one witness he appeared dazed, to another unconscious, lying back with his hands off the wheel. Various people present shouted to defendant to turn off the ignition of his car, and "within a matter of seconds the horn stopped blowing and the car did shut off."

Defendant was pulled out of the car by a number of bystanders and laid down on the sidewalk. To a policeman who came on the scene shortly he appeared "injured, dazed"; another witness said that "he looked as though he was knocked out..." An injured customer in the store, after receiving first aid, pressed defendant for an explanation of the accident and he told her: "I blacked out from the bridge." ***

Defendant [told] Dr. Wechter his past medical history, namely, that at the age of 7 he was struck by an auto and suffered a marked loss of hearing. In 1946 he was treated in this same hospital for an illness during which he had some convulsions. Several burr holes were made in his skull and a brain abscess was drained. Following this operation defendant had no convulsions from 1946 through 1950. In 1950 he had four convulsions, caused by scar tissue on the brain. From 1950 to 1954 he experienced about 10 or 20 seizures a year, in which his right hand would jump although he remained fully conscious. In 1954, he had 4 or 5 generalized seizures with loss of consciousness, the last being *** a few months before the accident. Thereafter he had more hospitalization, a spinal tap, consultation with a neurologist, and took medication daily to help prevent seizures.

On the basis of this medical history, Dr. Wechter made a diagnosis of Jacksonian epilepsy, [concluding] that defendant had a seizure at the time of the accident. . . . The testimony of Dr. Wechter [shows] that defendant had epilepsy, suffered an attack at the time of the accident, and had knowledge of his susceptibility to such attacks. ***

Issue

In choosing to drive a car, knowing that he was subject to epileptic seizures that would cause unconsciousness, did the defendant commit a voluntary act in driving the car?

Rule and Analysis

The indictment states essentially that defendant, *knowing* "that he was subject to epileptic attacks or other disorder rendering him likely to lose consciousness for a considerable period of time", was culpably negligent "in that he *consciously* undertook to and *did operate* his Buick sedan on a public highway"... and "while so doing" suffered such an attack which caused said automobile "to travel at a fast and reckless rate of speed, jumping the curb and driving over the sidewalk" causing the death of 4 persons. [T]his clearly states a violation of section 1053-a of the Penal Law. The statute does not require that a defendant must deliberately intend to kill a human being, for that would be murder. Nor does the statute require that he knowingly and consciously follow the precise path that leads to death and destruction. It is sufficient *** when his conduct manifests a "disregard of the consequences which may ensue from the act, and indifference to the rights of others. ***

[T]**his defendant knew he was subject to epileptic attacks and seizures that might strike** *at any time*. He also knew that a moving motor vehicle uncontrolled on a public highway is a highly dangerous instrumentality capable of unrestrained destruction. With this *knowledge*, and without anyone accompanying him, he deliberately took a chance by making a conscious choice of a course of action, in disregard of the consequences which he knew might follow from his conscious act, and which in this case did ensue. ***

His awareness of a condition which he knows may produce such consequences as here, and his disregard of the consequences, renders him liable for culpable negligence *** To have a sudden sleeping spell, an unexpected heart or other disabling attack, without any prior knowledge or warning thereof, is an altogether different situation . . . and there is simply no basis for comparing such cases with the flagrant disregard manifested here.

Conclusion

Since the defendant "deliberately took a chance" by choosing to drive, "in disregard of the consequences which he knew might follow from his conscious act," his resulting driving, even while physically unconscious, legally amounts to a voluntary act.[9]

The *Decina* court based criminal liability not on the fact that a person suffered from epilepsy, but on *how a person behaved knowing he had a condition that could cause unconsciousness at any moment.* Decina handled this risk by still choosing to drive even though he knew his car could become a driverless deadly weapon.

Emily Grant, in *While You Were Sleeping or Addicted: A Suggested Expansion of the Automatism Doctrine to Include an Addiction Defense*, 2000 U. Ill. L. Rev. 997 (2000), has identified many conditions that can cause "automatism," that state where we can be up and moving around as if we are in control of our actions when, in fact, we are unconscious automatons, committing actions not guided by our own will. Among the medical problems Grant cited were a panic attack from riding in an enclosed vehicle, hypoglycemia due to low blood sugar, brain injury, cerebral tumor, and carbon monoxide poisoning. Shouldn't persons who choose to drive knowing they risk such conditions occurring while driving be responsible for the foreseeable consequences of a driverless vehicle?

LEGAL SKILLS: How to Negotiate a Case for Plea Bargaining

I joined the Los Angeles District Attorney's Office to do jury trials. So, I had no real incentive to plead a case assigned to me for trial. I consistently stuck to the terms my boss, a Grade IV deputy district attorney with over a decade of experience in the office, gave me for taking a guilty plea. If, however, the defense attorney gave me genuinely new information, I would discuss it with my boss.

In plea bargaining, each lawyer makes a prediction about how his or her witnesses and evidence will impact a jury. The prosecutor and defense counsel argue over the strength of their case ("The victim will not even bother to show up" or "Your client will fall apart on the stand."). I myself simply did not say much. If the defendant was interested in a plea bargain, he or she could make the pitch.

If there was a genuine problem with the case, then the matter can be taken all the way up the chain of command to the Grade V deputy or even further. As always, the plea decision comes down to ensuring justice is done in the individual case. True justice does not mean maximizing punishment in every case—instead, the merits of the case, the defendant's future, the concerns of the victims, and the impact on society have to be weighed.

---

b) Involuntariness Due to Physical Injury

Suppose that someone who started a fight with you knocked you out. In this state of unconsciousness, you committed an act that, if you were awake, would be illegal. Could you argue in your defense that you suffered **involuntary unconsciousness** that **prevented you from committing a criminal act**? What if **you were the one who started** the fight?

---

9. Reprinted with the permission of LexisNexis.

LEGAL ANALYSIS

People v. Newton
8 Cal. App. 3d 359, 87 Cal. Rptr. 394 (1970).
Justice Rattigan, of the California Court of Appeal, wrote the unanimous opinion for the Court.

Facts

[A jury convicted Huey P. Newton of the voluntary manslaughter of Officer John Frey on October 28, 1967. Officer Frey stopped a "known Black Panther vehicle" in Oakland, California. Officer Heanes, hearing the radio call, went to the location. When Heanes asked defendant to get out of the car, Newton asked, "if there was any particular reason why he should." Heanes asked him "if there was any reason why he didn't want to." The defendant then exited and walked, "rather briskly" to the rear of the police cars. Frey followed.

Heanes then saw the defendant assume a shooting stance and heard a gunshot. As Heanes drew and raised his own gun in his right hand, a bullet struck his right forearm. Heanes saw Officer Frey and Newton wrestling on the trunk of his car (the third car in line). He next remembered being on his knees at the front door of Frey's (the second) car. Frey was "hanging onto" the defendant. Now holding his gun in his left hand, Heanes aimed at defendant and fired "at his midsection." Heanes then heard other gunshots from the area where Frey and the defendant were tussling. In actuality, Heanes fired another shot, and was himself shot two more times. He did not remember these events, testifying that he "blacked out," and had a "lapse of memory," after being shot in the arm.

Henry Grier, a bus driver, testified that when driving his empty bus, he saw three vehicles, two of which were police cars with flashing lights, parked on the curb. He then saw an officer and a "civilian" walk toward his bus. The officer was holding the civilian "sort of tugged under the arm." The third man in the street was another police officer, who was walking in the same direction about "ten paces" behind. The civilian pulled a gun from inside his shirt and "spun around."] The two struggled, and "the gun went off." The officer walking behind them "was hit and he fell"; after he was hit, he drew his gun and fired. [T]he first officer and the civilian were struggling near the front door of the bus and within a few feet of Grier. He saw the civilian, standing "sort of in a crouched position," fire several shots into the first officer as the latter was falling forward. These shots were fired from *** a distance of "four or five feet" from the midsection of the officer's body; the last one was fired "in the direction of his back" as he lay, face down, on the ground. [Grier reported] on the bus radio, "Get help, a police officer is being shot. Shots are flying everywhere; get help. Help, quick." [Grier positively identified defendant at trial as the "civilian" mentioned in his account of the shootings.]

Defendant arrived at the emergency desk of Kaiser Hospital at 5:50 a.m. on the same morning. He asked to see a doctor, stating "I have been shot in the stomach." A nurse called the police, [who arrived and arrested Newton. The defendant] had a bullet wound in his abdomen. The bullet had entered in the front and exited through the back of his body.

Officers Frey and Heanes were taken to Merritt Hospital, where Frey was dead on arrival. He had been shot five times. *** Officer Heanes had three bullet wounds: one in his right arm, one in the left knee, one in the chest. ***

Defendant, testifying in his own behalf, denied killing Officer Frey, shooting Officer Heanes, or carrying a gun on the morning of the shootings. [He testified that while driving a Volkswagen, he was pulled over by the police. When Officer Frey approached, he] said "Well, well, well, what do we have? The great, great Huey P. Newton." Frey asked for defendant's driver's license [which the defendant handed over.]

[After Officer Heanes arrived, Officer Frey] ordered defendant out of the car. He got out. [Officer Frey] ordered defendant to lean against the car. Frey then searched him, placing his hands inside defendant's trousers and touching his genitals. (Officer Heanes had testified that defendant was not searched at any time.) ***

Seizing defendant's left arm with his right hand, Officer Frey told him to go back to his patrol car. [Defendant said,] "You have no reasonable cause to arrest me." The officer [responded with a racial slur and striking the] defendant in the face, dazing him. Defendant stumbled backwards and fell to one knee. Officer Frey drew a revolver. Defendant felt a "sensation like . . . boiling hot soup had been spilled on my stomach," and heard an "explosion," then a "volley of shots." He remembered *** nothing else until he found himself at the entrance of Kaiser Hospital with no knowledge of how he arrived there. He expressly testified that he was "unconscious or semiconscious" during this interval, that he was "still only semiconscious" at the hospital entrance.

[The defense doctor testified that defendant's recollections were "compatible" with the gunshot wound he had received. A gunshot wound which penetrated into the abdominal or thoracic cavity could produce a "profound reflex shock reaction," resulting in loss of consciousness "for short periods of time up to half an hour or so."]

Issue

Should the jury have been instructed on the unconsciousness defense based on the defendant suffering a gunshot to his abdomen?

Rule and Analysis

Defendant asserts [the trial court should have instructed the jury on *unconsciousness* as a defense to a charge of criminal homicide. ***

Although the evidence of the fatal affray is both conflicting and confused as to who shot whom and when, some of it supported the inference that defendant had been shot in the abdomen before he fired any shots himself. [This sequence, along with the nature of the abdominal wound, supported the] inference that defendant was in a state of unconsciousness when Officer Frey was shot.

[Defendant's testimony suggested that Officer Frey wounded him with the first shot fired. However, the absence of powder deposits on his (defendant's) clothing would indicate that Officer Heanes, not Frey, shot him. Grier's testimony was explicit as to this sequence: i.e., that Heanes, struck by the first bullet fired, shot at defendant before the latter commenced firing at Frey . . . Heanes' account, while less precise on this subject . . . also supports the inference that he shot defendant (in the "midsection") before Officer Frey was shot by anyone.]

Where not self-induced, * unconsciousness is a complete defense to a charge of criminal homicide. ["Unconsciousness" need not reach the physical dimensions commonly associated with the term** (coma, inertia, incapability of locomotion or manual action, and so on); **it can exist**—and the above-stated rule can apply—**where the subject physically acts in fact but is not, at the time, conscious of acting.**] As was true of Officer Heanes, according to his testimony . . . during part of the shooting episode in the present case. Penal Code section 26 provides *** that "**All persons are capable of committing crimes except those belonging to the following classes: . . . Five-Persons who committed the act charged without being conscious thereof.**"

Where evidence of involuntary unconsciousness has been produced in a homicide prosecution, the refusal of a requested instruction on the subject . . . is prejudicial error. *** The fact . . . that such evidence does not inspire belief does not authorize the failure to instruct: "However incredible the testimony of a defendant may be he is entitled to an instruction based upon the hypothesis that it is entirely true." *** It follows that the evidence of defendant's unconsciousness in the present case was "deserving of consideration" upon a material issue. ***

Conclusion

[**We hold that the trial court should have given unconsciousness instructions, and that its failure to do so was prejudicial error because the omission deprived defendant of his "constitutional right to have the jury determine every material issue presented by the evidence.**]

The judgment of conviction is reversed.[10]

Questions

Who shot first? The answer to this question has legal significance. If the defendant Newton had fired the first shot, then he initiated the shootout. Being the aggressor causes any resulting unconsciousness (due to being shot) to be deemed "voluntary" because starting the fight places the defendant at fault for it. The defendant, as the first to resort to violence, would then have no "unconsciousness" defense. If instead one of the officers was the first to fire his weapon, then Newton's unconsciousness from the resulting "reflex shock reaction" would be deemed involuntary and thus a valid basis for a defense against the claim of performing a criminal act.

Note that Justice Rattigan offers no opinion that the defendant did indeed suffer unconsciousness, instead noting only that even if defendant's testimony "does not inspire belief," he was entitled to have the jury hear the instruction regarding involuntary unconsciousness. Before Newton's testimony can be dismissed, however, it must be remembered that Officer Heanes also testified that he himself suffered unconsciousness due to his own gunshot wound.

One relevant rule for unconsciousness asks, "Who started the fight that led to unconsciousness?

© Sarah Jessup/Shutterstock.com

Have You Ever Taken Ambien? Sleeping Pills and Other Sleep Dangers

If you rely on Ambien at times to fall asleep, Stephanie Saul writing for *The New York Times* on March 14, 2006 in her article, "Study Links Ambien Use to Unconscious Food Forays," at: http://www.nytimes.com/2006/03/14/health/14sleep.html offers news that could keep you up at night. Saul noted that Ambien releases a "primitive desire to eat" in some people that causes them to essentially sleep eat. Some Ambien users wake up the next morning with the circumstantial evidence of feasting on midnight snacks.

Sleeping might involve even greater risks having nothing to do with sleep aids. David Schwartz, in his article, "Man gets life for 'sleepwalking' murder," January 10, 2000, *Iol News*, at http://www.iol.co.za/news/world/man-gets-life-for-sleepwalking-murder-1.25487#.Uydj9K1dVfU, described one man in Phoenix, Arizona, who claimed to be sleepwalking when stabbing his wife forty-four times with a hunting knife, dragging her to the family swimming pool and holding her head underwater, changing his clothes, and hiding his weapon inside a plastic wrapper and placing it in the wheel well of his car. Dubious, the jury convicted him in spite of his sleepwalking claims.

---

10. Reprinted with the permission of LexisNexis.

Sleep Texting?

Breeanna Hare of *CNN* reported on February 22, 2013, in her article, "Don't recall sending that message? Maybe you're 'sleep texting'" that sleep-texting is a different kind of messaging mishap.

For video and full article, visit:

http://www.cnn.com/2013/02/22/tech/mobile/sleep-texting/

© offstocker/Shutterstock.com

Who really sleepwalks like this? As an involuntary form of unconsciousness, sleepwalking can be a valid defense.

Further reporting on this issue can be viewed in "Sleeptexting Is the New Sleepwalking: The line is blurring between wakefulness and sleep," an October 16, 2013, article in *The Atlantic* by Kayleigh Roberts at:

http://www.theatlantic.com/health/archive/2013/10/sleeptexting-is-the-new-sleepwalking/280591/

Do's and Don'ts for Hearings, Trials, and Appeals

D.A. Investigation Before and During Trial

Do take a D.A. investigator with you to interview witnesses. **Don't** go alone. With an investigator, you have someone you can later put up on the stand to testify regarding what the witness said to you in the field. Without the investigator, you are left with the unappealing prospect of placing yourself on the stand and becoming a witness in your own case. **Do** bring subpoena so you can have the investigator immediately serve the witness.

VIDEO: The Unlikely Friendship of Political Polar Opposites: Justices Ginsburg and Scalia

U.S. Supreme Court Justices Ruth Bader Ginsburg and Antonin Scalia discuss their unlikely close friendship despite differing on the law at:

https://www.youtube.com/watch?v=b-Gwg8t7j3s

Ruth Bader Ginsburg gave a eulogy at Justice Scalia's funeral, which can be seen at:

https://www.youtube.com/watch?v=jb_2GgE564A

Who Was the Driver and Who the Involuntary Passenger?
The Curious Case of Jennifer or Robin Grimsley

A judge, after a bench trial, convicted Ms. Grimsley of driving under the influence. Her blood alcohol, measured by the old-fashioned "intoxilyzer," was at 0.21 percent. The defendant challenged her conviction, and actually won a reversal for being erroneously denied a jury trial. One of her other claims of error was less successful, for she urged that she was not guilty due to her suffering "multiple personality disorder"—a condition now known as dissociative identity disorder.

As the Court of Appeals of Ohio noted in *State v. Grimsley*, 3 Ohio App. 3d 265 (1982),

> Appellant contends that she cannot be held liable for any offense because at the time of the offense she was dissociated from her primary personality (Robin) and in the state of consciousness of a secondary personality (Jennifer). She contends that she was not acting either consciously or voluntarily. [The Ohio statue provides] that a person who acts unconsciously and without volition, acts involuntarily and cannot be guilty of any offense.

> Appellant's contention is based on [her being diagnosed with] having a multiple personality disorder, meeting the following criteria: (1) she is dominated *** by two or more separate personalities; (2) the personality who is "in consciousness," or dominant, at any particular time controls her behavior; (3) the transition from one personality to another is involuntary, sudden, and generally without warning; and (4) each personality has unique characteristics, including behavior patterns, memories and social associations. She [argues that], psychological trauma (report of a lump on her breast) caused her to dissociate into the personality of Jennifer, who is impulsive, angry, fearful, [anxious, and alcoholic. Appellant] contends that when she is Jennifer, Robin is unaware of what is going on, has no control over Jennifer's actions, and no memory of what Jennifer did later on when she is restored to the primary personality of Robin. ***

> Appellant [argues] it was error to hold her legally responsible because being Jennifer on the day in question, Robin was not conscious of what was happening and lacked voluntary control over Jennifer's actions. This is not an insanity defense but a claim that appellant cannot be found guilty because during the commission of the offense, her acts were beyond the control of her primary personality and were therefore involuntary.

The Court was not convinced, dispatching defendant's argument quite neatly as follows:

> We disagree. Assuming *arguendo* that the evidence was sufficient to establish such a complete break between appellant's consciousness as Robin and her consciousness as Jennifer that Jennifer alone was in control (despite years of therapy), nevertheless the evidence fails to establish the fact that Jennifer was either unconscious or acting involuntarily. **There was only one person driving the car and only one person accused of drunken driving. It is immaterial whether she was in one state of consciousness or another, so long as in the personality then controlling her behavior, she was conscious and her actions were a product of her own volition.** The evidence failed to demonstrate that Jennifer was unconscious or otherwise acting involuntarily.[11]

Today, such a defense would run into even bigger problems. The very existence of dissociative identity disorder (DID) is now being called into question. An article that offers insight into this controversy, written by Dr. Charles Raison on February 23, 2010, for *CNNs Expert Q&A* can be visited at:

http://www.cnn.com/2010/HEALTH/expert.q.a/02/23/dissociative.identity.disorder.raison/index.html

---

11. Reprinted with the permission of Ohio courts.

4. Failure to Act: Omission

Suppose you are sunbathing on an empty beach. Suddenly, you see a drowning person who desperately calls out for your help. As a vigorous swimmer who would only have to wade a few feet to save the drowning person, you could easily save this person's life. You instead shake your head and callously watch the person drown. Are you a criminal? What if instead you were a lifeguard duty-bound by your employment contract to save anyone who was drowning in this part of the ocean?

The law recognizes **two kinds of criminal acts**: 1) **commissions** and 2) **omissions. A commission is an affirmative act where a criminal actually does something, such as contracting a muscle or burning a calorie**. Commissions are what most people think of when they envision a criminal act. In contrast, **an omission is the failure to act when one has a legal duty to do something**. A legal duty, however, is not equivalent to a moral duty. If a person fails to act in the face of a *moral* duty, he or she is merely a bad person. If the same person fails to act in the face of a *legal* duty, he or she is a criminal.

a) Duty Based on Relationship

A failure to act, known as an **"omission,"** only creates criminal liability when the person failing to act has a **legal duty to act** under the circumstances. One legal duty which can create criminal liability for an omission is a **parent's duty to care for his or her child**. Can a man be found guilty of child neglect for failing to get a child to a doctor even **when he is not the child's father or legal guardian**? Consider how the court below analyzed the common law doctrine of *in loco parentis* in deciding whether a man is guilty of neglect when a child **he invited to live in his home** dies.

Parents have a legal duty, based on relationship, to care for their children.

LEGAL ANALYSIS

State v. Sherman
266 S.W.3d 395 (2008).
Judge Wade wrote the opinion for the Supreme Court of Tennessee.

Facts

[In 2001, the defendant, Ariel Ben Sherman, moved to Tennessee and conducted "Universal Life Church" religious services. He allowed eight of his parishioners to move into his home, including Jacqueline Crank ("Crank"), her daughter Jessica Crank ("Jessica"). Jessica's father had died in 1995.]

The defendant and Crank took Jessica, then fourteen, to a chiropractor to examine Jessica's enlarged right shoulder. The chiropractor, expressing concern about Jessica's condition, recommended that she be examined at the University of Tennessee Medical Center. Jessica did not go to the hospital, and, instead, she was taken to Physician's Care, a walk-in clinic, [where] she was not treated by a specialist. According to the Defendant, Crank did not have adequate health insurance to pay for Jessica's medical care, and, in consequence, the church initiated an effort to raise the funds necessary to pay for future tests on her shoulder. In September of 2002, however, Jessica died of Ewing's Sarcoma, a type of bone cancer most commonly found in young people under twenty years of age.

*** A grand jury indicted [the defendant and Crank of] child abuse and child neglect, *** charging that the two had knowingly treated Jessica "in such a manner as to inflict injury or neglect . . . so as to adversely affect the child's health and welfare." ***

The actions that the State alleges constitute the offense in question are the failure by either defendant to pursue the medical evaluations and treatments recommended by the Chiropractor and the persons at Physician's Care. [Crank clearly] stood in a parental relationship with the victim. With regard to defendant Sherman, it is the State's position that he repeatedly *held himself out as her father and one of her caretakers*, thereby creating a duty on his part as well . . . The Defendant [argued] that because he had no legal or special duty to provide care for Jessica, he could not be held criminally liable for her death. ***

[The Defendant had no marital relationship with Crank. The trial judge dismissed the case because the Defendant was neither a parent, a stepparent, nor a legal guardian to Jessica.]

Issue

Whether a person standing in loco parentis to a child might have a legal duty of care, the breach of which may result in criminal culpability.

Rule and Analysis

At the time of Jessica's death, the legislation governing child abuse and neglect provided as follows:

> (a) Any person who knowingly, other than by accidental means, treats a child under eighteen (18) years of age in such a manner as to inflict injury or neglects such a child so as to adversely affect the child's health and welfare commits a *** misdemeanor [Tenn. Code Ann. § 39-15-401(a)].

[Neglect] is composed of three essential elements: (1) a person knowingly must neglect a child; (2) the child's age must be within the applicable range set forth in the statute; and (3) the neglect must adversely affect the child's health and welfare. *** The first element is at issue in this case. In order to establish neglect, the State must first prove that a defendant owes a legal duty to the child.

***In order to be found guilty of a criminal omission, one must have knowledge of the circumstances that give rise to the duty. *** "One cannot be said in any manner to neglect or refuse to perform a duty unless he has knowledge of the condition of things which require performance at his hands." *** **A defendant's duty to act must arise from a legal duty; a mere moral obligation will not suffice** [One commentator has identified six sources of legal duties in the criminal context]: (1) duty based on relationship; (2) duty based on statute; (3) duty arising from contract; (3) duty arising from a voluntary assumption of care; (4) duty to control others; (5) duty arising from creation of peril; and (6) duty of landowner. [Usually, a legal duty comes] from a relationship with a child victim. ***

[We will use the rules of the juvenile courts and the Department of Children's Services to interpret the child neglect criminal statute here. The] "primary purpose of these statutes, like that of the criminal child abuse statute, is to prevent acts of child neglect and to protect and care for children who are victims of neglect." *** In juvenile proceedings, a "dependent and *neglected child*" is one "[w]hose *parent, guardian or custodian* neglects or refuses to provide necessary medical, surgical, institutional or hospital care for such child." [Since] the Defendant was neither the parent nor legal guardian of the victim, the precise issue is whether the term "custodian" applics. Λ "custodian" is dcfincd as "a person, other than a parent or legal guardian, *who stands in loco parentis to the child* or a person to whom temporary legal custody of the child has been given by order of a court." *** "'**Where one is in loco parentis the rights, duties, and liabilities of such person are the same as those of the lawful parent.**'" *** We hold, therefore, that our criminal code envisions that **a person standing in loco parentis to a child may be subject to criminal liability for child neglect.** ***

["In loco parentis" is **Latin** for **"in the place of a parent."** Someone who is "in loco parentis" to a child assumes the traditional obligations of a parent without a formal adoption, and so takes on the full responsibilities of a parent.

The key element for determining the criminal liabilities of "in loco parentis" is one of intent. **Whether someone assumes in loco parentis "depends on whether that person *intends* to assume that obligation.**] A fact-finder may infer intent from circumstantial evidence. ***While not exclusive, some facts to consider when determining whether a person had the intent to establish an in loco parentis relationship may include the child's age, the child's dependence upon the person claimed to be in loco parentis, and whether that person supports the child and exercises the duties and obligations of a natural parent. ***

[The] only relevant undisputed facts in this case were that the Defendant was not the biological parent of Jessica Clark, not her legal guardian, and not married to her mother. This is simply not enough information to warrant a dismissal of the indictment. The State may present other circumstances that might establish a duty on the part of the Defendant arising out of an in loco parentis relationship. The Defendant's relationship with the mother may be circumstantial evidence of duty, but the ultimate question is the nature and degree of the Defendant's relationship with Jessica. In theory, the State might be able to establish that the Defendant failed to perform a statutory duty to provide adequate medical care for the child. [We hold that the trial court erred by granting the Defendant's motion to dismiss.]

Conclusion

A person who is *in loco parentis* to a child may have a duty of care, the violation of which may warrant criminal penalties.[12]

Question

Codefendant Crank offered a different argument for her failure to seek medical attention for her daughter. In her motion to dismiss, Crank claimed that she had lawfully chosen "spiritual treatment as opposed to taking her child" for traditional medical services and specifically cited Tennessee Code Annotated section 39-15-402(c), which provides, in part, as follows:

> Nothing in this chapter shall be construed to mean a child is neglected, abused, or abused or neglected in an aggravated manner for the sole reason the child is being provided treatment by spiritual means through prayer alone in accordance with the tenets or practices of a recognized church or religious denomination by a duly accredited practitioner thereof in lieu of medical or surgical treatment.

Is such an argument convincing?

---

12. Reprinted with the permission of LexisNexis.

Is Faith Healing a Valid Defense for the Omission of Providing Medical Care?

In the *Washington Post*, Amanda Murphy reported on February 19, 2014, in her article, "Pennsylvania parents sentenced in second faith-healing death," that a Pentecostal couple was sentenced to prison for neglecting to take their sick son to the doctor.

Read the full story here:

http://www.washingtonpost.com/national/religion/pennsylvania-parents-sentenced-in-second-faith-healing-death/2014/02/19/e7f24b8a-99b2-11e3-b1de-e666d78c3937_story.html

Yesterday and Today: Criminalizing the Failure to Act

Failing to act in the face of a legal duty has created criminal liability since the times of Common Law. William Blackstone noted: "A crime . . . is an act committed, or omitted, in violation of public law, either forbidding, or commanding it."

The Model Penal Code likewise condemns omissions in defiance of duty. In Section 2.01(1), the code, in pertinent part, provides:

> A person is not guilty of an offense unless his liability is based on conduct which includes a voluntary act or the omission to perform an act of which he is physically capable.

***

> (3) Liability for the commission of an offense may not be based on an omission unaccompanied by action unless:
>
> (a) the omission is expressly made sufficient by the law defining the offense; or
>
> (b) a duty to perform the omitted act is otherwise imposed by law.[13]

In Texas, Vernon's Texas Statutes and Codes Annotated (V.T.C.A.) Penal Code § 6.01 Requirement of Voluntary Act or Omission states:

> (c) A person who omits to perform an act does not commit an offense unless a law *** provides that the omission is an offense or otherwise provides that he has a duty to perform the act.

---

13. From *The Model Penal Code* by the American Law Institute. Copyright © 1962 by the American Law Institute. Used by permission.

Learn from My (and Others') Mistakes

Deputy D.A.'s Should Always Perform Field Investigations with D.A. Investigators

As a new deputy district attorney, I once investigated a crime scene at MacArthur Park in Los Angeles, California, without having a D.A. investigator accompany me. Walking through the park being the only person wearing a suit and tie, I took photos of a location of a prior drug deal. Suddenly, persons took offense to my taking pictures and started running toward me. They pursued me as I sprinted to my car. I was just able to escape by recklessly pulling away and darting into traffic. My mistake was foolish for two reasons: (1) A D.A. investigator always arms him or herself with a gun when going into the field to protect the D.A., and (2) The photos I took could not be entered into evidence without some witness besides myself authenticating them—a task that could easily be performed by a D.A. investigator who could take the witness stand.

VIDEO: Regarding Infant Abandonment

What if a woman is not aware that she is pregnant until thirty minutes before the birth of her child? Is such a thing even possible? What legal duties does she owe the newborn?
   Here is "A personal perspective on infant abandonment" on YouTube at

http://www.youtube.com/watch?v=RLntJXH8YgA.

Failing Our Most Vulnerable Victims:
of Roaches and "Babysitting" Pit Bulls

In *Jones v. United States*, 308 F.2d 307 (1962), gas company collectors entering Mary Jones' basement came upon a two-year-old and a ten-month-old child for which Jones had taken custody from an unwed mother. The eldest boy, Robert Lee Green, was inside a "crib" consisting of a wooden frame covered with wire screening. Robert Lee's crib was lined with newspaper stained by his feces and crawling with cockroaches. Anthony Lee Green, the ten-month-old, boy, weighing just over half the weight of a normally-fed baby his age, looked like a "small baby monkey." Malnourished and suffering severe diaper rash, he later died of malnutrition despite the authorities' best efforts.
   In a separate case, *CBS News* staff reported in an article entitled, "Pit bull left to 'babysit' 10-month-old child, Fla man arrested" on December 6, 2012, that prosecutors charged James Irvine with child neglect for allegedly leaving a baby with a pit bull when he went out drinking. The full article can be seen at:

http://www.cbsnews.com/8301-504083_162-57557534-504083/pit-bull-left-to-babysit-10-month-old-child-fla-man-arrested/

The omissions, or failures to act, in both of these cases, are clear and reprehensible. But are they criminal? In order to graduate from merely a bad person to a criminal, one must have a legal duty to act.

VIDEO: Should It Be a Crime to Neglect a Patient in a Hospital Room Who Possibly Dies of Neglect?

The YouTube video, "Video Shows Woman Dying on NY Hospital Floor," demonstrates the consequences of such neglect.

http://www.youtube.com/watch?v=9IKUwBCIBzA

Further, *Newsweek* reported on the details of this story in *Newsweek* July 21, 2008, Jeneen Interlandi, "The Woman Who Died in the Waiting Room: Instead of helping her, they ignored her. The story behind the videotape that shocked the country."

These media present the case of Esmin Elizabeth Green dying in a waiting room of a Brooklyn psychiatric hospital.

---

b) Duty Arising from Creation of Peril

Suppose, while hunting, you shoot a person because you mistook him for a deer. What happens if you essentially **leave the shooting victim in the woods** instead of staying and rendering the needed medical aid or calling for an ambulance? What if you are not the shooter, but you caused the victim to **detrimentally rely on a promise** that you would get an ambulance? The case below considers the **legal duties** of **creating peril** for a victim and **voluntarily assuming the duty of care of another and then placing the victim in a worse situation**.

Unfortunately, the victim of a hunting accident in the case below did not receive the needed first aid that this accident victim is getting.

© riopatuca/Shutterstock.com

LEGAL ANALYSIS

Flippo v. State
523 S.W.2d 390 (1975).
Justice Holt authored the opinion for the Supreme Court of Arkansas.

Facts

A jury found appellants guilty of involuntary manslaughter. ***

The appellants, Robert L. Flippo, Jr., and Robert M. Flippo, are respectively father and son. The father drove his son, Bobby, and the son's teenage friend, Terry Dunlap, to a field to look for deer tracks. Mr. Flippo stopped the truck in the field and the two youths got out. Bobby took [a new 30.06 rifle with him.] After walking about 150 yards, Bobby raised the rifle, which was equipped with a telescopic sight, and fired once thinking he saw a deer. The weather conditions impaired visibility since it was overcast and approaching nightfall.

*** Bobby returned to the truck and expressed his belief that he had killed a deer which he heard "bay." Terry, however, said he heard three small caliber rifle shots, which were later determined to be distress signals. *** Bobby convinced his father to return to the scene and search for the deer. Bobby and Terry found Roy Ralph Sharp ***. The victim was conscious and asking for help. He was a "big man," weighing 225 pounds, and he left leg was "almost off at the hip." He had "drug" himself approximately twenty paces out of the woods. Bobby administered no first aid although there was evidence that he had won a "National 4-H Safetyman" award based upon his knowledge of "all aspects of safety." He and Terry ran to a nearby residence, which happened to be the residence of the victim's 72 year old father. There they told Mr. Sharp that they had found a person who was wounded. The boys returned to the Flippo truck where they told Mr. Flippo about the accident. Bobby then told his father that Mr. Sharp was going to follow them back to the scene of the accident. When they arrived near the scene, Mr. Flippo and Bobby told Mr. Sharp that they were going to call an ambulance. Bobby gave Mr. Sharp directions as to the location of the victim. There was no offer of assistance to Mr. Sharp in removing the victim in one of the trucks for medical aid. After they had left, Mr. Sharp found the victim and then learned that he was his son. He asked his father to get assistance. Mr. Sharp told him "[S]on, some folks have gone to call an ambulance. You lay right still and it will be here in just a few minutes."

The Flippos left and drove to the Flippo home which was twelve or fourteen miles away. Mr. Flippo, who was told by Terry that the victim's leg was nearly severed, drove past numerous houses, some of which had telephones, and a cafe, which was only 2.3 miles from the wounded man. The cafe was open and an outside public telephone was plainly visible. Mr. Flippo stopped once at a residence to use a phone at Bobby's suggestion and when the motor almost stopped, they continued on to the Flippo residence where they were certain there would not be a party line. "[T]here was conversation about removing the rifle from the truck so nobody would know we had the rifle and was hunting out of season." At Mr. Flippo's direction, after reaching the residence, Bobby and Terry switched the high powered rifle and another rifle from the truck to a "shack" for a shotgun, which was placed on the gun rack in the truck. Then, Mr. Flippo called an ambulance which met him approximately 25 minutes later at the cafe, which he had passed en route to his residence. While Mr. Flippo waited at the restaurant for the ambulance, Terry and Bobby returned in the Flippo truck to the scene where they assisted Mr. Sharp in placing his son in the Sharp truck. A short distance down the road, they met the ambulance to which the victim was transferred. It appears Roy Sharp died either shortly before or after he was placed in the ambulance.

After giving up on the Flippos, Mr. Sharp left his son in the field and found someone at a nearby residence, who then had a neighbor call an ambulance. Mr. Sharp was only away from his son about four minutes. He further testified that from the time he found his son and Bobby and Terry returned, it was about forty minutes to an hour and fifteen minutes.

A pathologist testified that the victim bled to death, and it is possible that the victim "could have been saved" if he had been hospitalized while still conscious. He testified there were other things that could have possibly saved his life: i.e., "the quicker you get a person in the better their chances of living"; "if a shirt or anything had been put around the body, the thigh, above that point that would have stopped the bleeding." It was his opinion "[T]hat had proper treatment been initiated immediately at the site, he could have been saved."

Issues

1. **Is the son, Robert M. Flippo, guilty of omission for failing to act in the face of the legal duty arising out of creating a peril?**
2. **Is the father, Robert L. Flippo, Jr., guilty of omission for failing to act in the face of a legal duty arising from voluntary assumption of duty?**

Rule and Analysis

Ark. Stat. Ann. § 41-2209 (Repl. 1964), which defines involuntary manslaughter, reads:

> If the killing be in the commission of an unlawful act, without malice, and without the means calculated to produce death, or in the prosecution of a lawful act, done without due caution and circumspection, it shall be manslaughter.

In a prior case, the court affirmed a manslaughter conviction where a hunter fired at what he thought was a bear. There the shooter was not sure of his target. [There is substantial evidence] from which the jury could find that Bobby, who was hunting out of season, was criminally negligent by acting without due caution and circumspection when he fired at an object he mistakenly believed to be a deer and then failed, as charged, to discharge his duty *** to render aid.

A more difficult question is presented with respect to Mr. Flippo. *** In this case, Bobby, a college student who is knowledgeable in gun safety, cannot be said to have been within his father's control. Neither did Mr. Flippo acquiesce in the culpable manner in which Bobby fired. Bobby was out of and away from the truck. However, *** Mr. Flippo and his son had a duty to render aid to the wounded man, upon discovering him, and failed to do so causing death. "**For criminal liability to be based upon a failure to act it must be found that there was a duty to act—a legal duty and not simply a moral duty.**" ***

> **There are at least four situations in which the failure to act may constitute breach of legal duty. One can be held criminally liable**: first, where a statute imposes a duty to care for another; second, where one stands in a certain status relationship to another; third, where one has assumed a contractual duty to care for another; and fourth, *where one has voluntarily assumed the care of another and so secluded the helpless person as to prevent others from rendering aid.* ***

Mr. Flippo assured the victim's elderly father that he would call for an ambulance. The father kept vigil and delayed seeking assistance in the belief assistance would be procured promptly by appellants. In the meantime the victim, known by the appellants to be seriously wounded, was bleeding to death, asking his father not to leave him after being assured assistance was forthcoming. During this time, Mr. Flippo drove twelve to fourteen miles to reach his residence although phones were in the vicinity of the shooting. A public phone, which the appellants passed, was 2.3 miles from the scene of the tragedy. Mr. Flippo was told that the victim's leg was "nearly blown off." Upon reaching his home he instructed the youths to place the rifles in a "shack" and substitute a shotgun and then used his phone to call an ambulance. According to Mr. Sharp, after waiting in vain for prompt assistance, within four minutes he was able to have someone at a nearby residence summon aid. There was medical evidence that if help had arrived sooner or if aid had been administered at the site by appellants, it was probable that the victim would have survived. **The jury could infer that Mr. Flippo's delay caused the helpless victim to be secluded in the field awaiting the promised aid and prevented or hindered others from rending timely aid.** [There] is substantial evidence from which a jury could find appellants criminally negligent.

Conclusion

1. **In mortally wounding the victim, the son, Robert M. Flippo, can be guilty of committing the actus reus of omission for failing to act in the face of the legal duty arising out of his creating a peril to the shooting victim.**

2. **In leaving a helpless victim secluded in a field after promising aid and therefore preventing others from rendering timely aid, the father, Robert L. Flippo, Jr., can be guilty of omission for failing to act in the face of a legal duty arising from voluntary assumption of duty.**

Affirmed.[14]

Biography—Police

Leroy David ("Lee") Baca

- Born in East Los Angeles, Baca started at the bottom as a deputy in the Los Angeles Sheriff's Department.
- According to Shelby Grad of the *Los Angeles Times* in "The rise and fall of Lee Baca, L.A. County's onetime 'Teflon Sheriff,'" http://www.latimes.com/local/lanow/la-me-baca-story-20170315-story.html, Baca was widely considered a reformer who "required his deputies to memorize a pledge to fight against racism, sexism and homophobia."
- Baca discovered that an inmate was using a cellphone (considered contraband in jail) to report on beatings occurring in the jail.
- According to prosecutors, Baca responded by interfering with a federal investigation and attempting to discover the focus of the federal investigation.
- A jury **convicted** Baca of: (1) **Obstruction of justice**, (2) Conspiracy to obstruct justice, and (3) making a false statement to federal investigators (FBI).
- Was sentenced to three years in federal prison at age seventy-four.

---

c)   Duty Arising from Statute

LEGAL ANALYSIS

May v. State
295 Ga. 388 (2014).
Justice Blackwell delivered the opinion for the Supreme Court of Georgia.

Facts

Kristin Lynn May was employed as a teacher at River Ridge High School, a public secondary school in the Cherokee County School District. In January 2011, May spoke with a former student—P.M., then sixteen years of age—who no longer was enrolled as a student at River Ridge ***. As they spoke, P.M. disclosed that she previously had a sexual relationship with Robert Leslie Morrow, a paraprofessional at River Ridge. *** May, however, did not make any report of the sexual abuse.

When these circumstances later came to the attention of law enforcement, May was charged by accusation with a criminal violation of [Georgia statute, OCGA Section 19-7-5]. In pertinent part, the accusation alleged that May:

---

14. Reprinted with the permission of LexisNexis.

[I]n Cherokee County, Georgia, in January 2011, did unlawfully then and there commit the offense of FAILURE TO REPORT CHILD ABUSE, by being a school teacher, a mandatory reporter within the meaning [of the statute], and knowingly and willfully failing to report a case of suspected child abuse, to wit, sexual abuse, against a student, [P.M.]

[The defendant argued that she committed no crime.] Because P.M. was not then enrolled at River Ridge, May argued, she had no duty *** to make a report.

Issue

Whether the defendant had a mandatory duty to report sexual abuse of a student that she only learned about after the student was no longer enrolled at defendant's school.

Rule and Analysis

[When] we consider the meaning of a statute, we must presume that the General Assembly meant what it said and said what it meant. *** To this end, "we must read the statutory text in its most natural and reasonable way, as an ordinary speaker of the English language would." ***

[The statute states:]

> *If a person is required to report child abuse pursuant to this subsection because that person attends to a child pursuant to such person's duties as an employee of or volunteer at a hospital, school, social agency, or similar facility,* that person shall notify the person in charge of the facility. [An employee] who makes a report to the person designated pursuant to this paragraph shall be deemed to have fully complied with this subsection. [The statute] speaks of an employee or volunteer of an institutional facility having an obligation to make a report about the abuse of a child *because* she attends to that child at the facility. If [the statute] means exactly what it says—that attending to a child is the circumstance that *causes* the obligation to arise—then the obligation necessarily must be limited to children to whom a mandatory reporter attends. ***

As a general rule at common law, **"strangers . . . are under no obligation to keep watch and ward over the children of others."** *** A person who undertakes to supervise a child, whether or not for compensation, has a duty to use reasonable care to protect the child from injury." *** [Since the statute's purpose] is to protect abused children from further abuse, understanding the obligation to report as one limited to children to whom the mandatory reporter attends is consistent with the general approach of the common law.

Having identified the extent of the statutory obligation, we turn now to the facts of this case. *** **By the time May learned of the sexual abuse, P.M. no longer was her student, no longer was enrolled in the school** at which May taught, and no longer was enrolled at any school in the same school system. **In these circumstances, we cannot conceive any set of facts by which the State might prove that May— when she learned of the sexual abuse—was attending to P.M. pursuant to her duties as a school teacher at River Ridge.** ***

Conclusion

May had no legal obligation to report the sexual abuse, and the trial court erred when it sustained the accusation.

Judgment reversed.[15]

---

15. Reprinted from Westlaw, with permission of Thomson Reuters.

VIDEO: Justice Breyer Speaks about the Constitution and the Court

U.S. Supreme Court Justice Stephen Breyer discusses various matters about the Constitution, the history of the Court, and being a Supreme Court Justice at:

https://www.youtube.com/watch?v=ksuRCixAto8

Yesterday and Today: Demanding the Impossible

What if, back in 1864, you were the captain of the ship, "Charger," while she was at sea, with the responsibility to protect all the lives onboard? One of your crew, John P. Swainson, fell from the ship's mainmast into the water 110 feet below. Would you stop the ship and lower a lifeboat in order to attempt to save Swainson? Captain Knowles refused to do so, leaving the victim to die. The United States sought manslaughter charges against him for his "*omission*" or *failure to act* to save seaman Swainson.

The court, in *United States v. Knowles*, 26 F. Cas. 800 (1864), noted, **"[W]here death is the direct and immediate result of the omission of a party to perform a plain duty imposed upon him by law or contract, he is guilty of a felonious homicide."** Yet, any obligation to act must come from a *legal* duty and not merely a *moral* obligation. A person's "humanity, or his sense of justice or propriety" cannot alone create a legal obligation that triggers criminal liability for failing to act. Even though "it is undoubtedly the moral duty of every person to extend to others assistance when in danger; to throw, for instance a plank or rope to a drowning man," if a person failed to act when he had no legal duty to do so, he would, "draw upon himself the just censure and reproach of good men; but this is the only punishment to which he would be subjected by society." If an inhabitant of a nearby island could have swum to Swainson's aid and readily saved him yet callously chose not to do so, that island dweller would be morally wrong but not legally guilty.

Knowles, however, was the captain of the ship, and therefore owed a legal duty to preserve the lives of those in his charge. So Captain Knowles must have been guilty of failing his legal duty to do his best to save Swainson. Or was he? Even a legal duty has its limits. Captain Knowles claimed he was not guilty for committing an omission because Swainson was killed by his 110-foot drop into the ocean from the mainmast. **The law does not require a person to perform the impossible—the Captain could not save a dead man.** Further, Knowles offered two fallback arguments. Knowles urged that even if Swainson had somehow survived the fall, the captain still was under no legal duty to rescue him because any such effort was not humanly possible due to the severe conditions of the sea and weather. This argument was another formulation of the idea that the law cannot mandate the impossible. Finally, any attempt to save Swainson would have endangered the safety of the ship and the lives of the rest of the crew. The law could not require that a captain kill other crewmen in an effort to save one. Captain Knowles' arguments, however cold-blooded, were persuasive, for the jury returned a verdict of acquittal.

Arguing the impossibility of raising the dead in 1864 was clearly correct. It is a far cry from urging, in 2012, the impossibility of making payments when charged with the felony of failure to pay court-ordered child support. *People v. Likine*, 492 Mich. 367; 823 N.W.2d 50 (2012), however, held that actual impossibility could be a valid defense to a felony nonsupport charge.

The Supreme Court of Michigan viewed the impossibility defense for omission as the other side of the coin of involuntary commissions. The court reasoned: **"Just as a defendant cannot be held criminally liable for committing an act that he or she was powerless to prevent, so, too, a defendant cannot be held criminally liable for failing to perform an act that was genuinely *impossible* for the defendant to perform."**

Courts have accepted claims that an affirmative action a person committed was done so involuntarily, due to reflex, seizure, or sleepwalking. *Likine* noted, "The common thread running through these "involuntariness" defenses is that the act does not occur under the defendant's control, and thus the defendant was powerless to prevent its occurrence and cannot be held criminally liable for the act."

When a defendant is facing a charge of criminal omission for failing to act, he or she argues impossibility rather than involuntariness. *Likine* explained:

> Like its counterpart, involuntariness, the centuries-old defense of impossibility derives from [English common-law. For example, in 1843, an English court considered whether a defendant was liable for failing to repair a highway rendered impassable by the encroaching sea. Since every repair the defendant made was "swept away by the act of God," he could not be found guilty of failing to repair the road.]

A defendant cannot be found guilty for failing to perform an act that was genuinely *impossible* for the defendant to perform. *Likine* held, "to establish an impossibility defense for felony nonsupport, a defendant must show that he or she acted in good faith and made *all reasonable efforts* to comply with the family court order, but could not do so through no fault of his or her own." Here:

> [Defendants] charged with felony nonsupport must make *all reasonable efforts*, and use all resources at their disposal, to comply with their support obligations. For the payment of child support to be truly impossible, a defendant must explore and eliminate all the reasonably possible, lawful avenues of obtaining the revenue required to comply with the support order. Defendants must not only establish that they cannot pay, but that theirs are among the exceptional cases in which it was not reasonably *possible* to obtain the resources to pay. A defendant's failure to undertake those efforts reflects "an insufficient concern for paying the debt" one owes to one's child, which arises from the individual's responsibility as a parent.

"Seamless Web" Connection

Knowles, the 1864 case just discussed, can be connected through the seamless web to *Flippo*, the hunting accident case occurring over a century later in 1975 (and discussed earlier in this chapter). While the captain in *Knowles* argued he could not be guilty of failing to perform the impossible—saving a dead man—Robert L. Flippo, Jr., the hunter in *Flippo*, suffered no such limit on his abilities. As winner of the "National 4-H Safetyman award based upon his knowledge of all aspects of safety," he had the ability to render first aid to the victim he had shot. Unlike the helpless captain who was acquitted in *Knowles*, Flippo could be properly convicted for his failure to act.

5. Possession as an Act

How can passively possessing something be a criminal act, or any kind of act? William Blackstone, in the time of common law, might have asked the same question, for his only reference to possession occurs in his discussion of civil law. The law today answers this question by interpreting the action of possession broadly, thus finding it much more active than one might at first think.

Model Penal Code 2.01:

> (4) Possession is an act . . . if the possessor knowingly procured or received the thing possessed or was aware of his control thereof for a sufficient period to have been able to terminate his possession.

Possession is a criminal act not so much for the actual act of having an item, but also for **actively obtaining** the item **or failing to rid oneself of it**. The law might be straining here to identify possession as an act by including active behavior occurring before acquisition or the lack of behavior after obtaining an item. How can the government **prove the existence of possession?** The following case offers an example of such an issue playing out in court.

Mere possession of an object alone can amount to a criminal act.

LEGAL ANALYSIS

Hawkins v. State
89 S.W.3d 674 (2002).
Justice Radack delivered the opinion for the Texas Court of Appeals.

A jury found appellant, Clarence Edward Hawkins, guilty of unlawful possession of a firearm by a felon. [Appellant argues] the evidence is legally insufficient to support his conviction. *** We affirm.

Facts

Houston Police Officer David Thomas, [while working canine detail on January 8, 2001, saw a speeding car run red lights. When the driver of the car refused to stop, a high-speed chase ensued which only ended when Hawkins pulled into a parking lot.] Appellant got out of the car "very quickly as if he was going to run." [Hawkins only stopped and laid on the ground after Thomas warned he would release his dog.] Thomas saw, in plain view, a .410 gauge shotgun in the back seat of the car ***. The butt of the gun was pointed down towards the floor, and the barrel was pointed up towards the rear window of the back door. The gun was within reach of the driver's seat. Officer Thomas placed the gun in his trunk after removing one live round. Appellant was arrested for evading arrest and taken to the police station. When it was determined that appellant had a previous felony conviction, he was charged with possession of a firearm by a felon. ***

[Appellant] argues that the evidence is legally insufficient to support his conviction. Appellant contends that there was no attempt to take fingerprints on the gun, no attempt to "bag" his hands to determine if he had recently handled a gun, and no admission by him that the weapon belonged to him, [or that he knew it was there.] Appellant argues that the State presented no evidence to prove he exercised care, custody, control, or management over the gun.

Issue

Whether there enough evidence to support a conviction that the defendant possessed the gun found in his car.

Rule and Analysis

*** To establish unlawful possession of a firearm by a felon, the State must show that the accused was previously convicted of a felony offense and possessed a firearm after the conviction and before the fifth anniversary of his release from confinement from supervision under community supervision, parole, or mandatory supervision, whichever date is later. TEX. PEN. CODE ANN. § 46.04(a)(1). ***

Possession is a voluntary act if the possessor knowingly obtains or receives the thing possessed or is aware of his control of the thing for a sufficient time to permit him to terminate his control. *** **The State may accomplish its task by [showing] that the defendant was conscious of his connection with the thing and [knew] what it was.** *** The evidence used to satisfy these elements can be either direct or circumstantial. *** Some of the factors that may establish affirmative links to the contraband include whether: (1) the contraband was in a car driven by the accused; (2) the contraband was in a placed owned by the accused; (3) the contraband was conveniently accessible to the accused; (4) the contraband was in plain view; and (5) the contraband was found in an enclosed space. *** The number of factors present is not as important as the logical force the factors have in establishing the elements of the offense.

[The] gun, found in plain view, was in the backseat of a car driven by appellant and was within easy reach of appellant. Appellant tried to escape by evading the police during a highspeed chase. Further, appellant was the driver and sole occupant of the vehicle at the time it was stopped. Appellant's previous felony conviction was established by the introduction of a penitentiary packet into evidence.

Conclusion

We hold that this evidence was legally sufficient to support appellant's conviction for possession a firearm by a felon.

We overrule appellant's first point of error.[16]

Vernon's Texas Statutes and Codes Annotated (V.T.C.A.) Penal Code § 6.01 Requirement of Voluntary Act or Omission:

> (b) Possession is a voluntary act if the possessor knowingly obtains or receives the thing possessed or is aware of his control of the thing for a sufficient time to permit him to terminate his control.

---

16. Reprinted with the permission of LexisNexis.

6. Act as "Status" or "Condition"

Does the law punish criminals for **what they do or for who they are**? Can people be stigmatized and jailed simply because they are a certain gender, race, or ethnicity? What if the underlying condition is not one with which we are born but only occurred as the result of some act which itself was volitional and even illegal? For instance, most addicts, excepting crack babies, perform some purposeful act of ingesting a drug, while most persons, again with the exception of newborns, perform some act to become infected with a disease such as herpes, HIV, or hepatitis. Does such prior behavior expose the person now suffering from a condition to criminal liability? The courts have determined that, in both instances, imposing criminal punishment based

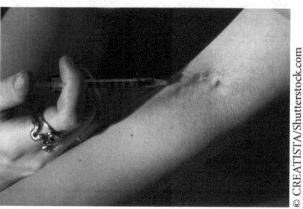

Police officers can find circumstantial evidence of use when they identify needle marks on a person's arm.

on **condition or status alone** is not a proper function of criminal law. In the following United States Supreme Court case, the justices consider if convicting a person for his or her "**status**" or "**condition**" **as a drug addict** violates the **Fourteenth Amendment** to the Constitution.

LEGAL ANALYSIS

Robinson v. California
370 U.S. 660 (1962).
Justice Stewart delivered the opinion for the United States Supreme Court.

Facts

A California statute makes it a criminal offense for a person to "be addicted to the use of narcotics." [The statute, § 11721 of the California Health and Safety Code, provides: "No person shall use, or be under the influence of, or be addicted to the use of narcotics, excepting when administered by or under the direction of a person licensed by the State to prescribe and administer narcotics . . ." This appeal questions the constitutionality of this statute.]

[At trial, Los Angeles Police Officer Brown testified that he observed "scar tissue and discoloration on the inside" of the appellant's right arm, and "numerous needle marks and a scab on the appellant's left arm.] The officer also testified that the appellant under questioning had admitted to the occasional use of narcotics. ***

Officer Lindquist testified that he had examined the appellant the following morning in the Central Jail in Los Angeles. The officer stated that [the discolorations and scabs] "were the result of the injection of hypodermic needles into the tissue into the vein that was not sterile." He stated that the scabs were several days old at the time of his examination, and that the appellant was neither under the influence of narcotics nor suffering withdrawal symptoms at the time he saw him. ***

The appellant testified in his own behalf, denying the alleged conversations with the police officers and denying that he had ever used narcotics or been addicted to their use. He explained the marks on his arms as resulting from an allergic condition contracted during his military service. His testimony was corroborated by two witnesses.

The trial judge instructed the jury that the statute made it a misdemeanor for a person *** to be addicted to the use of narcotics. *** That portion of the statute referring to 'addicted to the use' of narcotics is based upon a condition or status. *** **To be addicted to the use of narcotics is said to be a status or condition and not an act. It is a continuing offense and differs from most other offenses in the fact that [it] is chronic rather than acute. [It subjects the offender to arrest at any time before he reforms**. This chronic condition may be ascertained from a single examination.]

The judge further instructed the jury that the appellant could be convicted *** if the jury agreed *either* that he was of the "status" *or* had committed the "act" denounced by the statute. "All that the People must show is either that the defendant did use a narcotic in Los Angeles County, or that while in the City of Los Angeles he was addicted to the use of narcotics . . ." [The jury convicted the appellant.]

Issue

Whether convicting a person for his or her "status" or "condition" as a drug addict violates the Fourteenth Amendment to the Constitution.

Rule and Analysis

***There can be no question of the authority of the State in the exercise of its police power to regulate the administration, sale, prescription and use of dangerous and habit-forming drugs [A State can criminalize the unauthorized manufacture, prescription, sale, purchase, or possession of narcotics.] In the interest of discouraging the violation of such laws, or in the interest of the general health or welfare of its inhabitants, a State might establish a program of compulsory treatment, [including involuntary confinement] for those addicted to narcotics. And penal sanctions might be imposed for failure to comply with established compulsory treatment procedures. [The] range of valid choice which a State might make in this area is undoubtedly a wide one, and the wisdom of any particular choice within the allowable spectrum is not for us to decide. ***

[The judge instructed the jury that it could convict the appellant if it] found simply that the appellant's "status" or "chronic condition" was that of being "addicted to the use of narcotics." ***

This statute [is not limited to punishing] a person for the use of narcotics, for their purchase, sale or possession, or for antisocial or disorderly behavior resulting from their administration. [**This statute**] **makes the "status" of narcotic addiction a criminal offense, for which the offender may be prosecuted "at any time before he reforms."** California has said that a person can be continuously guilty of this offense, whether or not he has ever used or possessed any narcotics within the State, and whether or not he has been guilty of any antisocial behavior there.

It is unlikely that any State at this moment in history would attempt to make it a criminal offense for a person to be mentally ill, or a leper, or to be afflicted with a venereal disease. A State might determine that the general health and welfare require that the victims of these and other human afflictions be dealt with by compulsory treatment, involving quarantine, confinement, or sequestration. But *** a law which made a criminal offense of such a disease would doubtless be *** an infliction of cruel and unusual punishment in violation of the Eighth and Fourteenth Amendments.

We cannot but consider the statute before us as of the same category. [The] State recognized that **narcotic addiction is an illness**. [Thirty-seven years ago this Court recognized that persons addicted to narcotics "are diseased and proper subjects for medical treatment." Not only may addiction innocently result from the use of medically prescribed narcotics, but a person may even be a narcotics addict from the moment of his birth.] **We hold that a state law which imprisons a person thus afflicted as a criminal, even though he has never touched any narcotic drug within the State or been guilty of any irregular behavior there, inflicts a cruel and unusual punishment in violation of the Fourteenth Amendment**. *** Even one day in prison would be a cruel and unusual punishment for the "crime" of having a common cold. ***

We are not unmindful that the vicious evils of the narcotics traffic have occasioned the grave concern of government. There are, as we have said, countless fronts on which those evils may be legitimately attacked. We deal in this case only with an individual provision of a particularized local law as it has so far been interpreted by the California courts.

Conclusion

California's law, which imprisons an addict as a criminal, even though he has never touched any narcotic drug within the State or been guilty of any irregular behavior there, inflicts a cruel and unusual punishment in violation of the Fourteenth Amendment of the Constitution. *Reversed.*

Only six years later, the Supreme Court found itself having to limit the logic of *Robinson*. In *Powell v. Texas*, 392 U.S. 514 (1968), the Court was confronted with an appeal from a person convicted of intoxication in public in violation of Texas law, which read: "Whoever shall get drunk or be found in a state of intoxication in any public place, or at any private house except his own, shall be fined not exceeding one hundred dollars." Powell urged that, "his appearance in public [while drunk was] . . . not of his own volition, and therefore that to punish him criminally for that conduct would be cruel and unusual, in violation of the Eighth and Fourteenth Amendments to the United States Constitution" under the rule announced in *Robinson*.

The Court disagreed, noting,

> On its face the present case does not fall within that holding, since appellant was convicted, not for being a chronic alcoholic, but for being in public while drunk on a particular occasion. **[Texas] thus has not sought to punish a mere status, as California did in *Robinson*;** nor has it attempted to regulate appellant's behavior in the privacy of his own home. Rather, **it has imposed upon appellant a criminal sanction for public behavior which may create substantial health and safety hazards**, both for appellant and for members of the general public, and which offends the moral and esthetic sensibilities of a large segment of the community. This seems a far cry from convicting one for being an addict, being a chronic alcoholic, being "mentally ill, or a leper. . . ."

The Court worried about the logical implications of Powell's argument. Accepting the appellant's argument could have unsettling effects on criminal law, resulting in dangers to society. *Powell* warned:

> [Nothing in the logic of the defendant's argument] would limit its application to chronic alcoholics. If Leroy Powell cannot be convicted of public intoxication, it is difficult to see how a State can convict an individual for murder, if that individual, while exhibiting normal behavior in all other respects, suffers from a "compulsion" to kill, which is an "exceedingly strong influence," but "not completely overpowering." ***

> Traditional common-law concepts of personal accountability *** lead us to disagree with appellant. We are unable to conclude *** that chronic alcoholics in general, and Leroy Powell in particular, suffer from such an irresistible compulsion to drink and to get drunk in public that they are utterly unable to control their performance of either or both of these acts and thus cannot be deterred at all from public intoxication. ***

We cannot cast aside the centuries-long evolution of the collection of interlocking and overlapping concepts which the common law has utilized to assess the moral accountability of an individual for his antisocial deeds. The doctrines of *actus reus*, *mens rea*, insanity, mistake, justification, and duress have historically provided the tools for a constantly shifting adjustment of the tension between the evolving aims of the criminal law and changing religious, moral, philosophical, and medical views of the nature of man. This process of adjustment has always been thought to be the province of the States. ***

Affirmed.

While Simply Having an Illness is Not a Criminal Act, Knowingly Sharing an Illness Is

Assistant Criminal District Attorneys in Collin County, Curtis Howard and Lisa Milasky King, in an article entitled "I Love You to Death" for the Texas District and County Attorneys Association, at http://www.tdcaa.com/node/4922 offered the following:

> "The defendant's attorney referred to Philippe Padieu as a "lover" and "a modern-day Casanova." But we argued Padieu was a narcissistic predator who used his personality to attract and date several women simultaneously, ultimately infecting them with HIV. Not only did he fail to disclose his deadly secret, but he also lied to the women about his infection. In the end, 10 women from different walks of life and who had not known each other previously were forever connected by two things: They all dated Padieu and they all were infected with HIV. The courage of these women in coming forward to reveal the most intimate and sometimes embarrassing parts of their lives enabled us to bring Philippe Padieu to justice.

The successful prosecution "for aggravated assault with a deadly weapon" culminated in the jury taking "only two hours to sentence Padieu to 45 years in five cases and 25 years in one case (that being his long-term girlfriend, Barbara)." The prosecutors noted, "Because he will not be eligible for parole until he is around 75, we are very pleased with the verdict. Based on his age and the noticeable deterioration of his health, we are confident that he will never infect another woman again."

The *20/20* news report, "Women Recall HIV Criminal's Allure," on *ABC News* is available on YouTube at:

http://www.youtube.com/watch?v=Y3PA1x8JJkY

On the other hand, recall that merely suffering from an illness, even a potentially fatal one, is not itself a crime. For instance, having multi-drug-resistant tuberculosis, despite the fact that this disease can have the potential to cause devastating harm, does not constitute a criminal act. Yet, failure to maintain a course of treatment for one's own health could lead to state action that, to the infected individual, might closely resemble criminal prosecution and incarceration. An example of the severe measures that can be taken are offered in "Court-Ordered Treatment and Involuntary-Isolation Guidelines for the Control of Tuberculosis" at:

http://health.utah.gov/epi/diseases/TB/guidelines/court_ordered_treatment_tb.pdf

DISCUSSION QUESTIONS

1. What does it mean to commit an actus reus or criminal act?

2. Why are criminal acts required elements for all crimes?

3. What is the volitional act requirement and what does it mean to "voluntarily" commit an act?

4. What are the differences between voluntary and involuntary unconsciousness? Why is the difference between voluntary and involuntary unconsciousness legally important?

5. Can a person suffering unconsciousness due to a medical condition, such as epilepsy, be found to be voluntarily unconscious?

6. Can a person commit an actus reus by doing nothing?

7. What are the legal duties that can make a person a criminal for failing to act in a particular situation?

8. Can merely holding an item, such as a rock of cocaine that someone else placed in your hand, ever be considered an actus reus? Why or why not?

9. Can merely being addicted to a controlled substance be an actus reus? Why or why not?

WEB LINKS

1. Kevin Conlon and Doug Ganley of *CNN* reported on June 9, 2014, in "Police: Driver charged in Tracy Morgan crash was awake 24 hours" (Video can be viewed at: http://www.cnn.com/2014/06/09/showbiz/tracy-morgan-crash/) that: "A truck driver charged in a weekend crash that killed a man and injured comedian Tracy Morgan and others in New Jersey was awake for more than 24 consecutive hours before the incident, a criminal complaint filed in the case says. Kevin Roper, 35, is charged with vehicular homicide and assault by auto in the Saturday morning crash on the New Jersey Turnpike." Consider whether Roper suffered voluntary or involuntary unconsciousness in the case.

2. Arizona defines an "act" as meaning "a bodily movement." See: https://www.azleg.gov/ars/13/00105.htm at number 2.

3. Arizona defines "conduct" as "an act or omission and its accompanying culpable mental state." See: https://www.azleg.gov/ars/13/00105.htm at number 6.

4. Arizona defines an "omission" as "the failure to perform an act as to which a duty of performance is imposed by law." See number 28 at: https://www.azleg.gov/ars/13/00105.htm

CHAPTER III

"Mens Rea" or Criminal Intent: The Necessary Element for Most Crimes

A. WHAT IS MEANT BY CRIMINAL INTENT OR "MENS REA"?

1. Definition of "Mens Rea"

What makes a crime "criminal"? In most situations, **when a person commits a wrongful act, what makes the person a criminal**—someone who we find blameworthy and therefore truly worthy of being singled out for our collective blame—**is evil intent**. If instead someone performs a bad act only by innocent accident, ignorance, or even carelessness, most of us will at least partly empathize with that wrongdoer, thinking, "There but for the grace of God go I." But when a person intentionally acts, purposely meaning to wrong others, his or her guilty mind isolates the actor from our compassion and pity. Even members of other species know the difference between actions that are committed with evil intent and those that are not. As recognized in *Morissette v. United States*, 342 U.S. 246, 252 n. 9 (1952), "Even a dog distinguishes between being stumbled over and being kicked."

"Mens Rea" or criminal intent focuses on the criminal's mind.

Black's Law Dictionary, Ninth Edition, at 1075, defines **mens rea** as the "**guilty mind**," "**criminal intent**," or the "**state of mind that the prosecution, to secure a conviction, must prove that a defendant had when committing a crime**." This criminal intent is the element that causes the common reaction of revulsion and fear of criminals. This mental state is the focus of the punishment meted out to those who have committed crimes. **Mens rea is the second fundamental element of crime; it is required for *most* crimes**. Outside of a small class of crimes known as "strict liability" crimes that do not require an intent element, mens rea, or guilty intent, is an element of crime.

Is a Man Guilty of Bigamy When He Thinks His First Wife Divorced Him?

Congratulations! You have just married. Before you celebrate, consider the case, *People v. Vogel*, 46 Cal.2d 798 (1956), in which Robert S. Vogel found himself convicted of bigamy. Vogel first married Peggy Lambert and had two children with her. After serving in the Korean War, Vogel did not return to Peggy, who eventually took the children out of state. When Vogel later married Stelma Roberts, he was put on trial for bigamy. At trial, Vogel sought to testify that his first wife, Peggy, had told him she was going to divorce him "in a jurisdiction unknown to him so that he could not contest the custody of their children." He also offered to show that Peggy had married a new husband, Earl Heck. The trial judge rejected all of this evidence, concluding it would only show "a 'barnyard romance.'" The judge ruled that evidence showing Vogel's belief that Peggy had divorced and remarried was irrelevant.

The California Supreme Court disagreed, ruling that the "defendant is not guilty of bigamy, if he had a bona fide and reasonable belief that facts existed that left him free to remarry." The court, cited **Penal Code Section 20**, which provides, "**In every crime or public offense there must exist a union, or joint operation of act and intent, or criminal negligence**." *Vogel* declared, "As in other crimes, there must be a union of act and wrongful intent. So basic is this requirement that it is an invariable element of every crime unless excluded expressly or by necessary implication." The court also noted, "it is a universal doctrine that to constitute what the law deems a crime **there must concur both an evil act and an evil intent**."

The court explained that "guilty knowledge," which was once part of Penal Code 281 bigamy, was omitted only to shift the burden of proof. The prosecution now only has to make a "prima facie case upon proof that the second marriage was entered into while the first spouse was still living" to force the defendant to prove his "bona fide and reasonable belief that facts existed that left the defendant free to remarry." *Vogel* also reasoned, "The severe penalty imposed for bigamy, the serious loss of reputation conviction entails, the infrequency of the offense, and the fact that it has been regarded for centuries as a crime involving moral turpitude, make it extremely unlikely that the Legislature meant to include the morally innocent to make sure the guilty did not escape."

The court reversed the conviction because the trial judge did not allow the defendant to offer evidence of his belief that his first wife, Peggy, had divorced him before he chose to remarry. This deprived the defendant of "the defense of a bona fide and reasonable belief that facts existed that left him free to remarry."

Tips for Success for Future Law Enforcement

Stay Out of Hot Water by Telling the Truth

People thinking about joining law enforcement are exposing themselves to truth tests, whether polygraphs or cross-examination. So, successful careers are built by students who start their careers with the truth. A judge who taught classes at law school once told me the following joke, which has some relevance here:

A professor told her Chemistry students that they had to take the final because she would allow no makeup exams. Anyone missing the final, therefore, would receive an "incomplete" grade. Four of her students then returned so late from a Las Vegas trip that they missed the final. All four went into the professor to plead for a makeup exam, lying that their car had a flat tire on the way back into town. The professor relented, simultaneously giving each student a makeup final exam in a separate room. The exam questions were:

1. (For 10%) Describe Boyle's Law.
2. (For 90%) Specify precisely which tire on the car went flat.

2. Concurrence with Actus Reus

To commit a crime, it is not enough that there exist a criminal act and a criminal intent. The law requires **concurrence between mens rea and actus reus**—that the criminal be thinking guilty *while* he is doing guilty. Wayne LaFave, in *Criminal Law* at 341, believes the true meaning of concurrence is that the criminal's mental state "**actuate**," or **trigger**, the act or omission.

Difficulties in "concurrence" arise when a person forms a criminal intent before he acts but then abandons the intent by the time he actually commits an actus reus. The case below considers this crucial issue of **timing** and **actuation**.

In *State v. Rider,* the case below, evidence of a person's thoughts were gleaned from a damaged axe.

LEGAL ANALYSIS

State v. Rider
1 S.W. 825 (1886).
Chief Justice Henry delivered the opinion of the Supreme Court of Missouri.

Facts

[The defendant, Mart Rider, was convicted of killing R. P. Tallent, who had had a sexual relationship with the defendant's wife. On the day of the killing, Tallent had taken the defendant's wife away in a boat. The defendant therefore armed himself with a shotgun and went to Tallent's home with the intent to kill him.]

The defendant later testified that, upon meeting Tallent, "I spoke to Mr. Tallent and asked him if he knew where my wife was, and he made this remark: 'I have taken her where you won't find her'; and he says, 'God damn you, we will settle this right here.' He started at me with his axe in a striking position, and I bid Mr. Tallent to stop; then he advanced a few feet, and I fired. I fired one time."

Tallent's axe, later found on the ground, "had a shot in the handle near the end farthest from the blade, and on the same side as the blade." The condition of the axe corroborated the defendant's testimony because it showed "that the axe was pointing in the direction from which the shot came, and was held in an upright position."

Statements from the defendant's wife, Mrs. Rider, showed "that she was afraid Mart Rider would kill her." Mrs. Rider had once reported that Mart Rider "had beat her up with a club," and "she was as bloody as a hog." Mrs. Rider had said that she wanted Tallent to take her to Miami to get away from her husband.

The trial court instructed the jury that if they believed the defendant, prior to the killing, had armed himself with a gun in order to shoot or kill the victim, and then did actually, kill the victim, "then it makes no difference who commenced the assault, and the jury shall not acquit the defendant; and the jury are further instructed that in such case they shall disregard any and all testimony tending to show that the character or reputation of deceased for turbulency, violence, peace and quiet was bad, and they shall further disregard any and all evidence of threats made by deceased against the defendant."

Issue

Whether a person who initially intends to kill another person can be guilty of criminal homicide if he instead kills his initial target in self defense.

Rule and Analysis

The mere intent to commit a crime is not a crime. An attempt to perpetrate it is necessary to constitute guilt in law. One may arm himself with the purpose of seeking and killing an adversary, and may seek and find him, yet, if guilty of no overt act, commits no crime*** The above instruction authorized the jury to convict the defendant even though he had abandoned the purpose to kill the deceased when he met him, and was assaulted by deceased and had to kill him to save his own life. It does not follow because appearances would have excused deceased had he killed the accused, that the accused had no right to defend his life against the deceased, if in fact at the time he had made no assault upon the deceased and intended none. There was evidence of threats made by the deceased against the accused, and also of the turbulent and quarrelsome character of the deceased. *** **The jury had a right to consider the threats made by the deceased and his character as a turbulent, dangerous man in determining the question** as to who was the assailant, he or the defendant, and whether defendant had reasonable ground to apprehend, and did apprehend, that he was in imminent danger of sustaining great bodily harm at the hands of the deceased. ***

Conclusion

Since the judge improperly instructed the jury that it could convict the defendant even though he had abandoned the purpose to kill the deceased when he met him, the conviction must be reversed.
California Penal Code § 20. Crime; unity of act and intent, or criminal negligence:

> In every crime or public offense there must exist a union, or joint operation of act and intent, or criminal negligence.

The U.S. Supreme Court Overturned the Conviction of Arthur Andersen Due to Jury Instructions Failing to Supply a Mens Rea Requirement

According to a May 31, 2005, CNNMoney.com article entitled, "Andersen conviction overturned: Top court rules jury instructions flawed in Enron shredding case; other Enron cases to proceed," the U.S. Supreme Court overturned the conviction of the Arthur Anderson accounting firm due to inadequate jury instructions.

In this matter, the accounting firm destroyed documents. The case, *Arthur Andersen v. United States*, 544 U.S. 696 (2005), unanimously ruled that the criminal statutes defining the crime, 18 U.S.C. Section 1512(b)(2)(A) and (B) made it a crime to "knowingly . . . (and) corruptly persuad[e] another person . . . with intent to cause" the person to withhold or alter documents for use in a criminal proceeding. The court found that the statute therefore provided "knowingly" as part of the mens rea requirement. The jury instructions in the case were fatally flawed because they "simply failed to convey the requisite consciousness of wrongdoing." So, even in the most sophisticated of cases involving complex white collar crime, the basic element of mens rea can still be crucial to the entire prosecution.

The article explaining the court's ruling can be viewed at:

http://money.cnn.com/2005/05/31/news/midcaps/scandal_andersen_scotus/

The Botched Job That Is Somehow Still Completed

Imagine an attacker beating someone unconscious, intending to kill the victim but failing to actually cause death. Then, in an effort to clean up after what the would-be killer thought was murder, he or she buried the alive but unconscious victim, who then actually died from suffocation at being accidently buried alive? Could the attacker defend against a charge of murder by arguing a lack of concurrence? First, the defendant would argue that during the beating, while he had the mens rea to kill his or her victim, there was no actus reus (actual killing) in existence to concur with his guilty intent. Then, during the actus reus of the actual killing (burying a person who then died from lack of air), the killer lacked the mens rea (of intent to kill) needed to concur with his or her criminal act.

Courts have not looked kindly on such reasoning. In *Jackson v. Commonwealth*, 38 S.W. 422 (1896), the Court of Appeals of Kentucky was faced with a similar problem, although in the context of a jurisdictional issue. The question whether the Kentucky courts actually had jurisdiction over the homicide case depended on whether the killing in the case occurred in Ohio or Kentucky. In *Jackson*, "the headless body of a woman" was found on a Kentucky farm. The large quantity of blood at the scene along with signs that blood had spurted from the neck indicated that the victim had been decapitated. While, "[e]very effort to find the head proved futile," the shoes worn by the dead woman eventually led to her being identified as Pearl Bryan. Although ultimately found on a Kentucky farm, Pearl Bryan had earlier travelled to Cincinnati, Ohio, for an abortion. While in Ohio, she was poisoned with cocaine.

The court noted that the jury could have believed "from all the evidence beyond a reasonable doubt that the defendant, Scott Jackson, willfully, feloniously and with malice aforethought, himself attempted *** to kill Pearl Bryan [in Cincinnati, Ohio], but she was not thereby killed, and that said Scott Jackson, in this county and State [of Kentucky], *** though believing said Pearl Bryan was then dead, for whatever purpose, cut her throat with a knife or other sharp instrument so that she did then and there, and because thereof die, they will find said Scott Jackson guilty of murder."

For "concurrence" purposes, consider the following interpretation of the case: the defendant, Jackson, poisoned the victim with cocaine, intending to kill her. Then, mistakenly believing the victim to be dead, Jackson decapitated Pearl in an effort to prevent identification of her body. The victim, however, had survived the poisoning, only to actually die during the decapitation. Couldn't the defendant argue that, just as in the premature burial case, concurrence of act and intent never occurred? According to LaFave, *Criminal Law*, Fifth Edition at 345-46, courts have avoided the implications of such an argument by characterizing the two distinct acts as **part of a single overall transaction having a common intent and committed pursuant to a larger plan**.

LEGAL SKILLS:
How to Put on a Preliminary Hearing

Trials can ruin bank accounts and reputations, even when the defendant is acquitted. To prevent citizens from suffering these costs with every accusation, our founders required that federal cases be tested and that bad cases be filtered out before trial by having accusations considered by grand juries. Grand juries met behind closed doors to protect reputation and were streamlined (for example, no defense counsel were present at grand juries) so they were not as costly to the accused as trials. Many states, however, use a different way to test felony cases, called a preliminary hearing, to see if accusations merit a trial.

Since preliminary hearings test the strength of cases to see if they should go to trial, preliminary hearings cause a significant number of cases to either end in a plea bargain (when the case survives the test, the defendant would rather take a plea), or with a dismissal (although relatively rare, some cases do not survive the test, and so defendants are not "held to answer" at trial). This means that there are many more preliminary hearings, or "prelims," than actual trials.

A prosecutor has to be able to deal with many prelim cases, often fifteen to twenty, in a morning (my judge never liked having to deal with prelims after lunch). Getting through prelims takes on the feel of flipping burgers—you have to get many done quickly while making sure you accurately fill everyone's order. So, how can one successfully get through prelims? Go over the files before entering the courtroom. The first order of business is figuring out which cases will plead before prelim, so you do not even need to prepare them. Get to the courtroom early so you can meet with civilian witnesses. Civilians who see you arrive early have more time to tell their story when you interview them and will see you are doing your best if they have to wait for their case to be called. Be prepared to have to visit the room where officers working nights are sleeping to interview them for their prelim testimony. Wake them up early enough so they can review their report and answer your questions before taking the stand.

Above all, go with the flow of defense attorneys interrupting you with plea offers, witnesses asking questions, and staff trying to schedule matters. Embrace the chaos.

3. Distinguishing Mens Rea from Motive

Motive is the emotion behind or reason for committing a crime. *People v. Hillhouse*, 27 Cal.4th 469 (2002) explained, **"Motive describes the reason a person chooses to commit a crime. The reason, however, is different than a required mental state such as intent or malice."** Seeking the motive for a crime is based on so much common sense that television crime dramas often have a character assert, "We have found means, opportunity, and motive" against a suspect. Yet, motive is not an element of crime. Quite simply, many crimes are committed without any motive. A person will steal a candy bar even though he has a $20 bill in his wallet. Another will kill a friend who has done nothing to offend her attacker. These criminals fulfill all the elements of the crime even though no one can figure out why they did it in the first place.

How can motive not be needed for committing a crime when mens rea is a necessary element for most offenses? The answer is in the fact that **mens rea and motive are not the same thing**. Mens rea is a narrow legal concept that focuses only on the goal-oriented thinking of the criminal at the moment of his or her act, while motive causes the formation of intent—motive is the thinking behind mens rea.

Suppose a person is recorded on camera stealing peanuts from a street vendor. On the incriminating tape, the thief openly states aloud to himself, "I am stealing these nuts without intending to pay for them." At the later trial, the prosecution plays this tape to the jury as part of her case proving the defendant's guilt. Then, during the defense case, the defendant offers the fact that he has a fatal peanut allergy and thus would never expose himself to peanuts, let alone steal them. If the jury believes that the defendant did indeed take the peanuts with the intent to steal, it does not matter how irrational, or even self-destructive, the thief's actions were. The reason, or motive, for stealing the peanuts need not be established. The thief might have stolen the peanuts to feed his starving family, or for the thrilling adrenaline rush of exposing himself to danger, or to irritate the seller upon learning of the loss of inventory.

While in theory, the prosecutor who offers no explanation for a criminal's behavior is on firm legal ground, she might not be on such firm footing in an actual courtroom. Juries want things to make sense. Juries might come to doubt that a crime was committed without a reason, and therefore might acquit, despite the proof of all the elements to the crime. Thus, in trials, prosecutors often will do their best to supply the jury with a motive for the crime as a way to strengthen proof of mens rea and to remove doubt from the deliberation room.

4. Transferred Intent

What if a husband, say a John Saunders, intended to poison his wife so he could marry another woman? What if Saunders placed poison in an apple and gave it to his wife? Then, despite his best planning, his wife gave part of the apple to their young daughter who ate it and died. These facts, seemingly coming out of a *Grimms' Fairy Tale*, actually happened. As explained in *State v. Johnson*, 72 P.3d 343, 347 (2003), the court hearing this matter, *Regina v. Saunders,* recognized that the husband and father did not intend to kill his daughter. Still, "he was nonetheless guilty of her murder." The court "transferred" Saunder's intent to kill his wife to the death of his daughter. The resulting **"doctrine of transferred intent"** established criminal liability for those who, **while missing in directing harm toward one person, mistakenly cause the same injury to another.**

Yesterday and Today: Transferred Intent

Transferred intent is a doctrine as old as the bow and arrow. *Gladden v. State*, 330 A.2d 176 (1974), demonstrates that this controversial doctrine, often criticized as unnecessary, has been relied on by courts at least from 1576 to the present. In *Gladden*, Michael ("Box") Gladden tried to kill Walter Edward ("Rabbi") Siegel in the wake of a disagreement over a drug deal. Gladden, bringing a "revolver as a persuader," tracked Siegel down in order to shoot him. When Siegel ran away, Gladden chased him, "wildly" firing four or five shots "without hitting his intended target." One of these bullets went through the window of a nearby home and pierced the chest "of William Jeffrey Nixon, 12 years of age, a resident there, who was seated on the living room couch." The Court of Appeals of Maryland, affirming the resulting murder conviction, quoted with approval the following instructions read to the jury:

> **What is the situation where a person intends to kill one person but instead kills another person**? To put it a different way, **what is the situation when the deceased is not the intended victim**? The law is that such a homicide partakes of the quality of the original act so that the guilt of an accused is exactly what it would have been had the shots been fired at the intended victim instead of the person actually killed. The fact that the person actually killed was killed instead of the intended victim is immaterial and the only question is what would have been the degree of guilt if the result intended had actually been accomplished. The intent is transferred to the person whose death has been caused.

The Court of Appeals reasoned:

> The petitioner contends that in the absence of a specific intention to kill young Nixon the doctrine of transferred intent was improperly applied and cannot be used as a substitute for the willfulness, deliberation and premeditation required to constitute murder in the first degree. ***

> The so-called doctrine of "transferred intent" had its earliest roots firmly embedded in the English Common Law. As early as 1576, in *Reg. v. Saunders,* 2 Plowd. 473, 75 Eng. Rep. 706 (1576), it was stated:

> And therefore **it is every man's business to foresee what wrong or mischief may happen from that which he does with an ill-intention, and it shall be no excuse for him to say that he intended to kill another, and not the person killed**. For if a man . . . shoots an arrow at another with an intent to kill him, and a person to whom he bore no malice is killed by it, this shall be murder in him, for when he shot the arrow he intended to kill, and inasmuch as he directed his instrument of death at one, and thereby has killed another, it shall be the same offense in him as if he had killed the person he aimed at. ***

> Some courts succinctly analogize the doctrine by stating that "the intention follows the bullet," or "the malice was transferred or followed the bullet ***

> [Gladden's] *mens rea* for murder in the first degree was established, notwithstanding that the decedent was an unintended victim. All the elements of an intentional first degree killing were present. *** The purpose and malice with which the shots were fired are not changed in any degree by circumstances showing that they did not take effect—because of bad aim—upon Siegel. Gladden's culpability under the law and the resultant harm to society is the same as if he had accomplished the result he intended when he caused the death of the innocent youngster. ***[17]

---

17. Reprinted with the permission of LexisNexis.

"Seamless Web" Connection

In the 1576 case, *Reg. v. Saunders,* the transferred intent case discussed above, the court ruled, "it is every man's business to foresee what wrong or mischief may happen from that which he does with an ill-intention." This concept of foreseeability, here used to decide an issue of mens rea, is also crucial to determining if a person is responsible for having "proximately caused" some bad outcome. Three hundred years after *Reg. v. Saunders,* California, a state that did not exist when *Reg. v. Saunders* was decided, used foreseeability to decide if a drunken boater "caused" the death of his drowned passenger. The California court's proximate cause analysis, in *People v. Armitage,* can be found in Chapter 4.

Does "Success" in Killing the Original Target "Use Up" the Intent That Is Usually Transferred?

What if the killer actually succeeds in hitting his or her target? Is there any intent "left over" to concur with the killings of unintended bystanders? The doctrine of transferred intent might apply even when the wrongdoer actually succeeds in delivering harm to his or her original target. The court so ruled in *People v. Bland* (2002) 28 Cal. 4th 313; 48 P.3d 1107, in which the defendant, Jomo K. Bland, killed a driver of a car in a gang shooting. The driverless car then ran into a pole, injuring its passengers. The *Bland* court speculated about how transferred intent would have applied to the passengers had they too died in the accident. The court noted, "In its classic form, the doctrine of transferred intent applies when the defendant intends to kill one person but mistakenly kills another. The intent to kill the intended target is deemed to transfer to the unintended victim so that the defendant is guilty of murder." The *Bland* court then considered the "conceptual difficulties" that arose when the shooter was actually successful in killing his original target, yet causes further deaths to occur. In this scenario, the court concluded, **"(T)ransferred intent applies even when the person kills the intended target. Intent to kill is not limited to the specific target but extends to everyone actually killed."**

Tips for Success for Future Law Students and Lawyers

Think about What Law Schools Are Looking for in an Applicant When Preparing for Law School

Many law school professors still rely on the Socratic Method for teaching. Socrates taught by asking his students questions and using their answers to refine an inquiry to get ever closer to the truth. Similarly, law professors ask questions, relying on all the students' answers to hone in on a legal rule or argument. Since this process works best when you have a group of people with differing backgrounds, law schools have come to value diversity. So, law schools wish to have all sorts of students of various race, ethnicity, gender, geographic origin, and socio-economic class. Directors of Admission also want diversity in majors so that all kinds of subject expertise can be applied in a law school discussion. There are, therefore, no magic majors for law school.

Law schools happily accept any college major, from engineering to modern dance, so long as the applicant possesses strong reading, writing, and critical reasoning skills. Students hoping to study law should, therefore, take classes emphasizing reading, writing, and critical reasoning.

Unlike most graduate schools, law schools primarily focus on two numbers: (1) Law School Admissions Test (LSAT) score and (2) Cumulative undergraduate grade point average (GPA). Law schools are trying to foretell the future to figure out which applicants will promote the prestige of their institutions in the long term. Who will be the next great lawyers, judges, or legislators? Apparently the best crystal ball so far is a combination of LSAT and GPA. There is a strong correlation between successful LSAT/GPA and success in the first year of law school, all three years of law school, and passage of the licensing test, known as the State Bar Exam. Since the *U.S. News and World Report Law School Rankings* also consider LSAT/GPA, schools wishing for high ranking in this unofficial list have another reason to look for high LSAT/GPA.

5. General and Specific Intent

The concepts of general intent and specific intent confuse even lawyers and judges. Not only are mental states abstract concepts, but also the meaning of general and specific intent has changed over time. Originally, any crime that required the intentional commission of an act with an evil intent was deemed simply a general intent offense, while a crime that mandated the formation of a particular mental state, such as murder's "malice aforethought" or burglary's "intent to commit a felony therein," was labeled a specific intent crime.

However, as noted in the box below, the meanings of general and specific intent evolved over time. According to *People v. Hood* 1 Cal. 3d 444 (1969), the two terms came to mean the following:

1. **A general intent crime described as "a particular act, without reference to intent to do a further act or achieve a future consequence."**
2. **A specific intent crime described not only a particular act, but also "defendant's intent to do some further act or achieve some additional consequence."**

An example might clarify these abstractions. A person who committed California's HS 11350 Possession of a Controlled Substance is guilty of a general intent crime, because he or she simply intended to perform the present act of possession, thinking, "I am holding these drugs now." In contrast, a person who instead committed California's HS 11351 Possession of a Controlled Substance For Sale is guilty of a specific intent crime, because he or she is not only intending to commit the present act of holding the drugs, but is also entertaining an additional intent to sell those drugs to someone in the future. The law considers this future sale being contemplated to be "some further act or achieve some additional consequence." These differences in mental state might seem minor, but as we will see, they can have major consequences.

VIDEO: Ohio Highway Patrol Arrests a Police Officer and California Highway Patrol Arrests a Firefighter

An Ohio State Highway Patrol Officer arrested a police officer for driving under the influence at:

https://www.youtube.com/watch?v=oGH4Ee7Dhoo

The CHP arrested a firefighter for not moving his vehicle at:

https://www.youtube.com/watch?v=yNaXcYezt-8

The box below explains the importance of intoxication to the creation of the distinction between general intent and specific intent.

© Master305/Shutterstock.com

The Origin of the General-Versus-Specific Intent Distinction: Intoxication

The effect of alcohol on the mind of the offender played a crucial role in forming the doctrines of general and specific intent. *People v. Hood* (1969) 1 Cal. 3d 444 candidly explained the importance of intoxication in creating the general and specific intent concepts. In *Hood*, the defendant, David Keith Hood, after drinking for "several hours," went to the home of his former girlfriend and beat her so severely that neighbors heard her screams and called police. When police arrived, the defendant "directed a stream of obscenities" at one officer. The officer, in attempting to arrest the defendant, only got so far as to say, "Okay fella, you are . . . ," when defendant "swung at him with his fist." During the following struggle, the officer "fell with defendant on top of him in a corner of a pantry adjoining the kitchen . . ." The defendant ultimately shot the officer once in each of his legs.

The defendant's intoxication became an issue during the California Supreme Court's later discussion about whether assault was a general or a specific intent crime. The *Hood* court discussed the concepts of general and specific intent:

> The distinction between specific and general intent crimes evolved as a judicial response to the problem of the intoxicated offender. That problem is to reconcile two competing theories of what is just in the treatment of those who commit crimes while intoxicated. (The) moral culpability of a drunken criminal is frequently less than that of a sober person effecting a like injury. On the other hand, it is commonly felt that a person who voluntarily gets drunk and while in that state commits a crime should not escape the consequences. (Originally, courts refused to allow intoxication to lessen guilt.)

> (However, *Regina* v. *Monkhouse* [1849] 4 Cox C. C. 55, held) the burden was on the accused to show that his intoxication prevented him from using self-restraint or took away from him "the power of forming any specific intention." This opinion was apparently the first to use the words "specific intention."

> As if by accident, the 'specific intention' was seized upon as the important criterion. Yet the wording (in *Monkhouse* shows that the court) did not mean to weave any particular magic with these words. ***

> The theory that these judges explored was that (intoxication could negate intent. However,) such an exculpatory doctrine could eventually have undermined the traditional rule entirely,

since some form of *mens rea* is a requisite of all but strict liability offenses. *** To limit the operation of the doctrine and achieve a compromise between the conflicting feelings of sympathy and reprobation for the intoxicated offender, later courts both in England and this country drew a distinction between so-called specific intent and general intent crimes.

Specific and general intent have been notoriously difficult terms to define and apply, and a number of text writers recommend that they be abandoned altogether. *** Too often the characterization of a particular crime as one of specific or general intent is determined solely by the presence or absence of words describing psychological phenomena— "intent" or "malice," for example—in the statutory language defining the crime. **When the definition of a crime consists of only the description of a particular** act, without reference to intent to do a further act or achieve a future consequence, we ask whether the defendant intended to do the proscribed act. **This intention is deemed to be a general criminal intent. When the definition refers to defendant's intent to do some further act or achieve some additional consequence, the crime is deemed to be one of specific intent. There is no real difference, however, only a linguistic one**, between an intent to do an act already performed and an intent to do that same act in the future.

Hood did not then decide whether assault was a general or specific intent crime (although California would later deem assault to be a general intent crime). Instead, the Court reasoned:

A compelling consideration is the effect of alcohol on human behavior. A significant effect of alcohol is to distort judgment and relax the controls on aggressive and anti-social impulses. *** Alcohol apparently has less effect on the ability to engage in simple goal-directed behavior. (A) drunk man is capable of forming an intent to do something simple, such as strike another, unless he is so drunk that he has reached the stage of unconsciousness. What he is not as capable as a sober man of doing is exercising judgment about the social consequences of his acts or controlling his impulses toward anti-social acts. He is more likely to act rashly and impulsively and to be susceptible to passion and anger. It would therefore be anomalous to allow evidence of intoxication to relieve a man of responsibility for the crimes of assault with a deadly weapon or simple assault, which are so frequently committed in just such a manner. (Assault is not a crime) which requires an intent that is susceptible to negation through a showing of voluntary intoxication."

(On) retrial the court should not instruct the jury to consider evidence of defendant's intoxication in determining whether he committed assault with a deadly weapon on a peace officer or any of the lesser assaults included therein.[18]

Therefore, the important distinction between general and specific intent crimes might have more to do with an accident of history than with the genuine differences in these two mental states.

---

18. Reprinted with the permission of LexisNexis.

Biography—Judge

Justice Ginsburg

The following comes from *CNN* "Ruth Bader Ginsburg Fast Facts," February 26, 2017, http://www.cnn.com/2013/03/07/us/ruth-baderginsburg-fast-facts/index.html,

- Was born "Joan Ruth Bader" in Brooklyn, New York, March 15, 1933.
- Attended both Harvard Law School and Columbia Law School.
- Founded the American Civil Liberties (ACLU) Women's Rights Project.
- Was appointed Associate Justice to the Supreme Court by President Clinton in 1993.
- Dissented, along with three other justices in *Bush v. Gore*, which determined the 2000 presidential election in favor of George W. Bush and against Al Gore.
- Was the first Supreme Court justice to officiate at a same-sex marriage.
- Is the subject of "**Notorious RBG**: The Life and Times of Ruth Bader Ginsburg," by Irin Carmon and Shana Knizhnik, a play on the name of the rapper, "The Notorious B.I.G."

According to Charlotte Alter at *Time* magazine in "Here's Why Ruth Bader Ginsburg Is 'Notorious,'" (November 4, 2015), days before he died, Ginsburg's husband wrote her a note in which he declared, "You are the only person I have loved in my life." She corrected Marty Ginsburg's calculation of the years they had known each other from "56" to "almost 60."]

Are General and Specific Intents Even Real?

To further complicate matters, it must be acknowledged that neuroscientists and psychologists probably would not be impressed by the concepts of general and specific intent. Indeed, a general intent or a specific intent, as understood by lawyers and judges, might not actually ever exist in reality. If we could somehow measure a criminal's brain activity while he or she committed an offense (such as by some portable fMRI), the resulting images of the brain scan would, in all likelihood, show no difference in neural activity between a person committing a general intent crime and one committing a specific intent crime. This does not, unfortunately, get the student of law off the hook; whatever the truth about what actually occurs in the brain, these concepts have significant impact in many courtrooms in some jurisdictions, and therefore need to be understood.

6.   Proof of Mens Rea: Direct Versus Indirect (Circumstantial) Evidence

Prosecutors must prove the existence of mens rea or intent to a jury beyond a reasonable doubt just as they must prove every other fact of the People's case. **Mens rea can be proven,** just as every other fact can be established, **by offering either: (1) direct evidence or (2) indirect, or circumstantial, evidence**. For instance, California Penal Code Section 29.2(a) provides: "**The intent or intention is manifested by the circumstances connected with the offense.**"

Somewhere, circumstantial evidence gained a bad reputation. Perhaps the public began to question the use of circumstantial evidence when television shows had police officers complain that they had gathered "only circumstantial evidence" or lawyers declare in court, "Objection! That's circumstantial evidence!" It turns out that these shows improperly besmirched the reputation of perfectly good evidence.

Indirect or circumstantial evidence merely requires that the fact finder, usually the jury, draw an inference from the evidence. It can be as simple as connecting dots. In fact, **a child connecting numbered dots that form a picture, say on a breakfast menu in a family restaurant, involves the same process used to make sense of circumstantial evidence.**

Our everyday language speaks of the powerful proof of circumstantial evidence. When one laments that, in a particular situation, "there is no smoking gun," they are referring to indirect evidence. A "smoking gun" is the damning circumstantial evidence provided when one is caught standing over a recently killed body holding a gun that is still

Other than the smoke coming out of his ears, they couldn't tell what he thought of the quarterly numbers.

Everyone uses circumstantial evidence to sense the intent of others.

© Cartoon Resource/Shutterstock.com

smoking from being fired. Likewise, when a person is "caught red-handed," he is as guilty as a poacher found with the blood of a fresh kill still on his hands.

During voir dire, where attorneys question jurors to test for potential bias, prosecutors have been known to use the following hypothetical question to test an individual juror's ability to distinguish between direct and indirect evidence:

> Suppose it is raining. While you are walking down the street, you can see the rain falling in puddles and when you tilt back your head, you feel the drops hit your face. This is direct evidence that it is raining. If you were later called to the witness stand, you could testify that you perceived it was raining because you yourself saw and felt the rain.
>
> Now, in contrast, suppose you were standing in line waiting to buy tickets to see a movie in a theater. It is an overcast day with dark clouds above, yet it is not presently raining. You buy your tickets and see the movie. When you exit the theater, the streets are all wet. People walk past wearing dripping raincoats and hold closed umbrellas which drip onto the pavement. The cars that drive by have wet windshields with wedge-shaped clear areas where windshield wipers had scraped off water. Taking all these facts into account, what happened during the two hours you were in the movie theater? You use your common sense reason to surmise it rained when you were indoors. This is circumstantial evidence.
>
> After the prosecution has led a juror through this questioning, a defense counsel might then go up to the same juror and ask, "Is it possible that, while you were in the theater, an insane gardener soaked the entire neighborhood with a hose from a tall building while you were watching the movie?" This is possible, but certainly not likely.

The Arkansas Supreme Court in *Coggin v. State,* 156 S.W.3d 712 (2004) discussed circumstantial evidence when considering proof of mens rea. *Coggin* noted,

Circumstantial evidence may provide the basis to support a conviction, but it must be consistent with the defendant's guilt and inconsistent with any other reasonable conclusion . . . In other words, if you have two equally reasonable conclusions as to what occurred, this merely gives rise to a suspicion of guilt, which is not enough to support a conviction.

In *Coggin*, the court found enough evidence to support the jury's conclusion that the defendant had formed the most cold-blooded intent—premeditation and deliberation. The court explained that, **since we cannot read people's minds, "a criminal defendant's intent or state of mind is seldom capable of proof by direct evidence and must usually be inferred from the circumstances of the crime."** The court further noted that the intent needed in the murder case could be "inferred from the type of weapon used, the manner of its use, and the nature, extent, and location of the wounds. In addition, one is presumed to intend the natural and probable consequences of his actions." The *Coggin* court found that, while "the evidence supporting (Coggin's) conviction (was) of a circumstantial nature," it was "consistent with the sole conclusion" that he acted with "premeditation and deliberation in the murder of his wife." The couple had a "volatile relationship" and were experiencing "financial difficulties." Coggin's wife had told others she feared for her life. Further, Coggin had bought a drop cloth before the shooting, concealed evidence after the killing, and attempted to evade authorities. All of these facts offered enough circumstantial evidence of the defendant's mental state for a conviction.

VIDEO: What Was Going On in the Minds of Those Who Killed for Charles Manson?

WARNING: DISTURBING VIDEOS. A criminal defendant's statements about intent are one piece of evidence for mens rea. Prosecutors, judges, and juries are wise to consider all evidence in forming decisions regarding a person's criminal intent. Patricia Krenwinkel considered why she committed murder for Charles Manson at:

https://www.youtube.com/watch?v=U_hbIPJuiac

Susan Atkins discussed her killing of victims at:

https://www.youtube.com/watch?v=nOHJSFsJeIk

Patricia Krenwinkel, Leslie Van Houten, and Charles Manson discuss the killings at:

https://www.youtube.com/watch?v=uHQTuIrAS5Y

VIDEO: The Victim's Side of the Case: Sharon Tate's Sister Speaks

Patti Tate, Sharon Tate's sister, spoke at Patricia Krenwinkel's parole hearing at:

https://www.youtube.com/watch?v=1Cn4Hq_H-fE

What Is the Problem? True Motives Underlying Tensions between Courtroom Actors

Tensions between Police and Prosecutors

When an officer visits the filing deputy, there exists an institutional difference of interests. Police want the case to be filed because the D.A.'s decision to formally pursue the case represents a practical endpoint as far as the officers are concerned. Police view the filing of a case as a successful conclusion of their investigation, allowing them to pass the baton to the next agency in line. In short, a filing is a vindication of their hard work. In contrast, D.A.'s have no similar institutional interest in filing. For the prosecutor, a case filing is not the end but the beginning where all the challenges start. Some cases, therefore, become a hot potato, where the officer tries to leave the case with the D.A. while the D.A. either wishes to "reject" the filing or seek further investigation.

---

7.   Strict Liability Crimes

As previously noted, it is a fundamental rule of criminal law that most crimes require a concurrence of actus reus and mens rea. There is, however, a small class of crimes, known as "strict liability" crimes, which do not require such a concurrence because they lack the element of intent. With strict liability crimes, if one does a forbidden act, he or she is guilty regardless of the innocence of intention. If a person exceeds the speed limit by one mile an hour, he or she is guilty, even if this driver had been conscientiously looking at what turned out to be a faulty speedometer. Moreover, in most jurisdictions, if a person has intercourse with a seventeen-year-old, honestly and reasonably believing that the minor

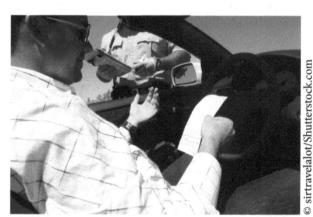

Many traffic offenses are strict liability crimes.

was over the age of majority, the mistaken person is guilty of statutory rape.

Yet, many strict liability crimes do not turn out to be a booby trap for the unwary. Most of these offenses are known as "**public welfare**" or "**regulatory**" **crimes.** They are designed to use regulations to signal to those in control of dangerous items or activities of their higher duties to the public. For example, when the Food and Drug Administration fines a food processor for unknowingly allowing the bacterium, E. coli, into its food, the government is aiming to combat the danger of food-borne illness regardless of the fact that the processor never intended to have such a toxin in the food. Often a food processor will commit a strict liability crime not by doing something wrong, but by failing to fulfill a particular duty. Further, the criminal sanction's harshness is lessened by the fact that the processor, working in a heavily regulated industry, was quite aware of the laws that existed prohibiting E. coli in food. Finally, the fine imposed generally does not constitute as severe a penalty or create as great a stigma as would a conviction and punishment for a traditional crime requiring mens rea. These **factors**: 1) **regulatory context**, 2) **failure to act in the face of a regulatory duty**, 3) the crime's **lessened penalty**, and 3) the crime's **lessened stigma**, were suggested in *Morissette v. United States*, 342 U.S. 246 (1952).

The following case involves a **strict liability crime**, and therefore does **not require mens rea**, or what the court calls "**scienter**." In this particular case, consider whether the defendant would have been guilty of this **regulatory offense** even if it were not a strict liability crime.

In *United States v. Smith*, the case below, the defendant violated the law by merely possessing the feathers of an eagle."

LEGAL ANALYSIS

United States v. Smith
29 F.3d 270 (1994).
Judge Bauer wrote the opinion for the United States Court of Appeals for the Seventh Circuit.

Facts

[Beverly Pickering sent a package from Canada to her friend, Debra Lynn Smith, in Decatur, Illinois. The package contained various times, including eagle feathers. U.S. Federal agents discovered the eagle feathers in the package at the O'Hare Airport international mail facility in Chicago. The U.S. Fish and Wildlife Service obtained a search warrant for Smith's house. U.S. Postal Inspector Rod Damery, dressed in a mailman's uniform, personally delivered the package. Smith signed for the package, took it inside her house, and and began opening it when armed federal agents came to her front door. The agents asked Smith how she came to possess the feathers.]

"My friend Bev sent them to me," Smith explained. "It's just a gesture of friendship. She thought I might like to have them."

[Smith admitted she knew it was illegal to possess eagle feathers because she once watched a television show that said as much. She knew the package contained eagle feathers and that she knew she was not supposed to possess them.]

"I might as well tell you," she admitted, "that I asked for some of these feathers [for] a macrame project."

Smith never attempted her proposed macrame project. Instead [a jury] found Smith guilty of possessing bald eagle feathers in violation of the Migratory Bird Treaty Act ("MBTA"), 16 U.S.C. § 703. [The MBTA] makes it "unlawful at any time, by any means or in any manner, to . . . possess . . . any migratory bird, any part . . . or any product . . . which consists, or is composed in whole or in part, of any such bird or any part . . . thereof." *** The bald eagle—our national symbol—is a migratory bird for purposes of the Migratory Bird Treaty Act. *** The magistrate judge sentenced Smith to probation and entered judgment on the conviction. ***

In this appeal, Smith argues *** that she did not have the requisite criminal intent to be convicted of a crime and that her conviction therefore violates the Due Process Clause. Smith also contends that she lacked any knowledge as to the contents of the package.

Issue

Whether the Migratory Bird Treaty Act is a "strict liability" crime.

Rule and Analysis

[The record shows that Smith knew that Pickering sent her a package containing eagle feathers. Smith asked Pickering to send her some eagle feathers that she planned to use as part of a macrame project. Smith knew she was not supposed to possess eagle feathers.]

Smith contends that, even so, she lacked **any *criminal* intent or scienter**. This is an interesting, though unavailing and somewhat confusing point. Smith urges us either to declare section 703 unconstitutional as violative of the Due Process Clause for this lack of requirement of scienter or, alternatively, to read the need for scienter into section 703. She does not claim, however, that . . . the MBTA requires a determination that she knew that possessing eagle feathers was illegal (although there is evidence that she in fact did so know).

Perhaps she means that she cannot be guilty if she did not know that she possessed eagle feathers. Smith accurately notes that scienter in some form is usually and traditionally a requirement of criminal responsibility. *** There are, however, many exceptions, especially in the regulation of activities involving public health, safety, and welfare . . . Such **regulatory offenses** often **do not and need not specify intent, particularly when the penalties for violations are small and do no grave harm to an offender's reputation**. [**Conduct alone, without regard to intent, is sufficient.**]

The plain language of . . . the MBTA makes it unlawful to "possess" bald eagle feathers. There is no scienter requirement expressly written into the statute. A number of courts have held that **the MBTA provides for strict liability** and that the provision does not offend the requirements of due process. ***

Smith's argument, if she could make it, runs counter to those opinions. We do not reach it, however, because that is not an argument she can make. There is evidence that she expected to receive eagle feathers that she hoped to use for a macrame project. The jury was instructed that it must find that she knowingly possessed eagle feathers. Criminal offenses generally require no more; a person commits the offense when he or she knowingly engages in the conduct constituting the offense. And the jury here so determined.

Conclusion

The Migratory Bird Act is a strict liability crime, and therefore the defendant need not have a criminal intent to be found guilty of violating this law.

*** Smith possessed migratory bird parts. She therefore broke the law.

Do's and Don'ts for Hearings, Trials, and Appeals

Interviewing and Preparing Witnesses for Preliminary Hearing Testimony

Don't "coach" a witness by telling him or her what to say. This could lead to suborning perjury, itself a crime. All lawyers, but particularly prosecutors, are "officers of the court" and so are not to support false testimony. The Wisconsin Supreme Court Rules, WI SCR Ch. 20 Preamble: A Lawyer's Responsibilities (1) notes, "an officer of the legal system and a public citizen having special responsibility for the quality of justice."

Instead, **do** learn the witness's weaknesses and prepare them to deal with the problems candidly. Proper preparation often involves getting a witness to candidly accept responsibility for something wrong, false, or embarrassing. Such open acknowledgment will protect your witness from being destroyed by opposing counsel when the sensitive subject arises.

Preliminary hearing testimony, which is given in a proceeding before trial, can become "prior testimony" which can then later be used to impeach a witness's credibility at trial. Therefore, **don't** let a preliminary hearing witness read the police report and simply parrot back to you what is written on it. Overburdened police, who often have less direct access to information than the witnesses themselves, sometimes write reports in haste. Unaware of this, witnesses will mistakenly defer to the authority of the police and the written word, believing it must be the "correct" version of events even though this is not so.

Don't believe everything your witness says just because he or she is your witness and is saying something you want to hear. **Don't** believe everything your witness says even if he or she is a police officer. Instead, test your witnesses before you put them on the stand by repeatedly having them tell their story. **Do** try to poke holes in their version and critically assess their statements in view of other evidence. For prosecutors, **don't** just try to win a case, **do** try to promote justice overall.

LEGAL ANALYSIS

In re Jennings
34 Cal.4th 254 (2004).
Justice Werdegar delivered the opinion for the Supreme Court of California.

Facts

On May 30, 2000, petitioner Michael Jennings, a supervisor for Armor Steel Company in Rio Linda, invited coworkers Charles Turpin, Curtis Fosnaugh, Daniel Smith and Donald Szalay to his home to view a videotape demonstrating some new machinery the company was to obtain. [Jennings had his wife purchase beer.] The five men sat in the garage and drank beer. [When the party broke up, Fosnaugh left driving a white Ford pickup truck. Turpin then left driving his Volkswagen Beetle, accompanied by Smith. [Fosnaugh and Turpin then got into a major collision, resulting in serious injuries to] Turpin, Smith and Fosnaugh. [Turpin had a blood-alcohol concentration of .124 percent.] Turpin was 19 years old. Fosnaugh was 20 years old.

Petitioner was charged with violating Section 25658(c), purchasing alcohol for someone under 21 years old who consumes it and "thereby proximately causes great bodily injury or death to himself, herself, or any other person." [Jennings argued that he was ignorant of Turpin's age and had once heard Turpin tell an officer he was 22 years old.]

Issue

Whether we should interpret the statute to require some mental state as a necessary element of the crime.

Rule and Analysis

[California actively regulates sale of alcoholic beverages to underage drinkers. Automobile] accidents by underage drinkers lead to the injuries and deaths of thousands of people in this country every year. ***

[Our laws shield young people from the dangers of excess alcohol consumption.] Our state Constitution establishes the legal drinking age at 21, three years past the age of legal majority [18]. The "likely purpose" of this constitutional provision "is to protect such persons from exposure to the 'harmful influences' associated with the consumption of such beverages." ***

[Section 25658(c) provides:] "Any person who [purchases] an alcoholic beverage for a person under the age of 21 years and the person under the age of 21 years thereafter consumes the alcohol and thereby proximately causes great bodily injury or death to himself, herself, or any other person, is guilty of a misdemeanor." [The offense is punishable by imprisonment in a county jail for a minimum of six months, by a fine of up to $1,000, or both. It does not explicitly require that the offender have knowledge, intent, or some other mental state when purchasing the alcoholic beverage.]

[The statute was meant to deal with] situation in which an underage person, loitering in front of a liquor store, asks an approaching adult to buy alcoholic beverages for him or her, commonly known as the "shoulder tap" situation. [Minors sometimes will] tap adults on the shoulder as they enter a market to get them to buy liquor for the minors.

To violate the statute,] one must not only *furnish* alcohol *to* an underage person, one must *purchase* the alcohol *for* that person. [The] generalized actions of the typical social party host, providing libations for his or her guests, do not run afoul of the [statute] because, as a general matter, such hosts cannot be said to have purchased alcohol "for" any particular guest. ***

The prevailing trend in the law is against imposing criminal liability without proof of some mental state where the statute does not evidence the Legislature's intent to impose strict liability. [However,] **for certain types of penal laws, often referred to as public welfare offenses, the Legislature does not intend that any proof of scienter or wrongful intent be necessary for conviction.** 'Such offenses generally are based upon *** statutes which are purely regulatory in nature and involve widespread injury to the public. *** "Under many statutes enacted for the protection of the public health and safety, e.g., traffic and food and drug regulations, criminal sanctions are relied upon even if there is no wrongful intent. These offenses usually involve light penalties and no moral obloquy or damage to reputation. [The] primary purpose of the statutes is regulation rather than punishment or correction. The offenses are not crimes in the orthodox sense, and wrongful intent is not required in the interest of enforcement." ***

[Section 25658(c) is a "public welfare offense" for which proof of knowledge or criminal intent is unnecessary. The statute does not expressly require a mental state, is aimed at avoiding widespread injury to the public, and imposes only "light penalties." The People need not prove knowledge or intent to establish a violation of the statute.]

[Although] the People must prove an accused "purchas[ed]" an alcoholic beverage "for" an underage person, the People need not also prove the accused knew that person was under 21 years of age.

Although the People need not prove knowledge of age in order to establish a violation of Section 25658(c), the question remains whether petitioner was entitled to raise a mistake of fact defense concerning Turpin's age. [Penal Code Section 26] provides: "All persons are capable of committing crimes except [those who committed the act or made the omission] under an ignorance or mistake of fact, which disproves any criminal intent." ***

[We conclude] that, although the prosecution need not prove an offender's knowledge of age in order to establish a violation of Section 25658(c), petitioner was entitled to raise an affirmative defense, for which he would bear the burden of proof, that he honestly and reasonably believed Turpin was at least 21 years old. [The] trial court erred in refusing petitioner's offer to prove he honestly and reasonably believed Turpin was over 21 years old.

[We conclude:] (1) **Section 25658(c) is not limited to the shoulder tap scenario, but applies whenever an offender *purchases* alcoholic beverages *for* an underage person;** (2) **Section 25658(c) does not apply in the typical social party host situation, because the host does not purchase alcohol for any particular guest;** (3) **the prosecution need not prove an offender knew (or should have known) the age of the person [*to*] whom he or she furnished alcohol** in order to prove a violation of Section 25658(c); (4) **the prosecution need not prove an offender knew (or should have known) the age of the person [*for*] whom he or she purchased alcohol** in order to prove a violation of Section 25658(c); and (5) **a person charged with violating Section 25658(c) may defend against the charge by claiming an honest and reasonable belief that the person for whom he or she purchased alcohol was 21 years of age or older.** The defendant bears the burden of proof for this affirmative defense.

Conclusion

Because the trial court refused to admit evidence that petitioner believed Turpin was over 21 years old, it erred. Reversed and remanded.[19]

Note

The *In Re Jennings* court seems to be trying to have it both ways here. It ruled that its statute forbidding the purchase of alcohol for minors was a strict liability crime. The court also ruled, however, that the defendant can use a mistake of fact defense to avoid conviction. Since a mistake of fact defense is only used to show the lack of a guilty intent, how can such a defense aid a defendant who is charged with a crime that does not need the proof of intent in the first place? Did the court provide Jennings with the mistake of fact defense because his situation was uncomfortably close to that of "the typical social party host situation, (where) the host does not purchase alcohol for any particular guest?"

---

19. Reprinted from Westlaw, with permission of Thomson Reuters.

Learn from My (and Others') Mistakes

Keep Your Client in the Loop about Your Strategy

During hearings outside the jury's presence at a PC 245 ADW jury trial (the case involved the defendant blinding the victim), I pushed to offer the jury evidence about the defendant's violent past. He had served time in state prison for voluntary manslaughter. The trial judge agreed with the public defender that such evidence was more prejudicial than probative—that the evidence was so damaging that the jury would use it to convict the defendant not for the blinding charged but for the prior killing. Therefore, the public defender successfully had the evidence excluded from the trial. Later, when she called the defendant to the stand, he volunteered that he had just gotten out of prison for killing a guy. The lesson this defense lawyer learned is that you must continually communicate with your client, even on things that might seem obvious. The Wisconsin Supreme Court Rules, WI SCR Ch. 20 Preamble: A Lawyer's Responsibilities demands that, "A lawyer should maintain communication with a client concerning the representation."

The History of Strict Liability Crimes

Morissette v. United States, 342 U.S. 246 (1952), in reviewing the history of strict liability crimes, recalled that under the **Anglo-American tradition** of criminal law, **no crime existed unless a wrongful act was accompanied by a guilty mind. Generally, crime was understood to be a compound concept, needing the concurrence of "an evil-meaning mind with an evil-doing hand."** *Morissette* explained that, originally, when statutes omitted an intent element, courts assumed that intent was so much a part of crime that it required no statutory mention. Courts would therefore interpret the statutes as requiring an element of intent even when they failed to mention mens rea.

    Over time, legislatures created new crimes consisting only of forbidden acts or omissions, and thus purposely lacking a mental element. Legislatures were responding to the increasing dangers created by the **industrial revolution.** The invention of more powerful factory machinery, the advent of faster and heavier traffic, the crowding of cities, and the increasingly wide distribution of goods (whether of "food, drink, drugs, [or] securities"), all led to a heightened danger to the public. *Morissette* explained that legislatures responded with "increasingly numerous and detailed regulations" meant to heighten "the duties of those in control of particular industries, trades, properties or activities that affect public health, safety or welfare." Legislatures aimed to make these regulations "more effective" by enforcing them with criminal penalties. The new criminal laws were known as "**public welfare offenses**." Instead of involving "positive aggressions or invasions," these strict liability crimes instead involved "neglect where the law require[d] care, or inaction where it impose[d] a duty." While these laws did not have an "intent" element, the offender, "if he does will the violation, usually is in a position to prevent it with no more care than society might reasonably expect and no more exertion than it might reasonably exact from one who assumed his responsibilities." These crimes typically imposed "relatively small" penalties and do no "grave damage to an offender's reputation." Judges eventually accepted that these public welfare offenses could be committed without criminal intent. Courts came to understand **the new strict liability laws were "regulatory measures" based on states' "police power" to achieve "some social betterment rather than the punishment of the crimes** as in cases of mala in se."

DISCUSSION QUESTIONS

1. What is mens rea or criminal intent? Why does criminal law require it for most crimes?

2. What is concurrence and is it required for all crimes?

3. What is motive and how does it differ from mens rea? Is motive even required to prove crimes?

4. Suppose Ann, aiming to kill Bud, shoots a gun but misses Bud, and instead accidentally kills Cathy. Would Ann be guilty of a crime or of just committing a tragic accident? How would the doctrine of "transferred intent" help answer this question?

5. What are the key legal differences between general intent crimes and specific intent crimes? Do these linguistic differences even exist in reality?

6. What are the four mental states identified by the Model Penal Code and how do they differ from each other?

7. Since mental states occur inside a person's head, how can they be proved in court? What kinds of evidence are offered to establish mental states?

8. What is a strict liability crime and what element is missing from it that is required in more traditional crimes?

WEB LINKS

1. New York's "Criminal Jury Instructions" provide a particularly apt discussion of proof of intent. The instructions state in part:

    "The question naturally arises as to how to determine whether or not a defendant had the intent required for the commission of a crime.

    To make that determination in this case, you must decide if the required intent can be inferred beyond a reasonable doubt from the proven facts.

    In doing so, you may consider the person's conduct and all of the circumstances surrounding that conduct, including, but not limited to, the following:

    - what, if anything, did the person do or say;
    - what result, if any, followed the person's conduct; and
    - was that result the natural, necessary and probable consequence of that conduct."

    The entire instruction can be seen at: https://www.nycourts.gov/judges/cji/1-General/CJI2d.Intent.pdf

2. New York's "Criminal Jury Instructions" define the mental state of "knowingly" at: http://www.nycourts.gov/judges/cji/1-General/CJI2d.Knowingly.pdf

3. The mens rea or intent requirement is all about blameworthiness. What society blames can change over time, as demonstrated in a June 13, 2014, *New Scientist* article by Jennifer Ouellette entitled, "Crime mining: Hidden history emerges from court data" at: http://www.newscientist.com/article/dn25724-crime-mining-hidden-history-emerges-from-court-data.html

4. California's jury instructions criminal (CALCRIM) number 250 discusses the "Union of Act and Intent" requirement for most crimes. See page 8 at: http://www.courts.ca.gov/documents/20110429itemb.pdf

CHAPTER
IV

Causation: The Element Required for Crimes Having a Forbidden Result

A.   WHAT IS MEANT BY "CAUSATION"?

1.   Definition

Before the Russian Revolution, many had feared and hated Gregory Rasputin, a monk who was said to have influence over the czar and czarina of Russia. As described by biographer Robert K. Massie in his book, *Nicholas and Alexandra*, at 373–76 (1967) Bantam Doubleday Dell Publishing Group, Inc.), conspirators lured Rasputin to a cellar where they offered him poisoned cakes. When Rasputin ate two, the would-be murderers expected him to collapse in agony. Rasputin, who suffered no ill effects, then drank two glasses of wine, which were also poisoned. After two and a half hours of Rasputin happily listening to music, the conspirators switched tactics, shooting the monk in the back. The conspirators now believed Rasputin to finally be dead. Instead, Rasputin ran from the house, only to be felled by two more bullets. One conspirator then kicked Rasputin in his temple with a booted foot while another beat him with a rubber club. The conspirators then tied Rasputin up and shoved him through a hole in the ice into the Neva River, where he finally drowned.

Causation is the process where one action makes another thing happen.

There is a lesson here regarding causation in homicide. No matter how many potentially awful and lethal attacks a person launches on a victim, the attacker will not be found guilty of homicide unless he or she actually causes the death of the victim. Before Rasputin drowned, his attackers were not murderers, but failures.

Tips for Success for Future Law Enforcement

Do Your Homework in Choosing a Career in Law Enforcement

Fully research the job before ever contacting the employer. (For a starting point, see Appendices listing agencies.) This will give you information about the employer's overall philosophy, job requirements, benefits, and disadvantages. Law enforcement is like no other job, so it is important to go in with your eyes open. Solid research will help you decide if you are a good fit or even want the job. All this homework will make you a much better interviewee, for you can tell your prospective employer which particular skills and character traits you have that will fit well with the specific job offered. Persons who have looked into the position they seek to fill impress interviewers. Interviewees who cannot even name the sheriff of the department to which they are applying do not.

2. Requirement for Crimes Having a Forbidden Result

Although causation can be an issue with infliction of great bodily injury, malicious mischief, or with arson causing great bodily injury, the most common crime where it is relevant is homicide, where the criminal must cause the death of the victim. **Causation is not a requirement for all offenses, for some crimes do not possess a forbidden result.**

3. Factual Cause or Cause-In-Fact

a) "But-For" Cause

What if death is the extraordinary outcome of a simple assault? If one violently attacks another, the aggressor can be liable for homicide if the victim ultimately dies, even if such a result was not the attacker's goal. As seen in the case below, if a person is about to hit another person with a blunt instrument, he should probably consider having the victim first visit a cardiologist.

Such was the case in *State v. Atkinson*, 259 S.E.2d 858 (1979), in which the defendant was involved in a robbery where the victim was severely beaten with a baseball bat. Dr. Hudson, the Chief Medical Examiner of the State of North Carolina, gave his opinion at trial that the victim's injuries "would have enormously stimulated the heart and his blood pressure and that Williamson's death was accelerated by this stress." The court noted:

Factual cause ensures that each event is linked with its prior event to form a connected chain of cause.

Dr. Hudson's internal examination of decedent's body revealed severe arteriosclerosis in the heart and the arteries of the heart as well as scar tissue in the heart muscle itself indicating that decedent had suffered a prior heart attack. Dr. Hudson observed that the injuries which decedent incurred would have stimulated the heart enormously, providing a great deal of stress to the heart and his blood pressure level. Dr. Hudson testified that *** the injuries and the stress which they brought about contributed to and in fact accelerated Mr. Williamson's death. On cross-examination, the doctor testified that "[I] would say that this man's heart was in terrible condition. . . . In part this man died from a heart attack. . . . Based upon my autopsy this man was a walking bombshell. Any severe stress could have caused his heart to stop. . . . His heart condition was such that he would have been susceptible to have his heart stop . . . if his heart was bothered, stimulated or irritated."

The court concluded:

> A person is criminally responsible for a homicide only if his act caused or directly contributed to the death of the victim. *** **The consequences of an assault which is the direct cause of the death of another are not excused nor is the criminal responsibility for the death lessened by a preexisting physical condition which made the victim unable to withstand the shock of the assault and without which preexisting condition the blow would not have been fatal**. *** The testimony of Dr. Hudson, coupled with the testimony of decedent's wife which outlined her husband's history of high blood pressure, was sufficient for the state's case to withstand defendant's motion for nonsuit.

(Please note that, on a separate issue [the test for admissibility of shoeprints in trial], *State v. Atkinson* has been abandoned as improper. This does not affect the viability of its causation rule.)

Tips for Success for Future Law Students and Lawyers

Carefully and Fully Complete the Application and Personal Statement

Your application to law school is likely one of thousands. Directors of admission or members of admission committees will happily shrink their piles of applications (and their workload) by quickly rejecting any incomplete or improperly filled-out application. So, follow instructions to the letter. You want to accurately present your best self, so take time and care in filling out the application.

Applicants typically have to write a personal statement that answers some broad question. First, precision is key. Write and rewrite your statement. Get specific feedback from professors and pre-law advisors on possible improvements for your statement. The personal statement should have no errors in spelling, grammar, or word choice. It should be absolutely truthful. Also, be clear and concise. Rather than saying, "I cogitated about the prospect of endeavoring to pursue the legal profession," say "I thought about attending law school." Contrary to popular belief, the most persuasive lawyer is the one people can actually understand. Finally, candidly deal with negative facts in your past, whether in the personal statement or in an addendum. Take responsibility by owning your mistakes rather than trying to blame "the system" which you are trying to join as an attorney. Try to create a "happy sandwich" by starting and ending your essay on a positive note. Negative facts should be candidly explained rather than minimized. If you genuinely accept responsibility for your error, there is an argument that you have become a stronger and better applicant because of it.

VIDEO: Can We Ever Say One Thing Causes Another?

Philosopher David Hume had his doubts about ever fully establishing that one event caused another event to happen, as seen at:

https://www.youtube.com/watch?v=_tDVm_X5eQo

Model Penal Code Section 2.03 Causal Relationship Between Conduct and Result

(1) Conduct is the cause of a result when:

(a) it is an antecedent but for which the result in question would not have occurred; and

(b) the relationship between the conduct and result satisfies any additional causal requirements imposed by the Code or by the law defining the offense.

a. Multiple Causes ("Substantial Factor" Cases)[20]

Suppose two people, Ann and Bud, attack a victim who ultimately dies. Ann blames Bud for causing the victim's death, while Bud blames Ann. Such a case brings up the issue of **concurrent causes**—the victim died from **multiple causes** of death. The following case offers a view into a court's reasoning when two people both shoot a victim, causing wounds that together result in death.

© kilukilu/Shutterstock.com

When a victim is shot by more than one person, who is responsible for the victim's death?

---

20. From *The Model Penal Code* by the American Law Institute. Copyright © 1962 by the American Law Institute. Used by permission.

LEGAL ANALYSIS

Radford Cox, Sr. and Radford Cox, Jr. v. State
808 S.W.2d 306 (1991).
Justice Dudley delivered the opinion for the Supreme Court of Arkansas.

Facts

[A jury convicted Radford Cox, Sr. and Radford Cox, Jr. of the capital murder of Freddie Harrison. Both were sentenced to life in prison without parole. We affirm the judgment of conviction.]

Radford Cox, Sr. and Radford Cox, Jr., commonly known as Big Rad and Little Rad, attended the Independence Day celebration at the Clear Creek Bridge *** on July 4, 1989. [When Little Rad set off some fireworks, Freddie Harrison, a war veteran, said the fireworks made him nervous and asked Little Rad to stop setting them off.] Little Rad refused, and Harrison started to shove him around. Big Rad said, "Stop it, if you all don't stop it, somebody's gonna get hurt." Harrison knocked Little Rad to the ground. Big Rad reached into his nearby van, grabbed a .25 caliber pistol, and fired three to five shots at Harrison; hitting him in the chest and side. Harrison fell to the ground near a road.

Jonathan Cox, a bystander, went to Harrison and attempted to aid him, but Little Rad kicked him away. Harrison was still breathing at the time. Little Rad dragged Harrison from the road over into some brush ***. He returned to the van and said, "It's not over with yet, we gotta finish it." Big Rad handed him the pistol. Little Rad then disappeared into the nearby brush where he left Harrison. A witness heard three more shots. Little Rad reappeared and gave the pistol back to Big Rad. Harrison's body was later found by the police. He had been shot six times. Three of the bullet wounds were in his chest and side, and three more, which had been fired from only a few inches away, were in his head. [A firearms tool marks examiner found that the bullets removed from Harrison's body had been fired from Big Rad's pistol.]

[Both] appellants contend that there was insufficient evidence to show which one of them caused the victim's death.

Issue

Whether the case presented sufficient evidence that the two defendants both caused the victim's death.

Rule and Analysis

Our law is well established that, **where there are concurrent causes of death, conduct which hastens or contributes to a person's death is a cause of death**. ***

In the case at bar, the medical examiner who performed the autopsy on the victim testified, "Mr. Harrison was shot six times and he died as a result of these six wounds, which entered the brain, internal organs and caused death of internal bleeding." The eyewitnesses to the murder described the manner in which the killing occurred. **The medical examiner's testimony, coupled with that of the eyewitnesses', was sufficient to prove that the victim died as a result of internal bleeding from the shots fired by the appellants. Thus, there was substantial evidence they caused the death of their victim.** ***

Conclusion

Each defendant's shots contributed to the victim bleeding to death, and so both are guilty of being a substantial factor in the victim's death.

Affirmed.[21]

Note

Sadly, killings by multiple shooters are all too common. *Commonwealth v. Soto*, 693 A.2d 226 (1997), presented the following facts:

> Angel Soto a/k/a Chino (Soto) and his cousin Luis Torres (Popo) savagely killed Nepomuceno Pacheco (Nepo). The murder, planned and openly discussed for at least one week prior to the actual execution, resulted from a drug dealing dispute. After the duo lured the victim to a desolate quarry, Popo shot Nepo five times throughout the body area. Apparently unsatisfied that these wounds would prove fatal, but out of ammunition, Soto and Popo quickly fled to [obtain more bullets]. This accomplished, the cohorts returned to the scene of the crime, after which Soto shot Nepo three times in the head and then fled the jurisdiction.

In his defense, Soto argued that he "either shot a dead body or a victim who was so near to death that the later wounds could not legally be a substantial and direct cause of death." The court rejected Soto's argument, explaining:

> In order for an act **to be a direct cause of death, it must be a substantial, although not the sole, cause of the death**. Criminal liability as a principal actor may attach provided that the defendant's actions in bringing about the victim's death were not overridden by an independent, overriding, factor. ["**An accused may not escape criminal liability on the ground that, prior to the criminal act, his victim was not in perfect health**."]
>
> Applied to the instant case, it is evident that, although the victim's very life-blood was seeping out of him and his pulse and breathing were strained, he was alive when appellant shot him three times in the face at close range. Appellant's argument that he is somehow less culpable because the victim was doomed to death at the time appellant shot him is specious and outlandish. To accept this argument, this Court would have to hold that either appellant or his cousin, but not both, was the principal killer. However, when faced with facts that prove that both men inflicted a total of eight fatal wounds to the victim within a very short time frame, it would belie reality and justice to allow one man to escape unscathed and unaccountable for his actions.[22]

VIDEO: Who Caused the Death? "Magnolia" —Sydney Barringer's Unsuccessful Suicide

The movie *Magnolia* offered a strange case involving convoluted questions of causation, as can be seen in this YouTube clip:

http://www.youtube.com/watch?v=Ec51smvcsDY

---

21. Reprinted with the permission of LexisNexis.
22. Reprinted with the permission of LexisNexis.

Do's and Don'ts for Hearings, Trials, and Appeals

Preserve Testimony of Shaky Witnesses

Not all witnesses are happy to testify. Many have mixed motives and loyalties in the case. If you have a witness that you suspect might not show up later to testify, or might change his or her story in the future or suddenly have a memory lapse, **do** preserve his or her testimony by having the person testify in the current proceeding. People usually act based on their relationships with others. If a person is a member of a gang or trapped in a domestic violence relationship, immediate preservation of testimony can preserve your options for the future. If the person is a victim of sexual assault or domestic violence, **don't** force them to testify but instead **do** check with your office to properly apply the policy in such cases.

b)   Proximate Cause or Legal Cause

Are we responsible for *all* the consequences we cause? Suppose that Al is found guilty of murdering Beth. Al is therefore guilty of causing Beth's death. Yet, Al's parents conceived and reared Al through childhood. Are Al's parents guilty of somehow contributing to Beth's death by having Al as a child in the first place? If so, wouldn't Al's grandparents also be guilty of contributing? How about Al's great-grandparents? Such thinking has caused the law to place limits on criminal liability when it comes to causation. To be found guilty of committing homicide, a person must not only **factually cause** the victim's death, but also **proximately cause** the victim's death. It is not enough for the law that a criminal's wrongful act physically caused a particular person's death. Instead, the death must be a **foreseeable** result of the criminal's wrongful act.

The following case considers an interesting question regarding proximate cause—what if a criminal commits a wrongful act, but after this wrong, the victim, through his or her own **carelessness**, or "**negligence**," himself commits a wrong that contributes to his own death? Would such "**contributory negligence**" prevent the original wrongdoer from proximately causing the victim's death? This case also introduces us to the concepts of **dependent** and **superseding intervening events**.

If you capsize a boat, is it foreseeable that one of its occupants might drown?

LEGAL ANALYSIS

People v. Armitage
194 Cal. App. 3d 405 (1987).
Justice Sparks wrote the opinion for the California Court of Appeal.

Facts

On a drunken escapade on the Sacramento River in the middle of a spring night, defendant David James Armitage flipped his boat over and caused his companion to drown. As a result of this accident, defendant was convicted of the felony of drunk boating causing death in violation of former Harbors and Navigation Code section 655, subdivision (c). [Armitage claims] that he cannot be held criminally responsible for the death because the victim, against his warning, turned loose of the overturned boat and drowned while foolhardily attempting to swim ashore. **We hold that the unreflective but predictable act of the victim to escape from a peril created by defendant did not break the causal connection between the drunken boating and the death of the victim**. ***

On the evening of May 18, 1985, defendant and his friend, Peter Maskovich, were drinking in a bar ***. In the early morning hours defendant and Maskovich wound up racing defendant's boat on the Sacramento River while both of them were intoxicated. The boat did not contain any personal flotation devices. About 3 a.m. Gary Bingham, who lived in a house boat in a speed zone (five miles per hour, no wake), was disturbed by a large wake. He went out to yell at the boaters and observed a small aluminum boat with two persons in it at the bend in the river. The boaters had the motor wide open, were zig-zagging, and had no running lights on at the time. About the same time, Rodney and Susan Logan were fishing on the river *** when they observed an aluminum boat with two men in it coming up the river without running lights. The occupants were using loud and vulgar language, and were operating the boat very fast and erratically.

[An autopsy revealed that at the time of his death Maskovich had a blood alcohol level of .25 percent. A blood sample taken from defendant revealed a blood alcohol level at that time of .14 percent.]

James Snook lives near the Sacramento River ***. Sometime around 3 a.m. defendant came to his door. Defendant was soaking wet and appeared quite intoxicated. He reported that he had flipped his boat over in the river and had lost his buddy. He said that at first he and his buddy had been hanging on to the overturned boat, but that his buddy swam for shore and he did not know whether he had made it. As it turned out, Maskovich did not make it; he drowned in the river.

Mr. Snook notified the authorities of the accident. [Deputy Snyder, an officer who normally worked on the river, met with the defendant.] Deputy Snyder attempted to question defendant about the accident and defendant stated that he had been operating the boat at a high rate of speed and zig-zagging until it capsized. Defendant also stated that he told the victim to hang on to the boat but his friend ignored his warning and started swimming for the shore. [Deputy Snyder then arrested defendant.]

Issue

Whether the defendant proximately caused the victim's death, even though the victim panicked and failed to follow the defendant's wise advice after the accident.

Rule and Analysis

[Defendant] contends his actions were not the proximate cause of the death of the victim. *** Defendant asserts that after his boat flipped over he and the victim were holding on to it and the victim, against his advice, decided to abandon the boat and try to swim to shore. According to defendant the victim's fatally reckless decision should exonerate him from criminal responsibility for his death.

We reject defendant's contention. *** Proximate cause of a death has traditionally been defined in criminal cases as "a cause which, in natural and continuous sequence, produces the death, and without which the death would not have occurred." ["Proximate] cause is clearly established where the act is directly connected with the resulting injury, with no intervening force operating." *** Defendant claims that the victim's attempt to swim ashore, whether characterized as an intervening or a superseding cause, constituted a break in the natural and continuous sequence arising from the unlawful operation of the boat. The claim cannot hold water. [In criminal prosecutions, the contributory negligence of the victim is not a defense. The relevant standard jury instruction reads: "**It is not a defense to a criminal charge that the deceased or some other person was guilty of negligence, which was a contributory cause of the death involved in the case.**"] In order **to exonerate a defendant the victim's conduct must not only be a cause of his injury, it must be a superseding cause**. "A defendant may be criminally liable for a result directly caused by his act even if there is another contributing cause. **If an intervening cause is a normal and reasonably foreseeable result of defendant's original act the intervening act is 'dependent' and not a superseding cause, and will not relieve defendant of liability.**" [An] obvious illustration of a dependent cause is the victim's attempt to escape from a deadly attack or other danger in which he is placed by the defendant's wrongful act." [**It is only an unforeseeable intervening cause, an extraordinary and abnormal occurrence, which rises to the level of an exonerating, superseding cause.** In] criminal law a victim's predictable effort to escape a peril created by the defendant is not considered a superseding cause of the ensuing injury or death. [An unreflective act in response to a peril created by defendant will not break a causal connection. "**When defendant's conduct causes panic an act done under the influence of panic or extreme fear will not destroy causal connection unless the reaction is wholly abnormal.**"]

Here defendant, through his misconduct, placed the intoxicated victim in the middle of a dangerous river in the early morning hours clinging to an overturned boat. The fact that the panic-stricken victim recklessly abandoned the boat and tried to swim ashore was not a wholly abnormal reaction to the perceived peril of drowning. Just as "[detached] reflection cannot be demanded in the presence of an uplifted knife" ***, neither can caution be required of a drowning man. Having placed the inebriated victim in peril, defendant cannot obtain exoneration by claiming the victim should have reacted differently or more prudently. ***

Conclusion

[The] evidence establishes that defendant's acts and omissions were the proximate cause of the victim's death. The judgment is affirmed.[23]

"Seamless Web" Connection

In the *Armitage* case just discussed, the court analyzed proximate cause in terms of foreseeability. If a person who is considering committing a wrongful act can foresee that a bad result of his or her conduct is likely, then that person should be held responsible for such a foreseeable consequence. This reasoning is directly connected to the criminal law's focus on morality and blame, discussed in Chapter 1. If a person could have foreseen the bad result of his or her actions, the law feels it is morally proper to blame him or her for that result.

---

23. Reprinted with the permission of LexisNexis.

> **VIDEO: *Magnolia's* Successful "Unsuccessful" Suicide of Sydney Barringer**
>
> The movie, *Magnolia*, has the following thought experiment regarding cause at:
>
> https://www.youtube.com/watch?v=Ec51smvcsDY

Biography—Prosecutor

Robert H. Jackson (also U.S. Supreme Court Justice):

- Born on February 13, 1892, in Spring Creek, Pennsylvania.
- According to the Robert H. Jackson Center, Jackson did not earn a college degree and did not earn the typical LL.B. or J.D. when attending Albany Law School.
- Served as U.S. Attorney General.
- According to Noah Feldman in "Scorpions: The Battles and Triumphs of FDR's Great Supreme Court Justices," by Twelve Hachette Book Group (2010), Jackson, while playing poker with President Roosevelt, learned that England was about to enter World War II.
- Was appointed Associate Justice to the Supreme Court by President Franklin Delano Roosevelt in 1941.
- According to the Robert H. Jackson Center at https://www.roberthjackson.org/, "During 1945-46, Justice Jackson was the architect of the international trial process and then the chief prosecutor of the surviving Nazi leaders at Nuremberg, Germany."
- **Left serving on the Supreme Court in order to prosecute Nazi war criminals**. Jackson's decision to prosecute the Nazis is dramatically described in Robert E. Conot's "Justice at Nuremberg," by Harper & Row Publishers (1983)."
- Joined the opinion in *Brown v. Board of Education* which ruled against segregation in schools.

Even jurists can demonstrate a lack of taste in discussing sensitive cases, such as a homicide. Thus, the court in *Armitage* did not choose the best possible language when, analyzing a drowning case; it declared that the defendant's "claim cannot hold water."

Yesterday and Today: If a Person Causes a Victim to Commit Suicide, Does This Constitute Murder?

The California Supreme Court, in *People v. Lewis* 124 Cal. 551 (1899), considered whether a person could be guilty of manslaughter in a case where the victim actually died by cutting his own throat. The court gave the facts as follows:

> Defendant [Lewis] and deceased [Farrell] were brothers-in-law, and not altogether friendly. [On the morning of the homicide the deceased visited] the defendant, was received in a friendly manner, but after a while an altercation arose, as a result of which defendant shot

deceased in the abdomen, inflicting a wound that was necessarily mortal. Farrell fell to the ground *** but soon got up and went into the house, saying: "Shoot me again; I shall die anyway." His strength soon failed him and he was put to bed. [In a few minutes,] the deceased procured a knife and cut his throat, inflicting a ghastly wound, from the effect of which, according to the medical evidence, he must necessarily have died in five minutes. The wound inflicted by the defendant severed the mesenteric artery, and medical witnesses testified that under the circumstances it was necessarily mortal, and death would ensue within one hour from the effects of the wound alone. Indeed, the evidence was that usually the effect of such a wound would be to cause death in less time than that. [The internal hemorrhage and other effects of the gunshot wound] produced intense pain. The medical witnesses thought that death was accelerated by the knife wound. Perhaps some of them considered it the immediate cause of death.

Lewis' jury heard other damaging evidence. The jury heard that, when Farrell asked whether his word was good with the defendant, Lewis responded, "No, not with me." The jury also heard that, when the defendant's wife asked for a doctor, Lewis responded, "Don't go for a doctor; damn him, let him die."

As heinous as the shooting might have been, the defendant argued that his own actions did not actually cause the victim's death. The victim, by slitting his own throat, committed an "independent intervening" event which "effectually prevented [the defendant] from killing ***." The defendant argued that he could only be guilty of attempted murder. The victim's cutting his own throat, as an intervening act, "was the cause of death, if it shortened the life of Farrell for any period whatever." The court ruled:

[The prosecution argued that the shooting] was the direct cause of the throat cutting, and, therefore, defendant is criminally responsible for the death. He illustrates his position by supposing a case of one dangerously wounded and whose wounds had been bandaged by a surgeon. He says, suppose through the fever and pain consequent upon the wound the patient becomes frenzied and tears away the bandage and thus accelerates his own death. Would not the defendant be responsible for a homicide? Undoubtedly he would be, for in the case supposed the deceased died from the wound, aggravated, it is true, by the restlessness of the deceased, but still the wound inflicted by the defendant produced death. ***

The attorney general seems to admit a fact which I do not concede, that the gunshot wound was not, when Farrell died, then itself directly contributory to the death. I think the jury [was] warranted in finding that it was. But if the deceased did die from the effect of the knife wound alone, no doubt the defendant would be responsible [because the jury could have found] that the knife wound was caused by the wound inflicted by the defendant in the natural course of events.

[Suppose one wounds another] intending to take life, but the wound, though painful, is not even dangerous, and the wounded man knows that it is not mortal, and yet takes his own life to escape pain, would it not be suicide only? [The] wound inflicted by the assailant would have the same relation to death which the original wound in this case has to the knife wound. The wound induced the suicide, but the wound was not, in the usual course of things, the cause of the suicide.

Here, when the throat was cut, Farrell was not merely languishing from a mortal wound. He was actually dying—and after the throat was cut he continued to languish from both wounds. **Drop by drop the life current went out from both wounds, and at the very instant of death the gunshot wound was contributing to the event.** ***

The judgment is affirmed.

VIDEO: U.S. Supreme Court Justice Elena Kagan Talks about Her Views of Her Colleague on the Court

Justice Kagan discloses her thoughts about her fellow justice, Chief Justice John Roberts at:

https://www.youtube.com/watch?v=RyIr0_ia030

LEGAL SKILLS: How to Preserve a Gesture for the Record

When witnesses are on the witness stand, they convey information not only by statements, but also by gestures. Witnesses will nod rather than say "yes," they will hold out their hands describing something as "this big," and they will say "he pointed the gun like this." These gestures are of little help when "building a record" in a case. Every word spoken is taken down "for the record" by a court reporter so that appellate courts, when considering defendants' appeals, can know what occurred in the courtroom. To "preserve" the record, an attorney will first ask a witness to provide a verbal response in order to help the court reporter in recording everything that is happening. Witnesses, often nervous, might continue to make gestures without explanations. The alert attorney will then explicitly note, "Let the record reflect that the witness nodded her head up and down indicating 'yes,'" or "Let the record reflect that the witness held his hands about one foot apart when indicating the size of the knife." Opposing counsel can offer his or her own refinements if need be. These efforts help provide a clearer picture of the case for all later courts.

---

c) **Proximate and Concurrent Causation**

LEGAL ANALYSIS

State v. Cox
2017 WL 1632635, No. COA16-1068 (May 2, 2017).
Judge Tyson wrote the opinion for Court of Appeals of North Carolina.

Facts

[After completing her second shift at work at about 1:00 a.m., on November 28, 2011, Hluon Siu picked up her four-year-old son, Khai, from her father's home. Siu, driving her white 2004 Nissan Altima sedan with Khai seated in a booster seat in the rear passenger seat, properly entered an intersection on a green light. Defendant, driving a 2000 gray Chevrolet Tahoe, struck the driver's side of Siu's vehicle.] The evidence tended to show Defendant *** failed to stop at a red light prior to entering the intersection. Ms. Siu was killed almost immediately by the impact.

[Witness Carmen Hayes testified that Defendant's vehicle "flew across" the intersection at between fifty and sixty miles per hour, in defiance of the posted thirty-five miles per hour speed limit.] Hayes testified Defendant got out of his vehicle, appeared to be uninjured, and "he just kind of stood there" and did "absolutely nothing." She stated, "He never once asked is she okay, he was not apologetic, he stood there. . . . No remorse."

[Witnesses Pamela Pittman and her daughter] both testified the light in Ms. Siu's lane of travel was green. Pittman immediately went to Ms. Siu's overturned vehicle to render assistance. She testified Defendant stood beside his vehicle and walked around with his hands in his pockets.

[The police department's Major Crash Unit investigated the crash. Officer Cerdan, assigned to evaluate Defendant for impairment, recognized him from an earlier DUI arrest.] Officer Cerdan observed Defendant's eyes to be red, watery and bloodshot. A strong odor of alcohol emanated from Defendant's breath. Defendant initially denied drinking alcohol, but later stated to Officer Cerdan he drank a glass of wine at 9:00 p.m. and had taken "DayQuil and NyQuil" earlier that day.

Officer Cerdan performed field sobriety testing on Defendant. On the horizontal gaze nystagmus test, Defendant manifested all six clues of impairment. *** After completing the field sobriety tests, Officer Cerdan formed the opinion that Defendant's mental and physical faculties were appreciably impaired by alcohol. Defendant was arrested for driving while impaired and for failure to comply with his .04 blood alcohol concentration restriction on his driver's license. [A chemical analysis of defendant's blood sample revealed a .17 blood alcohol concentration.]

Detective Sammis charged Defendant with second-degree murder and felonious serious injury by vehicle.

At the conclusion of his investigation of the crash, Detective Sammis determined that Defendant *** hit Ms. Siu's vehicle while traveling approximately 48.6 miles per hour. Ms. Siu was driving through a green light on The Plaza at approximately 36.8 miles per hour at the time Defendant struck her vehicle. There was no evidence of any "pre-impact braking" from tire marks on the road.

Detectives retrieved an iPhone from the driver's side floorboard of Defendant's vehicle. One of the text messages stored in Defendant's phone was sent about fourteen hours prior to the crash, and stated, "I might drink a little more than I should tonight." Defendant did not offer any evidence at trial.

Issue

Whether the trial judge committed error by failing to instruct the jury about the victim's "intervening negligence."

Rule and Analysis

Defendant argues the trial court's instruction on proximate cause was erroneous, [in] failing to instruct the jury on intervening negligence. We disagree.

The trial court instructed the jury [in part] as follows: "[T]he State must prove beyond a reasonable doubt only that the defendant's negligence was *a* proximate cause." *** Defendant contends [this] instruction suggests to the jury that they not consider the impact of any negligence on the part of Ms. Siu. Defendant acknowledges he did not request a jury instruction on intervening negligence.

[In a prior case, the court has correctly stated that, "**there may be more than one proximate cause of an injury. The State must prove beyond a reasonable doubt only that the defendant's negligence was *a* proximate cause.**" Here,] we find that the trial court did not err in denying defendant's requested instruction.

Even assuming [the decedent] was negligent, "[i]n order for negligence of another to insulate defendant from criminal liability, that negligence must be such as to break the causal chain of defendant's negligence; otherwise, defendant's culpable negligence remains a proximate cause, sufficient to find him criminally liable." In the instant case, [the **decedent's negligence, if any, would be, at most, a *concurring* proximate cause** of her own death].

[The record does not show] "the jury probably would have reached a different result" if the instruction on intervening negligence was given. *** Overwhelming evidence, including the testimonies of three eye witnesses, was presented to show Defendant drove through the red light, while grossly impaired and caused the crash. [The record shows] the only evidence to hint Ms. Siu may have been negligent in causing the crash is Defendant's off-handed comment to Officer Cerdan prior to the blood draw, when he asked if Officer Cerdan "tested the person that ran the red light." Defendant has failed to show plain error by the absence of a jury instruction on intervening negligence.

Even presuming Ms. Siu was somehow negligent, "her negligence, if any, would be, at most, a *concurring* proximate cause of her own death." *** The State's evidence tended to show that Defendant's blood alcohol content was over twice the legal limit. "This impairment inhibited defendant's ability to exercise due care and to keep a reasonable and proper lookout in the direction of travel." [The trial court's proximate cause instruction was an accurate statement of the law.]

Conclusion

The trial court's jury instructions on proximate cause were accurate and did not mislead the jury. Defendant has failed to show the trial court committed plain error by failing to give an instruction on intervening negligence.

It is so ordered. **NO PREJUDICIAL ERROR.**[24]

Does removal of a ventilator from an accident victim prevent a drunk driver from proximately causing an accident?

The Supreme Court of New Jersey considered this question in *State v. Pelham*, 176 N.J. 448 (2003). In *Pelham*, Sonney Pelham, driving a Toyota Camry, rear-ended William Patrick as he was driving his Chrysler LeBaron. "The LeBaron sailed over the curb and slid along the guardrail, crashing into a utility pole before it ultimately came to rest 152 feet from the site of impact." Police found Patrick, "unconscious and slumped forward in the driver's seat," making "gurgling" and "wheezing" sounds. Extracting Patrick with the "jaws of life," authorities took him to the hospital. Police determined that Pelham, who was "belligerent," had a blood alcohol content .19 and .22 at the time of the accident.

Patrick had a "spinal column fracture that left him paralyzed from the chest down." He had a "flailed chest," where multiple broken ribs cause "uneven chest wall movement during each breath." These and other injuries prompted doctors to place Patrick on a ventilator. Within days of the accident, Patrick's lungs began to fail. Since Patrick could not feed himself, doctors inserted a feeding tube directly into his stomach. He suffered inability to control his bladder or bowels, antibiotic-resistant infections, sepsis, pneumonia, and multi-organ system failure. Due to his injuries, Patrick became depressed, hallucinatory, psychotic, and "'significantly brain injured." Patrick "was aware of his physical and cognitive disabilities. During lucid moments, he expressed his unhappiness with his situation, and, on occasion, tried to remove his ventilator." Patrick's family "decided to act in accordance with his wishes and remove the ventilator." Two hours after doctors removed the ventilator, Patrick was pronounced dead.

The defendant was charged with aggravated manslaughter, which occurred when a person "recklessly causes death under circumstances manifesting extreme indifference to human life."

Pelham explained that causation had two parts: 1) "a **'but-for' test** under which **the defendant's conduct is 'deemed a cause of the event if the event would not have occurred without that conduct,'"** and, 2) a "culpability assessment" where "the actual result is of the same character, but occurred in a different manner from that designed or contemplated [or risked]. For this issue of **proximate cause**, a jury must decide "whether **intervening causes or unforeseen conditions lead**

---

24. Reprinted from Westlaw, with permission of Thomson Reuters.

to the conclusion," and so it would be "unjust to find that the defendant's conduct is the cause of the actual result." *Pelham,* noting the difference between "but for cause" and "proximate cause," recognized, "Although the jury may find that the defendant's conduct was a "but-for" cause of the victim's death . . . it may nevertheless conclude . . . that the death differed in kind from that designed or contemplated [or risked] or that the death was too remote, accidental in its occurrence, or dependent on another's volitional act to justify a murder conviction."

Proximate cause could be destroyed by an "intervening event" which is an "event that comes between the initial event in a sequence and the end result, thereby altering the natural course of events that might have connected a wrongful act to an injury." To "avoid breaking the chain of causation," the difference between the result a defendant intended or risked and the actual result of his conduct "must not be so out of the ordinary that it is unfair to hold defendant responsible for that result." Therefore, **an "independent intervening cause" can relieve a defendant of guilt.** *Pelham* identified the issue as whether the removal of the victim's life support constituted an "independent intervening cause."

Pelham explained that New Jersey had a "longstanding, clear policy" recognizing the "right of an individual to accept, reject, or discontinue medical treatment in the form of life supporting devices or techniques." **Since "a person's choice to have himself or herself removed from life support cannot be viewed as unexpected or extraordinary," the "removal of life support is not an independent intervening cause" used to remove the defendant's guilt.** The court therefore held a victim's decision to invoke his right to terminate life support may not, as a matter of law, be considered an independent intervening cause capable of breaking the chain of causation triggered by defendant's wrongful actions."[25]

Learn from My (and Others') Mistakes

Fully Investigate Your Own Witnesses

Not every victim is as pure as the driven snow. I prosecuted in a jury trial a large and powerful forty-year-old man who viciously pistol-whipped an elderly and frail victim into partial aphasia (brain damage which impairs the ability to speak). Although my victim had a crime on his record, his unidentified crime had happened so long ago that it was "manually stored" on paper files stuck in some warehouse. Since my victim was a sweet old gentleman, the records were beyond easy reach, and I had a trial deadline, I relied on his word that the crime was a small and inconsequential matter. The defense counsel did not make my mistake. When cross-examining my victim, the defense attorney calmly inquired as follows:

Atty.: "Have you ever committed a crime?"
Vict.: "Some small stuff long ago in my youth."
Atty.: "Only small stuff. Are you as sure about that as you are of all your testimony today?"
Vict.: "Yes, of course."
Atty.: "So you never stabbed a guy in the thigh while drinking at a bar, being convicted of ADW with a knife?"
Vict.: "That was different! That m----r f----r deserved it!"

So much for a kindly and sympathetic victim.

25. Reprinted from Westlaw, with permission of Thomson Reuters.

In *State v. Buckley*, 216 N.J. 249 (2013), Supreme Court of New Jersey considered a case where a veteran police officer lost control of a sports car. The defendant, Keith R. Buckley, had "served in the North Brunswick Police Department for fourteen years, and held the rank of lieutenant, supervising officers assigned to patrol responsibilities." Buckley borrowed a Dodge Viper, "a high-performance sports car," from his brother. While driving, Buckley saw a fellow police lieutenant named Zerby. Buckley "pulled up next to Zerby and asked him if he wanted an 'early lunch,' and Zerby said that he wanted a ride in the sports car." Zerby got in the vehicle. Buckley ultimately drove the Viper off the road and into a utility pole, killing Zerby.

Buckley was charged with second-degree vehicular homicide for causing "Zerby's death by driving recklessly." He claimed that Zerby failed to wear a seat belt as required by law. Had Zerby been wearing the seat belt, he "would have survived the accident." Zerby's failure to have a seat belt on prevented the prosecution from proving causation.

The court found Zerby's failure to wear the seat belt irrelevant to both "but for cause" and "proximate cause."

One might suppose that a jury would have little patience with a claim by a lieutenant who supervises patrol officers that he should be relieved of criminal responsibility for the consequences of such an auto accident.

Causing Homicide: The Guilty Verdict for Ice Cream

On July 9, 2013, Justin Peters, in his blog, *Crime: A Blog About Murder, Theft, and Other Wickedness*, wrote *When Ice Cream Sales Rise, So Do Homicides. Coincidence, or Will Your Next Cone Murder You?* discussing the question whether ice cream should be blamed for causing murders. His essay can be viewed by visiting:

http://www.slate.com/blogs/crime/2013/07/09/warm_weather_homicide_rates_
when_ice_cream_sales_rise_homicides_rise_coincidence.html

Nicholas Gerbis, in *howstuffworks, 10 Correlations That Are Not Causations*, stops the speculation. His article can be seen by visiting:

https://science.howstuffworks.com/innovation/science-questions/
10-correlations-that-are-not-causations.htm

DISCUSSION QUESTIONS

1. What does causation mean in criminal law? Why is it important?

2. Is causation a required element for all crimes? Why or why not?

3. What is factual cause? How can it be solved by reframing the issue with a "but for" question?

4. What is proximate cause and how does it differ from factual cause?

5. Can a wrongdoer still be guilty for causing a death if the carelessness of the decedent him or herself contributed to the fatal outcome?

6. What is foreseeability and how does it apply to proximate cause?

7. What are intervening events? How do intervening events affect causation?

8. What is the difference between a dependent intervening event and a superseding intervening event?

WEB LINKS

1. Who caused the death of President Garfield? Most would blame his assassin, Charles Guiteau. Author Candice Millard, in *Destiny of the Republic: A Tale of Madness, Medicine and the Murder of a President,* however, offers a different theory of causation—the president's own doctors. This discussion of causation can be seen at: http://www.nytimes.com/2011/10/02/books/review/ destiny-of-the-republic-by-candice-millard-book-review.html?pagewanted=all&_r=1&

2. How can we know if causation even exists? David Hume, the eighteenth century philosopher, doubted whether we could ever really know if one event truly "caused" another, or just happened at the same time. See the *Internet Encyclopedia of Philosophy* at: http://www.iep.utm.edu/hume-cau/

3. California's jury instructions criminal (CALCRIM) number 240 defines "causation" at page 61 at: http://www.courts.ca.gov/partners/documents/calcrim_juryins.pdf

4. California's jury instructions criminal (CALCRIM) number 640 discusses proximate cause issues at page 383 at: http://www.courts.ca.gov/partners/documents/calcrim_juryins.pdf

CHAPTER
V

Crimes against the Person and against Life: Homicide

A. MURDER

The law views human life as precious. In defending against a homicide charge, no one can diminish the value of another life, regardless of the victim's suffering or the brevity of the time he or she has left. Suppose you find a hospital patient who is suffering severe pain in the last stages of cancer. This patient has climbed out on the ledge of a high-rise hospital with the intent to jump to his death at noon. What if you shove the person off the ledge at 11:59? This shortening of life, or acceleration of death, is criminal homicide.

In *People v. Moan* 65 Cal. 532 (1884), the California Supreme Court explained, **"If a patient is lying in the last stages of consumption, with a tenure upon life that cannot possibly continue for a day, it is homicide to administer a poison to him by which his life is ended almost immediately."**

"He was a good boss, and we'll miss him ... go ahead and kick his briefcase down, too."

Did he fall or was he pushed? This explains why criminal law professors do not go on nature walks with their students.

© Cartoon Resource/Shutterstock.com

Likewise, if a victim, "by excessive indulgence in alcoholic drinks had reduced himself to a wreck and brought his life to the verge of the grave, it was a wrongful act for the defendant to accelerate his death by violence." Such crimes against the person, however brief a time they cut short, are still so severe that they can be included in the category of crimes against life.

1. Unlawful Killing

Not all homicide is criminal. For instance, killing the enemy in combat during war and killing another while defending one's own life from an illegal and fatal attack are lawful homicides. Manslaughter or murder—criminal homicide—is prosecuted because it falls outside of any lawful privilege to kill.

a) "Causing" Death: The Timing Issue

(1) Common Law

For most of human history, medicine was not something about which doctors could brag. Doctors, probing their patients with soiled hands and basing treatment decisions on balancing mythical bodily "humors," likely killed more patients than they cured. Traces of this legacy persist to this day. *The Lancet*, one of the most prestigious medical journals, is named after a device used to bleed patients, a practice doctors of old fell back on when they could think of no other treatment. At common law, in recognition of medicine's limitations, and the ever-increasing chance that with the passage of time other events might actually cause death, Blackstone, in *Commentaries*, Vol. IV, at 197, required that **"to make a killing murder, it is requisite that the party die within a year and a day after the stroke received, or cause of death administered."** United States jurisdictions adopted this arbitrary time limit. With the continual advances in modern medicine, support for the rule is waning.

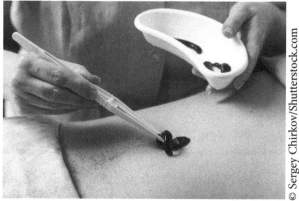

It once was so common for doctors to bleed patients that physicians were informally called 'leeches.'

© Sergey Chirkov/Shutterstock.com

The Supreme Court of Rhode Island discussed the history of the year and a day rule in *State v. Pine*, 524 A.2d 1104, 1105 (1987), in which Arthur Pine punched the victim in the jaw. The victim became unconscious when he fell against a curb. The court noted:

> The history of the common-law year-and-a-day rule is long but not altogether clear. The statutes made at Glocester on October 4, 1278, held that a suit for murder "shall not be abated for default of fresh suit, if the party shall sue within the year and the day after the deed done." [The Statute of Glocester therefore appears to have created the year and a day rule. This statute] appears to have provided a statute of limitations on the private form of murder prosecution, called an "appeal," measured from the date of the victim's death. *** The year-and-a-day rule that concerns us today is measured from the date of the assault rather than from the date of death. The latter rule, as part of the common law definition of murder, holds that **"in order also to make killing murder, it is requisite that the party die within a year and a day after the stroke received, or cause of death administered * * *."**

The following case, in considering **when a victim must die** in order for the law to deem that his or her death was a **homicide,** analyzes the common law's **year-and-a-day rule.**

LEGAL ANALYSIS

State v. Gabehart
114 N.M. 183 (1992).
Judge Donnelly delivered the opinion of the Court of Appeals of New Mexico.

Facts

Defendant [Tod G. Gabehart] appeals his conviction for involuntary manslaughter. [The issue] is whether the trial court erred in denying his motion to dismiss the charge against him under the "year-and-a-day" rule. We determine that the rule is applicable herein and reverse Defendant's conviction.

On April 11, 1988, Defendant was involved in an altercation with the victim. During the course of a fight between Defendant and the victim, the victim was thrown to the ground and struck his head on the pavement. Defendant called an ambulance and the victim was taken to a hospital. As a result of the injuries received in the altercation, the victim lapsed into a coma and never regained consciousness. On September 5, 1989, more than fifteen months following the altercation, the victim died. His death was attributable, in part, to his injuries received during his fight with Defendant. Following the death of the victim, Defendant was charged with voluntary manslaughter. He moved to dismiss the charges on the ground that the victim did not die within a year and a day of the time the injuries were sustained. The trial court denied the motion and Defendant was subsequently convicted of involuntary manslaughter.

Issue

Should the fact that the victim's death occurred after one year and one day from when the defendant threw him to the ground operate as a defense against a manslaughter charge?

Rule and Analysis

[**Under common law's year-and-a-day rule, if a person injured by an assailant survived beyond a year and one day after receiving the injuries, the defendant is excused from criminal culpability for the death**. Absent legislative or judicial abolition of such rule, a majority of jurisdictions] have determined that it constitutes a valid common-law defense to a charge of homicide. ***

Where there is no statute contravening the common-law rule that a party must die in a year and a day after the wound is inflicted to make the killing murder or manslaughter, the Legislature by its silence on the subject of time intended that the common-law rule should govern.

***Most American jurisdictions still follow the common-law rule that in order to constitute punishable homicide, death must ensue within a year and a day from the infliction of a mortal wound. ***

The State concedes that the New Mexico Legislature adopted the common law into this state's criminal jurisprudence. *** The State also admits that no statutory provision purports to change the year-and-a-day rule. However, the State argues that the rule should not be applied in this case because . . . the rule is anachronistic and should be abolished. ***

Courts in other jurisdictions have determined that at common law the year-and-a-day rule applied to all homicide cases. *** Review of these cases indicates that, at common law, the rule applied to manslaughter as well as murder cases.

The original reason for recognition of the rule was grounded upon the uncertainty of causation for the death of an individual where the death occurs more than a year and a day following the infliction of injuries upon the victim. [LaFave and Scott have noted that the] "difficulty in proving that the blow caused the death after so long an interval was obviously the basis of the rule." Recent precedent, however, points out that due to modern advances in medical and criminal science and technology, the rationale behind the rule no longer exists. [Retention] of the rule is inconsistent with demonstrable medical evidence in "lingering death" situations. Advances in medical technology now permit victims, although severely injured, to be kept alive for extended periods of time. We agree *** that **the basis for the rule has disappeared, and that it would be incongruous if developments in medical science that allow a victim's life to be prolonged were permitted to be used to bar prosecution of an assailant, where scientific evidence is presented to establish beyond a reasonable doubt that the defendant's acts proximately caused the victim's death**.

The debate in some courts as to the continuing viability of the rule has sometimes turned on the question of whether the courts or the legislature should take action to abolish the rule. *** In New Mexico, courts have not hesitated to abolish common-law doctrines that have proven anachronistic. [The] **common-law rule was judicially adopted, it is subject to abrogation by the courts, and the rule should be abolished and no longer recognized as a bar to prosecution for homicide in New Mexico**.

The remaining question before us then is whether abrogation of the common-law rule should be made applicable in the instant case. At the time Defendant committed the act for which he was convicted, the common-law rule was in effect in New Mexico, and Defendant could not have been convicted of homicide unless the victim died within a year and a day resulting from Defendant's wrongful act. ***

[Applying] **such a decision retroactively would violate the constitutional prohibition against *ex post facto* laws *** because the effect of the decision would be to aggravate a crime from a lesser offense to homicide. [We] conclude that abolition of such rule should be prospective in its effect**.

Conclusion

We hold that the common-law year-and-a-day rule should no longer be recognized in this jurisdiction and reject further application of the rule. The rule, although prospectively abolished, precludes the State from prosecuting Defendant for manslaughter herein. Accordingly, Defendant's conviction is reversed.[26]

"Seamless Web" Connection

In *State v. Gabehart*, the case just discussed, the court refused to overturn the common law's year and a day rule because the defendant committed his acts when that rule was in existence, and therefore might have relied upon it. The court, concerned about applying a new rule retroactively in a manner that would harm the defendant, warned against violating the "ex post facto" prohibition in the U.S. Constitution. This case therefore connects, through the seamless web, the common law's year and a day rule with Chapter 1's concept of ex post facto laws.

---

26. Reprinted by permission of LexisNexis and by the New Mexico Compilation Commission.

Tips for Success for Future Law Enforcement

Filling Out the Application

Tell the truth. Lies are not only wrong, but doom your prospects at this employer and potentially all other public safety employers—because law enforcement agencies communicate with each other. If sought, provide a carefully written writing sample. Any prior bad behavior or mistakes, placed in the middle of the statement, should be handled candidly and concisely. No employer in law enforcement wishes to hear that you once were railroaded by the system. Own your life mistakes by taking full responsibility—after all, you will have to do so when on duty.

VIDEO: Interviews with Serial Killers—Is a Serial Killer Ever Credible?

WARNING: POTENTIALLY DISTURBING VIDEOS. Ted Bundy blamed his murders on pornography at:

https://www.youtube.com/watch?v=Vlk_sRU49TI

Aileen Wuornos discusses her beliefs about police wrongdoing at:

https://www.youtube.com/watch?v=ilb4beZ_wQo

Jeffrey Dahmer and his family discuss his killings at:

https://www.youtube.com/watch?v=vPMBfX7D4WU

(2) Today's Law

Rather than entirely abolish common law's year and a day rule, some jurisdictions choose a compromise. California provides such an example.

PC 194: Murder and manslaughter: time of death; presumption

To make the killing either murder or manslaughter, **it is not requisite that the party die within three years and a day after the stroke received or the cause of death administered. If death occurs beyond the time of three years and one day, there shall be a rebuttable presumption that the killing was not criminal.** The prosecution shall bear the burden of overcoming this presumption. In the computational time, the whole of the day on which the act was done shall be reckoned the first.

b) Determining What Is "Death"

(1) Common Law

Traditionally, determining when "death" occurred was supposed to be a simple, if grim, matter. As noted by LaFave in *Criminal Law,* at 770, "When the heart stopped beating and the lungs stopped breathing, the individual was dead according to physicians and according to the law." In practice, however, deciding when a person had truly expired was not always so easy, as illustrated by the dying request of George Washington. Willard Sterne Randall in, *George Washington: A Life* at 502 (Henry Holt and Company 1997), quoted our first president as asking, "I am just going. Have me decently buried and do not let my body be put into the vault in less than three days after I am dead." Even the bravest of our founders did not relish the thought of being mistakenly sealed in a vault while still alive.

In the following case, the court considered the impact that medical advances should have on the traditional and limited definition of "death" for **homicide** purposes. The **common law definition of death required the permanent cessation of respiration and blood circulation. California expanded the definition of death** to include: (1) the **permanent cessation of respiration and blood circulation** or (2) **total and irreversible (permanent) cessation of brain function**.

(2) Today's Law

LEGAL ANALYSIS

People v. Mitchell
132 Cal. App. 3d 389 (1982).
Justice Work delivered the California Court of Appeal's decision.

Facts

Emmette Dize Mitchell appeals his [PC 187 murder] conviction for murdering his four-year-old nephew [arguing that, by "pulling the plug," the state participated in the killing while attempted murder charges were pending, thus, precluding it from later charging Mitchell with the murder].

When Diane Lewis left for school, she entrusted her four-year-old son to the care of Mitchell, who was living with them. Later, a police officer found the boy unconscious in the bathtub face up, completely submerged in water, barefoot and still clothed with a shirt and jeans. While paramedics attempted to revive him, the officer returned to his patrol car and found

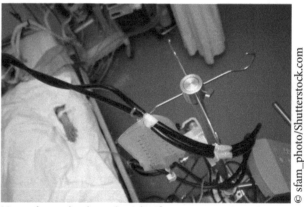

How does the law decide if a coma patient is alive or dead?

Mitchell sitting in the back seat. Mitchell was taken to the police station.

[The] victim was taken to Children's Hospital where, on entry, the attending doctor found no pulse (due to lack of oxygen) and dilated pupils showing a lack of brain function. The doctor determined the boy was a victim of "near drowning" and was not capable of breathing without the respiratory support system. Heroic measures eventually resulted in a measurable heart beat, and artificial ventilation induced some respiration. After 10 days the artificial life support equipment was removed, and the artificially induced heart beat and respiration ceased.

An autopsy performed the same day the systems were removed showed the boy was "brain dead" before removal. The autopsy surgeon ruled death was caused by softening of the brain tissue, consistent with "near drowning" (prolonged submersion in water, cutting off the oxygen flow to the brain).

*** Mitchell told the officer he had been babysitting the victim who was running around the house screaming, yelling and calling him names. When Mitchell noticed the victim had broken his headphones, he picked the boy up and hit his head against the ceiling. The victim threatened to tell his mother. Sometime later Mitchell "snapped and grabbed the victim around the neck in an attempt to strangle him." When the boy did not die, Mitchell decided to drown him in the bathtub. He filled the tub with 10 to 15 inches of water and held the victim's face down for about 5 minutes, then left the victim in the tub and went outside. He returned five minutes later, called the police and told them he had just murdered his nephew.

The trial court, sitting without a jury, found the murder to be of the first degree.

Issue

Since the defendant can only be responsible for deaths he causes, and since the defendant did not remove artificial life support from the victim, was the victim legally "dead" when doctors "pulled the plug"?

Rule and Analysis

[Health and Safety Code Section 7180, the statute defining death, reads:] "A person shall be pronounced dead if it is determined by a physician that the person has suffered a total and irreversible cessation of brain function. There shall be independent confirmation of the death by another physician. *** Nothing in this chapter shall prohibit the physician from using other usual and customary procedures for determining death as the exclusive basis for pronouncing a person dead." ***

[When there is no statutory law defining death, courts may apply the common law definition. The issue of death in homicide cases usually arises in tissue transplant cases. The public has shown approval of tissue transplant through Legislative adoption of the Uniform Anatomical Gift Act. The Uniform Anatomical Gift Act's definitions of death apply whether a person died naturally or at an aggressor's hand.]

[Life] support equipment can maintain an expired person's circulation and respiration artificially. A respirator can maintain physical breathing, as well as balance oxygen and carbon dioxide levels. However, if the victim has been without respiration long enough to have caused permanent and irreversible brain damage, the victim will forever remain in a vegetative state, a mere repository for organs capable of surviving if transplanted elsewhere, but incapable of regenerating the brain of the corpse in which they are contained. Under the common law definition of death, the patient is alive. [**The common law defines "death" as a total stoppage of the circulation of the blood and a cessation of the animal and vital functions consequent therein, such as respiration, pulsation, etc.**]

In the context of criminal homicide cases, brain death poses varied problems. That a transplant surgeon may become a superseding intervening cause of a homicide victim's death has led some hospitals to enforce a blanket prohibition of transplanting from victims of criminal acts. ***

Depending on the definition of death used, the crime would be murder or attempted murder. Where the accused intended to murder the victim but, using the common law definition of death, causation was interrupted by the transplant surgeon, the accused may be convicted of only attempted murder, battery or assault, all of which have much less severe punishments when compared to the punishment for criminal homicide. [Morally] reprehensible behavior of murder should be the focal point, not whether the accused was fortunate enough to have a subsequent intervention in causation. ***

Facts similar to ours appear in [the Massachusetts case, Commonwealth v. Golston.] Massachusetts had no statutory death definition and so the common law definition prevailed until this case. The trial judge charged the jury on brain death, and was upheld on appeal. [**California adopted a brain death** statute] providing: **"A person shall be pronounced dead if it is determined by a physician that the person has suffered a total and irreversible cessation of brain function.** There shall be independent confirmation of death by another physician. ***

[This definition seems unambiguous. However, in the *In re Benjamin C.*] case, the word "total" caused difficulty. A three-year-old child, struck by a car incurred irreversible brain damage, was comatose and on a respirator. His life expectancy on this equipment was one year, and off the equipment only minutes. However, the child did not have "total" cessation of brain function. His EEG showed some activity (unlike here where there was none), body temperature was acceptable and there was a pulse. *** His probability of recovery was nil due to irreversible brain damage. When the respirator was disconnected breathing stopped within 17 minutes. The brain death definition was upheld only after much controversy regarding the scope of the definition. ***

[The Kansas Supreme Court upheld a similar brain death statute.] Hospital surgeons declared the victim dead and transplanted a kidney. The Kansas Supreme Court upheld the statute as "based on practical medical considerations in keeping with advanced medical technology." *** Other states have followed in adopting a brain death definition.

Adopting brain death as the standard here does not intrude on Mitchell's rights. The prosecution must prove brain death occurred by proof beyond a reasonable doubt. *** The facts established sufficient evidence for the trier of fact to determine the issue of death occurring beyond a reasonable doubt. Mitchell could have cross-examined both doctors and presented his own experts on the issue if he desired. ***

Conclusion

[We] **hold substantial evidence shows there is no reasonable doubt the victim was "brain dead" when taken off life support. *** Defendant caused the brain death of the victim and therefore is liable for his murder.**

Affirmed.[27]

Biography—Defense Counsel

John Adams:

- Best known as a leader of the American Revolution and the second President of the United States.
- Was **defense counsel for the King's soldiers involved in the Boston Massacre,** achieving acquittals for six defendants. Adams' strong sense of duty in taking the unpopular case is described in David McCullough's biography, "John Adams" Simon & Schuster (2001).
- According to "The Official Website" of the "John Adams Historical Society" at http://www.john-adams-heritage.com/boston-massacre-trials/, John Adams argued in the soldiers' defense that, if **"a motley rabble of saucy boys"** had attacked the soldiers, they had a right to respond in self defense.

According to the John Adams Historical Society, Adams said that his role of defense counsel in the Boston Massacre "procured me Anxiety, and Obloquy enough." However, he considered it "one of the most gallant, generous, manly and disinterested Actions of my whole Life."

---

27. Reprinted with the permission of LexisNexis.

c)   The Right to Die and Assisted Suicide

Is there a **substantive due process right** to **assisted suicide**? In order to trigger the **Fourteenth Amendment Due Process Clause**, such a right would have to be a **fundamental part of our nation's law**. The following case considers this issue.

LEGAL ANALYSIS

Washington v. Glucksberg
521 U.S. 702 (1997).
Chief Justice Rehnquist delivered the opinion of the United States Supreme Court.

Facts

It has always been a crime to assist a suicide in the State of Washington. In 1854, Washington's first Territorial Legislature outlawed "assisting another in the commission of self-murder." Today, Washington law provides: "A person is guilty of promoting a suicide attempt when he knowingly causes or aids another person to attempt suicide." Wash. Rev. Code 9A.36.060(1) (1994). *** At the same time, Washington's Natural Death Act, enacted in 1979, states that the "withholding or withdrawal of life-sustaining treatment" at a patient's direction "shall not, for any purpose, constitute a suicide." Wash. Rev. Code § 70.122.070(1). ***

[Doctors, including Harold Glucksberg, M.D., who treat terminally ill patients, and who would assist these patients in ending their lives if not for Washington's assisted-suicide ban, along with three gravely ill plaintiffs and "Compassion in Dying," a nonprofit organization that counsels people considering physician-assisted suicide, sued Washington State] seeking a declaration that Wash Rev. Code 9A.36.060(1) (1994) was unconstitutional because it violated the Fourteenth Amendment's "liberty interest" which extends to a personal choice by a mentally competent, terminally ill adult to commit physician-assisted suicide."]

Issue

Whether Washington's prohibition against "causing" or "aiding" a suicide violates the Fourteenth Amendment. We hold that it does not.

Rule and Analysis

We begin, as we do in all due-process cases, by examining our Nation's history, legal traditions, and practices. [In virtually every State,] it is a crime to assist a suicide. The States' assisted-suicide bans [express] the States' commitment to the protection and preservation of all human life. [The majority of States in this country have laws imposing criminal penalties on one who assists another to commit suicide. Opposition to suicide and assisted suicide has been consistent and enduring.]

[For over 700 years, the Anglo-American common-law tradition has punished or disapproved of both suicide and assisting suicide.] In the 13th century, Henry de Bracton, one of the first legal-treatise writers, observed that "just as a man may commit felony by slaying another so may he do so by slaying himself." [Centuries later, Blackstone called this suicide "self-murder."]

[Although the American colonies abolished these harsh common-law penalties because it was unfair to punish the suicide's family for his wrongdoing, they still prohibited suicide. The] prohibitions against assisting suicide never contained exceptions for those who were near death or [hopelessly diseased or fatally wounded].

By the time the Fourteenth Amendment was ratified, it was a crime in most States to assist a suicide. [The Model Penal Code has prohibited aiding suicide.]

[Due to advances in medicine and technology, Americans today are increasingly likely to die in institutions, from chronic illnesses. The public is therefore focused] on how best to protect dignity and independence at the end of life. [Many States allow "living wills" and the withdrawal or refusal of life-sustaining medical treatment.] At the same time, however, voters and legislators continue for the most part to reaffirm their States' prohibitions on assisting suicide. ***

[In 1994, voters in Oregon enacted the "Death With Dignity Act," which legalized physician-assisted suicide for competent, terminally ill adults.]

Thus, the States are currently engaged in serious, thoughtful examinations of physician-assisted suicide and other similar issues. ***

The Due Process Clause guarantees more than fair process, and the "liberty" it protects includes more than the absence of physical restraint, [because it protects against government interference with certain fundamental rights and liberty interests. In] addition to the specific freedoms protected by the Bill of Rights, the "liberty" specially protected by the Due Process Clause includes the rights to marry, *** to have children, *** to direct the education and upbringing of one's children, ***to use contraception, *** to bodily integrity, *** and to abortion. [We have strongly suggested that Due Process protects the traditional right to refuse unwanted lifesaving medical treatment. We, however, must] "exercise the utmost care whenever we are asked to break new ground in this field," lest the liberty protected by the Due Process Clause be subtly transformed into the policy preferences of the members of this Court.

[We] have a tradition of carefully formulating the interest at stake in substantive-due-process cases. For example, although *Cruzan* is often described as a "right to die" case, [*Cruzan* was] in fact, more precise: we assumed that the Constitution granted competent persons a "constitutionally protected right to refuse lifesaving hydration and nutrition." [Washington's statute here prohibits "aiding another person to attempt suicide,"] and, thus, the question before us is whether the "liberty" specially protected by the Due Process Clause includes a right to commit suicide which itself includes a right to assistance in doing so. ***

We now inquire whether this asserted right has any place in our Nation's traditions. [We] are confronted with a consistent and almost universal tradition that has long rejected the asserted right, and continues explicitly to reject it today, even for terminally ill, mentally competent adults. To hold for respondents, we would have to reverse centuries of legal doctrine and practice, and strike down the considered policy choice of almost every State.***

In *Cruzan*, we considered whether Nancy Beth Cruzan, who had been severely injured in an automobile accident and was in a persistent vegetative state, "had a right under the United States Constitution which would require the hospital to withdraw life-sustaining treatment" at her parents' request. ["At] common law, even the touching of one person by another without consent and without legal justification was a battery." We then discussed the related rule that "informed consent is generally required for medical treatment." [We] concluded that "the common-law doctrine of informed consent is viewed as generally encompassing the right of a competent individual to refuse medical treatment." [A competent person has a constitutionally protected liberty interest in refusing unwanted medical treatment. The U.S. Constitution therefore granted] "a competent person a constitutionally protected right to refuse lifesaving hydration and nutrition." ***

The right assumed in *Cruzan*, however, was not simply deduced from abstract concepts of personal autonomy. Given the common-law rule that forced medication was a battery, and the long legal tradition protecting the decision to refuse unwanted medical treatment, our assumption was entirely consistent with this Nation's history and constitutional traditions. The decision to commit suicide with the assistance of another may be just as personal and profound as the decision to refuse unwanted medical treatment, but it has never enjoyed similar legal protection. Indeed, the two acts are widely and reasonably regarded as quite distinct. ***

[**The asserted "right" to assistance in committing suicide is not a fundamental liberty interest protected by the Due Process Clause.**]

[Washington] has an "unqualified interest in the preservation of human life." ***The State's prohibition on assisted suicide, like all homicide laws, both reflects and advances its commitment to this interest. [Washington's assisted-suicide ban] insists that all persons' lives, from beginning to end, regardless of physical or mental condition, are under the full protection of the law. ***

[All] admit that suicide is a serious public-health problem, especially among persons in otherwise vulnerable groups. [Suicide is a leading cause of death in Washington of those between the ages of 14 and 54, and is especially prevalent among the elderly.]

[Legal physician-assisted suicide could make it more difficult for the State to protect depressed or mentally ill persons, or those who are suffering from untreated pain, from suicidal impulses. [Physician-assisted suicide could erode the trust essential to the doctor-patient relationship by blurring the time-honored line between healing and harming.]

[The] State has an interest in protecting vulnerable groups—including the poor, the elderly, and disabled persons-—from abuse, neglect, and mistakes. [There is a] real risk of subtle coercion and undue influence in end-of-life situations. *** The risk of harm is greatest for the many individuals in our society whose autonomy and well-being are already compromised by poverty, lack of access to good medical care, advanced age, or membership in a stigmatized social group." *** If physician-assisted suicide were permitted, many might resort to it to spare their families the substantial financial burden of end-of-life health-care costs.

The State's interest here goes beyond protecting the vulnerable from coercion; it extends to protecting disabled and terminally ill people from prejudice, negative and inaccurate stereotypes, and "societal indifference." ***

Finally, the State may fear that permitting assisted suicide will start it down the path to voluntary and perhaps even involuntary euthanasia. *** Washington's ban on assisting suicide prevents such erosion. ***

Conclusion

[**The various interests**] **are unquestionably important and legitimate, and Washington's ban on assisted suicide is at least reasonably related to their promotion and protection. We therefore hold that Wash. Rev. Code § 9A.36.060(1) (1994) does not violate the Fourteenth Amendment, either on its face or "as applied to competent, terminally ill adults who wish to hasten their deaths by obtaining medication prescribed by their doctors." ***

Throughout the Nation, Americans are engaged in an earnest and profound debate about the morality, legality, and practicality of physician-assisted suicide. Our holding permits this debate to continue, as it should in a democratic society.**

*** *It is so ordered.*

Contrast Washington State's statute in *Glucksburg* with the statute from Washington's neighboring state, Oregon:

The Oregon Death with Dignity Act
ORS § 127.805 (2012).
127.805 §2.01. Who may initiate a written request for medication.

(1) An adult who is capable, is a resident of Oregon, and has been determined by the attending physician and consulting physician to be suffering from a terminal disease, and who has voluntarily expressed his or her wish to die, may make a written request for medication for the purpose of ending his or her life in a humane and dignified manner in accordance with ORS 127.800 to 127.897.

(2) No person shall qualify under the provisions of ORS 127.800 to 127.897 solely because of age or disability.

Triage or Murder?

Some doctors make life or death decisions without consent of the patient. An article in *Pro Publica* entitled, "Deadly Choices: Memorial Medical Center After Katrina," by Sheri Fink, offered insight into the doctors' decisions in administering lethal doses of morphine in the wake of hurricane Katrina.

To read "The Deadly Choices at Memorial" by Sheri Fink, August 27, 2009, visit:

https://www.propublica.org/article/the-deadly-choices-at-memorial-826

---

2. Human Being

When does life begin?

a) Common Law

At common law, killing a fetus was not homicide unless the fetus was "born alive." Blackstone declared in *Commentaries*, Vol. IV, at 198, "To kill a child in its mother's womb, is now no murder . . . But if the child be born alive, and dieth by reason of the potion or bruises it received in the womb, it is murder in such as administered or gave them. LaFave in *Criminal Law*, at 767–68 explained that the baby, being "fully brought forth" and having an "independent circulation, sometimes established by breathing, crying, or severing of the umbilical cord," satisfied the "born alive" rule.

The unborn rule can lead to injustice, as seen in *Keeler v. Superior Court* 2 Cal. 3d 619 (1970). In *Keeler*, Robert Harrison Keeler confronted his recently divorced wife of sixteen years, Teresa, by blocking her car on a road with his own. Having learned that Teresa was pregnant by another man, Keeler told her, "I hear you're pregnant." After getting Teresa out of her car and seeing her abdomen, Keeler became "extremely upset," stating, "You sure are. I'm going to stomp it out of you." He then shoved his knee into Teresa's abdomen and struck her several times in her face until she lost consciousness. Due to her severe injuries, doctors performed a caesarian section, delivering stillborn a five pound girl eighteen inches in length. Doctors concluded that before the attack, the fetus was viable and that "the cause of death was skull fracture with consequent cerebral hemorrhaging" caused by Keeler's attack to the mother's abdomen. When charged with murdering "Baby Girl Vogt," Keeler sought higher court review, arguing that an unborn, although viable, fetus was not a "human being" within the murder statute. The Supreme Court of California agreed, concluding, "the judicial enlargement of section 187 now urged upon us by the People would not have been foreseeable to this petitioner, and hence that its adoption at this time would deny him due process of law."

b)   Modern Law

As noted by the Supreme Court of California in the following case, "The Legislature reacted to the *Keeler* decision by amending the murder statute, section 187, subdivision (a), **to include within its proscription the killing of a fetus**." California's **PC 187** provides: "(a) **Murder is the unlawful killing of a human being, or a fetus, with malice aforethought**." This statutory amendment then prompted the question of **what legally constituted a "fetus"** for the murder law. In other words, did **a fetus have to be "viable"** in order for its killing to be considered "**murder**"?

LEGAL ANALYSIS

People v. Davis
7 Cal. 4th 797. 872 P.2d 591 (1994).
Chief Justice Lucas delivered the opinion for the Supreme Court of California.

Facts

On March 1, 1991, Maria Flores, who was between 23 and 25 weeks pregnant, and her 20-month-old son, Hector, went to a check-cashing store to cash her welfare check. As Flores left the store, defendant [Robert A. Davis] pulled a gun from the waistband of his pants and demanded the money ($378) in her purse. When she refused to hand over the purse, defendant shot her in the chest. Flores dropped Hector as she fell to the floor and defendant fled the scene.

Flores underwent surgery to save her life. Although doctors sutured small holes in the uterine wall to prevent further bleeding, no further obstetrical surgery was undertaken because of the immaturity of the fetus. The next day, the fetus was stillborn as a direct result of its mother's blood loss, low blood pressure and state of shock. Defendant was soon apprehended and charged with assaulting and robbing Flores, as well as murdering her fetus. ***

At trial, the prosecution's medical experts testified the fetus's statistical chances of survival outside the womb were between 7 and 47 percent. The defense medical expert testified it was "possible for the fetus to have survived, but its chances were only 2 or 3 percent." None of the medical experts testified that survival of the fetus was "probable."

Issue

Whether a fetus has to be "viable" in order for it's killing to be considered "murder" under California's PC 187.

Rule and Analysis

Penal Code section 187(a) provides that "**Murder is the unlawful killing of a human being, or a fetus, with malice aforethought**." [We] consider and reject the argument that viability of a fetus is an element of fetal murder under the statute**. [However,] we also conclude that this holding should not apply to defendant herein.

Although section 187, subdivision (a), does not expressly require a fetus be medically viable before the statute's provisions can be applied to a criminal defendant, the trial court *** instructed the jury that it must find the fetus was viable before it could find defendant guilty of murder under the statute. The trial court did not, however, give the standard viability instruction, CALJIC No. 8.10; which states that:

"A viable human fetus is one who has attained such form and development of organs as to be normally capable of living outside of the uterus." The jury, however, was given an instruction that allowed it to convict defendant of murder if it found the fetus had a possibility of survival: "A fetus is viable when it has achieved the capability for independent existence; that is, when it is *possible* for it to survive the trauma of birth, although with artificial medical aid."

The jury convicted defendant of murder of a fetus. ***The defendant was sentenced to life without possibility of parole, plus five years for the firearm use.

On appeal, defendant contended that the trial court prejudicially erred by not instructing the jury pursuant to CALJIC No. 8.10. He relied on United States Supreme Court decisions that have defined viability of a fetus in terms of "probabilities, not possibilities" when limiting a woman's absolute right to an abortion. (See *Roe* v. *Wade* (1973) 410 U.S. 113, 163 [35 L.Ed.2d 147, 182-183, 93 S.Ct. 705] [defining viability as that point in fetal development when a fetus, if born, would be capable of living normally outside the womb]; *Planned Parenthood* v. *Casey* (1992) 505 U.S. 833 [120 L.Ed.2d 674, 112 S.Ct. 2791] [reaffirming *Roe's* viability definition].) By analogy to the abortion cases, defendant asserted that a fetus is not viable under section 187, subdivision (a), unless "there is a reasonable likelihood of [its] sustained survival outside the womb, with or without artificial support." [Defendant] claimed, rather than defining viability as a "reasonable possibility of survival," the trial court should have instructed the jury under the higher "probability" threshold. ***

The People argued that no viability instruction was necessary because prosecution under section 187, subdivision (a), does not require that the fetus be viable. [The] Court of Appeal agreed with the People that contrary to prior California decisions, fetal viability is not a required element of murder under the statute. Nonetheless, the court reversed defendant's murder conviction and set aside the special circumstance finding, on the ground that application to defendant of its unprecedented interpretation of section 187, subdivision (a), would violate due process principles.

[We] agree with the People and the Court of Appeal that **viability is not an element of fetal murder under section 187, subdivision (a), and conclude therefore that the statute does not require an instruction on viability as a prerequisite to a murder conviction**. In addition, because every prior decision that had addressed the viability issue had determined that viability of the fetus was prerequisite to a murder conviction under section 187, subdivision (a), we also agree with the Court of Appeal that **application of our construction of the statute to defendant would violate due process and ex post facto principles**.*** [unforeseeable enlargement of a criminal statute operates in manner of ex post facto law].) [We] affirm the Court of Appeal judgment in its entirety (affirming the assault and robbery counts and reversing the judgment of murder). ***

In 1970, section 187, subdivision (a), provided: "Murder is the unlawful killing of a human being, with malice aforethought." [*Keeler v. Superior Court*] held that a man who had killed a fetus carried by his estranged wife could not be prosecuted for murder because the Legislature (consistent with the common law view) probably intended the phrase "human being" to mean a person who had been born alive.

The Legislature reacted to the *Keeler* decision by amending [PC section 187(a) to include within its proscription the killing of a fetus]. The amended statute reads: "Murder is the unlawful killing of a human being, or a fetus, with malice aforethought." ***The amended statute specifically provides that it does not apply to abortions complying with the Therapeutic Abortion Act, performed by a doctor when the death of the mother was substantially certain in the absence of an abortion, or whenever the mother solicited, aided, and otherwise chose to abort the fetus. ***

Conclusion

We conclude that viability is not an element of fetal homicide under PC 187(a). The third party killing of a fetus with malice aforethought is murder as long as the state can show that the fetus has progressed beyond the embryonic stage of seven to eight weeks.[28]

3.   Malice Aforethought

For centuries, a killing could only be "murder" if it was committed "with malice aforethought." Blackstone expressly stated that malice aforethought was "the grand criterion" which "distinguishes murder from other killing." Even in Blackstone's day, malice aforethought, also called "malice prepense," did not require "spite or malevolence to the deceased in particular." Instead, it meant a wicked heart in general.

Now, "malice aforethought" is a complex product of centuries of legal evolution, with each generation of judges adding to its meaning. Malice aforethought is a kind of legal fossil that traps rules of the past within it. Since malice aforethought carries the baggage of hundreds of cases, it now retains little of its original meaning.

Today, to kill "with **malice aforethought" actually means** to end a person's life in one of four different ways: **(1) to kill while having the intent to kill, (2) to kill while having the intent to commit serious bodily injury, (3) to kill while having a depraved, abandoned, or malignant heart, or (4) to trigger felony murder liability by killing during the commission of certain felonies.**

The Texas Penal Code provides a clear example of this list of various kinds of malice aforethought for murder.

Texas Penal Code Section 19.02 provides:

§ 19.02. Murder

(a) . . .

(b) A person commits an offense if he:

(1) intentionally or knowingly causes the death of an individual;

(2) intends to cause serious bodily injury and commits an act clearly dangerous to human life that causes the death of an individual; or

(3) commits or attempts to commit a felony, other than manslaughter, and in the course of and in furtherance of the commission or attempt, or in immediate flight from the commission or attempt, he commits or attempts to commit an act clearly dangerous to human life that causes the death of an individual.

The intent-to-kill kind of malice aforethought is precisely what it sounds like. If a person kills another person while having the intention to end the victim's life, this amounts to murder. **The intent to kill can be gleaned from the existence of a weapon or the kind of weapon used in a killing**. A person using a gun to shoot another is more likely to be seen as intending to kill than someone who picks up a paperweight to throw at another. **Intent to kill can also be inferred from the way or manner of use of a weapon**. A killer who shoots in the head or heart is more likely to be found to have intent to kill than a killer who happens to hit the femoral artery in the leg. Other circumstances, such as statements and actions of persons involved in the situation, can also offer insight into a killer's intent to kill.

---

28. Reprinted with the permission of LexisNexis.

One who **intends** only **to commit serious bodily injury**, but instead causes death, can also commit murder. As noted in *Comber v. United States*, 584 A.2d 26, 39 (1990), **serious bodily injury can be: "a serious impairment of physical condition, including, but not limited to, the following: loss of consciousness; concussion; bone fracture; protracted loss or impairment of function of any bodily member or organ; a wound requiring extensive suturing; and serious disfigurement."** According to Blackstone's *Commentaries*, Vol. IV, at 199–200, the eighteenth century's version of serious bodily injury was more gruesome: "As when a park-keeper tied a boy, that was stealing wood, to a horse's tail, and dragged him along the park; when a master corrected his servant with an iron bar, and when a schoolmaster stamped on his scholar's belly; so that each of the sufferers died."

For the third kind of malice aforethought, **depraved heart murder**, also known as killing in **"conscious disregard" of the risk to life**, *Comber v. United States*, 584 A.2d 26, 39 (1990) offered as examples: **"firing a bullet into a room occupied, as the defendant knows, by several people; starting a fire at the front door of an occupied building; shooting into . . . a moving automobile, necessarily occupied by human beings . . . ; playing a game of 'Russian roulette' with another person . . . ; selling 'pure' (i.e., undiluted) heroin."** According to Blackstone in his *Commentaries*, Vol. IV, at 200, at common law, "going deliberately with a horse used to strike, or discharging a gun, among a multitude of people" constituted depraved heart murder because it showed that the killer was "an enemy to all mankind in general."

The fourth kind of malice aforethought, felony murder, can arise from any killing during a felony or its attempt. Even if a person, say while committing the felony of robbery, *accidentally* kills his victim, the killing can be prosecuted as murder simply because it happened during a felony.

a)   Express Malice: Intent to Kill

How exactly can the mental state of intent to kill be proven to jurors beyond a reasonable doubt? We are generally not directly privy to the thoughts of others and we certainly do not wish to make a mistake when the stakes involve a murder charge. The Supreme Court of Utah dealt with this issue in *State v. Wardle*, 564 P.2d 764 (1977), a case where a jury found that Marvin Ray Wardle murdered with the intent to kill. Wardle and the victim, Justin E. Greed, had been friends, Wardle, however, became upset with Greed because "he believed Greed was contributing to defendant's wife's alcohol problem." Wardle went to Swanee's Lounge and "threatened an assault upon Greed." When Greed then left the bar, Wardle immediately followed him outside. A fellow bar patron, who checked on Greed, saw Wardle "had his hands braced upon the trunk of the vehicle and was jumping up and down on something." Wardle then reentered the bar and requested an ambulance. Greed was found "lying unconscious, behind the automobile. Greed was bleeding from the mouth, nose, and ears, and his breathing was labored."

> Mr. Greed was transported to the hospital. His hip and jaw were fractured, and he had multiple rib fractures which impaired breathing. His low blood pressure indicated internal bleeding. Emergency surgery was performed to remove his ruptured gall bladder and spleen and to repair his lacerated liver and other internal organs. A piece of his dental plate was lodged in his esophagus. Mr. Greed was removed from surgery to the intensive care unit where he died. *** The state medical examiner, who conducted a post mortem, testified multiple blunt blows to Mr. Greed's body caused his death.[29]

The defendant argued on appeal that the evidence was insufficient to prove the intent to kill needed for second degree murder, "since death is not the natural or probable result of a blow with the hand, no

---

29. Reprinted with the permission of LexisNexis.

intent to kill or malice will, under ordinary circumstances, be inferred, although death results from an assault thus committed." The *Wardle* court noted, however, that this rule did not apply "when the assault from which death resulted (occurred in) such circumstances of violence, excessive force, or brutality, an intent to kill or malice may be inferred." Here, the court relied on *Pine v. People*, a case in which the defendant not only used his fists but also, as the victim lay unconscious on the floor, jumped astride him and bounced his head "on and off the concrete floor about three times." With the violence in *Pine*, as well as that in *Wardle*, where the defendant appeared to be stomping on his victim, the jury could have found the intent to kill, among other kinds of malice aforethought. The *Wardle* court thus affirmed the murder conviction.

In *Reyes v. State*, 480 S.W.3d 70 (2015), the Texas Court of Appeals considered whether enough evidence existed to support the murder conviction of Colette Reyes for shooting her husband with the intent to kill. Reyes's husband, planning on divorcing Reyes the next day, stopped by their home to pick up some personal items. His daughter later found him "on the garage floor with a pool of blood around his head." Colette Reyes admitted to the police that she had "shot her husband and had placed the gun beside him." Over a month later, she tried to "collect on her husband's $250,000 life insurance policy."

A person commits murder if she intentionally or knowingly causes the death of an individual. *** A person acts intentionally when it is her conscious objective or desire to engage in the conduct or cause the result. *** A person acts knowingly when she is aware that her conduct is reasonably certain to cause the result. ***

Direct evidence of intent is not required. *** A jury may infer the intent to kill from any evidence that it believes proves the existence of that intent, including the accused's use of a deadly weapon. *** A jury may also infer intent or knowledge from circumstantial evidence such as acts, words, and the conduct of the defendant. [Since a person's acts are generally reliable circumstantial evidence of her intent, the jury could reasonably infer that the defendant intended to do exactly what she did.]

Appellant was aware her husband wanted a divorce and was afraid about her financial survival. She was the beneficiary of her husband's $250,000 life insurance policy. When asked, Appellant refused to turn her husband's handguns over to their daughter. Appellant shot her husband in the head at an intermediate range and killed him. Appellant then tried to collect on her husband's $250,000 life insurance policy. *** This was more than enough evidence from which the jury could have concluded Appellant murdered her husband for the life insurance policy rather than allowing the divorce to proceed and facing an uncertain financial future.

The *Reyes* court therefore affirmed the conviction.

Gunman Killed Worshippers in Texas Church Shooting

Devin P. Kelley allegedly killed twenty-six people in a shooting rampage at a Texas church. *CBS News* interviewed his ex-wife for a November 10, 2017, article, "Texas gunman Devin Kelley's ex-wife says he 'had a lot of demons.'" This article can be viewed at:

https://www.cbsnews.com/news/tessa-brennaman-devin-kelley-sutherland-springs/

Alex Horton of the *Washington Post* reported on December 5, 2017, in "The Air Force failed to alert the FBI about Devin Kelley. Other branches are worse at reporting violent criminals," that the Air Force failed to report Kelley's conviction for domestic violence, which would have prevented his purchasing a gun from a store. The article can be seen at:

https://www.washingtonpost.com/news/checkpoint/wp/2017/12/05/the-air-force-failed-to-alert-the-fbi-about-devin-kelley-other-branches-are-much-worse-at-reporting-violent-criminals/?utm_term=.f352c5028b03

b) Intent to Commit Serious Bodily Injury

LaFave in *Criminal Law,* at 778, noted, "English judges came to hold that one who intended to do serious bodily injury short of death, but who actually succeeded in killing, was guilty of murder in spite of his lack of an intent to kill." LaFave explained that this kind of murder has also been called "great bodily injury" and "grievous bodily harm."

Many examples of "serious bodily injury" come from cases that do not result in killings. In *State v. Perry*, 426 P.2d 415 (1967), for example, Eugene Perry was convicted of aggravated assault. One issue in the case was how severe an injury must be in order to be considered "serious bodily injury." In *Perry*, the defendant was placed in a "drunk tank" after being arrested in Winslow, Arizona, for fighting and intoxication. When a fellow inmate, King Naha, refused to give Perry a cigarette, Perry beat and kicked him and took off his belt and choked him. Police transported King Naha to the hospital, where it was found the beating victim sustained "a cut approximately two and one-half inches along on the back of his head, a black eye, and a broken rib. The cut was open and bleeding." The Court of Appeals of Arizona concluded that the beating sustained would "be within any definition that could be given by the court."

c) Implied Malice: Depraved Heart Murder

Murder can be committed by killing with "**implied malice**." Such "malice" is implied when a killing is caused by "**an act, the natural consequences of which are dangerous to life, which act was deliberately performed by a person who knows that his conduct endangers the life of another and who acts with conscious disregard for life**." In the following case, the court interprets this long phrase to mean, "**implied malice requires a defendant's awareness of engaging in conduct that endangers the life of another**—no more, and no less." The trick here is to avoid investing malice with "more" requirements or "less" requirements. As this case demonstrates, this task presents difficulty even for judges.

Can a person killing a victim with his or her dog be guilty of murder?

People v. Knoller
41 Cal. 4th 139 (2007).
Justice Kennard wrote the unanimous opinion for the California Supreme Court.

Facts

On January 26, 2001, two dogs owned by defendant Marjorie Knoller and her husband, codefendant Robert Noel, attacked and killed Diane Whipple in the hallway of an apartment building in San Francisco. Defendant Knoller was charged with [PC 189] second degree murder and [PC 192(b)] involuntary manslaughter; codefendant Noel, who was not present at the time of the attack on Whipple, was charged with involuntary manslaughter. ***

[Defendants Knoller and Noel were lawyers who owned four Presa Canario dogs named Bane, Isis, Hera, and Fury. This dog breed can be very large, weighing over 100 pounds, and reaching over five feet tall when standing on its hind legs. The Presa Canario is a gripping dog used and bred for combat, guard and fighting.]

[The dogs' prior owner warned Knoller that the dogs had killed sheep and that Hera and Fury should be shot. Knoller did not seem to care. A veterinarian who cared for the dogs warned Knoller of the dogs' lack of training and discipline and of his difficulty in vaccinating them. The veterinarian warned,] "these animals would be a liability in any household, reminding me of the recent [dog attack on a boy in Tehama County.] He lost his arm and disfigured his face." [Defendants considered opening a commercial breeding operation with such possible names as Wardog, or Dog-O-War.]

[About 30 incidents occurred where the dogs became uncontrollable or threatening from the time Noel and Knoller brought the dogs to their apartment to the Whipple's fatal mauling.]

[D]efendants' two dogs attacked or threatened people. David Moser, a fellow resident in the apartment building, [was bitten by Hera on the "rear end."] When he exclaimed, "Your dog just bit me," Noel replied, "Um, interesting." Neither defendant apologized to Moser or reprimanded the dog. Another resident, Jill Cowen Davis, was eight months pregnant when one of the dogs, in the presence of both Knoller and Noel, suddenly growled and lunged toward her stomach with its mouth open and teeth bared. Noel jerked the dog by the leash, but he did not apologize to Davis. Postal carrier John Watanabe testified that both dogs, unleashed, had charged him [in a snarling frenzy, making him terrified for his] life. Noel himself suffered a severe injury to his finger, requiring surgery, when Bane bit him during a fight with another dog.]

Mauling victim Diane Whipple and her partner Sharon Smith lived [across a lobby from defendants. In 2000, one of the dogs bit Whipple.] Whipple made every effort to avoid defendants' dogs, checking the hallway before she went out and becoming anxious while waiting for the elevator for fear the dogs would be inside. ***

On January 26, 2001, [Esther Birkmaier, a neighbor of Whipple's], heard dogs barking and a woman's "panic-stricken" voice calling, "Help me, help me." Looking through the peephole, [Birkmaier saw Whipple lying facedown on the floor with what appeared to be a dog on top of her.] Afraid to open the door, Birkmaier called 911, the emergency telephone number, and at the same time heard a voice yelling, "No, no, no" and "Get off." ***

[Officers found Whipple's body in the hallway with her clothing completely ripped off, her entire body covered with wounds, and bleeding profusely. When Knoller came out of her apartment, she did not ask about Whipple's condition.]

An emergency medical technician administered first aid to Whipple, who had a large, profusely bleeding wound to her neck. The wound was too large to halt the bleeding, and Whipple's pulse and breathing stopped as paramedics arrived. She was revived but died shortly after reaching the hospital.

An autopsy revealed over 77 discrete injuries covering Whipple's body "from head to toe." The most significant were lacerations damaging her jugular vein and her carotid artery and crushing her larynx, injuries typically inflicted by predatory animals to kill their prey. [Whipple had lost one-third or more of her blood at the scene. Molds of the neck bites were consistent with Bane's teeth.]

[An animal control officer] asked defendant Knoller to sign over custody of the dogs for euthanasia. Knoller, whom Runge described as "oddly calm," agreed to sign over Bane, but she refused to sign over Hera for euthanasia and she refused to help the animal control officers with the animals, saying she was "unable to handle the dogs." When tranquilizer darts malfunctioned and failed to quiet Bane, "come-along" poles were used by animal control officers backed up by officers with guns drawn. ***

[Both defendants appeared on the television show *Good Morning America* and basically blamed mauling victim Whipple for her own death.]

[Knoller testified that she] thought the dogs had no personality problems requiring a professional trainer. She avoided walking Bane, due to insufficient body strength to control him.] She said she had just returned from walking Bane [and had opened her apartment door], when Bane dragged her back across the lobby toward Whipple ***. The other dog, Hera, left defendants' apartment and joined Bane, who attacked Whipple. Knoller said she threw herself on Whipple to save her. *** She acknowledged not calling 911 to get help for Whipple.

Asked whether she denied responsibility for the attack on Whipple, Knoller gave this reply: "*** I had no idea that he would ever do anything like that to anybody. How can you anticipate something like that? It's a totally bizarre event. I mean how could you anticipate that a dog that you know that is gentle and loving and affectionate would do something so horrible and brutal and disgusting and gruesome to anybody?" ***

The jury found Knoller guilty of second degree murder. [It found both Knoller and Noel guilty of involuntary manslaughter. In granting Knoller's motion for a new trial on the second degree murder count, the trial court observed:] "There is no question [that defendants knew] that somebody was going to be badly hurt. I defy either defendant to stand up and tell me they had no idea that those dogs were going to hurt somebody one day. *But can they stand up and say that they knew subjectively *** that these dogs were going to stand up and kill somebody?*" ***

The Court of Appeal reversed [the order for new trial.] It disagreed with the trial court that a second degree murder conviction, based on a theory of implied malice, required that Knoller recognized "her conduct was such that a human being was likely to die." The Court of Appeal held that a second degree murder conviction can be based simply on a defendant's "subjective appreciation and conscious disregard of a likely risk of . . . serious bodily injury." ***

Issue

1) Whether the mental state required for implied malice includes only "conscious disregard for human life" or does implied malice instead require "actual awareness" (subjective knowledge) of a "*high probability*" of "*death*." [This issue involves the level of certainty of the result.]

And

2) Whether implied malice can be based merely on a defendant's awareness of the risk of "*serious bodily injury*" to another or instead requires an awareness of the risk that the defendant's conduct will result in the "*death*" of another. [This issue involves the kind of result (injury or death).]

Rule and Analysis

[The trial court believed that, to be guilty of second degree murder, Knoller must have known that her conduct involved *a high probability of resulting in the death of another*. The Court of Appeal believed instead that implied malice can be based simply on a defendant's conscious disregard of the risk of *serious bodily injury to another*.]

[Implied] malice requires a defendant's awareness of engaging in conduct that endangers the life of another—no more, and no less.

[The Court of Appeal set the bar too low, permitting a conviction of second degree murder, based on] implied malice, if the defendant knew his or her conduct risked causing death *or serious bodily injury*. But the trial court set the bar too high, ruling that implied malice requires a defendant's awareness that his or her conduct had a *high probability* of resulting in death. [Since the trial court used an incorrect test of implied malice,] it abused its discretion in granting Knoller a new trial on the second degree murder count. The case is remanded back to the trial court with directions to reconsider Knoller's new trial motion in light of the views set out in this opinion.]

Murder is the unlawful killing of a human being, or a fetus, with malice aforethought. (§ 187, subd. (a).) Malice may be express or implied. (§ 188.) At issue here is the definition of "implied malice."

Defendant Knoller was convicted of second degree murder as a result of the killing of Diane Whipple by defendant's dog, Bane. **Second degree murder is the unlawful killing of a human being with malice aforethought but without the additional elements, such as willfulness, premeditation, and deliberation, that would support a conviction of first degree murder.** *** Section 188 provides: "[M]alice may be either express or implied.** It is express when there is manifested a deliberate intention to take away the life of a fellow creature. **It is implied, when no considerable provocation appears, or when the circumstances attending the killing show an abandoned and malignant heart."**

The statutory definition of implied malice, a killing by one with an "abandoned and malignant heart" [does not require an evil disposition or a despicable character. Instead, **the focus should be on a defendant's awareness of the risk created by his or her behavior. [Implied] malice requires a defendant's awareness of the risk of death to another.**

*** Malice is implied when the killing is proximately caused by "an act, the natural consequences of which are dangerous to life, which act was deliberately performed by a person who knows that his conduct endangers the life of another and who acts with conscious disregard for life." ***

[A] killer acts with implied malice only when acting with an awareness of *endangering human life*. ***

[The] trial court properly viewed implied malice as requiring a defendant's awareness of the danger that his or her conduct will result in another's *death* and not merely in serious bodily injury. [But the trial court] stated that a killer acts with implied malice when the killer "*subjectively knows* *** that the conduct that he or she is about to engage in has a *high probability of death* to another human being." [The proper test does not require a defendant's awareness that his or her conduct has a *high probability* of causing death. Rather, it requires only that a defendant acted with a "conscious disregard for human life."]

Conclusion

[The trial mistakenly concluded that Knoller could not be guilty of murder, based on implied malice,] unless she appreciated that her conduct created a high probability of someone's death. [The Court of Appeal mistakenly reasoned that implied malice required only a showing that the defendant appreciated the risk of serious bodily injury.]

The [case is ultimately returned] to the trial court for reconsideration of defendant Knoller's new trial motion in accord with the views expressed in this opinion.[30]

Question

The prosecution offered evidence that the slight bruising on defendant Knoller's hands proved she did not come to the victim's rescue while her dog attacked. If the defendant "created peril" by allowing her dogs to attack the victim, it could be argued that her failure to remove the dogs, if she were able to do so, would be an "omission."

Do's and Don'ts for Hearings, Trials, and Appeals

Testifying as a Witness

As a witness, **do** dress for court because you are going to someplace important. This will immediately communicate respect for the judge and jury. A colleague of mine used to tell his witnesses, "Dress like you are going to church." As a witness, **do** listen carefully to the question asked. **Do** tell the truth. **Do** give responsive and clear answers. **Don't** guess a response when you do not know an answer—instead **do** admit that you do not know. **Don't** volunteer information or anticipate questions. **Don't** lose your temper or show contempt or disrespect for the questioner or proceedings. **Do** take your time to give the correct answer instead of rushing through just to get it over with.

The Frightening Variety of "Depraved Heart Murder" Killings

Sadly, the law offers many examples of depraved heart murder. **Probably the most common example of depraved heart murder is the shooting of a firearm into a crowd.** A variation of this risk-taking is shooting at public transportation, such as a train's caboose, as happened in *Banks v. State*, 211 S.W. 217 (1919). In *Banks*, Tom Banks shot Hawkins, a brakeman working at his post on a moving train. Banks admitted to shooting in the direction of the train, but claimed to be aiming at the ground. The Court of Criminal Appeals of Texas found "no reason" for the shooting, as it appeared that Banks was not acquainted with anyone on the train.

The court affirmed the murder conviction, using particularly dramatic language:

> One who deliberately uses a deadly weapon in such reckless manner as to evince a heart regardless of social duty and fatally bent on mischief, as is shown by firing into a moving railroad train upon which human beings necessarily are, cannot shield himself from the consequences of his acts by disclaiming malice. Malice may be toward a group of persons as well as toward an individual. It may exist without former grudges or antecedent menaces. **The intentional doing of any wrongful act in such manner and under such circumstances as that the death of a human being may result therefrom is malice.** ***

> An examination of (the defendant's) statement shows a deliberate unprovoked shooting into a moving train—an act which could reasonably result in the destruction of human life. No excuse or justification is pleaded, or shown in the evidence for the act. *** That man who

---

30. Reprinted with the permission of LexisNexis.

can coolly shoot into a moving train, or automobile, or other vehicle in which are persons guiltless of any wrongdoing toward him or provocation for such attack, is, if possible, worse than the man who endures insult or broods over a wrong, real or fancied, and then waylays and kills his personal enemy. The shame of the world recently has been the unwarranted killing of persons who were non-combatants and who were doing nothing and were not capable of inflicting injury upon their slayers. Of kindred spirit is he who can shoot in the darkness into houses, crowds or trains and recklessly send into eternity those whom he does not know and against whom he has no sort of reason for directing his malevolence.

Forcing a person to play Russian roulette can be depraved heart murder.

Some shootings implicating depraved heart murder involve Russian roulette. In *People v. Roe*, 542 N.E.2d 610 (1989), the defendant was convicted of "depraved indifference murder for the shooting death of a 13-year-old boy." The Court of Appeals of New York described the crime as follows:

> Defendant, a 15-1/2-year-old high school student, deliberately loaded a mix of "live" and "dummy" shells at random into the magazine of a 12-gauge shotgun. He pumped a shell into the firing chamber not knowing whether it was a "dummy" or a "live" round. He raised the gun to his shoulder and pointed it directly at the victim, Darrin Seifert, who was standing approximately 10 feet away. As he did so, he exclaimed, "Let's play Polish roulette" and asked "Who is first?" When he pulled the trigger, the gun discharged sending a "live" round into Darrin's chest. Darrin died as a result of the massive injuries.

The Court in *Roe* described "depraved indifference murder" in New York as:

> like reckless manslaughter is a *nonintentional* homicide. It differs from manslaughter, however, in that it must be shown that the actor's reckless conduct is imminently dangerous and presents a grave risk of death; in manslaughter, the conduct need only present the lesser "substantial risk" of death. Whether the lesser risk sufficient for manslaughter is elevated into the very substantial risk present in murder *** depends upon the wantonness of defendant's acts—i.e., whether they were committed "[under] circumstances evincing a depraved indifference to human life.

The court offered, as **examples of depraved heart murder, driving a car on a city sidewalk at excessive speeds and hitting a pedestrian without applying the brakes, firing several bullets into a house, and continually beating an infant over a five-day period**. The *Roe* court concluded, "The evidence of the objective circumstances surrounding defendant's point-blank discharge of the shotgun is, in our view, sufficient to support a finding of the very serious risk of death required for depraved indifference murder."

Roe's example of murder being committed by horribly dangerous driving actually occurred in California in *People v. Watson*, 30 Cal. 3d 290 (1981)(superseded by statute on a separate issue). In this case, Robert Lee Watson committed driving so dangerous that the resulting murder was named after him, and is thus now known as "*Watson* murder." Watson, after consuming "large quantities of beer" at a bar, ran a red light, only avoiding a collision with another car by skidding to a halt in the middle of the intersection. After this near collision, defendant sped away to another intersection and struck a Toyota sedan, ejecting its three passengers. The Toyota's driver and her six-year-old daughter were killed. Defendant had left 112 feet of skid marks prior to impact, and another 180 feet of skid marks after hitting the Toyota. Watson was estimated to be speeding 84 miles per hour in a 35 mile per hour zone. Defendant's blood alcohol content a half hour after the collision was .23 percent, more than twice the percentage necessary to support a finding that he was legally intoxicated under the law of the time and nearly three times the legal presumption today.

The Supreme Court of California, in allowing a murder case to proceed based on these facts, noted,

> [M[alice may be implied when a person, knowing that his conduct endangers the life of another, nonetheless acts deliberately with conscious disregard for life. ***Implied malice contemplates a subjective awareness of a higher degree of risk than does gross negligence, and involves an element of wantonness which is absent in gross negligence.

California continues to suffer deaths from outrageously dangerous driving. On August 4, 2013, a driver drove his car down the Venice boardwalk. No charges have been filed in the case and no jury has made any factual determinations. In the videos and interviews provided in the following videos from *CBS News* and *NBC News*, consider what mental state the driver might have harbored.

CBS News: Venice boardwalk rampage driver was "out for blood," witness says, at: http://www.cbsnews.com/8301-201_162-57596903/venice-boardwalk-rampage-driver-was-out-for-blood-witness-says/

NBC News: Alleged Venice Beach Boardwalk Driver Failed Sobriety Test: http://www.nbclosangeles.com/news/local/Venice-Beach-Boardwalk-Deadly-Crash-Nathan-Campbell-Sobriety-Test-218928121.html

Depraved heart murder can also be committed by use of poison, as seen in *State v. Davis*, 519 S.E.2d 852 (1999), in which a mother, Mary Beth Davis, who was a registered nurse, injected one child with insulin and the other with caffeine. A jury convicted Davis of the attempt to injure her infant son by poison and first degree murder of her infant daughter.

In 1981 in West Virginia, the Davises rushed their infant son, Seth, to the hospital after he appeared to have a seizure. Seth's condition was so grave that he was flown to another hospital in Pittsburgh, which determined "someone," likely the defendant, who was a registered nurse, "had injected Seth with insulin." Due to the large doses of insulin, Seth sustained massive brain damage, living in a vegetative state where he was unable to walk, speak, see, hear or eat solid food. The hospital physician reported her suspicions to Seth's treating physician in West Virginia, instructing him to report suspected child abuse to West Virginia officials. The West Virginia doctor failed to make such a report. The defendant had acted bizarrely after Seth took ill, at one point buying a casket for Seth and stating that if he did not die soon he would outgrow the casket.

Eleven years later, the defendant rushed her daughter, Tegan, to the hospital for vomiting. While at the hospital, a nurse saw the defendant injecting something into Tegan without a doctor's approval. After the injection, Tegan took a turn for the worse and ultimately died. The autopsy revealed a caffeine overdose caused by the child being fed diet pills over a short period of time. An empty pack of diet pills was found in the trash at the defendant's home. There was also evidence that the defendant had disposed of the contents of Tegan's stomach that had been previously sucked out by a tube. The Supreme Court of Appeals of West Virginia affirmed the conviction, concluding there was sufficient evidence to find defendant's conduct evinced a depraved heart.

The poison forming the basis for depraved heart murder can also be pure heroin, as it was in *State v. Randolph*, 676 S.W.2d 943 (1984). In this case, the defendant, Emmitt Eugene Randolph, an established dealer, employed a junkie, Kathy Barnhill, to sell uncut heroin to Hank W. Jones, who then died of a "self-injected overdose" the next day. Learning from the defendant that she was selling "pure" or "uncut," and therefore dangerous, heroin, Randolph's employee, Barnhill, warned the purchasers not to take quantities or injections as great as on previous occasions because she had not had an opportunity to dilute the heroin.

Later, Randolph, when discussing the victim's death with Barnhill on the tape, said that, "the same thing had happened" to one of his customers two weeks earlier. He said that he regretted this but that it was "... just one of those things, you don't force anybody to get on it and use drugs." He also stated that "the man that did it, he didn't care . . ." and that "anytime you do that you're subject to dying and he knew that . . . " The Court concluded that the defendant acted with "conscious indifference to the consequences of their highly unlawful activities as to evince malice."

Severe child abuse can create cases of depraved heart murder. In *Johnson v. United States*, 631 A.2d 871 (1993), Linda Johnson was charged with murder "for causing injuries to nine-month-old Jamie Banker, by shaking her, hitting her head against a wall, and dropping her, all of which resulted in the infant's death." Johnson pleaded guilty to voluntary manslaughter in exchange for dismissing the charges of cruelty to children and second-degree murder. The following facts supported the plea:

> One week after appellant began her employment with the Bankers, (Johnson) telephoned Jamie's mother at her job informing her that she had found Jamie breathing unnaturally with her eyes rolled back. Mrs. Banker told appellant to call Jamie's pediatrician, who instructed appellant to call an ambulance, which she did. After performing a CAT scan at Georgetown University Hospital, the doctors found that Jamie suffered multiple massive skull fractures, a cerebral edema, hematoma, and hemorrhaging. [T]he doctors suspected that Jamie's injuries were caused by severe physical abuse, and they notified the Youth Division of the Metropolitan Police Department. Appellant indicated to the Bankers, to the hospital personnel, and initially, to the police that "nothing had happened to the child." After further questioning, the appellant told the police that Jamie had rolled off the changing table several days earlier, but believed that she was not seriously injured. At the time of her arrest, appellant told police officers that Jamie had been crying, and in an effort to quiet her, appellant had thrown her approximately six feet up in the air a couple of times, and that on the third time, appellant dropped her and Jamie struck her head during the course of the fall.

> Two days after her arrival at the hospital, the doctors determined that Jamie was "brain dead" and terminated the life support measures. An autopsy on the infant revealed that the cause of death was blunt force injury to the head, including massive skull fractures with two distinct sites of impact. *** Evidence of retinal hemorrhaging in the eyes revealed severe shaking of the infant, and the other medical evidence was consistent with Jamie's head having been struck against a wall.***Appellant, however, denied having "slammed" Jamie against the wall, and in response to the court's question as to what appellant did do, she stated:

> After I had sit [sic] her up on the dressing table, I was talking to her and I shook her trying to ask her what was wrong with her; baby, what is the matter; why do you keep crying so much. Her head hit the wall. I didn't realize her head was hitting the wall until, I guess, I snapped back to myself, and when I realized what had happened, that is when I picked her up and felt her head.

Depraved heart murder can also be committed by omission, as occurred in *People v. Burden*, 72 Cal.3d 603(1977) in which failure to feed an infant resulted in the child effectively starving to death.

d)   The Felony Murder Rule

The felony murder rule is simple to state: **any killing during commission or attempted commission of a felony is automatically elevated to "murder."** It might not be so easy to defend. After all, the felon is a murderer under felony murder even if the killing was accidental. The lack of a link between criminal intent and punishment has led to harsh criticism of the rule. Nelson E. Roth and Scott E. Sundby have declared in *The Felony-Murder Rule: A Doctrine at Constitutional Crossroads*, 70 Cornell L. Rev. 446, (1985),

> Few legal doctrines have been as maligned and yet have shown as great a resiliency as the felony-murder rule. Criticism of the rule constitutes a lexicon of everything that scholars and jurists can find wrong with a legal doctrine: it has been described as "astonishing" and "monstrous," an unsupportable "legal fiction," "an unsightly wart on the skin of the criminal law," and as an "anachronistic remnant" that has "no logical or practical basis for existence in modern law."

Why is this so? Where did the felony murder rule come from? **Felony murder has existed since common law**. Blackstone stated, "**if two or more come together to do an unlawful act against the king's peace, of which the probable consequence might be bloodshed; as to beat a man, to commit a riot, or to rob a park; and one of them kills a man, it is murder in them all**, because of the unlawful act . . . or evil intended beforehand."

The Texas Court of Appeals discussed the felony murder rule and the reasons behind it in *Rodriguez v. State*, 953 S.W.2d 342 (1997). In the case, the defendant, Albert Ray Rodriguez, fired a pistol, perhaps as much as eight times, at a passing car, killing a passenger within. These facts did not present the typical felony murder case. Usually, felony murder charges occur during the perpetration of a felony that is entirely independent of the killing. For example, a killing might occur during a robbery, arson, or rape. The robbery, arson, or rape would clearly be felonies separate from the act of killing. Despite the particular facts, a jury convicted Rodriguez of murder based on the felony murder rule (rather than on some other theory of murder). He appealed, arguing that felony murder should not apply where the underlying felony, here "deadly conduct," was the very act that caused the homicide and thus not independent of the killing. In considering the defendant's contention, the *Rodriguez* court explained the history of felony murder:

> At early common law, an individual was held liable for murder when he caused a death, although unintentionally, while committing a felony. *** This concept is known as the felony murder rule. The first statement of the common law felony murder rule has frequently been attributed to the seventeenth century pronouncement of Lord Coke: "If the act be unlawful, it is murder." ***
>
> The felony murder doctrine, as developed at common law, provided that where a death occurs in the course of, or as a consequence of, the commission of another distinct felony, the felonious intent involved in the underlying felony may be transferred to supply the intent to kill necessary to characterize the death as murder. ***
>
> **The early felony murder rule lacked significance since all felonies in England at the time were punishable by death**. *** If the intended act was a felony, its felonious design was imputed to the act actually committed, if that act was a homicide, it became murder since it was immaterial whether the offender was hanged for one felony or the other. [The] felony murder doctrine was brought to the American colonies. After independence, the doctrine became a

part of the common law or statutory provisions of every American state. *** As the number of felonies multiplied so as to include a great number of relatively minor offenses, many of which involved no great danger to life or limb, it became necessary, in order to alleviate the harshness of the rule, to limit it in some fashion. *** In England, the courts came to limit the felony murder doctrine: (1) by requiring that the defendant's conduct in committing the underlying felony involve an act of violence in carrying out a felony of violence, or (2) by requiring that the death be the natural and probable consequence of the defendant's conduct in committing the felony. **In 1957, the [felony murder] rule was abolished in the country of its origin**. ***

In the United States, limitations on the doctrine have varied from state to state and often have depended on differently worded statutes. Some states limit the rule to certain enumerated felonies, others to felonies that are inherently or foreseeably dangerous to human life, or where the homicide is a natural consequence of the felonious act. Some states require that the underlying felony be *malum in se* rather than *malum prohibitum*. **Another limitation is that the underlying felony must be independent of the homicide. *** This latter limitation has become known as the merger doctrine.** *** (U)nder this doctrine the felony murder rule will not apply where the underlying felony sought to be used as a basis for the operation of the rule is an offense included in fact in the homicide itself. *** **Where the merger doctrine is applied, the felony murder rule is not invoked unless the slayer was engaged in some** *other felony* **so distinct as not to be an ingredient of the homicide itself.** ***[31]

After explaining merger, the *Rodriguez* court interpreted the Texas murder statute as rejecting the merger limit on felony murder. The court therefore affirmed the defendant's felony murder conviction despite the fact that he committed no felony "independent of" the killing itself.

The Greatest Loss over the Pettiest of Reasons

The *Philadelphia Inquirer* newspaper reported in "Man arrested in killing of neighbor in dispute over dog waste" by Joseph Gambardello and Morgan Zalot, on February 15, 2012, that police arrested Tyrirk Harris for allegedly shooting and killing Franklin Manuel Santana over a dispute about a Chihuahua's droppings. This article can be viewed at:

http://www.philly.com/philly/news/breaking/20120215_Man_arrested_
in_killing_of_neighbor_in_dispute_over_dog_waste.html

VIDEO: Former Prosecutor Vincent Bugliosi Talks about the Sharon Tate Murders

WARNING: POTENTIALLY DISTURBING VIDEO. Famous Los Angeles District Attorney Vincent Bugliosi discussed the "Helter Skelter" motive in the murders orchestrated by Charles Manson at:

https://www.youtube.com/watch?v=blVt5zLmur8

---

31. Reprinted with the permission of LexisNexis.

B. DEGREES OF MURDER

At common law, a person convicted of murder faced a death sentence. Since he or she was already going to die for the murder, there was no need to further determine the "degree" of murder. Today, many jurisdictions break various crimes into a series of degrees. Murder is often divided into first and second degree based on statutory standards.

California Penal Code Section 189: Murder, Degrees

All murder which is perpetrated by means of a destructive device or explosive, a weapon of mass destruction, knowing use of ammunition designed primarily to penetrate metal or armor, poison, lying in wait, torture, or by any other kind of willful, deliberate, and premeditated killing, or which is committed in the perpetration of, or attempt to perpetrate, arson, rape, carjacking, robbery, burglary, mayhem, kidnapping, train wrecking, or any act punishable under Section 206, 286, 288, 288a, or 289, or any murder which is perpetrated by means of discharging a firearm from a motor vehicle, intentionally at another person outside of the vehicle with the intent to inflict death, is murder of the first degree. All other kinds of murders are of the second degree. ***

To prove the killing was "deliberate and premeditated," it shall not be necessary to prove the defendant maturely and meaningfully reflected upon the gravity of his or her act.

1.   List of Means or Actions

As noted above, California's PC 189, provides that "all murder" which is perpetrated by any of a series of particularly heinous acts is first-degree murder. This code section lists those acts as follows: killings carried out by "means of a destructive device or explosive, a weapon of mass destruction, knowing use of ammunition designed primarily to penetrate metal or armor, poison, lying in wait, torture . . ."[32] Here, modern law shares with the common law recognition of the special danger of poisoning. In his commentaries, Blackstone labeled poisoning "the most detestable of all," since it was so difficult to prevent.[33] At one point, English statute even punished such poisoning by "boiling to death." Thus, killings carried out in certain ways have been singled out as murder in the first degree.

2.   Willful, Deliberate, Premeditated

First-degree murder also includes killing by those possessing the most cold-blooded intent. This mens rea is typically called "premeditation and deliberation."

Premeditation and Deliberation

First-degree murder includes killing with "**premeditation and deliberation**," the most cold-blooded intent in homicide. The following case considers the evidence that can prove deliberate, willful, and premeditated killing for first-degree murder. As noted by this case, **certain kinds of evidence are particularly relevant** for establishing this mental state: (1) the **defendant's planning activity prior to the homicide**; (2) the **defendant's motive to kill,** as gleaned from his prior relationship or conduct with the victim; and (3) the **manner of the killing**, from which it might be inferred the defendant had a preconceived design to kill.

---

32. From *Deering's California Codes* Annotated. Copyright © 2014 by Matthew Bender & Company, Inc., a member of the LexisNexis Group. Reprinted with the permission of LexisNexis.
33. Blackstone's *Commentaries*, Vol. IV, at 196.

LEGAL ANALYSIS

Acuna v. California
2012 WL 2865959 (2012).[34]
U.S. Magistrate Judge Stephen J. Hillman issued this Report and Recommendation.

Facts

[A Riverside County Superior Court jury found petitioner, George Michael Acuna, guilty of first degree murder.] In addition, the jury found true the special allegation that in the commission of the murder petitioner personally used a deadly and dangerous weapon, i.e., a bayonet. [Petitioner filed a Petition for Writ of Habeas Corpus challenging the sufficiency of the evidence to support his first degree murder conviction.]

In *Acuna v. California*, the defendant committed first degree murder with a bayonet.

On the evening of June 15, 2007, defendant stabbed and killed Shane MacLachlan. Defendant and his friend, Israel de la Cruz, had driven to Lake Elsinore to speak to de la Cruz's [homeless] father, Manuel. Israel [son] and Manuel [father] were somewhat estranged at the time because of Manuel's relapse into drug use. [Manuel] had previously lived in defendant's home, and defendant considered him a good friend and a part of his family. Israel wanted Manuel to spend Father's Day, which was the next day, at his home in Corona with Israel and his family.

[Defendant and Israel found Manuel outside the Suds R Us Laundromat.] As they were speaking to Manuel, Shane MacLachlan and Luis Chavez approached them. MacLachlan and his companions *** saw defendant and Israel engage in what appeared to them to be a loud argument or a confrontation with [a homeless man. Israel] told an investigator shortly after the incident that someone who walked in on the conversation could "probably" have perceived it as "something going on, something wrong."

According to both defendant and Israel, MacLachlan and Chavez approached them in an aggressive manner. *** Based on their demeanor, Israel thought they were looking for a fight. Chavez turned his cap around and said he was "old school," and "from L.A.," apparently intending to imply that he was or had been in a gang. He also had a "213" tattoo, which has gang implications. MacLachlan or Chavez or both said the words to the effect of "You mother-fucker" and "This is going to happen," or "You're going to get it." Defendant and Israel attempted to tell MacLachlan and Chavez that nothing was wrong, that it was just a family conversation. Nevertheless, a fight ensued. There was no evidence that either MacLachlan or Chavez was armed. ***

Defendant testified that after MacLachlan struck him in the face, he was "really pissed off." He went to his truck, which was parked nearby, to retrieve a knife which [he] had left in the truck after a camping trip. At that point, he looked back and saw that Israel was on the ground being kicked. He was very upset and angry. He grabbed the knife and walked back toward the fight. MacLachlan walked up to him and,

---

34. This ruling was accepted by District Court Judge Gary A. Feess in "ORDER ACCEPTING REPORT AND RECOMMENDATION OF UNITED STATES MAGISTRATE JUDGE" 2012 U.S. Dist. LEXIS 96925, July 10. (2012).

according to defendant, "took a swing at [him] and a kick." When MacLachlan threw a punch at him, defendant was very "pissed off." He "stuck" MacLachlan with the knife, stabbing him in the lower back. MacLachlan later died from his injury.

Kimberly Beckham, [a witness,] saw defendant involved in the melee. Then she saw him run to the truck. *** Then she saw him running back toward the fight, in which MacLachlan was still engaged. She thought she saw a knife in defendant's hand. He ran up to MacLachlan. It looked almost like they were hugging. Then MacLachlan stepped back and said, "I got stuck." He had a knife hanging out of his back.

[Another witness, Suzanna Fluornoy,] saw defendant take the knife from his truck, take the sheath off, and walk away from the truck holding the knife in his hand. She did not see the stabbing. She could see from defendant's manner and body language as he approached the truck that he was very angry. The others had ceased fighting as defendant walked back to the truck. She heard him say, "You better run or you're going to get shot." As defendant walked back toward the fight, Fluornoy's companion urged her to get into the car and she did not see what happened. ***

Defendant and Israel left in defendant's truck. As they drove off, Savannah and Kimberly heard defendant yell, "You don't fuck with family" or "It was a family issue."

Although most of the witnesses referred to the weapon as a knife, the police officer who found it at the scene described it as a military bayonet, "very sharp, double-edged [and with] some jagged edges on it." Further, he said, "When it goes in, it doesn't come out clean. When it goes in, it pulls internals [sic] out." ***

Issue

Whether there was sufficient evidence to support a first-degree murder conviction in this case.

Rule and Analysis

Habeas relief is not warranted with respect to petitioner's insufficiency of the evidence claim.

Petitioner contends that there was insufficient evidence that the murder was premeditated and deliberate. According to petitioner, the killing amounted to voluntary manslaughter because it resulted from a sudden quarrel and in the heat of passion or from an imperfect self-defense. ***

[Under California's PC 187,] murder is the unlawful killing of a human being with malice aforethought." The malice may be express or implied. Express malice exists "when there is manifested a deliberate intention unlawfully to take away the life of a fellow creature." *** Implied malice exists "when no considerable provocation appears, or when the circumstances attending the killing show an abandoned and malignant heart." *** **A killing is deliberate and premeditated only if the perpetrator acted "as a result of careful thought and weighing of considerations; as a deliberate judgment or plan; carried on coolly and steadily according to a preconceived design."** ['Premeditated'] means 'considered beforehand,' and 'deliberate' means 'formed or arrived at or determined upon as a result of careful thought and weighing of considerations for and against the proposed course of action." *** **The process of premeditation and deliberation "does not require any extended period of time" and can take place quickly. *** California applies a three-part test for determining the sufficiency of the evidence to support a finding of deliberation and premeditation: (1) the defendant's planning activity prior to the homicide; (2) the defendant's motive to kill, as gleaned from his prior relationship or conduct with the victim; and (3) the manner of the killing, from which it might be inferred the defendant had a preconceived design to kill.** First degree murder verdicts will typically be sustained when there is evidence of all three types or at least extremely strong evidence of (1) or evidence of (2) in conjunction with either (1) or (3). ***

Here, the evidence supports the inference that defendant acted deliberately, with premeditation and with the intent to kill. He testified that after MacLachlan hit him, he was "really pissed off" and went to his truck to retrieve his knife. He implied that he didn't think of getting his knife until he saw that Israel was on the ground being kicked—which also "pissed [him] off"—and claimed that he took the knife for protection and hoped not to have to use it. On cross-examination, however, he admitted that he went to the truck with the intention of retrieving his knife because he was angry. When he saw MacLachlan walking toward him, he removed the knife from its sheath. Rather than brandishing the knife as a warning to MacLachlan, he walked toward MacLachlan as MacLachlan approached him, apparently not displaying the knife. When MacLachlan threw a punch at him, he "got pissed off" and "stuck" MacLachlan with the knife. He did not claim that MacLachlan was armed or that he thought he was.

Defendant emphasized throughout his testimony that he was "pissed off" by what he viewed as the unprovoked assault on him and on Israel. Presumably, he sought to convey to the jury that the decision to stab MacLachlan arose out of the heat of passion engendered by the assault. However, **although jurors can view an act done in anger as rash and impulsive, thus negating premeditation and deliberation *** and possibly negating malice as well, *** anger can also be viewed as a motive to commit murder. *** And, an act committed out of anger can be deliberate and premeditated, as long as the evidence supports the conclusion that the defendant weighed the considerations and decided in advance to kill. *****

Here, the evidence supports the conclusion that defendant, angered by the assault, went to his truck to retrieve the knife and that either as he retrieved it or as he walked or ran back toward MacLachlan, he reached a decision to stab and kill MacLachlan. The time it took him to walk from the truck to where he encountered MacLachlan was sufficient. . . . The evidence also supports the conclusion that defendant intended to kill MacLachlan because by its nature, the weapon he used was extremely likely to cause serious injury or death. ***

Conclusion

[The] Court finds that a rational trier of fact could have found beyond a reasonable doubt that petitioner was guilty of premeditated and deliberate murder. ***

[I]t is recommended that the court issue an Order: (1) approving and accepting this Report and Recommendation; (2) directing that Judgment be entered dismissing the action with prejudice.

Note

The three-part test—(1) defendant's planning activity prior to killing, (2) motive to kill based on prior relationship with victim, and (3) manner of killing that is "deliberately calculated to result in death"— was created in *People v. Anderson* 70 Cal.2d 15 (1968). Unfortunately, California has been less than consistent in applying its own "*Anderson* Rule." For instance, in *Anderson*, the Court overturned a first-degree murder conviction after strictly applying its three-part test. In the case, Robert Arthur Anderson, an unemployed cabdriver, had been living with a woman and her three children for eight months. He was left at home one day with the youngest child, Victoria, aged 10 years. Later, when blood was found on the kitchen floor, Anderson responded to inquires about the blood with ever-changing stories (he first claimed he cut himself, then changed to the assertion that Victoria's brother, Kenneth, cut himself, and finally said Victoria cut herself). Kenneth, having a "'weird'" feeling," looked in Victoria's room and found her "nude, bloody body under some boxes and blankets on the floor near her bed." Police were called.

The arresting officer found Victoria's body on the floor near her bed. He found defendant's blood-spotted shorts on a chair in the living room, and a knife and defendant's socks, with blood encrusted on the soles, in the master bedroom. The evidence established that the victim's torn and bloodstained dress had been ripped from her, that her clothes, including her panties out of which the crotch had been ripped, were found in various rooms of the house, that there were bloody footprints matching the size of the victim's leading from the master bedroom to Victoria's room, and that there was blood in almost every room including the kitchen, the floor of which appeared to have been mopped.

Over 60 wounds, both severe and superficial, were found on Victoria's body. The cuts extended over her entire body, including one extending from the rectum through the vagina, and the partial cutting off of her tongue. Several of the wounds, including the vaginal lacerations, were post mortem.

Despite the gruesome circumstances, and the fact that the defendant procured a knife and killed when "the shades were down on all the windows and the doors were locked," the *Anderson* Court reduced the crime to second-degree murder because it ruled the case simply did not fulfill its three-part test. As for planning activity, one would surmise that if the defendant had planned the killing, he would have laid down a tarp to catch the blood from the stabbing or would have taken the girl to a bathroom tub for the attack. At the very least, someone who had planned the killing would have created a cover story for the blood rather than fumble through three versions of a lame lie. For motive, the court expected more of a prior relationship to have been established between the killer and his victim than the mere fact that they both lived in the same home. Finally, for manner of killing, the court viewed sixty-plus wounds as evidence of a frenzied attack rather than a cold-blooded killing.

The California Supreme Court reached quite a different conclusion when applying the *Anderson* rule twenty-four years later in *People v. Perez* 2 Cal.4th 1117 (1992). In *Perez*, the defendant, Arthur Richard Perez, repeatedly stabbed Victoria Mesa, who was four months pregnant, to death, while she was getting ready for work one morning. The court noted:

According to the pathologist who performed the autopsy, Victoria bled to death. She had sustained blunt force trauma to her eyes, nose and lips, probably from a fist. There were about 38 knife wounds, including 26 stab and slash wounds and 12 puncture wounds. There were deep stab and slash wounds about the head, face, and neck, in the carotid artery, around the spinal column, and on the back of the arms. There were defensive wounds on her forearms, wrists, and hands. The injuries to the front part of the body were inflicted before the injuries to the back of the body. Two different knives were used.

In this case, the *Perez* Court affirmed the first degree murder conviction, despite the frenzied nature of the attack and the fact that:

The only connection between defendant and the victim and her husband was that they had attended the same high school some 10 years earlier. Defendant had played sports with Michael Mesa. Defendant lived about two and a quarter miles away and would drive by the Mesa house about twice a week in the early evening and wave to Michael as the latter was working in the yard.

Perhaps the facts better supported *Anderson's* three-part test; Arthur Perez's manner of killing pointed to premeditation and deliberation because he hunted about for a second knife after he had snapped off the blade of the first knife while attacking the victim. The court likened the use of a second knife to reloading a gun after firing all the rounds in the weapon into the victim. The reloading of the gun, or second knife, demonstrates the intent to finish the job of killing the victim—ample evidence of premeditation and deliberation. Another factor might have been the simple fact that the California Supreme Court, experiencing a change in membership over the decades, viewed the *Perez* case with different eyes.

Las Vegas Shooter Planned Extensively before Committing the Deadliest Mass Shooting in U.S. History

Matt Zapotosky, Devlin Barrett, and Mark Berman reported on October 3, 2017, in the *Washington Post* article, "Police say Las Vegas gunman planned 'extensively,' used cameras to monitor officers as they approached," that Stephen Paddock performed much planning activity in preparing for his shooting of victims at a concert venue in Las Vegas. Such planning activity, as explained in the *People v. Anderson* case, can establish strong evidence for willful premeditated and deliberate murder. The full article can be visited at:

https://www.washingtonpost.com/news/post-nation/wp/2017/10/03/as-las-vegas-grieves-investigators-struggle-to-piece-together-the-motives-behind-shooting/?utm_term=.43c07d1db888

---

3.   Felony Murder in First Degree

Legislatures can choose to identify certain felonies that are so heinous or dangerous that killings, which occur during their commission, are deemed first-degree murder. The killings can amount to first-degree murder even though the deaths were actually accidental or if the underlying felonies were merely attempted rather than successfully completed. California Penal Code Section 189 lists the following felonies for first-degree felony murder:

> All murder which is…committed in the perpetration of, or attempt to perpetrate, arson, rape, carjacking, robbery, burglary, mayhem, kidnapping, train wrecking, or any act punishable under Section 206, 286, 288, 288a, or 289, or any murder which is perpetrated by means of discharging a firearm from a motor vehicle, intentionally at another person outside of the vehicle with the intent to inflict death, is murder of the first degree.[35]

C.   CAPITAL MURDER: KILLING MERITING THE DEATH PENALTY

As the following case illustrates, imposition of a **death sentence** has been **restricted by state legislatures** to ensure that this most severe penalty is **meted out uniformly**. For a murderer to receive the death penalty, the fact finder must determine that certain "**aggravating factors**" exist in the case. Such aggravating factors are listed in state statutes. Consider whether the two aggravating factors in the following case, "**witness elimination murder**," and "**intentional murder in the course of . . . second degree burglary**" have been proven.

---

35. From *Deering's California Codes Annotated*. Copyright © 2014 by Matthew Bender & Company, Inc., a member of the LexisNexis Group. Reprinted with the permission of LexisNexis.

LEGAL ANALYSIS

People v. Cahill
2 N.Y.3d 14 (2003).
Justice Rosenblatt delivered the opinion for the New York Court of Appeals
(the highest court in the state).

Facts

Under New York's capital punishment scheme (in Penal Law Section 125.27[1][a][i]–[xiii], a person who commits an intentional] murder is eligible for a death sentence if any one of 13 aggravating factors is proved. In the case before us, a jury found defendant guilty of two counts of first degree murder, based on two aggravating factors (witness elimination murder, Penal Law § 125.27 [1] [a] [v], and intentional murder in the course of and in furtherance of second degree burglary, Penal Law § 125.27 [1] [a] [vii]). At the penalty phase of the trial, the jury determined that defendant should be sentenced to death on both counts. [We] conclude that neither of the aggravating factors was proved. This being so, the penalty phase was conducted without legal foundation and the resulting death sentences must be vacated. ***

What homicides land persons on death row?

[Defendant, James F. Cahill, III, and his wife, Jill, although legally separated, continued to live in the same home. During] a pre-dawn heated argument, defendant struck Jill repeatedly on the head with a baseball bat. The couple's two young children were nearby and Jill called out, urging them to call the police because their father was trying to kill her. *** Having been summoned to the scene, the police found Jill lying on the kitchen floor. She was covered in blood, writhing in pain and moaning incoherently. Her left temple was indented from the injury.

[During questioning, defendant first stated] that Jill had instigated the argument and attacked him with a knife, causing some cuts and scratches on his body. He claimed he struck her in self-defense. Defendant later admitted that he struck Jill with the bat when she was unarmed and that he cut himself, making it look like self-defense. ***

[A grand jury indicted defendant for assault in the first degree and a family court] issued orders of protection prohibiting defendant from seeing his children or entering University Hospital, where Jill was confined.

*** Jill had been hit at least four times in the skull. At the hospital, she underwent emergency surgery to remove a blood clot from her brain. In the ensuing weeks, Jill suffered from brain swelling and a number of life-threatening infections. She began to improve and eventually moved from intensive care to the coma rehabilitation unit, and later to the general rehabilitation unit. Her recovery was slow and by no means complete. [Six months after the assault,] Jill was able to recall the names of her children and had regained some ability to speak, but could use only short, simple words.

[After] the hospital was closed to visitors, defendant entered the premises, [disguised with] a wig and glasses, posing as a maintenance worker, complete with a mop and falsified name tag. [A nursing assistant also testified that about a week before the murder she saw defendant in the hospital, disguised as a janitor. When she saw defendant enter Jill's hospital room, she followed him in and asked if she could help him. He answered that he "just came down to say hi to Jill" and left the room.] Shortly after 10:00 P.M., a nurse detected a strong odor in the room and saw Jill having trouble breathing. The nurse also observed a waxy-looking substance on Jill's chest and that Jill's hospital gown caused a burning sensation when touched. Despite efforts to revive her, Jill died the next morning. She had been poisoned. An autopsy revealed that potassium cyanide was administered through her mouth or feeding tube.

Police promptly arrested defendant for Jill's murder. [Officers] recovered data from Cahill's home computer revealing Internet searches for "cyanide" and "ordering potassium cyanide." Cahill had also ordered potassium cyanide through the mails. In the area near the shed on the Cahill property police found a half-burned wig and a bottle containing potassium cyanide. Further investigation produced eyewitnesses who saw defendant intercept [a] delivery of cyanide. ***

Issue

Whether there was sufficient evidence to support the aggravating factors triggering the death penalty in this case.

Rule and Analysis

[The] first degree murder conviction based on witness elimination was against the weight of the evidence; and that the first degree murder conviction premised on burglary was legally insufficient to support a conviction.

[**A conviction for witness] elimination murder is committed when a defendant intentionally kills a victim who "was a witness to a crime committed on a prior occasion and the death was caused** *for the purpose of* **preventing the intended victim's testimony in any criminal action"** *** Defendant argues that the crime is not made out unless a defendant kills the victim for the *sole* purpose of preventing the victim's testimony. He argues, in essence, that the verdict cannot stand if there was proof that he had any motive for the murder other than his desire to prevent Jill's testimony. The People contend that evidence of multiple motives may support a conviction for witness elimination murder. ***

[The] statute would have to be read too expansively to authorize a conviction when a defendant's motivation to eliminate a witness is insubstantial or incidental. [We] cannot imagine that the Legislature intended to exclude a defendant—whose motivation to eliminate a witness was a substantial reason for the murder—merely because the defendant may have had other reasons or motives for the murder. Accordingly, **the statute is satisfied if defendant's motivation to eliminate Jill as a witness was a substantial factor in murdering her, even though he may have had mixed motives**. [The verdict is against the weight of the evidence. The defendant] wanted to kill Jill at the hospital for reasons that had virtually nothing to do with her ability to testify against him. **The weight of the evidence does not support witness elimination as a substantial motive for the murder**, and we therefore hold that the conviction for murder in the first degree *** must be vacated.

[The defendant was also convicted of capital-eligible murder for killing with the "intent to cause the death of another person" and] the victim was killed while the defendant was in the course of committing or attempting to commit and in furtherance of *** burglary in the first or second degree." [The] **conviction cannot stand because the burglary carried no intent other than to commit the murder**.

[To find a defendant eligible for the death penalty, the trier of fact must convict the defendant of murder and find one 'aggravating circumstance.']

The Legislature drew up a list of aggravating factors to create a subclass of defendants who, in contrast to others who commit intentional murder, it thought deserving of the death penalty. By this device, the lawmakers saw to it that the death penalty could not fall randomly on all murder defendants.

The Legislature's factors govern the discretion of courts and juries by limiting capital punishment to certain enumerated categories of intentional killings. [**The factors ensure**] **that the State follows its "constitutional responsibility to tailor and apply its law in a manner that avoids the arbitrary and capricious infliction of the death penalty."** ***

Penal Law § 125.27 (1) identifies death-eligible defendants as those who commit intentional murders in the context of one or more of 13 aggravating factors. Five aggravating factors relate to the killing of a member of a specific group (police officers, peace officers, corrections employees, witnesses and judges) ***, two relate to the present or past circumstances of the offender (defendants serving life sentences and defendants previously convicted for murder) ***, four address the circumstances of the killing or criminal transaction (murder committed in furtherance of certain enumerated felonies, multiple murders as part of the same criminal transaction, murder by torture and terrorism) ***. The remaining two involve contract killing and serial murder. ***

Among other arguments, defendant contends that he cannot be convicted under Penal Law § 125.27 (1) (a) (vii) because the statute requires that the underlying felony (here, burglary in the second degree) have an objective apart from the intentional murder and that the burglary was merely an act that enabled the murder, one of many anticipatory steps along the way. [There is legally insufficient evidence that the burglary had an objective apart from the intentional murder of the victim.]

Conclusion

[**The court order**] **should be modified by reducing defendant's conviction of two counts of murder in the first degree to one count of murder in the second degree and remitting to that court for resentencing on the second degree murder as well as the remaining counts and, as so modified, affirmed.**[36]

Learn from My (and Others') Mistakes

Do Not Forget That the Defendant You Are Prosecuting Might Not Be Convicted

The pistol-whipping PC245 ADW case involving the elderly victim (discussed in Mistake #3) not only resulted in an acquittal, but in the defendant returning to court seeking the return of his gun. I learned about this hearing to return evidence only by stepping into an elevator one day and coming face-to-face with the defendant who was on his way to court. We nodded to each other and rode the elevator in silence while I recalled all the awful things I said about him to the jury.

Texas has performed the most executions of any state since the reimposition of the death penalty. The following is Texas' statute defining capital murder.

V.T.C.A., Penal Code § 19.03 Capital Murder

(a) A person commits an offense if the person commits murder as defined under Section 19.02(b) (1) and:

(1) the person murders a peace officer or fireman who is acting in the lawful discharge of an official duty and who the person knows is a peace officer or fireman;

---

36. Reprinted with the permission of LexisNexis.

(2) the person intentionally commits the murder in the course of committing or attempting to commit kidnapping, burglary, robbery, aggravated sexual assault, arson, obstruction or retaliation, or terroristic threat ***;

(3) the person commits the murder for remuneration or the promise of remuneration or employs another to commit the murder for remuneration or the promise of remuneration;

(4) the person commits the murder while escaping or attempting to escape from a penal institution;

(5) the person, while incarcerated in a penal institution, murders another:

(A) who is employed in the operation of the penal institution; or

(B) with the intent to establish, maintain, or participate in a combination or in the profits of a combination;

(6) the person:

(A) while incarcerated for an offense under this section or Section 19.02, murders another; or

(B) while serving a sentence of life imprisonment or a term of 99 years ***, murders another;

(7) the person murders more than one person:

(A) during the same criminal transaction; or

(B) during different criminal transactions but the murders are committed pursuant to the same scheme or course of conduct;

(8) the person murders an individual under 10 years of age; or

(9) the person murders another person in retaliation for or on account of the service or status of the other person as a judge or justice of the supreme court, the court of criminal appeals, a court of appeals, a district court, a criminal district court, a constitutional county court, a statutory county court, a justice court, or a municipal court.

(b) An offense under this section is a capital felony.

Special Circumstances in High Profile Cases

The Associated Press, in its article, "Details of What Timothy McVeigh's Jury Must Consider," on June 12, 1997, provided the specific aggravating circumstances (which point toward imposition of the death penalty) and mitigating circumstances (which point away from imposition of the death penalty) the jury had to weigh in deciding whether to impose the death penalty on Oklahoma City Bomber Tim McVeigh.

http://www.apnewsarchive.com/1997/ Details-of-what-Timothy-McVeigh-s-jury- must-consider/id-72ed362ba72abdcb824 39361a92a8097

© Jacob Clausnitzer/Shutterstock.com

Oklahoma City Memorial Chairs.

Stanford Law School's Robert Crown Law Library offered the California Supreme Court's opinion in serial murderer Richard Ramirez's case, *People v. Ramirez*, 50 Cal.3d 1158, 270 Cal. Rptr. 286, 791 P.2d 965 (1990). This case, which discusses the special circumstances meriting the death penalty in the case, can be viewed at:

http://scocal.stanford.edu/opinion/people-v-ramirez-30982

Cornell University Law School Legal Information Institute offers "18 USC Section 3592: Mitigating and aggravating factors to be considered in determining whether a sentence of death is justified" which lists aggravating factors supporting imposition of the death penalty. This can be viewed at:

http://www.law.cornell.edu/uscode/text/18/3592

D. MANSLAUGHTER

What exactly is manslaughter, where did it come from, and how does it differ from murder? These questions were considered in *Comber v. United States*, 584 A.2d 26 (1990), in which Gilbert J. Comber punched a man unconscious for secretly marrying Comber's sister. The punching victim, who was "extremely intoxicated," fell down, lapsed into unconsciousness, and ultimately died from "bleeding in the part of the brain which controls the heartbeat and respiration."

Since common law defined manslaughter in Washington D.C., the Court of Appeals reviewed the common law history of manslaughter:

"What we now know as murder and manslaughter constituted just one offense under the common law of England." R. PERKINS & R. BOYCE, CRIMINAL LAW 125 (3d ed. 1982). At the turn of the sixteenth century, all homicides, with the exception of accidental homicides, homicides committed in self-defense, or homicides committed "in the enforcement of justice," "were deemed unlawful and were punished by death." [The harsh effects of this rule were lessened by the extension of ecclesiastic (church) jurisdiction.] Ecclesiastic courts, which retained jurisdiction to try clerics accused of criminal offenses ***, did not impose capital punishment. [Under] ecclesiastic law, a person who committed an unlawful homicide "received a one-year sentence, had his thumb branded and was required to forfeit his goods." [Transferring a case from secular to church jurisdiction by a procedure known as "benefit of clergy," caused a dramatic reduction of sentence. By] the fifteenth century, the courts began to accept proof of literacy as the test for clerical status, with the result that benefit of clergy became a 'massive fiction' that 'tempered in practice the harshness of the common law rule that virtually all felonies were capital offenses.' ***

[Eventually.] England's monarchs, beginning in the late fifteenth century and into the first half of the sixteenth, enacted a series of statutes which excluded a class of the most heinous homicides from benefit of clergy. *** These killings were referred to in the various statutes as "willful prepense murders," "murder upon malice prepensed," and "murder of malice prepensed." 3 J. STEPHEN, A HISTORY OF THE CRIMINAL LAW OF ENGLAND 44 (1883). *** "Unlawful homicides that were committed without such malice were designated 'manslaughter,' and their perpetrators remained eligible for benefit of clergy." *** The offenses encompassed by the new statutes were designated "murder"; perpetrators of these offenses were subject to secular jurisdiction and capital punishment. This distinction between murder and manslaughter persisted "[even after ecclesiastic jurisdiction was eliminated for all secular offenses."] These early statutory developments thus led to the division of criminal homicides into murder, which retained its status as a capital crime, and the lesser offense of manslaughter. The courts defined murder in terms of the evolving concept of "malice aforethought" and treated manslaughter as a residual category for all other criminal homicides. ***

Thus, manslaughter, "in its classic formulation . . . consisted of homicide without malice aforethought on the one hand and without justification or excuse on the other." [The District of Columbia has adopted this definition.] **A homicide which constitutes manslaughter is distinguished from murder by the absence of malice*****, and **is distinguished from a killing to which no homicide liability attaches by the absence of factors which would excuse or justify the homicide. Manslaughter is thus a "catch-all" category, defined essentially by reference to what it is not.** ***"[37]

Committing Manslaughter by Text

As reported by Ray Sanchez and Natisha Lance for CNN in, "Judge finds Michelle Carter guilty of manslaughter in texting suicide case" on June 16, 2017, a person has now been found guilty of homicide even though the contact causing death was by text.

The video can be seen by visiting:

http://www.cnn.com/2017/06/16/us/michelle-carter-texting-case/index.html

---

1. Voluntary

Provocation Once Considered Sufficient for Manslaughter

The common law recognized voluntary manslaughter. Blackstone in his *Commentaries*, Vol. IV, at 191, described the "voluntary branch" of manslaughter as:

> [I]f upon a sudden quarrel two persons fight, and one of them kills the other, this is manslaughter: and so it is, if they upon such an occasion go out and fight in a field; for this one continued act of passion: and the law pays that regard to human frailty, as not to put a hasty and a deliberate act on the same footing with regard to guilt. So also if a man be greatly provoked, as by pulling his nose, or other great indignity, and immediately kills the aggressor, though this is not excusable [as self defense], since there is no absolute necessity for doing it to preserve himself; yet neither is it murder, for there is no previous malice; but it is manslaughter.

What leaps out of Blackstone's discussion is the seriousness that the common law attached to the wounding of a gentleman's honor. Pulling on another person's nose could escalate into a deadly duel in a field. The resulting killing, while criminal, was not seen as so disproportionate to the nose-pulling as to mandate murder charges. At common law, a person's dignity was not to be trifled with.

---

37. Reprinted with the permission of LexisNexis.

Generally, **voluntary manslaughter occurs when the malice aforethought for murder is negated, or destroyed, by** either (1) **"heat of passion" which overrides the killer's self-control leading him or her to kill,** or (2) **an "unreasonable" belief in the need for self-defense, which can trigger a claim of imperfect self-defense,** a subject explored in Chapter 13 involving defenses.

The "heat of passion" leading to voluntary manslaughter has been described in a case from Kansas, *State v. Ritchey*, 223 Kan. 99 (1977), where the defendant, Mark E. Ritchey, beat a man to death with a pool cue. The *Ritchey* Court explained:

> "Heat of passion" includes an emotional state of mind characterized by anger, rage, hatred, furious resentment, or terror. *** It must be of such a degree as would cause an ordinary man to act on impulse without reflection. *** The emotional state must have arisen from circumstances constituting sufficient provocation. ***

California's Two Ways to Voluntary Manslaughter

In *People v. Lee* 20 Cal. 4th 47 (1999), the California Supreme Court described **manslaughter, under PC 192**, as **"the unlawful killing of a human being without malice."** *Lee* explained, "manslaughter has been considered a lesser, necessarily included, offense of intentional murder. Generally, an intent to unlawfully kill reflects malice ... An unlawful killing with malice is murder. Nonetheless, **an intentional killing is reduced to voluntary manslaughter if other evidence negates malice." This negation of malice can occur in the following ways: (1) when the defendant acts upon a sudden quarrel or heat of passion on sufficient provocation, or (2) kills in the unreasonable, but good faith, belief that deadly force is necessary in self-defense.**

Lee also required that the "provocation which incites the defendant to homicidal conduct in the heat of passion must be caused by or be conduct reasonably believed by the defendant to have been engaged in by the victim."

a) Upon Sudden Quarrel or Heat of Passion

The California Supreme Court, in *People v. Rountree*, 56 Cal.4th 823, 855 (2013), ruled:

> **The heat of passion requirement for manslaughter has both an objective and a subjective component.** *** **The defendant must actually, subjectively, kill under the heat of passion.** *** But the circumstances giving rise to the heat of passion are also viewed objectively. **[This] heat of passion must be such a passion as would naturally be aroused in the mind of an ordinarily reasonable person under the given facts and circumstances.**

The Court of Appeal in *People v. Mercado*, 216 Cal.App.4th 67, 81 (2013) affirmed the importance of the requirement that the killing occur under circumstances that would provoke an objectively reasonable person:

> [No] defendant may set up his own standard of conduct and justify or excuse himself because in fact his passions were aroused, unless further the jury believe that the facts and circumstances were sufficient to arouse the passions of the ordinarily reasonable man.

In the *Mercado* case, Monica Mercado, appealed her conviction of attempted murder (of a pregnant woman) and murder (of her unborn fetus). Mercado and Porsche Davis were rivals for the affection of a man named Bryant Waller. When Mercado was driving Waller down a street, she saw Davis, eight months pregnant with Waller's child. Mercado then ran Davis over "in a jealous rage." As described by the court:

> Davis put her hands on the car hood, curled into a ball and held her stomach. The next thing she knew she was underneath the Range Rover: "I just felt my baby go in my back and that was it . . . And my stomach just went flat instantly." The front and back tires of the Range Rover had driven over her. Davis testified the car did not swerve before it hit her, and she never heard any sound to indicate Mercado had applied the brakes.

> Davis was taken to a hospital [where her baby] was born critically injured and did not survive. Davis suffered a cracked pelvis, broken ribs and injuries to her spine and shoulder.

While *Mercado* found ample evidence fulfilling the subjective element of the heat-of-passion defense, evidence for the objective element was simply missing. The court confirmed the convictions.

California's heat of passion defense was fully explained in *People v. Berry* 18 Cal.3d 509 (1976)(*Berry's* diminished capacity analysis, an issue different from heat of passion, has been superseded by PC 25(a), which abolished the diminished capacity defense). In *Berry*, Albert Joseph Berry, a forty-six-year-old cook, married a twenty-year-old woman from Israel named Rachel Pessah. As with all homicide cases, the jury might have received a one-sided view of the crime, for the homicide victim could not testify as to her version of events. According to the defendant, only three days after their marriage, Rachel left for Israel, where she became romantically involved with a man named Yako. Immediately upon her return to the defendant, she told him about her love for Yako, which provoked a "brawl" where the defendant choked Rachel and she repeatedly scratched him. Berry claimed that, "Rachel kept taunting defendant with Yako and demanding a divorce. She claimed she thought she might be pregnant by Yako. She showed defendant pictures of herself with Yako." The defendant later described "a tormenting two weeks in which Rachel alternately taunted defendant with her involvement with Yako and at the same time sexually excited defendant, indicating her desire to remain with him."

At the end of this period, defendant choked Rachel into unconsciousness. At the hospital where Rachel was treated, she reported her strangulation to police, who issued a warrant for defendant's arrest. While Rachel was at the hospital, defendant removed his clothes from their apartment and stored them in a Greyhound Bus Depot locker, staying overnight at the home of a friend.

The defendant then returned to the apartment to talk to Rachel. Since she was out, he slept there overnight. The Court described defendant's version of Rachel's return to the apartment as follows:

> Rachel returned around 11 a.m. the next day. Upon seeing defendant there, she said, "I suppose you have come here to kill me." Defendant responded, "yes," changed his response to "no," and then again to "yes," and finally stated "I have really come to talk to you." Rachel began screaming. Defendant grabbed her by the shoulder and tried to stop her screaming. She continued. They struggled and finally defendant strangled her with a telephone cord.

Berry claimed he was provoked into killing Rachel because of "a sudden and uncontrollable rage so as to reduce the offense to one of voluntary manslaughter." The trial court, however, refused to instruct the jury on the heat of passion defense. On appeal, the California Supreme Court agreed with Berry that he was legally entitled to have the jury consider the heat of passion defense because, "In the present condition of our law *it is left to the jurors* to say whether or not the facts and circumstances in evidence are sufficient to lead them to believe that the defendant did, or to create a reasonable doubt in their minds as to whether or not he did, commit his offense under a heat of passion." Since the reasonable people of the jury can decide what is reasonable, the judge should have allowed them to decide if Berry killed in the heat of passion.

The "passion" in heat of passion did not have to be the kind found in romance novels, nor mean "rage" or "anger." Instead, it could be any "[violent], intense, high-wrought or enthusiastic emotion."

The *Berry* Court's approach represented a departure from earlier law that only trusted jurors to weigh facts of cases already determined by trial judges to be eligible for the heat of passion defense. At one time, defendants had to pigeonhole the provocation into various previously approved categories, such as mutual combat or finding a spouse in the act of infidelity. *Berry* instead ruled, "there is no specific type of provocation required by section 192 and that verbal provocation may be sufficient." Further, the stimulus creating the passion need not arise all at once from a single event, but could simmer over time as a pot boils over. In *Berry*, defendant claimed to be "aroused to a heat of 'passion' by a series of events over a considerable period of time." Examples of various stimuli that could build over time to "arouse a passion of jealousy, pain and sexual rage in an ordinary man of average disposition such as to cause him to act rashly from this passion" were Rachel's "admissions of infidelity by the defendant's paramour," and her "taunts to him and other conduct." A jury could decide such evidence supported a finding that the "defendant killed in wild desperation induced by [the woman's] long continued provocatory conduct."

The prosecution argued that, "the killing could not have been done in the heat of passion because there was a cooling period, defendant having waited in the apartment for 20 hours." The Court responded that Rachel's scream during their final conflict might have acted essentially as the straw that broke the camel's back: "the long course of provocatory conduct, which had resulted in intermittent outbreaks of rage under specific provocation in the past, reached its final culmination in the apartment when Rachel began screaming." The Court found the failure to give the heat of passion instruction to the jury doomed the case.

The California Supreme Court considered killing in heat of passion or upon sudden quarrel in *People v. Lee* (1999) 20 Cal. 4th 47, 971 P.2d 1001. In *Lee*, Steven B. Lee, and the victim, his wife Mee Nor, hosted a Chinese New Year's party at which the defendant drank most of a bottle of cognac. Being depressed at losing his job, Steven appeared, with his blank stare, as if he were "possessed by a spirit." When the defendant got into an argument with his wife, he went to the bedroom and returned with a gun.

> He pulled Mee Nor from the kitchen sink, where she was washing dishes, into the hallway, where the couple continued to push each other with the gun between them. (The couple's 12-year-old daughter) heard her parents arguing, and then heard a shot. When she came out of her room, she saw her father holding Mee Nor who was lying on the floor, begging her not to die. The gun was on the floor. Mee Nor had died instantly from a contact or near contact gunshot to the head just above her eye.

Lee noted that voluntary manslaughter could occur when the killing is "upon a sudden quarrel or heat of passion." *Lee* explained, "**The provocative conduct by the victim may be physical or verbal**, but the conduct must be sufficiently provocative that it would cause an ordinary person of average disposition to act rashly or without due deliberation and reflection. *Lee* found such provocation simply lacking in this case.

> [Even though defendant and Mee Nor were in an argument prior to the shooting, there] was no direct evidence that Mee Nor did or said anything sufficiently provocative that her conduct would cause an average person to react with deadly passion. Nor was there direct evidence that defendant acted under the influence of such passion.

> [Lee argues that something Mee Nor said to him after the dinner guests left angered him] as he and his wife argued and pushed each other for five minutes before the gun was fired. [Lee argues that he] may have been prone to emotional instability and [was intoxicated,] increasing the possibility that he reacted strongly to only modest provocation.

> The test of adequate provocation is an objective one, however. The provocation must be such that an average, sober person would be so inflamed that he or she would lose

reason and judgment. Adequate provocation and heat of passion must be affirmatively demonstrated.[38]

b)   Imperfect Self-Defense—Actual but Unreasonable Belief in Need to Defend

In *People v. Flannel* 25 Cal.3d 668 (1979), the California Supreme Court created the *"Flannel* defense" by ruling that an actual belief in the need to defend, even if unreasonable, could negate malice aforethought and thus reduce murder to voluntary manslaughter. In this case, Charles M. Flannel formed part of a "hostile and violent" three-way relationship involving his girlfriend (later wife) and Charles Daniels, the common-law father of Flannel's girlfriend/wife. At one time, resenting Daniels' "interference with his romance," Flannel attacked Daniels, kicking him in the chest and head and hitting him with a glass.

On the afternoon of the killing, Flannel happened to see Daniels. In defiance of his friends' reassurances and suggestions he simply leave the area, the defendant retrieved his gun from the trunk of his car and approached Daniels.

> Defendant walked up to Daniels and, standing directly in front of him with his hand on the gun in his right front pocket, asked him what was "happening." Daniels graphically told defendant to "stop messing" with him, that they were not supposed to be around each other, and asked him to "get goin."

> Daniels began backing away . . . waving defendant away with his left hand while his right hand remained near his back pocket where he was known to have kept his knife. Defendant followed, saying "Was you going to stick me in the side with a knife?" "Come on pull your knife." He then drew the gun from his pocket, extended his arm full length and fired one shot into Daniels' temple from a distance of approximately two feet. As Daniels fell, his switchblade knife flew into the air, landing on the ground where it spun around and popped open. No one observed the knife in Daniels' hand.

> Defendant immediately told his friends not to touch Daniels but to "leave him right there." He said, "He pulled a knife on me," adding that Daniels "deserved to be dead, nobody cares." Defendant dropped his weapon and waited until the police arrived.

Flannel ruled that, **"An honest but unreasonable belief that it is necessary to defend oneself from imminent peril to life or great bodily injury negates malice aforethought, the mental element necessary for murder, so that the chargeable offense is reduced to manslaughter."** Although the *complete* defense of self-defense requires *both* an honest *and* reasonable belief in the need to defend, **a defendant can seek to reduce the crime from murder to voluntary manslaughter when "his belief, although honestly held, fails to meet the standard of a 'reasonable person.'"** The Court explained,

> an honest belief, if unreasonably held, (cannot) be consistent with malice. No matter how the mistaken assessment is made, an individual cannot genuinely perceive the need to repel imminent peril or bodily injury and simultaneously be aware that society expects conformity to a different standard. Where the awareness of society's disapproval begins, an honest belief ends. It is the honest belief of imminent peril that negates malice.[39]

A portion of the *Flannel* case was later superseded by passage of Penal Code Section 25 (a) and (c), which abolished diminished capacity. This legislation did not affect *Flannel's* imperfect self-defense ruling.

38. Reprinted with the permission of LexisNexis.
39. Reprinted with the permission of LexisNexis.

Three Girls Charged in Death of Man Allegedly Dragged by a Car

Sarah Schulte of Channel 7 ABC Eyewitness News reported on May 2, 2017 in "Father of 7 dragged by car, killed while trying to sell his phone, 3 teens charged," that three teen girls allegedly shorted a man who had agreed to sell his iPhone to them for $450. The girls sped away while the victim was still leaning inside the vehicle, allegedly causing him to fall and strike his head. The full article can be viewed by visiting:

http://abc7chicago.com/news/father-of-7-killed-while-trying-to-sell-iphone-to-teens/1944493/

What Is The Problem? True Motives Underlying Tensions between Courtroom Actors

Tensions between Police and Prosecutors

When an officer visits the filing deputy, there exists an institutional difference of interests. Police want the case to be filed because the D.A.'s decision to formally pursue the case represents a practical endpoint as far as the officers are concerned. Police view the filing of a case as a successful conclusion of their investigation, allowing them to pass the baton to the next agency in line. In short, a filing is a vindication of their hard work. In contrast, D.A.'s have no similar institutional interest in filing. For the prosecutor, a case filing is not the end but the beginning where all the challenges start. Some cases, therefore, become a hot potato, where the officer tries to leave the case with the D.A. while the D.A. either wishes to "reject" the filing or seek further investigation.

2. Involuntary

In contrast to the intentional killing involved in voluntary manslaughter, **involuntary manslaughter can occur when a person: (1) acts with "criminal negligence" by creating a highly unreasonable risk of death that kills the victim,** or (2) commits **"misdemeanor manslaughter" by committing an "unlawful act not amounting to a felony."** The following case involves a defendant who was prosecuted for both kinds of manslaughter.

LEGAL ANALYSIS

People v. Oliver
210 Cal. App. 3d 138 (1989).
Justice Strankman wrote the opinion for the Court of Appeal of California.

Facts

[Appellant, Carol Ann Oliver, met the victim, Cornejo, at a bar. She bought jewelry from Cornejo. When Oliver left the bar, she drove Cornejo, who was intoxicated, to her home. At her house, Cornejo] asked her for a spoon and went into the bathroom. [Knowing Cornejo wanted the spoon to take drugs, Oliver gave him one.] Cornejo "shot up" in the bathroom. He then came out and collapsed onto the floor in the living room. She tried but was unable to rouse him.

[Appellant then returned to the bar. Appellant's daughter then came home] with two girlfriends. They found Cornejo unconscious on the living room floor. When the girls were unable to wake him, they searched his pockets, [finding no] wallet or identification. The daughter then [phoned Oliver, who] told her to drag Cornejo outside in case he woke up and became violent. The girls dragged Cornejo outside and put him behind a shed so that he would not be in the view of the neighbors. He was snoring when the girls left him there. [Appellant later returned home. She and the girls went outside to look at Cornejo.]

The next morning, Oliver told her daughter that Cornejo might be dead. Cornejo was purple and had flies around him. Telling the girls to call the police, Oliver left for work.]

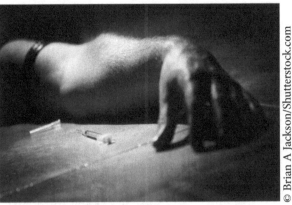

Helping an intoxicated person overdose on heroin can lead to manslaughter liability.

© Brian A Jackson/Shutterstock.com

[Police arrived and searched the home, finding in the bathroom] some tissue stained with blood. In the kitchen, [police] found a spoon with a blackish-gray residue on it, [a flat rubber strap in a kitchen drawer, and] drug paraphernalia.

[Oliver] told the police that Cornejo was extremely drunk when she drove him to her home. He went into the bathroom and asked for a spoon, which she gave him. Cornejo "shot up" and then collapsed. She said she believed that he had collapsed from the injection of drugs.

[Later, appellant delivered jewelry to a friend, telling her that] she had taken the jewelry off a man who had died of a drug overdose at her house. She asked her friend to keep the jewelry for her temporarily. The friend delivered the jewelry to the police.

An autopsy revealed that Cornejo died of morphine poisoning. The heroin (which shows up in the blood as morphine) was injected shortly before his death. Cornejo also had a .28 percent blood-alcohol level. The forensic pathologist who testified at trial was reasonably certain that Cornejo's death was not caused by the alcohol.

Issue

Whether the defendant was guilty of committing involuntary manslaughter either by 1) being criminally negligent about the victim's safety or 2) aiding and abetting the commission of a misdemeanor, during which the victim died.

Rule and Analysis

[PC 192 (b)] defines **involuntary manslaughter** as manslaughter (1) **in the commission of an unlawful act not amounting to a felony [misdemeanor manslaughter]; or** (2) in the commission of a lawful act which might produce death, in an unlawful manner, or **without due caution and circumspection [criminal negligence]**. [The People prosecuted under both theories here. For the first theory, the prosecution argued] appellant had aided and abetted Cornejo in the commission of a violation of Health and Safety Code section 11550 (use of controlled substance). [For the second theory, the prosecution argued] that appellant was criminally negligent when she failed to summon medical aid for Cornejo and then abandoned him, when she must have known he needed medical attention. ***

[After the trial court instructed the jury on the two theories of involuntary manslaughter, the jury found the defendant guilty.]

As to the criminal negligence theory, the evidence supports the trial court's determination that appellant owed a duty to seek medical attention for Cornejo, and there was substantial evidence of criminal negligence. **Criminal negligence is premised on conduct more reckless and culpable than that of "ordinary," or civil negligence. The conduct must be such a sharp departure from the conduct of an ordinarily prudent person that it evidences a disregard for human life, and raises a presumption of conscious indifference to the consequences.** ***

A necessary element of negligence [is a duty owed to a person and a breach of that duty.] Appellant claims that [she did not cause Cornejo's condition and therefore] did not owe him any duty to seek medical care. *** **Generally, one has no legal duty to rescue or render aid to another in peril, even if the other is in danger of losing his or her life, absent a special relationship which gives rise to such duty.*****

[An affirmative duty to act can be created by a defendant committing some act or omission that either created or increased the risk of injury to a person, or created a dependency relationship inducing reliance or preventing assistance from others.] Where, however, the defendant took no affirmative action which contributed to, increased, or changed the risk which would otherwise have existed, and did not voluntarily assume any responsibility to protect the person or induce a false sense of security, courts have refused to find a special relationship giving rise to a duty to act. ***

If the actor does an act, and subsequently realizes or should realize that it has created an unreasonable risk of causing physical harm to another, he is under a duty to exercise reasonable care to prevent the risk from taking effect. [Also,] "One who, being under no duty to do so, takes charge of another who is helpless adequately to aid or protect himself is subject to liability to the other for any bodily harm caused to him by . . . the failure of the actor to exercise reasonable care to secure the safety of the other while within the actor's charge." ***

[The events which occurred between the time Oliver left the bar with Cornejo through the time he fell to the floor unconscious, established] a relationship which imposed upon appellant a duty to seek medical aid. At the time appellant left the bar with Cornejo, she observed that he was extremely drunk, and drove him to her home. In so doing, she took him from a public place where others might have taken care to prevent him from injuring himself, to a private place—her home—where she alone could provide such care. To a certain *** extent, therefore, she took charge of a person unable to prevent harm to himself. *** She then allowed Cornejo to use her bathroom, without any objection on her part, to inject himself with narcotics, an act involving the definite potential for fatal consequences. When Cornejo collapsed to the floor, appellant should have known that her conduct had contributed to creating an unreasonable risk of harm for Cornejo—death. At that point, she owed Cornejo a duty to prevent that risk from occurring by summoning aid, even if she had not previously realized that her actions would lead to such risk. *** Her failure to summon any medical assistance whatsoever and to leave him abandoned outside her house warranted the jury finding a breach of that duty.

Appellant [argues that] there is no substantial evidence which supports a finding of *gross* negligence necessary to impose criminal liability. ***

We disagree. "The fundamental requirement fixing criminal responsibility is knowledge, actual or imputed, that the act of the accused tended to endanger life." *** Here, the evidence established that appellant knew that Cornejo wanted a spoon to administer drugs, that he then "shot up," i.e., injected himself with drugs, and then collapsed to the floor unconscious. There was also evidence that appellant believed that Cornejo had collapsed because he had "hotshotted," from which the jury could infer that she believed he had injected a dangerous dose, if not a fatal dose, of drugs. Such evidence constitutes substantial evidence that appellant either knew or should have known that Cornejo's condition was critical, that immediate medical aid was necessary, and that the failure to summon aid tended to endanger Cornejo's life. Such finding is particularly warranted by the evidence that appellant's ex-husband had died of a drug overdose, and that appellant believed that the persons who were with him at the time had delayed too long in seeking medical help.

Aiding and abetting. Appellant contends there was insufficient evidence to support a finding that she aided and abetted Cornejo's use of heroin. ***A person aids and abets the commission of a crime when he or she, with knowledge of the unlawful purpose of the perpetrator, and with the intent or purpose of committing, encouraging, or facilitating the commission of the offense, by act or advice aids, promotes, encourages or instigates the commission of the crime.** ***

Here, the evidence establishes that appellant was aware of Cornejo's criminal purpose when he asked for a spoon. The evidence of appellant's act of giving Cornejo a spoon and allowing him to use her bathroom to inject drugs, with the evidence of the flat rubber strap and other drug paraphernalia found by the police at appellant's house, support the finding that appellant facilitated the commission of Cornejo's use of heroin. [This] evidence, and all reasonable inferences drawn therefrom, also support the finding that appellant intended to facilitate Cornejo's use of drugs. The law presumes that an aider and abettor intends the natural and reasonable consequences of the acts he intentionally performs. ***

People v. *Hopkins* (1951) 101 Cal.App.2d 704 [226 P.2d 74] *** supports our conclusion. There the decedent purchased heroin with the defendant's money. They then prepared the narcotic for injection in the defendant's car and injected themselves, the defendant helping to manipulate a handkerchief-tourniquet around the decedent's arm while he did so. When the decedent fell unconscious, the defendant rushed him to the hospital where he died. The court held there was sufficient evidence to hold the defendant to answer a charge of manslaughter based upon aiding and abetting the decedent's use of heroin. [Even if the defendant had not touched decedent's arm, but had merely stood by and kept a lookout for passers-by he could still be charged as a principal.]

Conclusion

We conclude the record supports the trial court's denial of the section 1118.1 motion, and the conviction of involuntary manslaughter on both theories presented to the jury. ***

The judgment is affirmed.[40]

"Seamless Web" Connection

In *People v. Oliver*, the case just discussed, the court carefully explained the reasons for affirming the defendant's conviction for manslaughter. However, this case has other issues that connect it through the seamless web to other parts of the law. First, the court recognized a legal duty creating criminal liability for the defendant's omission in failing to help the unconscious victim. *Oliver* ruled, "One who, being under no duty to do so, takes charge of another who is helpless adequately to aid or protect himself is subject to liability to the other." The defendant's failure to do anything connects this case to the omission form of actus reus, discussed in Chapter 2.

Second, in finding that the defendant "should have known that her conduct had contributed to creating an unreasonable risk" of harm or death for the victim, the court is referring to foreseeability and causation, an issue explored in Chapter 4.

Third, in basing the defendant's guilt on the fact that she aided and abetted in the commission of heroin use, a misdemeanor, the court relied on accomplice liability, discussed in Chapter 14.

---

40. Reprinted with the permission of LexisNexis.

Manslaughter in the News—
Michael Jackson's Doctor Is Released from Prison

An October 28, 2013, *CBS News* article, "Conrad Murray released: Doctor convicted in Michael Jackson's death reportedly heckled as he's released from jail," reported on the greeting given Conrad Murray after he served almost two years of a four-year sentence. The piece can be viewed at:

http://www.cbsnews.com/8301-504083_162-57609591-504083/conrad-murray-released-doctor-convicted-in-michael-jacksons-death-reportedly-heckled-as-hes-released-from-jail/

---

3. Vehicular

In the following case, the court notes that **the mens rea for vehicular manslaughter is recklessness or criminal negligence**. When reading this case, consider whether the fact that a person is **driving under the influence** automatically makes the driver guilty of manslaughter for any killing his or her driving causes.

LEGAL ANALYSIS

State v. Cheney
55 A.3d 473 (2012).
Justice Alexander delivered the opinion of the Supreme Judicial Court of Maine.

Facts

Garrett Cheney appeals from a judgment of conviction of manslaughter [under 17-A M.R.S. § 203(1)(A) (2011).]

On January 30, 2010, between 2:30 a.m. and 3:00 a.m., the victim, a junior at the University of Maine, was walking in Orono. Around the same time, Cheney, who was visiting a family member in the area and had consumed alcohol to the point of significant intoxication, decided to drive his Chevrolet Silverado pick-up truck. As the victim walked south along Middle Street, Cheney drove north. Cheney crossed over the center of the street and struck the victim. She was projected, and her head struck the ground. She died at the scene.

Driving under the influence can cause vehicular homicide.

© Jonathan Weiss/Shutterstock.com

Cheney did not remain at the scene. [He left Orono and drove south on I-95, eventually driving his truck off the side of the highway.] A driver stopped to assist and advised Cheney to call 911 for assistance. When Cheney did so, the dispatcher instructed him to stay at the scene; however, Cheney asked the driver to take him to a gas station down the highway in Newport. At approximately 4:00 a.m., a trooper found Cheney eating breakfast at a restaurant attached to the gas station.

The trooper administered a breathalyzer test that indicated Cheney then had a blood-alcohol content of 0.15 grams of alcohol per 210 liters of breath. The trooper charged Cheney with operating under the influence. [Pieces of the defendant's truck were located at the accident scene.]

Issue

Whether there was sufficient evidence to prove the defendant committed vehicular manslaughter.

Rule and Analysis

Cheney contends that [there was insufficient evidence that he had the required mens rea for manslaughter at the time of the criminal conduct].

To be guilty of [vehicular manslaughter, a person must have recklessly or with criminal negligence caused the death of another human being.] A person acts "recklessly" when "the person consciously disregards a risk that the person's conduct will cause such a result." *** A person acts with "criminal negligence" when "the person fails to be aware of a risk that the person's conduct will cause such a result." *** Both culpable mental states encompass "a gross deviation from the standard of conduct that a reasonable and prudent person would observe in the same situation." ***

Whether a person was operating under the influence [is relevant in considering whether the operator of a motor vehicle is guilty of criminal negligence. But,] "a death caused by one operating a motor vehicle while under the influence is not *ipso facto* the result of recklessness or criminal negligence." ***

Here, the record evidence indicated that Cheney decided to drive a motor vehicle while heavily intoxicated. The jury could infer from the accident reconstruction testimony that Cheney crossed the centerline of the road to strike the victim. These facts permitted the jury to find beyond a reasonable doubt that Cheney's operation of his truck constituted a gross deviation from the standard of conduct that a reasonable and prudent person would observe in the same situation.

Conclusion

This evidence, along with the State's other evidence concerning Cheney's whereabouts and intoxication . . . are sufficient to permit a rational fact-finder to find, beyond a reasonable doubt, that, operating his vehicle with criminal negligence, Cheney caused the death of the victim.
[*Judgment affirmed.*][41]

The Fatal Consequences of Drunk Driving

The *Los Angeles Times* reported about Matthew Cordle's sentencing in an October 23, 2013, article by Michael Muskal entitled, "Ohio man who confessed online gets 6 1/2 years for drunk driving."
   This article can be viewed at:

http://www.latimes.com/nation/nationnow/la-na-nn-ohio-man-get-65-years-in-deadly-drunk-driving-confession-case-20131023,0,576.story#axzz2j2JPnmWD

The "I killed a man" YouTube video confession is at:

http://www.youtube.com/watch?v=MmpK_EshSL4#action=share

---

41. Reprinted with the permission of LexisNexis.

DISCUSSION QUESTIONS

1. Suppose Al hits Beth in the head and Beth dies from Al's blow—fifty years later. Can it be said that Al is guilty of "homicide" for killing Beth?

2. How is "death" defined for purposes of homicide?

3. Is there a right to die in the United States? Why or why not?

4. What is a human being for purposes of homicide? Does the term human being include the fetus within a pregnant woman?

5. What is malice aforethought and what is its relevance for murder?

6. What are the four kinds of malice aforethought?

7. How does the felony murder rule operate? Is it fair?

8. How is first-degree murder distinguished from second-degree murder?

9. What special circumstances cause a killer to be sentenced to death?

10. What are the various kinds of manslaughter?

11. What distinguishes manslaughter from murder?

WEB LINKS

1. Ohio man broadcasted his killing of an elderly man on Facebook live, ABC Action News, YouTube. This video, which might be disturbing for some viewers, can be seen at: https://www.youtube.com/watch?v=CfSG1WhVMp0

2. The Oklahoma State Courts Network provides Oklahoma's jury instructions. The jury instruction "OUJI-CR 4-64" defines "Murder in the first degree by felony murder," which can be viewed at: http://www.oscn.net/applications/oscn/DeliverDocument.asp?CiteID=81118

3. Oklahoma's jury instructions define certain terms for death penalty cases. The instruction, "OUJI-CR 4-73 Death Penalty Proceedings—Heinous, Atrocious, Cruel Defined" states:

   "you are instructed that the term 'heinous' means extremely wicked or shockingly evil; the term "atrocious" means outrageously wicked and vile; and the term "cruel" means pitiless, designed to inflict a high degree of pain, or utter indifference to or enjoyment of the suffering of others."

   The full instruction can be seen at: http://www.oscn.net/applications/oscn/DeliverDocument.asp?CiteID=81128

4. In *People v. Mitchell*, the case involving the definition of "death" for homicide, the Court referred to the "Uniform Anatomical Gift Act" involved in organ donation. The Uniform Law Commission, as part of the National Conference of Commissioners of Uniform State Laws, can be visited at: http://www.uniformlaws.org/ActSummary.aspx?title=Anatomical%20Gift%20Act%20(2006)

5. Jason Hanna and Ed Payne reported for *CNN* in their July 10, 2014, piece, "Authorities: Man kills 4 children, 2 adults in Texas shooting," that "A man shot and killed four children and two adults Wednesday at a Houston-area home belonging to relatives of his estranged wife, authorities said." It is speculated that he will face the death penalty. See: http://www.cnn.com/2014/07/09/justice/texas-shooting/index.html

CHAPTER VI

Crimes against the Person: Assaultive Conduct

Crimes against the person impose criminal liability for wrongful intrusions upon the "person," or body, of a victim. Perhaps the simplest and most common such crime is battery.

A. BATTERY

California Penal Code § 242: Battery

A battery is any willful and unlawful use of force or violence upon person of another.

Battery requires one person to **unlawfully touch** (make **contact** or use "**force or violence**") on another person. Can a person commit a **battery** by mere **careless** contact or must he or she **intentionally mean to cause contact** with another person? What if instead a person makes contact with "**conscious disregard of human life and safety**"? The following case considers what **intent** is needed for battery.

© Evannovostro/Shutterstock.com

LEGAL ANALYSIS

People v. Lara
44 Cal. App.4th 102 (1996).
Justice Yegan delivered the opinion for the California Court of Appeal.

Facts

[A jury convicted Pete Lara, Jr. of PC 242 and 243(d) battery with serious bodily injury. Appellant Lara had argued with his girlfriend, Michelle M., after he had watched two teenage girls walking in front of the house while Michelle did housework.]

Michelle told appellant to leave. They argued while appellant gathered his belongings. Appellant removed $60 from Michelle's purse. [When Lara was about to leave,] Michelle stood behind him, asked him to stay, and asked for the return of her money. Appellant swung around to face her and the side of his right hand struck Michelle, breaking the bone in her nose. Appellant looked shocked and said: "Your nose," or "I broke your nose."

[Michelle called 911, asking that Lara be arrested. Michelle then drove herself to the hospital, where she gave a tape-recorded statement to police.] Michelle stated that she did not touch appellant before he hit her. When asked whether appellant had been "physical" with her before, Michelle answered: "Actually, . . . he has never hit me. OK, the guy he pushed me . . . It's always when I tell him to leave, you know I tell him to leave, and he'll, you know, be getting ready to leave but I start running off at the mouth. . . . I don't shut up so he flips out on me, you know."

[At] the district attorney's office, Michelle stated this was the first time appellant struck her and that she had mixed feelings about the prosecution. Toward the end of the interview, Michelle claimed, for the first time, that appellant might have hit her by accident.

At trial, Michelle testified that, before appellant hit her, she grabbed the back of his Pendleton shirt with such force that most of the buttons popped off the front of the shirt. Appellant turned around to free himself from her grasp and hit her in the nose by accident.

Issue

Whether a battery can be committed with criminal negligence rather than intentional touching.

Rule and Analysis

***No reported California case has ever said that a battery can be committed with "criminal negligence." We shall not be the first to so hold. *** We reverse because the trial court instructed the jury that appellant could be convicted of battery if he acted with "criminal negligence." ***

[**Battery is a general intent crime**. This] excludes criminal liability when the force or violence is accomplished with a "lesser" state of mind, i.e., "criminal negligence." As with all general intent crimes, "the required mental state entails only an intent to do the act that causes the harm." [**Battery**] **requires that the defendant actually intend to commit a "willful and unlawful use of force or violence upon the person of another."** ***

Reckless conduct alone does not constitute a sufficient basis for [battery.] However, if an act "'inherently dangerous to others' . . . [is] done 'with conscious disregard of human life and safety,' the perpetrator must be aware of the nature of the conduct and choose to ignore its potential for injury, i.e., act willfully. If these predicates are proven to the satisfaction of the trier of fact, the requisite intent is [established by the evidence.]

Acting with "conscious disregard" . . . is not the equivalent of "criminal negligence." [Conscious disregard] requires proof that the defendant subjectively intended to engage in the conduct at issue. General criminal intent may be inferred by the conduct of the defendant if he or she acts with a "conscious disregard." On the other hand, "criminal negligence" requires jurors to apply an objective standard and to ask whether a reasonable person in the defendant's position would have appreciated the risk his or her conduct posed to human life. ***

"Criminal negligence" requires proof of "aggravated, culpable, gross, or reckless conduct, which is such a departure from the conduct of an ordinarily prudent person under the same circumstances as to demonstrate an indifference to consequences or a disregard of human life." [Where liability is based on "criminal negligence," the defendant may be found to have acted with "criminal negligence" without proof that he or she intended to commit the act.]

Here, *** the jury was…instructed that it could convict appellant if it found that he acted with the "lesser" mental state of "criminal negligence." This was error. ***

Conclusion

Appellant is entitled to a trial without reference to "criminal negligence."
The judgment is reversed.[42]

Battery requires some kind of contact with the victim; California calls it **"force or violence." How much or what kind of contact is needed for battery?** Does a person actually have to **"hurt"** the victim to commit a battery?

LEGAL ANALYSIS

People v. Martinez
3 Cal. App.3d 886 (1970).
Justice Stephens delivered the opinion for the California Court of Appeal.

Facts

Defendant [Carlos Maritnez was charged with violation of PC 243 (battery on a peace officer) and with PV 148 (obstructing public officers in the discharge of their duties.)

[On July 7, 1968, Officer Erland E. Polson, a uniformed Manhattan Beach police officer, with six other policemen, attempted to shut down a loud party.] While Officer Polson was standing next to a police vehicle helping a fellow officer arrest another person, defendant *** came to within two feet of the officers and shouted in a very loud tone of voice, "Who do you think you are? You can't do this. Where are you taking him?" Defendant kept repeating these statements and Officer Polson advised him to go back to the sidewalk and stop interrupting the officers. [Defendant] backed up onto the sidewalk, continuing "to yell [abuses at Officer Polson]." The officer, who was wearing motorcycle boots, said, "Now, what are you going to do about it?" *** Defendant, who was barefooted, kicked him twice in the shin. Officer Polson did not suffer any injury. "The most I would say it smarted due to the fact I was wearing motorcycle boots."

---

42. Reprinted with the permission of LexisNexis.

Issue

Whether kicking a person wearing motorcycle boots with a bare foot amounts to "use of force or violence" for a battery?

Rule and Analysis

[Defendant argued that when a barefooted young man kicks a police officer's booted leg after the officer has asked "What are you going to do about it?" and the officer suffers no injury, there has not been a battery on a police officer.] However, section 243 does not change the definition of battery, it only provides for a greater penalty when acts otherwise constituting a battery are committed upon a peace officer engaged in the performance of his duties. To paraphrase Gertrude Stein, "A battery is a battery is a battery." *** "A battery is a battery whoever may be the victim. It is simply that section 243 of the Penal Code increases the punishment if the victim is a peace officer and certain other requirements are satisfied."

The definition of battery in Penal Code section 242, **any willful and unlawful use of force or violence upon the person of another**, remains the same. **Any harmful or offensive touching constitutes an unlawful use of force or violence.** *** We are not prepared to say that a barefooted kick is unoffensive. Given the appropriate circumstances and the appropriate barefoot, it may be more than ordinarily offensive.

Defendant could not argue that the officer's words justified the battery. No conduct or words, no matter how offensive or exasperating, are sufficient to justify a battery. ***

Conclusion

Since any offensive or rude touching suffices for "use of force or violence" for battery, the defendant, in kicking the officer with a bare foot, fulfilled the elements of battery.[43]

Aggravated Battery: Due to Subject of Attack

Common law considered "one species of battery," the "beating of . . . a clergyman," to be "more atrocious and penal than the rest" because the batterer attacked someone of "sacred character" and a "minister and embassador of peace."[44]

Modern statutes also perceive batteries as more severe, or "aggravated," when the attack is focused on certain victims. California Penal Code 243 provides an example:

Penal Code § 243. Punishment for battery generally; Punishment for battery against specified officers or others

(a) A battery is punishable by a fine not exceeding two thousand dollars ($2,000), or by imprisonment in a county jail not exceeding six months, or by both that fine and imprisonment.

(b) **When a battery is committed against the person of a peace officer, custodial officer, firefighter, emergency medical technician, lifeguard, security officer, custody assistant, process server, traffic officer, code enforcement officer, animal control officer, or search and rescue member** engaged in the performance of his

---

43. Reprinted with the permission of LexisNexis.
44. Blackstone, *Commentaries,* Vol. IV, at 217.

or her duties, whether on or off duty, including when the peace officer is in a police uniform and is concurrently performing the duties required of him or her as a peace officer while also employed in a private capacity as a part-time or casual private security guard or patrolman, or a nonsworn employee of a probation department engaged in the performance of his or her duties, whether on or off duty, or a physician or nurse engaged in rendering emergency medical care outside a hospital, clinic, or other health care facility, and the person committing the offense knows or reasonably should know that the victim is a peace officer, custodial officer, firefighter, emergency medical technician, lifeguard, security officer, custody assistant, process server, traffic officer, code enforcement officer, animal control officer, or search and rescue member engaged in the performance of his or her duties, nonsworn employee of a probation department, or a physician or nurse engaged in rendering emergency medical care, the battery is punishable by a fine not exceeding two thousand dollars ($2,000), or by imprisonment in a county jail not exceeding one year, or by both that fine and imprisonment.

Battery By Adulterating Someone's Drink

It has been widely reported that Bill Cosby has been accused by dozens of women for having nonconsensual intercourse with them. Some of Cosby's accusers have alleged that he put drugs, such as Quaaludes, into beverages they were drinking. Separate from rape issues, the very fact of purposely adulterating another person's drink without that person's knowing consent is a battery when the victim then ingests the tainted beverage. On July 7, 2015, Holly Yan, Eliott C. McLaughlin, and Dana Ford reported for CNN in "Bill Cosby admitted to getting Quaaludes to give to women" regarding testimony Cosby gave during a deposition. This article can be viewed in full at:

http://www.cnn.com/2015/07/07/us/bill-cosby-quaaludes-sexual-assault-allegations/index.html

B.   ASSAULT

While **battery requires contact**—a "battering," **assault does not**. This lack of a "contact" element can raise some subtle issues that do not arise in battery cases.

1.   Common Law

Can a person ever be convicted of **"assault"** when the victim **neither suffered harm nor was ever aware of the attack**? The following Maryland case provides the **common law rule** regarding assault and defines the two types of assault recognized by some jurisdictions: (1) **attempted battery** and (2) **putting another in fear**.

© Max Sky/Shutterstock.com

Assault does not require contact.

LEGAL ANALYSIS

Harrod v. State
499 A.2d 959 (1985).
Justice Alpert delivered the opinion for the Court of Special Appeals of Maryland.

Facts

The facts in the instant case present this court with an excellent opportunity to explain the distinctions between these two different types of assault (at common law).

The assault charges arose out of a confrontation among appellant, John G. Harrod, his wife Cheryl, and her friend Calvin Crigger. The only two witnesses at trial were appellant and Cheryl Harrod.

[Cheryl testified that Calvin visited when she thought appellant had gone to work. "All of a sudden" appellant came out of the bedroom with a hammer in his hand, swung it around, and came after Cheryl and Calvin. Calvin ran out of the house. Appellant threw the hammer over top of Christopher's port-a-crib and it went into the wall.]

[Appellant testified that, having missed his ride to work, he came back home and went to sleep in a back room. Awakened by Calvin's deep voice, appellant picked up his hammer and, walking into the living room, told Calvin,] "Buddy, if you want your head busted in, stand here; if you want to be healthy and leave, go." Appellant said that Calvin just stood there, so he swung the hammer, Calvin moved his head back, and the hammer struck the wall over Christopher's crib, which was near the door.

[The trial court convicted appellant, stating:]

Mr. Harrod came after Cheryl and Calvin. He came out of his room swinging a] hammer, and ultimately threw it, not too far from the child, Christopher. [He] is guilty of two counts of Assault; one against Cheryl and one against the minor child.

Defense counsel inquired of the court: "On the second count of the Information, is the Court finding specific intent on behalf of the Defendant to injure his child?" The court responded, "Yes. Threw that hammer within a very short distance—sticking it—it was still sticking in the wall."

Issue

Whether a person can be convicted of assaulting another who has suffered no harm and was never aware of the alleged assault.

Rule and Analysis

The common law crime of assault encompasses two definitions: (1) an attempt to commit a battery or (2) an unlawful intentional act which places another in reasonable apprehension of receiving an immediate battery. ***

Two Types of Assault

Appellant [argues that there was insufficient evidence] that he harbored a specific intent to injure Christopher when he threw the hammer. [He] notes that there was no evidence that Christopher was injured by the hammer or that he was even aware that a hammer was thrown. [Appellant claims that the trial court's finding that he criminally assaulted Christopher was erroneous. We agree.]

[An] assault "is committed when there is *either* an attempt to commit a battery *or* when, by an unlawful act, a person is placed in reasonable apprehension of receiving an immediate battery."

*** These **two types of assaults**—*attempted battery* and *putting another in fear*—are indeed two distinct crimes that have been inadvertently overlapped and confused. One commentator explained this confusion:

> In the early law the word "assault" represented an entirely different concept in criminal law than it did in the law of torts. As an offense it was an attempt to commit a battery; as a basis for a civil action for damages it was an intentional act wrongfully placing another in apprehension of receiving an immediate battery. The distinction has frequently passed unnoticed because a misdeed involving either usually involves both. If, with the intention of hitting X, D wrongfully threw a stone that X barely managed to dodge, then D would have been guilty of a criminal assault because he had attempted to commit a battery, and he would also have been liable in a civil action of trespass for assault because he had wrongfully placed X in apprehension of physical harm.

Attempted Battery

[In] an attempted battery-type assault, the victim need not be aware of the perpetrator's intent or threat. If a person be struck from behind, or by stealth or surprise, or while asleep, he is certainly the victim of a battery. [Because] there may be committed a battery without the victim first being aware of the attack, an attempted battery-type assault cannot include a requirement that the victim be aware. ***

The facts in the case . . . do not support a finding that appellant committed an attempted battery towards the infant, Christopher. An attempt to commit any crime requires a specific intent to commit that crime. **[An attempted battery-type assault] requires that the accused harbor a specific intent to cause physical injury to the victim . . . and take a substantial step towards causing that injury.** ***

Nowhere does the record indicate that appellant threw the hammer with the specific intent to injure Christopher. The court expressly stated that it found specific intent on behalf of appellant because he "[threw] that hammer within a very short distance" of the child. The court here is merely inferring a criminal intent from reckless or negligent acts of the appellant. This is not sufficient . . . especially where all of the evidence tends to the contrary: that appellant's intent was to injure Calvin.

Assault by Placing One in Fear

There is likewise insufficient evidence that appellant, by an unlawful intentional act, placed Christopher in reasonable apprehension of receiving an immediate battery. **By definition of [Assault by Placing One in Fear the victim must be aware of the impending contact.]** "Since the interest involved is the mental one of apprehension of contact, it should follow that the plaintiff must be aware of the defendant's act at the time, and that it is not an assault to aim a gun at one who is unaware of it." ***

There is no evidence in the record before us that Christopher was in fact aware of the occurrences in his home on the morning in question. Therefore, there was insufficient evidence to find appellant guilty of the putting victim in fear-type assault.

Conclusion

Because the trial court was clearly erroneous in finding appellant guilty of an assault on Christopher, we must reverse that conviction.[45]

---

45. Reprinted with the permission of LexisNexis.

Why Was Senator Rand Paul Assaulted?

Jen Kirby, in her November 20, 2017, *Vox* article, "Did Rand Paul Really Get Beat Up over Lawn Clippings?" reported that the senator's neighbor, Rene Boucher, tackled Rand Paul while he was mowing his lawn. The alleged assault broke Paul's ribs. The article can be viewed at:

https://www.vox.com/policy-and-politics/2017/11/6/16612734/rand-paul-neighbor-assault

---

2. Current Law

California Penal Code § 240: Assault

An assault is an unlawful attempt, coupled with a present ability, to commit a violent injury on the person of another.

VIDEO: A Florida Criminal Defense Attorney Discusses How Criminal Cases Are Filed

Criminal Defense attorney Jonathan Blecher talks about how the prosecution files a case in Florida for felonies and misdemeanors at:

https://www.youtube.com/watch?v=n-krbFlNcBQ

What exactly is meant by **"an unlawful attempt"**? **Must the attacker specifically intend to make contact** with the victim, or is it enough that the defendant merely **generally intend to willfully commit an *act* the direct, natural, and probable consequences of which if successfully completed would be the injury to another?** The California Supreme Court case below considers these alternatives.

LEGAL ANALYSIS

People v. Trujillo
181 Cal.App.4th 1344 (2010).
Justice King.

Facts

While riding in a car, defendant Angel Trujillo fired numerous shots from a semiautomatic rifle at another moving car. The other car had two occupants, a driver and a backseat passenger. At least two bullets hit the car, but neither occupant of the car was hit. Defendant was charged with two counts of [PC 664/187 attempted murder and two counts of PC 245(b) assault with a semiautomatic firearm. A jury acquitted Trujillo of the attempted murder charges and convicted him of the assault charge].

On appeal, defendant contends *** the evidence is insufficient to convict him of two counts of assault because he had no knowledge of the backseat passenger in the car he was shooting at. [We] conclude the evidence is sufficient to support convictions for assault with a semiautomatic firearm as to both occupants of the car even if defendant did not actually see the backseat passenger.

Issue

Whether a person can form the required mental state for assault even when he or she lacks actual knowledge of each specific victim of his assault.

Rule and Analysis

[Defendant argues that he did not have the required mental state for assault as to the passenger] because he was not actually aware that there was a second person in the Civic when he shot at the car. [We conclude that defendant had the required mental state for assault even if he did not have actual knowledge of each specific victim of his assault.]

The California Supreme Court has [attempted to clarify the nature of the mental state for assault in *People v. Rocha*, *People v. Colantuono*, and *People v. Williams*. *Rocha* held, **"the criminal intent required for assault] is the general intent to wilfully commit an act the direct, natural and probable consequences of which if successfully completed would be the injury to another**. Given that intent it is immaterial whether or not the defendant intended to violate the law or knew that his conduct was unlawful. **The intent to cause any particular injury *** to severely injure another, or to injure in the sense of inflicting bodily harm is not necessary."** [*Colantuono* explained that intent for assault is measured by: 1) the character of the defendant's willful conduct, with 2) its direct and probable consequences. For] assault, as with any general intent crime, the nature of the defendant's *present willful conduct* alone suffices to establish the necessary mental state without inquiry as to an intent to cause further consequences. [To prove assault's intent, one need only to prove a willful act that by its nature will directly and immediately cause the least touching. The defendant need not intend to violate the law or intend to cause any particular injury to another.] **The pivotal question is whether the defendant intended to commit an act likely to result in such physical force, not whether he or she intended a specific harm.** [The necessary mental state for assault] is 'an intent merely to do a violent act.'] Once the violence is commenced, 'the assault is complete.' [*Williams* explained, for a defendant to be guilty of assault, she] must be aware of the facts that would lead a reasonable person to realize that a battery would directly, naturally and probably result from his conduct." ***

[A defendant who has the required mental state for assault while committing one or more criminal acts so] that a direct, natural, and probable result is a battery against two persons may be convicted of assault against each. Here, there is no dispute that the firing of multiple gunshots from a semiautomatic weapon at the Civic is an "action [or are actions] enabling him to inflict a present injury" on anyone inside the Civic, thus constituting [the criminal act(s) of assault. The defendant had the requisite mental state for assault. He] was actually aware that he was shooting at an occupied car in a manner that would lead a reasonable person to realize that a battery against another would directly, naturally, and probably result. *** Even if he was not actually aware of the second person in the Civic, his mental state can be [readily combined with the criminal act or acts of shooting at the car with two people inside. Just as a person maliciously intending to kill is guilty of the murder of all persons actually killed, a person who has the required intent for assault is guilty of the assault of all persons actually assaulted. For assault, there are as many crimes as there are victims].

Conclusion

[The victim, sitting in the backseat of the car nearest to defendant's fusillade of gunshots, was no less a victim of defendant's assault than the driver. Therefore, defendant can be convicted of assault against both occupants of the car even if defendant did not actually see the passenger in the backseat. The evidence was sufficient to support the conviction for assault against the passenger.] The judgment is modified [and] affirmed.[46]

What does "**present ability**" mean for purposes of **assault**? Can an assailant fulfill present ability even when his **gun**, though loaded and fully operational, is **pointed away** from the victim?

LEGAL ANALYSIS

People v. Chance
44 Cal. 4th 1164 (2008).
Justice Corrigan delivered the opinion of the California Supreme Court.

Facts

[On November 29, 2003, sheriff's officers drove to a house in a rural area] to arrest defendant pursuant to felony warrants. The officers had information that defendant was there and armed with a handgun. Defendant, evidently alerted to their approach, ran from the house. Sergeant Tom Murdoch pursued him on foot. Murdoch wore a vest marked with a large yellow star and the word "SHERIFF" on the front and back. Defendant saw Murdoch and kept running.
*** Murdoch twice shouted, "Sheriff's Department, stop." From a distance of 30 to 35 feet, Murdoch saw that defendant was carrying a handgun. Defendant ran around the front end of a trailer. Murdoch approached, looking and listening for any indication that defendant was still fleeing. Detecting none, and anticipating that defendant might be lying in wait for him, Murdoch advanced to his left, around the back of the trailer. Carefully peering around the corner, he saw defendant pressed against the trailer, facing the front end. He was holding the gun in his right hand, extended forward and supported by his left hand. ***
Defendant looked back over his right shoulder at Murdoch, who had his own gun trained on defendant. Murdoch repeatedly told defendant to drop the weapon. The officer testified, "I was in fear of my life. I was afraid . . . he was going to try to shoot me any second." After some hesitation, defendant brought the gun toward the center of his body, then flipped it behind him. *** Defendant was arrested and the gun recovered. It was fully loaded with 15 rounds in the magazine. There was no round in the firing chamber, but defendant could have chambered one by pulling back a slide mechanism. The safety was off.
A jury convicted defendant of [PC 245(d)(1) assault with a firearm on a peace officer.]

Issue

Whether the defendant, Chance, had the "present ability" to commit assault even though he was pointing his gun in a direction opposite to the victim and the victim had already pointed his weapon at the defendant.

---

46. Reprinted from Westlaw, with permission of Thomson Reuters.

Rule and Analysis

[*Colantuono* reaffirmed that assault is a general intent crime. Attempt crimes require specific intent. But,] the "unlawful attempt" term of section 240 is different. **Assault requires an act that is closer to the accomplishment of injury than is required for other attempts. Other criminal attempts, because they require proof of specific intent, may be more remotely connected to the attempted crime.** ***

[Defendant argues that he lacked the present ability to commit assault because his conduct did not immediately precede a battery. We reject this argument. **Present ability] is satisfied when "a defendant has attained the means and location to strike immediately."** ["Immediately"] **does not mean "instantaneously." It simply means that the defendant must have the ability to inflict injury on the present occasion. [An] assault may be committed even if the defendant is several steps away from actually inflicting injury,** or if the victim is in a protected position so that injury would not be "immediate," in the strictest sense of that term. ***

[Back at common law, the original concept of criminal assault developed before the doctrine of criminal attempt in general.] Assault 'is not simply an adjunct of some underlying offense [like criminal attempt], but an independent crime [defined in terms of certain unlawful conduct immediately antecedent to battery.']

Unlike criminal attempt where the [act constituting an attempt may be more remote, an assault is an act done toward the commission of a battery and must "immediately" ' precede the battery.]

[Criminal] attempt and assault require different mental states. Because the act constituting a criminal attempt 'need not be the last proximate or ultimate step toward commission of the substantive crime,' criminal attempt has always required 'a specific intent to commit the crime.' *** In contrast, the crime of assault has always focused on the nature of the act and not on the perpetrator's specific intent. An assault occurs whenever ' "[t]he next movement would, *at least to all appearance*, complete the battery." ' *** Thus, assault 'lies on a definitional . . . *continuum of conduct* that describes its essential relation to battery: An assault is an incipient or inchoate battery; a battery is a consummated assault.' ***

[It] is a defendant's action enabling him to inflict a present injury that constitutes the actus reus of assault. **There is no requirement that the injury would necessarily occur as the very next step in the sequence of events, or without any delay.** *** "**There need not be even a direct attempt at violence; but any indirect preparation towards it, under the circumstances mentioned, such as drawing a sword or bayonet, or even laying one's hand upon his sword, would be sufficient.**" ***

[When] a defendant equips and positions himself to carry out a battery, he has the "present ability" required by section 240 if he is capable of inflicting injury on the given occasion, even if some steps remain to be taken, and even if the victim or the surrounding circumstances thwart the infliction of injury.

[In *People v. Ranson*,] Ranson aimed a rifle at a police car. After the police shot and disarmed him, it was discovered that there was no round in the chamber because a cartridge was jammed in the magazine. [*Ranson* explained] that while an unloaded gun does not confer "present ability," the element is satisfied if the defendant wields an automatic rifle with cartridges in the magazine, even if the firing chamber is empty. [Assault cannot be committed with an unloaded gun, unless the weapon is used as a bludgeon.] The court continued: "The instant case presents a unique fact situation. The rifle held by appellant was definitely loaded and operable; however, the top cartridge that was to be fired was at an angle that caused the gun to jam. There was evidence from which the trial court could infer that appellant knew how to take off and rapidly reinsert the clip. *** Time is a continuum of which 'present' is a part. 'Present' can denote 'immediate' or a point near 'immediate.' ***

Here, defendant was further along the continuum of conduct toward battery than Ranson was. ***The *Ranson* court held the evidence of present ability sufficient, even though Ranson had to do much more than turn around to use his weapon against the police. He had to remove the clip, dislodge a jammed cartridge, reinsert the clip, chamber a round, point the weapon, and pull the trigger. ***

Defendant contends he lacked the present ability to inflict injury not only because he was aiming in the opposite direction from Murdoch, but also because Murdoch had him covered and would have shot him first. However, this argument cannot be squared with cases demonstrating that an assault may occur even when the infliction of injury is prevented by environmental conditions or by steps taken by victims to protect themselves.

[In People v. *Valdez*,] the defendant was convicted of assault with a firearm for shooting at a gas station attendant who was behind a bulletproof window. *** He contended he lacked the present ability to injure the attendant because of the protective glass. *** The Court of Appeal disagreed. We do not adopt all the *Valdez* court's reasoning, but the following discussion is sound:

"Nothing suggests this 'present ability' element was [meant] to excuse defendants from the crime of assault where they have acquired the means to inflict serious injury and positioned themselves within striking distance merely because, unknown to them, external circumstances doom their attack to failure. This proposition would make even less sense where a defendant has actually launched his attack—as in the present case—but failed only because of some unforeseen circumstance which made success impossible. [California] decisions holding a defendant lacks 'present ability' when he tries to shoot someone with an unloaded gun or a toy pistol do not support any such proposition. In those situations, the defendant has simply failed to equip himself with the personal means to inflict serious injury even if he thought he had." ***

"**Once a defendant has attained the means and location to strike immediately he has the 'present ability to injure.'** The fact an intended victim takes effective steps to avoid injury has never been held to negate this 'present ability.'" [An "immediate" injury for purposes of assault is one that is threatened on the present occasion.]

Here, defendant's loaded weapon and concealment behind the trailer gave him the means and the location to strike "immediately" at Sergeant Murdoch, as that term applies in the context of assault. Murdoch's evasive maneuver, which permitted him to approach defendant from behind, did not deprive defendant of the "present ability" required by section 240. Defendant insists that . . . he never pointed his weapon in Murdoch's direction. That degree of immediacy is not necessary. [In People v. *Lee Kong*, a police officer observed the defendant's gambling operation from a hole he had bored in the roof of the defendant's building. When the defendant discovered the officer's presence, he fired his gun where he believed the officer to be. At that moment, however, the officer was at a different spot on the roof.]

[The *Lee Kong* court concluded,] "the appellant had the present ability to inflict the injury. He knew the officer was upon the roof, and knowing that fact he fired through the roof. . . . The fact that he was mistaken *** as to the exact spot where his intended victim was located is immaterial. [Lee Kong's] mistake as to the policeman's exact location upon the roof affords no excuse for his act, and causes the act to be no less an assault." ***

Here too, defendant's mistake as to the officer's location was immaterial. He attained the present ability to inflict injury by positioning himself to strike on the present occasion with a loaded weapon. This conduct was sufficient to establish the actus reus required for assault.

Conclusion

The defendant had the "present ability" required for assault. We reverse the Court of Appeal's judgment, insofar as it held the evidence insufficient to support a conviction for assault with a firearm on a peace officer.[47]

---

47. Reprinted with the permission of LexisNexis.

Biography—Criminal

Geoffrey Dahmer—Serial Killer and Cannibal

- Born on May 21, 1960, in Wisconsin.
- Dahmer had been placed on probation in May of 1991 due to a "1988 conviction for sexual abuse of a male child."
- The case, *Estate of Sinthasomphone*, 785 F.Supp. 1343 (1995), reported the following:
- Chief Judge Terence Evans called Dahmer a "31-year-old chocolate factory worker, a killing machine who committed the most appalling string of homicides in this city's history."
- Dahmer had been holding 14-year-old Sinthasomphone captive in his apartment where he "drugged him, stripped him of his clothing, and committed acts of physical and sexual abuse. All the while, the remains of previous victims of Dahmer's madness lay decaying in another room of the apartment."
- Sinthasomphone "although he was drugged, naked, and bleeding," escaped the apartment and tried to get help.
- A witness then called 911 and reported, "there is this young man. He's buck naked. He has been beaten up . . . He is really hurt . . . He needs some help."
- The plaintiffs in the case claimed that the police who responded to the 911 call failed to heed witnesses' warnings that one of Dahmer's victims, Sinthasomphone, was in danger, and delivered the victim back into Dahmer's custody.
- Dahmer then killed Sinthasomphone.
- Dahmer later "terrorized" another of his victims, Tracy Edwards who "escaped and led the police to Dahmer, who was finally arrested on July 22, 1991."
- Dahmer confessed to killing seventeen males ranging in age from fourteen to twenty-eight.
- "The case is incredibly gruesome and bizarre; **the dismembered bodies of many of the victims—hearts in the freezer, heads in the fridge**—were preserved in Dahmer's . . . apartment. The leftovers were deposited in a barrel of acid, conveniently stationed in the kitchen."
- Dahmer committed cannibalism of some of his victims.
- After he pleaded guilty to fifteen of his sixteen murders, the judge sentenced Dahmer to life imprisonment without the possibility of parole.
- In 1994, a fellow prisoner killed Dahmer while he was in a Wisconsin prison.[48]

Situations Where Present Ability Can Exist Despite Factual Impossibility

People v. Chance referred to *People v. Valdez* 175 Cal. App.3d 103(1985). In *Valdez*, Rogelio Valdez, a shooter, fired three bullets at a self-serve gas station cashier, Kenneth McKinley, as the victim sat behind bullet-resistant glass. *Valdez* noted that the case presented the issue:

> Is the "present ability" element of the crime of assault satisfied where some outside circumstance unknown to the defendant makes it impossible for the chosen means of attack to actually inflict injury on the victim? Or, more specific to the facts of this case, does a man who fires a loaded gun at another have a "present ability" to inflict injury where the victim is behind a bulletproof window?

---

48. Reprinted from Westlaw, with permission of Thomson Reuters.

Valdez then concluded that:

> "The 'present ability' referred to in the definition of assault relates *solely to the ability of the person* attempting the unlawful injury and does not refer to the fact that, by reason of some fact or condition not controlled by the defendant, the intended injury cannot be inflicted. If one person rush at another in an attempt to strike him but is prevented from carrying out his intention by being seized by a third person or by the intended victim; or *if the person fired at were protected by a bullet proof vest* or if the cartridge misfired or if the defendant slipped and fell and the gun were discharged into the ground, *there would still be the present ability* even though the attempt was unsuccessful. ***

The *Valdez* court also cited *People v. Yslas* 27 Cal. 630 (1865), in which a victim ran away and hid from a hatchet-wielding attacker who had approached within seven or eight feet of her. Even though he could not reach his victim with a swing of his hatchet from seven feet away, the defendant in *Yslas* was still found guilty of assault.

Valdez thus concluded that present ability was not nullified by the victim's successful attempt to avoid injury or even by situations where the attempt to render injury was "impossible." The court found assault occurred when, "one who knows of the bulletproof barrier yet blazes away like some perverted Don Quixote in the *hope* he might realize his impossible dream—and the victim's worst nightmare."

Video of One Football Fan Punching Another

Marissa Payne reported on October 13, 2017, in her *Washington Post* article, "Fan who left 62-year-old bloodied after 'sucker punch' incident at Panthers game arrested," that police had arrested a man for assault. Charlotte-Mecklenburg Police reported that a Carolina Panthers fan, who they identified as Kyle Adam Maraghy, punched a 62-year-old man in the face. The incident, caught on video, occurred at a Panthers football game against the Philadelphia Eagles. Authorities charged Maraghy with assault.

For the full article describing the attack, see the link below. Please note that the video accompanying the article contains images of graphic violence that might disturb some viewers.

https://www.washingtonpost.com/news/early-lead/wp/2017/10/13/nfl-investigating-sucker-punch-incident-that-left-panthers-fan-bleeding-in-the-stands/?undefined=&utm_term=.bd9a90bc9917&wpisrc=nl_most&wpmm=1

Dodgers Fans Brutally Assault Man Wearing Giants Clothing

CBS News Los Angeles and *KNX News Radio* reported on June 6, 2012, in "Friend Gives Disturbing Account of Bryan Stow's Beating At Dodger Stadium" that:

> A paramedic who was off-duty at the time Giants fan Bryan Stow was severely attacked at Dodger Stadium gave graphic details of the incident in court Wednesday.

For the full article and video describing the attack, see:

http://losangeles.cbslocal.com/2012/06/06/off-duty-paramedics-gives-disturbing-account-of-bryan-stow-beating/

The entire report and video can be viewed at:

http://espn.go.com/los-angeles/mlb/story/_/id/10489372/two-men-admit-guilt-dodger-stadium-attack-bryan-stow

Model Penal Code § 211.1: Assault

(1) **Simple Assault.** A person is guilty of assault if he:

(a) attempts to cause or purposely, knowingly or recklessly causes bodily injury to another; or

(b) negligently causes bodily injury to another with a deadly weapon; or

(c) attempts by physical menace to put another in fear of imminent serious bodily injury.[49]

Can a Hand or Foot Be Considered a "Deadly Weapon" for Purposes of Assault with a Deadly Weapon?

The Ninth Circuit Court of Appeals considered this issue in *United States v. Rocha*, 598 F.3d 1144 (2010). In this case, the defendant, Victor Rocha, left off ironing clothes in the Victorville prison to join a fight captured on a security videotape. The victim, Fischer, was backing away from his attackers, "when Rocha came up from behind him, reached down, grabbed the six-foot-seven, three hundred pound Fischer by his feet, and pulled his feet out from under him, causing Fischer's body to slam down onto the concrete floor." Inmates kicked the victim and even tried to throw him over a railing. When Fischer later died, an autopsy revealed four stab wounds and various bruises and abrasions. The *Rocha* court refused to find a body part to be a "deadly weapon," and thus reversed the defendant's conviction for assault with a deadly weapon.

Rocha explained that state courts were divided over "whether body parts can constitute dangerous or deadly weapons" for purposes of assault and battery. The court noted, "**Most states have determined that body parts cannot be considered a dangerous or deadly weapon.**" *Rocha* relied on the New York case, *People v. Owusu*, 93 N.Y.2d 398 (1999), in which:

the New York Court of Appeals addressed whether the defendant, who nearly severed the victim's finger by biting it, had used a "dangerous instrument." *** The court read the statute to "[increase criminal liability when an actor has upped the ante by employing a device to assist in the criminal endeavor."] Here, "Mr. Owusu's teeth came with him," and the court declined to find his teeth a dangerous instrument.

Other courts in the majority have rejected body parts as deadly weapons, such as Tennessee (fists and feet not deadly weapons), Nebraska (teeth not deadly weapons), Alabama (fists or other body parts not deadly weapons), Illinois (sharp fingernail not a deadly weapon), and Idaho, Missouri, Utah, and Michigan (hands not deadly weapons).

Rocha also noted that, "Other states, although a clear minority, have allowed body parts to be considered dangerous or deadly weapons." North Carolina, South Carolina, Colorado, Rhode Island, and Texas recognize hands to be deadly weapons, while Mississippi recognizes fists and teeth as deadly weapons. Thus, whether a body part can be a deadly weapon depends on where in the country a person finds him or herself when arrested.

49. From *The Model Penal Code* by the American Law Institute. Copyright © 1962 by the American Law Institute. Used by permission.

VIDEO: Police Subdue a Suspect Armed with a Knife

WARNING: GRAPHIC VIDEO. A body camera filmed two officers subduing a suspect wielding a knife at:

https://www.youtube.com/watch?v=wTtGmodTCSc

What Is the Difference Between "Great Bodily Injury" and "Serious Bodily Injury"?

The California Supreme Court, in *People v. Santana* 56 Cal. 4th 999 (2013), noted, "We recognize that the terms 'serious bodily injury' and 'great bodily injury' have been described as 'essential[ly] equivalent.'" Such a description, however, is less than accurate. *People v. Taylor* 118 Cal. App.4th 11 (2004) clarified the distinctions between "great bodily injury" and "serious bodily injury:"

> Although the terms "great bodily injury" and "serious bodily injury" have been described as being "essentially equivalent" *** or having "substantially the same meaning," *** they have separate and distinct statutory definitions. Serious bodily injury is defined [in PC 243(f)(4)] as "a serious impairment of physical condition, including, but not limited to, the following: loss of consciousness; concussion; *bone fracture*; protracted loss or impairment of function of any bodily member or organ; a wound requiring extensive suturing; and serious disfigurement." By contrast, great bodily injury is defined [in PC 12022.7(f)] as "a significant or substantial physical injury." Unlike serious bodily injury, the statutory definition of great bodily injury does not include a list of qualifying injuries and makes no specific reference to bone fractures.

The above passage once again illustrates that, for judges and lawyers, words matter. Precision in language is crucial in determining who is incarcerated and who goes free.

Can a Carnival Ride at a Fair Become a "Deadly Weapon"?

ABC World News reported, in an October 26, 2013, article by Dean Schabner, Anthony Castellano, Rebecca Lee, and Michael Howard, entitled, "NC Ride Operator Charged With Assault With Deadly Weapon" that the ride operator was charged with felony assault.
    The full article is at:

http://abcnews.go.com/US/nc-ride-operator-charged-assault-deadly-weapon/story?id=20692984

Chris Brown Charged with Felony Assault

Alan Duke of CNN reported on October 27, 2013, in "Chris Brown jailed on felony assault charge" that Washington DC Metropolitan Police explained that Chris Brown was arrested and charged with felony assault for allegedly punching a man. Duke reported that Brown allegedly said, "I'm not down with that gay s—t" and "I feel like boxing."

The article can be viewed at:

http://www.cnn.com/2013/10/27/showbiz/chris-brown-arrested/index.html

---

C.   MAYHEM

1.   Common Law

At common law, Blackstone, in *Commentaries*, Vol. IV, at 205, described **mayhem as an offense that directly undermined the power of the king**, because mayhem was "an atrocious breach of the king's peace, and an offense tending to deprive him of the aid and assistance of his subjects." This was because mayhem involved "**violently depriving another of the use of such of his members, as may render him the less able in fighting, either to defend himself, or to annoy his adversary**." The logic here seemed to be that if a fight broke out in a tavern, a person was not supposed to cut off the arm or leg of a fellow Englishman because such injury would prevent the victim from boarding a boat to France to cut off the arm or leg of a Frenchman during time of war.

This reasoning explains the original limits placed on mayhem at common law. Mayhem included "the cutting off, or disabling, or weakening a man's hand or finger, or striking out his eye or foretooth, or depriving him of those parts, the loss of which in all animals abates their courage." Mayhem, however, originally did not include "cutting off his ear, or nose, or the like," because such injuries only disfigured a person rather than lessening his fighting ability.

Common law's original punishment for mayhem was a "sentence to lose the like part." So, if a criminal cut off the ring finger on the victim's left hand, the government would cut off the wrongdoer's same finger. Interestingly, this punishment, although draconian, proved to provide insufficient deterrence. In fact, it was discontinued "partly because upon repetition of the offense the punishment could not be repeated." Once the State cuts off a man's ring finger for removing one victim's ring finger, it cannot cut off the defendant's same finger when he removes another victim's ring finger.

The Supreme Court of Appeals of West Virginia analyzed common law mayhem in *State v. McDonie*, 109 S.E. 710 (1921). In that case, Joe McDonie maimed his six-year-old stepson, James Gibson. The victim was in shock due to emaciation and bruises and cuts all over his body, many of which were infected. The six-year-old's feet were so severely burned that gauze had to be kept between the toes to prevent them from growing together. When considering the defendant's appeal from his conviction for mayhem, the court **defined the term "maim"** for purposes of mayhem to mean "**to violently inflict a bodily injury upon a person so as to make him less able to defend himself or to annoy his adversary**." The court explained:

> To so injure a fighting member of the body that it cannot be used, or cannot be used as effectively as it could theretofore, is as much maiming as it is to entirely sever the member . . . The principal offense alleged against the defendant was the scalding of the boy's

feet. This might not result in the boy losing his feet, or either of them, but it can very well be seen that it might result in them being of less use to him in repelling or making an attack. In fact, the nurse says that if he had not received attention when he did the toes of one of his feet would have grown together. This . . . would in fact be maiming in the legal sense of the term.

At common law, mayhem was crafted as a crime against the sovereign who needed to be able to field a fighting force.

2.   Current Law

What is "**mayhem**" and where did it come from? The following case shows that mayhem is a particularly brutal crime with **ancient common law** origins based on **maintaining military fitness**. Mayhem can be committed in one of two ways: (1) severing or damaging a "**member**" (essentially a limb) of the victim's body, or (2) by **attacking features of the victim's face**.

LEGAL ANALYSIS

People v. Newble
120 Cal. App. 3d 444 (1981).
Justice Carr delivered the opinion of the California Court of Appeal.

Facts

The facts demonstrate the potential for violent encounter when romance wanes and is displaced by hostility. Defendant and Berline Kizzie, the victim herein, had lived together for several months. Upon their separation, Berline saw defendant quite frequently but the relationship was not friendly and defendant had on two occasions threatened Berline, the last threat being "I'm going to get you, and I'm going to fix you where won't nobody have you."

[Berline attended a party where she ran into the defendant.] Defendant testified on his own behalf; there is a wide variance between his testimony and that of Berline, he stating she called him names all evening, and she testifying they did not speak until he prepared to leave at which time defendant began swearing at her and calling her bad names. When he persisted in such conduct after she told him to leave her alone, she became angry and either dropped her drink glass or threw it at defendant. Defendant then grabbed her by the hair and turned her around. When she put her hand to her face, she found she had been cut.

She was treated at the emergency hospital for a three-inch laceration with a maximum depth of one-half inch on the left side of her face. The injury, caused by a slash from a sharp object [the evidence indicates defendant's fingernail file], severed a small portion of one of the salivary glands. A doctor testified the wound required double layer suturing and was likely to leave a scar. ***

Issues

1. **Whether, for mayhem, a person's head is a "member" of the body.**

2. **Whether the infliction of a three-inch facial laceration that extends from the bottom of the left ear to just below the chin, which is likely to leave a permanent scar, constitutes PC 203 mayhem.**

Rule and Analysis

[Defendant argues that the head is not a member of the body. The head is a member of the body within the meaning of the mayhem statute.]

Section 203 provides: **"Every person who unlawfully and maliciously deprives a human being of a member of his body, or disables, disfigures, or renders it useless, or cuts or disables the tongue, or puts out an eye, or slits the nose, ear, or lip, is guilty of mayhem."** ***

[In *People v. Page*,] defendants were found to have committed mayhem by forcibly tattooing "the letters 'M.F.F.M.' (representing a club slogan, Misfits Forever, Forever Misfits) over an area measuring four by two and one-half inches on [the female victim's] left breast. They then tattooed 'Property of G.P.' (Gordon Page) *** on her abdomen." *** A plastic surgeon testified that the tattoos on the victim's breast and abdomen were permanent, [because attempting to remove them would "leave permanent scarring for life."]

Defendant urged that tattooing of a woman's abdomen or breast could not constitute mayhem since the torso is not a member of the body within the meaning of section 203. [The court disagreed, explaining that **"member" is defined as 'a bodily part or organ (such as a limb) that projects from the main mass of the body**.] The court concluded that there might be a question about the abdomen qualifying, but clearly a female breast was a body member by any definition, dictionary, common or legal.

[The head, the uppermost extremity of the body, certainly projects from the mass of the body and so qualifies as a member of the body.]

Defendant urges the statutory delineation of types of injury to specific parts of the head demonstrates a legislative intent that unenumerated parts of the head were not meant to be included within the scope of mayhem. Further, that under the maxim of *expressio unius est exclusio alterius* the enumeration of things coming within the operation of the statute necessarily involves the exclusion of things not expressly enumerated. Since the statute specifically sets forth eyes, ears, tongue, nose and lips, other parts of the head are excluded. ["*Expressio unius est exclusio alterius* should not apply where it would operate against legislative intent, or where it would lead to absurd and undesirable consequences or manifest injustice.]

[PC 203 should be interpreted in light of mayhem's origin.] "To cut off, or permanently to cripple, a man's hand or finger, or to strike out his eye or foretooth, were all mayhems at common law, if done maliciously, because any such harm rendered the person less efficient as a fighting man (for the king's army). But an injury such as cutting off his ear or nose did not constitute mayhem, according to the English common law, because it did not result in permanent disablement, but merely disfigured the victim. This was corrected by an early English statute. It seems that an assault was made upon Sir John Coventry on the street by persons who waylaid him and slit his nose in revenge for obnoxious words uttered by him in Parliament. This emphasized the weakness of the law of mayhem. [A new statute extended the English common law crime of mayhem to include intentional disfigurement, such as as the following:] 'cut out or disable the tongue, put out an eye, slit the nose, cut off a nose or lip, or cut off or disable any limb or member of any subject. *** Hence a true definition of the crime according to the English law must be [essentially]: *Mayhem is malicious maiming or maliciously and intentionally disfiguring another.*" ***

Although it is apparent section 203 contains verbal vestiges of English Common law ***, "**the modern rationale of the crime may be said to be the preservation of the natural completeness and normal appearance of the human face and body, and not, as originally, the preservation of the sovereign's right to the effective military assistance of his subjects.**" ***

In light of the stated rationale of the crime of mayhem we conclude **there is no tenable reason for distinguishing prominent facial wounds to a nose, ear or lip, from comparable wounds which happen to miss one of those areas of the head specifically mentioned in section 203.** The opposite conclusion would lead to a result which is undesirable, if not absurd.

[The fact that various parts of the head are mentioned in section 203 is probably attributable more to historical happenstance than to a current legislative intent to exclude from the purview of mayhem areas of the head not specifically mentioned. If Sir John Coventry had been injured as the victim in the instant case was injured, it is possible the issue under discussion would not have arisen in the context of this case.]

Conclusion

Since, under PC 203, the head is a member of the body, and disfiguring portions of the face not listed in the statute can constitute mayhem, the defendant's conviction is affirmed.[50]

The California Supreme Court, in *People v. Santana* (2013) 56 Cal. 4th 999, has offered the following examples of injuries amounting to mayhem:

1. Cigarette burns to both breasts
2. A breast nearly severed by a box cutter
3. A five-inch facial wound from a knife
4. Forcible tattoos on the breast and abdomen
5. Blinding of an eye from a kick
6. Severe facial trauma requiring metal plates and wires to keep the facial bones together
7. A bitten-through lower lip
8. A broken ankle that had not completely healed after six months
9. An eye "put out" by a machete

"Seamless Web" Connection

People v. Taylor's effort to carefully parse the legal terms "great bodily injury" and "serious bodily injury" and *People v. Newble's* caution in defining what is a "member" of the body for purposes of mayhem are practical examples of the courts' efforts to provide adequate notice to citizens about their duties under criminal law. The concern about ensuring that people understand the law connects to *Kolender's* refusal, in Chapter 1, to enforce unconstitutionally vague laws.

---

50. Reprinted with the permission of LexisNexis.

Wives Maiming Husbands Could Face Mayhem Charges

In an article at *Legally Weird*, Cynthia Hsu reports in "CA Woman Cut off Husband's Penis, Tossed in Garbage Disposal," on July 13, 2011, that a woman could face, among other charges, aggravated mayhem for her attack on her husband. See the article at:

http://blogs.findlaw.com/legally_weird/2011/07/ca-woman-cut-off-husbands-penis-tossed-in-garbage-disposal.html

Another article in "Legally Weird, entitled Woman Bit Off Husband's Tongue During Kiss," by Tanya Roth on December 9, 2010, tells of a wife who bit off her husband's tongue while grabbing his genitals. See the article at:

http://blogs.findlaw.com/blotter/2010/12/woman-bit-off-husbands-tongue-during-kiss.html

---

D.   TORTURE

California Penal Code § 206: Torture

> **Every person who, with the intent to cause cruel or extreme pain and suffering for the purpose of revenge, extortion, persuasion, or for any sadistic purpose, inflicts great bodily injury** as defined in Section 12022.7 **upon the person of another, is guilty of torture. The crime of torture does not require any proof that the victim suffered pain.**

People v. Barrera, 14 Cal. App. 4th 1555, 1559 (1993) explained that, in 1990, California passed Proposition 115, the "Crime Victims Justice Reform Act" to create "a system . . . in which violent criminals receive just punishment." To carry out this aim, California enacted PC 206, defining the crime of torture. *People v. Barrera* determined, "'Torture' has a long-standing, judicially recognized meaning: **'Torture' has been defined as the 'Act or process of inflicting severe pain, esp. as a punishment in order to extort confession, or in revenge.'"** *Barrera* found its facts supported the jury's conviction for torture.

> Barrera shot Rodarte at close range as a means of inflicting enough pain upon the victim to gain the victim's cooperation and property. The bullet broke the victim's leg and he bled profusely. The life of the victim's son was threatened in the victim's presence and the immediate capability of carrying out that threat was evident: a sawed-off shotgun was held against his son's head. Again, the cooperation of the victim was behind the threat. The victim was forced to walk on his broken leg, described as an open fracture, in order to assist Barrera in locating the money he sought. Barrera [attempted] to minimize the offense, labeling it merely an aggravated assault, but under these facts his conduct was manifestly more than that. His actions were cold-blooded, calculated, motivated by financial gain, and resulted in a great cost to his victim.

Torture was also committed in *People v. Baker*, 98 Cal. App.4th 1217 (2002), a case in which Guy Leslie Baker lit his wife, Jasmine, on fire. Despite the fact that he had threatened his wife before his attack by saying, "Problems. Lots of problems for you," the defendant contended, "he did not have the requisite intent to cause Jasmine cruel or extreme pain and that she was burned accidentally in his failed suicide attempt." The Court disagreed, describing the facts in the case that fulfilled torture's elements:

> Jasmine graphically described and physically demonstrated how Baker forcibly held her by the waist with his left hand, poured gasoline over her head with his right hand, discarded the plastic container, used both hands to drag her toward the stove, fumbled to turn on the stove, and ultimately used a lighter to set her hair on fire. Jasmine described the sensation of burning hair and her frantic efforts to quench the flames with dishwater—while Baker did nothing but watch her burn.

Further, "Jasmine suffered second and third degree burns over her extremities, neck, and torso that required skin grafts to repair and left severe scarring and disfigurement." The court concluded, "there is substantial evidence that Baker inflicted great bodily injury on Jasmine with the requisite intent and purpose."

People v. Hale 75 Cal. App.4th 94 (1999) also considered torture. In this case, the defendant, Godoy Anthony Hale, entered his girlfriend's bedroom late at night with a ball-peen hammer. Sleeping with her three-year-old daughter at her side, the victim, Roanne Bracks, "was awakened by a loud cracking sound from a hammer hitting her face." When she screamed, the defendant "shouted angrily 'Die, bitch' and something to the effect of 'That's what you get' or 'You're going to get it.' Hale struck Bracks in the face with the hammer a second time." The court noted, "Hale contends there was insufficient evidence to show he intended to cause cruel or extreme pain and suffering. Although Hale concedes the evidence shows he intended to assault Bracks, possibly even kill her, Hale contends there was not sufficient evidence he intended to torture her."

The *Hale* court disagreed, because:

> **Intent to cause cruel or extreme pain can be established by the circumstances of the offense.** ***We note a ball peen hammer is a machinist's hammer, and it has "a hemispherical peen" for beating metal. *** It is reasonable to infer when Hale twice aimed and struck the ball peen hammer at Bracks's face, he intended to cause her to suffer extreme or cruel pain. Moreover, the injuries suffered by Bracks also support such an inference. Multiple teeth were cracked and broken, her lip was split and she sustained a cut under her eye. Immediately after the attack, Bracks had difficulty talking because her face was "all broken."

Finally, a court found torture's elements fulfilled in the bizarre case of *People v. Jung* 71 Cal. App.4th 1036 (1999). The case presented the following facts:

> Fifteen-year-old Donald Hyon was a member of an Asian street gang called Jef-Rox. (Defendants Jung and Nguyen were members of gangs that were rivals of victim Hyon's gang. In a gang altercation, Hyon had attacked one the defendants. Then, defendants) beat and kicked Hyon, grabbed him by his hair and forced him to disrobe. They (pushed) the naked and struggling Hyon . . . into the backseat of defendant Jung's car, a black Acura Integra, where he was bound hand and foot and blindfolded. Defendant Nguyen beat Hyon with his fists. After some minutes of driving, they stopped the car, removed Hyon from the backseat, and placed him in the trunk. They drove for an additional period. Hyon was removed from the car and taken to a room in a residence.

The five to eight occupants of the room were laughing and jeering. They told Hyon he was going to die. They shoved Hyon onto a couch. They used his body as an ashtray, burning him with cigarettes on both shoulders three to four times. They beat him with their fists and kicked him. They repeatedly hit him on the head and in the face and slapped him. They laid him on the floor and five or six of them jumped on him from the couch. They forced him to drink urine. They bit him on his upper thighs and scratched him. They gave him hickeys on his neck. They put Ben-Gay on his penis, which hurt. They tattooed his back, legs, and arms extensively with a tattoo machine. The needle was painful. After tattooing him, they poured rubbing alcohol over his fresh wounds, which stung. They wrote on his body with magic markers. They shaved the hair on his head. They hit him with hard objects on his backside and legs. They whipped him with a cloth. They placed a hard object between his buttocks. They rubbed and played with his penis and attempted to have him ejaculate. They photographed him and forced him to dance and pose. They dressed him in girl's clothing. They continued to beat him. Hyon curled into a protective fetal position, yet they continued to kick him . . . The attacks continued for several hours, after which they put Hyon in a van, drove him to another location, and released him, still bound, blindfolded, and dressed in girl's clothing. They threatened to kill him and his family and burn his house down if he went to the police. . . . Hyon had been in fear.

Defendants argued the evidence established only intent to humiliate rather than intent to cause severe pain and suffering. The court responded:

Although some of the abuse inflicted on Hyon appears to have been intended to humiliate him, such as dressing him in women's clothing, forcing him to drink urine, and forcing him to dance and pose for photographs, the evidence also supports an intent to cause severe pain and suffering. Indeed, there can be no other explanation for the cigarette burns, the application of Ben-Gay to Hyon's penis, the pouring of rubbing alcohol over Hyon's fresh wounds, the beating, the biting, and the kicking. **That defendants may have intended to humiliate Hyon, as well as cause him severe pain and suffering, does not defeat their convictions for torture.** *** The evidence clearly supports a finding that in retaliation for Hyon's earlier attack on defendant Nguyen, defendants intended to cause Hyon severe pain and suffering.[51]

People v. Misa, 140 Cal.App.4th 837 (2006) analyzed the mental state needed for torture. *Misa* explained **that the "intent necessary for torture, that is, to cause cruel or extreme pain, does not require that the defendant acted with premeditation or deliberation or had the intent to inflict prolonged pain."** *Misa* ruled that its case had enough circumstantial evidence to prove that Misa acted with "the cold-blooded intent to inflict pain for personal gain or satisfaction." In this case, Misa, a man who stood 6 foot, 3 inches tall and weighed approximately 300 pounds, suspected that the victim, Hoock, had stolen from him. Misa used a golf club (a driver with a substantial head), to strike Hoock's head with such force that he cracked Hoock's skull where it was close to a half-inch thick. Hoock's skull "cracked like an egg, exposing brain tissue." Even though he had caused the victim "substantial and visible injuries," Misa "continued to taunt Hoock, poking and prodding him with the golf club and swinging the club in the air around Hoock." Misa yelled profanities and made threats against Hoock "for an additional 30 minutes." The court ruled that Misa's statements, "you're going to pay for this" and "I'm going to teach you a fucking lesson," proved "that Misa intended to inflict cruel or extreme pain

---

51. Reprinted with the permission of LexisNexis.

on Hoock." Misa's "callousness" in refusing to allow others to take the victim to the hospital and "in sitting across from Hoock, who was vomiting and lapsing in and out of consciousness" demonstrated a "calculated purpose of causing Hoock to suffer." The "totality of circumstances," including: 1) "the level of violence," 2) "the nature of Hoock's injuries," 3) "the manner in which Misa inflicted them," and 4) "Misa's callous indifference in the face of Hoock's obvious need for medical intervention," supported an "inference of an intent to cause cruel pain and suffering." The court therefore upheld Misa's conviction for torture.

The California Crime of "Torture" is Not the Same as the Geneva Convention's Definition of "Torture"

The Council on Foreign Relations offers an article by Lionel Beehner, last updated September 20, 2006, called *The United States and the Geneva Conventions*, which helps explain how international law defines torture. This article can be seen at:

http://www.cfr.org/international-law/united-states-geneva-conventions/p11485

Tips for Success for Future Law Enforcement

Job Interview

For just about any interview, you should aim to be alert yet relaxed. If you have followed the previous tips of researching your employer before the interview and of resolving to stick with the truth, you can enter the interview with calm confidence. The key is composure—employers ask questions not only to test your knowledge but your reaction to being placed in an uncomfortable situation with no easy or clearly correct answers. Prior to the interview, gain information not only from websites but also from people—seek out professors or other contacts who have law enforcement experience or have even worked for the particular agency for which you are interviewing.

Since people communicate so much outside of direct speech, be aware of all the signals you send to your interviewer. Dress appropriately so the employer knows you take the interview and the career seriously. Show a courteous frankness by looking your questioner in the eye and offering direct and honest answers to any questions. Be sure to actually listen to your interviewer to demonstrate you care about his or her concerns and so you can fully and appropriately answer the questions. At the end, thank your interviewer for their time.

Since the career you're seeking can trigger moral issues, be on alert for questions testing your ethics and morals. Seriously consider the values you wish to promote as an officer before these questions are even asked.

E.   FALSE IMPRISONMENT

People v. Fosselman, 33 Cal.3d 572 (1983) presents an example of false imprisonment. In this case, the defendant, Jerome Fosselman, approached a woman named Carla Z. from behind as she walked down a street to board a bus. After failing to strike up a conversation with the victim, the defendant "placed his hand on her shoulder, put a knife to her back, and told her to 'get behind the building.' She reached behind her back and felt the knife, which slightly cut her middle finger. As defendant seized her jacket she pulled away, lost her balance, and fell to her knees. She then arose and made her way to the middle of the road." When she flagged down a car for help, Fosselman ran away.

The California Supreme Court found sufficient evidence to prove felony false imprisonment, noting, "By his own admission defendant held Ms. Z. against her will; the jury further found on the basis of her testimony that in doing so he put a knife to her back. The evidence thus supports the implied finding that his conduct constituted an 'unlawful violation of [her] personal liberty.'" The defendant therefore fulfilled California Penal Code Section 236: "**False imprisonment is the unlawful violation of the personal liberty of another.**" The court further concluded that the false imprisonment "was felonious because it was effected by 'violence' or 'menace' within the meaning of Penal Code section 237." **Felony false imprisonment occurs when it is "effected by violence, menace, fraud, or deceit."**[52]

Model Penal Code § 212.3: False Imprisonment

A person commits a misdemeanor if he knowingly restrains another unlawfully so as to interfere substantially with his liberty.[53]

VIDEO: The Rescue of One of a Serial Killer's Captives

WARNING: DISTURBING VIDEO. As video shows rescue of one victim, convicted serial killer Todd Kohlhepp warned of more victims than those already known to police at:

https://www.washingtonpost.com/news/true-crime/wp/2017/12/10/a-serial-killers-creepy-post-conviction-message-there-are-more-victims/?utm_term=.822d0861959e

---

Do Storeowners Commit False Imprisonment of Shoplifters? The "Shopkeeper's Privilege"

Does the storeowner, him or herself a victim of shoplifting, become a criminal when detaining the shoplifting suspect? This issue arose in *Commonwealth v. Rogers,* 945 N.E.2d 295 (2011), in which the defendant, Daniel Rogers, was convicted of first-degree murder and armed robbery. In this case, three CVS drugstore employees chased the defendant after finding him shoplifting toothpaste. After

---

52. From *Deering's California Codes Annotated.* Copyright © 2014 by Matthew Bender & Company, Inc., a member of the LexisNexis Group. Reprinted with the permission of LexisNexis.
53. From *The Model Penal Code* by the American Law Institute. Copyright © 1962 by the American Law Institute. Used by permission.

capturing the defendant outside the store and telling him that they were taking him back to the store because he had been shoplifting, Rogers stabbed one of the employees, who later died from his injuries.

The defendant argued he should not have been convicted of robbery because the force he used was in response to improper force the employees employed in detaining him for the shoplifting. This contention prompted the Supreme Judicial Court of Massachusetts to review **the shopkeeper's privilege**, which provided merchants the "right to detain shoplifters . . . on or in the immediate vicinity of the premises." **This right permits "store employees with suspicion based on reasonable grounds to detain a suspected shoplifter for a reasonable time and by reasonable means."**

The shopkeeper's privilege did not, however, explicitly discuss the use of force to enforce the privilege. The *Rogers* court found that "cases in other jurisdictions suggest that **force may be a component of a reasonable detention so long as the force used is itself reasonable**." In fact, *Rogers* went even further, declaring, "the privilege is meaningless if reasonable force cannot be used. It makes no sense to assume that shoplifters caught in the act will simply comply with a request to wait for the police to arrive. [Shopkeepers] may use reasonable force appropriate to the circumstances in detaining suspected shoplifters." The court thus affirmed the conviction of the defendant.

F.   KIDNAPPING

1.   Common Law

Blackstone, in *Commentaries*, Vol. IV, at 219, defined **kidnapping at common law as "being the forcible abduction or stealing away of man, woman, or child from their own country, and selling them into another."** Blackstone deemed kidnapping **"a very heinous crime, as it robs the king of his subjects, banishes a man from his country,** and may in its consequences be productive of the most cruel and disagreeable hardships."

© BlueSkyImage/Shutterstock.com

2.   Current Law

As with so many other common law crimes, the crime of kidnapping has expanded over the centuries to cover more behavior. Specifically, modern statutes have greatly eased the movement requirement of kidnapping so that kidnappers can commit their crimes without leaving the country. Courts have differed on the question of how much movement, or "asportation," kidnapping requires.

The Supreme Court of Oregon tried to clarify what movement is needed to fulfill asportation for kidnapping in *State v. Sierra*, 254 P.3d 149 (2010). In this case, the defendant, Joaquin Sierra, pointing a loaded crossbow at a convenience store employee's head, moved him inside the store, and forced him to kneel. In assessing whether there was enough movement of the employee, as well as other kidnap victims in this case, the court was burdened with a vaguely written statute. Oregon's kidnapping statue, ORS 163.225(1), provided:

(1) A person commits the crime of kidnapping in the second degree if, with intent to interfere substantially with another's personal liberty, and without consent or legal authority, the person:

(a) Takes the person from one place to another; or

(b) Secretly confines the person in a place where the person is not likely to be found.

An earlier Oregon court had complained that the statute prompted a "question of what is included in the concept of 'taking' a person 'from one place to another'" which was "at bottom, an exercise in metaphysics." The court had decided that, "in the final analysis," defining kidnapping came down to "the question of how one is to define the term 'place.'"

The *Sierra* court therefore aimed to clarify the phrase "from one place to another" by explaining:

First, because the wording selected by the legislature requires movement from one place to a second, distinct place, **it generally is problematic to suggest or conclude that minimal movement that effectuates little change in the victim's position—such as, for example, movement requiring one to step to the side, or move from a standing position to a sitting or lying position—is movement "from one place to another."** Second, because the asportation element is defined in terms of relative movement, **the degree of force or threat used by a defendant to effectuate the victim's movement ordinarily is not relevant to a determination whether a victim has been "taken from one place to another."** Third, the degree by which the movement in question increases defendant's control over the victim, or isolates the victim from the view of others, is relevant to the determination whether a defendant has moved a victim "from one place to another" only to the extent that those considerations tend to demonstrate the qualitative difference between where the victim started ["from one place"] and where the victim was as a result of the defendant's conduct ["another place"]. However, because neither isolation nor control of the victim is required by the wording of ORS 163.225(1)(a), those considerations cannot be substituted for the ultimate inquiry whether the victim was moved from one place to another.

The California Supreme Court came to a conclusion quite different from Oregon, for it did consider factors other than mere distance as relevant in determining whether asportation occurred in a case. In *People v. Martinez*, 20 Cal. 4th 225 (1999), the court ruled "that **factors other than actual distance are relevant to determining asportation**" in simple kidnapping cases under Penal Code 207(a). *Martinez* explained:

[**For simple kidnapping asportation the movement must be "substantial in character,"**] **but hold that the trier of fact may consider more than actual distance.** "[S]ection 207 does not speak in terms of a movement of any specific or exact distance." [Nothing in] section 207(a) limits the asportation element solely to actual distance. Section 207(a) proscribes kidnapping or forcible movement, not forcible movement for a specified number of feet or yards. [For] both aggravated and simple kidnapping, limiting a trier of fact's consideration to a particular distance is rigid and arbitrary, and ultimately unworkable.

***The two prongs of aggravated kidnapping are not distinct, but interrelated, because a trier of fact cannot consider the significance of the victim's changed environment without also considering whether that change resulted in an increase in the risk of harm to the victim. **[For] simple kidnapping asportation, movement that is "substantial in character" arguably should include some consideration of the "scope and nature" of the movement or changed environment, and any increased risk of harm.**

Martinez noted that "**a primary reason forcible asportation is proscribed by the kidnapping statutes is the increase in the risk of harm to the victim because of the diminished likelihood of discovery, the opportunity for the commission of additional crimes, and the possibility of injury from foreseeable attempts to escape.**" The court thus concluded:

> [In simple kidnapping cases,] the instructions currently provide that the victim must have been moved "for a substantial distance, that is, a distance more than slight or trivial." [It] would also be proper for the court to instruct that, in determining whether the movement is "'substantial in character'" *** the jury should consider the totality of the circumstances. [The] jury might properly consider not only the actual distance the victim is moved, but also such factors as whether that movement increased the risk of harm above that which existed prior to the asportation, decreased the likelihood of detection, and increased both the danger inherent in a victim's foreseeable attempts to escape and the attacker's enhanced opportunity to commit additional crimes.[54]

VIDEO: Fire Scene, Kidnapping Scene, or Both?

Police were called to the scene of a fire that curiously turned into a kidnapping investigation at:

https://www.youtube.com/watch?v=H35K67OLdG8

Model Penal Code § 212.1: Kidnapping

A person is guilty of kidnapping if he unlawfully removes another from his place of residence or business, or a substantial distance from the vicinity where he is found, or if he unlawfully confines another for a substantial period in a place of isolation, with any of the following purposes:

(a) to hold for ransom or reward, or as a shield or hostage; or
(b) to facilitate commission of any felony or flight thereafter; or
(c) to inflict bodily injury on or to terrorize the victim or another; or
(d) to interfere with the performance of any governmental or political function[55]

---

54. Reprinted with the permission of LexisNexis.
55. From *The Model Penal Code* by the American Law Institute. Copyright © 1962 by the American Law Institute. Used by permission.

Kidnapper Ariel Castro

A July 13, 2013, *USA Today* article entitled, "Ariel Castro Faces 977 charges in Cleveland Kidnappings," by reporter Donna Leinwand Leger, along with an accompanying video, discuss the legal implications of the case. The article noted:

> The indictment covers the entire period of captivity, from the Aug. 22, 2002, disappearance of Knight to May 6, when Amanda Berry, missing since April 21, 2003, and her child escaped Castro's Cleveland house and led police to Knight and Gina DeJesus, missing since April 2, 2004.

The article and video are at:

> http://www.usatoday.com/story/news/nation/2013/07/12/
> ariel-castro-charged-with-kidnapping-rape/2513199/

The sentencing hearing can be viewed at:

> http://www.youtube.com/watch?v=HyX_nxUxn60 and
> http://www.youtube.com/watch?v=I4zXBU68JTw

Ariel Castro was later found dead in his cell. An article by *CBS News* and the *Associated Press* on October 10, 2013, entitled, "Ariel Castro May Have Died from Auto-Erotic Asphyxiation, Not Suicide, State Says," discussed the circumstances of his death. This article is at:

> http://www.cbsnews.com/8301-201_162-57606900/

The "Merger" Issue

In defining asportation, courts have asked the question "How much must the criminal move the victim in order to establish kidnapping?" Kidnapping has also presented courts with a related but distinct issue—merger. **Merger** becomes a problem in situations similar to the following hypothetical question. Suppose a kidnapper kidnaps a person in order to rob them at another location. The distinction between the kidnapping and robbery is clear when the criminal actually moves the victim a significant distance, say several miles by car, and then robs the victim. With the ever-shrinking distance requirement some courts have created for kidnapping, however, a problem arises when the robber forcibly moves the victim only a small distance. **Was the small movement really a separate kidnapping, or was it just a movement incidental to the "real" crime of robbery?**

In *People v. Hanley*, 987 N.E.2d 268 (2013), New York's highest court, the Court of Appeals, considered kidnapping's "merger" problem. In this case, Kirk Hanley, a mentally troubled twenty-one-year-old student at City College in Manhattan, went to his school's campus intending to kill "at least five persons at the school." When police approached Hanley,

> he brandished the fully-loaded handgun, yanked a nearby woman out of her seat, pointed the pistol at her head and threatened to kill her if anyone moved. Defendant begged the

police to shoot him and, when that didn't occur, he freed the hostage and pointed the gun at himself. Two police officers eventually convinced defendant to relinquish the firearm. When taken into custody, defendant reiterated his desire for the police to kill him and declared that the Columbine killers were his heroes.

Convicted of reckless endangerment and kidnapping, Hanley appealed, "arguing that his restraint of the female hostage was allegedly incidental to the conduct constituting reckless endangerment and, therefore, the kidnapping count 'merged' with the reckless endangerment offense." The Court explained **the merger doctrine as a judicial response to the concern that prosecutors would abuse the kidnapping charge by filing it whenever the defendant happened to forcibly move a victim, even if the movement was trivial and really performed as part of committing some other crime**. *Hanley* explained that kidnapping:

> could 'literally overrun several other crimes'—most notably robbery or rape—'since detention and sometimes confinement, against the will of the victim, frequently accompany' those offenses. [The minimum sentence for kidnapping was once] 20 years to life, a punishment more severe than that permitted for rape or robbery. [Prosecutors would] charge a defendant with kidnapping "in order to expose him to the heavier penalty" even if the underlying criminal conduct constituted a robbery, rape or some other offense carrying a lesser term of incarceration. ***

> This Court created the merger doctrine to rectify this problem of overcharging. *** **The aim of merger is to prohibit a 'conviction for kidnapping based on acts which are so much the part of another substantive crime that the substantive crime could not have been committed without such acts' and independent criminal responsibility for kidnapping may not fairly be attributed to the accused.** *** Although each case should be considered independently, a kidnapping is generally deemed to merge with another offense only 'where there is minimal asportation immediately preceding' the other crime or 'where the restraint and underlying crime are essentially simultaneous.' *** But where 'the abduction and underlying crime are discrete' or 'the manner of detention is egregious, regardless of other circumstances,' there is no merger and the kidnapping conviction should be sustained.[56]

For procedural reasons (the defendant had failed to raise his merger claim at trial), the *Hanley* court rejected the defendant's merger defense. If the defendant had raised the issue in the trial court, however, he seemingly would have had a valid argument, since the movement (yanking the victim from a seat) involved only a short distance and was wholly for the purpose of threatening a victim as a means to provoke the police into killing him.

In *Hickey v. State*, 2010 Ark. 109 (2010), the Supreme Court of Arkansas developed a list of factors to assess merger. *Hickey* had to decide if evidence existed to support George Hickey's conviction for both rape and kidnapping. Hickey was drinking at his home with his friend, Derrick Baker, and the victim,

---

56. Reprinted with the permission of LexisNexis.

Gayle Miller. When Baker passed out, Hickey made disrespectful comments toward Miller, who then expressed her intention to leave. The defendant slammed his front door shut, telling Miller, "You ain't going nowhere, bitch." Miller called out to Baker, who was unresponsive. Hickey told Miller to get in his room. "When Miller refused [Hickey] slapped her in the face and told her, "Get in the room, bitch." He also stated, "I got a .380 bitch," and threatened to kill her if she said anything. [The defendant] walked Miller through the house to his room. Once she entered the room, Appellant closed the door to the room. Hickey then forced Miller to participate in a series of sex acts.

In weighing whether there was sufficient evidence for kidnapping, *Hickey* noted:

> Arkansas Code Annotated § 5-11-102 defines when a kidnapping has occurred and states that:
>
> (a) A person commits the offense of kidnapping if, without consent, the person restrains another person so as to interfere substantially with the other person's liberty with the purpose of:
>
> [among other purposes]
>
> (5) Engaging in sexual intercourse, deviate sexual activity, or sexual contact with the other person . . .

The Court listed **factors relevant in deciding, "whether a separate kidnapping conviction is supportable."** These included **"whether the movement or confinement (1) prevented the victim from summoning assistance; (2) lessened the defendant's risk of detection; or (3) created a significant danger or increased the victim's risk of harm."** *Hickey* concluded:

> [We hold that there was sufficient evidence to support Appellant's kidnapping conviction.] On the night of the crime, Miller had voiced her decision that she was leaving, thus expressing her intention and revoking her consent to remain at Appellant's home. Appellant then stood up and slammed the door, telling Miller that she was not going anywhere. He then told her to go to his bedroom. When she refused, he slapped her and told her that he had a .380 pistol and would kill her if she said anything. At this point, Appellant had taken action sufficient to satisfy the elements of the crime of kidnapping. He substantially interfered with her liberty interest by physically threatening her and impeding her egress from the home. In addition, . . . he (1) prevented the victim from summoning assistance from Baker, who was passed out in the chair in the room; (2) he lessened his risk of being detected by taking Miller to a separate room where they would not be seen; and (3) he created a significant danger and increased the victim's risk of harm by secreting her away in his bedroom where he was able to inflict physical injury on her and engage in deviate sexual activity at increased risk to Miller. Thus, based on the lack of consent and the factors listed above, there was substantial evidence to sustain the separate conviction of kidnapping.[57]

---

57. Reprinted with the permission of LexisNexis.

G. STALKING

What precisely needs to occur for **stalking**, a relatively recently defined crime, to be committed? The following case relies upon both **explicit statements** and **inferences from conduct**.

© LCohelan/Shutterstock.com

LEGAL ANALYSIS

People v. Uecker
172 Cal.App.4th 583 (2009).
Justice Robie delivered the opinion of the California Court of Appeals.

Facts

[Defendant Danny Greg Uecker was charged with stalking two victims. *People v. Lopez*, 240 Cal.App.4th 436 (2015) provided the following factual summary.]

For months, the defendant expressed his interest in going out with the first victim, [M.], by leaving notes on her car and appearing at the car every day when she went to lunch, even if her lunchtime varied and after she told him she was not interested and moved to a different parking location. *** His last note called her an "'immature trouble making brat'" for trying to avoid him, asked, "'What's a guy gotta do to get a call from a beautiful woman?'" and stated he would "be here tomorrow if you want to see me," noting that she had "funny lunch hours." *** After she started parking a distance away and having people walk her to her car, the defendant was seen in his truck, positioned with a good view of the parking lot entrance and employee entrance. ***

The defendant contacted the second victim, a real estate agent, multiple times a day in the guise of looking for a property but never provided the information she pressed him for to help him qualify for a loan; he told her she had a "'really cool voice' and he could "[probably talk to her all day,"]" hinted she should take him to look at properties "in the boonies," became irate when she did not return a call, and after she told him she was leaving the residential real estate market, insisted he wanted to "'finish this with [her]', wanted her to 'handle [his] issues', and he wanted 'out of Dodge and by now, [she] probably kn[e]w why.'" *** The last of these comments indicated he knew the victim had learned he was a sex offender. ***

Issue

Whether there was sufficient evidence that the defendant committed Penal Code Section 646.9 Stalking against victims M. and J.

Rule and Analysis

The Legislature has defined the crime of stalking as follows: "Any person who willfully, maliciously, and repeatedly follows or willfully and maliciously harasses another person and who makes a credible threat with the intent to place that person in reasonable fear for his or her safety, or the safety of his or her immediate family." ***

"'[H]arasses' means engages in a knowing and willful course of conduct directed at a specific person that seriously alarms, annoys, torments, or terrorizes the person, and that serves no legitimate purpose." ***

"'[C]ourse of conduct' means two or more acts occurring over a period of time, however short, evidencing a continuity of purpose. Constitutionally protected activity is not included within the meaning of 'course of conduct.'" ***

"'[C]redible threat' means a verbal or written threat, including that performed through the use of an electronic communication device, or a threat implied by a pattern of conduct or a combination of verbal, written, or electronically communicated statements and conduct, made with the intent to place the person that is the target of the threat in reasonable fear for his or her safety or the safety of his or her family, and made with the apparent ability to carry out the threat so as to cause the person who is the target of the threat to reasonably fear for his or her safety or the safety of his or her family. It is not necessary to prove that the defendant had the intent to actually carry out the threat. The present incarceration of a person making the threat shall not be a bar to prosecution under this section. Constitutionally protected activity is not included within the meaning of 'credible threat.'" ***

Defendant argues there was insufficient evidence of all three elements of stalking, namely: (1) following or harassing another person; (2) making a credible threat; and (3) intending to place the victim in reasonable fear for her safety. We [find] sufficient evidence supported all three.

[There was sufficient evidence to support the first element of stalking, "willfully, maliciously, and repeatedly following or willfully and maliciously harassing another person."] After M. told defendant firmly she was not interested in him, he got mad. The next day after she had taken a much later lunch hour than normal, defendant left a note calling her derogatory names. The day after this note, defendant positioned himself in his car with a good view of the employee entrance. From this evidence, a reasonable jury could have found defendant purposefully (i.e., willfully) followed M. on more than one occasion (i.e., repeatedly) with the intent to disturb or annoy her (maliciously) after she told him she was not interested in him and refused to acquiesce in his requests to go out with him.

The second element is "mak[ing] a credible threat," which includes a threat implied by a pattern of conduct or a combination of verbal and written communicated statements and conduct. *** Here, defendant's pattern of conduct, his written notes, and verbal statements implied he was going to do whatever it took to get M. to go out with him, reasonably causing M. to fear for her safety. Almost every work day for approximately seven months, defendant followed M. and/or placed notes on her car. He would always find her or her car no matter what time she had taken her lunch hour or what location she had parked her car. When she told him firmly she was not interested in him, he got mad. The next day, defendant tracked her car down yet again, left her a note stating he did not like to keep leaving notes on her car, she was an "immature trouble making brat" and asking, "Now what" and what he had to do to get a call from a beautiful woman. When M. read this note, she "really freaked out," "starting parking way down the road" so defendant would not see her car and had people walk her to her car. The next day, he returned again and positioned himself with a good view of the employee entrance. From this evidence, a reasonable jury could have found that defendant made an implied threat to her safety in that he was going to do whatever he needed to get M. to go out with him and that she reasonably feared for her safety. His persistence lasted seven months with no signs of abating, his last conversation with M.

and his last note to her evidenced hostility toward her, and his final action of positioning himself where he could see her comings and goings at work signaled he was not going to take no for an answer.

The third element of stalking is intending to place the victim in reasonable fear for safety. Here, defendant's intent was evidenced by comments in two notes he left for M. explicitly alerting her he had been tracking her. The first was when he mentioned her new car within the first week she purchased it. The second was when he mentioned she had "funny lunch hours." From these comments, a reasonable jury could conclude defendant wanted M. to know he had been watching her while she was parked at work and keeping track of her schedule to place her in fear of her safety.

Taken as a whole, therefore, there was sufficient evidence to support the jury's verdict that defendant stalked M. within [PC section 646.9.]

Defendant makes a similar sufficiency-of-the-evidence argument with respect to J., challenging all three elements of the crime. Again, we find sufficient evidence to support the stalking conviction.

As to the first element, there was no evidence defendant followed J., so we focus on the evidence he harassed her within the meaning of the statute. Defendant called J. under the guise of searching for a "livable shack in the boonies for less than 60,000 dollars." It was apparent defendant's contact with J. was not directed toward the legitimate purpose of buying real estate, as he refused her request to provide her information to help him qualify for a loan, would not give her the correct spelling of his name, and would not tell her the truth about how he got her contact information. When she tried to cut off contact with him, defendant kept calling her, leaving her one irate message about realtors dropping customers and another message that he wanted to "finish this with [her]" and wanted her to "handle [his] issues." Defendant left her feeling afraid and trapped. This evidence was sufficient to support the element of harassment.

The second element is making a credible threat. Here, defendant's pattern of conduct in calling J. over 30 times in three weeks despite her desire to cut off contact with him, and his verbal statements in those calls, implied a threat that caused her to reasonably fear for her safety. He left messages for J. that were "a little too comfortable and playful," ones that left her with a "haunting and violating feeling," and ones that scared her. He told her he wanted a house in the boonies and then hinted she should take him out in her car to look at the properties. He told J. that she had a "really cool voice" and he could "'[p]robably talk to [her] all day.'" He left a message saying he had something to tell her, laughed, and then told her if she was curious enough, she would call back. When she did not, he asked her if she liked surprises. He left a message saying he wanted to come by the office. She changed her parking habits and dress to hide from defendant and would not hold open houses. When she did not return this call, he left her an irate message about realtors dropping their clients. When she told him that she was quitting the residential real estate market, he still persisted calling her. In his last messages, he cryptically told her he wanted to "finish this with [her]," wanted her to "handle [his] issues," and he wanted "out of Dodge and by now, [she] probably kn[e]w why." It was after this series of calls that J. contacted law enforcement.

Taken as a whole, this conduct implied a threat to J.'s safety. She knew defendant is a sex offender and defendant's last comment to J. indicated he knew that she knew. He intimated he wanted to be alone with her, made suggestive comments about her voice, asked if she liked surprises, told her he wanted to come by the office, was irate when she tried to get rid of him, and left cryptic messages on her answering machine. Simply put, this pattern of unrelenting conduct over the course of three weeks that toward the end became hostile and demanding, perpetrated by someone who is a sex offender and had no legitimate interest in real estate, was sufficient to satisfy this element.

The third element is intending to place the victim in reasonable fear for safety. Here, it can be inferred defendant intended to place J. in reasonable fear for her safety from his persistent phone contacts with her despite her attempts to end them, his apparent knowledge that she knew he is a registered sex offender, and his hostile and demanding tone in one of his last messages. This evidence supported not only the conclusion J. reasonably feared defendant and had reason to fear him but also that he acted with the intent to induce that fear. ***

Conclusion

[There was Sufficient evidence defendant stalked both victims M. and J.]
The judgment is affirmed.[58]

California Penal Code § 646.9: Stalking

(a) Any person who willfully, maliciously, and repeatedly follows or willfully and maliciously harasses another person and who makes a credible threat with the intent to place that person in reasonable fear for his or her safety, or the safety of his or her immediate family is guilty of the crime of stalking, punishable by imprisonment in a county jail for not more than one year, or by a fine of not more than one thousand dollars ($1,000), or by both...

(b) Any person who violates subdivision (a) when there is a temporary restraining order, injunction, or any other court order in effect prohibiting the behavior described in subdivision (a) against the same party, shall be punished by imprisonment in the state prison for two, three, or four years. ***

(e) For the purposes of this section, "harasses" means engages in a knowing and willful course of conduct directed at a specific person that seriously alarms, annoys, torments, or terrorizes the person, and that serves no legitimate purpose.

(f) For the purposes of this section, "course of conduct" means two or more acts occurring over a period of time, however short, evidencing a continuity of purpose. Constitutionally protected activity is not included within the meaning of "course of conduct."

(g) For the purposes of this section, "credible threat" means a verbal or written threat, including that performed through the use of an electronic communication device, or a threat implied by a pattern of conduct or a combination of verbal, written, or electronically communicated statements and conduct, made with the intent to place the person that is the target of the threat in reasonable fear for his or her safety or the safety of his or her family, and made with the apparent ability to carry out the threat so as to cause the person who is the target of the threat to reasonably fear for his or her safety or the safety of his or her family. It is not necessary to prove that the defendant had the intent to actually carry out the threat. The present incarceration of a person making the threat shall not be a bar to prosecution under this section. Constitutionally protected activity is not included within the meaning of "credible threat."

(h) For purposes of this section, the term "electronic communication device" includes, but is not limited to, telephones, cellular phones, computers, video recorders, fax machines, or pagers. ***

(l) For purposes of this section, "immediate family" means any spouse, parent, child, any person related by consanguinity or affinity within the second degree, or any other person who regularly resides in the household, or who, within the prior six months, regularly resided in the household. ***

North Carolina Penal Code § 14–196.3: Cyberstalking

(a) The following definitions apply in this section:

(1) Electronic communication.—Any transfer of signs, signals, writing, images, sounds, data, or intelligence of any nature, transmitted in whole or in part by a wire, radio, computer, electromagnetic, photoelectric, or photo-optical system.

58. Reprinted from Westlaw, with permission of Thomson Reuters.

(2) Electronic mail.—The transmission of information or communication by the use of the Internet, a computer, a facsimile machine, a pager, a cellular telephone, a video recorder, or other electronic means sent to a person identified by a unique address or address number and received by that person.

© Balefire/Shutterstock.com

(b) It is unlawful for a person to:

(1) Use in electronic mail or electronic communication any words or language threatening to inflict bodily harm to any person or to that person's child, sibling, spouse, or dependent, or physical injury to the property of any person, or for the purpose of extorting money or other things of value from any person.

(2) Electronically mail or electronically communicate to another repeatedly, whether or not conversation ensues, for the purpose of abusing, annoying, threatening, terrifying, harassing, or embarrassing any person.

(3) Electronically mail or electronically communicate to another and to knowingly make any false statement concerning death, injury, illness, disfigurement, indecent conduct, or criminal conduct of the person electronically mailed or of any member of the person's family or household with the intent to abuse, annoy, threaten, terrify, harass, or embarrass.

(4) Knowingly permit an electronic communication device under the person's control to be used for any purpose prohibited by this section.

(c) Any offense under this section committed by the use of electronic mail or electronic communication may be deemed to have been committed where the electronic mail or electronic communication was originally sent, originally received in this State, or first viewed by any person in this State.

(d) Any person violating the provisions of this section shall be guilty of a Class 2 misdemeanor.

(e) This section does not apply to any peaceable, nonviolent, or nonthreatening activity intended to express political views or to provide lawful information to others. This section shall not be construed to impair any constitutionally protected activity, including speech, protest, or assembly.

Do's and Don'ts for Hearings, Trials, and Appeals

Voir Dire

Do show great respect for jurors by learning how to pronounce their names, and by respecting their time by avoiding calling unnecessary witnesses, asking unneeded questions, or making too many objections. Jurors are quite sensitive to the clock. **Do** look at the jury from time to time to see if your information is sinking in or if you are boring them into yawns. **Don't** make jokes because they could bomb and they undermine your dignity or credibility. Further, prosecutors should never joke for it reduces the dignity of the proceedings and the seriousness of the defendant's crime. If a juror says something outrageous, **do** "rehabilitate" that juror in order to educate the other jurors and then promptly kick that juror off the panel to signal other jurors about inappropriate behavior. **Do** employ hypothetical questions to probe jurors' understanding (and to therefore educate) jurors about the law.

Source: North Carolina General Statutes.

Cyberstalking Can Be Deadly

Trial Judge Moniz found Michelle Carter guilty of manslaughter for, at age 17, allegedly telling her 18-year-old friend, Conrad Roy III, to follow through with his suicide. The full article, reported by Katharine Q. Seelye and Jess Bidgood on June 16, 2017, in their *New York Times* article, "Guilty Verdict for Young Woman Who Urged Friend to Kill Himself," can be viewed at:

https://www.nytimes.com/2017/06/16/us/suicide-texting-trial-michelle-carter-conrad-roy.html

As reported by Ray Sanchez, Natisha Lance, and Eric Levenson for CNN on August 3, 2017, in "Woman sentenced to 15 months in texting suicide case," the judge sentenced Carter to fifteen months in jail. This article can be viewed at:

http://www.cnn.com/2017/08/03/us/michelle-carter-texting-suicide-sentencing/index.html

A video explaining the case was created by Barbara Demick on June 16, 2017, for the *Los Angeles Times*, entitled "Michelle Carter found guilty in Massachusetts texting suicide case." This video can be viewed at:

http://www.latimes.com/nation/la-na-text-suicide-20170616-story.html

What Can Be Done about Cyberstalking and Cyberbullying?

Want to stop cyberbullying? Information to prevent this dangerous action can be viewed at:

https://www.stopbullying.gov/

The National Crime Prevention Council: Cyberbullying, at:

http://www.ncpc.org/resources/files/pdf/bullying/cyberbullying.pdf

H.   CRIMINAL OR TERRORIST THREATS

The law considers it a crime to "**willfully threaten**" to commit a crime which will "**result in death or great bodily injury**" to someone else, if the speaker **specifically intends** his or her statement **to be taken as a threat**. Such a threat, however, has to be "so **unequivocal, unconditional, immediate, and specific**" that it "**conveys**" a "**gravity of purpose and an immediate prospect of execution of the threat**" that causes the victim to be in reasonable "**sustained fear for his or her own safety.**" In interpreting this statute, just how **unconditional** does a threat have to be in order to qualify as a "**criminal threat**"?

© AFPics/Shutterstock.com

LEGAL ANALYSIS

People v. Bolin
18 Cal. 4th 297 (1998).
Justice Brown delivered the opinion of the California Supreme Court.

Facts

A jury convicted defendant Paul Clarence Bolin of [murder with special circumstances and set the penalty at death].

[During the penalty phase,] the trial court admitted evidence of a threatening letter defendant sent to Jerry Halfacre while in jail awaiting trial. [The letter read as follows:]

"Jerry 6/25/90

"Well I finally heard from Paula [defendant's daughter and mother of Halfacre's child] and what I heard from her I'm not to[o] pleased with. I heard her side of things w[h]ich are real different from what you had to say. I'm only going to say this one time so you better make sure you understand. If you ever[] touch my daughter again, I'll have you permanently removed from the face of this Earth. You better thank your lucky stars you['re] Ashley's father or you[']d already have your fucking legs broke.

"I found out what happen[e]d to most of the money from the van, and I also found out you got 1500 for the truck not 1300 like you said. I'm still going to find out how much you got for the Buick and if it's 1 cents over 1000 you can kiss your ass good by[e]. I also found out it was running like a top and the burnt valves was a bunch of bull shit, just like I thought in the first place. You sounded a little shak[]y over the phone and gave yourself away.

"I told you a long time ago don't play fucking games with me. You're playing with the wrong person asshole. I've made a couple of phone calls to San Pedro to some friends of mine and the[y're] not to[o] happy with your fucking game playing with other people's money and especially you hitting Paula.

"What I want done and it better be done. Everything that's mine or hers tools, clothes, books, gun, TV, VCR, I don't fucking care if it's a bobby pin, you better give it to Paula. I want all my shit given to her and I mean every fucking thing. You have a week to do it or I make another phone call. I hope you get the fucking message. Your game playing is eventually going to get you in more than a poo butt game player can handle.

"1 week asshole.

"And keep playing your game with [my granddaughter] and see what happens."

Issue

Whether defendant's statements in the letter amount to a criminal threat under PC 422, even though his threats were "conditional."

Rule and Analysis

[PC section 422 makes it a crime to "willfully threaten] to commit a crime which will result in death or great bodily injury to another person, with the specific intent that the statement is to be taken as a threat, even if there is no intent of actually carrying it out, which, on its face and under the circumstances in which it is made, is so unequivocal, unconditional, immediate, and specific as to convey to the person threatened, a gravity of purpose and an immediate prospect of execution of the threat, and thereby causes that person reasonably to be in sustained fear for his or her own safety . . . ."** [Defendant contends that because the letter did not contain an unconditional threat, it did not constitute a violation of section 422 as a matter of law.]

In *People v. Brown*, the defendant accosted two women approaching their apartment and made several menacing statements as he pointed a gun at the head of one of the women. *** When the other said they should call the police, the defendant said he would kill them if they did. [The Court of Appeal reversed the defendant's PC 422 conviction,] construing the statute to preclude conviction when the threat is conditional in any respect. "The plain meaning of an 'unconditional' threat is that there be no conditions. '*If* you call the police . . .' is a condition. [Several courts have] expressly disagreed with this strict interpretation of section 422. *** We find the reasoning of these subsequent cases more persuasive and now hold that prosecution under section 422 does not require an unconditional threat of death or great bodily injury. ***

[This court invalidated former section 422 as unconstitutionally vague in 1981. The Legislature then enacted a revised version, adopting almost verbatim language from *United States v. Kelner*.] In *Kelner*, the defendant, a member of the Jewish Defense League, had been convicted under a federal statute for threatening to assassinate Palestinian leader Yasser Arafat, who was to be in New York for a meeting at the United Nations. Kelner argued that without proof he specifically intended to carry out the threat, his statement was political hyperbole protected by the First Amendment rather than a punishable true threat. ***

The reviewing court disagreed and concluded threats are punishable [so] long as the threat on its face and in the circumstances in which it is made is so unequivocal, unconditional, immediate and specific as to the person threatened, as to convey a gravity of purpose and imminent prospect of execution, the statute may properly be applied." [*Kelner* relied on *Watts v. United States*,] in which the United States Supreme Court reversed a conviction for threatening the President of the United States. Defendant Watts had stated, in a small discussion group during a political rally, "And now I have already received my draft classification as 1-A and I have got to report for my physical this Monday coming. I am not going. If they ever make me carry a rifle the first man I want to get in my sights is L.B.J.'" *** Both Watts and the crowd laughed after the statement was made. *** The Supreme Court determined that taken in context, and considering the conditional nature of the threat and the reaction of the listeners, the only possible conclusion was that the statement was not a punishable true threat, but political hyperbole privileged under the First Amendment. ***

[As *Kelner* understood,] the Supreme Court was not adopting a bright line test based on the use of conditional language but simply illustrating the general principle that punishable true threats must express an intention of being carried out. *** "In effect, the Court was stating that **threats punishable consistently with the First Amendment were only those which according to their language and context conveyed a gravity of purpose and likelihood of execution so as to constitute speech beyond the pale** of protected [attacks on government and political officials]." [The purpose of the

Watts] definition of the term 'threat' is to insure that **only unequivocal, unconditional and specific expressions of intention immediately to inflict injury may be punished**—only such threats, in short, as are of the same nature as those threats which are . . . 'properly punished every day under statutes prohibiting extortion, blackmail and assault.'" ***

[PC section 422's reference to an "unconditional" threat is not absolute.] As the court in *People v. Stanfield* noted, "By definition, extortion punishes conditional threats, specifically those in which the victim complies with the mandated condition. [*Kelner's*] use of the word 'unconditional' was not meant to prohibit prosecution of all threats involving an 'if' clause, but only to prohibit prosecution based on threats whose conditions precluded them from conveying a gravity of purpose and imminent prospect of execution." *** "Most threats are conditional; they are designed to accomplish something; the threatener hopes that they *will* accomplish it, so that he won't have to carry out the threats."

Moreover, imposing an "unconditional" requirement ignores the statutory qualification that the threat must be "*so . . . unconditional . . . as to convey to the person threatened, a gravity of purpose and an immediate prospect of execution . . . .*" ***

"The use of the word 'so' indicates that unequivocality, unconditionality, immediacy and specificity are not absolutely mandated, but must be sufficiently present in the threat and surrounding circumstances to convey gravity of purpose and immediate prospect of execution to the victim." *** "If the fact that a threat is conditioned on something occurring renders it not a true threat, there would have been no need to include in the statement the word 'so.'" *** This provision "implies that there are different degrees of unconditionality. A threat which may appear conditional on its face can be unconditional under the circumstances . . . Language creating an apparent condition cannot save the threatener from conviction when the condition is illusory, given the reality of the circumstances surrounding the threat. **A seemingly conditional threat contingent on an act highly likely to occur may convey to the victim a gravity of purpose and immediate prospect of execution.**" ***

Conclusion

Since a threat need not be unconditional to satisfy PC 422, and because the jury likely based its sentence on the wealth of other aggravating circumstances, the death sentence was affirmed.[59]

Learn from My (and Others') Mistakes

Do Not Let Your Witness Testify While Under the Influence of PCP

This is one mistake I avoided. When prosecuting a defendant for PC 664/261 attempted rape, I interviewed a witness who was supposed to testify as to the victim's actions immediately following the attack. I was told that she would describe that the victim, traumatized by the attack, ran back and forth in a bar in a vain attempt to get away from herself. Instead, when I asked this witness about the victim's movements, she stared at me with a vacant expression, offering words of gibberish. When I gave her pen and paper to draw the victim's movements, the witness just leaned her weight on the pen. By this time, I noticed the smell of some volatile chemical in my office. I excused myself on the pretext of getting the witness some coffee and invited other D.A.'s to enter my office to identify the smell. Since the consensus was that my witness was likely on PCP, I thanked her for her time, wisely choosing to prove my case without her.

---

59. Reprinted with the permission of LexisNexis.

I.   HATE CRIMES

In these next three sections (hate crimes, child abuse, and elder abuse), the criminal activity involved is defined in part by the identity of the victim. In fact, with all three kinds of crimes, the victim is somehow vulnerable, whether due to being singled out as a target of violence due to bigotry or due to age (children and the elderly). First, we will consider hate crimes, where the victims are attacked simply because of real or perceived differences.

California Penal Code Section § 422.55: Hate Crime Defined

(a) "Hate crime" means a criminal act committed, in whole or in part, because of one or more of the following actual or perceived characteristics of the victim:

(1)   Disability.
(2)   Gender.
(3)   Nationality.
(4)   Race or ethnicity.
(5)   Religion.
(6)   Sexual orientation.
(7)   Association with a person or group with one or more of these actual or perceived characteristics.

Roof's Killing of Nine Churchgoers Was Based on Race Hatred

Jay Croft and Tristan Smith of CNN reported in their April 10, 2017, article, Dylann "Roof pleads guilty to state charges in church massacre," that Dylann Roof killed nine victims in a church because, he was recorded as saying, "black people are killing white people every day." He pleaded guilty and was sentenced to death for these killings motivated by hate. The full article can be viewed at:

http://www.cnn.com/2017/04/10/us/dylann-roof-guilty-plea-state-trial/index.html

As reported by Lindsey Bever in the May 17, 2017, *Washington Post* article, "'I'm just a sociopath,' Dylann Roof declared after deadly church shooting rampage, court records say," Dylann Roof failed to show any remorse for shooting nine African American parishioners to death in a South Carolina church. A psychological evaluation reported that Roof was preoccupied with racism. The full article can be viewed at:

https://www.washingtonpost.com/news/post-nation/wp/2017/05/17/im-just-a-sociopath-dylann-roof-declared-after-deadly-church-shooting-spree-court-records-say/?utm_term=.b2c63a1b0599

Cross burning has a frighteningly violent history in our country. People committing hate crimes have been known to burn crosses. Does this mean that the act of **cross burning**, even **without any "intent to intimidate,"** can be **constitutionally prosecuted** as a crime?

© ProstoSvet/Shutterstock.com

LEGAL ANALYSIS

Virginia v. Black
538 U.S. 343 (2003).
Justice O'Connor delivered portions of the plurality opinion of the United States Supreme Court.

Facts

[Respondents Barry Black, Richard Elliott, and Jonathan O'Mara were convicted of violating Virginia's cross-burning statute, § 18.2–423, which provided:]

"It shall be [a felony] for any person or persons, with the intent of intimidating any person or group of persons, to burn, or cause to be burned, a cross on the property of another, a highway or other public place. ***

"Any such burning of a cross shall be prima facie (on its face) evidence of an intent to intimidate a person or group of persons."

On August 22, 1998, Barry Black led a Ku Klux Klan rally in Carroll County, Virginia. Twenty-five to thirty people attended this gathering, which occurred on private property with the permission of the owner, who was in attendance. The property was located on an open field. ***

[At the rally, Klan members spoke about "what they were" and "what they believed in." They] "talked real bad about the blacks and the Mexicans." [One speaker said] that "he would love to take a .30/.30 and just randomly shoot the blacks." [A witness testified that this language made her "very . . . scared."]

At the conclusion of the rally, the crowd circled around a 25- to 30-foot cross. The cross was between 300 and 350 yards away from the road. [The cross "then all of a sudden . . . went up in a flame."] As the cross burned, the Klan played "Amazing Grace" over the loudspeakers. ***

Black was charged with burning a cross with the intent of intimidating a person or group of persons. At his trial, the jury was instructed that "intent to intimidate means the motivation to intentionally put a person or a group of persons in fear of bodily harm. Such fear must arise from the willful conduct of the accused." *** The trial court also instructed the jury that "the burning of a cross by itself is sufficient evidence from which you may infer the required intent." [The jury convicted Black.]

On May 2, 1998, respondents Richard Elliott and Jonathan O'Mara, as well as a third individual, attempted to burn a cross on the yard of James Jubilee. Jubilee, an African-American, was Elliott's next-door neighbor in Virginia Beach, Virginia. Four months prior to the incident, Jubilee and his family had moved from California to Virginia Beach. Before the cross burning, Jubilee spoke to Elliott's mother to inquire about shots being fired from behind the Elliott home. Elliott's mother explained to Jubilee that her son shot firearms as a hobby, and that he used the backyard as a firing range.

On the night of May 2, respondents drove a truck onto Jubilee's property, planted a cross, and set it on fire. Their apparent motive was to "get back" at Jubilee for complaining about the shooting in the backyard. *** The next morning, as Jubilee was pulling his car out of the driveway, he noticed the partially burned cross approximately 20 feet from his house. After seeing the cross, Jubilee was "very nervous" because he "didn't know what would be the next phase," and because "a cross burned in your yard . . . tells you that it's just the first round." ***

Elliott and O'Mara were charged with attempted cross burning and conspiracy to commit cross burning. O'Mara pleaded guilty to both counts, reserving the right to challenge the constitutionality of the cross-burning statute. ***

Issue

Whether Virginia's statute banning cross burning without "an intent to intimidate a person or group of persons" violates the First Amendment.

Rule and Analysis

[While] a State, consistent with the First Amendment, may ban cross burning carried out with the intent to intimidate, the provision in the Virginia statute treating any cross burning as prima facie (on its face) evidence of intent to intimidate renders the statute unconstitutional in its current form. ***

Cross burning originated in the 14th century as a means for Scottish tribes to signal each other. *** Sir Walter Scott used cross burnings for dramatic effect in The Lady of the Lake, where the burning cross signified both a summons and a call to arms. *** Cross burning in this country, however, long ago became unmoored from its Scottish ancestry. Burning a cross in the United States is inextricably intertwined with the history of the Ku Klux Klan.

The first Ku Klux Klan began in Pulaski, Tennessee, in the spring of 1866. *** The Klan fought Reconstruction and the corresponding drive to allow freed blacks to participate in the political process, [imposing] "a veritable reign of terror" throughout the South. *** The Klan employed tactics such as whipping, threatening to burn people at the stake, and murder. *** The Klan's victims included blacks, southern whites who disagreed with the Klan, and "carpetbagger" northern whites.

*** In 1871, "President Grant sent a message to Congress indicating that the Klan's reign of terror in the Southern States had rendered life and property insecure." *** Congress passed what is now known as the Ku Klux Klan Act. *** By the end of Reconstruction in 1877, the first Klan no longer existed.

The genesis of the second Klan began in 1905, with the publication of Thomas Dixon's [sympathetic portrait of the first Klan, The Clansmen: An Historical Romance of the Ku Klux Klan.] Although the first Klan never actually practiced cross burning, Dixon's book depicted the [first Klan burning crosses.] When D. W. Griffith turned Dixon's book into the movie The Birth of a Nation in 1915, the association between cross burning and the Klan became indelible. ***

[The second Klan used cross burnings to communicate both threats of violence and messages of shared ideology.] The first known cross burning in the country had occurred . . . when a Georgia mob celebrated the lynching of Leo Frank by burning a "gigantic cross" on Stone Mountain that was "visible throughout" Atlanta. ***

[The new Klan violently promoted racism. It] used cross burnings as a tool of intimidation and a threat of impending violence. [In 1939 and 1940, the Klan burned crosses in front of synagogues and churches.] After one cross burning at a synagogue, a Klan member noted that if the cross burning did not "shut the Jews up, we'll cut a few throats and see what happens." ***

[*Brown v. Board of Education*, along with the civil rights movement, sparked another outbreak of Klan violence, including] bombings, beatings, shootings, stabbings, and mutilations. *** Members of the Klan burned crosses on the lawns of those associated with the civil rights movement, assaulted the Freedom Riders, bombed churches, and murdered blacks as well as whites whom the Klan viewed as sympathetic toward the civil rights movement.

*** The burning cross became a symbol of the Klan itself and a central feature of Klan gatherings. According to the Klan constitution (called the kloran), the "fiery cross" was the "emblem of that sincere, unselfish devotedness of all klansmen to the sacred purpose and principles we have espoused." ***

For its own members, the cross was a sign of celebration and ceremony. During a joint Nazi-Klan rally in 1940, the proceeding concluded with the wedding of two Klan members who "were married in full Klan regalia beneath a blazing cross." *** In short, a burning cross has remained a symbol of Klan ideology and of Klan unity.

To this day, regardless of whether the message is a political one or whether the message is also meant to intimidate, the burning of a cross is a "symbol of hate." [When] a cross burning is directed at a particular person not affiliated with the Klan, the burning cross often serves as a message of intimidation, designed to inspire in the victim a fear of bodily harm. Moreover, the history of violence associated with the Klan shows that the possibility of injury or death is not just hypothetical. The person who burns a cross directed at a particular person often is making a serious threat, meant to coerce the victim to comply with the Klan's wishes unless the victim is willing to risk the wrath of the Klan. ***

In sum, while a burning cross does not inevitably convey a message of intimidation, often the cross burner intends that the recipients of the message fear for their lives. And when a cross burning is used to intimidate, few if any messages are more powerful. ***

The First Amendment *** provides that "Congress shall make no law . . . abridging the freedom of speech." The hallmark of the protection of free speech is to allow "free trade in ideas"—even ideas that the overwhelming majority of people might find distasteful or discomforting. ["If there is a bedrock principle underlying the First Amendment, it is that the government may not prohibit the expression of an idea simply because society finds the idea itself offensive or disagreeable.]" Thus, the First Amendment "ordinarily" denies a State "the power to prohibit dissemination of social, economic and political doctrine which a vast majority of its citizens believes to be false and fraught with evil consequence." *** The First Amendment affords protection to symbolic or expressive conduct as well as to actual speech. ***

The protections afforded by the First Amendment, however, are not absolute, and we have long recognized that the government may regulate certain categories of expression consistent with the Constitution. *** The First Amendment permits "restrictions upon the content of speech in a few limited areas."***

[For] example, a State may punish those words "which by their very utterance inflict injury or tend to incite an immediate breach of the peace." *** We have consequently held that fighting words—"those personally abusive epithets which, when addressed to the ordinary citizen, are, as a matter of common knowledge, inherently likely to provoke violent reaction"—are generally proscribable under the First Amendment. ***

[The First Amendment permits a State to ban a "true threat," with which] the speaker means to communicate a serious expression of an intent to commit an act of unlawful violence to a particular individual or group of individuals. *** The speaker need not actually intend to carry out the threat.

Rather, a prohibition on true threats "protects individuals from the fear of violence" and "from the disruption that fear engenders," in addition to protecting people "from the possibility that the threatened violence will occur." *** Intimidation in the constitutionally proscribable sense of the word is a type of true threat, where a speaker directs a threat to a person or group of persons with the intent of placing the victim in fear of bodily harm or death. [Some cross burnings fit within this meaning of intimidating speech.]

The First Amendment permits Virginia to outlaw cross burnings done with the intent to intimidate because burning a cross is a particularly virulent form of intimidation. Instead of prohibiting all intimidating messages, Virginia may choose to regulate this subset of intimidating messages in light of cross burning's long and pernicious history as a signal of impending violence. ***

The Supreme Court of Virginia [ruled] that "the act of burning a cross alone, with no evidence of intent to intimidate, will nonetheless suffice for arrest and prosecution." *** The court in Barry Black's case . . . instructed the jury that the provision means: "The burning of a cross, by itself, is sufficient evidence from which you may infer the required intent." ***

The prima facie evidence provision, as interpreted by the jury instruction, renders the statute unconstitutional. [The provision allows the government to convict] a person based solely on the fact of cross burning itself.

It is apparent that the provision as so interpreted "would create an unacceptable risk of the suppression of ideas." *** **The act of burning a cross may mean that a person is engaging in constitutionally proscribable intimidation. But that same act may mean only that the person is engaged in core political speech.** The prima facie evidence provision in this statute blurs the line between these two meanings of a burning cross. [The] provision chills constitutionally protected political speech because of the possibility that a State will prosecute—and potentially convict—somebody engaging only in lawful political speech at the core of what the First Amendment is designed to protect.

As the history of cross burning indicates, a burning cross is not always intended to intimidate. Rather, sometimes the cross burning is a statement of ideology, a symbol of group solidarity. It is a ritual used at Klan gatherings, and it is used to represent the Klan itself. Thus, "burning a cross at a political rally would almost certainly be protected expression." *** Indeed, occasionally a person who burns a cross does not intend to express either a statement of ideology or intimidation. Cross burnings have appeared in movies such as *Mississippi Burning*, and in plays such as the stage adaptation of Sir Walter Scott's *The Lady of the Lake*.

The prima facie provision makes no effort to distinguish among these different types of cross burnings. *** It does not distinguish between a cross burning at a public rally or a cross burning on a neighbor's lawn. It does not treat the cross burning directed at an individual differently from the cross burning directed at a group of like-minded believers. It allows a jury to treat a cross burning on the property of another with the owner's acquiescence in the same manner as a cross burning on the property of another without the owner's permission. ***

It may be true that a cross burning, even at a political rally, arouses a sense of anger or hatred among the vast majority of citizens who see a burning cross. But this sense of anger or hatred is not sufficient to ban all cross burnings *** **The prima facie evidence provision in this case ignores all of the contextual factors that are necessary to decide whether a particular cross burning is intended to intimidate.** The First Amendment does not permit such a shortcut.

For these reasons, the prima facie evidence provision, as interpreted through the jury instruction and as applied in Barry Black's case, is unconstitutional on its face. [All] we hold is that because of the interpretation of the prima facie evidence provision given by the jury instruction, the provision makes the statute facially invalid at this point. ***

Conclusion

With respect to Barry Black . . . his conviction cannot stand, and we affirm the judgment of the Supreme Court of Virginia. With respect to Elliott and O'Mara, we vacate the judgment of the Supreme Court of Virginia, and remand the case for further proceedings. [It is so ordered.]

The Matthew Shepard Case

The crime against Matthew Shepard, as described below, shocked the nation. For background on the Matthew Shepard and James Byrd, Jr., Hate Crimes Prevention Act of 2009, visit U.S. Department of Justice website at:

http://www.justice.gov/crt/about/crm/matthewshepard.php

United States Attorney General Eric H. Holder Jr. testified as follows regarding the Matthew Shepard case:

> This bill is named in honor of Matthew Shepard, a gay man who was brutally murdered ten years ago in Laramie, Wyoming, in a case that shocked the nation. Matthew Shepard was murdered by two men, Russell Henderson and Aaron McKinney, who set out on the night of October 6, 1998, to rob a gay man. After going to a gay bar and pretending to befriend him, the killers offered their young victim a ride home, but instead drove him away from the bar, repeatedly pistol-whipped him in his head and face, and then tied him to a fence and left him to die. The passerby who found Shepard the next morning, tied to the fence and struggling to survive, initially thought that Matthew was a scarecrow. He was rushed to the hospital, where he died on October 12 from massive head injuries. At the defendants' murder trial, Henderson and McKinney initially tried to use a "gay panic" defense, claiming that they killed Shepard in an insane rage after he approached them sexually. At another point, they claimed that they intended only to rob Shepard, but not to kill him. Both men were sentenced to serve two consecutive life terms in prison.

This testimony can be viewed at:

https://www.justice.gov/sites/default/files/testimonies/witnesses/attachments/ 2009/06/25//2009-06-25-ag-holder-s-909.pdf

The Mathew Shepard Foundation can be visited at:

http://www.matthewshepard.org/

Was the Infamous Hate Crime Case Victimizing Matthew Shepard Really a Hate Crime?
Questions about the true motive behind the infamous crime are discussed in Stephen Jimenez's article, "The Myths of Matthew Shepard's Infamous Death," published in *The Daily Beast* on Sep 22, 2013, 4:45 AM EDT. For this article and a book excerpt, see:

http://www.thedailybeast.com/articles/2013/09/22/the-myths-of- matthew-shepard-s-infamous-death.html

---

The Victim of a Beating by White Men in Charlottesville, Virginia, Was Himself Charged with Felony Assault

A WAVY.com video, "Man with ties to Hampton Roads injured in Charlottesville clashes," on YouTube, shows DeAndre Harris suffering a beating by a mob. The video, which shows graphic violence and so could be disturbing to viewers, can be seen at:

https://www.youtube.com/watch?v=C2i0p6wJX_8

Trymaine Lee reported on October 10, 2017, for NBC News in "Man Attacked in Charlottesville Charged With Assault in Unexpected Turn" that DeAndre Harris, who was filmed being beaten by white men at a "Unite the Right" rally was charged with felony assault. His attackers had been charged with malicious wounding. For the full story, visit:

https://www.nbcnews.com/news/nbcblk/man-attacked-charlottesville-charged-assault-unexpected-turn-n809576

J.   CHILD ABUSE

Child abuse is a particularly heinous crime because the victims are so vulnerable. Should the prohibition against **child abuse** be extended to include **prosecuting pregnant mothers for drug use during pregnancy** that could cause **child endangerment**?

© Sinisha Karich/Shutterstock.com

LEGAL ANALYSIS

State v. Wade
232 S.W.3d 663 (2007).
Justice Hardwick wrote the opinion for the Court of Appeals of Missouri.

Facts

The State of Missouri appeals from the circuit court's dismissal of a child endangerment charge against Janet Wade. [We affirm the dismissal judgment.]

Janet Wade gave birth to her son, T.L.W., on August 21, 2005. The following day, both Wade and the child tested positive for marijuana and methamphetamine.

The State filed a felony information charging Wade with first-degree child endangerment, Section 568.045.1, R.S.Mo., for causing a substantial risk to T.L.W.'s health by using marijuana and methamphetamine during her pregnancy. Wade moved to dismiss the charge. [The] circuit court found the information was deficient because the child endangerment statute could not be applied to parental conduct involving an unborn child. ***

Issue

Whether the child endangerment statute applies to parental conduct involving an unborn child.

Rule and Analysis

Section 568.045 provides that a person commits the felony of first-degree child endangerment by "knowingly [acting in a manner that creates a substantial risk to the life, body, or health of a child less than seventeen years old.]" The State charged Wade with violating this statute by using illegal drugs while she was pregnant and thereby creating "a substantial risk to the life and body and health of T.L.W., a child less than seventeen years old." The circuit court dismissed the charge because it determined the child endangerment statute could not be applied to a mother's conduct against her unborn child. The State contends the court erred *** because the term "a child less than seventeen years old" necessarily includes an unborn child from the moment of conception until birth.

[The goal of statutory] interpretation is to ascertain the intent of the legislature from the language of the statute, considering the words used in their plain and ordinary meaning, and to give effect to that intent, if possible.

Section 568.045 does not define the word "child" beyond the description of "less than seventeen years old." The only definition for "child" in . . . dealing with Crimes Against the Family relates to cases involving criminal nonsupport. [Section 568.040 RSMo. states that a "'Child' means any biological or adoptive child, or any child whose relationship to the defendant has been determined, by a court of law in a proceeding for dissolution or legal separation, to be that of child to parent.]" This definition does not appear to include a child in-utero. [The] context of the nonsupport statute indicates that it strictly applies to children who have already been born. [We] find nothing to suggest that the legislature intended the term "child" to refer to a fetus.

The State argues Missouri courts have previously relied on Section 1.205 in determining that an unborn child is a person . . . Section 1.205.1 provides that "[t]he life of each human being begins at conception" and "[u]nborn children have protectable interests in life, health, and well-being." Section 1.205.2 further states that Missouri laws shall be interpreted to acknowledge that an unborn child has "all the rights, privileges, and immunities available to other persons." Consistent with these provisions, Missouri courts have upheld murder and manslaughter convictions, as well as wrongful death judgments, against *third parties* for causing the death of an unborn child. *** **Although Section 1.205 generally provides legal authority for protecting the rights of unborn children, the statute creates an exception in situations when a mother allegedly causes harm to her unborn child.** Section 1.205.4 provides:

Nothing in this section shall be interpreted as creating a cause of action against a woman for indirectly harming her unborn child by failing to properly care for herself or by failing to follow any particular program of prenatal care.

This provision precludes any effort to prosecute a mother who causes indirect harm to her fetus by ingesting illegal drugs during her pregnancy and, thereby, fails to properly care for herself. The statute indicates the legislature's intent to avoid criminalizing the lack of proper prenatal care. Consistent with the exception provided in Section 1.205.4, we have found no Missouri cases allowing criminal or civil actions to proceed against a mother whose pregnancy-related misconduct allegedly caused harm to her unborn child.

*** Missouri is not alone in barring the prosecution of mothers who fail to exercise proper prenatal care. Of fifteen state courts addressing this issue, fourteen have ruled that a mother cannot be held criminally liable for conduct harmful to her fetus. One reason why courts have disallowed such criminal charges is that it would be difficult to determine what types of prenatal misconduct should be subject to prosecution. Here, the State argues that criminal liability should arise when an unborn child is injured as a result of the mother's unlawful conduct, such as the use of illegal drugs. However, the mother is already subject to prosecution for such unlawful activity, and the only purpose of allowing additional pregnancy-related charges would be to protect the interest of the fetus. **Given that goal of protection, the logic of allowing such prosecutions would be extended to cases involving smoking, alcohol ingestion, the failure to wear seatbelts, and any other conduct that might cause harm to a mother's unborn child.** It is a difficult line to draw and, as such, our legislature has chosen to handle the problems of pregnant mothers through social service programs instead of the court system. ***

[The] circuit court correctly determined that Wade could not be prosecuted for child endangerment based on her pregnancy-related conduct. The felony indictment was properly dismissed. ***

Conclusion

While it may be clear that Wade's misconduct has created substantial health risks for T.L.W., the questions of whether and how the State can intervene to protect the child's rights are governed by legislative authority. We must apply the law as written and . . . avoid criminal prosecution of mothers in favor of providing education, treatment, and protection of the child through social services.
The judgment of dismissal is affirmed.[60]

Note

Not all courts have reached the same conclusion as *Wade* above. In *Ankrom v. State,* 152 So.3d 373 (2011), the Court of Criminal Appeals of Alabama considered a case where the defendant, Hope Elisabeth Ankrom, pleaded guilty to chemical endangerment of a child under Alabama Code Section 26-15-3.2(a) (1). The court noted, "Hope Ankrom, gave birth to a son, [B.W.], at Medical Center Enterprise. Medical records showed that the defendant tested positive for cocaine prior to giving birth and that the child tested positive for cocaine after birth." On appeal, the court, recognizing Alabama's public policy to protect unborn life that was capable of living outside the womb, ruled that the defendant was properly convicted.

---

60. Reprinted with the permission of LexisNexis.

What Really Happens to "Crack Babies"?

Surprisingly, according to a May 28, 2013, article in *Time* magazine entitled "'Crack Babies' Don't Necessarily Turn Into Troubled Teens" by Maia Szalavitz, "Exposure to crack cocaine in the womb does not increase the risk of later criminal behavior or school dropout— although the drug may have some lasting effects on behavior and development, according to a new review of the research."

To read the entire article, visit:

http://healthland.time.com/2013/05/28/crack-babies-dont-necessarily-turn-into-troubled-teens/

Can Leaving a Child in a Locked Car be Child Abuse?

For a video potentially involving an allegation of child abuse or neglect, see *NBC News* "Good Samaritans Rescue Child Locked in Sweltering Truck" at:

http://www.nbcnews.com/search/good%20samaritans%20rescue%20child%20locked

K. ELDER ABUSE

Elder abuse is another detestable crime due to the vulnerability of its victims. The following case considers the question of just how far the law should go in creating criminal liability for those who **knowingly allow elder abuse**. Should the law declare as criminal **all children who are aware** that their parents are being abused or neglected, or just those who have a **special legal duty** to care for their parents or control those who do?

© mrmohock/Shutterstock.com

LEGAL ANALYSIS

People v. Heitzman
9 Cal.4th 189 (1994).
Justice Lucas delivered the opinion for the California Supreme Court.

Facts

The egregious facts of this case paint a profoundly disturbing family portrait in which continued neglect of and apparent indifference to the basic needs of the family's most vulnerable member, an elderly dependent parent, led to a result of tragic proportion. Sixty-seven-year-old Robert Heitzman resided in the Huntington Beach home of his grown son, Richard Heitzman, Sr., along with another grown son, Jerry Heitzman, and Richard's three sons. [In 1990, police] discovered Robert dead in his bedroom. His body lay on a mattress that was rotted through from constant wetness, exposing the metal springs. The stench of urine and feces filled [the entire house.]

Police learned that Jerry Heitzman was primarily responsible for his father's care, rendering caretaking services in exchange for room and board. Jerry admitted that he had withheld all food and liquids from his father for the three days preceding his death, [explaining that he was expecting company for dinner and did not want his father, who no longer had control over his bowels and bladder, to defecate or urinate because it would cause the house to smell.]

[At death, decedent had large] bed sores, covering one-sixth of his body. An autopsy revealed *** a yeast infection in his mouth, and showed that he suffered from congestive heart failure, bronchial pneumonia, and hepatitis. The forensic pathologist *** attributed decedent's death to septic shock due to the sores which, he opined, were caused by malnutrition, dehydration, and neglect.

Twenty years earlier, decedent had suffered *** strokes that paralyzed the left side of his body. Defendant, 31-year-old Susan Valerie Heitzman, another of decedent's children, had previously lived in the home and had been her father's primary caregiver at that time. In return, defendant's brother Richard paid for her room and board. ***

One year prior to her father's death, defendant decided to move away from the home. After she moved out, however, she continued to spend time at the house visiting her boyfriend/nephew Richard, Jr. Since leaving to live on her own, she noticed that the entire house had become filthy. She was aware that a social worker had discussed with Jerry the need to take their father to a doctor. ***

In the last six weekends before her father died, defendant had routinely visited the household. She was last in her father's bedroom five weeks prior to his death, at which time she noticed the hole in the mattress and feces-soiled clothing lying on the floor. ***

*** On the day decedent died, defendant awoke midmorning and left the house to return to her own apartment. Around one o'clock in the afternoon, Jerry discovered decedent dead in his bedroom.

In a two-count indictment, the Orange County District Attorney jointly charged Jerry and Richard, Sr., with involuntary manslaughter (§ 192), and Jerry, Richard, Sr., and defendant with violating section 368(a). ***

Issue

Whether the defendant, Susan Heitzman, had a duty to control the conduct of the individuals who were directly causing or inflicting abuse on the elder or dependent adult.

Rule and Analysis

Penal Code section 368, subdivision (a), is one component of a multifaceted legislative response to the problem of elder abuse. The statute imposes felony criminal liability on "[a]ny person who, under circumstances or conditions likely to produce great bodily harm or death, willfully causes or permits any elder or dependent adult, with knowledge that he or she is an elder or dependent adult, to suffer, or inflicts thereon unjustifiable physical pain or mental suffering, or having the care or custody of any elder or dependent adult, willfully causes or permits the person or health of the elder or dependent adult to be injured, or willfully causes or permits the elder or dependent adult to be placed in a situation such that his or her person or health is endangered . . . " ["Elder" is defined as "any person who is 65 years of age or older." (§ 368, subd. (d).) Section 368, subdivision (e), defines "dependent adult" as any person between 18 and 64 years of age "who has physical or mental limitations which restrict his or her ability to carry out normal activities or to protect his or her rights."]

[To avoid finding the statute unconstitutionally vague, the court limited the reach of the law. The court interpreted the statute cover only those who have a particular legal duty. The legal obligation for this statute was the] duty to control the conduct of the individual who is directly causing or inflicting abuse on the elder or dependent adult. Because the evidence in this case does not indicate that defendant had the kind of "special relationship" with the individuals alleged to have directly abused the elder victim that would give rise to a duty on her part to control their conduct, she was improperly charged with a violation of section 368(a). ***

Section 368(a) purportedly reaches two categories of offenders: (1) *any person* who willfully causes or permits an elder to suffer, or who directly inflicts, unjustifiable pain or mental suffering on any elder, and (2) the elder's *caretaker or custodian* who willfully causes or permits injury to his or her charge, or who willfully causes or permits the elder to be placed in a dangerous situation. The statute may be applied to [active] assaultive conduct, as well as passive forms of abuse, such as extreme neglect. ***

Defendant here was charged *** with willfully *permitting* her elder father to suffer the infliction of unjustifiable pain and mental suffering. It was thus her *failure to act*, i.e., her failure to prevent the infliction of abuse on her father, that created the potential for her criminal liability under the statute. **[When] an individual's criminal liability is based on the *failure* to act, it is well established that he or she must first be under an existing legal duty to take action.** ***

Defendant claims that the statute is unconstitutionally vague (in violation of the Fourteenth Amendment to the United States Constitution) because it [imposes a legal duty to prevent the infliction of abuse on an elder on those] who might not reasonably know they have such a duty. ***

[We reject the argument] that the statute itself imposes a blanket duty on everyone to prevent the abuse of any elder. The wide net cast by a statutory interpretation imposing such a duty on every person is apparent when we consider that it would extend the potential for criminal liability to, for example, a delivery person who, having entered a private home, notices an elder in a disheveled or disoriented state and purposefully fails to intervene. ***

[Since the first report on elder abuse by the House of Representatives in 1981, the subject has received much congressional attention and national publicity.] California lawmakers responded to the newly documented evidence of elder abuse in 1982 with legislation recognizing "that dependent adults may be subject to abuse, neglect, or abandonment and that this state has a responsibility to protect such persons." ***

[Legislators modeled the elder abuse law on existing child abuse statutes because] similar to children, dependent adults could neither speak for, nor protect, themselves. [Improvements] in geriatric medicine had resulted in a growing number of older persons who cannot properly care for themselves. [Dependent adults were] analogous to . . . children, in that the disabilities of age or a physical or mental condition may make them as helpless at the hands of a caretaking adult as is a small child.

In some respects, their position may be even worse than a child's because they are likely to understand fully what is happening, yet lack sufficient control of their circumstances to be able to do anything about it." ***

[Section 368(a) was enacted] to protect the members of a vulnerable class from abusive situations in which serious injury or death is likely to occur. [This law] fails to provide adequate notice as to the class of persons who may be under an affirmative duty to prevent the infliction of abuse.***

*** Before declaring a statute void for vagueness [we must] determine whether its validity can be preserved by "giv[ing] specific content to terms that might otherwise be unconstitutionally vague." [We] cannot invalidate a statute as unconstitutionally vague if "any reasonable and practical construction can be given to its language." ***

[The] constitutionally offensive portion of the statute is indeed susceptible of a clarifying construction. [The Court found a "duty to control" can form if "one who takes charge of a third person."] From this it follows that one (the defendant/daughter) will be *criminally* liable for the abusive conduct of another [the son's in the house watching over the father] only if he or she has the *ability* to control such conduct. ***

Conclusion

Based on their status as Robert Heitzman's caretakers, felony criminal liability was properly imposed on Richard, Sr., and Jerry pursuant to section 368(a). ***

[Given] defendant's failure to intercede on her father's behalf under the egregious circumstances presented here, we can well understand the prosecution's decision to charge defendant under section 368(a). Because the People presented no evidence tending to show that defendant had a *legal duty* to control the conduct of either of her brothers, however, we * reinstate the trial court's order dismissing the charges against defendant.[61]**

Florida Elder Abuse Statutes

Fla. Stat. § 784.08: Assault or battery on persons 65 years of age or older; reclassification of offenses; minimum sentence

(1) A person who is convicted of an aggravated assault or aggravated battery upon a person 65 years of age or older shall be sentenced to a minimum term of imprisonment of 3 years and fined not more than $10,000 and shall also be ordered by the sentencing judge to make restitution to the victim of such offense and to perform up to 500 hours of community service work. Restitution and community service work shall be in addition to any fine or sentence which may be imposed and shall not be in lieu thereof.

(2) Whenever a person is charged with committing an assault or aggravated assault or a battery or aggravated battery upon a person 65 years of age or older, regardless of whether he or she knows or has reason to know the age of the victim, the offense for which the person is charged shall be reclassified as follows:

(a) In the case of aggravated battery, from a felony of the second degree to a felony of the first degree.

(b) In the case of aggravated assault, from a felony of the third degree to a felony of the second degree.

(c) In the case of battery, from a misdemeanor of the first degree to a felony of the third degree.

(d) In the case of assault, from a misdemeanor of the second degree to a misdemeanor of the first degree.

61. Reprinted with the permission of LexisNexis.

(3) Notwithstanding the provisions of s. 948.01, adjudication of guilt or imposition of sentence shall not be suspended, deferred, or withheld.

Florida Statute § 825.103: Exploitation of an elderly person or disabled adult; penalties

(1) "Exploitation of an elderly person or disabled adult" means:

(a) Knowingly, by deception or intimidation, obtaining or using, or endeavoring to obtain or use, an elderly person's or disabled adult's funds, assets, or property with the intent to temporarily or permanently deprive the elderly person or disabled adult of the use, benefit, or possession of the funds, assets, or property, or to benefit someone other than the elderly person or disabled adult, by a person who:

    1. Stands in a position of trust and confidence with the elderly person or disabled adult; or

    2. Has a business relationship with the elderly person or disabled adult;

(b) Obtaining or using, endeavoring to obtain or use, or conspiring with another to obtain or use an elderly person's or disabled adult's funds, assets, or property with the intent to temporarily or permanently deprive the elderly person or disabled adult of the use, benefit, or possession of the funds, assets, or property, or to benefit someone other than the elderly person or disabled adult, by a person who knows or reasonably should know that the elderly person or disabled adult lacks the capacity to consent; or

(c) Breach of a fiduciary duty to an elderly person or disabled adult by the person's guardian or agent under a power of attorney which results in an unauthorized appropriation, sale, or transfer of property.

Florida recognizes that elder victims do not have the luxury of time to pursue justice. Thus, state law allows to advance a trial date in consideration of the health of the victim, as seen below.

Florida Statute § 825.106: Criminal actions involving elderly persons or disabled adults; speedy trial

In a criminal action in which an elderly person or disabled adult is a victim, the state may move the court to advance the trial on the docket. The presiding judge, after consideration of the age and health of the victim, may advance the trial on the docket. The motion may be filed and served with the information or charges or at any time thereafter.[62]

California Elder Abuse Statutes

Cal Pen Code § 368 Crimes against elders and dependent adults; Legislative findings; Infliction of pain, injury or endangerment; Theft, embezzlement, forgery, fraud, or identity theft; False imprisonment

(a) The Legislature finds and declares that crimes against elders and dependent adults are deserving of special consideration and protection, not unlike the special protections provided for minor children, because elders and dependent adults may be confused, on various medications, mentally or physically impaired, or incompetent, and therefore less able to protect themselves, to understand or report criminal conduct, or to testify in court proceedings on their own behalf.

(b)

---

62. Reprinted with the permission of LexisNexis.

(1) Any person who knows or reasonably should know that a person is an elder or dependent adult and who, under circumstances or conditions likely to produce great bodily harm or death, willfully causes or permits any elder or dependent adult to suffer, or inflicts thereon unjustifiable physical pain or mental suffering, or having the care or custody of any elder or dependent adult, willfully causes or permits the person or health of the elder or dependent adult to be injured, or willfully causes or permits the elder or dependent adult to be placed in a situation in which his or her person or health is endangered, is punishable by imprisonment in a county jail not exceeding one year, or by a fine not to exceed six thousand dollars ($6,000), or by both that fine and imprisonment, or by imprisonment in the state prison for two, three, or four years.

(2) If in the commission of an offense described in paragraph (1), the victim suffers great bodily injury, as defined in Section 12022.7, the defendant shall receive an additional term in the state prison as follows:

(A) Three years if the victim is under 70 years of age.

(B) Five years if the victim is 70 years of age or older.

(3) If in the commission of an offense described in paragraph (1), the defendant proximately causes the death of the victim, the defendant shall receive an additional term in the state prison as follows:

(A) Five years if the victim is under 70 years of age.

(B) Seven years if the victim is 70 years of age or older.[63]

Want to Help Prevent Elder Abuse?

The National Center on Elder Abuse at the Department of Health and Human Services provides the following recommendations:

"Response and prevention strategies for elder and vulnerable adult abuse are numerous and varied. We've summarized and collected information about some of the most well-known interventions and response systems. It's important to remember that **anyone** can help at some level.

- Learn when and how to report abuse
- Get help for commonly seen "suspicious situations" involving possible abuse of elders and adults with disabilities
- Learn about the agencies and organizations that respond to reports of abuse
- Learn what some communities and multidisciplinary teams are doing to prevent abuse from occurring
- Explore how the many fields and organizations that serve elders and adults with disabilities may play a role in abuse intervention and prevention"

For this and more information, visit:

https://ncea.acl.gov/suspectabuse/index.html

---

63. From *Deering's California Codes Annotated.* Copyright © 2014 by Matthew Bender & Company, Inc., a member of the LexisNexis Group. Reprinted with the permission of LexisNexis.

DISCUSSION QUESTIONS

1. What or who is the "person" in crimes against the person?

2. What is battery and how does it differ from assault?

3. What are the elements of assault? What are the two definitions of assault recognized in some jurisdictions?

4. What is mayhem, why was it created at common law, and how does it differ from simple assault?

5. What must be done to commit the crime of torture?

6. How do the crimes of false imprisonment and kidnapping differ?

7. What are the actus reus elements and mens rea elements of stalking?

8. Can a person commit criminal threats or terrorist threats just by speaking words? What else, if anything, is required to commit this crime?

9. Does the passage and prosecution of hate crime legislation violate the protections provided in the First Amendment right of free speech? Why or why not?

10. What is the similarity between the victims of child abuse and elder abuse?

WEB LINKS

1. Massachusetts's Court System has created a definition for "Assault and Battery by Means of a Dangerous Weapon G.L. c. 265, § 15A" that can be viewed at: http://www.mass.gov/courts/docs/courts-and-judges/courts/district-court/jury-instructions-criminal/6000-9999/6300-assault-and-battery-by-means-of-a-dangerous-weapon.pdf

2. Massachusetts's Court System has created a jury instruction for a crime it recognizes as "Assault and Battery on a Pregnant Woman" at Instruction 6.200 at: http://www.mass.gov/courts/docs/courts-and-judges/courts/district-court/jury-instructions-criminal/6000-9999/6200-assault-and-battery-on-a-pregnant-woman.pdf

3. For statistics on "hate crime incidents" in New York state, visit: http://www.criminaljustice.ny.gov/crimnet/ojsa/stats.htm

4. For more information on elder abuse, visit the National Council on Aging at: https://www.ncoa.org/public-policy-action/elder-justice/elder-abuse-facts/

5. Deborah Ziff of *The Albuquerque Journal* reported on April 14, 2013, that "N.M. among worst in child abuse deaths." For full article visit: https://www.abqjournal.com/

CHAPTER VII

Crimes against the Person: Sex Crimes

Sexual Assault Awareness Demonstration at the University of Oregon

Sex crimes such as rape, spousal rape, and sodomy involve violent invasions of bodily integrity and therefore are categorized as crimes against the person. Unfortunately, these brutal crimes have existed for ages, as illustrated by the fact that rape and sodomy were defined as crimes long ago at common law.

213

A. RAPE

1. Common Law

Common law commentators were hardly forthcoming in seeking to help the victims of rape. Blackstone, in his *Commentaries,* Vol. IV, at 213, was reticent to discuss the elements of rape, noting that "As to the material facts requisite to be given in evidence and proved upon an indictment of rape, they are of such nature (that) they are highly improper to be publicly discussed, except only in a court of justice." While Blackstone acknowledged that a rape victim was "a competent witness," he suggested the following factors be consulted when assessing the victim's credibility:

> For instance, if the witness be of good fame (meaning reputation); if she presently discovered the offence (meaning that she made a prompt complaint), and made search for the offender; if the party accused feld for it; there and the like are concurring circumstances, which give greater probability to her evidence. But, on the other side, if she be of evil fame, and stands unsupported by others; if she concealed the injury for any considerable time after she had opportunity to complain; if the place, where the fact was alleged to be committed, was where it was possible she might have heard, and she made no outcry; there and the like circumstances carry a strong, but not conclusive presumption that her testimony is false or feigned.

Blackstone declared, "**rape is a most detestable crime, and therefore ought severely and impartially to be punished with death**; but it must be remembered, that it is an accusation easy to be made, hard to be proved, but harder to be defended by the party accused, though innocent."

VIDEO: A Prosecutor Talks about Proving a Sexual Assault Case

WARNING: POTENTIALLY DISTURBING VIDEO. Deputy Prosecutor Mike Perry discussed the practical problems that occur when there is a delay in reporting a sexual assault at:

https://www.youtube.com/watch?v=n-krbFlNcBQ

---

2. Current Law

California Penal Code § 261: Rape: "Duress"; "Menace"

(a) Rape is an act of sexual intercourse accomplished with a person not the spouse of the perpetrator, under any of the following circumstances:

(1) Where a person is incapable, because of a mental disorder or developmental or physical disability, of giving legal consent, and this is known or reasonably should be known to the person committing the act. [Even if a conservatorship exists,] the prosecuting attorney shall prove, as an element of the crime, that a mental disorder or developmental or physical disability rendered the alleged victim incapable of giving consent.

(2) Where it is accomplished against a person's will by means of force, violence, duress, menace, or fear of immediate and unlawful bodily injury on the person or another.

(3) Where a person is prevented from resisting by any intoxicating or anesthetic substance, or any controlled substance, and this condition was known, or reasonably should have been known by the accused.

(4) Where a person is at the time unconscious of the nature of the act, and this is known to the accused. As used in this paragraph, "unconscious of the nature of the act" means incapable of resisting because the victim meets any one of the following conditions:

(A) Was unconscious or asleep.

(B) Was not aware, knowing, perceiving, or cognizant that the act occurred.

(C) Was not aware, knowing, perceiving, or cognizant of the essential characteristics of the act due to the perpetrator's fraud in fact.

(D) Was not aware, knowing, perceiving, or cognizant of the essential characteristics of the act due to the perpetrator's fraudulent representation that the sexual penetration served a professional purpose when it served no professional purpose.

(5) Where a person submits under the belief that the person committing the act is someone known to the victim other than the accused, and this belief is induced by any artifice, pretense, or concealment practiced by the accused, with intent to induce the belief.

(6) Where the act is accomplished against the victim's will by threatening to retaliate in the future against the victim or any other person, and there is a reasonable possibility that the perpetrator will execute the threat. As used in this paragraph, "threatening to retaliate" means a threat to kidnap or falsely imprison, or to inflict extreme pain, serious bodily injury, or death.

(7) Where the act is accomplished against the victim's will by threatening to use the authority of a public official to incarcerate, arrest, or deport the victim or another, and the victim has a reasonable belief that the perpetrator is a public official. As used in this paragraph, "public official" means a person employed by a governmental agency who has the authority, as part of that position, to incarcerate, arrest, or deport another. The perpetrator does not actually have to be a public official.

(b) As used in this section, "duress" means a direct or implied threat of force, violence, danger, or retribution sufficient to coerce a reasonable person of ordinary susceptibilities to perform an act which otherwise would not have been performed, or acquiesce in an act to which one otherwise would not have submitted. The total circumstances, including the age of the victim, and his or her relationship to the defendant, are factors to consider in appraising the existence of duress.

(c) As used in this section, "menace" means any threat, declaration, or act which shows an intention to inflict an injury upon another.[64]

Model Penal Code § 213.1: Rape

(1) *Rape.* A male who has sexual intercourse with a female not his wife is guilty of rape if:

    (a) he compels her to submit by force or by threat of imminent death, serious bodily injury, extreme pain or kidnapping, to be inflicted on anyone; or

    (b) he has substantially impaired her power to appraise or control her conduct by administering or employing without her knowledge drugs, intoxicants or other means for the purpose of preventing resistance; or

    (c) the female is unconscious; or

    (d) the female is less than 10 years old.[65]

---

64. From *Deering's California Codes Annotated.* Copyright © 2014 by Matthew Bender & Company, Inc., a member of the LexisNexis Group. Reprinted with the permission of LexisNexis.

65. From *The Model Penal Code* by the American Law Institute. Copyright © 1962 by the American Law Institute. Used by permission.

What is required to fulfill the element of "sexual intercourse"?

California Penal Code § 263: Penetration

The essential guilt of rape consists in the outrage to the person and feelings of the victim of the rape. Any sexual penetration, however slight, is sufficient to complete the crime.

The Court of Appeal in *People v. Minkowski* (1962) 204 Cal. App.2d 832, in discussing penetration, has explained,

> While penetration is an essential ingredient of the offense ["**any sexual penetration, however slight, is sufficient to complete the crime**."] Penetration may be proved by circumstantial evidence.

In contrast, the Supreme Court of Ohio once required not only penetration but emission of semen in order to establish intercourse, as noted in *Williams v. State*, 14 Ohio 222 (1846):

> Rape is defined to be the having unlawful and carnal knowledge of a woman, by force and against her will. To constitute this carnal knowledge, there must be both penetration and emission; both these are necessary elements in the crime of rape. Hence, before an infant has arrived at the age of puberty, or before, by the physical laws of human nature, he can emit seed, he is incapable of committing the crime of rape.

Ohio has since expanded its definition of the sexual intercourse needed for rape. In *In Re Washington*, 662 N.E.2d 346 (1996), the Supreme Court of Ohio ruled, "A rule which requires proof of the capacity to emit a seed when there is proof of penetration by force against the victim's will is archaic and has no place in today's society." The Court of Appeals of Ohio, in *In Re Wilson*, 1988 WL 129176 (1988), when discussing "sexual conduct," noted, "Penetration, however slight, is sufficient to complete vaginal or anal intercourse."

What exactly is sexual intercourse "accomplished with a person"?

People v. Sellers (1988) 203 Cal. App.3d 1042 considered whether Robert Lloyd Sellers had actually performed intercourse with a "person." The defendant had appealed from a conviction of murder in the first degree, rape, and a "special circumstance allegation that the murder was committed while the defendant was engaged in the commission of the crime of rape." The court declared, "We find ourselves in the unfortunate position of having to reverse this conviction for a most heinous murder and remand for a new trial because the jury was improperly instructed on the law of rape."

Sellers, a security guard in the victim Anderson's apartment complex, climbed through the victim's bedroom window. "Defendant beat Anderson savagely over her head and shoulders with his baton or nightstick. He also strangled her, probably with the Sam Browne belt he was wearing." After killing her, Sellers,

> carried her into the bathroom and tried to clean her off in the sink, but it was too small. He took her clothes off and put her in the shower. He turned down the covers on the bed, put the body back on the bed, and covered the face. He had intercourse with the body, got dressed and left through the front door, locking it after him.

The *Sellers* court concluded:

> [That PC 261 rape requires a live victim. Rape is] "an act of sexual intercourse accomplished with *a person* not the spouse of the perpetrator." [For PC 261(2), intercourse "is accomplished against a *person's will* by means of force, violence, or fear of immediate and unlawful bodily injury on the person or another."] **Rape must be accomplished with a person, not a dead body**. It must be accomplished against a person's will. A dead body cannot consent to or protest a rape, nor can it be in fear of immediate and unlawful bodily injury. [PC 263 provides, "the essential guilt of rape consists in the outrage to the person and feelings of the victim of the rape."] A dead body has no feelings of outrage.

The court reversed the conviction and remanded the case back to the trial court.[66]

TIPS FOR SUCCESS FOR FUTURE LAW ENFORCEMENT

Background Investigations

Public safety positions, by their very nature, involve a loss of a certain amount of privacy. Applicants providing information for background investigators should avoid reading questions too narrowly in an effort to hide damaging information. Here, omissions could be seen as dishonesty. Further, you should resolve to tell the truth before even sitting for the polygraph. Departments have been known to share failed polygraph results with other departments.

a) Rape by Fear

Since **rape** can be committed by use of **"fear of immediate and unlawful bodily injury,"** courts have had to define what might seem obvious—**the meaning of "fear."** As seen in the case below, defining fear can be a more nuanced and complicated endeavor than one might imagine.

LEGAL ANALYSIS

People v. Iniguez
7 Cal.4th 847 (1994).
Justice Arabian delivered the opinion for the California Supreme Court.

Facts

[On the eve of her wedding,] 22-year-old Mercy P. arrived at the home of Sandra S., a close family friend whom Mercy had known for at least 12 years and considered an aunt. Sandra had sewn Mercy's wedding dress, and was to stand in at the wedding the next day for Mercy's mother. [That evening, Mercy met defendant, Hector Guillermo Iniguez, Sandra's fiancé, for the first time.]

---

66. Reprinted with the permission of LexisNexis.

Around 11:30 p.m., Mercy went to bed in the living room. She slept on top of her sleeping bag. She was wearing pants with an attached skirt, and a shirt. [Mercy was awakened around 1:30 a.m.] when she heard some movements behind her. She was lying on her stomach, and saw defendant, who was naked, approach her from behind. Without saying anything, defendant pulled down her pants, fondled her buttocks, and inserted his penis inside her. Mercy weighed 105 pounds. Defendant weighed approximately 205 pounds. Mercy "was afraid, so I just laid there" [without trying to resist or escape]. Less than a minute later, defendant ejaculated, got off her, and walked back to the bedroom. Mercy had not consented to any sexual contact.

[Mercy had not resisted defendant's sexual assault because, "She knew that the man had been drinking and he was a complete stranger to her. She panicked and froze. Fearing violence, she decided just to lay still, wait until it was over with and then get out of the house as quickly as she could.]

Mercy immediately telephoned her fiancé Gary and left a message for him. She then telephoned her best friend Pam, who testified that Mercy was so distraught she was barely comprehensible. Mercy asked Pam to pick her up, grabbed her purse and shoes, and ran out of the apartment, [hiding in the bushes outside the house for a half hour because she was terrified defendant would look for her. Gary called the police.]

The following day, Mercy and Gary married. *** Neither Sandra nor defendant participated in the wedding. [Police arrested the defendant the same day.]

[A psychologist, testifying as an expert on "rape trauma syndrome," stated that victims respond in a variety of ways to the trauma of being raped.] Some try to flee, and others are paralyzed by fear. This latter response he termed "frozen fright."

Defendant conceded at trial that the sexual intercourse was nonconsensual, [but argued that the element of force or fear was absent. The defendant thought he could get away with it and "his judgment flew out the window." Nothing indicated] "using fear ever entered his mind. What he was doing was taking advantage, in a drunken way, of a situation where somebody appeared to be out of it."

The jury was instructed on both rape *** and sexual battery. [Sexual battery is defined [in part in PC section 243.4(a):]

"Any person who touches an intimate part of another person while that person is unlawfully restrained by the accused or an accomplice, and if the touching is against the will of the person touched and is for the purpose of sexual arousal, sexual gratification, or sexual abuse, is guilty of sexual battery.]

The jury found defendant guilty of rape. [He was sentenced to six years in prison.]

Issue

Whether there was sufficient evidence that the intercourse was without consent for purposes of PC 261 rape, even though the victim did not resist.

Rule and Analysis

[The Court of Appeal reversed defendant's rape conviction, finding the evidence of force or fear of immediate and unlawful bodily injury to be insufficient. We reverse the Court of Appeal.]

Prior to 1980, [a rape victim was required to either resist or be prevented from resisting because of threats. In 1980, PC 261 was amended] to eliminate both the resistance requirement. ***

["Studies have shown] that while some women respond to sexual assault with active resistance, others 'freeze,'" and "become helpless from panic and numbing fear." "[**The Legislature has made the decision whether a sexual assault should be resisted a personal choice.**"] "By removing resistance as a prerequisite to a rape conviction, the Legislature has brought the law of rape into conformity with other crimes such as robbery, kidnapping and assault, which require force, fear, and nonconsent. *** In these crimes, the law does not expect falsity from the complainant who alleges their commission and thus demand resistance as a corroboration and predicate to conviction." ***

[Section 261(a)(2) currently provides:

"(a) Rape is an act of sexual intercourse accomplished with a person not the spouse of the perpetrator, under any of the following circumstances:

"(2) Where it is accomplished against a person's will by means of force, violence, duress, menace, or fear of immediate and unlawful bodily injury on the person or another."]

[The 1980 amendment's deletion of the resistance language changed] the purpose of evidence of fear of immediate and unlawful injury. Prior to 1980, evidence of fear was directly linked to resistance; the prosecution was required to demonstrate that a person's *resistance* had been overcome by force, or that a person was prevented from resisting by threats of great and immediate bodily harm. *** As a result of the amendments, evidence of fear is now directly linked to the overbearing of a victim's will; the prosecution is required to demonstrate that the act of sexual intercourse was accomplished against the person's *will* by means of force, violence, or fear of immediate and unlawful bodily injury.

[Even a complainant's unreasonable fear of immediate and unlawful bodily injury can be enough to sustain a rape conviction], "if the accused knowingly takes advantage of that fear in order to accomplish sexual intercourse." [The trier of fact should look at both the acts of the alleged attacker and the response of the alleged victim to measure consent.]

[**The element of fear of immediate and unlawful bodily injury has two parts, one subjective and one objective.** The **subjective part** asks **whether a victim genuinely felt a fear sufficient to induce her to submit to sexual intercourse against her will**. To satisfy this part, the seriousness of physical force inducing fear is not relevant. It may consist in the taking of indecent liberties or of embracing and kissing her against her will].

[The **prosecution must also satisfy the objective part**,] which asks **whether the victim's fear was reasonable under the circumstances, or, if unreasonable, whether the perpetrator knew of the victim's subjective fear and took advantage of it. [We] conclude that the evidence that the sexual intercourse was accomplished against Mercy's will by means of fear of immediate and unlawful bodily injury was sufficient to support the verdict.** *** First, there was substantial evidence that Mercy genuinely feared immediate and unlawful bodily injury. Mercy testified that she froze because she was afraid, and the investigating police officer testified that she told him she did not move because she feared defendant would do something violent.

"Fear" may be inferred from the circumstances of a case. [Immediately] after the attack, Mercy was so distraught her friend Pam could barely understand her. Mercy hid in the bushes outside the house waiting for Pam to pick her up because she was terrified defendant would find her; she subsequently asked Pam if the word "rape" was written on her forehead, and had to be dissuaded from bathing prior to going to the hospital.

[There was also substantial evidence that Mercy's fear of immediate and unlawful bodily injury was reasonable.] Defendant, who weighed twice as much as Mercy, accosted her while she slept in the home of a close friend, thus violating the victim's enhanced level of security and privacy. [A person inside a private home, whether their own or that of an acquaintance, feels a sense of privacy and security not felt when outside, providing an attacker with the advantages of shock and surprise which may incapacitate the victims]. Defendant, who was naked, then removed Mercy's pants, fondled her buttocks, and inserted his penis into her vagina for approximately one minute, without warning, without her consent, and without a reasonable belief of consent. Any man or woman awakening to find himself or herself in this situation could reasonably react with fear of immediate and unlawful bodily injury. Sudden, unconsented-to groping, disrobing, and ensuing sexual intercourse while one appears to lie sleeping is an appalling and intolerable invasion of one's personal autonomy that, in and of itself, would reasonably cause one to react with fear. ***

The Court of Appeal's suggestion that Mercy could have stopped the sexual assault by screaming and thus eliciting Sandra S.'s help, disregards [the elimination of the resistance requirement.] It effectively guarantees an attacker freedom to intimidate his victim and exploit any resulting reasonable fear so long as she neither struggles nor cries out. *** **"The law has outgrown the resistance concept; a person demanding sexual favors can no longer rely on a position of strength which draws no physical or verbal protest."** *** **There is no requirement that the victim say, "I am afraid, please stop," when it is the defendant who has created the circumstances that have so paralyzed the victim in fear and thereby submission.** ***

Conclusion

The jury could reasonably have concluded that under [these circumstances,] instigated and choreographed by defendant, created a situation in which Mercy genuinely and reasonably responded with fear of immediate and unlawful bodily injury, and that such fear allowed him to accomplish sexual intercourse with Mercy against her will. ***

The judgment of the Court of Appeal is reversed.[67]

VIDEO: An Explanation of Rape Kits

WARNING: POTENTIALLY DISTURBING VIDEO. Salt Lake City Police Chief Chris Burbank discusses his department's "Code R Kits Project" at:

https://www.youtube.com/watch?v=OvsDyFaDlE0

California Penal Code § 261.6: "Consent"; Effect of current or previous relationship

In prosecutions under Section 261, 262, 286, 288a, or 289, in which consent is at issue, "consent" shall be defined to mean positive cooperation in act or attitude pursuant to an exercise of free will. The person must act freely and voluntarily and have knowledge of the nature of the act or transaction involved.

A current or previous dating or marital relationship shall not be sufficient to constitute consent where consent is at issue in a prosecution under Section 261, 262, 286, 288a, or 289.

USA Gymnastics Doctor Larry Nassar Pleaded Guilty to Molesting Gymnasts

Nicole Chavez and Eric Levenson reported for *CNN* in their November 22, 2017, article, "Ex-USA Gymnastics doctor apologizes, pleads guilty to criminal sexual conduct," that Larry Nassar, who used

---

67. Reprinted with the permission of LexisNexis.

to be the USA Gymnastics doctor, had pleaded guilty to seven counts of sexually abusing underage females. The article can be viewed at:

http://www.cnn.com/2017/11/22/us/us-gymnastics-doctor-plea-hearing/index.html

Mark Osborne, in his October 18, 2017, *ABC News* article, "Olympic gymnast McKayla Maroney describes years of alleged abuse by team doctor," reported that McKayla Maroney, a member of the USA Olympic gymnast team, revealed Nassar's assault of her. This article can be seen at:

http://abcnews.go.com/US/olympic-gymnast-mckayla-maroney-shares-allegations-sexual-assault/story?id=50554470

Shouldn't "No" Mean "No"?

Commonwealth v. Berkowitz, 641 A.2d 1161 (1994) made a ruling regarding rape that was so controversial that it caused a change in state legislation. Rosemary J. Scalo, in her article, "What Does 'No' Mean in Pennsylvania? The Pennsylvania Supreme Court's Interpretation of Rape and the Effectiveness of the Legislature's Response," 40 Vill. L. Rev. 193, 195–96 (1995), noted:

Quite simply, 'No' means 'No.'

© Amir Ridhwan/Shutterstock.com

> [The Pennsylvania Supreme Court, in *Commonwealth v. Berkowitz*, held] that a woman is not raped when a man penetrates her despite her repeated and clearly-expressed lack of consent. ***

> **As a result of public discontent with the *Berkowitz* court's holding and as part of a broad attempt to reform Pennsylvania's outdated rape law, the Pennsylvania General Assembly has enacted a law that purports to remedy the court's decision**. [While this statute is hailed] as the **"'no means no' provision,"** a critical review of the statute suggests imperfections and unresolved issues that make its impact on rape and the Berkowitz decision dubious.

Berkowitz's facts are as follows:

> [The victim, a college student, entered an unlocked dorm room looking for a friend. The friend's roommate, the appellant, was lying on his bed. He asked the victim to "hang out for a while" and she agreed. The victim declined the appellant's request for a back rub, explaining that she did not "trust" him. When he asked her to sit on his bed, she instead sat on the floor. The appellant got down on the floor, pushed the victim back and kissed her. When the victim said, "Look, I gotta go. I'm going to meet my boyfriend," the appellant lifted up her shirt and bra and began fondling her. The victim then said "no." The appellant then "undid his pants," prevented the victim from moving, and, despite her still saying "no," tried to put his penis in her mouth. Although the victim did not physically resist, she continued to protest, saying "No, I gotta go, let me go." Disregarding the victim's continual complaints that she "had to go," appellant locked the door, placed the victim on the bed,

straddled her, and removed her sweatpants and underwear.] The victim did not physically resist in any way while on the bed because appellant was on top of her, and she "couldn't like go anywhere." *** She did not scream out at anytime because, "[i]t was like a dream was happening or something." ***

Appellant then used one of his hands to "guide" his penis *** into her vagina. [When] appellant was inside her, the victim began saying "no, no to him softly in a moaning kind of way . . . because it was just so scary." *** After about thirty seconds, appellant pulled out his penis and ejaculated onto the victim's stomach. ***

Immediately thereafter, appellant got off the victim and said, "Wow, I guess we just got carried away." *** To this the victim retorted, "No, we didn't get carried away, you got carried away." *** The victim then quickly dressed, grabbed her school books and raced downstairs to her boyfriend who was by then waiting for her in the lounge.

Once there, the victim began crying. Her boyfriend and she went up to his dorm room where, after watching the victim clean off appellant's semen from her stomach, he called the police.

[The victim had previously attended a school seminar entitled, "Does 'no' sometimes means 'yes'?" The lecturer at this seminar had discussed the average length and circumference of human penises. During a phone conversation, the victim had asked appellant the size of his penis. When the appellant suggested that the victim "come over and find out," she declined.]

Appellant [testified that the penis size discussion led him to suspect that the victim wanted to pursue a sexual relationship with him.] He believed that his suspicions were confirmed when she came by his room. He] conceded that she continually whispered "no's," but claimed that she did so while "amorously . . . passionately" moaning. *** When asked why he locked the door, he explained that "that's not something you want somebody to just walk in on you [doing." The appellant viewed these and other actions providing consent to intercourse.]

Berkowitz aimed to answer what "degree of force [is] necessary to prove the 'forcible compulsion' element of the crime of rape." Pennsylvania defined rape as:

A person commits a felony of the first degree when he engages in sexual intercourse with another person not one's spouse:

(1) by forcible compulsion;
(2) by threat of forcible compulsion that would prevent resistance by a person of reasonable resolution;
(3) who is unconscious; or
(4) who is so mentally deranged or deficient that such person is incapable of consent.

The *Berkowitz* court then reasoned as follows:

The victim of a rape need not resist. "The force necessary [for rape] need only be such as to establish lack of consent and to induce the [victim] to submit without additional resistance. [The amount of force required to constitute rape depends on the facts and particular circumstance of the case."]

[The] complainant's testimony is devoid of any statement which clearly or adequately describes the use of force or the threat of force against her. In response to defense counsel's question, "Is it possible that [when Appellee lifted your bra and shirt] you took no physical action to discourage him," the complainant replied, "It's possible." When asked, "Is it possible that [Appellee] was not making any physical contact with you . . . aside from attempting to untie the knot [in the drawstrings of complainant's sweatpants]," she answered, "It's possible." She testified that "He put me down on the bed. It was kind of like—He didn't throw me on the bed. It's hard to explain. It was kind of like a push but not—I can't explain what I'm trying to say." *** She agreed that Appellee's hands were not restraining her in any manner during the actual penetration, and that the weight of his body on top of her was the only force applied. She testified that at no time did Appellee verbally threaten her. The complainant did testify that she sought to leave the room, and said "no" throughout the encounter. [The complainant] never attempted to go to the door or unlock it.

[The fact that complainant said "no" throughout the encounter, is relevant to the issue of consent, not to the issue of force. Where] there is a lack of consent, but no showing of either physical force, a threat of physical force, or psychological coercion, the "forcible compulsion" requirement [is not met.]

(T)he complainant's testimony simply fails to establish that the Appellee forcibly compelled her to engage in sexual intercourse as required. [Even] if all of the complainant's testimony was believed, the jury, as a matter of law, could not have found Appellee guilty of rape. [We] hold that the Superior Court did not err in reversing Appellee's conviction of rape. ***

Accordingly, the order of the Superior Court reversing the rape conviction is affirmed. ***[68]

Biography—Police

William Bratton

- Boston Police Commissioner (1992–1993), New York City Police Commissioner (1994–1996 & 2014–2016), and Los Angeles Police Chief (2002–2009). An in-depth look into Chief Bratton's life is offered by the *New York Times* by Al Baker and J. David Goodman in their July 25, 2016 article, "Bratton, Who Shaped Era in Policing, Tries to Navigate a Racial Divide," at https://www.nytimes.com/2016/07/26/nyregion/william-bratton-new-york-city-police-commissioner.html
- Started as a Boston PD patrol officer in 1970.
- Was arguably responsible for a dramatic decrease in crime while New York Police Commissioner.
- When in New York, applied the **"Broken Windows" theory of policing,** which posits that crime is most effectively limited when police, in pursuit of low-level crimes, prevent more serious crime from occurring.

SEMAPHORE ALPHABET

© Denis Dubrovin/Shutterstock.com

Those wishing to engage in intercourse carry a burden of establishing clear communication.

---

68. Reprinted with the permission of LexisNexis.

- Was commissioner when Eric Garner died while New York police had him in a chokehold, one of the incidents prompting the Black Lives Matter movement.
- According to LAPDonline.org, at http://www.lapdonline.org/history_of_the_lapd/content_basic_view/1120, Bratton "led the development of COMPSTAT," which was a "command accountability metric system" that combined "computer-mapping technology" with "timely crime analysis to target emerging crime patterns and coordinate police response."
- While LA Police Chief, oversaw the implementation of the consent decree to fight racial bias in the LAPD.
- U.S. Attorney, Preet Bharara, said of Bratton, "Over a long career, on both coasts, no one has done more for policing and public safety in America's largest cities than Bill Bratton." According to Vera Haller, William Bratton, stepping down as New York police commissioner, says, "I wish I had more time," *Los Angeles Times*, August 2, 2016, http://www.latimes.com/nation/la-na-bratton-resigns-20160802-snap-story.html.

b)   Rape of an Intoxicated Person

LEGAL ANALYSIS

People v. Braslaw
233 Cal.App.4th 1239 (2015).
Justice Banke delivered the opinion for the California Court of Appeal.

Facts

Defendant and Jane Doe were classmates at a vocational school in St. Helena.

[Doe and her friend,] M.H., attended a party at defendant's house. Doe became "really drunk." One moment she was hanging out with friends; the next thing she recalled was being unclothed in a shower.

[While playing a drinking game, Doe became so intoxicated that] M.H.'s boyfriend took Doe upstairs so she could sleep. Doe then vomited, and M.H., the boyfriend, and defendant assisted with cleanup. M.H. and her boyfriend got Doe undressed and into the

© Cool Pictures/Shutterstock.com

shower. Doe *** was "completely gone"—just dead weight, not really aware of anything. Defendant was also drunk, but his level of intoxication was not comparable to Doe's, as defendant was coherent and functional.

While in the shower, Doe saw M.H. and the boyfriend leave the bathroom, and saw that defendant had entered. Defendant, also unclothed, came into the shower and asked if it was "gonna be awkward." Doe recalled saying "no" and being confused about what defendant intended to do, but thought he might help her bathe. She remembered nothing else in detail about what happened in the shower. Afterwards, M.H. dressed Doe in a sweater, nothing more, and placed her in a spare trundle bed in the boyfriend's bedroom. Doe had no recollection of being dressed in the sweater or placed in the bed.

M.H. and her boyfriend then retired to his bed. Although the lights in the bedroom were out, M.H. saw defendant enter the bedroom and [go] onto Doe's bed. M.H. asked her boyfriend to get a condom. Overhearing, defendant asked, in what M.H. perceived as a joking tone, if he could have one too. The boyfriend got out of bed, asked if Doe and defendant were okay, and returned to bed with a condom. M.H. and her boyfriend began having sex when, "[a] short amount of time" later, M.H. heard Doe scream "no, no, no." M.H. got up and saw defendant "jump" back, heard him say something like "okay, okay, I'll stop," and saw him run out of the room.

Doe had no recollection of anything going on in the bedroom until "looking up" and seeing defendant "on top of me." He was "moving back and forth," and she felt his penis inside her vagina. She recalls "crying and just like—he left."

[Defendant was convicted of rape of an intoxicated person] and the trial court sentenced him to three years in state prison.

Issue

Whether the trial court should have instructed the jury a defendant is not guilty of rape of an intoxicated person if he reasonably believed the person had the capacity to consent.

Rule and Analysis

The trial court instructed the jury [with CALCRIM No. 1002 which provides the elements of rape of an intoxicated person:

(1) defendant had sexual intercourse with a person; (2) defendant and the person were not married; (3) the effects of intoxicants prevented the person from resisting; and (4) "defendant knew or reasonably should have known that the effect of an intoxicating substance prevented [his alleged victim] from resisting." An] intoxicating substance prevents resistance when it prevents the giving of legal consent— that is, "consent given freely and voluntarily by someone who knows the nature of the act involved." Over defendant's objection, the trial court omitted CALCRIM No. 1002's bracketed, optional portion,] which reads:

The defendant is not guilty of this crime if he actually and reasonably believed that the [alleged victim] was capable of consenting to sexual intercourse, even if that belief was wrong. The People have the burden of proving beyond a reasonable doubt that the defendant did not actually and reasonably believe that the [alleged victim] was capable of consenting. If the People have not met this burden, you must find the defendant not guilty. [The trial court found the evidence insufficient to support instructing the jury on defendant's reasonable-belief-in-the-capacity-to-consent theory.]

The trial court did not err in refusing to give the optional language of the instruction. The key evidence defendant marshals in support of his reasonable-belief-in-the-capacity-to-consent theory does not show a reasonable belief in Doe's *capacity* to consent.

Defendant [argued that his naked entry into the shower, his asking Doe if this is] "gonna be awkward," and her response of "no"] was sufficient for him to reasonably believe Doe was giving consent to intercourse sometime later that night.

Even apart from the fact such [an interpretation by the defendant] of the shower exchange is manifestly unreasonable, whether defendant believed Doe was consenting to intercourse sometime later in the evening is irrelevant if he did not also reasonably believe she was *capable of giving consent* to intercourse despite her intoxication. **It is a reasonable belief in the victim's capacity to consent, not the consent, that provides a defense to rape of an intoxicated person.** ["If] the victim is so unsound of mind that he or she is incapable of giving legal consent, the fact that he or she may have given actual consent does not prevent a conviction of rape." ["The] **actual consent of the victim is not a defense to a charge of rape by intoxication,** *a belief in the existence of such actual consent is irrelevant.*" ***

Even if there was an evidentiary basis for giving the additional language regarding actual and reasonable belief in the capacity to consent, the trial court's decision to omit it was not prejudicial error in light of the adequacy of the instructions it did give. [The jury was instructed] on the elements of the crime, including the fourth element, which requires proof the defendant *"knew, or reasonably should have known, that [the alleged victim] was unable to resist due to her intoxication."* ***

Conclusion

Had defendant wanted to argue * that he had a reasonable belief the victim could consent, he was free to do so. [The jury,] by finding the fourth element true, necessarily found any belief by defendant that the victim had capacity to consent was unreasonable. We *** reject defendant's claim the trial court prejudicially erred by not giving the full CALCRIM No. 1002 instruction.[69]**

VIDEO: Should Victims Report a Sexual Assault?

WARNING: POTENTIALLY DISTURBING VIDEO. The City of Madison Police Department explains the options after suffering sexual assault at:

https://www.youtube.com/watch?v=Oy3feXJeLjl

Alleged Rape by Intoxication: Bill Cosby is Put on Trial for Sexual Assault

CNN Entertainment reported on June 19, 2017, that, "more than 50 women have accused comedian Bill Cosby of sexual misconduct." This article, "Who are Cosby's accusers?" can be viewed at:

http://www.cnn.com/2014/12/13/showbiz/gallery/cosby-accusers/index.html

Further information is offered in a December 30, 2015, article by CNN reporters Eliott C. McLaughlin, Michael Martinez, and Ben Brumfield entitled "Bill Cosby facing litany of allegations," at:

http://www.cnn.com/2014/11/20/showbiz/bill-cosby-allegations-repercussions/index.html

As reported by Jia Tolentino on June 14, 2017, in her article for *The New Yorker*, "Bill Cosby's Defense and Its Twisted Argument About Consent," Bill Cosby has been tried for allegedly sexually assaulting Andrea Constand. The full article can be viewed at:

https://www.newyorker.com/culture/jia-tolentino/bill-cosbys-defense-and
-its-twisted-argument-about-consent

---

69. Reprinted from Westlaw, with permission of Thomson Reuters.

"Me Too" Suffering in a Culture Enabling Sexual Exploitation

The allegations that movie producer Harvey Weinstein has sexually harassed and abused women could serve as a wake-up call to the frequency and intensity of sexual violence in society in general. Several celebrities are hoping to raise awareness by initiating a Twitter campaign known as "Me too." *The New York Times* has reported extensively on this story. For an investigation of the larger issues in this matter, visit the October 16, 2017, *New York Times* article, "Harvey Weinstein's Fall Opens the Floodgates in Hollywood" at:

https://www.nytimes.com/2017/10/16/business/media/harvey-weinsteins-fall-opens-the-floodgates-in-hollywood.html

In the October 23, 2017, issue of *The New Yorker* magazine, Ronan Farrow reported that multiple women have accused Harvey Weinstein of sexual assault. The full article can be viewed by visiting:

https://www.newyorker.com/news/news-desk/from-aggressive-overtures-to-sexual-assault-harvey-weinsteins-accusers-tell-their-stories?mbid=social_twitter

Time's October 12, 2017, cover story, "How Do You Solve a Problem Like Harvey Weinstein?" written by Stephanie Zacharek, can be viewed at:

http://time.com/magazine/us/4979222/october-23rd-2017-vol-190-no-16-u-s/

c)   Rape by Fraud

When Does a Lie Destroy Consent and When Does It Not?

People v. Minkowski (1962) 204 Cal. App.2d 832 considered rape by fraud. The defendant, William Louis Minkowski, faced three charges of rape under Penal Code 261 (5) "[where the female] is at the time unconscious of the nature of the act, and this is known to the accused," for actions involving "three young women" referred to as "Miss X, Miss Y and Mrs. Z." The jury found the defendant guilty regarding Miss X and Mrs. Z. The defendant argued that the evidence failed to prove rape. The court rejected all of the defendant's arguments, as follows:

> The defendant was a physician with offices in Palo Alto, California. On January 7, 1961, Miss X, who was 16 years old, accompanied by her mother went to the defendant's office for the treatment of menstrual cramps. *** She went into the examination room, removed her clothing and put on a hospital gown. She and the defendant were the only persons in the room. He told her to lean over a table with her feet spread apart, giving as a reason that it was an easier position for the test. As she did so, the gown would slip off her shoulders. While she was in this position, the defendant used an instrument for a few seconds, and then something else. The first object was cold and "the second time it wasn't at all." The second object "didn't pinch like the first one did. It wasn't as uncomfortable." The second object "kept coming in and out" of her vagina; "[it] didn't go in and stay like the first one did." During the examination the defendant exercised her breasts, telling her it was necessary to help stimulate the glands. He used both hands doing this, while the second object was being inserted during the second part of the test. Right before the second part of the test

and at the end, she thought she heard a zipper. She also felt clothing against the back of her legs during the second part of the test. She estimated that the whole test would last about three minutes.

Miss X returned to the defendant's office for similar examinations on six or eight other occasions. *** After the tests he would tell her to go home and be sure to wash off because the test might cause an infection or she might be allergic to it in some way. ***

It was after the last examination that Miss X was sure that the defendant was using himself during the second part of the test.

Mrs. Z was 19 years of age at the time of the events involving the defendant. [She testified to activity similar to that experienced by Miss X. Miss Z. She] told the defendant she was financially unable to continue with the examination, whereupon he answered that it would not cost her anything as he was interested in seeing how her system changed from the last examination. He told her when she got home to douche immediately. *** It was not until the last visit that she suspected anything, [for on this visit she felt the defendant's penis inside of her and "knew that it was him and not an instrument."]

[The defendant admitted two officers] that he first used on [a victim] a proctoscope, an instrument usually used for rectal examinations, because it was shaped like a penis; that after he used the protoscope, he would insert his penis into the vaginal region. ***

[The prosecution an obstetrician/gynecologist, who testified that the position taken by the prosecuting witnesses was not the proper one. He] had never heard nor read that the exercise of a woman's breasts was a known medical treatment for menstrual cramps; and that the most commonly used instrument for vaginal examinations is a Gray speculum rather than a proctoscope.]

We are persuaded that *** the strangeness of the circumstances, the unusual behavior of the doctor, the method of his examination, and the differences between the two parts of the examination, the grand jury could have reasonably inferred *** that the defendant had accomplished an act of sexual penetration. [Mrs. Z's testimony similarly supported a reasonable inference of intercourse.]

We conclude *** the grand jury had "some rational ground for assuming the possibility that an offense [had] been committed. Judgment affirmed.][70]

The sexual intercourse in *Minkowski* constituted rape because the victims, trusting their doctor to be performing merely a medical procedure, were not conscious that the act committed upon them was sexual intercourse. They therefore did not and could not legally provide consent. Further, intercourse with Miss X, who was only sixteen, could constitute unlawful sexual intercourse with a minor legally unable to provide consent. This was a separate issue in the case.

What if the defendant has intercourse with a victim *who knows* the nature of the act, but, in fear from a diagnosis of a terrible disease, submits to intercourse as a "cure"? To protect victims in these situations, California's rape law now includes Penal Code section 261(4)(D), which covers a person who:

Was not aware, knowing, perceiving, or cognizant of the essential characteristics of the act due to the perpetrator's fraudulent representation *that the sexual penetration served a professional purpose when it served no professional purpose* (emphasis added).[71]

---

70. Reprinted with the permission of LexisNexis.
71. Reprinted with the permission of LexisNexis.

People v. Icke, 9 Cal.App.5th 138 (2017) involved a similar issue. A jury convicted Brian Steven Icke, a chiropractor, of PC Section 289(d)(4) sexual penetration by fraudulent misrepresentation of professional purpose. Icke had been treating his patient, Jane Doe, for injuries she received in a car accident. At Doe's last session, Icke locked the office door, led her to a back room and closed the door. Doe was not worried because she was with her doctor and so "was safe." After performing the usual parts of Doe's treatment, Icke pulled down her pants and underwear and massaged her thighs with Benzocaine. Icke then digitally penetrated Doe. She told Icke, "You're getting a little too close down there." When Icke stopped and apologized, Doe believed she was still under treatment and just wanted to complete the session. When Icke then inappropriately touched her breasts and spoke of his marital problems, she realized his behavior was not part of his medical treatment. "Doe felt very scared and told Icke she had to leave for a lunch appointment."

The court reviewing Icke's conviction listed the elements for sexual penetration: 1) An act of sexual penetration (by any foreign object or body part, except a sexual organ), 2) The victim unconsciousness of the nature of the act and, 3) the defendant's knowledge of the victim's unconsciousness of the nature of the act.

To be "unconscious of the nature of the act," the victim had to be unaware "of the essential characteristics of the act due to the perpetrator's fraudulent representation that the sexual penetration served a professional purpose when it served no professional purpose."

Section 289(d)(4) was enacted "to expand the circumstances under which a defendant may be prosecuted for fraudulently inducing a victim to consent to sexual conduct." The legislature "wanted to ensure that 'sex offenses committed by fraudulent inducement involving a purported professional purpose can be prosecuted,' even without proof of the victim's fear." Consent required "positive cooperation" in the "exercise of free will." **Consent can only occur when a person has "*knowledge of the nature of the act* or transaction involved." Consent is not legally given "where it is obtained through deceit."**

To fulfill "the statute's intent to criminalize sexual acts committed under the guise of professional services, it only makes sense to consider the totality of the defendant's conduct— not just his verbal statements—in determining whether he fraudulently represented the nature of his actions." The court declared, "[When] it comes to treating their patients, physicians occupy a position of implicit trust." Patients place confidence in doctors when allowing "access to the most intimate parts of the body."

Icke argued that the evidence or fraudulent misrepresentation was lacking because "he never claimed any medical necessity for touching her 'too close' to her vaginal area," and "never claimed that touching that area was part of any treatment." The court rejected this argument, reasoning,

> [The] representation need not be an express verbal statement; physical circumstances and a course of conduct may indirectly communicate a false professional purpose. [The] representation also need not be specific as to the sexual touching. Here, Icke never specifically told Doe that he touched her labia for a professional purpose, but the context in which the touching occurred—an appointment with Icke for the specific purpose of providing Doe a final chiropractic treatment session as the culmination of a several-month course of such treatment that included regular chiropractic massage—was sufficient to communicate a purported professional purpose for *all* of the touching Icke engaged in while Doe lay on a treatment table.

The court affirmed Icke's conviction.[72]

---

72. Reprinted from Westlaw, with permission of Thomson Reuters.

d)   Rape of the Developmentally Disabled

LEGAL ANALYSIS

People v. Vukodinovich
238 Cal.App.4th 166 (2015).
Presiding Justice Robie delivered the opinion for the California Court of Appeal.

Facts

Statistics show that 1 percent of the United States population has developmental disabilities. ***
Given this percentage, there has been a "movement toward the normalization and mainstreaming of
. . . individuals [with developmental disabilities]" in our society. *** "Greater integration into society
has created opportunities in education, vocational training, and recreational activities." *** It has
"also led to more opportunities to develop consensual intimate relationships that are often positive.
While opportunities for consensual relationships have increased, the sexual exploitation and abuse of
[individuals with developmental disabilities] continues to be a major problem."

[Defendant Thomas Michael Vukodinovich was the 73-year-old bus driver for Yolo Employment
Services, a nonprofit agency providing work activity programs, job training, and job retention for
individuals with disabilities, who was entrusted with taking clients to and from work. L. was a 49-year-
old female client of Yolo Employment Services with a mental age of three or four and an IQ of 37 who
rode defendant's bus. From 2009 through 2012, defendant and L. carried on a sexual relationship, mostly
in the bus consisting of sexual intercourse, oral copulation, and digital penetration. The sex acts usually
took place when all the other passengers were off the bus, except sometimes the sex acts occurred while
a gentleman who could not speak and another gentleman who was often asleep remained on the bus.
Defendant told L. to "be quiet" about the sex acts and not to tell anybody because defendant *** did
not want to be fired. Oftentimes, L. would say she did not want to engage in the sex acts, but defendant
persisted. Defendant was prosecuted for the sex acts on the sole theory that L. was incapable of giving
legal consent.

The jury found defendant guilty of one count of sexual intercourse, one count of attempted sexual
intercourse, five counts of oral copulation, and four counts of digital penetration, all with a person
who "is incapable, because of a mental disorder or developmental or physical disability, of giving legal
consent." (Sections 261(a)(1) [sexual intercourse], 288a(g) [oral copulation], 289(b) [penetration by a
foreign object].) The court sentenced defendant to 14 years in prison.

Issue

**Whether statutes criminalizing sexual acts with people incapable of consent due to a developmental
disability are unconstitutional because they violate a federal and state rights to privacy.**

Rule and Analysis

Defendant contends that the statutes criminalizing sexual conduct with people incapable of consent due
to a developmental disability *** are unconstitutional because they violate his federal and state rights to
privacy. [He] relies on *Lawrence v. Texas*, 539 U.S. 558 (2003), in which the United States Supreme Court
held the "[p]etitioners' criminal convictions for adult consensual sexual intimacy in the home," which

consisted of sodomy, violated "their vital interests in liberty and privacy protected by the Due Process Clause of the Fourteenth Amendment." ***

[*Lawrence* made clear that its decision] did not extend beyond protecting the private sexual conduct of two *consenting* adults: " [*Lawrence* noted that its case did "*not involve persons who might be injured or coerced or who are situated in relationships where consent might not easily be refused.*" ***

["The] principle that rape may be committed by having sex with a person so mentally incapacitated as to be incapable of consenting is hardly novel. 'Under English common law this situation was considered no different from intercourse with an unconscious person. . . .' *** In California law, the phrase 'incapable . . . of giving legal consent' dates back at least as far as the original Penal Code of 1872. ***

Were we to accept the alternative conclusion that defendant had a constitutional right to engage in sexual conduct with a person who had developmental disabilities and who lacked the legal capacity to consent, we would render the state incapable of protecting individuals with disabilities. "Obviously, it is the proper business of the state to stop sexual predators from taking advantage of developmentally disabled people."

We therefore reject defendant's contention that the penal laws at issue here designed to protect individuals with developmental disabilities from sexual exploitation, when there is evidence that the victim lacked the legal ability to consent, violate his right to privacy.

Conclusion

The judgment of conviction is affirmed.[73]

"Seamless Web" Connection

In *People v. Vukodinovich*, the case discussed above, the court was concerned about the "sexual exploitation and abuse of" persons with developmental disabilities. The intercourse which occurred in the case was problematic not only because a developmental disability can undermine an individual's ability to provide legally recognized consent, but also because the perpetrator is intruding upon the rights of a person who might be particularly vulnerable. This latter concern connects this case with crimes against the person in Chapter 6 which are defined as involving victims in a particular category, such as child abuse and elder abuse offenses.

Rape in Steubenville, Ohio

As reported by CNN Staff in the November 25, 2013, article, *"Four more school employees charged in Steubenville rape case,"*

> A grand jury investigating the 2012 rape of a 16-year-old girl in Steubenville, Ohio, has indicted four school employees, including the school superintendent, who faces felony charges, Ohio Attorney General Mike DeWine announced Monday.

---

73. Reprinted from Westlaw, with permission of Thomson Reuters.

The article and video can be viewed at:

http://www.cnn.com/2013/11/25/justice/ohio-steubenville-rape-case/

The *Christian Science Monitor*, in a March 13, 2013, article by Stacy Teicher Khadaroo entitled, "Steubenville rape trial: Where were 'courageous bystanders'? (+video)" noted:

> The Steubenville rape trial has highlighted the widespread problem of students not intervening to stop dating and sexual violence among peers. But awareness is growing.

The article can be viewed at:

http://www.csmonitor.com/USA/Education/2013/0313/Steubenville-rape-trial-Where-were-courageous-bystanders-video

---

Consensual Sex or Rape?

Nina Golgowski of the *New York Daily News* reported on October 16, 2013, in an article entitled, "Photo of couple engaging in public sex act actually picture of rape, female student says," that:

> As many as 10 witnesses tweeted photos and video of a man having oral sex with a woman outside of a bank according to students who broadcast the scene on Twitter. The woman photographed now tells police that she was a victim of sexual assault and no one intervened. A website claiming to have seen a video of the incident says it appears consensual.

The full article can be read at:

http://www.nydailynews.com/news/national/photo-public-sex-act-rape-woman-article-1.1487092

Do's and Don'ts for Hearings, Trials, and Appeals

Opening Statement

Do keep your opening statement simple. Explain to the jury that an opening statement is a "roadmap" for your case and offer a brief summary of what your witnesses will tell the jury. **Don't** be too specific in predictions about what each witness will say because witnesses, following human nature, tend to change their stories somewhat. Any changes, even if minor, could undermine your credibility with the jury.

---

e)   Timing of Consent

A legal issue can arise regarding the **timing of consent**. What if a person **initially consents** to having intercourse and then, **during the act of sex**, changes her mind and **withdraws her consent**? Would the male, **having heard and understood that the female had said "no"** to further intercourse, and who **continued anyway** in spite of her withdrawal of consent, be guilty of **rape**? This question is considered in the following case.

LEGAL ANALYSIS

In Re John Z.
29 Cal.4th 756 (2003).
Justice Chin delivered the opinion of the California Supreme Court.

Facts

[Laura T. drove Juan G., whom she had met two weeks earlier, to a party at defendant John Z's home. When Laura and Juan were in the defendant's parents' bedroom, Juan indicated he wanted to have sex. Laura told him she was not ready for that kind of activity. Later, when the defendant John Z. asked her why she "wouldn't do stuff," Laura repeated that she was not ready.]

[Defendant] and Juan asked Laura if it was her fantasy to have two guys, and Laura said it was not. Juan and defendant began kissing Laura and removing her clothes, although she kept telling them not to. [The] boys removed Laura's pants and underwear and began "fingering" her, "playing with [her] boobs" and continued to kiss her. Laura enjoyed this activity in the beginning, but objected when Juan [put on a condom. The defendant then left the room and Juan had intercourse with Laura even though she] told him she did not want to have intercourse. [Juan G. admitted to sexual battery and unlawful sexual intercourse.]

[While Laura searched for her clothes, the defendant, who had removed his clothing,] entered the bedroom and walked to where Laura was sitting on the bed. [He pushed Laura back down on the bed.] Laura did not say anything and defendant began kissing her and telling her that she had "a really beautiful body." Defendant [put his penis into Laura's vagina and rolled her over so that she was sitting on top of him.] Laura [kept trying to sit up to get it out but he grabbed her hips and pushed her back down. The defendant] kept saying, "will you be my girlfriend." Laura "kept like trying to pull away" and told him that "if he really did care about me, he wouldn't be doing this to me and if he did want a relationship, he should wait and respect that I don't want to do this." After about 10 minutes, defendant got off Laura, and helped her dress and find her keys. She then drove home.

On cross-examination, Laura testified [that when the defendant began kissing her, she kissed him back. During intercourse,] Laura told him that she needed to go home, but he would not stop. He said, "just give me a minute," and she said, "no, I need to get home." He replied, "give me some time" and she repeated, "no, I have to go home." Defendant did not stop, "[h]e just stayed inside of me and kept like basically forcing it on me." After about a "minute, minute and [a] half," defendant got off Laura.

Defendant testified, [claiming] he discontinued the act as soon as Laura told him that she had to go home.

Issue

Whether the crime of forcible rape [PC 261(a)(2)] is committed if the female victim consents to an initial penetration by the male, and then withdraws her consent during an act of intercourse, but the male continues against her will.

Rule and Analysis

[A] withdrawal of consent effectively nullifies any earlier consent and subjects the male to forcible rape charges if he persists in what has become nonconsensual intercourse. ***

Although the evidence of Laura's initial consent to intercourse with John Z. was hardly conclusive, we will assume for purposes of argument that Laura impliedly consented to the act, or at least tacitly refrained from objecting to it, until defendant had achieved penetration. [But see § 261.6, which defines consent as "positive cooperation in act or attitude pursuant to an exercise of free will". **Forcible] rape occurs when, during apparently consensual intercourse, the victim expresses an objection and attempts to stop the act and the defendant forcibly continues despite the objection.**

[The *Vela* Court of Appeals case] held that where the victim consents to intercourse at the time of penetration but thereafter withdraws her consent, any use of force by her assailant past that point is not rape.

Vela [reasoned] that "the essence of the crime of rape is the outrage to the person and feelings of the female resulting from the nonconsensual violation of her womanhood. When a female willingly consents to an act of sexual intercourse, the penetration by the male cannot constitute a violation of her womanhood nor cause outrage to her person and feelings. If she withdraws consent during the act of sexual intercourse and the male forcibly continues the act without interruption, the female may certainly feel outrage because of the force applied or because the male ignores her wishes, [but the sense of outrage] could hardly be of the same magnitude as that resulting from an initial nonconsensual violation of her womanhood. [The essential guilt of rape is lacking in the withdrawn consent scenario.]

[We find *Vela*'s] reasoning unsound. First, contrary to *Vela*'s assumption, we have no way of accurately measuring the level of outrage the victim suffers from being subjected to continued forcible intercourse following withdrawal of her consent. We must assume the sense of outrage is substantial. [SPC 261(2) defines rape as "an act of sexual intercourse accomplished with a person not the spouse of the perpetrator where it is accomplished against a person's will by means of force, violence, duress, menace, or fear of immediate and unlawful bodily injury on the person or another."] Section 263 states that "[t]he essential guilt of rape consists in the outrage to the person and feelings of the victim of the rape. Any sexual penetration, however slight, is sufficient to complete the crime." But no California case has held that the victim's outrage is an element of the crime of rape. ***

[Forcible rape occurs when] sexual intercourse is accomplished against the will of the victim by force or threat of bodily injury and **it is immaterial at what point the victim withdraws her consent, so long as that withdrawal is communicated to the male and he thereafter ignores it.** [Assuming arguendo that Laura initially consented to intercourse,] substantial evidence shows that she withdrew her consent and, through her actions and words, communicated that fact to defendant. [No] reasonable person in defendant's position would have believed that Laura continued to consent to the act. ***

Vela [assumes] that, to constitute rape, the victim's objections must be raised, or a defendant's use of force must be applied, *before* intercourse commences, but that argument is clearly flawed. One can readily imagine situations in which the defendant is able to obtain penetration before the victim can express an objection ***. Surely, if the defendant thereafter ignores the victim's objections and forcibly continues the act, he has committed "an act of sexual intercourse accomplished [against a person's will by means of force].

Defendant, *** contends that, in cases involving an initial consent to intercourse, the male should be permitted a "reasonable amount of time" in which to withdraw, once the female raises an objection to further intercourse. As defendant argues, "By essence of the act of sexual intercourse, a male's primal urge to reproduce is aroused. It is therefore unreasonable for a female and the law to expect a male to cease having sexual intercourse immediately upon her withdrawal of consent. It is only natural, fair and just that a male be given a reasonable amount of time in which to quell his primal urge."

We disagree. [Defendant's "primal urge" theory is contrary to the language of PC 216(a)(2).] Nothing in the language of section 261 or the case law suggests that the defendant is entitled to persist in intercourse once his victim withdraws her consent.

Conclusion

We disapprove _Vela_, * to the extent that decision is inconsistent with our opinion. The judgment of the Court of Appeal is affirmed.**[74]

Note

The California Supreme Court, in "_assuming arguendo_" that the victim initially consented to intercourse, is _not_ actually concluding that she did in fact ever consent to intercourse, even at its outset. Instead, by "_assuming arguendo_," the court is, for the purpose of argument, simply not contesting the defendant's claim of initial consent so that it can reach the main issue in the case—whether the defendant's continuance in having sex after the withdrawal of consent during the act of intercourse amounts to rape.

In fact, _John Z._ does not provide the court with the best facts to reach this issue because the circumstances clearly demonstrate that the victim never consented to intercourse with anyone when she was raped. The fact that the court used this case to decide this issue demonstrates the institutional passivity of courts. Courts, unlike Congress or the President, cannot simply choose to address a wrong in their midst. Instead, courts have to passively wait for "cases or controversies" to reach them. This means that, no matter how strongly a court feels about a particular injustice, it cannot change the law on its own. It waits, sometimes years, for the "right" case, which presents the relevant issue, to come along. Perhaps the _John Z._ court took the case not so much because it thought the victim initially consented, but because it wished to change the improper rule created in _Vela_. This shows a weakness in courts and judges—they must wait for a case to come along on an issue they care about. Yet, at the same time, having to wait often means that courts and judges have the power to offer the _last_ word on a matter.

North Carolina Law Is the Opposite of California's Ruling in _In Re John Z._

As reported by Molly Redden on June 24, 2017, in _The Guardian_ article, "'No doesn't really mean no': North Carolina law means women can't revoke consent for sex: Recent rape cases highlight legal loophole resulting from 1979 state supreme court ruling, prompting renewed campaign for change," a person cannot withdraw consent for sex once intercourse is taking place. The full article can be visited at:

https://www.theguardian.com/us-news/2017/jun/24/north-carolina-rape-legal-loophole-consent-state-v-way

Further information is available in the July 5, 2017, article in Motto: From the Editors of TIME, "In North Carolina, Sexual Consent Cannot Be Withdrawn," reported by Areva Martin, at:

http://motto.time.com/4842845/sexist-laws-explained-north-carolina-sexual-consent-law/

---

74. Reprinted with the permission of LexisNexis.

Can a Woman Be Guilty of "Rape"?

In *State v. Medrano*, 321 N.E.2d 97 (1974), the defendant Derlis Medrano argued that Illinois' rape statute denied "equal protection on the basis of sex" because it provided "that only a male person may be guilty of rape." The Appellate Court of Illinois countered, "that a female may be guilty of rape as an accessory, an aider or an abettor." *Medrano* ruled, "the statute here in question is both rationally related to a legitimate governmental objective, namely the protection of females." The court sought support from the Arizona Supreme Court, which ruled:

> Defendant argues that the statutes make it a crime for a man to commit a sexual act upon a woman without her consent while a woman, however, who commits the same sexual act upon a man without his consent, cannot be charged with the crime of rape.

> [The] need for treating males and females differently in enacting the rape statute is clearly reasonable. The statute satisfies the real, if not compelling, need to protect potential female victims from rape by males.

> However, for obvious physiological as well as sociological reasons we perceive no need by males for protection against females from rape ***. The fact that the law does not provide the same protection to males as it does to females does not deny the male perpetrator the equal protection of the law. The classification is logical and rational. *** We do not find the statutes constitutionally infirm.

Medrano Court also relied on the Supreme Court of Wisconsin's ruling:

> The sex classification is reasonable and bears a fair and substantial relationship to the object of the law. Sec. 944.01 is intended to protect women against sexual attack and forced pregnancy. ***

Medrano found that Illinois' limiting rape to being committed only by a male constitutional.

Perhaps *Medrano* protested too much, for the law later changed in that state. *People v. Andersen*, 604 N.E.2d 424 (1992) later declared: "Although sexual assault statutes now provide for conviction of either males or females *** under earlier statutes, only a male could be directly guilty; females could be found guilty of rape, but as an accessory, an aider or an abettor."

In the Ohio case, *In Re Wilson*, 1988 WL 129176 (1988),

> (A)s late as 1973, the statutory definition of rape required the element of "carnal knowledge." In 1974, a sweeping reform of the criminal code changed the definition of rape to what is presently R.C. 2907.02. This new definition of "rape" replaced the term "carnal knowledge" with the term "sexual conduct." "Sexual conduct" is defined in R.C. 2907.01(A) to mean "vaginal intercourse, between male and female, and anal intercourse, fellatio, and cunnilingus between persons regardless of sex." Also, 2907.02 changed the requirement that the actor be male. Now, any person of either sex may commit rape.

B. SPOUSAL RAPE

Is a **wife** the "**property**" of her husband? Does she "**merge**" into his being to become a part of him? When marrying her husband, does the wife give **irrevocable consent to intercourse** at any time? The following case, occurring during a transition in Wyoming from **common law** to **modern law**, demonstrates the significant distinctions between the common law and current statutes.

LEGAL ANALYSIS

Shunn v. State
742 P.2d 775 (1987).
Justice Brown delivered the opinion for the Supreme Court of Wyoming.

Facts

In December of 1985, the victim, Connie Shunn, filed a divorce action against appellant Laverne "Sonny" Shunn, and moved into a separate residence. A mutual restraining order was obtained prohibiting any contact between appellant and the victim. On March 8, 1986, nine days before the actual divorce, [Appellant confronted the victim in her bedroom,] striking the victim with a wooden baton, drawing blood. Appellant] sexually assaulted her with the baton; and then had sexual intercourse with the victim.

Appellant was found guilty of both sexual assault and aggravated assault. ***

Issue

Whether Wyoming's sexual assault statute is unconstitutionally vague in it's wording, "The fact that the actor and the victim are married to each other is not by itself a defense to a violation of W.S. 6-2-302(a) (i)."

Rule and Analysis

[§ 6-2-302(a) (i), W.S.1977 states in part:]

"(a) Any actor who inflicts sexual intrusion on a victim commits a sexual assault in the first degree if:

"(i) The actor causes submission of the victim through the actual application, reasonably calculated to cause submission of the victim, of physical force or forcible confinement." [The fact that the actor and the victim are married to each other is not by itself a defense to a violation of W.S. 6-2-302(a) (i)."]

[Appellant argues that this language creates a spousal exception to sexual assault in Wyoming and renders the statute unconstitutional when applied to a person convicted of sexually assaulting his spouse.]

"An ordinance or statute is void for vagueness if it fails to give a person of ordinary sensibility fair notice that the contemplated conduct is forbidden." ***

Appellant contends that the phrase "not by itself a defense" [is vague.] We disagree. The standard by which conduct is to be measured is clearly outlined ***. Section 6-2-307 clearly puts an assailant on notice that marriage to the victim of a sexual assault is not a complete defense, but may be considered along with other evidence in deciding the guilt of the defendant. ***

Appellant also argues that [finding the current statute unconstitutional would return Wyoming to] the common law spousal exception to rape. [17th Century English jurist Sir Matthew Hale is] the source for the spousal exception to rape. He has stated, "But the husband cannot be guilty of a rape committed by himself upon his lawful wife, for by their mutual matrimonial consent and contract the wife hath given up herself [to her husband, which she cannot retract."] With the adoption of the English common law, this rule was followed in this country for almost 200 years. [Three justifications have been identified as the reason for the spousal exception to rape.]

The first belief was that the woman was considered to be property of her husband or father. [The] early rape laws sought compensation for the husband or father, rather than the victim, for the damages incurred to the "property." The second premise is that the wife had no separate legal identity. [Blackstone commented that] "The very being or legal existence of the woman is suspended during this marriage, or at least is incorporated and consolidated into that of the husband: under whose wing, protection and [cover] she performs everything." [This] merger prevented a husband from being convicted of, in effect, raping himself. The third justification evolved from the belief that upon entering marriage, the wife consents to sexual intercourse with her husband. This irrevocable consent negated an essential element of the crime of rape, lack of consent.

[The appellant is incorrect] that the common law marital exception to rape would be reinstated if the challenged statute is found to be void for vagueness. The common law is the law of Wyoming unless abrogated by statute. [Statutes remedy defects in the common law and adapt it to changes of time and circumstance.]

To allow a spousal exception to rape would be inconsistent with the history of legislation in this state. When the legislature enacted § 6-2-307 and repealed the statutory spousal exception, *** it removed the common law spousal exception to rape in Wyoming. ***

Statutory and societal changes have significantly affected the appropriateness of a marital rape exception. Today, Hale's theory is both unrealistic and unreasonable.

Conclusion

[No] rational basis exists for distinguishing between marital and nonmarital rape. The degree of violence is no less when the victim of a rape is the spouse of the actor. We therefore see no justification to reinstate the common law marital exception to sexual assault. Affirmed.[75]

Police Officer Accused of Rape of Motorist

Ben Gittleson reported for *ABC News* in a November 26, 2013, article, "Texas Police Officer Accused of Raping Woman During Traffic Stop," that an officer assaulted a woman after stopping her for a traffic violation.

The full article can be viewed at:

http://abcnews.go.com/US/texas-police-officer-accused-traffic-stop-rape/story?id=21010823

C. STATUTORY RAPE OR "UNLAWFUL SEXUAL INTERCOURSE"

The **majority of jurisdictions** hold a male who has sexual intercourse with a female under the age of majority **strictly liable** for his actions **regardless of any mistake of fact he might have about the victim's age**. The Supreme Court of Idaho followed this approach in *State v. Stiffler*, 788 P.2d 220 (1990), where the defendant, Jason Ray Stiffler, was charged with statutory rape of a fifteen-year-old female. He pleaded guilty only after the trial court rejected his contention that, "a mistake as to the female's age should be a defense." He appealed to the Supreme Court, which affirmed his conviction. The court noted that "Statutory rape in this state 'is an act of sexual intercourse accomplished with a female . . . under the age of eighteen (18) years.' I.C. § 18-6101(1) (1987)." The *Stiffler* court explained that, "In the early part of this century this Court stated that the purpose of our statutory rape law was 'to protect girls under the age of eighteen years from conscienceless men, as far as possible.'" The court continued, "More recently

---

75. Reprinted with the permission of LexisNexis.

we noted that "the **prevention of illegitimate teenage pregnancies** is one of the objectives behind the statute and that the state has a strong interest in furthering this important governmental objective." The court thus ruled, in capital letters no less, that: "**MISTAKE OF AGE IS NOT A DEFENSE TO A CHARGE OF STATUTORY RAPE.**"

Other jurisdictions have chosen instead to **allow the defense of mistake of fact as to the victim's age** in such cases. California, as noted in the case below, was one of the first to so rule. Consider these questions when reading the following case: When an **underage female** agrees to have intercourse, is she **capable of giving voluntary "consent"**? Or, should the **law always presume** that she is **too innocent and naive to understand the implications of agreeing to sexual intercourse?**

LEGAL ANALYSIS

People v. Hernandez
61 Cal.2d 529 (1964).
Justice Peek wrote the opinion for the California Supreme Court.

Facts

[The defendant and the prosecuting witness were not married and had been companions for several months prior to the date of the commission of the offense.] Upon that date the prosecutrix [victim] was 17 years and 9 months of age and voluntarily engaged in an act of sexual intercourse with defendant. [The defendant was convicted of misdemeanor statutory rape by the court sitting without a jury.]

Section 261 of the Penal Code [at one time provided]: "Rape is an act of sexual intercourse, accomplished with a female not the wife of the perpetrator, under either of the following circumstances: 1. Where the female is under the age of eighteen years . . ."

[The defendant argues that the trial court erred in refusing to allow him to give evidence showing that he had in good faith a reasonable belief that the victim was 18 years or more of age.]

Issue

Whether an actual and reasonable good faith belief that the underage victim was 18 years or more of age constitutes a defense to statutory rape [now known in California as "unlawful sexual intercourse"].

Rule and Analysis

[With statutory rape, in one sense, the lack of consent of the female is not an element of the offense. In a broader sense, the lack of consent remains an element but the law conclusively presumes a lack of consent because young females are presumed too innocent and naive to understand the implications and nature of sex. It is popularly believed that social and moral values are preserved by making young females abstain from sex.] An unwise disposition of her sexual favor is deemed to do harm both to herself and the social mores. [Statutory] rape intervenes in an effort to avoid such a disposition. This goal, moreover, is not accomplished by penalizing the naive female but by imposing criminal sanctions against the male, who is conclusively presumed to be responsible for the occurrence. ***

The assumption that age alone will bring an understanding of the sexual act to a young woman is of doubtful validity. Both learning from the cultural group to which she is a member and her actual sexual experiences will determine her level of comprehension. The sexually experienced 15-year-old may be far more acutely aware of the implications of sexual intercourse than her sheltered cousin who is beyond the age of consent. *** [Even where a girl's actual comprehension contradicts the law's presumption, the male is deemed criminally responsible for the act.]

[The issue in the instant case] goes to the culpability of the young man who acts *without* knowledge that an essential factual element exists and has, on the other hand, a positive, reasonable belief that it does not exist.

The [*mens rea* requirement expresses the principle that the law is concerned with not conduct alone but conduct accompanied by certain specific mental states. The mens rea requirement means that commission of a crime requires a "joint operation of act and intent." Recently,] this court has moved away from the imposition of criminal sanctions in the absence of culpability where the governing statute [mentions no legislative policy to be served by imposing strict liability.]

[California law now rests, as it did in 1896, with *People* v. *Ratz*, 115 Cal. 132, where it ruled, "The purpose of the law is] too plain to need comment, the crime too infamous to bear discussion. The protection of society, of the family, and of the infant, demand that one who has carnal intercourse under such circumstances shall do so in peril of the fact, and he will not be heard *** to urge his belief that the victim of his outrage had passed the period which would make his act a crime." The age of consent at the time of the *Ratz* decision was 14 years, and it is noteworthy that the purpose of the rule, as there announced, was to afford protection to young females therein described as "infants." ***

[*Ratz*, rather than eliminating intent as an element of the crime, held that the wrongdoer assumed the risk. The wrongdoer, when committing the act, consciously intended to proceed regardless of the age of the female.] There can be no dispute that a **criminal intent exists when the perpetrator proceeds with utter disregard of, or in the lack of grounds for, a belief that the female has reached the age of consent. But if he participates in a mutual act of sexual intercourse, believing his partner to be beyond the age of consent, with reasonable grounds for such belief, where is his criminal intent?** In such circumstances he has not consciously taken any risk. Instead he has subjectively eliminated the risk by satisfying himself on reasonable evidence that the crime cannot be committed. ***

[At common law an honest and reasonable belief in the existence of circumstances, which, if true, would make the act for which the person is indicted an innocent act, has always been held to be a good defense. Our departure from *Ratz*] is in no manner indicative of a withdrawal from the sound policy that it is in the public interest to protect the sexually naive female from exploitation. No responsible person would hesitate to condemn as untenable a claimed good faith belief in the age of consent of an "infant" female whose obviously tender years preclude the existence of reasonable grounds for that belief. However, the prosecutrix in the instant case was but three months short of 18 years of age and there is nothing in the record to indicate that the purposes of the law as stated in *Ratz* can be better served by foreclosing the defense of a lack of intent.

Conclusion

[Statutory rape is defensible wherein a criminal intent is lacking. *Ratz* is overruled.] We conclude that it was reversible error to [not allow the defendant to offer a defense based on actual and reasonable good faith belief as to the victim's age. The judgment is reversed.]

Note

The law's curious view of female sexuality in 1964 can be gleaned from the following footnote in the *Hernandez* case:

The inequitable consequences to which we may be led are graphically illustrated by ***
State v. *Snow* (Mo. 1923) 252 S.W. 629, 632: "We have in this case a condition and not a

theory. This wretched girl was young in years but old in sin and shame. A number of callow youths, of otherwise blameless lives ... fell under her seductive influence. They flocked about her, ... like moths about the flame of a lighted candle and probably with the same result. The girl was a common prostitute. ... The boys were immature and doubtless more sinned against than sinning. They did not defile the girl. She was a mere 'cistern for foul toads to knot and gender in.' Why should the boys, misled by her, be sacrificed? What sound public policy can be subserved by branding them as felons? Might it not be wise to ingraft an exception in the statute?"[76]

The passage of time has hopefully undermined the societal notion that females are either uniquely promiscuous or are members of the only gender who is vulnerable to sexual advances from older persons. This change is seen in the current version of California's Penal Code section 261.5, which has been amended to provide that **the crime can be committed by either a female of the age of majority against a minor male or a male of the age of majority against a minor female**.

California Penal Code § 261.5: Unlawful Sexual Intercourse with a Minor

(a) Unlawful sexual intercourse is an act of sexual intercourse accomplished with a person who is not the spouse of the perpetrator, if the person is a minor. For the purposes of this section, a "minor" is a person under the age of 18 years and an "adult" is a person who is at least 18 years of age.

(b) Any person who engages in an act of unlawful sexual intercourse with a minor who is not more than three years older or three years younger than the perpetrator, is guilty of a misdemeanor.

(c) Any person who engages in an act of unlawful sexual intercourse with a minor who is more than three years younger than the perpetrator is guilty of either a misdemeanor or a felony, and shall be punished by imprisonment in a county jail not exceeding one year, or by imprisonment pursuant to subdivision (h) of Section 1170.

(d) Any person 21 years of age or older who engages in an act of unlawful sexual intercourse with a minor who is under 16 years of age is guilty of either a misdemeanor or a felony, and shall be punished by imprisonment in a county jail not exceeding one year, or by imprisonment pursuant to subdivision (h) of Section 1170 for two, three, or four years.[77]

Learn from My (and Others') Mistakes

Be Courteous to Courtroom Personnel and Learn the Habits of a Particular Courtroom

D.A.'s and public defenders are in the courtroom every day and, so come to know every employee in it and the judge's particular peeves. Private defense counsel, often seen as brilliant, expensive, and accomplished, often do not know the specifics of this daily courtroom culture. One private attorney, known as an expert in big narcotics cases, came to court wearing expensive suits and having perfectly manicured nails. Arrogant, he did not bother to inquire about the courtroom particulars. I felt no need to enlighten him. During the case, when, without notice or permission, he entered "the well"—the area in front of the bench where the judge sits, the judge blew up at him in front of the jury. Any expertise he had evaporated in front of those twelve jurors.

---

76. Reprinted with the permission of LexisNexis.
77. From *Deering's California Codes Annotated*. Copyright © 2014 by Matthew Bender & Company, Inc., a member of the LexisNexis Group. Reprinted with the permission of LexisNexis.

Another defense attorney failed to be courteous, and served some time for his trouble. Just before lunch, this defense attorney, who was disliked by court staff, asked to be let into "lockup," the cells in courthouses where defendants await the calling of their cases. A bailiff let him in, closed the door, and then immediately went to lunch. When the attorney knocked on the door to be let out, there was no bailiff to respond. As the knocking turned to desperate pounding, the court clerk shuffled his papers as if nothing was happening. When I asked if anyone could let him out, the clerk shrugged and said he had no key. When I called the bailiff's office for help, it took quite some time to find someone to let the attorney out.

D. SODOMY

1. Common Law

If Blackstone was circumspect about rape, he spoke even more obliquely about **sodomy**, calling it "the infamous *crime against nature*, committed with man or beast." (Italics in the original.) About sodomy, Blackstone darkly stated, "it is an offense of so dark a nature, so easily charged, and the negative so difficult to be proved, that the accusation should be clearly made out: for if false, it deserves a punishment inferior only to that of the crime itself."

Historically, "sodomy" has been subject to many different definitions, as noted by Christopher R. Leslie in, *Creating Criminals: The Injuries Inflicted by "Unenforced" Sodomy Laws* 35 Harv. C.R.-C.L. L. Rev. 103, 110–11 (2000). Some states crafted "gender-specific" laws prohibiting "only same-sex sodomy." Under these laws, Leslie noted, "while the woman who performs fellatio is expressing herself sexually, the man who performs fellatio is a felon." Other states wrote "gender-neutral" statutes prohibiting "all fellatio and cunnilingus whether performed by a man or a woman."

The following case demonstrates how the **evolution of social norms can directly influence not only criminal law but also constitutional law.** In *Lawrence*, the Supreme Court considered whether a law that **criminalized sexual intimacy by same-sex couples, but not identical behavior by different-sex couples, violated the Fourteenth Amendment.**

2. Current Law

LEGAL ANALYSIS

Lawrence v. Texas
539 U.S. 558 (2003).
Justice Kennedy delivered the opinion of the United States Supreme Court.

Facts

The question before the Court is the validity of a Texas statute making it a crime for two persons of the same sex to engage in certain intimate sexual conduct.

In Houston, Texas, [police officers] were dispatched to a private residence in response to a reported weapons disturbance. They entered an apartment where one of the petitioners, John Geddes Lawrence, resided. [The officers found Lawrence and another man, Tyron Garner, engaging in a sexual act. The two petitioners were arrested, charged, and convicted] before a Justice of the Peace.

The complaints described their crime as "deviate sexual intercourse, namely anal sex, with a member of the same sex (man)." [Texas Penal Code Section 21.06(a)(2003)] provides: "A person commits an offense if he engages in deviate sexual intercourse with another individual of the same sex." The statute defines "deviate sexual intercourse" [as:]

(A) any contact between any part of the genitals of one person and the mouth or anus of another person; or

(B) the penetration of the genitals or the anus of another person with an object." ***

The petitioners *** challenged the statute as a violation of the Equal Protection Clause of the Fourteenth Amendment. [Petitioners' arguments were rejected. They entered *nolo contendere* pleas and were each fined $200 and assessed court costs. ***

The petitioners were adults at the time of the alleged offense. Their conduct was in private and consensual.

Issues

1. **Whether Petitioners' criminal convictions under the Texas "Homosexual Conduct" law— which criminalizes sexual intimacy by same-sex couples, but not identical behavior by different-sex couples—violate the Fourteenth Amendment guarantee of equal protection of laws?**
2. **Whether Petitioners' criminal convictions for adult consensual sexual intimacy in the home violate their vital interests in liberty and privacy protected by the Due Process Clause of the Fourteenth Amendment?**

Rule and Analysis

We conclude the case should be resolved by determining whether the petitioners were free as adults to engage in the private conduct in the exercise of their liberty under the Due Process Clause of the Fourteenth Amendment to the Constitution. ***

[There] is no longstanding history in this country of laws directed at homosexual conduct as a distinct matter. Beginning in colonial times there were prohibitions of sodomy derived from the English criminal laws [which included] relations between men and women as well as relations between men and men.] Nineteenth-century commentators similarly read American sodomy, buggery, and crime-against-nature statutes as criminalizing certain relations between men and women and between men and men. *** The absence of legal prohibitions focusing on homosexual conduct may be explained in part by noting that according to some scholars the concept of the homosexual as a distinct category of person did not emerge until the late 19th century. ["The modern terms *homosexuality* and *heterosexuality* do not apply to an era that had not yet articulated these distinctions"]. Thus early American sodomy laws were not directed at homosexuals as such but instead sought to prohibit nonprocreative sexual activity more generally. [Homosexual conduct] was not thought of as a separate category from like conduct between heterosexual persons.

Laws prohibiting sodomy do not seem to have been enforced against consenting adults acting in private. A substantial number of sodomy prosecutions and convictions *** were for predatory acts against those who could not or did not consent, as in the case of a minor or the victim of an assault. *** Instead of targeting relations between consenting adults in private, 19th-century sodomy prosecutions typically involved relations between men and minor girls or minor boys, relations between adults involving force, relations between adults implicating disparity in status, or relations between men and animals.

[Far from possessing "ancient roots," American laws targeting same-sex couples did not develop until the last third of the 20th century. *** It was not until the 1970's that any State singled out same-sex relations for criminal prosecution, and only nine States have done so. [Over the last] decades, States with same-sex prohibitions have moved toward abolishing them. ***

In *Planned Parenthood of Southeastern Pa. v. Casey,* 505 U.S. 833, 120 L. Ed. 2d 674, 112 S. Ct. 2791 (1992), the Court reaffirmed the substantive force of the liberty protected by the Due Process Clause. The *Casey* decision again confirmed that our laws and tradition afford constitutional protection to personal decisions relating to marriage, procreation, contraception, family relationships, child rearing, and education. *** In explaining the respect the Constitution demands for the autonomy of the person in making these choices, we stated as follows:

> "These matters, involving the most intimate and personal choices a person may make in a lifetime, choices central to personal dignity and autonomy, are central to the liberty protected by the Fourteenth Amendment. At the heart of liberty is the right to define one's own concept of existence, of meaning, of the universe, and of the mystery of human life. Beliefs about these matters could not define the attributes of personhood were they formed under compulsion of the State." ***

Persons in a homosexual relationship may seek autonomy for these purposes, just as heterosexual persons do. ***

The stigma this criminal statute imposes *** is not trivial. The offense, [although a misdemeanor,] remains a criminal offense with all that imports for the dignity of the persons charged. The petitioners will bear on their record the history of their criminal convictions. *** [If] Texas convicted an adult for private, consensual homosexual conduct under the statute here in question the convicted person would come within the registration laws of at least four States were he or she to be subject to their jurisdiction. *** This underscores the consequential nature of the punishment and the state-sponsored condemnation attendant to the criminal prohibition. ***

[The] fact that the governing majority in a State has traditionally viewed a particular practice as immoral is not a sufficient reason for upholding a law prohibiting the practice; neither history nor tradition could save a law prohibiting miscegenation from constitutional attack. [Individual decisions by married and unmarried] persons, concerning the intimacies of their physical relationship, even when not intended to produce offspring, are a form of "liberty" protected by the Due Process Clause of the Fourteenth Amendment. ***

The present case does not involve minors, [persons who might be injured or coerced, those who are situated in relationships where consent might not easily be refused, or public conduct or prostitution.] The case does involve two adults who, with full and mutual consent from each other, engaged in sexual practices common to a homosexual lifestyle. **The petitioners are entitled to respect for their private lives. The State cannot demean their existence or control their destiny by making their private sexual conduct a crime. Their right to liberty under the Due Process Clause gives them the full right to engage in their conduct without intervention of the government. "It is a promise of the Constitution that there is a realm of personal liberty which the government may not enter."** *** The Texas statute furthers no legitimate state interest which can justify its intrusion into the personal and private life of the individual. ***

Conclusion

Since "petitioners were free as adults to engage in the private conduct in the exercise of their liberty under the Due Process Clause of the Fourteenth Amendment to the Constitution," the sodomy statute is unconstitutional. [The judgment of the Court of Appeals is reversed,] and the case is remanded for further proceedings not inconsistent with this opinion.

Note

As noted by the Supreme Court above, forcing sexual acts upon another person poses quite a different issue, as discussed in the Box below, involving a brutal act of violence.

Officer Pleads Guilty to Sodomizing Abner Louima with a Broom Handle

In *United States v. Volpe*, 78 F.Supp.2d 76 (1999), Judge Eugene H. Nickerson provided the following facts supporting the officer's guilty plea in the case:

[On August 9, 1997, New York City Police Officers] were summoned to Club Rendez-Vous, a Brooklyn nightclub.] Among them were Officers Justin Volpe, Thomas Bruder, Charles Schwarz, and Thomas Wiese, and Sergeant Michael Bellomo.

The officers attempted to disperse a large crowd. [Some people] became unruly, yelling and throwing bottles at the officers. During the fracas, Volpe struggled with an intoxicated patron named John Rejouis and eventually pushed Rejouis to the ground. Rejouis held up his badge as a New York City Corrections Officer. Volpe slapped Rejouis's hand and knocked the badge to the ground.

*** Abner Louima confronted Volpe and began yelling at him regarding his treatment of Rejouis. Volpe attempted to push Louima away from the club, but Louima refused to move and the confrontation escalated. [When Volpe was struck hard on the side of his head and knocked to the ground, he thought Louima had hit him.] In fact, Jay Nicholas, Louima's cousin, struck Volpe and then fled.

[Schwarz and Wiese arrested Louima. They also mistakenly believed he assaulted Volpe. On the way to the precinct, they stopped the patrol car and beat Louima, handcuffed, about the body and head.]

[Later,] Volpe approached Louima, who was still in handcuffs in the back of the patrol car. Volpe taunted Louima and beat him on his head and face with a closed fist and a radio. Louima sustained lacerations and abrasions on his face and swelling in his mouth and around his eye.

Schwarz and Wiese [then processed Louima at the precinct's front desk, where Louima's pants and underwear fell to his ankles.]

[Volpe, seeing Louima at the front desk, grabbed a wooden broom stick and broke it over his knee. He hid the upper section in the bathroom.] Volpe then went to the front desk where he borrowed a pair of leather gloves.]

Louima testified that when police [finished processing him, they grabbed him by the handcuffs and took him to the bathroom.]

Volpe then picked up the stick he had put behind the garbage can and told Louima, "I'm going to do something to you. If you yell or make any noise, I'll kill you." Volpe pushed Louima to the ground, with his head near a toilet bowl, and kicked him in the groin. When Louima began screaming, Volpe put his foot over Louima's mouth. Louima testified that the two officers began to punch him about the head and body, and that the driver of the car then grabbed Louima by his handcuffs and lifted him from the ground.

Volpe then forced the broken broomstick approximately six inches into Louima's rectum. He removed the stick, which was covered with Louima's feces, and held it in front of Louima's mouth and taunted him. Volpe then slammed the stick against the wall, leaving behind traces of feces.

With Louima crying and in severe pain, Volpe lifted him to his feet and took him to a holding cell, leaving Louima's pants and underwear around his ankles. Before putting him in the cell, Volpe told Louima that if he told anybody what had happened, Volpe would kill him. Volpe then returned the leather gloves, now covered with Louima's blood ***.

[Later] Volpe was overheard telling fellow officers that "I broke a man down." Volpe later [told] Sergeant Kenneth Wernick what he had done to Louima, saying "I took a man down tonight." Volpe took Wernick to the bathroom and showed him the stick used in the sexual assault, which Volpe had left in the bathroom. Shortly thereafter, Volpe showed the stick to Officer Michael Schoer. Smelling Louima's feces on the stick, Schoer said, "What is that, dog shit?" Volpe responded, "No, human shit." ***

Approximately four hours after the bathroom assault, Louima [was] taken to Coney Island Hospital in Brooklyn, New York. [Tests] showed internal injuries to his bladder and rectum. [Doctors] surgically repaired a two-centimeter perforation to Louima's rectum and a three-centimeter perforation to his bladder. Doctors also performed colostomy and cystostomy procedures.

Louima [suffered was an intestinal blockage and two surgeries for implantation and removal of a colostomy bag.] Louima received medical and psychiatric treatment on an outpatient basis and continued to suffer severe headaches, abdominal pain and insomnia.

[The Internal Affairs Bureau of the New York City Police Department began an investigated these events. Volpe ultimately] pleaded guilty to six counts, including conspiring to deprive Abner Louima of his civil rights by aggravated assault and aggravated sexual abuse, assaulting Louima in a police car, and sexually abusing Louima in a restroom at the 70th Precinct. The Court sentenced Volpe to 360 months.] Upon Appeal, the United States Court of Appeals for the Second Circuit ruled, in *United States v. Volpe*, 224 F.3d 72 (2000), that, "Judge Nickerson did not err in sentencing the defendant."

DISCUSSION QUESTIONS

1. What are the elements of rape at common law? Could a husband rape his wife at common law?

2. What are the elements of rape today? How has the crime of rape evolved?

3. What is "consent" for purposes of rape? Is mere acquiescence the same as consent for purposes of rape?

4. What are the seven ways to destroy consent in California's rape law? Do they all require application of force or violence or is consent destroyed in other ways?

5. Is having intercourse with an unconscious person rape?

6. Is resistance to intercourse an element of rape today? Why or why not?

7. What is the difference between rape and statutory rape or unlawful sexual intercourse?

8. What is sodomy? Is all sodomy prosecuted as criminal today?

WEB LINKS

1. New York's "Criminal Jury Instruction" for "Rape First Degree (B Felony) (Forcible Compulsion) Penal Law 130.35(1)" is at: http://www.nycourts.gov/judges/cji/2-PenalLaw/130/130.35%281%29.pdf

2. New York's "Criminal Jury Instruction" for "Predatory Sexual Assault (A-II Felony) Penal Law 130.95(1)(a)" is at: http://www.nycourts.gov/judges/cji/2-PenalLaw/130/130.95%281%29%28a%29.pdf

3. Massachusetts's Court System has a jury instruction entitled, "Instruction 6.600 Annoying and Accosting Persons of the Opposite Sex," which is at: http://www.mass.gov/courts/docs/courts-and-judges/courts/district-court/jury-instructions-criminal/6000-9999/6600-annoying-and-accosting-persons-of-opposite-sex.pdf

4. California's jury instructions for criminal trials (CALCRIM) provides instructions at number 1030 for "Sodomy by Force, Fear, or Threats (Pen. Code, § 286(c)(2), (3), (k))" at: https://www.justia.com/criminal/docs/calcrim/1000/1030.html

5. California's jury instructions for criminal trials (CALCRIM) provides instructions at number 1015 for "Oral Copulation by Force, Fear, or Threats (Pen. Code, § 288a(c)(2) & (3), (k))" at: https://www.justia.com/criminal/docs/calcrim/1000/1015.html

CHAPTER
VIII

Crimes against Property

© DDekk/Shutterstock.com

Thieves are amazingly creative in discovering new ways to steal. All of the differing theft crimes, however, share certain concepts from larceny formed at common law centuries ago in England. In short, when talking about theft, it all starts with larceny.

A. LARCENY

1.   Common Law

John Wesley Bartram, in *Pleading for Theft Consolidation in Virginia: Larceny, Embezzlement, False Pretenses and § 19.2-284,* 56 Wash & Lee L. Rev. 249, 258–59 (1999), defined **larceny at common law** as: **"(1) trespassory (2) taking and (3) carrying away of the (4) personal property (5) of another (6) with intent to steal it."** Blackstone, in *Commentaries,* Vol. IV, at 230, expanded on some of these elements. He explained that larceny's second element, "taking," occurred when "the consent of the owner (was) wanting." Therefore, when a thief takes an item without the owner's consent, he or she is wrongfully taking the property, which fulfills the first element of larceny—that the taking be "trespassory." Not only must the larcenist take property, but also he or she must "carry it away," albeit for a slight distance. "A bare removal from the place in which he found the goods, though the thief does not quite make off with them, is sufficient asportation, or carrying away." Blackstone offered as an example "a thief, intending to steal plate, takes it out of a chest in which it was, and lays it down upon the floor, but is surprized before he can make his escape with it; this is larciny." To satisfy larceny's fourth element, the item taken must amount to property. Taking wild animals, such as deer, hares, and other "beasts" in the forest, or "fish in an open river or pond, or wild fowls at their natural liberty," did not amount to larceny because all these animals were free and so not the subject of property. Only a certain kind of property qualified for larceny—the "personal goods of another." Real estate, such as land or the buildings on land, were considered real property, and therefore "could not be taken and carried away." Therefore, any taking of real property was not larceny.

VIDEO: The Woman Might Be Naked But it's the Officer Who Winds Up "Losing His Shirt"

WARNING: POTENTIALLY DISTURBING VIDEO. A woman steals a Maricopa County Sheriff Deputy's police vehicle in Arizona at:

https://www.youtube.com/watch?v=YXGcDRhPt1U

---

2.   Current Law

Over the centuries, thieves created different kinds of theft. Traditionally, victims could be wrongfully separated from their property by **larceny, larceny by trick, theft by false pretenses, and embezzlement. What are all these different theft crimes, where did they come from, and how do they differ from each other? What do the different theft crimes mean for theft today?** If there are differences, do they even matter? The California Supreme Court answered these questions in the case below.

The following case involves a **robbery** charge that explains the **specific differences between larceny and theft by false pretenses.** This is because **robbery is actually "aggravated larceny"—larceny committed with "force or fear."** The court was called upon to decide if robbery could be committed not only with the **"trespassory taking"** of larceny, but also with the **"consensual taking"** of theft by false pretenses. The meaning of these concepts and the importance of the differences between them are explored on the following pages.

LEGAL ANALYSIS

People v. Williams
57 Cal.4th 776 (2013).
Justice Kennard delivered the opinion of the Supreme Court of California.

Facts

[Defendant] Demetrius Lamont Williams entered a Walmart department store in Palmdale. Using either a MasterCard or a Visa payment card, which was re-encoded with a third party's credit card information, defendant bought a $200 Walmart gift card from a recently hired cashier, who was filling in for a cashier on a break. Defendant then tried to buy three more gift cards from the same cashier. At that point, the regular cashier came back and, after learning of the previous transaction, told defendant of Walmart's policy prohibiting the use of credit cards for purchases of gift cards. Defendant was permitted to keep the $200 gift card he had initially bought.

Defendant then went to a different cash register and again presented a re-encoded payment card to buy another $200 gift card. [Two Walmart security guards who saw the transaction] asked defendant for the receipt and payment card used. Defendant complied. When told that the payment card's last four digits did not match those on the receipt, defendant produced two other re-encoded payment cards, but their numbers did not match those on the receipt either.

Defendant began walking toward the exit, followed by the two security guards. When defendant was told to stop, he produced yet another re-encoded payment card, but this card's last four digits also did not match those on the receipt. As defendant continued walking toward the exit, he pushed one of the guards, dropped some receipts, and started running away. [The guards wrestled defendant to the ground, handcuffed him, and recovered from his possession four payment cards issued by MasterCard and Visa.] Also retrieved from defendant were several gift cards from Walmart and elsewhere.

Defendant was charged with [PC 211 robbery, fraudulent use of an access card, grand theft, and other charges]. The jury found defendant guilty as charged, and the trial court sentenced him to a total prison term of 23 years eight months. The Court of Appeal *** affirmed *** defendant's robbery convictions.

[Defendant] argues his robbery convictions should be reversed because robbery requires theft by larceny, whereas the theft he committed was by false pretenses. We agree. ***

Issue

At issue here is the meaning of "felonious taking." Can that element of robbery be satisfied only by the crime of theft by larceny, or can it also be committed through theft by false pretenses?

Rule and Analysis

[PC 211] **Robbery is "the *felonious taking* of personal property in the possession of another, from his person or immediate presence, and against his will, accomplished by means of force or fear."** The term "felonious taking" originated in the common law and was later adopted in California's robbery statute.

[What type of theft constitutes a "felonious taking"? Is it only theft by larceny or can it also be theft by false pretenses? The Court of Appeal upheld defendant's robbery convictions by ruling that theft by false pretenses can satisfy the "felonious taking" requirement of robbery. We reverse.]

[To understand the meaning that the Legislature intended when it used the words "felonious taking" in California's robbery statute, we examine that statute's common law roots.] Part A. discusses the common law origins and development of the related crime of larceny. Part B. discusses the British Parliament's enactment in the 18th century of the two statutory offenses of theft by false pretenses and embezzlement, both of which were later adopted in the early criminal laws of the American states. Part C. discusses the elements of robbery, larceny, and theft by false pretenses, and their application to this case.

Crime of Larceny

[California's PC 484 defines **the crime of theft by larceny as the felonious stealing, taking, carrying, leading, or driving away of the personal property of another**. This statutory definition reflects its English common law roots.]

The common law defined larceny as the taking and carrying away of someone else's personal property, by trespass, with the intent to permanently deprive the owner of possession. [Larceny was less serious than robbery because of robbery's additional requirement of personal violence against, or intimidation of, the victim. Under common law, robbery and larceny, being felonies, were punishable by death.]

[In 1275, the English Parliament created] a sentencing distinction between "grand" and "petit" larceny, making grand larceny a more serious offense than petit larceny, involving property valued at greater than 12 pence (the approximate price of a sheep). [Grand larceny remained punishable by death, but petit larceny became punishable only by imprisonment, whipping, or forfeiture of goods. Larceny remained a felony, whether it was grand or petit.] Therefore, larceny was, in essence, a felonious taking. ***

Until the latter part of the 18th century, death was the punishment for all theft offenses except petty larceny. [English judges, becoming troubled by the harshness of the death penalty for theft crimes, limited the scope of larceny.] For instance, it was held not to be larceny—and not a crime at all—if someone in lawful possession of another's property misappropriated it for personal use (the later offense of embezzlement), or if someone acquired title to another's property by fraud (the later offense of false pretenses). *** These limitations [on] larceny made sense in light of that crime's original purpose of preventing breaches of the peace; because embezzlement and false pretenses lacked larceny's requirement of a "trespass in the taking," they were viewed as less likely to result in violence. ***

Although common law larceny was [narrowed to limit punishment by death it was also broadened to provide greater protection of private property.] For instance, in 1799 an English court decision introduced the concept of "larceny by trick" [which involved taking possession of another's property by fraud].

[Larceny required a *trespassory* taking, which is a taking without the property owner's consent.] Although a trespassory taking is not immediately evident when larceny occurs "by trick" because of the crime's fraudulent nature, English courts held that a property owner who is fraudulently induced to transfer possession of the property to another does not do so with free and genuine consent, so "the one who thus fraudulently obtains possession commits a trespass." "[The fraud takes the place of the trespass and the defendant is guilty of larceny by trick or device." In cases of larceny by trick] the owner is deemed still to retain a constructive possession of the property. ***

The reasoning supporting larceny by trick's inclusion within the crime of larceny—that fraud vitiates the property owner's consent to the taking—was not extended, however, to cases involving the fraudulent transfer of title. [Blackstone defines "title" as the right to possess property.] Under the common law, if title was transferred, there was no trespass and hence no larceny. *** The theory was that once title to property was voluntarily transferred by its owner to another, the recipient owned the property and therefore could not be said to be trespassing upon it. *** Similarly, under the common law there was no trespass, and hence no larceny, when a lawful possessor of another's property misappropriated it to personal use. *** These subtle limitations on the common law crime of larceny spurred the British Parliament in the 18th century to create the separate statutory offenses of theft by false pretenses and embezzlement. ***

Crimes of Theft by False Pretenses and Embezzlement

[The British Parliament enacted statutes prohibiting theft by false pretenses and embezzlement. Each crime was distinct from larceny.] **Unlike larceny, the newly enacted offense of theft by false pretenses involved acquiring title over the property, not just possession. *** Unlike larceny, the newly enacted offense of embezzlement involved an initial, lawful possession of the victim's property, followed by its misappropriation. *****

Britain's 18th century division of theft into the three separate crimes of larceny, false pretenses, and embezzlement made its way into the early criminal laws of the American states. [Things would have been simpler if Parliament had stretched larceny rather than creating new crimes.]

For instance, it was difficult at times to determine whether a defendant had acquired title to the property, or merely possession, a distinction separating theft by false pretenses from larceny by trick. [It was difficult to determine] whether a defendant, clearly guilty of some theft offense, had committed embezzlement or larceny, as [the 1867 Massachusetts case, *Commonwealth v. O'Malley*, illustrates]. There, a defendant was first indicted for larceny and acquitted; later, on the same facts, he was indicted for embezzlement and convicted; and thereafter, on appeal, his conviction was set aside on the ground that his offense was larceny, not embezzlement. ***

[**In 1927, the California Legislature consolidated the three crimes of larceny, false pretenses, and embezzlement into "theft" to remove the technicalities existing in these crimes at common law.**] Indictments and informations charging the crime of 'theft' can now simply allege an 'unlawful taking'. *** Juries need no longer be concerned with the technical differences between the several types of theft, and can return a general verdict of guilty if they find that an 'unlawful taking' has been proved. *** The elements of the several types of theft included within section 484 have not been changed, however, and a judgment of conviction of theft, based on a general verdict of guilty, can be sustained only if the evidence discloses the elements of one of the consolidated offenses." ***

[California's consolidation of larceny, false pretenses, and embezzlement into the single crime of theft did not change the elements of those offenses, a fact that is significant to our analysis.]

Elements of Robbery, Larceny, and Theft by False Pretenses and Their Application Here

We now consider the issue here: whether robbery's element of "felonious taking" can be satisfied through theft by false pretenses, the type of theft defendant committed. Robbery [requires "felonious taking. The taking required in larceny, as in robbery, must be "felonious."]

[By using the phrase "felonious taking"—the same language that was used at common law for both robbery and larceny—the Legislature intended to attach to "felonious taking" the same meaning the phrase had under the common law.]

[All larceny at common law was a felony, and so the common law defined larceny as a "felonious taking."] "'Felonious taking' means a taking with intent to commit the crime of larceny." **Because California's robbery statute uses the common law's phrase "felonious taking," and because at common law "felonious taking" was synonymous with larceny, we conclude that larceny is a necessary element of robbery.** [Larceny and robbery are similar—the one being merely an aggravated form of the other.] Each is the felonious taking of the personal property of another, although in robbery the felonious taking is accomplished by force or threats. [Robbery is larceny, committed by violence, from the person of another.]

Two differences in the crimes of larceny and theft by false pretenses tend to support our conclusion that only theft by larceny, not by false pretenses, can fulfill the "felonious taking" requirement of robbery.

First, *larceny* **requires "asportation,"** which is a carrying away of stolen property. [Asportation is satisfied by only the slightest movement.] Asportation is what makes larceny a continuing offense. *** **Because larceny is a continuing offense, a defendant who uses force or fear in an attempt to escape with property taken by larceny has committed robbery.** *People v. Estes* (1983) 147 Cal. App. 3d 23, 27-28. Similarly, the Attorney General asserts that defendant committed robbery because he shoved the Walmart security guards during his attempt to flee the store after acquiring the store gift cards through theft by false pretenses.

But *theft by false pretenses,* **unlike larceny, has no requirement of asportation. The offense requires only that "(1) the defendant made a false pretense or representation to the owner of property; (2) with the intent to defraud the owner of that property; and (3) the owner transferred the property to the defendant in reliance on the representation." [Theft] by false pretenses ends at the moment title to the property is acquired, and thus cannot become robbery by the defendant's later use of force or fear.** Here, when defendant shoved the store security guards, he was no longer engaged in the commission of theft because he had already acquired title to the Walmart gift cards; therefore, defendant did not commit robbery. ***

We now consider another significant difference between larceny and theft by false pretenses. **[Larceny requires a "trespassory taking," which is a taking without the property owner's consent.]** This element of larceny, like all its other elements, is incorporated into California's robbery statute. *** **By contrast, theft by false pretenses involves the *consensual* transfer of possession as well as *title* of property; therefore, it cannot be committed by trespass.** This is illustrated by *People v. Beaver,* where the defendant staged an accident at his place of employment, a ski resort, to obtain medical expenses for a preexisting injury to his knee. [*Beaver* essentially held that because the ski resort consented to paying for the defendant's medical treatment, the defendant did not commit a trespassory taking, and hence did not commit larceny. He instead committed theft by false pretenses.]

Here too defendant did not commit larceny. Walmart, through its store employees, consented to transferring title to the gift cards to defendant. Defendant acquired ownership of the gift cards through his false representation, on which Walmart relied, that he was using valid payment cards to purchase the gift cards. Only after discovering the fraud did the store seek to reclaim possession. Because [PC 211's "felonious taking" must be *without the consent* of the property owner,] and Walmart *consented* to the sale of the gift cards, defendant did not commit a *trespassory* (nonconsensual) taking, and hence did not commit robbery. Moreover, unlike the offense of larceny by trick, in which a defendant's fraud vitiates the consent of the victim as a matter of law, the acquisition of title involved in the crime of theft by false pretenses precludes a trespass from occurring. *** **Therefore, theft by false pretenses cannot satisfy the "felonious taking" element of robbery.** ***

The logic and fairness of this conclusion may be open to question because a thief who uses force to resist capture may be equally culpable whether the theft was committed by larceny (for example, ordinary shoplifting) or by false pretenses (as occurred here). Nevertheless, our task is simply to interpret and apply the laws as the Legislature has enacted them, not to revise or reform them to better reflect contemporary standards.

Conclusion

We reverse the Court of Appeal's judgment upholding defendant's four robbery convictions.

Note

The United States Supreme Court gave its own history lesson about theft in *Bell v. United States*, 462 U.S. 356 (1983). *Bell* explained:

> In the 13th century, **larceny was limited to trespassory taking: a thief committed larceny only if he feloniously "took and carried away" another's personal property *from his possession*. The goal was more to prevent breaches of the peace than losses of property, and violence was more likely when property was taken from the owner's actual possession.**
>
> As the common law developed, protection of property also became an important goal. The definition of larceny accordingly was expanded by judicial interpretation to include cases where the owner merely was deemed to be in possession. Thus when a bailee of packaged goods broke open the packages and misappropriated the contents, he committed larceny. *** The bailor was deemed to be in possession of the contents of the packages, at least by the time of the misappropriation. Similarly, a thief committed "larceny by trick" when he obtained custody of a horse by telling the owner that he intended to use it for one purpose when he in fact intended to sell it and to keep the proceeds. *** The judges accepted the fiction that the owner retained possession of the horse until it was sold, on the theory that the thief had custody only for a limited purpose. ***
>
> By the late 18th century, courts were less willing to expand common-law definitions. Thus when a bank clerk retained money given to him by a customer rather than depositing it in the bank, he was not guilty of larceny, for the bank had not been in possession of the money. *** **Statutory crimes such as embezzlement and obtaining property by false pretenses therefore were created to fill this gap.** ***
>
> The theoretical distinction between false pretenses and larceny by trick may be stated simply. If a thief, through his trickery, acquired *title* to the property from the owner, he has obtained property by false pretenses; but if he merely acquired *possession* from the owner, he has committed larceny by trick. ***

VIDEO: The Fatal Consequences of Fleeing a Shoplifting Arrest

WARNING: GRAPHIC VIDEO. A driver suspected of shoplifting suffers a fatal accident in fleeing police at:

https://www.youtube.com/watch?v=ateexj96TWM

Is It Possible to Commit Theft by Stealing Money from a Public Fountain? Is This the Kind of Case that Should Even Be Pursued?

An article entitled, "Woman Charged With Stealing Fountain Change," *10 TV.com* ("Central Ohio's News Leader") reported on October 17, 2013, that prosecutors accused Deidre Romine of petty theft for taking $2.87 out of a courthouse fountain.

The crime apparently could result in a maximum fine of $1,000 and also comes with potential jail time. Is this the best way to deal with someone desperate enough to take money out of a fountain?

The article and video can be viewed at:

http://www.10tv.com/content/stories/2013/10/17/Bellefontaine_Fountain_Change.html

Tips for Success for Future Law Students and Lawyers

Law School Letters of Recommendation

When choosing a person to write your letter, it is best to ask a professor rather than an employer or friend. Law schools, knowing you will be a law student before you are a lawyer, want to know about your academic abilities. Also, professors will likely be more candid than an employer, who might write a mere "puff piece." The status or rank of the professor is not as important as the enthusiasm and knowledge of the recommender.

When officers and district attorneys want a judge to sign off on a search warrant, they write up the actual warrant so it is easy for the judge to approve the warrant with a simple signature. Although students should not have to write their own letters of recommendation for law school, they should make the process as easy as possible for professors to write the best of letters. Ask professors for letters early in the application process so that professors will not be rushed into writing a shortened or unenthusiastic letter to meet a looming deadline. Provide the professor with a package possibly including: (1) a cover letter giving your full name and contact information as well as the classes—complete with titles, numbers, and semesters taken with the professor, (2) a writing sample from the classes, (3) your personal statement to the law school, and (4) a resume. Make your request with the proper amount of respect. If you have maintained contact with the professor by dropping in for brief visits over the semesters or by e-mailing your progress in careers after graduation, the professor will be more likely to remember you.

B. EMBEZZLEMENT

People have long recognized that theft can occur not only by taking something *from* another's possession, but also by taking something that *is already in* one's possession. Often, a victim entrusts an item to a person who, being a thief, then takes the item. As Stephen Greenblatt noted in *The Swerve: How the*

World Became Modern, at 30 (Norton & Company 2011), one medieval monastery facing this ancient problem attempted to ward off theft of one of its manuscripts by placing the following curse on it, directed against "him that stealeth, or borroweth and returneth not, this book from its owner":

> Let it change into a serpent in his hand and rend him. Let him be struck with palsy, and all his members blasted. Let him languish in pain crying aloud for mercy, and let there be no surcease to his agony till he sing in dissolution.

John Wesley Bartram, in *Pleading for Theft Consolidation in Virginia: Larceny, Embezzlement, False Pretenses and § 19.2-284,* 56 Wash & Lee L. Rev. 249, 269 (1999), explained: "Embezzlement is the conversion of lawfully possessed property. However, unlike larceny, embezzlement was not a crime at common law. Larceny required a trespassory taking. As a result, **those individuals who had lawfully acquired possession of property could not be guilty of larceny for subsequently misappropriating that property. In order to mend these [loopholes], the English Parliament created the statutory crime of embezzlement.**"

Common law judges could have simply expanded larceny to include takings of property already in lawful possession. As explained in *Commonwealth v. Ryan*, 155 Mass. 523, 527 (1892), the judges chose not to because they did not relish expanding larceny, which was a capital offense. The creation of two separate theft crimes was therefore a "historical accident." The case below provides a recent example of embezzlement.

Another difference between **embezzlement** and **larceny** is the **intent needed to commit each crime.** While **larceny requires** that the thief stole "**with the intent to permanently deprive**" the owner of the property, **embezzlement does not**, instead requiring "**fraudulent appropriation.**" Therefore, as noted by the court below, **although an intent to return property can be a defense to larceny, it is not a defense to embezzlement.**

Possible Embezzlement by City Council Candidate

Felicia Gans reported for *The Boston Globe* on October 10, 2017, in her article, "Former City Council Candidate Charged with Larceny, Embezzlement," that Cornell Mills was arraigned on charges involving $50,000. Asking alleged victims to have him hold money "in escrow," he is charged with having spent it instead. The full article can be viewed at:

https://www.bostonglobe.com/metro/2017/04/24/former-city-council-candidate-charged-with-larceny-embezzlement-after-allegedly-posing-real-estate-broker/jlg8XJM0MQ2Y0fTglcri7L/story.html

LEGAL ANALYSIS

People v. Sisuphan
181 Cal. App. 4th 800 (2010).
Justice Jenkins delivered the opinion for the California Court of Appeals.

Facts

As the director of finance at Toyota of Marin [the dealership], Sisuphan managed the financing contracts for vehicle sales, [ensured] that the proper paperwork was completed for each sale, [and] supervised two finance managers who prepared sales contracts, received payments from customers, and issued receipts for car purchases. Sisuphan complained repeatedly to management about *** one of the finance managers, Ian McClelland, [saying McClelland] made frequent mistakes in preparing paperwork and refused to follow his direction. *** General manager Michael Christian [Christian] opted not to terminate McClelland "because he brought a lot of money into the dealership."

On July 3, 2007, McClelland accepted a large payment [$22,600 in cash and two checks totaling $7,275.51 from customer Jill Peacock for the vehicle she purchased]. McClelland prepared a receipt, placed the cash, both checks, and a copy of the receipt in a large manila envelope [and tried to jam the envelope into] the company safe in Sisuphan's office. *** The envelope, which was stuffed with a large amount of cash, did not drop all the way down into the safe and became lodged, with a portion "sticking out." McClelland could not retrieve the envelope or push it completely into the safe, so he decided to cut it and transfer the contents to two envelopes. He paged another salesman for assistance but received no response and asked Sisuphan to keep an eye on the envelope while he went to the showroom. While McClelland was gone, Sisuphan "wiggled" the envelope free, extracted it from the safe, and kept it. [Sisuphan was not authorized to remove money from the safe and did not have the combination.] When McClelland returned, Sisuphan told him "Hey, no problem, [the envelope] dropped into the safe."

[When a bookkeeper found that the payment for the Peacock purchase was missing, she repeatedly asked Sisuphan], "Where's money?" [He "said they were looking into it."]

The bookkeeper [left Sisuphan messages about the missing money.] Christian followed up with the customer, made a police report, and filed a claim with the dealership's insurer. [He told all the managers that he would not bring criminal charges if the money was returned within 24 hours.]

[Sisuphan finally admitted to Christian] that he had taken the money. He claimed he had no intention of stealing it and had taken it to get McClelland fired. He said he had not returned the money during the 24-hour amnesty period because he did not believe Christian's assurance that no punitive action would be taken. [Sisuphan said] he had taken the money to prove a point—that McClelland was "sloppy" in handling the dealership's money. [Christian had trusted Sisuphan and was] shocked that he had taken the money.

The next day, Christian terminated Sisuphan's employment. [Although Sisuphan] repaid the entire sum of cash he had taken [the checks were lost, prompting the customer to stop payment on them.]

[The district attorney charged Sisuphan with theft by embezzlement. When a jury convicted Sisuphan, he appealed.]

Sisuphan [argued that his return of the money to the company showed] he never intended to keep it and therefore lacked the requisite intent for the crime. We reject these contentions and affirm the judgment.

Issue

Whether returning embezzled property or having the intent to return embezzled property is a valid defense to a charge of embezzlement.

Rule and Analysis

[The intent] to permanently deprive the owner of the property is not required to establish embezzlement [People v. Talbot, 220 Cal. 3, 14. 16 (1934). **Restoration of the property is not a defense because the offense is complete at the time of the taking.**] Sisuphan's "no harm, no foul" interpretation contradicts this authority and flies in the face of public policy protecting the rights of property owners. Such a construction would allow an agent to take property without the owner's permission or knowledge and keep it indefinitely, without consequence, until the owner filed criminal charges. [A] "thief may not purge himself of guilt, by giving back the plunder, before or after arrest."

***Sisuphan contends that evidence of repayment was relevant to show he lacked fraudulent intent at the time he took the money. ***

Fraudulent intent is an essential element of embezzlement. *** Although restoration of the property is not a defense, evidence of repayment may be relevant to the extent it shows that a defendant's intent at the time of the taking was not fraudulent. *** The question before us, therefore, is whether evidence that Sisuphan returned the money reasonably tends to prove he lacked the requisite intent at the time of the taking. ***

Section 508 ***: "Every clerk, agent, or servant of any person who fraudulently appropriates to his own use, or secretes with a fraudulent intent to appropriate to his own use, any property of another which has come into his control or care by virtue of his employment . . . is guilty of embezzlement." Sisuphan denies he ever intended "to use the [money] to financially better himself, even temporarily" and contends the evidence he sought to introduce showed "he returned the [money] without having appropriated it to his own use in any way." He argues that this evidence negates fraudulent intent because it supports his claim that he took the money to get McClelland fired and acted "to help his company by drawing attention to the inadequacy and incompetency of an employee." We reject these contentions.

In determining whether Sisuphan's intent was fraudulent at the time of the taking, the issue is not whether he intended to spend the money, but whether he intended to use it for a purpose other than that for which the dealership entrusted it to him. ["That the property was never 'applied to the embezzler's personal use or benefit'" is no defense. ***] **The offense of embezzlement contemplates a principal's entrustment of property to an agent for certain purposes and the agent's breach of that trust by acting outside his authority in his use of the property.** [See § 503: "**Embezzlement is the fraudulent appropriation of property by a person to whom it has been [e]ntrusted.**"] "It is the immediate breach of trust that makes the offense; *** ["The gist of embezzlement is the appropriation to one's own use of property delivered to him for devotion to a specified purpose other than his own enjoyment of it." An] employee who intentionally deprives his employer of property, even temporarily, and uses it for a purpose outside the scope of the trust, fraudulently appropriates it "to his own use" within the meaning of section 508. [The intent essential to embezzlement is the intent to fraudulently appropriate the property to a use and purpose other than that for which it was entrusted, in other words, the intent to deprive the owner of his property [even though only temporarily. An intent to permanently deprive the owner of the property is not required]. **Sisuphan's undisputed purpose—to get McClelland fired—was beyond the scope of his responsibility and therefore outside the trust afforded him by**

the dealership. Accordingly, even if the proffered evidence shows he took the money for this purpose, it does not tend to prove he lacked fraudulent intent, and the trial court properly excluded this evidence.

Conclusion

Neither returning embezzled property nor having the intent to return embezzled property is a valid defense to a charge of embezzlement. [Judgment affirmed.][78]

Note

What if the embezzler does return the money stolen? The *Sisuphan* Court quoted California Penal Code Section 513 as follows:

> **Whenever**, prior to an information laid before a magistrate, or an indictment found by a grand jury, charging the commission of embezzlement, **the person accused voluntarily and actually restores or tenders restoration of the property alleged to have been embezzled**, or any part thereof, **such fact is not a ground of defense**, but it authorizes the court to mitigate punishment, in its discretion.

Sisuphan then noted that Penal Code 513 only benefitted the embezzler by establishing that, "a defendant's subsequent restorative action, if timely and voluntarily made, [is] a mitigating factor at sentencing."

Robin Hood Embezzlement: Can people commit embezzlement even if they do not intend to enrich themselves?

In *State v. Lassiter*, 796 S.E.2d 401 (2017), the Court of Appeals of North Carolina, in an unpublished opinion, considered whether the following facts amounted to embezzlement. Dana Alton Lassiter, as office manager for Carolina Women's Physicians, "was responsible for monitoring the business's finances and accounts and paying bills." Without authorization, Lassiter used the business's credit card to make some purchases, including buying two flower arrangements that he presented as gifts to other employees. The owner of the business later "testified that Lassiter was the only employee with access to the business credit card, that the charges were not for business purposes, and that Lassiter was not authorized to use the business credit card for any other purposes without first obtaining approval from the owner." A jury convicted Lassiter of embezzlement. The *Lassiter* court found sufficient evidence to support the conviction. The court noted:

> The essential elements of embezzlement are:
>
> (1) the defendant, older than 16, acted as an agent or fiduciary for his principal, (2) he received money or valuable property of his principal in the course of his employment and through his fiduciary relationship, and (3) he fraudulently or knowingly and willfully misapplied or converted to his own use the money of his principal which he had received in a fiduciary capacity.

---

78. Reprinted with the permission of LexisNexis.

Lassiter [argued] that the State failed to show that he purchased the flowers for his own use or misapplied the funds with fraudulent intent. Lassiter contends that he *** did not personally benefit from the transaction.

There is no dispute that Lassiter gave the flowers to other employees, and nothing suggests that he had an improper motive for doing so. However, the State is under no obligation to prove that Lassiter used the embezzled money in a way that enriched him personally. **If, like a modern-day Robin Hood, an office manager knowingly and willfully siphoned funds from a business and gave the money away to random strangers without any personal gain, that is still embezzlement.** [Embezzlement] requires only the defendant's "misapplication of her employer's funds by paying bills she knew to be not for [her employer's] benefit and specifically not authorized by her employer." ***

Here, Dr. Ferguson, the owner of the business, testified that there are a limited set of authorized expenses for which Lassiter was permitted to spend the business's money; that this fact was part of Lassiter's job description; and that flowers for other employees were not among those authorized expenses unless Lassiter first obtained approval from the owner. She also testified that Lassiter did not obtain approval before buying the flowers. [This testimony is sufficient for a reasonable juror to infer all the elements of embezzlement.]

C.   THEFT BY FALSE PRETENSES

John Wesley Bartram offered, in *Pleading for Theft Consolidation in Virginia: Larceny, Embezzlement, False Pretenses and § 19.2-284,* 56 Wash & Lee L. Rev. 249, 281–82 (1999), the following regarding theft by false pretenses:

"Obtaining property by false pretenses," shortened to merely "false pretenses," was not a crime at English common law. As was the case with embezzlement, **the English Parliament created the crime of false pretenses to fill a loophole in the law of larceny.** At common law, a person who, with intent to steal, fraudulently induced another to pass possession of some property, and subsequently converted that property, was guilty of larceny by trick. However, **one who, by fraudulent inducement, obtained both possession and title to the property in question was guilty of no crime at all. The wrongful acquisition of title to another's property merely gave rise to civil action . . . In response to this gap in the common law, Parliament enacted the first general false pretenses statute in 1757.**

***In a majority of the American jurisdictions, false pretenses consists of five basic elements: "(1) a false representation of a material present or past fact (2) which causes the victim (3) to pass title to (4) his property to the wrongdoer, (5) who (a) knows his representation to be false and (b) intends thereby to defraud the victim."**

MPC 223.2 Theft by Deception

A person is guilty of theft if he purposely obtains property of another by deception. A person deceives if he purposely:

(1) creates or reinforces a false impression, including false impressions as to law, value, intention or other state of mind; but deception as to a person's intention to perform a

promise shall not be inferred from the fact alone that he did not subsequently perform the promise; or

(2) prevents another from acquiring information which would affect his judgment of a transaction; or

(3) fails to correct a false impression which the deceiver previously created or reinforced, or which the deceiver knows to be influencing another to whom he stands in a fiduciary or confidential relationship; or

(4) fails to disclose a know lien, adverse claim, or other legal impediment to the enjoyment of property which he transfers or encumbers in consideration for the property obtained . . .

The term "deceive" does not, however, include falsity as to matters having no pecuniary significance, or puffing by statements unlikely to deceive ordinary persons in the group addressed.[79]

Biography—Judge

Chief Justice John Marshall

- Born on September 24, 1755, in Germantown, Virginia, and appointed to the Supreme Court by John Adams.
- **Was a staunch Federalist and antagonist of President Thomas Jefferson, but was also Jefferson's cousin.**
- **Wrote the opinion for *Marbury v. Madison*,** 1 Cranch 137 (1803), the case creating the Doctrine of Judicial Review, making the U.S. Supreme Court the final word on interpreting the U.S. Constitution.
- Was Secretary of State when President John Adams made his "midnight appointments" of Federalist partisans to the federal judicial bench in an effort to deny the next administration, Thomas Jefferson's Democratic Republicans, the chance to fill the positions.
- As Secretary of State, failed to deliver some of the new commissions, including that of William Marbury, leaving it to the Secretary of State of the new Administration to do so. The new Secretary of State, James Madison, refused to deliver the commission to Marbury, who then sued, starting the litigation for *Marbury v. Madison*, the very case upon which Marshall would make his famous ruling.
- The *Marbury v. Madison* ruling, by finding Congress violated the Constitution in passing the legislation by which the case came to the court, not only strengthened the institutional power of the court, it also allowed Marshal to avoid the lose-lose situation of ruling in the favor of Jefferson, his political rival, or ruling against Jefferson, only to see the new president ignore the court's ruling and thus weaken its authority.
- Was quite persuasive with other justices, particularly because the **members of the court at that time lived in the same lodging house and broke bread and drank wine together**—making it easier to reach consensus on some of the court's decisions.

---

79. From *The Model Penal Code* by the American Law Institute. Copyright © 1962 by the American Law Institute. Used by permission.

D.   MODERN TREND TO CONSOLIDATE THEFT CRIMES INTO ONE OFFENSE

If you are having trouble distinguishing between the theft crimes of larceny, embezzlement, and false pretenses, you are not alone. As noted by legal commentators B. E. Witkin and Norman L. Epstein, in *California Criminal Law*, Third Edition, Vol. II, at 19 (Witkin Legal Institute) (2000):

> These legalistic distinctions were hard to apply to fact situations. Great inconvenience was encountered in selecting the proper offense to be charged and the appropriate instructions to be given to the jury; and variance sometimes resulted in the reversal of a conviction for the wrong crime. Hence **modern legislation typically abolishes the procedural distinctions and combines the crimes under one general heading, such as theft**.

California offers an example of such consolidation statutes in Penal Codes 490a and 484, below.

California Penal Code § 490a: Substitution of "Theft" for Other Terms

Wherever any law or statute of this state refers to or mentions larceny, embezzlement, or stealing, said law or statute shall hereafter be read and interpreted as if the word "theft" were substituted therefor.

California Penal Code § 484: What Constitutes Theft; Determination of Value of Property . . .

(a) Every person who shall feloniously steal, take, carry, lead, or drive away the personal property of another, or who shall fraudulently appropriate property which has been entrusted to him or her, or who shall knowingly and designedly, by any false or fraudulent representation or pretense, defraud any other person of money, labor or real or personal property, or who causes or procures others to report falsely of his or her wealth or mercantile character and by thus imposing upon any person, obtains credit and thereby fraudulently gets or obtains possession of money, or property or obtains the labor or service of another, is guilty of theft. In determining the value of the property obtained, for the purposes of this section, the reasonable and fair market value shall be the test, and in determining the value of services received the contract price shall be the test . . .[80]

When Is a Theft So Serious That It Should Be "Grand Theft?"

California defines "grand theft" by statute in PC 487 as follows:

West's Ann. California Penal Code § 487. "Grand theft" defined

Grand theft is theft committed in any of the following cases:

(a) When the money, labor, or real or personal property taken is of a value exceeding nine hundred fifty dollars ($950), except as provided in subdivision (b).
(b) Notwithstanding subdivision (a), grand theft is committed in any of the following cases:
(1)(A) When domestic fowls, avocados, olives, citrus or deciduous fruits, other fruits, vegetables, nuts, artichokes, or other farm crops are taken of a value exceeding two hundred fifty dollars ($250).

---

80. From *Deering's California Codes Annotated.* Copyright © 2014 by Matthew Bender & Company, Inc., a member of the LexisNexis Group. Reprinted with the permission of LexisNexis.

(B) For the purposes of establishing that the value of domestic fowls, avocados, olives, citrus or deciduous fruits, other fruits, vegetables, nuts, artichokes, or other farm crops under this paragraph exceeds two hundred fifty dollars ($250), that value may be shown by the presentation of credible evidence which establishes that on the day of the theft domestic fowls, avocados, olives, citrus or deciduous fruits, other fruits, vegetables, nuts, artichokes, or other farm crops of the same variety and weight exceeded two hundred fifty dollars ($250) in wholesale value.

(2) When fish, shellfish, mollusks, crustaceans, kelp, algae, or other aquacultural products are taken from a commercial or research operation which is producing that product, of a value exceeding two hundred fifty dollars ($250).

(3) Where the money, labor, or real or personal property is taken by a servant, agent, or employee from his or her principal or employer and aggregates nine hundred fifty dollars ($950) or more in any 12 consecutive month period.

(c) When the property is taken from the person of another.

(d) When the property taken is any of the following:

(1) An automobile.

(2) A firearm.

Meanwhile, Massachusetts's law on grand theft is evolving. Katie Lannan of the *State House News Service* reported on March 11, 2016, in "Senate acts to raise threshold for felony larceny" on masslive.com that the state is moving the threshold for felony theft from $250 to $1,500. The full article can be viewed at:

http://www.masslive.com/politics/index.ssf/2016/03/senate_acts_to_raise_threshold.html

E.   ROBBERY

1.   Common Law

Blackstone, in his *Commentaries*, Vol. IV, at 241, defined robbery as "Open and violent larciny from the *person* . . . the *rapina* of civilians." **To commit robbery at common law required "felonious and forcible taking, from the person of another, of goods or money to any value, by putting him in fear."** Robbery could occur by taking directly from the victim's person (body), or from "his presence only; as where a robber by menaces and violence puts a man in fear, and drives away his sheep or his cattle before his face." Blackstone declared, "It is immaterial of what value the thing taken is: a penny as well as a pound, thus forcibly extorted, makes a robbery." Robbery could be committed with use of only fear, such as when "a person with

Robbery is a centuries-old crime.

© Everett Historical/Shutterstock.com

a sword drawn begs an alms, and I give it him through mistrust and apprehension of violence." Robbery could also be committed with use of only force, as when "a man be knocked down without previous warning, and stripped of his property while senseless, though strictly he cannot be said to be *put in fear*, yet this is undoubtedly robbery."

VIDEO: Suspected Robber Evades Police and Then Shoots at Officers

WARNING: GRAPHIC VIDEO. A police dashcam video shows a suspected robber evading police, firing a gun at them, and then running, at:

https://www.youtube.com/watch?v=dQGgEAqurSs

---

2. Current Law

Robbery has been called "compound larceny" or "aggravated larceny" because it is essentially larceny compounded with or aggravated by "force or fear." The California Supreme Court, in *People v. Clary* 72 Cal. 59 (1887), has simply stated, "Robbery is larceny, with the element of force or intimidation added."

a) What Is "Force" for Robbery?

How Much Force Is Needed to Elevate Mere Theft to Robbery?

The "force" necessary for robbery typically causes one to think of shootings or beatings of victims in order to obtain their property. What about situations, however, where the application of force is more subtle, as with getting a victim intoxicated so that property can be taken from the person when he or she becomes unconscious? *People v. Kelley* 220 Cal. App.3d 1358 (1990) considered this issue in a case where the defendant, Robert Kelley, was convinced of conspiracy to commit robbery and murder.

Kelley and Proceso Serrato, who both lived in an abandoned Pacific Bell building in San Diego, agreed to steal money from some sailors. The defendant and others invited two sailors, one of whom was named Brian Farr, back to the Pacific Bell building. Serrato and Kelley planned to get Farr involved in the drinking game, "quarters," get him drunk, "have him pass out and then take his money and leave." The next day, Farr's body was found face down, beaten to death with a rod or pipe. Farr suffered "a skull fracture and intracranial hemorrhage due to blunt trauma to the head." The evidence indicated that the beating occurred after the drinking game. "Farr's wallet was found about 12 or 15 inches from his head. There was no money in the wallet. Farr's pockets had apparently been searched, his left front pocket had been turned inside out."

Focusing on the conspiracy to commit robbery charge, Kelley contended he was entitled to jury instructions on conspiracy to commit theft as a lesser included offense of conspiracy to commit robbery. The Court of Appeal agreed, reasoning as follows:

> To sustain a conviction for conspiracy to commit a particular offense, the prosecution must show not only that the conspirators intended to agree but also that they intended to commit the elements of that offense. ***The elements of robbery are (1) a taking of personal property, (2) from the person or immediate presence of another, (3) through the use of force or fear, (4) with an intent to permanently deprive the owner of his property.** [Theft is a lesser included offense of robbery.]

> When Farr's body was discovered, his blood alcohol level was .21 percent. There were 11 empty or nearly empty beer cans and other evidence indicating the game of "Quarters" had been played. Farr's pockets had been searched and his money taken. There was evidence suggesting he had been assaulted in a different place from where his body was found.

From this evidence, the jury could conclude [that] Kelley and Serrato agreed to intoxicate Farr by the drinking game but planned to take his money only after he had passed out. Kelley argues [this] does not show an agreement to commit robbery because it does not show an agreement to use force or fear against Farr. The Attorney General responds the force element was satisfied by Kelley's and Serrato's plan to use alcohol to overcome Farr's resistance and cites *People v. Dreas* (1984) 153 Cal.App.3d 623 [200 Cal.Rptr. 586] in support.

In *Dreas*, the defendant was convicted of multiple robberies based on his conduct of patronizing a bar, striking up a conversation with an individual patron, suggesting that they leave to get some coffee, going to the victim's home where he surreptitiously put lorazepam, a hypnotic sedative and tranquilizer, into the victim's coffee and then taking the victim's property while the victim was unconscious. ***

The *Dreas* [found that administering drugs to overcome the victim's resistance to constitute force within the purview of section 211.] 'Just as battery may be committed by the administration of poison, so the force used to obtain property from a person against his will may be applied internally.' *** **'One may commit robbery by striking his victim** with fist or weapon and then, having thus rendered the victim unconscious or dazed or unwilling to risk another blow, taking property away from him. **One may also render one's victim helpless by more subtle means, as by administering intoxicating liquors or drugs in order to produce a state of unconsciousness or stupefaction; to act in this way is to use force for purposes of robbery.'** ***"

The *Dreas* court concluded: "A showing of 'force or fear' is not (and cannot be) limited to external forces such as bludgeoning the victim or displaying a lethal weapon to overcome his will and resistance. A poison or intoxicant, although internally applied, may also serve as a potent means to achieve the same goal and may also render the felonious taking of personal property a taking against the will of the victim, thereby constituting robbery." ***

[*Dreas's* facts] are very different from the situation presented here. [*Dreas*] administered a drug to an unsuspecting victim and the victim was involuntarily intoxicated. Here, Kelley's and Serrato's plan was not to secretly administer a drug to an unsuspecting victim but to openly play a drinking game with a sailor who agreed to play the game. In other words, their plan involved voluntary intoxication by the victim. This is a crucial distinction. [*Dreas's* "force" findings] depended on the surreptitious use of the drugs to overcome the victim's resistance. [The test for finding force "is the overcoming of resistance *without the voluntary co-operation* of the subject whose resistance is repressed."] Here, the plan was to have the subject, Farr, voluntarily cooperate by participating in the drinking game. Thus, the "administering of an intoxicating liquor" here did not involve force by Kelley and Serrato, Farr knowingly "administered" the intoxicating liquor to himself.

In cases **where the victim's lack of resistance or unconsciousness is not due to the defendant surreptitiously drugging the victim, but due to the victim's own actions, [the force element is] lacking when the defendant takes property from an unconscious victim.** *** "It is not robbery, however, to steal from the person or presence of one for whose helplessness through drugs or drink the thief was not responsible."

Since the facts here could support a finding Kelley's and Serrato's plan was to get Farr so drunk that he would pass out and thus they would not need to use any force or fear to take Farr's money and that a charged overt act occurred making a culpable conspiracy complete, the jury should have been instructed on conspiracy to commit theft as a lesser included offense of conspiracy to commit robbery.[81]

The Court of Appeal therefore reduced Kelley's conviction for conspiracy to commit robbery to conspiracy to commit theft.

People v. Burns, 172 Cal. App.4th 1251(2009), considered the minimum amount of violence needed to fulfill the "force" element of robbery. In this case, the victim, Dora Hollowell, after having visited an ATM machine, found herself being followed by the defendant, Samuel Alexander Burns, and his accomplice, Carnethia Adams. Burns and Adams followed their victim to the stairwell of an apartment building. As Ms. Hollowell began to climb the staircase, Burns:

> entered the building and grabbed her purse. The purse was on Ms. Hollowell's elbow and he "grabbed it down." She tried to clutch the purse, but appellant stepped on her toe and grabbed the purse. Ms. Hollowell was unable to hold onto it any longer. Appellant pulled the purse down and forcibly took it away from Ms. Hollowell's grip, then ran out the door with the purse. Ms. Hollowell saw him as he ran off and yelled that "he was going to pay for what he did."

Upon conviction for robbery, the defendant appealed, arguing that [the trial court should have instructed the jury on PC 487(c) grand theft from the person as a lesser included offense of robbery.] The Court of Appeal found no error, deeming this "purse snatch" to be a robbery. The *Burns* court reasoned:

> Theft in any degree is a lesser included offense to robbery, since all of its elements are included in robbery. The difference is that robbery includes the added element of force or fear. ***

> [The] seizure in this case did not involve shoving, striking or pulling with such force as to break the purse strap. [Burns] points out that Ms. Hollowell testified that she let go of the purse because she "couldn't hold it any longer" and, based on her testimony, "the jury, properly instructed on both theft and robbery, could readily have concluded that appellant did not use more force than that necessary to take the purse from Ms. Hollowell, and thus he committed theft, not robbery."

> We do not agree. We hold, instead, that **where a person wrests away personal property from another person, who resists the effort to do so, the crime is robbery, not merely theft**.

> *** We have found no California case holding that a purse snatch cannot qualify as a robbery. As we shall explain, whether it does depends on the force used. ***

> The robbery statute, **Penal Code section 211, describes robbery as "the felonious taking of personal property in the possession of another, from his person or immediate presence, and against his will, accomplished by means of force or fear."** ***

> *** In *People v. Morales, supra*, 49 Cal.App.3d 134, the court observed that no case had purported to precisely define that amount of force. "However, it is established that **something more is required than just that quantum of force which is necessary to accomplish the mere seizing of the property**." ["When] actual force is present in a robbery, at the very least it must be a quantum more than that which is needed merely to

81. Reprinted with the permission of LexisNexis.

take the property from the person of the victim, and is a question of fact to be resolved by the jury taking into account the physical characteristics of the robber and the victim." ['All the force that is required to make the offense a robbery is such force as is actually sufficient to overcome the victim's resistance.']

In this case, appellant came up to Ms. Hollowell and grabbed the purse she was holding; she tried to hold onto it but his strength and his act in stepping on her foot overcame her resistance, and he got away with the purse. That was robbery, and there is no basis in the record for a jury to find that it was nothing more than grand theft from the person.[82]

Burns therefore affirmed the defendant's robbery conviction.

Not all purse snatchings have such violence as to rise to the level of robbery. In *People v. Patton*, 389 N.E.2d 1174 (1979), the Supreme Court of Illinois considered a case of a quick and efficient thief. In the case, Ray Patton snatched the purse of Rita Alexander as she and her family were hurrying along the sidewalk to church. As the court noted:

Mrs. Alexander was carrying her purse "[i]n the fingertips of my left hand down at my side." She noticed the defendant cross the street in front of the Alexanders and thought that perhaps he too was going to the service. Instead, the defendant changed direction and walked toward the Alexander family. As he came abreast of Mrs. Alexander, he "swift[ly] grab[bed]" her purse, throwing her arm back "a little bit," she said, and fled. She testified that the purse was gone before she realized what had happened. Once she overcame her momentary shock, Mrs. Alexander screamed and Mr. Alexander unsuccessfully chased the defendant.

The Supreme Court considered whether "the simple taking or 'snatching' of a purse from the fingertips of its unsuspecting possessor in itself constitutes a sufficient use of force, or threat of the imminent use of force, to warrant a conviction of robbery." Although the prosecution argued that "any amount of physical force whatsoever, employed to overcome the force exerted by the person to maintain control over the object in hand, is sufficient to bring the act of taking within the robbery statute," the court was not convinced. *Patton* reasoned:

Our statute defines robbery:

"A person commits robbery when he takes property from the person or presence of another by the use of force or by threatening the imminent use of force." (Ill. Rev. Stat. 1975, ch. 38, par. 18 -- 1.)

Thus, if no force or threat of imminent force is used in the taking, there is no robbery, although the act may constitute a theft. *** Mrs. Alexander did not realize what was happening until after the defendant had begun his flight, and it is clear there was no robbery through the "threatening [of] the imminent use of force." The People maintain that the defendant's act of grabbing was a "use of force" such as is contemplated by the robbery statute, and that no minimum amount of force need be shown to constitute robbery under the statute. ***

[When an article is taken] "without any sensible or material violence to the person, as snatching a hat from the head or a cane or umbrella from the hand" the offense will be held to be theft from the person rather than robbery.

***

---

82. Reprinted with the permission of LexisNexis.

> Mrs. Alexander testified her arm was thrown back "a little bit," but [w]here it is doubtful under the facts whether the accused is guilty of robbery…it is the duty of the court and the jury to resolve that doubt in favor of the lesser offense."[83]

b)   What Is "Fear" for Robbery?

Since **robbery** can be committed by use of **"force" or "fear," exactly how much fear must the victim experience for robbery to occur?** Is absolute terror required, or can the state of fear be less?

LEGAL ANALYSIS

Ross v. State
237 P. 469 (1925).
Justice Edwards delivered the opinion for the Court of Criminal Appeals of Oklahoma.

Facts

[Two persons went into the Bank of Adair,] which was in charge of Faye Godsey, assistant cashier. [The two robbers] pointed a pistol at her and ordered her to "stick 'em up." One of them went behind the rail, ordered her to step out of the way, and she did so, and sat down in a chair. They then took the money from the tray, inquired if there was anything in the safe, and, on being told there was, one of them went outside the rail with her and took the money out of the safe, during which time one of the robbers kept her covered with a pistol. When she had given them the money out of the safe, they ordered her to go into the vault, and they then shut the door and left. $2,100 was taken from the bank. ***

[The defendant, Watie Ross, argued that the testimony is insufficient to support a conviction because there was no proof of the use of force or fear.]

Issue

Whether there was sufficient evidence of "fear" for robbery purposes even thought the victim was not in fear of her life so long as she complied with the persons pointing guns at her.

Rule and Analysis

Robbery is a wrongful taking of personal property in the possession of another from his person or immediate presence and against his will, accomplished by means of force or fear."

*** **The fear which constitutes robbery may be either:**

"First. The fear of an unlawful injury, immediate or future, to the person or property of the person robbed or of any relative of his, or member of his family; or,

"Second. The fear of an immediate and unlawful injury to the person or property of anyone in the company of the person robbed, at the time of the robbery." ***

[No force was employed. Faye Godsey testified that the two men told her that they were not going to hurt her. She was not afraid of them so long as she did what they told her to do. She turned the money over to them because their guns were in evidence. Defendant argues that this may prove larceny, but not robbery.]

This witness displayed great poise and coolness under the circumstances. She apparently was imbued with the idea that the persons who came into the bank, pointing a gun at her, with the command "stick 'em up," were after the money in the bank, and that if they could procure the money there would be no reason to hurt her. This is common sense. She also apparently realized that, if she attempted to resist, violence sufficient to overcome her resistance would be made. [If there is an assault which would furnish a reasonable ground for fear, the robbery is complete.]

In this case **it was not essential to constitute robbery that the custodian of the money taken become hysterical** and believe that she would meet death if she failed to immediately respond to the demands made. **It is sufficient if the demand, with the display of firearms as shown by the evidence, caused her to stand aside and permit the money in her custody to be taken in the manner disclosed by the evidence.** The delivery or taking the money is not rendered voluntary because the witness did not see fit to endanger her safety by attempting to resist. A threat may be made and be just as potent by some act or gesture as if made by words; and fear in a legal sense may result from such a threat, although the person threatened may maintain composure. A defendant will hardly be heard to say that, by holding up another at the point of a gun, and taking property from his person or immediate presence, he is not guilty of robbery, merely because the person robbed was able to exercise self-control.

Robbery's 'fear' element does not require that the victim be placed in extreme terror.

Conclusion

The case is affirmed.[84]

---

84. Reprinted with the permission of LexisNexis.

Robbery Due to Snapchat: Beware of Meeting Up with Old Friends

Anna Conkey, Brie Stimson, and Cassia Pollock reported for *NBC News San Diego* in, "Woman Believes Snapchat Friend Set Her Up for Armed Robbery Near Oak Park Elementary: The friend added her on Snapchat and asked her to meet in a park," that meeting up with an old friend by Snapchat led to her being robbed. Visit the article at:

https://www.nbcsandiego.com/news/local/Woman-Robbed-in-Car-Near-Elementary-School-449998313.html

The "Fear" Needed for California's Robbery

People v. Moorehead 191 Cal. App.4th 765 (2011) ruled, "**The element of fear for purposes of robbery is satisfied when there is sufficient fear to cause the victim to comply with the unlawful demand for his property.**" *Moorehead* considered a series of bank robberies in which the defendant, Melwatt Morehead, Jr., wearing a beanie and sunglasses in an attempt to hide his identity, presented notes to tellers demanding money. The court concluded Moorhead's actions constituted robbery, explaining:

> **It is not necessary that there be direct proof of fear; fear may be inferred from the circumstances in which the property is taken. *** If there is evidence from which fear may be inferred, the victim need not explicitly testify that he or she was afraid**. [The jury may infer fear "from the circumstances despite even superficially contrary testimony of the victim."] The requisite fear need not be the result of an express threat or the use of a weapon. *** Resistance by the victim is not a required element of robbery *** and the victim's fear need not be extreme to constitute robbery [All that is needed is that the record show conduct, words, or circumstances reasonably calculated to produce fear.] **An unlawful demand can convey an implied threat of harm for failure to comply, thus supporting an inference of the requisite fear**. ***

Moorehead thus provided a list of things that were *not* required to legally establish fear for robbery. Just how little does a robber have to do to instill fear for robbery? An answer to this question was provided in *People v. Davison* 32 Cal. App.4th 206 (1995), in which the defendant, Herbert N. Davison, and an accomplice approached the victim, Charlotte Rosebrough at a bank ATM. The court noted:

> On the evening of February 10, 1993, Charlotte Rosebrough drove to a bank in Berkeley, parked her car in the bank's parking lot, and went to one of the bank's automatic teller machines [ATM]. While Rosebrough was waiting for the ATM to dispense her money, appellant and another man [approached from the rear to her right, seemingly out of nowhere. The] two men began "fiddling with the envelope drawer" and "staring" at Rosebrough. *** Appellant, who was closest to Rosebrough, told her to "[s]tand back." According to Rosebrough, appellant spoke in "a calm . . . but . . . firm voice," "a voice like he really meant business." As appellant spoke, he "sort of had a smirk on his face, a strange smile . . . ."

> Upon hearing appellant's words, Rosebrough "felt [she] was in big trouble" and that she "was being robbed . . . ." She "responded immediately" by stepping back from the ATM. She followed the instructions because she "felt they meant business when they said 'Stand back,'" and she "didn't know if they were going to hit [her] or pull a weapon on [her] or what

was their plan." Given her concerns, she "wanted to get some distance between these two men and [herself] just as a matter of personal safety." She therefore moved back 20 to 30 feet in the direction of her car, which she believed "would be safety for" her. As she did so, she "muttered an obscenity."

After Rosebrough retreated, the two men moved over to the ATM she was using. *** Rosebrough eventually retrieved a receipt from the ATM; her bank card and the money were gone.

Davison explained, "Section 211 defines robbery as 'the felonious taking of personal property in the possession of another, from his person or immediate presence, and against his will, accomplished by means of force or fear.'" The Court, in reviewing the evidence presented at trial, found the jury properly convicted the defendant.[85]

Prosecutors can even prove robbery occurred when the victim himself refuses to admit to a jury that the robber frightened him. This was the case in *People v. Renteria* 61 Cal. 2d 497 (1964), where the following occurred:

The . . . defendant entered a liquor store owned by Betty Sandlow, with a gun and a paper bag in his hands and, with the gun pointed at the clerk, told him to fill the bag. The clerk complied with defendant's demand, and put $25 or $30 in the bag. Betty Sandlow was in the store at the time.

At the trial the clerk was asked if he was in fear that defendant would use the gun, and he said, "No, I didn't have any fear of him."

Renteria affirmed the robbery conviction, explaining:

The People are not "bound" by the clerk's testimony that he was not in fear, since there is other evidence which will support the conclusion that he acted in fear and would not have disgorged the contents of his employer's till except in fear of the harm which might come to him or his employer if he failed to comply with defendant's demands. ***

*** "Prompt compliance with the commands of an armed person, who by words or demonstration threatens bodily harm for failure to do so, furnishes some evidence of fear. The very prompt relinquishing of the money in the cash register is also evidence of fear. Men do not ordinarily give up their hard-earned cash to a stranger who threatens them with a gun, except for fear of bodily injury in the event of a refusal to do so. In spite of the bravado of the merchant in declaring that he was not much afraid, we are inclined to believe he meant he was not afraid of receiving bodily harm so long as he complied with the demands of the robber." ***

The circumstances *** fully support the trial court's conclusion that the clerk would not have given his employer's money to defendant unless he was in fear, in spite of his "bravado" answer in court, and that the clerk said he was not in fear because he felt certain no harm would result to him or his employer if he complied with the demand, as he did.

It is not reasonable to suppose that, particularly with his employer in the store, the clerk would have given the employer's money to an unauthorized stranger who demanded possession at the point of a gun, had the clerk not been in fear that injury to himself or his employer would result if he failed to comply with the demand.[86]

---

85. Reprinted with the permission of LexisNexis.
86. Reprinted with the permission of LexisNexis.

"Seamless Web" Connection

In *People v. Renteria,* the case discussed in the box above, the court considered whether the prosecution could prove a robbery victim's fear in the face of his denials on the witness stand that he was frightened for his life. In recognizing that the prosecution could prove the victim's fear by establishing his actions and the circumstances surrounding his actions, the court was relying on "circumstantial evidence" or "indirect evidence." Proving a person's thoughts by offering circumstantial evidence connects this case to the similar rule in Chapter 1 that mens rea or criminal intent can be proven by circumstantial evidence.

Since Robbery Is a Crime of Confrontation, Where Exactly Must the Taking Occur? What Is Meant by the "Immediate Presence" of the Victim?

People v. Hayes 52 Cal.3d 577 (1990) defined "immediate presence" for robbery. *Hayes* noted:

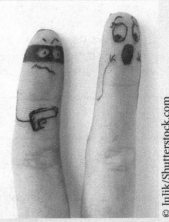
© Jujik/Shutterstock.com

The generally accepted definition of immediate presence, as stated by the Massachusetts Supreme Court, is that"'**[a] thing is in the [immediate] presence of a person, in respect to robbery, which is so within his reach, inspection, observation or control, that he could, if not overcome by violence or prevented by fear, retain his possession of it.'"** *Commonwealth* v. *Homer* (1920) 235 Mass. 526, 533 [127 N.E. 517]. [Property may be found to be in the victim's immediate presence "even though it is located in another room of the house, or in another building on [the] premises."] A taking can be accomplished by force or fear and yet not be from the victim's immediate presence. For example, a person might enter the victim's home and there, by the use of force or fear, compel the victim to reveal the combination of a safe located many miles away in the victim's office. The culprit at the victim's house could then relay the combination to a confederate waiting in or near the office, who could use it to open the safe and take its contents before the victim could reach the office or otherwise interfere with the taking. In such a case, the criminals would have accomplished the taking by force or fear and yet not have taken property from the person or immediate presence of the victim. The perpetrators of the taking would be guilty of several offenses—conspiracy, burglary, assault, and grand theft at the least—but they would not be guilty of robbery as defined in section 211 because the taking would not be from an area over which the victim, at the time force or fear was employed, could be said to exercise some physical control.[87]

The Supreme Court, relying in part on *Hayes* in *People v. Gomez* 43 Cal.4th 249 (2008), further explained:

"immediate presence" is "an area over which the victim, at the time force or fear was employed, could be said to exercise some physical control" over his property. *** "Under this definition, **property may be found to be in the victim's immediate presence 'even though it is located in another room of the house, or in another building on [the] premises.'** ***

[PC 211's "person or immediate presence" requirement] describes a spatial relationship between the victim and the victim's property, and refers to the area from which the property is taken." [The] decisions addressing the 'immediate presence' element of robbery have focused on whether the taken property was located in an area in which the victim could have expected to take effective steps to retain control over his property.

In *People v. Abilez* 41 Cal. 4th 472 (2007), the Supreme Court concluded that "immediate presence" was satisfied:

by evidence defendant took electronic equipment from the victim's bedroom, the same location in which she was killed. Moreover, even taking her car or items from another bedroom would qualify: "**The zone of immediate presence [for purposes of robbery] includes the area 'within which the victim could reasonably be expected to exercise some physical control over his property.**" [For example, when a victim is killed in the bedroom, items in her kitchen would be in her "'immediate presence'" for robbery purposes.]

VIDEO: 1968 FBI Training Film on Bank Robbery

The FBI made a film instructing victims on what to do during a bank robbery at:

https://www.youtube.com/watch?v=EXMQICltnRg

Do's and Don'ts for Hearings, Trials, and Appeals

Direct Examination

Do tell the jury your version of the case three times: Once by leading the witness through his or her memory of the facts, a second time with a map, and a third time with pictures. **Don't** put words in your witness's mouth. Even if you do not trigger an objection from opposing counsel, the jury will sense that you are feeding your witness a story, undermining your credibility.

---

87. Reprinted with the permission of LexisNexis.

F.   EXTORTION

1.   Common Law

Not just anyone could commit extortion back in England's **common law** days. Blackstone, in his *Commentaries*, Vol. IV, at 141, defined **extortion as "the abuse of public justice, which consists in any officer's unlawfully taking, by color of his office, from any man, any money or thing of value, that is not due to him, or more than his due, or before it is due."** Since extortion required the abuse of public office, to commit this crime one had to have a public office to abuse. The punishment for extortion at common law was imposition of "fine and imprisonment." Curiously, punishment only "sometimes" included loss or "forfeiture" of the office.

2.   Current Law

As with robbery, extortion possesses a "force or fear" element. This similarity with robbery is not accidental, for, as La Fave noted in *Criminal Law*, at 1067, **extortion was "created in order to plug a loophole in the robbery law by covering sundry threats which will not do for robbery."** Extortion's threats often are less immediate than those of robbery and need not involve physical danger. While a robber will threaten "Give me your money or I will kill you now!" an extortionist could instead speculate that, "If you do not give me money for 'fire insurance,' your business could suddenly catch fire, if not this month, then sometime soon." Further, robbery envisions a confrontation between robber and victim while an extortionist can communicate a threat to a victim without even being in the same room.

Model Penal Code § 223.4: Theft by Extortion

A person is guilty of theft if he purposely obtains property of another by threatening to:
    (1) inflict serious bodily injury on anyone or commit any other criminal offense; or
    (2) accuse anyone of a criminal offense; or
    (3) expose any secret tending to subject any person to hatred, contempt or ridicule, or to impair his credit or business repute; or
    (4) take or withhold action as an official, or cause an official to take or withhold action; or
    (5) bring about or continue a strike, boycott or other collective unofficial action . . . ; or
    (6) testify or provide information or withhold testimony or information with respect to another's legal claim or defense; or
    (7) inflict any other harm which would not benefit the actor.[88]

California Penal Code § 518

Extortion is the obtaining of property from another, with his consent, or the obtaining of an official act of a public officer, induced by a wrongful use of force or fear, or under color of official right.[89]

> **What exactly is "sextortion" and can it be prosecuted under the existing extortion laws?**
> The following case, *People v. Bollaert*, considers these questions.

---

88. From *The Model Penal Code* by the American Law Institute. Copyright © 1962 by the American Law Institute. Used by permission.
89. From *Deering's California Codes Annotated.* Copyright © 2014 by Matthew Bender & Company, Inc., a member of the LexisNexis Group. Reprinted with the permission of LexisNexis.

People v. Bollaert
248 Cal.App.4th 699 (2016).
Justice O'Rourke delivered the opinion of the California Court of Appeal.

Facts

A jury convicted Kevin Christopher Bollaert of extortion [based on] his operation of Web sites, "UGotPosted.com," through which users posted private, intimate photographs of others along with that person's name, location and social media profile links, and "ChangeMyReputation.com," through which victims could pay to have the information removed. ***

In 2012, 2013 and 2014, a number of individuals discovered that photographs of themselves, including nude photographs, as well as their names, hometowns, and social media addresses, had been posted without their permission on a Web site, UGotPosted.com. Most of the pictures were taken by or for former significant others or friends. Some of the pictures the victims had taken on their own phones or placed on personal webpages for private viewing by themselves or select others. Some had been taken while the victim was drugged and in a compromised state or otherwise unaware of the photographing. Victims received harassing and vulgar messages from strangers. Many of the victims contacted the Web site administrator at UGotPosted.com to try to get their photographs and information removed, without success. *** The UGotPosted Web site contained a link to another Web site, ChangeMyReputation.com, where victims were told that for payment of a specified amount of money, their pictures and information would be taken down. Six of the victims paid money to an account on ChangeMyReputation.com to have their pictures removed from the Web site.

Bollaert was the administrator and registered owner of the UGotPosted Web site. *** Bollaert was in control of the Web site, and he managed and maintained it; changed, added and deleted content; and updated software that operated the site. He designed the Web site so that he had to review the content before it was posted, and it had "required fields" by which a user who wanted to post pictures of another person had to input that other person's full name, age, location ("city, state, country") and Facebook link. Bollaert had the only user account on the computer; he looked at every single post that came through the Web site and decided what would get posted on it, placed watermarks on each photograph to discourage others from stealing the pictures, and accessed the site remotely. He kept a spreadsheet recording every single post. ***

Bollaert also set up and managed the Web site ChangeMyReputation.com, to which individuals who had pictures posted on the UGotPosted.com site would be directed and told they could pay money to have the information removed. [Victims paid a total of $30,147.73, which was forwarded to Bollaert's personal PayPal account.]

At trial, victim Rebecca testified that *** she discovered that intimate photographs of herself and her ex-fiancée, as well as her full name, work location, Facebook link and age, were posted on UGotPosted. com without her consent. Rebecca felt "extremely violated" by the situation, which was very hurtful and embarrassing to her. She e-mailed the Web site and demanded the photographs be taken down, but received no response. She also e-mailed ChangeMyReputation.com, and within minutes received a response directing her to pay $249.99 via PayPal. Rebecca paid the money because she felt the images were disgusting and, though her manager and others had already seen them, she was worried the images would be exposed to more people. ***

Victim Alaina testified that after she discovered her own nude pictures, full name, age, city and school were posted on UGotPosted.com without her consent, she sent five to 10 messages to the Web site in an effort to have the content removed, without response. Alaina testified she then "paid the blackmail fee of $350" to ChangeMyReputation.com, which stated it would take photographs down upon payment. The content was removed the next day. Alaina was "devastated" by the situation; she changed her appearance because she lived in a small town, was afraid of being stalked, and still suffered psychological trauma at the time of trial.

[Bollaert argued there was no extortion because he did not threaten any of the victims to expose any secret. Also, the alleged secrets—the photographs—were already in the public domain. The People argued that Bollaert used the implicit threat of *continued* exposure of the victims' pictures and information to extort money from them, and that a secret can remain a secret despite being made known to others, even many others, as long as there are some who do not know it. Because the evidence is sufficient to support Bollaert's extortion convictions, we affirm the judgment.]

Issue

1. **Whether there was sufficient evidence of defendant making threats for extortion.**
2. **Whether a secret can remain a secret despite being made known to others, for purposes of extortion.**

Rule and Analysis

[PC 518 **Extortion is the obtaining of property from another, with his consent . . . induced by a wrongful use of force or fear**. Under PC 519, **fear for purposes of extortion may be induced by a threat to accuse the individual threatened of a crime or to expose a deformity, disgrace or crime or expose a secret affecting the victim**.]

[To establish extortion, the wrongful use of force or fear must be the operating or controlling cause compelling the victim's consent to surrender the thing to the extortionist. **The 'secret' referred to in the statute is a matter 'unknown to the general public, or to some particular part thereof which might be interested in obtaining knowledge of the secret.** The] secret must affect the threatened person in some way so far unfavorable to the reputation or to some other interest of the threatened person, that threatened exposure thereof would be likely to induce him through fear to pay out money or property for the purpose of avoiding the exposure.' *** No precise or particular form of words is necessary in order to constitute a threat under the circumstances. **Threats can be made by innuendo and the circumstances under which the threat is uttered and the relations between [the defendant and the target of the threats] may be taken into consideration.**] 'The more vague and general the terms of the accusation the better it would [serve] the purpose of the accuser in magnifying the fears of his victim, and the better also it would serve to protect him in the event of the failure to accomplish his extortion and of a prosecution for his attempted crime.'***

[The] threats were inherent and implied in the very structure and content of Bollaert's Web sites, which Bollaert himself created and operated. When victims were directed via UGotPosted.com to the ChangeMyReputation.com Web site, they were informed *** they could have their photos removed for a fee, from which victims could infer that if they did not pay, the offensive content would remain on the site in further public view. Those victims who communicated with Bollaert before they paid were told the content would only be removed upon payment, and Bollaert only removed the content when the victims paid the requested fee ***. There is no question based on the victims' testimony that the display of their private images and information subjected them to shame, disgrace and embarrassment as to their reputation and character, and they would continue to be exposed to other people if the content was not removed. The fact Bollaert did not *** seek out or contact the victims, but merely responded to the victims' pleas to remove their content, does not render the threat element unsupported by the evidence.

[There] is ample evidence from which the jury could conclude Bollaert's joint operation and connection of the two Web sites in this manner, as well as his communications to the victims, was a means to obtain their money by wrongful use of fear, namely the threat to "impute to [them disgrace"] by continued display of their private nude images and further humiliation, embarrassment, and damage to their reputation, unless they paid.

[There is substantial evidence that the victims' photographs and personal identifying information constituted a secret within the meaning of the crime of extortion, notwithstanding its posting on the Internet and viewing by some individuals.]

[To] **suffice for extortion, the "'thing held secret must be unknown to the general public, *or to some particular part thereof which might be interested in obtaining knowledge of the secret*'"** in addition to affecting the threatened person in some way so far unfavorable to the reputation, or to some other interest of the threatened person, that threatened exposure would be likely to induce the victim through fear to pay money so as to avoid the exposure.

[Here, the fact the victims' photographs were placed on the Internet and exposed to the public did not mean that some other "particular part of the public"]—namely, family members, classmates, coworkers, or employers who might be interested—had seen them. The People presented direct testimony from some of the six victims concerning their fear that others would see their images if they did not pay to have them removed, as well as evidence as to all of the victims that they quickly paid for removal, from which the jury could readily infer the victims were fearful of continued exposure. The jury could reasonably conclude the photographs therefore remained a secret to persons who had not viewed the Web site, and reasonably found it was the victims' fear that others would see the content, causing further humiliation or damage to their reputation, that compelled them to pay Bollaert's fee. ***

Conclusion

There was sufficient evidence to prove both the defendant's threats and exposure of a secret. The judgment is affirmed.[90]

Can Threatening to Expose a Criminal for His Crime Be Extortion?

In *People v. Beggs* 178 Cal. 79 (1918), the California Supreme Court considered whether threatening to accuse a person of a crime for a criminal act he or she committed could be extortion. In *Beggs*, Joseph Steining discovered that his employee, Joseph N. Da Rosa, was stealing from his store. Steining had Da Rosa arrested "by a detective and taken to the police station, where, in the absence of a complaint filed, he was 'booked' as charged with [theft]." When arrested, Da Rosa freely admitted that he had stolen clothes and offered to pay Steining the $50 he owed him. Instead, Steining hired the defendant, Beggs, as his attorney. Beggs learned from interviewing Da Rosa at the police station that the employee had $2,500 in the bank. Beggs "impressed upon [Da Rosa] the gravity of his offense" and threatened that he would send him to San Quentin, "for seven to ten years" unless he immediately paid defendant two thousand dollars to settle with Steining. Induced by this fear, Da Rosa paid $2000 "to compensate Steining for loss due to thefts committed by Da Rosa." At trial, the judge told the jury:

> the law does not permit the collection of money by the use of fear induced by means of threats to accuse the debtor of crime. It makes no difference whether Da Rosa stole any goods from Steining, nor how much he stole"; and that "it is your duty to convict the

---

90. Reprinted from Westlaw, with permission of Thomson Reuters.

defendant, even though you should also find that he believed that Da Rosa was guilty of the theft of Steining's goods in an amount either less than, equal to, or greater than any sum of money obtained from Da Rosa.

When Beggs was convicted, the court affirmed, explaining:

> [The trial judge did not let the jury consider] the good faith with which defendant acted in . . . enforcing payment of the money alleged to be due to Steining. [PC 518 provides,] "Extortion is the obtaining of property from another, with his consent, induced by a wrongful use of force or fear, or under color of official right."

> The consent of the injured party in surrendering his property must, in the language of the statute, be "induced by the wrongful use of fear." This implies there may be a rightful use of fear. What meaning is to be ascribed to the word wrongful? Is it wrongful for A, from whom B has stolen goods, to threaten the latter with prosecution unless he pay the value thereof, and thus, by means of the fear induced by such threat, obtain from B that which is justly due to A? [**The use of fear induced by such threats as a means of collecting a debt, is wrongful**. PC 519 provides that fear for extortion may be induced by a threat to accuse the victim of any crime.][91]

> [Assuming Da Rosa had in fact stolen two thousand dollars worth of goods from Steining, defendant's threats to prosecute Da Rosa unless he paid the two thousand dollars, by reason of fear induced by such threat,] constitutes the crime of extortion. **It is the means employed which the law denounces, and though the purpose may be to collect a just indebtedness arising from and created by the criminal act for which the threat is to prosecute the wrongdoer, it is nevertheless within the statutory inhibition. The law does not contemplate the use of criminal process as a means of collecting a debt.** [Good faith,] or the fact that the end accomplished by such means is rightful, cannot avail one as a defense in such prosecution, any more than such facts would constitute a defense where one compels payment of a just debt by the threat to do an unlawful injury to the person of his debtor. ***

Beggs noted that the South Dakota Supreme Court agreed that the word, "wrongful," had ""no reference whatever to the question of the justness of the ultimate result sought, but relates solely to the methods used to obtain such results." The South Dakota Courts have ruled, "A person whose property has been stolen cannot claim the right to punish the thief himself, without process of law, and to make him compensate him for the loss of his property by maliciously threatening to accuse him of the offense." Interestingly, South Dakota reasoned that the "**moral turpitude of threatening, for the purpose of obtaining money, to accuse a guilty person of the crime which he has committed, is as great as it is to threaten for a like purpose an innocent person of having committed a crime**. The intent is the same in both cases, to acquire money without legal right by threatening a legal prosecution."

Beggs concluded:

> [**To threaten a thief with an accusation and prosecution unless he pays the value of property stolen, with the resulting payment made in fear, is PC 518 extortion, regardless of the good faith in exacting the amount justly due**. The jury was so instructed. There was no error.]

---

91. From *Deering's California Codes Annotated.* Copyright © 2014 by Matthew Bender & Company, Inc., a member of the LexisNexis Group. Reprinted with the permission of LexisNexis.

To constitute extortion the wrongful use of fear must be the operating cause which produces the consent. *** "If some other cause were the primary and controlling one in inducing the consent, then there would be no extortion." ***

The Model Penal Code disagrees with *Beggs*. Model Penal Code Section 223.4 provides:

It is an affirmative defense to prosecution based on (a threat to accuse the extortion victim of a criminal offense, to expose a secret, or to take or withhold official action) that the property obtained by threat of accusation, exposure, lawsuit or other invocation of official action was honestly claimed as restitution or indemnification for harm done in the circumstances to which such accusation, exposure, lawsuit or other official action relates, or as compensation for property or lawful services.

Can Extortion Be Based on Something Other Than "Property," Such as "Anything of Value"?

The Supreme Court of Iowa, in *State v. Crone*, 545 N.W.2d 267 (1996), considered whether **extortion, a property crime, can be committed by obtaining something other than property**. *Crone* had to decide a fundamental question: What else, besides material things, has value? In this case, Crone was convicted of extortion for threatening to circulate compromising photos of his former girlfriend, Andrea Forman, unless she met with him. Crone had taken pictures of Forman when she was intoxicated and unclothed. Crone made "more than fifty 8 1/2 by 11-inch fliers which displayed Crone's photographs of Forman and a message giving Forman's name, place of employment and phone number and inviting one and all to call her." He told Forman that if she did not meet with him, he would circulate the pictures. Crone's fliers then "appeared in a variety of public places: tacked on telephone poles, distributed throughout the University of Iowa student union and placed on the windshields of parked cars. Copies were also mailed to Forman's friends and family, as well as her mother's co-workers."

The *Crone* Court noted that Iowa defined extortion as:

A person commits extortion if the person does any of the following with the purpose of obtaining for oneself or another anything of value, tangible or intangible, including labor or services *** Threatens to expose any person to hatred, contempt, or ridicule.

The prosecution and defense argued over whether "a meeting with Forman was something of value to Crone" for extortion purposes. The court noted that Iowa's extortion statute was amended from prohibiting malicious threats done "with intent to extort any money or pecuniary advantage whatever, or to compel the person so threatened to do any act against his will" to prohibit threats made "with the purpose of obtaining for oneself or another anything of value, tangible or intangible, including labor or services." *Crone* recognized that the change "*broadened* the crime of extortion" since extortion was no longer limited to attempts to extort "money or pecuniary advantage." With the amendment, "extortion of 'anything' of value is now sufficient." Therefore, "if a defendant's conduct is done for the purpose of obtaining something of value for himself or another, that conduct falls within the scope of the statute." The court concluded, "Crone's threats were intended to extort a personal meeting with Forman."

Crone then considered whether a meeting with Forman had "value" to the defendant. The amended extortion statute expanded "value" to include "*anything* of value, tangible *or intangible*," which covered a "broader definition of 'value,'—'*relative* worth, utility, or importance,' not the narrow definition—'the *monetary* worth of something.'" The term 'value' in the extortion statute meant "the particular importance attached to something by the person making the threat." The face-to-face meeting had this "value" to the defendant because "Crone was relentless in his efforts to exact such a meeting. He called Forman numerous times; he consistently asked her to meet with him." Crone speculated that the defendant's "wish for a personal meeting may have been as simple as a desire to witness the look on Forman's face when she saw the photographs." The court therefore affirmed the extortion conviction.[92]

Does the Criminal Actually Need to Obtain the Property to Commit Extortion?

The short answer to this question is that it depends on the jurisdiction where the crime occurs. In states following the **Model Penal Code**, **the crime is committed only when the extortionist actually "obtains" the property he or she seeks**.

In contrast, **in Washington**, as noted by *State v. Martinez*, 884 P.2d 3 (1984), **actual possession of the property by the extortionist is not required**. *Martinez* explained:

> [In Washington, what is "punished is the extorsive threat whether anything was obtained thereby or not".] Martinez completed the crime of first degree extortion as defined in Washington law when he communicated his threat to cause E.L. bodily injury in the future if she did not sign over her car. That E.L. wrote out the bill of sale in the hope of avoiding further bodily injury is an evidentiary fact that tends to substantiate the extorsive nature of the threat, but E.L.'s compliance or attempted compliance with Martinez's threatening demand was not an essential element of the crime. In sum, in Washington, the *victim's* conduct in response to the extorsive threat is not an element of this crime.

G. CARJACKING

Unlike larceny or robbery, carjacking is a relatively new crime. There were no carjackers at common law. Explaining its absence amounts to more than merely pointing out that cars themselves did not exist centuries ago. The creation of laws to combat carjacking in the 1990s pointed to a larger problem facing society.

The authors of California's Penal Code Section 215 have discussed the larger context surrounding carjacking. As explained by the Court of Appeals in *People v. Medina* (1995) 39 Cal. App.4th 643:

> [There] has been considerable increase in the number of persons who have been abducted, many have been subjected to the violent taking of their automobile and some have had a gun used in the taking of the car.

© plantic/Shutterstock.com

Why is there a gun pointing toward the robber in the side view mirror?

---

92. Reprinted with the permission of LexisNexis.

"This relatively 'new' crime appears to be as much thrill-seeking as theft of a car. If all the thief wanted was the car, it would be simpler to hot-wire the automobile without running the risk of confronting the driver. People have been killed, seriously injured, and placed in great fear, and this calls for a strong message to discourage these crimes. Additionally, law enforcement is reporting this new crime is becoming the initiating rite for aspiring gang members and the incidents are drastically increasing.

Carjacking has often replaced auto theft as the crime of choice not in spite of its danger, but because of it. The confrontation with the victim required in carjacking provides the rush of adrenaline sought by some criminals and its increased risk gives those willing to commit it more status among gangs they wish to join.

The legislation creating carjacking also plugged a loophole found in robbery. Since robbery is simply "compound larceny," it shares larceny's mens rea element of "intent to *permanently* deprive" the owner of the property. As explained below by Penal Code 215's drafters, many carjackers commit their crimes with no intent to keep the car:

[Many] carjackings cannot be charged as robbery because it is difficult to prove the intent required of a robbery offense (to permanently deprive one of the car) since [many] of these gang carjackings are thrill seeking thefts. There is a need to prosecute this crime.

Can carjacking be committed when **the driver is not actually in the car at the time of taking?** After all, isn't carjacking essentially a crime against a driver or passenger in a car? **If a victim need not be in the car at the time of the taking, how near must he or she be to be within "immediate presence" of the vehicle?** What if the reason the victim is not within the car is because the **defendant tricked him to leave it?** These questions are explored in the following case.

LEGAL ANALYSIS

People v. Medina
39 Cal. App.4th 643 (1995).
Justice Vartabedian delivered the opinion for the California Court of Appeal.

Facts

[The victim, Luis Larios, testified that while he was stopped at an intersection, the defendant, Medina, grabbed Larios by the neck and got into his car. Defendant held what felt like a knife against Larios's ribs. Another man and a woman got in the car. While ordered to drive, Larios felt something like a gun being held against him. The assailants ordered Larios to stop driving, got him out of the car, and beat him with a stick-like object. They handcuffed Larios and took his wallet and car keys.] The three assailants drove off.

Shani Moschetti, the female assailant, testified to a different version of the facts. [Moschetti was on] the street pretending to be a prostitute. Larios picked her up, and they agreed to an act of prostitution. Moschetti directed Larios to room 12 of the Lullaby Motel. Larios parked his car directly in front of the motel room, went into the room, and put his car keys in his pocket.

Defendant and his brother, Flavio, came out of the bathroom of the motel room with sticks. Larios crouched down in the corner of the room. Moschetti handcuffed Larios, took his keys, [and removed money from his wallet.] Moschetti tied up Larios's feet with the cord defendant had cut from the television set in the room. Defendant and Flavio hit Larios with sticks and Moschetti kicked him numerous times. They left, taking Larios's car with them.

Moschetti testified that Larios's car was probably 20 feet away from Larios when he was in the room. [The son of the owner of the Lullaby Motel confirmed that the cord was cut from the television in room 12.]

Issue

Whether taking a car from a victim who is located in a hotel room and is 20 feet from his car constitutes "immediate presence" for PC 215 carjacking.

Rule and Analysis

Defendant was convicted of carjacking. Carjacking is a relatively new crime, created in 1993. Section 215 provides:

"(a) 'Carjacking' is the felonious taking of a motor vehicle in the possession of another, from his or her person or immediate presence, or from the person or immediate presence of a passenger of the motor vehicle, against his or her will and with the intent to either permanently or temporarily deprive the person in possession of the motor vehicle of his or her possession, accomplished by means of force or fear.

"(b) Carjacking is punishable by imprisonment in the state prison for a term of three, five, or nine years.

"(c) This section shall not be construed to supersede or affect Section 211. A person may be charged with a violation of this section and Section 211 [robbery."]

The trial court instructed the jury:]

"The meaning of the term 'immediate presence' depends upon the circumstances of each case. *** **"A thing is in the immediate presence of a person if it is so within his reach or control that he could, if not overcome by violence or prevented by fear, retain possession of it."**

[The] jury was confronted with two distinct factual scenarios as the basis for the crime of carjacking. The first scenario was the victim's version, a "classic" carjacking where the victim is accosted while in his vehicle and the vehicle is forcibly taken from him. The second scenario, as testified to by Moschetti, involves the victim not being in his car; more specifically, he was inside a motel room when his keys were forcibly taken and his nearby car was driven away.

*** Defendant argued that if the jurors believed Moschetti's testimony, then they should acquit him of carjacking because the car parked outside the motel room door was not within his immediate presence. [Defendant argues that actual physical proximity of the victim to the vehicle is required.]

[**The victim need not actually be physically present in the vehicle when the confrontation occurs.**]

[The instruction was proper.] It defines immediate presence to encompass an area in proximity to the vehicle. We thus next focus on whether there is substantial evidence to show the vehicle was purloined from the victim's "immediate presence," as provided in the statute. ***

[The] jury believed Moschetti's version of events and not Larios's version. Thus we analyze this issue based on the motel room carjacking version as substantially the version accepted by the jury.

[The] clear nature of the theft involved here as one committed by "trick or device" makes it unnecessary for us to any more specifically define the parameters of "immediate presence" in the context of a carjacking. Moschetti testified that in posing as a prostitute she planned to take Larios's car; defendant and Flavio knew of this and went along with the plan. Moschetti then lured Larios to the motel room, robbed him, took his car keys, and took his car. [***The trick or device by which the physical*** *presence of the victim was detached from the property* under his *possession* and control should not avail defendant in his claim that the property was not taken from the 'immediate presence' of the victim.]

Here the defendant planned a forceful taking of Larios's car from Larios. The only reason Larios was not in the car when it was taken and this was not a "classic" carjacking, was because he had been lured away from it by trick or device. ***

Conclusion

The immediate presence requirement was satisfied. Substantial evidence supports the conviction. * The judgment is affirmed.**[93]

Note

People v. Coryell 110 Cal. App.4th 1299 (2003) also considered carjacking's "immediate presence" element. In *Coryell*:

> Omar Garcia and his girlfriend, 16-year-old Iman O., drove to a liquor store in Lake Elsinore. Iman remained in Garcia's car while Garcia used a pay telephone. While Iman was waiting, another car pulled up and parked in the store parking lot. Four young men got out. [One of the four, defendant Darden, approached Garcia at the telephone kiosk and asked Garcia where he was from i.e., his gang affiliation].

> He pushed Garcia's shoulder and punched him in the face. Garcia tried to get away as Darden pulled out a knife and tried to stab him.

> Garcia ran away; Darden gave chase. Fearing that either she or Garcia would be hurt, Iman fled from Garcia's car. Darden, having chased Garcia away, returned to Garcia's car. Iman had left the car with the keys in the ignition. Darden got in, started the car, and drove away. ***

In *Coryell*, Darden argued that "the evidence failed to establish the element that Garcia's car was taken 'from the person or immediate presence of a victim,' because neither Garcia nor his girlfriend, Iman O., were in the car when he drove it away." Darden noted that the victim Garcia had run "over a block away" when the taking occurred. The court disagreed, noting:

> The argument proves too much: Of course Garcia was no longer near the car—Darden's knife wielding was sufficient to drive him away from it. Darden accosted Garcia near the car, made a gang challenge, grabbed him, punched him, and threatened him with a knife. The force and fear accomplished the taking from Garcia.

Darden next urged that, since the girlfriend, Iman O., had abandoned the car before he took it, he did not commit carjacking against her. The court again disagreed, noting that Iman O., having seen "the vicious attack on Garcia," fled from the car because she "immediately feared for her safety." The court thus affirmed Darden's conviction.

---

93. Reprinted with the permission of LexisNexis.

Learn from My (and Others') Mistakes

Do Not Throw Your Colostomy Bag at a Judge

People can get in heated disagreements with judges. When I was a prosecutor decades ago, I was told that an attorney, in a fit of pique, detached his colostomy bag and threw it at the judge. The judge promptly found the lawyer in criminal contempt of court and had him placed in custody. As stated in Business and Professions Code Section 6068(b). Duties of attorney, "It is the duty of an attorney to . . . maintain the respect due to the courts of justice and judicial officers."

Carjacking must be committed **against the will** of the victim, or "**without the victim's consent.**" **Can carjacking ever be committed against the will of an infant? Do infants**, for that matter, **have free will?** Does this even matter for carjacking when an infant is in the car? The following case considers the victims' lack of consent in the context of a carjacking and kidnapping.

LEGAL ANALYSIS

People v. Hill
23 Cal.4th 853 (2000).
Justice Chin delivered the opinion of the California Supreme Court.

Facts

[January R. drove home] with her seven-month-old daughter Marissa, exited the car, and reached into the passenger side to take the child from her seat. While she was unbuckling the child, defendant and William Dabney, wearing hooded jackets with bandannas over their faces, accosted her. Dabney told January to give him money. She said they could have the car but asked them to let her and the baby go. She gave Dabney her jewelry. He demanded her keys, grabbed them from her, and tossed them to defendant. Dabney and January got into the backseat, with Marissa still in the front passenger seat but no longer buckled. Defendant drove the car with all four inside.

When the car stopped, Dabney [demanded that January] take off her clothes or he would shoot the baby. Believing that Dabney and defendant would let her go if she complied, January partially undressed. Dabney pushed her onto the seat and raped her. During this time, the baby "was crying. She was in the front seat rolling back and forth because the seat wasn't buckled in." January then managed to push Dabney away, grab the baby, open the car door, and flee. Defendant and Dabney drove away. ***

A jury convicted defendant of [PC 207 kidnapping and PC 215 carjacking of] both January and Marissa. On appeal, defendant argued the evidence did not support the convictions for kidnapping and carjacking Marissa because the evidence was insufficient that he acted against the victim's will and by means of force or fear. ***

Issue

1. **Whether there was sufficient evidence that the PC 207 kidnapping of the mother and her infant daughter were "against the victim's will."**
2. **Whether there was sufficient evidence that the PC 215 carjacking of the mother and her infant daughter were "against the victim's will."**

Rule and Analysis

Conviction of kidnapping and carjacking generally requires proof that the perpetrator committed the criminal acts against the will of the victim, i.e., without the victim's consent. This requirement presents special problems when the victim is an infant too young to give or withhold consent. [**The against-the-will requirement is] satisfied as to a person unable to give legal consent if the criminal act "is done for an illegal purpose or with an illegal intent."** [An] analogous rule is appropriate for carjacking. [Substantial evidence supports defendant's convictions for kidnapping and carjacking as to both an infant and the infant's mother.]

A. *Kidnapping*

[**PC 207(a)] provides: "Every person who forcibly, or by any other means of instilling fear, steals or takes, or holds, detains, or arrests any person in this state, and carries the person into another country, state, or county, or into another part of the same county, is guilty of kidnapping."** [The statute generally requires that the defendant use force or fear.] "If a person's free will was not overborne by the use of force or the threat of force, there was no kidnapping." ***

[An analytical problem arises when the person taken, for example a baby, lacks free will.] How can a baby's will be overborne? We confronted this problem in [*People v. Oliver*, where] the defendant was convicted of kidnapping and lewd conduct with a two-year-old child. So far as the evidence showed, "the baby went willingly with defendant" *** but we also noted that "the baby was too young to give his legal consent to being taken by the defendant." [We were concerned that a defendant might be convicted of kidnapping a person unable to give consent even if the defendant acted for a good purpose such as carrying the person to safety. We] concluded that **"section 207, as applied to a person forcibly taking and carrying away another, who by reason of immaturity or mental condition is unable to give his legal consent thereto, should . . . be construed as making the [actor] guilty of kidnapping only if the taking and carrying away is done for an illegal purpose or with an illegal intent."** ***

[Defendant argues PC 207 still requires proof of force or fear] even as to a child.

[Here] ample evidence of force or fear exists. Defendant and Dabney accosted January and forced her and the child to go with them. *** This behavior constituted the use of both force and fear. Defendant contends the force and fear was directed at January, not the baby. [**In kidnapping cases the requirement of force may be relaxed where the victim is a minor who is 'too young to give his legal consent to being taken' and the kidnapping was done for an improper purpose.**] Here, defendant snatched the baby as well the mother. The baby certainly did not move herself. Dabney also threatened to shoot the baby, thus using her as leverage to force the mother's cooperation. Additionally, the car seat was unbuckled, and Marissa was rolling around on the front seat while defendant drove. We are unaware of any authority that to suffer kidnapping, a baby must apprehend any force used against her.

[We find] sufficient evidence to support the conviction for kidnapping Marissa as well as January.

B. *Carjacking*

[**PC 215(a)] defines carjacking as "the felonious taking of a motor vehicle in the possession of another, from his or her person or immediate presence, or from the person or immediate presence of a passenger of the motor vehicle, against his or her will and with the intent to either permanently** or temporarily deprive the person in possession of the motor vehicle of his or her possession, accomplished by means of force or fear." The Court of Appeal found [that Marissa could not be a victim of carjacking because at seven months, she was unaware that her mother's car was being taken and had no will which was overcome.]

The Attorney General argues that the Court of Appeal [wrongly assumed that some individuals are incapable of experiencing 'will' simply because they are unable to effectively convey it or are too young. As is manifested in an infant's first cries for food and comfort, 'free will' exists from the moment of birth.]

We need not engage in a philosophical discussion of whether, or when, a young child is imbued with a "will." [The Legislature did not intend to preclude an infant from being the victim of a carjacking.] In the usual case of carjacking involving multiple occupants, all are subjected to a threat of violence, all are exposed to the high level of risk *** and all are compelled to surrender their places in the vehicle and suffer a loss of transportation. All are properly deemed victims of the carjacking." ***

As with kidnapping, an analytical problem arises when the victim is an infant. But we do not believe the solution is to conclude that an infant, lacking an independent will, cannot be the victim of a carjacking. ***

"[Carjacking] is a particularly serious crime that victimizes persons in vulnerable settings and *** raises a serious potential for harm to the victim, the perpetrator and the public at large." *** The potential for harm is not less because the victim is an infant who, we may assume, is incapable of giving or withholding consent. Here, for example, Marissa faced great potential harm. A baby of seven months and unbuckled from her car seat, she was rolling around the front of a vehicle in motion. [In both practical and legal terms, Marissa, like her mother, was a carjacking victim. **An infant, like any person, *may* be the victim of a carjacking.**]

When applied to an infant, ["against his or her will" means] merely the absence of lawful consent, not an affirmative act of free will. [For carjacking, a taking will be considered against the "will" of an infant if it is without lawful consent.]

[**The Legislature expanded carjacking's taking element to include a taking from the person or immediate presence of *either* the possessor *or* any passenger.**] By extending carjacking to include a taking from a passenger, even one without a possessory interest[,] the Legislature has made carjacking more nearly a crime against the person than a crime against property. [If the defendant used force or fear, as we found he did here, he is guilty of carjacking whether or not the victim was aware of that force or fear.]

In this case, defendant had no lawful consent from Marissa. The "against his or her will" requirement is thus satisfied as to her. ***

Conclusion

[**The] evidence was sufficient to support the convictions for kidnapping and carjacking both January and Marissa.**[94]

---

94. Reprinted with the permission of LexisNexis.

DISCUSSION QUESTIONS

1. What was the original theft crime at common law? How is it relevant to this day?

2. What are the differences between larceny and embezzlement?

3. How does theft by false pretenses differ from larceny and embezzlement?

4. What did the states do when they consolidated the theft offenses? Why did they make this change in crimes against property?

5. What is meant by "force" in robbery?

6. What is meant by "fear" in robbery?

7. What are the differences between robbery and extortion?

8. Why was the crime of carjacking created?

9. Does a victim of carjacking have to actually be in his or her car at the time of the carjacking? Why or why not?

WEB LINKS

1. For New York's jury instructions on "grand larceny of a specified amount," see: http://www.ny courts.gov/judges/cji/2-PenalLaw/155/155.30%281%29.155.35.155.40%281%29.155.42. Larceny.Revision.pdf

2. For New York's jury instructions on robbery, see: http://www.nycourts.gov/judges/cji/2-PenalLaw/160/160.pdf

3. In a Dec 27, 2013, *UPI* article, "Woman hypnotizes priest, steals church donations," was the criminal applying sufficient "force" to have committed robbery?

4. See: http://www.upi.com/Odd_News/2013/12/27/Woman-hypnotizes-priest-steals-church-donations/UPI-61551388180606/

5. For Michigan's Model Criminal Jury Instructions defining retail fraud, see, "M Crim JI 23.13 Retail Fraud—Theft" at: http://courts.mi.gov/Courts/MichiganSupremeCourt/criminal-jury-instructions/Documents/HTML/Criminal%20Jury%20Instructions-Responsive%20HTML5/index.html#t=Criminal_Jury_Instructions%2FCrim_Jury_Ch_23%2FM_Crim_JI_23_13_Retail_Fraud%25E2%2580%2594Theft.htm

6. For Michigan's Model Criminal Jury Instructions defining robbery, see, "M Crim JI 18.2 Robbery" at: http://courts.mi.gov/Courts/MichiganSupremeCourt/criminal-jury-instructions/Documents/HTML/Criminal%20Jury%20Instructions-Responsive%20HTML5/index.html#t=Criminal_Jury_Instructions%2FCrim_Jury_Ch_18%2FM_Crim_JI_18_2_Robbery.htm

CHAPTER
IX

Crimes against Habitation

Burglary is a crime against habitation.

The law separated crimes against habitation from property crimes for good reason, for crimes against habitation involve wrongs beyond the mere taking of someone else's possessions. In such crimes as burglary and arson, the criminal is attacking a person's home. The house possessed a special place in English law as a man's castle free from intrusions by strangers and even by government officials. The crimes against habitation thus intruded upon this precious English right.

A. BURGLARY

Burglary is not a simple crime against property. The creation of the crime of burglary was originally meant to punish some of the most frightening and heinous behavior. Burglary involved the breaking into and invasion of a person's home—the one safe place where we can let down our guard and feel completely safe. **Burglaries were originally limited to entries at night in an era when electricity had not been invented and so most people were at their most vulnerable, being asleep.** Further, burglaries were not limited to those intending to commit theft, for the crime included the intent to commit any felony—even the most horrible felonies of rape, mayhem, robbery, or murder.

Burglaries today pale in comparison to their common law ancestors. Many states do not require a breaking element while some prosecute those who remain on premises rather than those who at least unlawfully entered. Burglary's nighttime element has been essentially abandoned. Further, some jurisdictions expanded burglary to include intention to commit merely a misdemeanor. Burglary provides a dramatic example of a larger trend in criminal law. While the common law crafted crimes to deal with particular problems, the centuries have expanded the definition of crimes to include ever more behavior. The expansion of burglary has received severe criticism. Helen A. Anderson, in *From the Thief in the Night to the Guest Who Stayed Too Long: The Evolution of Burglary in the Shadow of the Common Law,* 45 Ind. L. Rev. 629, (2012), has argued, "burglary's evolution has finally gone too far, and no longer necessarily describes a distinct offense. It is only the memory of the common law offense that keeps courts and lawmakers from recognizing how empty the crime has become."

1.   Common Law

Blackstone, in *Commentaries* Vol. IV, at 223, described common law burglary as follows:

> Burglary, or nocturnal housebreaking . . . has always been looked upon as a very heinous offence: not only because of the abundant terror that it naturally carries with it; but also as it is a forcible invasion and disturbance of that right of habitation, which every individual might acquire in a state of nature; an invasion, which in such a state, would be sure to be punished with death, unless the assailant were the stronger.

Blackstone explained that burglary occurs when "he that by night breaketh and entreth into a mansion-house, with intent to commit a felony." In assessing burglary, Blackstone isolated "four things to be considered; the *time*, the *place*, the *manner*, and the *intent*." Each of these factors highlighted the seriousness of **common law burglary**:

1. **Time:**
   "**The time must be at night, and not by day**; for in the day time there is no burglary." Night was the time when daylight was so lacking that one could not "discern a man's face withal." In other words, **nighttime was so dark that the features of a person's face could not be made out.** It stands to reason then that if an occupant could not recognize the features of a face, which is usually how we recognize friend or foe, the victim was at a disadvantage because he did not know whether or not he needed to defend against an intruder. Blackstone emphasized the "malignity" of burglary because it could occur at "the dead of night" when "all creation, except beasts of prey, are at rest" and "sleep has disarmed the owner."

2. **Place:**
Although **burglary at common law was limited to the dwelling or mansionhouse**, the definition of this residence was expanded to include "the barn, stable, or warehouse" if these structures were "parcel of the mansionhouse, though not under the same roof or contiguous." A home was considered a dwelling house even if the owner was gone for a "short season." Moreover, a "chamber (room) in a college or an inn of court, where each inhabitant hath distinct property," was considered a "mansionhouse of the owner."

3. **Manner:**
The manner of **burglary required both breaking and entry**. "Breaking" was not satisfied by some legal fiction of crossing over "invisible ideal boundaries," but by an actual creation of an opening, such as actually breaking or "taking out the glass of, or otherwise opening, a window; picking a lock, or opening it with a key; nay, by lifting up the latch of a door, or unloosing any other fastening which the owner has provided." If an owner leaves his door open "it is his own folly and negligence," and so no burglary can occur upon entry. Still, Blackstone would find "breaking" satisfied if someone knocked on a door only to rush in with felonious

Burglary at common law required 'breaking,' which was 'the creation of an opening.'

intent, or entered pretending to seek lodgings and instead robbed the landlord, because "the law will not suffer itself to be trifled with by such evasions."

4. **Intent:**
Blackstone mandated that "breaking and entry must be with felonious intent, otherwise the crime was only trespass." Once the intent was formed upon entry, the burglary had occurred, regardless of whether any of the intended felonies were carried out or not. The felonies intended were not limited to only larceny or theft, but included any felony, such as robbery, murder, or rape.

2. Current Law

Model Penal Code §221.1: Burglary

(1) *Burglary Defined.* A person is guilty of burglary if he enters a building or occupied structure, or separately secured or occupied portion thereof, with purpose to commit a crime therein, unless the premises are at the time open to the public or the actor is licensed or privileged to enter. It is an affirmative defense to prosecution for burglary that the building or structure was abandoned.[95]

---

95. From *The Model Penal Code* by the American Law Institute. Copyright © 1962 by the American Law Institute. Used by permission.

California Penal Code § 459: Burglary Defined

Every person who enters any house, room, apartment, tenement, shop, warehouse, store, mill, barn, stable, outhouse or other building, tent, vessel, *** floating home, *** railroad car, locked or sealed cargo container, whether or not mounted on a vehicle, trailer coach, *** any house car, *** inhabited camper, *** when the doors are locked, aircraft *** or mine or any underground portion thereof, with intent to commit grand or petit larceny or any felony is guilty of burglary. As used in this chapter, "inhabited" means currently being used for dwelling purposes, whether occupied or not. A house, trailer, vessel designed for habitation, or portion of a building is currently being used for dwelling purposes if, at the time of the burglary, it was not occupied solely because a natural or other disaster caused the occupants to leave the premises.

New York: McKinney's Penal Law § 140.20: Burglary in the Third Degree

A person is guilty of burglary in the third degree when he knowingly enters or remains unlawfully in a building with intent to commit a crime therein.

Burglary in the third degree is a class D felony.

Tips for Success for Future Law Students and Lawyers

Research the Law Schools You Are Considering Attending

Traditionally, the most important standard law schools must meet is American Bar Association (ABA) accreditation. Law school graduates of ABA accredited schools are eligible to take a state's bar exam. Students should also consider the law school's general reputation in the legal profession, its ranking in the *U.S. News and World Report* (even though this is an unofficial ranking, admission directors pay quite close attention to it), bar passage rate, and employment—within the profession—one year after graduation. Also, call ahead to the school and ask to attend a law class to get a feel of the school's campus and philosophy.

---

a) Entry

Since modern statutes require "entry" of a building as a requirement for **burglary, what precisely amounts to "entry"** for purposes of burglary? **What would be the minimum a burglar would have to do to fulfill this "entry" element?** Can a person "enter" a building when only an **instrument** he or she holds actually goes into the structure? The following case considers such issues with a variety of examples.

LEGAL ANALYSIS

Magness v. Superior Court
54 Cal.4th 270 (2012).
Justice Liu delivered the opinion of the Supreme Court of California.

Facts

Defendant Christopher Magness was charged [with attempted first degree burglary of an inhabited dwelling PC 664, 459, 460(a)] and second degree burglary of an automobile [PC 459, 460(b). On] the evening of July 24, 2010, Timothy Loop was at home with his wife when he heard the garage door of their house opening. Loop ran into the garage and saw defendant standing near the end of the driveway. [Loop summoned the sheriffs, who arrested defendant.]

[Loop and the sheriff deputy] found the remote control for the garage door near the end of the driveway where defendant had been standing. Loop had locked the remote control in his car, which was parked in the driveway. The door seal on one of the car's windows had been "peeled back a little bit" and the window "was down a couple of inches."

[In court, the magistrate that defendant had committed a completed burglary of the residence,] reasoning that opening the garage door constituted an entry into the residence. [The superior court denied defendant's motion to reduce the charge to attempted burglary.]

Issue

Whether a person standing in the driveway of a residence who uses a remote control to open a motorized garage door has entered the residence within the meaning of the burglary statute.

Rule and Analysis

[Under PC 459, a person who "enters any house . . . with intent to commit . . . larceny or any felony is guilty of burglary." The] **slightest entry by any part of the body or an instrument is sufficient: "As for the entry, any the least degree of it, with any part of the body, or with an instrument held in the hand, is sufficient**: as, to step over the threshold, to put a hand or a hook in at a window to draw out goods, or a pistol to demand one's money, are all of them burglarious entries." [**A burglary may be committed by using an instrument to enter a building—whether that instrument is used solely to effect entry, or to accomplish the intended larceny or felony as well.** Using a tire iron to pry open a door, using a tool to create a hole in a store wall, or using an auger to bore a hole in a corn crib is a sufficient entry to support a conviction of burglary. Entry requires a part of the body or an instrument to penetrate the outer boundary of the building.]

In *People v. Osegueda*, [a defendant entered] an electronics store for purposes of burglary by using tools to create a small hole in the wall. Osegueda [was] arrested at 2:30 a.m. outside the electronics store. [A three-foot by four-foot section of the wall had been removed and a small six by four to five inch hole existed in the inner wall leading into Rees Electronics. One could see into the store through the hole.] "Instruments were discovered adjacent" to the hole. [This was enough evidence to support the jury's finding that the air space of Rees Electronics was penetrated and thus the defendant had entered the store.]

[*People v. Ravenscroft* applied this "air space test" to hold that the defendant had entered two banks for purposes of burglary by inserting a stolen automatic teller machine (ATM) card into two ATMs that were "mounted inside the banks and secured flush with the exterior walls of those banks." We disapproved *Ravenscroft* in *People v. Davis*] in which we held that inserting a forged check into a chute in the walkup window of a check-cashing business did not constitute an entry for purposes of burglary. *** Although we agreed with [*Ravenscroft* "that the ATM card in that case was inserted into the air space of the ATM",] we concluded that this was not an entry for purposes of burglary because neither that act nor inserting the forged check into the chute in *Davis* "violates the occupant's possessory interest in the building as does using a tool to reach into a building and remove property." ***"Inserting a stolen ATM card into the designated opening in an ATM is markedly different from the types of entry traditionally covered by the burglary statute, as is passing a forged check through a chute in a walk-up window. In each situation the defendant causes an object to enter the air space of a building, but it is not apparent that the burglary statute was meant to encompass such conduct. It is important to establish reasonable limits as to what constitutes an entry by means of an instrument for purposes of the burglary statute. Otherwise the scope of the burglary statute could be expanded to absurd proportions." ***

[A burglary remains an entry that invades a possessory right in a building.] "Burglary laws are **based primarily upon a recognition of the dangers to personal safety created by the usual burglary situation—the danger that the intruder will harm the occupants in attempting to perpetrate the intended crime or to escape and the danger that the occupants will in anger or panic react violently to the invasion, thereby inviting more violence.** The laws are primarily designed, then, not to deter the trespass and the intended crime, which are prohibited by other laws, so much as **to forestall the germination of a situation dangerous to personal safety.**" [PC 459 in short, is aimed at the danger caused by the unauthorized entry itself.]

People v. Calderon *** held that kicking in the door of a residence constituted an entry for purposes of burglary. The defendant and two accomplices went to the victim's home to collect a debt. One of the defendant's accomplices [kicked in the victim's door, but before anyone in the group had gone inside, the victim came running out. Defendant tried to stab the victim in the chest, but the victim grabbed the knife blade.]

[For burglary, a person enters a building if some part of his body or some object under his control penetrates the area inside the building's outer boundary.]

[*Calderon* reached the correct result. Just as it reasonably could be inferred in *Osegueda*] that, in creating the hole in the wall, some portion of the tools had entered the building," *** it reasonably could be inferred in *Calderon* that, in kicking the door and causing it to open, some portion of the accomplice's foot had crossed the outer boundary of the residence. [Kicking in a door invades the occupant's possessory interest and is likely to provoke a violent response.]

["Entry is an indispensable element in the crime of burglary at common law." The defendant in *Walker v. State*] committed burglary by using an auger to bore a hole in the bottom of a corn crib. The Supreme Court of Alabama acknowledged that boring a hole in the corn crib certainly constituted a breaking, but recognized if "an *entry* is not effected, burglary has not been committed." [The defendant had used an instrument to enter the corn crib when the auger "was intruded into the crib."]

In California, the requirement of a breaking has long been eliminated from our burglary statute. *** Here, defendant may well have committed a common law breaking by using the remote control to open the garage door. **But whether or not he committed a breaking, he did not commit burglary because he did not enter the residence. Nothing penetrated the outer boundary of the residence.** ***

There is no question that "an intruder's use of a garage door opener to open a garage door violates the occupant's possessory interest and fosters a situation that can be extremely dangerous to personal safety." But not all conduct that implicates the interests underlying the burglary statute constitutes a completed burglary. *** The line we adopt—**something outside must go inside for an entry to occur**—is simple, workable, and consistent with common sense. It is also consistent, to our knowledge, with every case that has found a completed burglary.

Conclusion

[Using] **a remote control to open a garage door does not constitute an entry into the residence. [While defendant may be charged with attempted burglary, he cannot be charged with a completed burglary.]**[96]

---

96. Reprinted with the permission of LexisNexis.

Note

The Court of Appeals of Alaska, in *Sears v. State*, 713 P.2d 1218 (1986), defined "enters" in a manner similar to that of California. In *Sears*, the defendant, Raymond Sears, was:

[in the Gavora Shopping Mall in Fairbanks.] The "Sew'n Vac" store was closed, with a sliding iron gate pulled across the entrance to prevent patrons still in the mall from entering.

[Sears straightened a clothes hanger and used it] to reach through the Sew'n Vac iron gate to obtain a hand-held vacuum cleaner worth approximately $100. The state did not dispute that only the clothes hanger, or at the most Sears' arm, entered the Sew'n Vac store.

The court affirmed the conviction, reasoning:

Raymond Sears was convicted, following a jury trial, of burglary in the second degree, AS 11.46.310. Alaska Statute 11.46.310 provides: "(a) A person commits the crime of burglary in the second degree if the person enters or remains unlawfully in a building with intent to commit a crime in the building."

[Enters" in Alaska . . . means that the intruder enters by entry of his whole body, part of his body, or by insertion of any instrument that is intended to be used in the commission of a crime.**

Do's and Don'ts for Hearings, Trials, and Appeals

Presenting Exhibits

Don't have the officer bring certain volatile controlled substances to the courtroom as evidence, because the intoxicants can leak through the bag, overdosing the officer.

California Penal Code § 459.5: Shoplifting

(a) Notwithstanding Section 459, **shoplifting is defined as entering a commercial establishment with intent to commit larceny while that establishment is open during regular business hours, where the value of the property that is taken or intended to be taken does not exceed nine hundred fifty dollars ($950).** Any other entry into a commercial establishment with intent to commit larceny is burglary. Shoplifting shall be punished as a misdemeanor, [with certain exceptions for persons with prior convictions].

(b) Any act of shoplifting as defined in subdivision (a) shall be charged as shoplifting. No person who is charged with shoplifting may also be charged with burglary or theft of the same property.

The Legal Impact of Consent to Enter

Generally, **one commits "entry" for purposes of burglary when his or her body, body part, or, in some instances, an instrument under his or her control, goes into one of the structures (crosses some kind of threshold) covered in a burglary statue**. But, what if the person entering receives *consent* to do so from the building's owner or occupant? Can the occupant *limit* the scope of his or her consent? For instance, suppose an occupant limited the **place of entry** by giving someone consent to enter a building but not a particular room within the building. Would burglary occur if the person exceeded the limits of consent by entering the forbidden room? Or perhaps the occupant limited the **purpose of the entry**, permitting entry to fix a faucet but not to commit theft while inside the home. Finally, an occupant might **limit the time or duration of consent to enter** by allowing entry but not permitting the person to remain on the premises. The courts have crafted a variety of rules to address these various issues.

Depending on the Jurisdiction, Consent to Enter Can Negate the "Unauthorized Entry" Element of Burglary

The Supreme Court of Louisiana, in *State v. Lockhart*, 438 So.2d 1089 (1983), reversed a burglary conviction after concluding that the victim had consented to the defendant's entry. In *Lockhart*, Libby B. Carter, a woman in her sixties, recognized Lockhart as her distant cousin when he knocked on her door asking to use the bathroom. When she consented to Lockhart's entry, he first used the bathroom and then attempted to rape Carter, stating, "Give me some of this . . . ," and "Don't make me kill you." Upon his conviction for burglary, the defendant appealed, contending that the victim's consent negated burglary's "unauthorized entry" element in Louisiana. The Court agreed, reasoning:

> [To prove burglary, the State must prove that the defendant made an unauthorized entry of a structure with the intent to commit a theft or a felony.]

> [There] was no proof of an unauthorized entry. The victim let defendant into her house. Lockhart was a distant cousin; Ms. Carter recognized him. He asked to use the bathroom; Ms. Carter pointed in the appropriate direction. The victim's own testimony was to the effect that she consented to allow defendant into her house. ***

> The consent was valid. The State did not prove the essential element of unauthorized entry. ***

Consent to Enter for a Legitimate Purpose

In *State v. Hall*, 14 P.3d 404 (2000) Supreme Court of Kansas considered whether a person given consent to enter a store to legitimately shop could be found guilty of burglary when he committed the illegitimate activity of stealing items from a stockroom.

> Hall, who was not an employee, was recorded on video surveillance on three separate occasions entering the stockroom of a K-Mart store and stuffing merchandise into his trousers. From the public retail area of the store, there were two closed doors that Hall had to pass through to get to the stockroom. The stockroom had three separate doors, two of which were locked. *** K-Mart did not intend for its customers to enter into the stockroom.

> During Hall's third foray into the stockroom, he was observed on the video camera taking cellular phones, a Sega Saturn game system, and a stack of prepaid calling cards. [When

employees apprehended and searched Hall, they found he] did not have a checkbook, cash, or credit cards to purchase the items from K-Mart.

Defendant appealed his three burglary convictions under K.S.A. 21-3715 (one conviction for each entry of the storeroom). The Supreme Court reversed Hall's convictions, reasoning:

> The elements of burglary relevant to this case are knowingly and without authority entering into or remaining within any building, manufactured home, mobile home, tent or other structure which is not a dwelling, with intent to commit a felony, theft or sexual battery therein. ***

> In concluding that Hall had not committed the crime of burglary, the Court of Appeals queried: "The consent of K-Mart extended to the members of the general public to enter the K-Mart building for the purpose of shopping. As a member of the general public, Hall had the authority of K-Mart to enter the retail store building. Being inside the building with authority, did Hall's entry into the storeroom portion of the same building constitute a burglary?" ***

[Kansas has] rejected the "California Rule," under which a defendant's criminal intent upon entry renders an authorized entry unlawful.

> In [*State v. Harper*, Harper's employer had given him] a key and permission to enter the employer's building for a variety of purposes at all hours of the day and night. [Even] though Harper had authority to enter the maintenance building where he worked, he had no authority to remove papers by forced entry into a locked file cabinet within the building.

> The *Harper* court noted California had broadly interpreted its burglary statute and had determined that a defendant's criminal intent upon entry renders the authorized entry into the building an "unlawful" burglary. [The] California rule has been criticized by other jurisdictions. For example, the Colorado Supreme Court had noted that under the California rule, "one who enters a building, even with the permission of the owner, but with intent to commit a theft therein, would a fortiori be guilty of burglary. Intent at the time of entry in Colorado is not the sole element of burglary under our statute." ***

> The *Harper* court observed that under the California rule, any theft that occurs inside a building would be elevated to a burglary because no one would authorize an entry into a building for an individual to commit theft. It noted that the Kansas Legislature could have omitted the element in the burglary statute that the entry must occur "without authority," thereby making all entries to commit a felony or theft a burglary, but it did not do so. [*Harper*] found that Harper's authority to enter the building was not negated because he entered into the building for an unlawful purpose. ***

K.S.A. 21-3715(b), under which Hall was charged, **defines burglary as "knowingly and without authority entering into or remaining within any: . . . building, manufactured home, mobile home, tent or other structure which is not a dwelling, with intent to commit a felony, theft or sexual battery therein."** ***

Hall's illegal intent to commit a theft when entering the stockroom is evidenced by the presence of stockroom merchandise in Hall's trousers, the lack of funds or other means to pay for the merchandise, and Hall's prior thefts of items in the stockroom. However, we are required to strictly construe penal statutes in favor of the accused, subject to the rule that judicial interpretation must be reasonable and sensible to effect legislative design and intent. ***

> "**A broad construction of K.S.A. 21-3715 would blur the line between burglary and crimes such as shoplifting and criminal trespass.** We are not free to adapt the statute defining burglary by construing it to fit a set of facts presented to us. The facts must support the crime as it is defined by the legislature. If the statute is to be changed, it must be changed by the legislature, not the courts." ***[97]

Kansas correctly interpreted California law by noting that an occupant's consent in California will not negate the "entry" element from forming when a person enters for improper purposes. **Consent does not negate entry for those who intend to steal rather than to purchase goods in California. California, however, has recently limited the reach of its burglary law by creating the separate and lesser crime of "shoplifting"** to cover entry into "a commercial establishment with intent to commit larceny while that establishment is open during regular business hours," where the value of the stolen property "does not exceed nine hundred fifty dollars ($950)."

Consent to Enter Building but Not Room

In California, a person can commit burglary under Penal Code 459 when he or she "enters . . . a room." The California Supreme Court, in *People v. Sparks,* 28 Cal.4th 71 (2002), determined precisely what "room" meant for burglary purposes. In *Sparks,* the victim, Ana I., answered the defendant Michael Joseph Sparks' knock on the door of her single family home only to politely refuse his pitch for magazines. When he asked for a glass of water, Ana supplied him one. The defendant asked if he could enter the home and did so, though Ana I. could not recall at trial whether she invited him to enter. Once inside, the defendant would not leave, despite Ana I.'s requests he do so. Knowing she had to leave to pick up her niece, Ana I. went to her bedroom to get her shoes so she could leave the house. "Although Ana did not ask defendant to go with her into the bedroom, he followed her into that room." As the court noted,

> Defendant blocked Ana's exit, diverted her attention by telling her to look out a window, and then shoved her face down onto the bed, pressing a pillow on top of her head as she began to scream. During her struggles, Ana began to see white spots and had difficulty breathing. Ultimately, defendant raped her.

The case presented the issue of "whether a defendant's entry into a bedroom within a single-family house with the requisite intent can support a burglary conviction if that intent was formed only after the defendant's entry into the house." *Sparks* reasoned:

> The Attorney General asserts that (since) the plain words of section 459 (define) as burglary the entry of "any . . . room . . . with intent to commit . . . larceny or any felony," . . . the elements of the offense of burglary were established in this case.

> Defendant [argues that the term "any room" was intended to encompass only certain types of rooms—for example, a locked room within a single-family house or a separate dwelling unit within a boarding house.]

> During the past few decades, the legislatures of many of our sister states have been quite active in amending their respective burglary statutes in ways that either clarify or limit the meaning of the term "room," or otherwise narrow the circumstances in which entry of a room can constitute burglary. **[Statutes] in most jurisdictions, consistent with the recommendation of the Model Penal Code, make clear that the burglary statutes in these jurisdictions apply only to entry of a "room" that constitutes a "separate unit" or**

---

97. Reprinted with the permission of LexisNexis.

a "separately secured" or "separately occupied" portion of a building or structure. [A typical statute provides that, for purposes of the offense of burglary, "each unit of a building consisting of two or more units separately secured or occupied is a separate building."]

*** California decisions applying section 459 have upheld burglary convictions based upon entry into diverse types of rooms—among them ticket offices, liquor cages, business offices, enclosed counter areas, school classrooms, hotel rooms, apartments, a kitchen in a single-family home, and, *** a bedroom within a single-family home.

[Although the legislatures of many of our sister states have enacted statutes that have narrowed and confined the type of room that will qualify as the subject of a burglary,] the California Legislature, when presented with legislation that proposed similar amendments, did not adopt any similar amendment to our burglary statute. [Legislative proposals that would have incorporated the *same* limitations enacted in other states were introduced in the California Legislature on four occasions but never enacted.]

[This history reveals that although there have been some relatively recent attempts to limit the term "room" in section 459, to date no such proposal has been adopted.]

[The] trial court did not err in defining burglary to include entry into the victim's bedroom with the specific intent to commit rape.[98]

After *Sparks*, California might have interpreted *State v. Hall* (the case discussed above) as presenting an issue of scope of consent as to *place* of entry (building v. room). California courts, in light of *Sparks*, could rule that a person commits burglary even when given consent to enter a *building* (a K-Mart store), but not given consent to enter a *room* in the building (a non-public stockroom for employees only).

Consent to Enter but Not to Stay

The Supreme Court of Washington, in *State v. Collins*, 751 P.2d 837 (1988), considered the effect of an occupant's consent to entry on the state's "unlawfully remain" element of burglary. *Collins* declared: "This case presents the question whether the element of 'entering or remaining unlawfully' in our first degree burglary statute, RCW 9A.52.020, is satisfied where the accused receives an invitation to the premises which is not expressly qualified as to area or purpose, and commits a crime while on the premises." The case presented the following facts:

> On March 13, 1985, John F. Collins appeared at the door of Charlotte Dungey, 72. Mrs. Dungey's mother-in-law, Ellah Dungey, 84, answered the door. Collins asked if a Mr. Thatcher lived in the house. Ellah answered that he did not, and asked her daughter-in-law if the Thatchers lived nearby. Charlotte knew the Thatchers had previously lived in the house. Noticing that Collins had a slip of paper with the incorrect address and a phone number on it, Charlotte said, "Wouldn't you like to call him, use the phone?" She then turned and went into the front room with Collins following her. She picked up the receiver and handed it to him.
>
> Collins called the number and apparently received no answer. He then grabbed Charlotte by the arm and Ellah by the wrist. He dragged them into a bedroom and threw them on the bed. While he pinned Charlotte to the bed with his right leg, he pulled off Ellah's panty hose and inserted a finger in her vagina. *** In the struggle with Charlotte, he dislocated her shoulder.

---

98. Reprinted with the permission of LexisNexis.

Collins was convicted of rape and burglary in the first degree because the trial court found that the "'unlawfully remaining' element of the crime was proved by evidence that Collins formed the intent to commit the assault and rape once he had gained entry to the house." The trial judge stated:

> So I'm going to find that you went into the building lawfully, upon invitation, that while you were lawfully in the building you—your mind's purpose, or your purpose, changed to one of an unlawful nature, an intent to either rape or to assault, and that constitutes unlawfully remaining within the building.

The Washington Supreme Court ruled:

> The record supports an inference that the invitation or license extended to Collins was limited to a specific area and a single purpose. Collins was a total stranger. Charlotte made an offer only of the use of her telephone. She led him to one particular telephone and handed it to him herself. No reasonable person could construe this as a general invitation to all areas of the house for any purpose.

> A second theory, likewise to be applied on a case by case basis, supports the same result. Once Collins grabbed the two women and they resisted being dragged into the bedroom, any privilege Collins had up to that time was revoked.

In so ruling, the Washington Court rejected the "California rule" that a person's wrongful intent upon entry can simply invalidate consent. Instead, it held: **"on a case by case basis, an implied limitation on the scope of an invitation or license may be recognized**. We find such a limitation in the subject case." The conviction was therefore affirmed.[99]

b) Structures Subject to Entry

Where Exactly Must "Entry" Occur? Considering Balconies, Window Screens, Fenced-In Yards, and Rooms

California's Penal Code section 459 has broadly expanded burglary beyond the common law's "dwelling house" to include entry into all sorts of structures, including:

> any house, room, apartment, tenement, shop, warehouse, store, mill, barn, stable, outhouse or other building, tent, vessel (including "ships of all kinds, steamboats, steamships, canal boats, barges, sailing vessels, and every structure adapted to be navigated from place to place for the transportation of merchandise or persons"), floating home . . . railroad car, locked or sealed cargo container, whether or not mounted on a vehicle, trailer coach . . . , any house car . . . , inhabited camper . . . , vehicle

© suksawad/Shutterstock.com

In California, it is possible to burglarize a room of a house.

---

99. Reprinted with the permission of LexisNexis.

as defined by the Vehicle Code, when the doors are locked, aircraft . . . , or mine or any underground portion thereof."[100]

© Robert Hoetink/Shutterstock.com

California's burglary statue has even listed "or other building" in an effort to include structures the legislature could not have foreseen when crafting the law. To carry out the legislature's intent of broadly defining burglary, the courts have expansively interpreted "building." The Supreme Court of California, in *People v. Yarbrough,* 54 Cal.4th 889 (2012), did so when considering whether a balcony could be subject to being burglarized. In this case, Jammal Haneef Yarbrough "was charged with residential burglary after climbing onto a second-story apartment's private balcony, which was surrounded by a metal railing some four feet in height and accessible only through the single bedroom's sliding glass door." *Yarbrough's* facts were as follows:

> Salvador Deanda and his family lived in a one-bedroom unit on the second floor of an apartment building. The bedroom had a sliding glass door opening onto a balcony that was five feet wide by three feet deep and surrounded by a metal railing that Deanda, an adult, said came to his stomach. The balcony's floor was eight or nine feet above the ground.

> On August 5, 2009, two bicycles were on the balcony and visible from the street. Around midnight, Deanda was awakened by the barking of his dog. He saw defendant standing on the balcony outside its railing. The toes of defendant's shoes protruded under the railing, and defendant's fingers were clutching the top of the railing. Deanda grabbed a stick and rushed at defendant, who either fell or jumped to the ground.

The court determined that the balcony did fit within burglary's "building" element. *Yarbrough* explained that when burglary was created back at common law, it was seen as a crime against habitation. **Common law burglary therefore included as part of a "dwelling" not just a building but "also any structure that was 'within the curtilage or courtyard surrounding the house' and used in connection with the house."** Since the focus was on the criminal's intrusion on habitation, **the "concern underlying the offense of burglary was that an intruder's entry into the curtilage of a dwelling would pose a 'human risk,' as 'the dweller or some member of his household might hear a prowler' and then 'go to investigate.'"**

While California's PC 459 retained many of the concepts of common law burglary, it eliminated certain elements. A burglar did not need to commit "breaking" or enter at "nighttime." Further, as noted above, California greatly expanded the list of buildings beyond "dwelling house."[101] After this review of burglary's history, *Yarbrough* ruled:

> ***Whenever a private, residential apartment and its balcony are on the second or a higher floor of a building, and the balcony is designed to be entered only from inside

100. From *Deering's California Codes Annotated.* Copyright © 2014 by Matthew Bender & Company, Inc., a member of the LexisNexis Group. Reprinted with the permission of LexisNexis.

101. California did recognize the importance of entry into a "dwelling house" for purposes of degrees of burglary. As noted by *Yarbrough,*

> Section 460 sets out two degrees of burglary: Burglary of an inhabited dwelling (residential burglary) is burglary of the first degree. (Id., subd. (a).) "All other kinds of burglary are of the second degree." (Id., subd. (b).)

the apartment (thus extending the apartment's living space), the balcony is part of the apartment. The railing of such a balcony marks the apartment's "outer boundary" ***, any slight crossing of which is an entry for purposes of the burglary statute.

In reaching its conclusion, *Yarbrough* criticized an earlier California Supreme Court case, *People v. Valencia*, 28 Cal. 4th 1 (2002), which had declared that an "unenclosed balcony" could not be "reasonably" viewed as being part of a building's outer boundary. The *Yarbrough* court noted that the *Valencia* case had "nothing to do with a balcony," and therefore anything it said about balconies could be dismissed as worthless "dictum."[102]

What *Valencia* did decide, and what was still good law (despite its errant balcony dictum), dealt with the issue of window screens. In *Valencia*, Cuahtemoc Sanchez Valencia "used a screwdriver to remove a bathroom window's screen and to pull back a bedroom window's screen, but he was unable to open either window." Valencia was convicted of residential burglary and appealed. The Supreme Court upheld the conviction, ruling:

> We recognize that penetration into the area behind a window screen without penetration of the window itself usually will effect only a minimal entry of a building in terms of distance. But it has long been settled that "[a]ny kind of entry, complete or partial, [will] suffice.] All that is needed is entry "inside the premises" *** not entry inside *some inner part of* the premises. Furthermore, there is little doubt that even the minimal entry effected by penetration into the area behind a window screen—without penetration of the window itself—is "the type of entry the burglary statute was intended to prevent." ***
>
> **[Penetration] into the area behind a window screen amounts to an entry of a building within the meaning of the burglary statute even when the window itself is closed and is not penetrated.**

The Supreme Court of New Mexico, in *State v. Holt*, 368 P.3d 409 (2016), also found that entry was fulfilled when a person intruded beyond a window screen. In this case, "Anthony Holt had partially removed a window screen from a residential dwelling when he was detected by the homeowner and fled." The court determined, "In the process of removing the screen, he placed his fingers behind the screen and inside the outer boundary of the home." *Holt* ruled this amounted to the "unauthorized entry" needed for burglary.

California does have limits when it comes to burglary. In *People v. Chavez* 205 Cal. App.4th 1274 (2012), for instance, the court ruled that a "building" means an actual building. *Chavez* explained:

> Burglary requires entry into a building, but the jury was instructed that entry into the yard was sufficient. **Although our Supreme Court has defined "building" broadly for purposes of burglary, it has still generally limited the meaning of "building" to a structure with walls and a roof.** We know of no California case that has gone so far as to hold that a fenced yard surrounding a building is itself a building or part of a building, and case law from other states in which a burglar must enter a "building" in the ordinary sense, without a special statutory definition, rejects the view that a fenced yard can be burglarized. The plain meaning of the word "building" also does not include a fenced yard.

---

102. Reprinted with the permission of LexisNexis.

A Husband Can Be Found Guilty of Burglarizing the Home He Once Shared with His Estranged Wife

In the Georgia case, *Polanco v. State*, 340 Ga.App. 292 (2017), the defendant, Deivi M. Polanco, was charged with burglary (and stalking) for entering a home he used to share with his estranged wife. The couple's relationship had "deteriorated into [a] lot of fights, arguing, hitting [and] insults." When his wife said she would leave him, Polanco threatened he would "put [her] four meters under the ground." When Polanco was incarcerated for domestic violence, his wife moved all of his possessions to his mother's house and changed the locks. Although Polanco then lived with his mother, he appeared at his wife's house, which involved his "crouching below the window, hiding in a storage closet, and entering the residence and hiding under the bed." The victim had a temporary protective order ("TPO") served on Polanco, which ordered him to "not contact the victim, leave and stay away from the family residence, and surrender all keys and other items associated with the residence." Later:

> the victim arrived home and found flowers, a ring, and a note from Polanco inside her apartment. Polanco then approached her from where he had been hiding in the back of the apartment, and fearing for her safety, the victim told him to leave. Polanco eventually left, and the victim called the police. The responding officers discovered that Polanco had gained access to the apartment from a bedroom window and that "[t]he window was off the hinge and the blinds were disarrayed." Fearing that Polanco might come back, the victim and her children stayed in a hotel that night.

A person commits burglary under OCGA 16-7-1(b) when, "without authority and with the intent to commit a felony or theft therein, he or she enters or remains within the dwelling house of another." Polanco argued that he did not commit an "essential element of burglary," namely, entering "the dwelling house of another." Polanco urged that he could not be guilty of burglary because "he was authorized to enter his own residence." The *Polanco* court ruled that an **"entry into the separate residence of an estranged spouse, without authority and with the intent to commit a felony or theft therein, constitutes burglary."** The fact that Polanco had once lived in the victim's home did not, "in itself, give the defendant subsequent authority to enter." *Polanco* noted:

> Here, the evidence demonstrated that Polanco had been arrested for domestic violence against the victim, and that the victim so feared for her safety that a TPO had been issued which required that Polanco leave and stay away from the family residence. Further, Polanco's name was not on the lease for the residence. During Polanco's incarceration, the victim changed the locks to the residence. When he was released from jail, Polanco moved in with his mother and did not live at the residence, and when Polanco later entered the residence, he did so through a bedroom window. Given these circumstances, the jury was entitled to conclude that Polanco no longer lived at the residence and was no longer authorized to enter it. Moreover, "in light of [Polanco's] forcible entry, the jury could infer that [Polanco] knew that he was without authority to be in [his wife's] house."

The court therefore confirmed his burglary and stalking convictions.[103]

---

103. Reprinted from Westlaw, with permission of Thomson Reuters.

A "Polite" Burglar Apologizes for Breaking into the Wrong Home

Kelly Bliss for *NBC 10 Philadelphia News* reported on June 30, 2011, in "Polite Burglar Offers to Repair Damage: Cops," that, "Police say the suspect apologized to the victim, claiming he broke into the wrong home." The news report can be seen at:

http://www.nbcphiladelphia.com/news/local/Polite-Burglar-Offers-to-
Fix-Broken-Screen-Cops-124777974.html

---

c)   Intent Upon Entry

The mens rea of burglary—the intent to commit a felony therein—must be formed upon entry. This requirement can be explored with two hypothetical situations.

1. Suppose a person intends to enter her neighbor's house in order to steal the silverware and so has the intent to commit theft upon entry. Once inside, however, the person learns that the silverware is not made of sterling silver and so abandons her plans to steal the silverware, simply leaving without doing anything else. Since the would-be thief had the relevant intent upon entry, she committed burglary. Proving her intent when she did not commit her target crime of theft might be challenging. Suppose, however, that she brought a bag with her to commit the crime. Equipping oneself with a bag for the loot is circumstantial evidence of intent upon entry.

2. Suppose instead that a person has no intent to commit a crime upon entry. He enters a home simply to get away from a rabid dog. Once inside, however, he finds the occupant and rapes her. This would not be burglary because the intruder did not have the felonious intent to rape when he entered the home. Even though not guilty of burglary, the intruder could be charged with the rape he committed.

Learn from My (and Others') Mistakes

Do Not Get into a Car That You Suspect Might Be Wired with an Explosive

In the early days of gang prosecution before there were special "gang" units (Los Angeles's gang unit is called "Hard Core"), the D.A.'s office assigned each courtroom its own "gang deputy." For a short while, I had this assignment because no one else wanted it (no one at that early time knew it would be the fast-track to promotion). I remember prosecuting one gang member in particular that seemed to take personal offense with my arguments at jury trial. Coincidentally, at the end of one day of the trial, I found my car broken into in the parking lot. Wires were hanging out of the dashboard. I stopped a passing police cruiser and told the officers in it of my fears that my car might be rigged with a bomb. Without leaving the patrol car, the officers within shrugged and suggested I get in the car, turn on the ignition, and see what happened. Unbelievably, I followed their advice, turned the car on and when it did not explode, drove home. Apparently, thieves had tried to steal the car or its stereo. I, of course, cringe at my stupidity each time I tell this story.

A burglar must form **intent "upon entry." How can the prosecution prove what was in a person's mind as he or she entered? What if the defendant argues that no criminal intent was created until after he or she had already entered?** The following case considers these questions.

LEGAL ANALYSIS

People v. Gaines
74 N.Y.2d 358 (1989).
Judge Kaye delivered the opinion of the Court of Appeals of New York.

Facts

[In] the early morning of February 2, 1985, defendant was arrested as he emerged from the window of a building supply company. Over his own clothes defendant was wearing coveralls and a jacket that belonged to a company employee; pens bearing the company name were in the jacket pocket. Inside the building, several desks were in disarray. [No burglar's tools were found.]

[Defendant testified that he left the homeless shelter where he had been staying because he had inadequate funds to remain there. He walked] until he reached the building supply company, pushed in a window and entered the building for refuge from the cold and heavy snow that fell that night. Defendant claimed that he did not touch the desks, file cabinets or safe but simply put on the jacket and coveralls to keep warm and stayed near a heating vent until he heard police officers approaching.

[Defense] counsel requested that the jury be instructed that, where there is an unlawful entry, in order for a burglary to occur the intent to commit a crime within the building must exist at the time of the entry. [The judge refused the request and charged] that the jury could find defendant guilty of burglary if, at the time of his knowingly unlawful entry [or] remaining, defendant intended to commit a crime in the building.

[The jury convicted the defendant. Concluding that the trial court erred in denying defendant's requests, we now reverse his burglary conviction.]

Issue

Whether a defendant must have intent to commit a crime in the building *at the time* of his entry, or whether the burglary statute's "remains unlawfully" element means that such intent may be formed *after* defendant's unlawful entry.

Rule and Analysis

[We conclude that **Penal Law 140.20 third degree burglary requires the intent to commit a crime in the building exist at the time of the unlawful entry**. Penal Law 140.20 third degree burglary occurs when a person "knowingly enters or remains unlawfully in a building with intent to commit a crime therein."]

At common law, burglary was defined "as the breaking and entering of a dwelling of another, at night, with intent to commit a felony therein." *** Unless the intent to commit a felony existed at the time of the breaking and entry, there was no burglary. Similarly, under the former Penal Law, a defendant who broke and entered with no intent to commit a crime was not guilty of burglary, though later deciding to commit a crime on the premises. ***

When the Penal Law was revised in 1965, burglary in the third degree was defined as "knowingly enters *or remains* unlawfully in a building with intent to commit a crime therein." *** The People's contention in essence is that the addition of "remains unlawfully"—a concept unknown at common law or in the former Penal Law—abrogates the requirement of intent to commit a crime at the time of unlawful entry. All that is now required, according to the People, is that defendant commit a crime while unlawfully on the premises. ***

This interpretation is *** not consistent with the purpose of classifying burglary as a separate and relatively more serious crime. [Burglary] is in fact a form of attempt crime, since the crime the unlawful intruder intended to commit need not be completed. The development of burglary as an independent felony resulted from two deficiencies in the early law of attempt: that an attempt could not be penalized until the last act short of completion had occurred, and that the conduct was [punishable only as a misdemeanor.]

These gaps in the laws of attempt have now been remedied. An attempt need not encompass the final act toward the completion of the offense *** and is punishable as an offense of the same grade or a single lesser grade of severity as the completed crime. *** Nonetheless, the Legislature has continued to penalize burglary as a serious felony—rather than simply punish the trespass and the attempted or consummated crime within a building—because of the heightened danger posed when an unlawful intrusion into a building is effected by someone bent on a criminal end. A defendant who simply trespasses with no intent to commit a crime inside a building does not possess the more culpable mental state that justifies punishment as a burglar.

[The Legislature did not intend to change the long-standing rule requiring intent upon entry. The] Legislature was plainly addressing a different factual situation—not one of unlawful entry but of unauthorized remaining in a building after lawful entry (as a shoplifter who remains on store premises after closing). [The word "remain" in the phrase "enter or remain" is designed to be applicable to cases in which a person enters with "license or privilege" but remains on the premises after termination of such license or privilege.]

[**To be guilty of burglary for unlawful remaining, a defendant must have entered legally, but remained for the purpose of committing a crime after authorization to be on the premises terminates. To be guilty of burglary for unlawful entry, a defendant must have had the intent to commit a crime at the time of entry.**]

Conclusion

[**Defendant**] **was entitled to a charge clearly stating that the jury must find that he intended to commit a crime at the time he entered the premises unlawfully.**

[**Reversed.**][104]

Can burglary be avoided by gaining consent to enter based on subterfuge, fraud, deceit, or false pretenses? The case below considers the implications of this question.

---

104. Reprinted from Westlaw, with permission of Thomson Reuters.

LEGAL ANALYSIS

State v. Newton
294 Ga. 767 (2014).
Justice Benham delivered the opinion of the Supreme Court of Georgia.

Facts

[A jury convicted David Allen Newton of burglary and theft] for taking jewelry while touring a home that he claimed he was interested in purchasing and using a fictitious name on a brokerage agreement. [Newton challenged the sufficiency of the evidence to support his burglary conviction.]

[A] man identifying himself as David Flynn contacted Jessica Harris, a real estate agent in Douglas County, and told her that he was relocating from New Jersey and wanted to look at houses in the $600,000 to $1,000,000 price range. Harris met with the potential buyer and presented him with a buyer's brokerage agreement, which he signed as David Flynn. He provided a driver's license with his picture and the name David Flynn. They spent two full days looking at houses. At trial, Harris identified the defendant, David Newton, as the potential buyer she had known as David Flynn.

[Defendant toured a house owned by Cynthia Murphy. Harris, the real estate agent, had briefly left Newton alone in the master bedroom. When they later got back to the agent's car,] Harris saw Newton reach into the back seat where he had stored a canvas tote bag and do something with the bag before getting into her car.

[Later, Murphy found her jewelry boxes were empty.] The value of her missing jewelry was approximately $20,000. ***

Shay Brooks with the Douglas County Sheriff's Office investigated the theft from Murphy's home. After obtaining the paperwork Harris had on David Flynn, Brooks determined that the New Jersey license in the name of David Flynn was fake and received information that David Flynn was actually David Newton.

The State introduced similar transaction evidence of a theft from a home in Sandy Springs.

*** Newton argued that the evidence was insufficient to support the burglary conviction because there was no evidence that he entered the house without authority. The trial court denied the motion, noting that Newton never had authority to enter the house because only a person named David Flynn was so authorized. ***

[The court instructed that jury that:

a] person commits the offense of burglary when, without authority and with the intent to commit a theft therein, he enters a room in the dwelling house of another. To constitute the offense of burglary, it is not necessary that it be shown that a break-in occurred or that an actual theft was accomplished.

Issue

Whether a person enters a home 'without authority' when he enters with the consent of the owner, which was obtained by fraud, deceit, or false pretense.

Rule and Analysis

Despite the fact that appellee engaged in subterfuge to gain permission to enter Murphy's home, the Court of Appeals reversed appellee's burglary conviction, concluding the evidence was insufficient to show that appellee was "without authority" to be in the victim's house. ***

"At common law burglary was defined as the breaking and entering of a dwelling house at night with the intent to commit a felony inside that dwelling. Although all modern statutes enlarge the scope of the crime, essentially they vary around this definition." *** [Georgia's pre–1968 statutory law required a "breaking and entering" to establish the crime of burglary. In 1968, Georgia did away with the breaking requirement. The] statutory language was changed to require that the entry be " without authority," coupled, of course, with the intent to commit a felony or theft within the dwelling or building of another. [OCGA 16-7-1(a) provided] as follows:

A person commits the offense of burglary when, without authority and with the intent to commit a felony or theft therein, he enters or remains within the dwelling house of another or any building, vehicle, railroad car, watercraft, or other such structure designed for use as the dwelling of another or enters or remains within any other building, railroad car, aircraft, or any room or any part thereof.

[**The term "without authority" has been defined to mean "without legal right or privilege or without permission of a person legally entitled to withhold the right."**]

[We] see no meaningful difference between gaining entry by force and gaining consent to enter by artifice:

The purpose of the burglary statute is to protect against the specific dangers posed by entry into secured premises of intruders bent on crime. **The intruder who breaches the barrier with a lie or deception, by pretending to deliver a package or to read a meter, is no less dangerous than his more stealthy cohorts, and nothing in the statute suggests an intent to exempt him from liability.**

The evolution of Georgia's statutory law concerning burglary has been to broaden rather than restrict the parameters within which it may be applied. Here, the evidence showed appellee staged an elaborate ruse to pose as a potential home buyer. Not only did he use an alias, but he used false identification and gave false information concerning his true identity all to bolster his pretense of being a bona fide potential home buyer. [Since the consent to enter the home was procured by fraud, appellee's entry into the home was "without authority."]

Conclusion

[The Court of Appeals' decision is reversed, and appellee's conviction for burglary is reinstated.][105]

---

105. Reprinted from Westlaw, with permission of Thomson Reuters.

When a car is burglarized, such "auto burglary" occurs only when the doors are locked and the windows are secured.

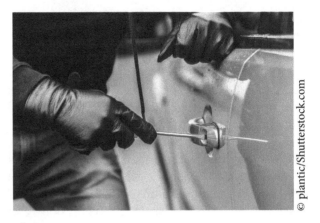

© plantic/Shutterstock.com

Breaking and Entering Alone Do Not Amount to Burglary

Can a person commit burglary by entering a home without consent merely for the purpose of cleaning up? As Stephanie Rabiner noted in her article, "'Cleaning Fairy' Charged with Breaking and Tidying," on June 4, 2012, in *Legally Weird*, such an intruder lacks the intent for burglary, and therefore will probably face a charge of trespass. The full article can be seen at:

http://blogs.findlaw.com/legally_weird/2012/06/cleaning-fairy-charged-with-breaking-and-tidying.html

---

Biography—Criminal

John Wayne Gacy—Killer Clown

- Born March 17, 1942, in Chicago, Illinois.
- According to Sophie Gilbert in her October 9, 2014 article in *The Atlantic*, "How Clowns Became Terrifying," **Gacy once told police, "clowns can get away with murder."**
- The case, *People v. Gacy*, 103 Ill.2d 1, 468 N.E.2d 1171 (1984), reported the following:
- On December 11, 1978, "Robert Piest, a 15–year–old boy," who had told his mother that he was going to visit a contractor about a promised job, went missing.
- Police suspicion focused on Gacy, who "had a record of sexually assaulting young men and had been convicted in Iowa for an assault on a teenage boy."
- A jury convicted John Wayne Gacy of 33 counts of murder, one count of deviate sexual assault, and one count of indecent liberties with a child.
- Gacy admitted to killing about 30 people, burying some "in the crawl space under his home" and throwing 5 "into the Des Plaines River."
- "Excavation of the crawl space and the area surrounding defendant's home recovered 29 bodies" while "four bodies were recovered from the Des Plaines and Illinois rivers, downstream from the place where defendant had told the police that he threw the bodies."
- Gacy was executed by lethal injection on May 10, 1994.[106]

---

106. Reprinted from Westlaw, with permission of Thomson Reuters.

B.   ARSON

1.   Common Law

Blackstone, in *Commentaries,* Vol. IV, at 220, described **common law arson as "the malicious and willful burning of the house or outhouses of another man."** He argued that **arson was "much more pernicious to the public than simple theft"** because (1) "it is an offense against that right, of habitation, which is acquired by the law of nature as well as by the laws of society," (2) it caused "terror and confusion," and (3) with theft, "the thing stolen only changes its master," with burning, "the very substance is absolutely destroyed." Blackstone deemed arson "frequently

more destructive than murder itself, of which too it is often the cause; since murder, atrocious as it is, seldom extends beyond the felonious act designed; whereas fire too frequently involves in the common calamity persons unknown to the incendiary, and not intended to be hurt by him, and friends as well as enemies." Blackstone's fear of arson was fully justified, given the vulnerability of the closely spaced wooden buildings of the time to quickly spreading fires.

Given the danger posed by arson, the common law took great care in defining what qualified as a "house" and what amounted to "burning" for arson. A "house" included not only the dwelling house, but all outhouses, barns, and stables, even though not under a single roof. Burning a barn standing alone in a field was arson "if filled with hay or corn." Willfully setting fire to one's own home was arson if a neighbor's home was thus also burned. The "burning" element could not be satisfied with a mere attempt to burn, but "the burning and consuming of any part is sufficient," even if the fire was later extinguished. As for intent, the fire had to be set maliciously. Thus, "an unqualified person, by shooting with a gun, happens to set fire to a house" did not commit arson.

VIDEO: Things to Look for at a Fire Scene

An arson expert explains the things to be on the lookout for when arriving at the scene of a fire at:

https://www.youtube.com/watch?v=jYaLO-BITSU

---

2.   Current Law

Arson is categorized as a crime against habitation because the common law originally defined it as the burning of a house. Current law has expanded arson to involve other kinds of burnings. As explained in *People v. Labaer* 88 Cal. App. 4th 289 (2001):

> The arson statutes provide different levels of punishment, depending on the subject matter of the arson. (§ 451.) These statutory categories, in descending level of punishment, are: (1) arson resulting in great bodily injury (five, seven, or nine years); (2) arson to "an inhabited structure or inhabited property" (three, five, or eight years); (3) arson of a "structure or forest land" (two, four, or six years); and (4) arson to other types of property (16 months, two, or three years). (§ 451, subds. (a), (b), (c) & (d).) By creating these different levels of punishment, the Legislature intended to impose punishment "'in proportion to the seriousness of the offense,'" and, in particular, "according to the injury or potential injury to human life involved . . . ."

a)   Statutes Defining Arson

Florida § 806.01. Arson

(1) Any person who willfully and unlawfully, or while in the commission of any felony, by fire or explosion, damages or causes to be damaged:

(a) Any dwelling, whether occupied or not, or its contents;

(b) Any structure, or contents thereof, where persons are normally present, such as: jails, prisons, or detention centers; hospitals, nursing homes, or other health care facilities; department stores, office buildings, business establishments, churches, or educational institutions during normal hours of occupancy; or other similar structures; or

(c) Any other structure that he or she knew or had reasonable grounds to believe was occupied by a human being,

is guilty of arson in the first degree, which constitutes a felony of the first degree, punishable as provided in s. 775.082, s. 775.083, or s. 775.084.

(2) Any person who willfully and unlawfully, or while in the commission of any felony, by fire or explosion, damages or causes to be damaged any structure, whether the property of himself or herself or another, under any circumstances not referred to in subsection (1), is guilty of arson in the second degree, which constitutes a felony of the second degree, punishable as provided in s. 775.082, s. 775.083, or s. 775.084.

(3) As used in this chapter, "structure" means any building of any kind, any enclosed area with a roof over it, any real property and appurtenances thereto, any tent or other portable building, and any vehicle, vessel, watercraft, or aircraft.

A Lawyer's Pants Catch on Fire in Court—Really

In an incident that will confirm everyone's worst suspicions about lawyers, defense attorney Stephen Gutierrez's pants caught fire during his closing argument in an arson trial. Articles from the *Miami Herald* and *NBC News* can be visited at:

http://www.miamiherald.com/news/local/crime/article137317553.html and
https://www.nbcnews.com/news/us-news/lawyer-s-pants-catch-fire-
during-florida-arson-trial-n731161

California Penal Code § 451: What Constitutes Arson; Term of Imprisonment

A person is guilty of arson when he or she willfully and maliciously sets fire to or burns or causes to be burned or who aids, counsels, or procures the burning of, any structure, forest land, or property.

(a) Arson that causes great bodily injury is a felony punishable by imprisonment in the state prison for five, seven, or nine years.

(b) Arson that causes an inhabited structure or inhabited property to burn is a felony punishable by imprisonment in the state prison for three, five, or eight years.

(c) Arson of a structure or forest land is a felony punishable by imprisonment in the state prison for two, four, or six years.

(d) Arson of property is a felony punishable by imprisonment in the state prison for 16 months, two, or three years. For purposes of this paragraph, arson of property does not include one burning or causing to be burned his or her own personal property unless there is an intent to defraud or there is injury to another person or another person's structure, forest land, or property.

(e) In the case of any person convicted of violating this section while confined in a state prison, prison road camp, prison forestry camp, or other prison camp or prison farm, or while confined in a county jail while serving a term of imprisonment for a felony or misdemeanor conviction, any sentence imposed shall be consecutive to the sentence for which the person was then confined.

California Penal Code § 450: Definitions Regarding Arson

In this chapter, the following terms have the following meanings:

(a) "Structure" means any building, or commercial or public tent, bridge, tunnel, or powerplant.

(b) "Forest land" means any brush covered land, cut-over land, forest, grasslands, or woods.

(c) "Property" means real property or personal property, other than a structure or forest land.

(d) "Inhabited" means currently being used for dwelling purposes whether occupied or not. "Inhabited structure" and "inhabited property" do not include the real property on which an inhabited structure or an inhabited property is located.

(e) "Maliciously" imports a wish to vex, defraud, annoy, or injure another person, or an intent to do a wrongful act, established either by proof or presumption of law.

(f) "Recklessly" means a person is aware of and consciously disregards a substantial and unjustifiable risk that his or her act will set fire to, burn, or cause to burn a structure, forest land, or property. The risk shall be of such nature and degree that disregard thereof constitutes a gross deviation from the standard of conduct that a reasonable person would observe in the situation. A person who creates such a risk but is unaware thereof solely by reason of voluntary intoxication also acts recklessly with respect thereto.[107]

Model Penal Code § 220.1: Arson

(1) A person is guilty of arson, a felony of the second degree, if he starts a fire or causes an explosion with the purpose of:

(a) destroying a building or occupied structure of another; or

(b) destroying or damaging any property, whether his own or another's, to collect insurance for such loss[108]

---

107. From *Deering's California Codes Annotated*. Copyright © 2014 by Matthew Bender & Company, Inc., a member of the LexisNexis Group. Reprinted with the permission of LexisNexis.
108. From *The Model Penal Code* by the American Law Institute. Copyright © 1962 by the American Law Institute. Used by permission.

b)   What Intent Is Needed for Arson?

The **intent** required for **arson** varies with the jurisdiction. Some courts have moved further away from common law than others. **The case below interpreted arson as a general intent crime.** Therefore, arson, which the court noted is often committed by persons who have been drinking, is **not a specific intent crime that is subject to an intoxication defense**. In reading the case, consider the court's analysis of the two kinds of intent needed for arson: **"willfully"** and **"maliciously."**

© Angelina Babii/Shutterstock.com

LEGAL ANALYSIS

People v. Atkins
25 Cal.4th 76 (2001).
Justice Chin delivered the opinion for the California Supreme Court.

Facts

[Defendant Robert Nelson Atkins] told his friends that he hated Orville Figgs and was going to burn down Figgs's house. [Defendant and his brother David drove by Figgs's home on the Ponderosa Sky Ranch and "flipped the bird" at Figgs as they passed by. Later, a fire started which came within 150 feet of Figgs' house.]

The county fire marshal, Alan Carlson, responded to the fire around 1:30 a.m. and saw a large fire rapidly spreading in the canyon below the ranch. He described fire conditions on that night as "extreme." Both the weather and the vegetation were particularly dry. The wind was blowing from 12 to 27 miles per hour, with gusts up to 50 miles per hour. The canyon had heavy brush, trees, grass, and steep sloping grades. The fire could not be controlled for three days and burned an area from 2.5 to 2.8 miles long.

[Later, defendant told the fire marshal] that he and his brother had spent much of the day drinking. [Noticing that the Ponderosa Sky Ranch was in poor condition, he decided to burn some of the weeds.] He pulled out the weeds, placed them in a small pile in a cleared area, retrieved a plastic gasoline jug from David's truck, and from the jug poured "chainsaw mix" on the pile of weeds. Defendant put the jug down a few feet away and lit the pile of weeds with a disposable lighter. The fire quickly spread to the jug and got out of hand. He and David tried to put the fire out, unsuccessfully. They panicked and fled while the jug was still burning. Defendant told the marshal that he meant no harm [and claimed the fire was an accident.]

The marshal testified that the fire had not been started in a cleared area. The area was covered with vegetation, and there was no evidence that the fire started accidentally during a debris burn or that someone had tried to put it out. The marshal opined that the fire was intentionally set.

[A jury convicted the defendant of arson of forest land. (§ 451, subd. (c).)].

Issue

Whether arson's "willfully" and "maliciously" constitute general intent and therefore are not vulnerable to the voluntary intoxication defense.

Rule and Analysis

[PC 22] provides: "(a) No act committed by a person while in a state of voluntary intoxication is less criminal by reason of his or her having been in that condition. ***"(b) Evidence of voluntary intoxication is admissible solely on the issue of whether or not the defendant actually formed a required specific intent, (but) is inadmissible to negate the existence of general criminal intent. ***

[**Arson requires only a general criminal intent** and] the specific intent to set fire to or burn *** the relevant structure or forest land is not an element of arson.

*** **A person is guilty of arson when he or she willfully and maliciously sets fire to or burns or causes to be burned or who aids, counsels, or procures the burning of, any structure, forest land, or property.**" *** "Maliciously" is defined in the arson chapter as "a wish to vex, defraud, annoy, or injure another person, or an intent to do a wrongful act." ["Willfully" implies simply a purpose or willingness to commit the act, or make the omission referred to. It does not require any intent to violate law, or to injure another, or to acquire any advantage.]

*** "Willfully implies no evil intent; ' "it implies that the person knows what he is doing, intends to do what he is doing and is a free agent." ["Willfully" in a penal statute usually defines a general criminal intent. "Maliciously," in the context of arson, requires no specific intent.]

[The] proscribed acts within the statutory definition of arson are to (1) set fire to; (2) burn; or (3) cause to be burned, any structure, forest land, or property. *** Language that typically denotes specific intent crimes, such as "with the intent" to achieve or "for the purpose of" achieving some further act, is absent from section 451. ***

Arson's * willful and malice requirement ensures that the setting of the fire must be a deliberate and intentional act, as distinguished from an accidental or unintentional ignition.** [There] must be a general intent to willfully commit the act of setting on fire under such circumstances that the direct, natural, and highly probable consequences would be the burning of the relevant structure or property. [The different] offense of unlawfully causing a fire covers reckless accidents or unintentional fires, which, by definition, is committed by a person who is "aware of and consciously disregards a substantial and unjustifiable risk that his or her act will set fire to, burn, or cause to burn a structure, forest land, or property." (§§ 450, subd. (f), 452.) For example, such reckless accidents or unintentional fires may include those caused by a person who recklessly lights a match near highly combustible materials. ***

In arson, as with assault, there is generally no complex mental state, but only relatively simple impulsive behavior. A typical arson is almost never the product of pyromania. [**It often is an angry impulsive act, requiring no tools other than a match or lighter, and possibly a container of gasoline.**] "Arson is one of the easiest crimes to commit on the spur of the moment . . . it takes only seconds to light a match to a pile of clothes or a curtain." ***

The *** legislative policy concerns are consistent with studies that have shown *** that revenge and vindictiveness are principal motives for arson *** that **there is a strong relationship between alcohol intoxication and arson** *** [55 percent of arsonists intoxicated on alcohol and more than 60 percent of arsonists under influence of some intoxicant during arson] ***; and that recidivist arsonists committing chronic or repetitive arson have high levels of alcohol dependence ***. Thus, the motivations for most arsons, the ease of its commission, and the strong connection with alcohol reflect the crime's impulsiveness. "It would therefore be anomalous to allow evidence of intoxication to relieve a man of responsibility for [arson], which [is] so frequently committed in just such a manner."

Conclusion

[Evidence of voluntary intoxication is not admissible because arson is a general intent crime. We reverse the judgment of the Court of Appeal.][109]

Note

Florida reduced the level of intent even further than California, substituting "unlawfully" for the traditional and more severe "maliciously" mental state. The Court of Appeal of Florida discussed this change in *Lofton v. State*, 416 So.2d 522 (1982). The *Lofton* court noted that under the old law, "arson convictions were difficult to obtain because of the problems inherent in proving malice, i.e., the defendant's evil intent." *Lofton* explained:

> In order to alleviate this problem, **the Legislature substituted the word "unlawfully" for the word "maliciously." Under this new wording the State need not prove an evil intent on the part of the perpetrator. It need only be shown that the willful act was done without a legitimate, lawful purpose**.

VIDEO: An NYFD Investigator Discusses a Fire Scene

A New York City Fire Department Investigator leads viewers through an arson scene at:

https://www.youtube.com/watch?v=FdfxMTaT-jY

"Seamless Web" Connection

In *People v. Atkins*, the case discussed above, the court considers what intent a person must have in order to be found guilty of arson. The court's analysis causes it to consider general and specific intent, issues regarding the fundamental element of mens rea discussed in Chapter 3. Further, the defendant wished to rely on voluntary intoxication, a defense that connects this case to the "excuse" defenses explored in Chapter 16.

Is Arson Underreported?

Scripps News and *41 Action News KSHB.com* report in "Arson in America: An alarming reality?" that the crime of arson is severely underreported in the United States.
The video reporting this can be viewed at:

http://www.kshb.com/dpp/news/national/arson-in-america-an-alarming-reality

---

109. Reprinted with the permission of LexisNexis.

Are Enough Resources Committed to Arson Investigations?

One city, Detroit, has suffered great difficulty in investigating all of its suspicious fires. Jeff Wattrick of *Deadline Detroit* reported in the November 26, 2013, article, "Arson Investigations Overwhelm Understaffed Detroit Fire Dept.," that:

> Detroit has six certified arson investigators to handle a caseload that usually includes about 5000 suspicious fires every year. The result is the Detroit Fire Department has a tough time proving arson.

The video of this piece can be viewed at:

http://www.deadlinedetroit.com/articles/7363/arson_investigations_overwhelms_
understaffed_detroit_fire_dept#.UpVxjijR1Fl

What Exactly Does Arson Require for "Burn"?

Does arson mandate that actual flames appear when it refers to "burns"? Or, instead, is it enough to satisfy the burning element that there was "charring," "scorching," "wasting," "shriveling," or causing "soot" or "discoloration"? Although choosing among such words might seem to involve something as trivial as picking terms out of a thesaurus, nothing could be further from the truth. According to John S. Baker, Jr. in *Criminal Law*, 46 La. L. Rev. 431, 431–32 (1986), determining the actual "degree of damage" that arson requires "could mean the difference between guilt or innocence."

The California Supreme Court considered the issue in *People v. Haggerty* 46 Cal. 354 (1873), where the defendant set fire to oily rags lying on the floor of a house. He urged that he did not commit arson because little damage occurred as the fire was quickly put out. *Haggerty* rejected his argument and affirmed the conviction, because:

> ["Burn" for arson at common law] **means to consume by fire. If the wood is blackened, but no fibers are wasted, there is no burning**; yet the wood need not be in a blaze. **[The] burning of any part, however small, completes the offense, the same as of the whole.** [If the floor of the house is charred in a single place, so as to destroy any of the fibers of the wood, this is a sufficient burning in a case of arson.] There was evidence tending to show that a spot on the floor was charred, so as to destroy the fibers of the wood by the fire set by the defendant; and there was no evidence directly contradicting that fact.

In contrast, **Louisiana**, in both *State v. Williams*, 457 So.2d 610 (1984) and *State v. Smith*, 988 So.2d 861 (2008) **has found that mere "scorching" is sufficient to support an arson charge**. Similarly, Indiana, in *Williams v. State*, 600 N.E.2d 962 (1992), found that, "smoke damage and the soot on the basement wall were enough to support a conviction for arson under IC 35-43-1-1(a)." The Indiana Court of Appeals so ruled even though it was fully aware of the common law requirement of charring:

> Traditionally the common law rigidly required an actual burning. The fire must have been actually communicated to the object to such an extent as to have taken effect upon it. [At common law,] **any charring of the wood of a building, so that the fiber of the wood was destroyed, was enough to constitute a sufficient burning to complete the crime of arson.** *** However, merely singeing, smoking, scorching, or discoloring by heat were not considered enough to support a conviction. ***

The Indiana statute, however, requiring only "damaging," was not limited to common law restrictions.

c)   Arson of a "Structure"

What counts as part of a "**structure**" for purposes of arson of a structure? Would a person be guilty of this crime if his or her fire only burned **wallpaper**, or melted the plastic covers of **fixtures** such as lights? The case below not only provides the answers, but the reasons for the lines the court chooses to draw in this case.

© Gorb Andrii/Shutterstock.com

LEGAL ANALYSIS

In Re Jesse L.
221 Cal. App.3d 161 (1990).
Justice Martin delivered the opinion of the California Court of Appeal.

Facts

[The administration building at Roosevelt High School in Fresno caught fire.] [Fire investigator John Salveson] testified that entry into the administration building had been obtained by breaking a window next to a door, reaching around, and pressing the panic bar on the locked door, allowing it to open. Appellant's fingerprints and palm prints were found in three different places on the window. [Three] fires had been ignited, two on the tops of desks and one on the floor, by heaping files and papers, dousing them with a flammable liquid and igniting them.

[The estimated cost] of the "equipment and supplies that were destroyed as well as the damages to the structure itself" was approximately $250,000. [In front of a group of students, appellant claimed responsibility for the fire.]

Acknowledging that the evidence supports the burning of *property* in violation of [PC 451(d), appellant claims there was insufficient evidence that a structure as required by PC 451(c) was burned.]

Issue

Whether there was sufficient evidence that the defendant burned a "structure" within the meaning of California's arson statute.

Rule and Analysis

Appellant was charged with [violating PC 451(c), which provides]: **"A person is guilty of arson when he or she willfully and maliciously sets fire to or burns or causes to be burned or who aids, counsels or procures the burning of, any structure, forest land or property."** [Arson of a *structure* is punishable by imprisonment in the state prison for two, four, or six years. Arson of *property* is punishable by imprisonment in the state prison for 16 months, two, or three years. The setting of a fire which does not burn the structure itself does not violate this subsection of the statute.]

[John Salveson testified that inside] the building he observed fire damage on two desk tops, computers, typewriters, telephones, and other items of property and paper had been damaged by the fire. Plastic light covers had melted and the "formica covered wood" of a counter top had been charred by fire. [He discovered "burn patterns" on the floor, on the bottom edge of the counter, and on the face of the doors.]

Appellant contends that the foregoing evidence is insufficient to support a finding that arson of a structure occurred. We must disagree. [Salveson's] uncontradicted testimony of "burn patterns" on the floor of the building and the bottom edge of the counter and on the face of the doors was sufficient to establish that an area on the floor and a door were charred so as to destroy the fibers of the wood by the fire set by the appellant. Mr. Salveson's testimony clearly distinguished between smoke damage and these so-called "burn patterns." To illustrate, he used the term "burn pattern" to describe the burning of both the desks and the counter which he specifically testified were charred as opposed to "smoke stains" around the entrance doors.

[Plastic light covers had melted and some of them had fallen on the ground, while others were hanging from the metal framework. A] further question is presented whether the destruction by fire of a light fixture is sufficient evidence of structural fire damage to support a conviction of arson.

[A "fixture" is defined as "a thing that is] affixed to land when it is attached to it by roots, as in the case of trees, vines, or shrubs; or embedded in it, as in the case of walls; or permanently resting upon it, as in the case of buildings; or permanently attached to what is thus permanent, as by means of cement, plaster, nails, bolts or screws." [**A fixture is a thing, originally personal property, but later affixed to realty, so that it is considered real property**. An out-of-state case found] the prosecution sufficiently established a "burning" of a county jail within the meaning of arson in the first degree with evidence of "damage to paint and light fixtures" as well as other factors. ***

[Evidence for arson was sufficient when a structure's wallpaper was burned. Wallpaper affixed to an interior wall is a part of the dwelling's framework.]

[A Utah court] held that acoustical tile is an integral part of a building within the rule that a charring of a part of the building is all that is required to constitute a burning sufficient for the crime of arson. ***

[A] **fixture, i.e., personal property affixed to the realty so that it becomes an integral part of the structure, becomes part of the structure to the extent that a burning or charring or destruction by fire is all that is required to constitute a burning sufficient to support a conviction of [PC 451(c). The evidence of "burn patterns" which indicates at least minor charring of the structure together with the damage to the light fixtures is ample evidence of a violation of [PC 451(c).]**

Conclusion

There was sufficient evidence that the defendant burned a "structure" within the meaning of Penal Code Section 451. The order of the juvenile court is affirmed.[110]

---

110. Reprinted with the permission of LexisNexis.

The following case considers the crime of **arson** due to burning the **"contents" of a dwelling. If a person sets clothes in a closet on fire, the crime would be fulfilled. What if, instead, the person sets the clothing on fire when another person in the home is wearing them?** Does the fact that a person is currently wearing the clothes make them any less "contents" of a dwelling?

LEGAL ANALYSIS

State v. Harrington
782 So. 2d 505 (2001).
Justice Campbell delivered the opinion of the Court of Appeal of Florida.

Facts

The State challenges the dismissal of the arson count of the indictment that charged Johnny Harrington with first-degree murder and first-degree arson. We reverse.

[Harrington and Gwendolyn Bell had a long "on again, off again" relationship over many years. At] the time of the alleged offenses, Ms. Bell and Harrington were living together in Harrington's apartment.

On July 25, 1999, [Ms. Bell and Harrington, argued] over the use of crack cocaine. It is alleged that Harrington forced Ms. Bell to smoke crack cocaine by holding a knife to her throat. As the argument increased, Harrington poured lamp oil over Ms. Bell and her clothing, struck a match, and set Ms. Bell and her clothing on fire. Ms. Bell subsequently died from her burn injuries. The only damage from the fire to Harrington's apartment was soot damage to the ceiling that would require repainting to correct.

A person is guilty of arson as defined in section 806.01, Florida Statutes when they willfully and unlawfully, by fire, damage or cause to be damaged any dwelling or its contents. The trial judge dismissed the arson count against Harrington finding that . . . the burning of the clothing Ms. Bell was wearing could not be considered "contents" of the apartment for purposes of the arson charge. We disagree ***. The arson statute requires that a dwelling or its contents be damaged as a result of an intentional and unlawful fire. ***

Issue

Whether the burning of a person's clothing while the person is wearing them inside a home can be considered "contents" of the dwelling for purposes of arson.

Rule and Analysis

Clearly, if Harrington had gone to a closet and set fire to any of Ms. Bell's clothing hanging in the closet, we would not be faced with this issue. Merely because Ms. Bell was wearing the clothing at the time Harrington set the clothing on fire does not make them any less "contents" of the dwelling. ***

Conclusion

[Ms.] **Bell's clothing qualified as "contents" of the dwelling. Reversed and remanded.**

A Curious Reason for Committing Arson

Lock Yourself Out of Your Car? It Is Not Worth Starting a Fire

A woman lit a hillside on fire in an attempt to get someone's attention when she found she was locked out of her car.

This article can be viewed at:

http://www.signalscv.com/archives/46023/

Can Trash Be "Property" for Purposes of Arson?

In the California case, *In Re L.T.* 103 Cal. App.4th 262 (2002), L.T., a minor, was charged with arson under PC 451(d), based on the following facts:

> Walter J., a student who attended Charles Drew Middle School with L.T., testified that he saw L.T., who was holding a lighter, put her hand inside a trash can that was located on school premises. He said that his friend "saw the whole trash can burn," but Walter J. said that he only saw cardboard inside of the trash can on fire.

L.T. moved to dismiss the case, arguing that she did not commit arson because she "burned only the cardboard inside the trash can, and the cardboard was not the property of another." The court reasoned:

> L.T. argues that she did not commit arson because she did not burn the property of another. She contends that she merely burned trash, and that trash is not "property" that belongs to anyone. The People contend that the trash L.T. burned was "property" that did not belong to her; hence, she committed arson when she burned it. We agree with the People.

© Big Pants Production/Shutterstock.com

Someone else's trash can be "property" for arson.

[PC 451 provides:] "A person is guilty of arson when he or she willfully and maliciously sets fire to or burns or causes to be burned or who aids, counsels, or procures the burning of, any structure, forest land, or property. **[Arson] of property does not include one burning or causing to be burned his or her own personal property unless there is an intent to defraud or there is injury to another person or another person's structure, forest land, or property.** [Arson] is committed when the "property" burned does not belong to the person causing the fire. **The trash burned [constitutes "property" in the arson statute.] The Penal Code defines "property" to include "personal property," which, in turn, includes "money, goods, chattels, things in action, and evidences of debt."** *** Trash fits within

this definition. "Goods" and "chattels" are things that are "visible, tangible, movable" and are "objects of the senses." ***

["Property" is all-embracing, including every intangible benefit and prerogative susceptible of possession or disposition.] Trash is a "thing of which there may be ownership." ***

The trash did not belong to L.T. The trash was in a container on school property. There is no evidence that L. T. did any act causing the trash to become her property before she set fire to it. L.T.'s theory that by burning the trash, it became her property, is meritless. Whether the trash L.T. burned belonged to the school, the city, or the city trash collectors or was abandoned property does not alter the fact that the trash did not belong to L.T.

By burning property not belonging to her, L.T. committed [PC 451 arson.] The judgment is affirmed.[111]

DISCUSSION QUESTIONS

1. What makes burglary a "crime against habitation" instead of a "crime against property"?

2. What makes common law burglary so much more heinous than burglary today?

3. Can a person fulfill the "entry" element of burglary today if he or she has "consent" to enter from the owner? Why or why not?

4. When and where must a burglar form his or her intent in order to be guilty of burglary? Why?

5. Is "breaking and entering" the same as burglary? Why or why not?

6. What is a "building" for purposes of arson?

7. What is "property" for purposes of arson? Does property include trash?

8. Why is arson an underreported crime?

WEB LINKS

1. Michigan defines terminology for arson at: http://www.legislature.mi.gov/(S(0jwdjlzwdfp5 mklzbm33ozs3))/mileg.aspx?page=getObject&objectName=mcl-750-72&highlight=arson and http://www.legislature.mi.gov/(S(0jwdjlzwdfp5mklzbm33ozs3))/mileg.aspx?page=getObject& objectName=mcl-750-71&highlight=arson

---

111. Reprinted with the permission of LexisNexis.

2. Mississippi's jury instructions for: "3412 Burglary—Breaking and Entering a Dwelling House—Under Circumstances Likely to Terrorize," can be viewed at: https://courts.ms.gov/mmji/Proposed%20Plain%20Language%20Model%20Jury%20Instructions%20-%20Criminal.pdf at page 358 (Mississippi Plain Language Model Jury Instructions—Criminal 2012). Further, Mississippi's jury instructions for "3417 Burglary—Breaking and Entering a Place of Worship" can be viewed at the same website at page 364.

3. For arson, Nevada instructs its juries that property must be "scorched, charred or burned." See the "Brief Bank" for the "Washoe County District Attorney's Office" at: http://nvpac.nv.gov/uploadedFiles/nvpacnvgov/Content/Attorneys/JuryInstructions.pdf

4. For New York's jury instructions on arson generally, see: http://www.nycourts.gov/judges/cji/2-PenalLaw/150/art150hp.shtml. For the particular crime of arson first degree (Intentionally Damaging a Building and Causing Serious Physical Injury to Another Person Under Penal Law 150.20), see: http://www.nycourts.gov/judges/cji/2-PenalLaw/150/150-20-2.pdf.

CHAPTER X

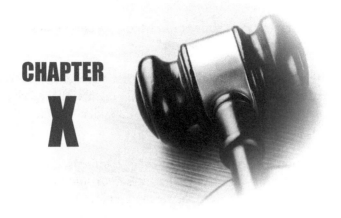

White-Collar Crime

While white-collar crime can be committed by those wearing white collars, it is perhaps better understood by looking at the resources of the criminal or the damage done.

A. WHAT IS "WHITE-COLLAR CRIME"?

Zvi D. Gabbay, in *Exploring the Limits of the Restorative Justice Paradigm: Restorative Justice and White-Collar Crime* 8 Cardozo J. Conflict Resol. 421, 428 (2007), described the origin of the term "white-collar crime" as follows:

> The first to coin the phrase and offer a definition was Edwin Sutherland in a famous address to the American Sociological Society in Philadelphia on December 27, 1939. **Sutherland**

defined white-collar crime as "a crime committed by a person of respectability and high social status in the course of his occupation."

Gabbay explained that **Sutherland's definition** has been characterized as flawed. First, it **singled out for liability "a particular social stature and class,"** which violated criminal law's aim to punish criminal acts rather than the qualities or status of the offender. Second, it was simply **not accurate** because, as one study found,

> Contrary to the common perception of white-collar criminals, the (study) sample consisted mostly of "offenders who are very similar to average or middle class Americans." In fact, eight percent of the offenders in the sample were unemployed at the time they committed the offense, and only a third were officers or owners of businesses.

Gabbay noted that the United States **Department of Justice (DOJ)** has offered an **alternative definition for white-collar crime** as:

> **nonviolent crime for financial gain committed by means of deception by persons whose occupational status is entrepreneurial, professional or semi-professional and utilizing their special occupational skills and opportunities**; also, nonviolent crime for financial gain utilizing deception and committed by anyone having special technical and professional knowledge of business and government, irrespective of the person's occupation.

Trotter Hardy, in *Prosecuting White-Collar Crime: Criminal Copyright Infringement* 11 Wm. & Mary Bill of Rts. J. 305 (2002), has offered still other ways to think of white-collar crime. He explained:

> Current thinking, however, has changed the meaning of "white-collar crime." [C]ontemporary views generally shift the emphasis away from the status of the wrong-doer. One view, for example, emphasizes the resources available for use in the commission of a crime. Not that the presence of resources, such as accounting records and the corporate treasury in an embezzlement scheme, should be taken to *define* "white-collar crime," but rather that the amount of resources that the defendant controls should be understood to correlate closely with the seriousness and scope of white-collar offenses. [Therefore "white-collar crime" could mean] a crime committed by someone using sophisticated resources that are readily available, typically at the place of employment.

Alternatively, **other commentators emphasize the scope of the harm done by white-collar criminals, coupled with the absence of physical violence and a corresponding reliance on fraud or deceit as defining characteristics.** The "fraud and deceit" elements, in fact, may be the common thread in modern analysis, as they frequently appear in both the scholarly literature and in law enforcement.

"Ah, those were great days, The Pre-Accountabilty Era."

© Cartoon Resource/Shutterstock.com

Tips for Success for Future Law Enforcement

Academy

Some police or sheriff academies are "stress" academies where instructors yell at those going through the program about seemingly insignificant trivialities. The philosophy behind such an approach is to test or strengthen a person's response to stress. Policing can be a thankless job with persons shouting all sorts of unpleasant accusations at an officer. Persons entering law enforcement need an inner reserve of patience, calm, and self-worth.

Academies are also physically demanding. Certainly try your best but also weigh the consequences of continuing with an injury. I have had students tell me that they ignored an injury so they could continue through the academy only to cause worse harm to the injury. The law enforcement employer, learning of the severe injury, then disqualified them from active duty even though the injury was caused during academy training. The key here is the importance of sticking to common sense about any long-term damage to your body.

Federal Jury Convicted C. Ray Nagin, Mayor of New Orleans during Hurricane Katrina, of Bribery

Matt Smith and Deanna Hackney of *CNN* reported on February 14, 2014, in "Ex-New Orleans Mayor Ray Nagin Guilty after Courtroom 'Belly Flop'" that a jury found Nagin guilty of taking bribes and other favors.

The full article can be seen at:

http://www.cnn.com/2014/02/12/justice/louisiana-nagin-convicted/

B.   MAIL FRAUD

18 USCS § 1341: Frauds and Swindles

Whoever, having devised or intending to devise any scheme or artifice to defraud, or for obtaining money or property by means of false or fraudulent pretenses, representations, or promises, or to sell, dispose of, loan, exchange, alter, give away, distribute, supply, or furnish or procure for unlawful use any counterfeit or spurious coin, obligation, security, or other article, or anything represented to be or intimated or held out to be such counterfeit or spurious article, for the purpose of executing such scheme or artifice or attempting so to do, places in any post office or authorized depository for mail matter, any matter or thing whatever to be sent or delivered by the Postal Service, or deposits or causes to be deposited any matter or thing whatever to be sent or delivered by any private or commercial interstate carrier, or takes or receives therefrom, any such matter or thing, or knowingly causes to be delivered by mail or such carrier according to the direction thereon, or at the place at which it is directed to be delivered by the person to whom it is addressed, any such matter or thing, shall be fined under this title or imprisoned not more than 20 years, or both. If the violation occurs in relation to, or involving any benefit authorized, transported, transmitted, transferred, disbursed, or paid in connection with, a presidentially declared major disaster or emergency (as those terms are defined in section 102 of the

Robert T. Stafford Disaster Relief and Emergency Assistance Act (42 U.S.C. 5122)), or affects a financial institution, such person shall be fined not more than $1,000,000 or imprisoned not more than 30 years, or both.

If the point of punishing **mail fraud is that a person has abused our postal system by using the mails to commit fraud, does the act of mailing have to be a central part of the fraud or further the fraud?** The following case considers what **link is needed to the mail** in order to satisfy the federal law.

LEGAL ANALYSIS

Schmuck v. United States
489 U.S. 705 (1988).
Justice Blackmun delivered the opinion for the Supreme Court of the United States.

Facts

[Petitioner Wayne T. Schmuck, a used-car distributor, was indicted in the U.S. District Court for the Western District of Wisconsin on 12 counts of mail fraud, in violation of 18 U. S. C. §§ 1341 and 1342.]

Schmuck purchased used cars, rolled back their odometers, and then sold the automobiles to Wisconsin retail dealers for prices artificially inflated because of the low-mileage readings. These unwitting car dealers, relying on the altered odometer figures, then resold the cars to customers, who in turn paid prices reflecting Schmuck's fraud. To complete the resale of each automobile, the dealer who purchased it from Schmuck would submit a title-application form to the Wisconsin Department of Transportation on behalf of his retail customer. The receipt of a Wisconsin title was a prerequisite for completing the resale; without it, the dealer could not transfer title to the customer and the customer could not obtain Wisconsin tags. The submission of the title-application form supplied the mailing element of each of the alleged mail frauds.

*** Schmuck moved to dismiss the indictment on the ground that the mailings at issue—the submissions of the title-application forms by the automobile dealers—were not in furtherance of the fraudulent scheme and, thus, did not satisfy the mailing element of the crime of mail fraud. [The jury convicted Schmuck on all 12 counts.]

Issue

Whether the mailing of the title-application forms by unwitting dealers to the Wisconsin Department of Transportation on behalf of his retail customer amounted to "mailing" envisioned in the mail fraud statute.

Rule and Analysis

"The federal mail fraud statute does not purport to reach all frauds, but only those limited instances in which the use of the mails is a part of the execution of the fraud, leaving all other cases to be dealt with by appropriate state law." [The statute provides in relevant part: "Whoever, having devised or intending to devise any scheme or artifice to defraud, or for obtaining money or property by means of false or fraudulent pretenses, representations, or promises . . . for the purpose of executing such scheme or artifice or attempting so to do . . . knowingly causes to be delivered by mail according to the direction thereon, or at the place at which it is directed to be delivered by the person to whom it is addressed, any such matter or thing, shall be fined not more than $1,000 or imprisoned not more than five years, or both." 18 U. S. C. § 1341.] **To be part of the execution of the fraud, however, the use of the mails need not be an essential element of the scheme. [It is enough for the mailing to be "incident to an essential part of the scheme," or "a step in the] plot."]**

Schmuck *** argues that mail fraud can be predicated only on a mailing that affirmatively assists the perpetrator in carrying out his fraudulent scheme. The mailing element of the offense, he contends, cannot be satisfied by a mailing, such as those at issue here, that is routine and innocent in and of itself, and that, far from furthering the execution of the fraud, occurs after the fraud has come to fruition, is merely tangentially related to the fraud, and is counterproductive in that it creates a "paper trail" from which the fraud may be discovered. *** We disagree both with this characterization of the mailings in the present case and with this description of the applicable law.

Schmuck was charged with devising and executing a scheme to defraud Wisconsin retail automobile customers who based their decisions to purchase certain automobiles at least in part on the low-mileage readings provided by the tampered odometers. *** Schmuck had employed a man known only as "Fred" to turn back the odometers on about 150 different cars. *** Schmuck then marketed these cars to a number of dealers, several of whom he dealt with on a consistent basis over a period of about 15 years. *** Thus, Schmuck's was not a "one-shot" operation in which he sold a single car to an isolated dealer, [but] an ongoing fraudulent venture. A rational jury could have concluded that the success of Schmuck's venture depended upon his continued harmonious relations with, and good reputation among, retail dealers, which in turn required the smooth flow of cars from the dealers to their Wisconsin customers.

[A] rational jury could have found that the title-registration mailings were part of the execution of the fraudulent scheme, a scheme which did not reach fruition until the retail dealers resold the cars and effected transfers of title. Schmuck's scheme would have come to an abrupt halt if the dealers either had lost faith in Schmuck or had not been able to resell the cars obtained from him. These resales and Schmuck's relationships with the retail dealers naturally depended on the successful passage of title among the various parties. Thus, although the registration-form mailings may not have contributed directly to the duping of either the retail dealers or the customers, they were necessary to the passage of title, which in turn was essential to the perpetuation of Schmuck's scheme. A mailing that is "incident to an essential part of the scheme," satisfies the mailing element of the mail fraud offense. The mailings here fit this description.]

The mailing of the title-registration forms was an essential step in the successful passage of title to the retail purchasers. Moreover, a failure of this passage of title would have jeopardized Schmuck's relationship of trust and goodwill with the retail dealers upon whose unwitting cooperation his scheme depended. ***

We also reject Schmuck's contention that mailings that someday may contribute to the uncovering of a fraudulent scheme cannot supply the mailing element of the mail fraud offense. The relevant question at all times is whether the mailing is part of the execution of the scheme as conceived by the perpetrator at the time, regardless of whether the mailing later, through hindsight, may prove to have been counterproductive and return to haunt the perpetrator of the fraud. The mail fraud statute includes no guarantee that the use of the mails for the purpose of executing a fraudulent scheme will be risk free. Those who use the mails to defraud proceed at their peril.

Conclusion

[The] mailings in this case satisfy the mailing element of the mail fraud offenses. [Schmuck's] conviction was consistent with the statutory definition of mail fraud. [Affirmed.]

Justice Scalia, with whom Justice Brennan, Justice Marshall, and Justice O'Connor join, dissenting.

***The purpose of the mail fraud statute is "to prevent the post office from being used to carry [fraudulent schemes] into effect." *** The law does not establish a general federal remedy against fraudulent conduct, with use of the mails as the jurisdictional hook, but reaches only "those limited instances in which the use of the mails is *a part of the execution of the fraud*, leaving all other cases to be dealt with by appropriate state law." *** In other words, it is mail fraud, not mail and fraud, that incurs liability. This federal statute is not violated by a fraudulent scheme in which, at some point, a mailing happens to occur—nor even by one in which a mailing predictably and necessarily occurs. The mailing must be in furtherance of the fraud.

Corruption in the U.S. Navy? "Fat Leonard" Might Have Bribed Sailors and Admirals

In a November 5, 2017 *Washington Post* article, "'Fat Leonard' probe expands to ensnare more than 60 admirals", Craig Whitlock reported that a defense contractor might have compromised Navy officials with alcohol, dinner and prostitutes. The article can be viewed at:

https://www.washingtonpost.com/investigations/fat-leonard-scandal-expands-to-ensnare-more-than-60-admirals/2017/11/05/f6a12678-be5d-11e7-97d9-bdab5a0ab381_story.html?utm_term=.83d87347cf47

VIDEO: U.S. Supreme Court Justice Antonin Scalia Discussed *Roe v. Wade*

Supreme Court Justice Scalia criticized the "substantive due process" argument supporting the abortion case at:

https://www.youtube.com/watch?v=Rj_MhS2u-Pk

C. SECURITIES VIOLATIONS AND INSIDER TRADING

The United States Securities and Exchange Commission (SEC), which polices activities involving stocks, offered the following **explanation for illegal "insider trading":**

> **Illegal insider trading refers generally to buying or selling a security (such as a stock in a corporation), in breach of a fiduciary duty (which is a special duty of trust) or other relationship of trust and confidence, while in possession of material, nonpublic information about the security. Insider trading violations may also include "tipping" such information,** securities trading by the person "tipped," and securities trading by those who misappropriate such information.

Examples of insider trading cases that have been brought by the SEC are cases against:

- ▶ Corporate officers, directors, and employees who traded the corporation's securities after learning of significant, confidential corporate developments;

- ▶ Friends, business associates, family members, and other "tippees" of such officers, directors, and employees, who traded the securities after receiving such information;

- ▶ Employees of law, banking, brokerage and printing firms who were given such information to provide services to the corporation whose securities they traded;

- ▶ Government employees who learned of such information because of their employment by the government; and

- ▶ Other persons who misappropriated, and took advantage of, confidential information from their employers.

"We want to beat the system, but we want the system to keep playing."

The crimes involving securities can have dollar damages far greater than those of 'street crime.'

© Cartoon Resource/Shutterstock.com

Because insider trading undermines investor confidence in the fairness and integrity of the securities markets, the SEC has treated the detection and prosecution of insider trading violations as one of its enforcement priorities.

Anyone can check up on the latest cases the SEC is pursuing. The SEC lists its current "enforcement actions" at:

https://www.sec.gov/spotlight/insidertrading/cases.shtml

For a slide show and summary of "Famous Insider Trading Cases," including Ivan Boesky, Raj Rajaratnam, Enron's Jeffrey Skilling, and ImClone's Samuel Waksal (and Martha Stewart), visit CNBC.com at:

http://www.cnbc.com/id/40319986/page/1

Tips for Success for Future Law Students and Lawyers

As an Officer of the Court, Always Tell the Truth

People always say that there are too many lawyers, but in reality, law is a small town where everybody knows everybody else. If you want to be happy with your job and wish to succeed over the long haul, you have to tell the truth. Being a good lawyer is all about persuading others. Once you lie or even shave the truth, you have lost your audience forever. If you lied in one case, why wouldn't you lie in all the others? Lawyers gossip, so if you tell a stretcher to one attorney, all will find out. The lesson is that you are only as strong as your word. According to the Rules of Professional Conduct, Rule 3.3, 42 Pennsylvania C.S.A. Rule 3.3.(a)(1) Candor Toward the Tribunal, "A lawyer shall not knowingly . . . make a false statement of material fact or law to a tribunal or fail to correct a false statement of material fact or law previously made to the tribunal by the lawyer." Section 3 of this rule forbids a lawyer from offering "evidence that the lawyer knows to be false."

Martha Stewart—The Most Famous Insider Trading Case Did Not End in a Conviction for Insider Trading

In *New York Magazine*, Vanessa Grigoriadis wrote on April 1, 2012, in her article entitled, "I Just Want to Focus on My Salad: Insider trading—not a good thing," April 1, 2012 (Copyright © 2012 by New York Magazine):

> Before Imclone, everything was just perfect for Martha Stewart. Her story had been one of ever-increasing power, from the admittance to Barnard in the fifties from Nutley, New Jersey, where she grew up as the eldest daughter in a Polish family of eight, to almost single-handedly building the domestic-bliss industry in the eighties, harnessing the rise in disposable income and backlash against the arid feminism of the previous decade; to say nothing of her role atop Martha Stewart Living Omnimedia, a publicly traded company encompassing all things Martha, from tart-making, to tips on pruning trees, which she liked to do in the middle of the night.

> Then the American icon of flawlessness made a mistake. On December 27, 2001, when the young assistant to her debonair Merrill Lynch broker told her on his orders that she should sell all her 3,928 shares in ImClone Systems, a biotech company run by Sam Waksal, because the company was about to implode, she jumped at the opportunity. She would never have felt the loss—she was coming up on a billion dollars, and by selling those shares she avoided a loss of $45,673—but she couldn't resist the chance to daub at the blot on her investment record. "Isn't it nice to have brokers who tell you these things?" she reportedly said. It was a good thing—and then it became a very bad thing.

The SEC responded by investigating Martha Stewart and her broker, as described on the SEC's website:

> *Washington, D.C., June 4, 2003*—The Securities and Exchange Commission today filed securities fraud charges against Martha Stewart and her former stockbroker, Peter Bacanovic. The complaint, filed in federal court in Manhattan, alleges that Stewart committed illegal insider trading when she sold stock in a biopharmaceutical company, ImClone Systems, Inc., on Dec. 27, 2001, after receiving an unlawful tip from Bacanovic, at

the time a broker with Merrill Lynch, Pierce, Fenner & Smith Incorporated. The Commission further alleges that Stewart and Bacanovic subsequently created an alibi for Stewart's ImClone sales and concealed important facts during SEC and criminal investigations into her trades. In a separate action, the United States Attorney for the Southern District of New York has obtained an indictment charging Stewart and Bacanovic criminally for their false statements concerning Stewart's ImClone trades.

The Commission seeks, among other relief, an order requiring Stewart and Bacanovic to disgorge the losses Stewart avoided through her unlawful trades, plus civil monetary penalties. The Commission also seeks an order barring Stewart from acting as a director of, and limiting her activities as an officer of, any public company. Stewart has been Chairman and Chief Executive Officer of Martha Stewart Living Omnimedia, Inc.

Stephen M. Cutler, the SEC's Director of Enforcement, said: "It is fundamentally unfair for someone to have an edge on the market just because she has a stockbroker who is willing to break the rules and give her an illegal tip. It's worse still when the individual engaging in the insider trading is the Chairman and CEO of a public company."

The full account can be viewed at:

https://www.sec.gov/news/press/2003-69.htm

Martha Stewart, however, was never actually convicted for insider trading, but for lying about it to the authorities, as noted by *Fox News* and the *Associated Press* in the March 8, 2004, article, "Martha Stewart Convicted on All Four Counts." The report noted:

Martha Stewart was convicted Friday of obstructing justice and lying to the government about a superbly timed stock sale — a devastating verdict that probably means prison for the woman who epitomizes meticulous homemaking and gracious living.

Stewart, 62, grimaced and her eyes widened slightly upon hearing the verdict, and she later released a statement maintaining her innocence and promising an appeal.

The entire article can be viewed at:

http://www.foxnews.com/story/2004/03/08/martha-stewart-convicted-on-all-four-counts/

D. MONEY LAUNDERING

What Is Money Laundering?

Money laundering amounts to taking money that has been obtained illegally and investing it so that it appears to have been obtained legally. The U.S. Department of the Treasury, on its website describes money laundering as follows:

Money laundering generally refers to financial transactions in which criminals, including terrorist organizations, attempt to disguise the proceeds, sources or nature

of their illicit activities. Money laundering facilitates a broad range of serious underlying criminal offenses and ultimately threatens the integrity of the financial system.

© Billion Photos/Shutterstock.com

The United States Department of the Treasury is fully dedicated to combating all aspects of money laundering at home and abroad, through the mission of the Office of Terrorism and Financial Intelligence (TFI). TFI utilizes the Department's many assets—including a diverse range of legal authorities, core financial expertise, operational resources, and expansive relationships with the private sector, interagency and international communities—to identify and attack money laundering vulnerabilities and networks across the domestic and international financial systems.

For more information, visit:

http://www.treasury.gov/resource-center/terrorist-illicit-finance/Pages/Money-Laundering.aspx

In the article, *Money Laundering*, 39 Am. Crim. L. Rev. 839, 839–40 (2002), the following was offered as a characterization of money laundering:

> **Money laundering is "the process by which one conceals the existence, illegal source, or illegal application of income, and disguises that income to make it appear legitimate."** Laundering criminally derived proceeds has become a lucrative and sophisticated business, and is an indispensable element of organized criminal activities. Although money laundering occurs in various and creative media, money laundering typically effectuated through a three-step process: (1) the criminally derived money is "placed" into a legitimate enterprise; (2) the funds are "layered" through various transactions to obscure the original source; and (3) the newly laundered funds are integrated into the legitimate financial world "in the form of bank notes, loans, letters of credit," or other recognizable financial instruments.

Money laundering has an enormous negative impact on society. The "Money Laundering" article above noted that money laundering "is an indispensable element of organized criminal activities." Shawn Turner, in *U.S. Anti-Money Laundering Regulations: An Economic Approach to Cyberlaundering* 54 Case W. Res. 1389 (2004), has noted:

> The International Monetary Fund estimates that at least $600 billion is laundered annually, representing between two and five percent of the world's gross domestic product. While "primarily a paperless crime, without physical violence directed at individuals," money laundering can have a widespread detrimental impact on a nation's economy.

> Laundering undermines and manipulates legitimate businesses by allowing considerations other than sound business practice to influence decisions. It corrupts public officials, perhaps even entire governments, by buying votes and influencing the actions of politicians and career officials. It distorts macroeconomic estimates, skews currency markets, and destabilizes financial institutions through the creation of illegal economies.

For an in-depth description of money laundering, see Julia Layton's explanation in "How Money Laundering Works" on the "How Stuff Works?" website at:

http://money.howstuffworks.com/money-laundering.htm

Source: Case Western Reserve Law Review.

For an example of money laundering in drama, see Walter and Skyler White's laundering of their meth money through a car wash on *AMC's Breaking Bad* at:

http://www.amctv.com/shows/breaking-bad

Biography—Police

David Brown

- Came to national prominence on July 7, 2016, when he approved the use of a robot to use a bomb to kill Micah Xavier Johnson, who shot five police officers to death.
- Was the first police chief to use a **robot to apply lethal force** to a suspect.
- According to David A. Graham of *The Atlantic* magazine in "The Dallas Shooting and the Advent of Killer Police Robots," on July 8, 2016, https://www.theatlantic.com/news/archive/2016/07/dallas-police-robot/490478/, Chief Brown justified his decision by saying, "We saw no other option but to use our bomb robot" because "Other options would have exposed our officers to grave danger."
- According to WFAA.com, ABC on Channel 8, http://www.wfaa.com/news/local/dallas-county/dallas-police-chief-david-brown-announces-retirement/312529582, Chief Brown was controversial even before his use of the robot because he dramatically shifted officers' scheduling ("Six hundred officers were asked to move into the field for an evening shift and 700 more were rotated to foot patrol") to respond to the increasing murder rate. The Police union sought his resignation for this action.
- According to Belinda Luscombe, 8 Questions With David Brown, Former Dallas Police Chief, at Time magazine, June 7, 2017, http://time.com/4810491/former-dallas-police-chief-david-brown/, Chief Brown believes that protests against police shootings alone are not enough if "that's the only thing you do." Instead, persons must vote because, "Policing is controlled by local governments, and 90% of people don't participate in those elections."

Too Little Law: Is the U.S. Government Serious about Punishing Money Laundering Banks?

In a March 31, 2013, editorial for *Bloomberg* in the opinion section entitled, "Money-Laundering Banks Still Get a Pass From U.S.," Simon Johnson declared it has reached epidemic proportions.
    To view the entire article, visit:

http://www.bloomberg.com/news/2013-03-31/money-laundering-
banks-still-get-a-pass-from-u-s-.html

Dylan Murphy, in a May 13 2013, article for *Global Research* entitled, "Money Laundering and The Drug Trade: The Role of the Banks," Global Research, (Copyright © 2013 Dylan Murphy, Centre for Research on Globalization), declared:

> Mexico is in the grip of a murderous drug war that has killed over 150,000 people since 2006. It is one of the most violent countries on earth. This drug war is a product of the transnational drug trade which is worth up to $400 billion a year and accounts for about 8% of all international trade.
>
> The American government maintains that there is no alternative but to vigorously prosecute their zero tolerance policy of arresting drug users and their dealers. This has led to the incarceration of over 500,000 Americans. Meanwhile the flood of illegal drugs into America continues unabated.
>
> One thing the American government has not done is to prosecute the largest banks in the world for supporting the drug cartels by washing billions of dollars of their blood stained money. As Narco sphere journalist Bill Conroy has observed banks are "where the money is" in the global drug war.

The full article can be viewed at:

> http://www.globalresearch.ca/money-laundering-and-the-drug-trade-the-role-of-the-banks/5334205

Can a person be charged with money laundering if the acts he committed in laundering money "overlapped" with (in other words, were essentially the same as) the acts that he performed to commit the underlying crime? Or would prosecution for money laundering in such a case constitute improper double punishment for one wrongful act? Would it make a difference if the money laundering statute had an **additional requirement** that money had to be laundered **with the intent to promote further illegal activity**, or that the laundering was **designed to conceal illegal activity**? The following case considers this issue.

LEGAL ANALYSIS

United States v. Omoruyi a/k/a Charles Oloro a/k/a Bobby Pierce
260 F.3d 291 (2001).
Justice Greenberg delivered the opinion for the United States Court of Appeals.

Facts

In February 1999, a person not known to the authorities stole seven blank "convenience checks" attached to the bottom of First USA credit card statements from the mail in Texas. [In] April 1999, a similarly unknown person stole three blank American Express convenience checks from the mail in New York. In approximately March and April 1999, Omoruyi opened three savings accounts at banks in the Middle District of Pennsylvania in the names of "Charles Oloro" or "Robert Pierce." Thereafter, all ten of the stolen checks were made payable to Pierce or Oloro in amounts varying between $5,100 and $9,890, and deposited in the savings accounts, nine via the mail and the tenth at a teller's window.

After the banks credited the accounts with the deposits, Omoruyi began withdrawing funds from the accounts via automatic teller machine ("ATM") and teller window withdrawals. Most of the ATM withdrawals took place in New York and New Jersey, while most of the teller window withdrawals took place in Pennsylvania. ***

[Postal inspectors determined that Omoruyi was "Robert Pierce" and "Charles Oloro. " Inspectors] established a surveillance on a Brooklyn mail drop Omoruyi had opened. When Omoruyi arrived at the mail drop on June 1, 1999, the inspectors arrested him.

[A grand jury charged] Omoruyi with six counts of mail fraud affecting a financial institution and eight counts of money laundering. The six counts of mail fraud stemmed from the mailing of the counterfeit check as well as five of the ten checks to banks in the Harrisburg area. The money laundering counts were based on eight teller window withdrawals by Omoruyi, utilizing false identification, at Harrisburg-area banks.

[Omoruyi] pled guilty to the mail fraud counts and submitted to a bench trial on the money laundering counts. The trial was premised almost entirely upon stipulated testimony and exhibits establishing that Omoruyi "opened [three] savings accounts and withdrew funds using the false names under which the savings accounts were established." [Omoruyi was convicted on all money laundering counts.]

Issue

Whether there was sufficient evidence to support a money laundering conviction.

Rule and Analysis

[Omoruyi argued there was insufficient evidence of] money laundering because he did not conduct a financial transaction with "proceeds" of the mail fraud. He argues that the mail fraud was not complete, and therefore did not yield "proceeds "until he took possession of the cash credited to the accounts. [In his view, the cash withdrawals could not serve as the basis for the money laundering counts.]

On this appeal, we are concerned with the construction of 18 U.S.C. § 1956(a)(1) which defines illegal money laundering as:

> Whoever, knowing that the property involved in a financial transaction represents the proceeds of some form of unlawful activity, conducts or attempts to conduct such a financial transaction which in fact involves the proceeds of specified unlawful activity—
> (A)(i) with the intent to promote the carrying on of specified unlawful activity; or . . .
> (B) knowing that the transaction is designed in whole or in part—
> (i) to conceal or disguise the nature, the location, the source, the ownership, or the control of the proceeds of specified unlawful activity . . .

Accordingly, section 1956(a)(1) sets forth the **four elements of a money laundering** offense: (1) **an actual or attempted financial transaction**; (2) **involving the proceeds of specified unlawful activity**; (3) **knowledge that the transaction involves the proceeds of some unlawful activity**; and (4) **either an intent to promote the carrying on of specified unlawful activity or knowledge that the transactions were designed in whole or in part to conceal the nature, location, source, ownership, or control of the proceeds of specified unlawful activity.** ***

[*United States v. Conley*] considered whether the deposit of illegal gambling proceeds could support a conviction for the money laundering object of a conspiracy. There the defendant argued that the government failed to establish the essential elements of money laundering because the conduct upon which the government based the charge was essentially the same as that supporting the illegal gambling charges. [*Conley* explained]:

> McGrath contends before us that a wide variety of transactions involving the money placed into the video poker machines is necessarily part of the illegal gambling business, including collecting and counting money, dividing up money, transferring and transporting money, depositing money into banks and withdrawing money from banks. McGrath contends that this same conduct cannot be properly alleged to be money laundering.

We disagreed. *** In doing so, we acknowledged that "obviously, whenever a defendant makes money from criminal activity he has something to do with it," and that "Congress did not enact money laundering statutes simply to add to the penalties for various crimes in which defendants make money." [But,] section 1956(a)(1) addressed this concern, and therefore delineated clearly between the underlying offense and the money laundering offense, by including an **intent requirement**. *** We stated:

> Section 1956(a)(1), quite clearly, does not prohibit all financial transactions that are conducted with the proceeds of specified unlawful activity. **It only proscribes those transactions that are conducted with the intent to promote certain further illegal activity, under subsection (A), or that are designed to conceal under subsection (B).**
> These requirements [prevent the statute from applying] to non-money laundering acts such as a defendant's depositing the proceeds of unlawful activity in a bank account in his own name and using the money for personal purposes. ***

[The conduct constituting the underlying offense] may overlap with the conduct constituting money laundering. [The money, when collected from the video] poker machines, became "'proceeds of specified unlawful activity'" within *** the money laundering statute, even though there may have been some overlap in the acts alleged to constitute the conduct of an illegal gambling business and money laundering. ***

Applying *Conley* here, it is clear that there was substantial evidence supporting Omoruyi's money laundering conviction. Omoruyi contends, in an argument similar to that of the defendant in *Conley*, that the conduct charged as money laundering was the same conduct constituting mail fraud. Nevertheless, inasmuch as the money was deposited in bank accounts under false names, and Omoruyi used false identification to withdraw it, he clearly conducted the transactions charged with the intent to conceal or disguise the nature, source, ownership and control of the proceeds of the mail fraud. [Section 1956] would not apply to a defendant's depositing the proceeds of unlawful activity in a bank account "in his own name" and using the money for personal purposes, as neither the "promote" or "conceal" aspects of the money laundering statute would be met. *** Here, however, there is sufficient evidence of concealment, and of Omoruyi's intent to conceal, to sustain his conviction. ***

Conclusion

[There] was substantial evidence supporting Omoruyi's convictions for money laundering which we thus affirm.

"Seamless Web" Connection

The concern about "overlap," creating an issue of double punishment in *United States v. Omoruyi a/k/a Charles Oloro a/k/a Bobby Pierce*, the case discussed above, involves double jeopardy concerns, which were considered in Chapter 1.

Do's and Don'ts for Hearings, Trials, and Appeals

Interacting with Jurors During Courtroom Breaks

As a prosecutor or defense counsel, **don't** start conversations with jurors when seeing them in the hallway or bathroom on break. **Don't** discuss the case with jurors or even place yourself in a position where others can mistakenly believe you are having such conversations with jurors. **Do** be polite with jurors, but steer any conversation you must have to a quick conclusion. **Do** report any contact with jurors to the judge and anything the juror said about the case to you. Jurors talking to you about the case are not ignorantly innocent—they are defying an explicit instruction from the judge to leave you alone. As provided in Texas C.C.P. Art. 36.22. [671] [748] [728] Conversing with jury, "No person shall be permitted to converse with a juror about the case on trial except in the presence and by the permission of the court."

Too Much Law: Will Anti-Money Laundering Regulations Cost Somalia Banking Services?

Tim Worstall, a contributor to *Forbes*, argues in his August 8, 2013, article entitled, "HSBC's $1.9 Billion Money Laundering Fine And the Somalian Cost Of Bank Regulation," that money laundering regulation is so costly to banks that these institutions are terminating services to Somalia for fear of running afoul of the law.

The full article can be viewed at:

http://www.forbes.com/sites/timworstall/2013/08/08/hsbcs-1-9-billion-money-laundering-fine-and-the-somalian-cost-of-bank-regulation/

Martin Shkreli Jailed

Martin Shkreli, the executive who dramatically increased the price of Daraprim, was jailed for offering $5000 online if someone obtained a strand of Hillary Clinton's hair. An August 19, 2016, *NBC News* article, by Ben Popken, entitled, "Martin Shkreli Weighs in on EpiPen Scandal, Calls Drug Makers 'Vultures'," discussing the EpiPen price increase can be viewed at:

https://www.nbcnews.com/business/consumer/martin-shkreli-weighs-epipen-scandal-calls-drug-makers-vultures-n634451

A September 14, 2017, *Washington Post* article by Renae Merle, entitled, "Martin Shkreli jailed after Facebook post about Hillary Clinton," discusses Shkreli's conviction for defrauding investors and his incarceration for "solicitation of assault." This article can be viewed at:

https://www.washingtonpost.com/news/ business/wp/2017/09/13/ martin-shkreli-apologizes-for- facebook-post-about-hillary- clinton/?utm_term=.62d982ec1d4c

"We're getting back to first principles ... which means we're going to have some."

© Cartoon Resource/Shutterstock.com

E. ANTITRUST

At various times in our country's history, companies have merged together to make ever-larger corporations. Over one hundred years ago, John D. Rockefeller combined various oil companies and refineries together to form Standard Oil. Today, banks, airlines, and cable companies merge, creating fewer, yet larger, corporations in the marketplace. When two or more corporations combine, consumers may benefit from the cost savings that come from efficiencies and economies of scale. Customers, however, can also be harmed by the resulting decrease in competition.

Suppose the many cable companies that provide television and other services continually merge with each other until there are only two companies, "Cable West" and "Cable East" in all of the United States. Cable West agrees with its competitor that it will only provide service to the states west of the Mississippi River while Cable East will limit itself to providing service to those east of the Mississippi. Customers in say, Colorado, will have no choice but to deal with Cable West. Cable West, enjoying a "monopoly" over cable services in Colorado, will have no competitors forcing it to provide the best

Teddy Roosevelt is known as the Trust-Busting President.

© Everett Historical/Shutterstock.com

services at the lowest prices. Cable West therefore might hike its prices, fail to fix problems in a timely fashion, and force its customers to subscribe to packages including channels they do not wish to watch. The resulting "restraint of trade" created by Cable West and Cable East agreeing to carve the cable market into "territories" hurts the customer and prevents innovation that should occur in a free market.

To remedy this problem, the government could sue or even prosecute the cable companies for their illegal agreement to form territories in restraint of trade. The cable companies, in turn, could offer a defense that they are not monopolists in the market, even though they control all the cable in their territories. Their defense would hinge on how a judge should define "the market." While the prosecutors would argue that there is no competition from other cable providers, the cable companies would say that they do not have monopoly control of the market because they face competition from content providers who send programs by satellite dish or telephone fiber optics or Internet. If customers do not like the cable company's service or price, they can simply opt instead for satellite, fiber optic, or Internet access.

The merits of such arguments are litigated in antitrust cases. Antitrust laws were created in the Progressive Era to fight the great "trusts" created in the wake of the Civil War, such as Rockefeller's Standard Oil. Antitrust is still a concern with our current corporations. About a century after the government broke up the Standard Oil Company into such separate entitles as Mobile, Exxon, and Chevron, the United States challenged Microsoft, contending it violated the antitrust statute known as the Sherman Act. This litigation is discussed in the box below.

Legal Skills: How to Cross-Examine Opposing Counsel's Witness

Cross-examination is the questioning an attorney performs of opposing counsel's witnesses. Since these witnesses often give testimony harmful to the questioning attorney's side of the case, the aim is to poke holes in these witnesses' version of events. As a prosecutor, I cross-examined defendants and defense witnesses, including percipient (eye) witnesses, character witnesses, and experts. In law school, I was taught that cross-examination was "the engine of truth" because its proper use would expose the inaccuracies, mistakes, and outright lies given during direct examination. So, how can cross-examination be used to perform such miracles?

My old evidence professor drilled into us that cross-examination attacks the witness's: (a) perception, (b) memory, (c) narrative, and (d) bias. When an attorney tests a witness's perception, he or she is questioning whether the witness could accurately take in the events in question ("There was a tree on the street that was right in front of you—didn't that block your view of the defendant's act?" "I notice you are wearing hearing aids—were you wearing them when you heard the victim respond to the defendant?"). If the witness could not accurately see, hear, feel, or smell the events (taste is not usually an issue), then the information was distorted when it was improperly gathered from the start, and so cannot be fully believed.

Even if a witness accurately gained information, perhaps it was not properly stored, leading to questioning the witness's memory ("The car theft occurred five years ago—how can you be so certain that you locked your car on that particular day?"). Attacking a witness's narrative ability focuses on the witness's failure to accurately describe what actually occurred ("When you say the victim 'consented' to sex, don't you really mean that she did not put up any fight when the defendant had intercourse with her?"). Bias is prejudice, whether based on factors such as gender or race, or based on personal experience ("My client stole your girlfriend and so you have just been waiting to get back at him with your testimony against him.").

The tools of cross-examination are not typically used in a relentless frontal attack. Usually, the questioner will ask some easy questions to set up the attack by lulling the witness into a box out of which he or she cannot escape.

VIDEO: Senator Asks Professor Some Antitrust Questions about Google

Senator Blumenthal asks Professor Tim Wu about antitrust issues with Google at:

https://www.youtube.com/watch?v=dFpqo1jBBZk

---

15 USCS § 1 (This law is popularly known as the Sherman Antitrust Act)

§ 1. Trusts, etc., in restraint of trade illegal; penalty

Every contract, combination in the form of trust or otherwise, or conspiracy, in restraint of trade or commerce among the several States, or with foreign nations, is hereby declared to be illegal. Every person who shall make any contract or engage in any combination or conspiracy hereby declared to be illegal shall be deemed guilty of a felony, and, on conviction thereof, shall be punished by fine not exceeding $100,000,000 if a corporation, or, if any other person, $ 1,000,000, or by imprisonment not exceeding 10 years, or by both said punishments, in the discretion of the court.

§ 2. Monopolization; penalty

Every person who shall monopolize, or attempt to monopolize, or combine or conspire with any other person or persons, to monopolize any part of the trade or commerce among the several States, or with foreign nations, shall be deemed guilty of a felony, and, on conviction thereof, shall be punished by fine not exceeding $ 100,000,000 if a corporation, or, if any other person, $1,000,000, or by imprisonment not exceeding 10 years, or by both said punishments, in the discretion of the court.

LEARN FROM MY (AND OTHERS') MISTAKES

Do Not, as a Defense Lawyer, Take on the Task of Defining "Reasonable Doubt" to the Jury

Attorneys argue and judges instruct the jury on the law. When a lawyer starts defining the law to jurors, he is usurping the judge's role and could easily be spouting bad law. A defense lawyer in one of my jury trials once pulled out a Webster's Dictionary during closing argument and tried to define "reasonable doubt," "abiding," and "conviction" for the jury. When I objected, the judge rightly said to the defense lawyer in front of the jury, "Counsel, I am disappointed in you." That took all the air out of the lawyer's closing argument.

By the way, "reasonable doubt" is such an unknown quantity that trial judges steer clear of trying to define it, instead reading previously approved standard instructions about it to the jury. The lawyer was, therefore, way out of bounds.

Remember When Microsoft Software Automatically Came Installed When You Bought a PC? Why Doesn't That Happen Anymore?

As you use your iPhone and iPad and happily count your shares in Apple, which, according to the August 21, 2012, article in *Forbes,* is "Now the Most Valuable Company in History ("Apple Now Most Valuable Company in History," *Forbes*, August 21, 2012, at: http://www.forbes.com/sites/benzingainsights/2012/08/21/apple-now-most-valuable-company-in-history/) you might not recall that not long ago, before Steve Jobs rejoined it, Apple was fighting a seemingly losing battle with the software giant, Microsoft. It could be argued that the change of fortunes was not only due to Job's genius, but also to the antitrust cases brought by the United States government.

Amanda Cohen, in her article, "Surveying the Microsoft Antitrust Universe," 19 Berkeley Tech. L.J. 333 (2004)(© 2004 by the Regents of the University of California. Reprinted from "Surveying the Microsoft Antitrust Universe" by Amanda Cohen, *Berkeley Technology Law Journal*—19 Berkeley Tech. L.J. 333 (2004). By permission of the Regents of the University of California), offered an illuminating picture of the antitrust litigation involving Microsoft. Cohen noted, "antitrust actions against Microsoft have brought to light the problems of applying traditional antitrust law to a high-technology industry" because this litigation has "underscored the disconnect between a legal system that works over the course of years and an industry in which a shift in the technology standard can set in motion the downfall of a monopolist in a matter of months." In one of the several cases brought against Microsoft, the court found:

> Microsoft liable for violations of both section 1 and section 2 of the Sherman Act. Section 1 governs combinations, and prohibits those that restrain trade. Agreements to fix prices, divide markets, and tie unrelated goods are most likely in violation of section 1. When a company forces the sale of two separate products together, it is liable for a section 1 tying violation, as long as the company has market power in the tying product market (the market of the principal good, to which another good is attached), offers consumers no option to purchase the products separately, and affects a significant share of commerce with its arrangement.

> Section 2 proscribes certain behavior by monopolists, companies that can profitably charge a supra-competitive price in a defined market. Under section 2, monopolists may not intentionally garner their market power, nor may they willfully maintain market power achieved by superior business sense or accident. Finally, a firm is liable for attempted monopolization if, intending to monopolize, it engages in anticompetitive behavior and has a dangerous probability of success.

In *United States v. Microsoft*, 231 F. Supp. 2d 144 (2002), the U.S. District Court for the District of Columbia discussed the events that led to Microsoft's dominance in the marketplace. The court noted that Microsoft was, in part, a victim of its own success:

> Microsoft's lawfully acquired monopoly is naturally protected by a "structural barrier," known as the "applications barrier to entry." [This barrier stems] from two characteristics of the software market: (1) most consumers prefer operating systems for which a large number of applications have already been written; and (2) most developers prefer to write for operating systems that already have a substantial consumer base." [This creates a "chicken-and-egg"] situation, which perpetuates Microsoft's operating system dominance because "applications will continue to be written for the already dominant Windows, which in turn ensures that consumers will continue to prefer it over other operating systems."

[Since] "every operating system has different APIs," applications written for one operating system will not function on another operating system unless the developer undertakes the "time consuming and expensive" process of transferring and adapting *** the application to the alternative operating system.

The court also indicated that Microsoft's own behavior, once it had obtained a dominant position in the market, caused it to maintain that position of strength. The Court explained that, in working with computer makers, or "original equipment manufacturers (OEMs)," Microsoft had "three license provisions 'prohibiting the OEMs from: removing any desktop icons, folders, or 'Start' menu entries; (2) altering the initial boot sequence; and (3) otherwise altering the appearance of the Windows desktop.'" Microsoft also integrated "[Internet Explorer ('IE')] and Windows." Microsoft saw the integration of IE into its Windows as offering a benefit to its customers rather than being a restraint of trade. The court, however, also noted that, "the appellate court's final imposition of liability arose out of a 'threat' by Microsoft directed at Intel." The court explained:

> "Intel is [a firm] engaged principally in the design and manufacture of microprocessors." *** A segment of Intel's business develops software, with the primary focus upon "finding useful ways to consume more microprocessor cycles, thereby stimulating demand for advanced Intel microprocessors." *** The appellate court recounted that in 1995, Intel was in the process of "developing a high performance, Windows-compatible JVM." *** Furthering its efforts to combat the cross-platform threat of Java to the Windows platform, Microsoft repeatedly "urged Intel not to help Sun by distributing Intel's fast, Sun compliant JVM." *** Eventually, Microsoft "threatened Intel that if it did not stop aiding Sun . . . then Microsoft would refuse to distribute Intel technologies bundled with Windows." *** Intel capitulated after Microsoft threatened to support an Intel competitor, AMD, if Intel's efforts with Java continued. ***

As a result of such findings, a settlement was eventually reached. Looking back on the Microsoft litigation with the benefit of years of hindsight, can we say that Microsoft had a point? The company repeatedly urged that, in such a dynamic and technology-driven industry as computers, software, and the Internet, market dominance might simply not be possible in a practical sense. Microsoft might have been king in the age of the PC, but it did not dominate the growing market of handheld devices such as the phone and tablet. What is the result of all of this litigation?

Seattle Times technology reporter Sharon Pian Chan wrote in her article entitled, "*Long antitrust saga ends for Microsoft,*" that Microsoft's antitrust battles with the U.S. government are ending after twenty-one years.

The full article can be viewed at:

http://seattletimes.com/html/microsoft/2015029604_microsoft12.html

The case below involved theft with stolen credit cards.

F.   IDENTITY FRAUD

Identity fraud, by its nature, is committed by people who are hiding their true selves, and therefore are attempting to avoid accountability for their actions. How can such a crime be proven? As discussed below, courts not only allow the prosecution to use circumstantial evidence in such cases, but also have upheld convictions based on **nothing but circumstantial evidence**.

LEGAL ANALYSIS

United States v. Savarese
686 F.3d 1 (2012).
Justice Howard wrote the opinion for the United States Court of Appeals.

Facts

Defendants-appellants Dennis Savarese and James DeSimone were indicted, along with [alleged co-conspirators, on charges arising from their participation in a credit card fraud scheme.] Savarese was convicted after a six-day jury trial. ***

In early August 2007, Dennis Savarese and James DeSimone were arrested outside the Prairie Meadows Racetrack in Altoona, Iowa. Found in their possession were *** six stolen credit cards, each with a corresponding false identification bearing the cardholder's name, but Savarese's or DeSimone's picture. The arrests marked the culmination of a lengthy investigation, which uncovered a fraud operation spanning more than a dozen states and involving hundreds of stolen identities.

[The operation involved several co-defendants. From 2005 to 2007, Savarese visited nearly 150 different Bally Total Fitness clubs across the United States to] steal credit cards from the storage lockers of unsuspecting gym members. *** Savarese compiled and faxed to his associates a list which identified the name on each stolen credit card, forged attempted replicas of the cardholders' signatures, and specified which co-defendant would ultimately use the cards in the scheme's subsequent phases.

Armed with this list, one or more of the defendants *** would commission [photographers] to manufacture corresponding false identifications, each of which contained a name from one of the stolen cards, a picture of one of the defendants, and otherwise fictional biographical information. When enough credit cards and identifications were collected, a select group of the defendants would congregate at racetracks and various other gambling establishments of Savarese's choosing throughout the country. There, they used the false documentation to withdraw significant cash advances, to the tune of almost $430,000 over the life of the scheme.

Issue

Whether there was sufficient evidence to support the defendant's identity fraud conviction under 18 U.S.C. § 1028(a)(7).

Rule and Analysis

Congress defined **the essential elements of identity fraud as "knowingly [transferring, possessing, or using], without lawful authority, a means of identification of another person with the intent to commit, or to aid and abet, or in connection with, any unlawful activity that constitutes a violation of Federal law, or that constitutes a felony under any applicable State or local law."** 18 U.S.C. § 1028(a)(7). Pursuant to that provision, the indictment alleged the following: that on July 13, 2007, Savarese stole a credit card from "T.M.'"s locker at a Bally's gym in Houston, Texas; that on the same day, James DeSimone purchased a false identification from Dana Ross Studios containing T.M.'s name, and DeSimone's picture; and that DeSimone then flew to Arizona, where he met Savarese and used T.M.'s credit card to withdraw $2,000 at the Phoenix Greyhound Racetrack.

Savarese submits that because the government offered no evidence that he used T.M.'s stolen credit card, and insufficient evidence to prove beyond a reasonable doubt that he was the individual who stole it (i.e., possessed or transferred it), the district court should have granted his motion for acquittal. We disagree. *** The government adduced compelling evidence of identity fraud ***.

That Savarese possessed and transferred T.M.'s means of identification (T.M.'s name and credit card) in furtherance of the scheme is plainly inferable from the evidence. Donald DeSimone Jr. testified that Savarese acquired, by theft, all of the credit cards used in the fraud. [Richard Regnetta similarly] described the scheme's (and Savarese's) methods of operation. Further, the victim (T.M.) testified that his credit card vanished shortly after he visited a Houston-area Bally's on a Friday in July of 2007, and both documentary and testimonial evidence indicated that Savarese's membership card was scanned at two different Bally's locations in that vicinity on Thursday, July 12 and Friday, July 13, 2007. ***

Records and security camera footage additionally showed that a person using the name "Dennis Savarese," and using Savarese's personal credit card, rented a car at the Phoenix airport on July 14, 2007—the same day that James DeSimone, with an unidentified accomplice, withdrew a $2,000 cash advance at the Phoenix Greyhound Racetrack using T.M.'s credit card. Other evidence, including transaction records and copies of false identifications containing Savarese's picture, demonstrated that Savarese was actively participating in the scheme during this general time frame. ***

*** Although the evidence is largely circumstantial, the jury reasonably could have concluded that Savarese stole, transferred, and aided and abetted DeSimone's fraudulent use of T.M's name and credit card. [**Circumstantial evidence, in and of itself, is often enough to ground a conviction.**]

The proof as a whole was enough to support Savarese's conviction for identity fraud, and the district court therefore did not err in denying his motion for acquittal on that count. ***

Conclusion

The conviction for identity fraud was based on sufficient evidence, even though it was largely circumstantial. [Affirmed.]

Equifax Data Breach

The credit reporting agency, Equifax, suffered an enormous data breach that could have compromised the private information, including Social Security Numbers, of 143 million consumers. Allen St. John, in a September 21, 2017, *Consumer Reports* article, "Equifax Data Breach: What Consumers Need to Know," offered insight for those concerned about identity theft. The article can be viewed at:

https://www.consumerreports.org/privacy/what-consumers-need-to-know-
about-the-equifax-data-breach/

The Federal Trade Commission has information for those concerned that Equifax's data breach could expose them to identity theft, which can be viewed at:

https://www.ftc.gov/equifax-data-breach

What Is the Problem? True Motives Underlying Tensions between Courtroom Actors

Tension between Defendants and Public Defenders

In America we are taught that you get what you pay for. Indigent defendants who cannot afford to hire their own attorneys sometimes wrongly apply this notion to their public defenders. On the contrary, public defenders can be brilliant lawyers who daily hone their cross-examination skills and who learn all the cultural nuances of their courtrooms. Defendants who see their lawyers relax or joke with prosecutors might reasonably suspect that the public defender is too chummy with the D.A. and is about to sell him out. Instead, public defenders are building long-term relationships with prosecutors so that they have shared experiences and credibility when negotiating the close cases. All lawyers, continually trained to be zealous advocates, are generally able to form friendships with opposing counsel, understanding that the gloves come off at trial.

"Acquitted. Acquitted. Acquitted. Very impressive."

© Cartoon Resource/Shutterstock.com

"Recent Massive Data Breach" at Target Stores

Ken Harney of *The Seattle Times* reported in a February 1, 2014, article entitled, "The long reach of identity theft," that:

> Massive data breaches recently at retailers like Target and Neiman Marcus leave millions vulnerable to identity theft and could turn into credit-report trouble for consumers seeking mortgages or trying to close home purchases.

The full article can be viewed at:

> http://seattletimes.com/html/businesstechnology/2022797871_bizharney02xml.html

Aimee Picchi, in her article for a January 22, 2014, report for *CBSNews.com*, "As Target Fallout Continues, Incidents of Fraud Emerge," noted that thieves stole more than payment card numbers. The video and article are at:

> http://www.cbsnews.com/news/as-target-fallout-continues-incidents-of-fraud-emerge/

Mitch Lipka, in a January 14, 2014, article for *Reuters* entitled, "What Target customers should know about identity theft protection," reported:

> In the wake of a massive data breach that affected up to 100 million shoppers over the holidays, Target Corp has offered all of its customers—whether or not they were directly affected—a year of free credit monitoring.

He answers the question, "Is it an offer you should take?" at:

> http://www.reuters.com/article/2014/01/14/us-target-data-idtheftprotection-
> idUSBREA0D12M20140114

The hacking of Target accounts was so significant that it received international attention. In England's newspaper, *The Guardian*, Jana Kasperkevic reported on December 19, 2013, in an article entitled: "Target data breach: what you need to know about identity theft—Identity theft is much more common than you think. The Target data breach is one of many, and you don't have to be a victim:"

> Millions of people are dealing with the possibility that their personal information, including their names, credit and debit card numbers might have been stolen in a recently uncovered cyber breach.

The full article can be viewed at:

> http://www.theguardian.com/money/us-money-blog/2013/dec/19/
> target-identity-theft-credit-card-breach

G.   ENVIRONMENTAL CRIMES

What should be the mens rea for the crime of violating the Clean Air Act by improperly handling and disposing of asbestos? Should the defendant be found guilty if he **knew he was dealing with asbestos** and therefore was on notice that he should check federal regulations, or should he be guilty **only if he knew that the particular asbestos with which he was dealing was a "regulated kind"** of asbestos? The following case considers this important issue.

"Is it possible that toxic dumping could create a vile organism? Nah."

Environmental crimes can have devastating consequences.

LEGAL ANALYSIS

United States v. Duane L. O'Malley, aka Butch
739 F.3d 1001 (2014).
Justice Tinder delivered the opinion for the United States Court of Appeals.

Facts

*** Duane "Butch" O'Malley was convicted of removing, transporting, and dumping asbestos-containing insulation. A jury was convinced beyond a reasonable doubt that O'Malley knew the insulation contained asbestos. O'Malley appeals [arguing that the Clean Air Act required the government prove that O'Malley knew that the asbestos] was a regulated type of asbestos. [The jury was correctly instructed on, and the government proved, the correct *mens rea* for the violations.]

Michael Pinski, a real estate developer, purchased a building in Kankakee, Illinois, [aware] that the building contained approximately 2,200 linear feet of asbestos-containing insulation material wrapped around pipes. [Pinski hired Origin Fire Protection, a company run by O'Malley, to convert the sprinkler system.]

[O'Malley] offered to remove the insulation for an additional payment. Pinski, [told] O'Malley that some of the insulation-wrapped pipes contained asbestos. O'Malley, however, convinced Pinski that he would remove the insulation properly and dispose of it in a proper landfill, and even save Pinski money in the process. O'Malley insisted on a cash payment for the $12,000 contract price, and provided no written contract for the insulation removal work, even though he gave Pinski a written contract for the installation of the sprinkler system. [O'Malley wanted cash payments from Pinski so "there wouldn't be a paper trail."] O'Malley and his business did not hold a license to remove asbestos. ***

Almost everyone in the cast of characters recognized the asbestos for what it was. James Mikrut, one of O'Malley's employees *** told O'Malley that "[t]his is probably all asbestos in this building."

[O'Malley hired Jeff Franc, who] stripped dry asbestos insulation off the pipes using [O'Malley's circular saw.] O'Malley did not [train] Franc and his workers in the proper way to remove asbestos. He did not make available to Franc's crew water or equipment for wetting the asbestos. Predictably, the circular saw produced large amounts of asbestos dust that filled the room. The workers were equipped only with a few paint suits, simple dust masks, and useless respirators with missing filters. The workers donned the dust masks initially, but they quickly became clogged and the workers were unable to breathe through them. Franc's crew stopped working after a day or two because they inhaled a large amount of dust, and they claimed the dust made them sick. O'Malley did not notify the federal EPA or the Illinois EPA about the asbestos removal.

The discarded asbestos insulation was packed into more than 100 large, plastic garbage bags. [When an asbestos-abatement company refused to accept the load of asbestos waste, O'Malley asked Franc to dispose of some of the bags] at an abandoned farmhouse a couple of miles from O'Malley's property; O'Malley also enlisted Lietz to dispose of garbage bags, which Lietz placed in a dumpster near a Hobby Lobby store.

[The Illinois EPA, inspecting the field where the bags of asbestos had been dumped, observed open and torn bags in the field, with] some of the contents spilling out onto the bare ground. EPA Superfund contractors later spent more than $47,000 to properly remove and dispose of the bags of asbestos and to clean up the contaminated soil. ***

[O'Malley instructed his employee, Mikrut, to tell the EPA that he did not remove any insulation but only did alarm work. When the federal EPA's criminal investigation division interviewed Mikrut,] he admitted to the truth and agreed to make recorded calls to O'Malley. The calls revealed O'Malley coaching Mikrut to mislead federal agents if asked further about the asbestos removal and disposal. O'Malley also came up with the clever scheme to pin the illegal asbestos removal on Franc. When confronted by the agents, O'Malley admitted *** that he had failed to stop the illegal asbestos removal even after he suspected the material was asbestos. [O'Malley's material contained a regulated type of asbestos at concentrations ranging from 4% to 48%.]

Issue

Whether the trial court properly instructed the jury that a conviction under the Clean Air Act here required that the defendant "knew that asbestos-containing material was in the building."

Rule and Analysis

O'Malley is correct that not all forms of asbestos are subject to regulation. The Clean Air Act authorizes the regulation of hazardous air pollutants, one of which is asbestos. [The EPA's work-practice standard for the handling of asbestos in building demolition and renovation applies] only to the six types of "regulated asbestos-containing material (RACM)," defined as:

> (a) Friable asbestos material, (b) Category I nonfriable ACM that has become friable, (c) Category I nonfriable ACM that will be or has been subjected to sanding, grinding, cutting, or abrading, or (d) Category II nonfriable ACM that has a high probability of becoming or has become crumbled, pulverized, or reduced to powder by the forces expected to act on the material in the course of demolition or renovation operations regulated by this subpart. ***

"Friable asbestos material" is defined as "any material containing more than 1 percent asbestos *** that, when dry, can be crumbled, pulverized, or reduced to powder by hand pressure." [There] is no question that the material in question—which was both friable and contained asbestos at concentrations ranging from four percent to forty-eight percent—was indeed "regulated asbestos-containing material.

The Clean Air Act makes it a crime for any person to "knowingly [violate any requirement or prohibition of the Act. [The court instructed the jury on the knowledge elements as follows: "The government must prove ... the defendant knew that asbestos-containing material was in the building."] The district court [defined] "regulated asbestos-containing material", [as including] "any material containing more than one-percent (1%) asbestos *** that, when dry, can be crumbled, pulverized, or reduced to powder by hand pressure." ***

O'Malley argues that the knowledge element instruction should have required the government to prove that the defendant knew that regulated asbestos-containing material, not simply asbestos-containing material, was in the building. But this cannot be correct. As a general rule, "unless the text of the statute dictates a different result, **the term 'knowingly' merely requires proof of knowledge of the facts that constitute the offense.**" [*United States v. International Minerals & Chemical Corp.*] held that the phrase "knowingly violates" does not "carv[e] out an exception to the general rule that ignorance of the law is no excuse." *** The *mens rea* required by the phrase is one that is higher than strict liability, such that "[a] person thinking in good faith that he was shipping distilled water when in fact he was shipping some dangerous acid would not be covered." ***But it is certainly much lower than specific intent, especially when, as here, "dangerous or deleterious devices or products or obnoxious waste materials are involved," because "the probability of regulation is so great that anyone who is aware that he is in possession of them or dealing with them must be presumed to be aware of the regulation." *****The very fact that O'Malley was knowingly working with asbestos-containing material met the *mens rea* requirement** outlined in *International Minerals*, **as asbestos is certainly a dangerous material of a type where "the probability of regulation is so great that anyone who is aware that he is in possession of [it must be presumed to be aware of the regulation."]**

[**The scienter required by the Clean Air Act in the asbestos context is mere knowledge of the presence of asbestos**. In] the context of asbestos regulations under the Clean Air Act, "the phrase 'knowingly violates' requires knowledge of facts and attendant circumstances that comprise a violation of the statute, not specific knowledge that one's conduct is illegal." ***

Conclusion

[T]he district court's instructions on scienter were proper. [Affirmed.]

"Seamless Web" Connection

In *United States v. O'Malley*, the case discussed above, the court considered what precise knowledge was needed in order to be guilty of "knowingly" handling asbestos. This issue focuses on mens rea or criminal intent, one of the basic elements of crime that cause it to differ from all other behavior. This case is, therefore, connected to mens rea, a subject fully explored in Chapter 3.

H. OCCUPATIONAL SAFETY CRIMES

Violations of occupational health and safety codes can lead to loss of life and therefore can be quite serious. One job filled with danger is mining. The lethality of this occupation was brought home in 2010 when an explosion in the Upper Big Branch mine in West Virginia claimed the lives of twenty-nine miners. Ian Urbina reported for the *New York Times* in an April 9, 2010, article entitled, "No Survivors Found After West Virginia Mine Disaster," that the wait ended tragically.

The full article can be viewed at:

> http://www.nytimes.com/2010/04/10/us/10westvirginia.html?_r=0

The disaster led to criminal convictions. As reported by Sandy Smith in *EHS Today Magazine* in her September 13, 2013, article, "Another Massey Energy Official Sentenced on Federal Criminal Charges" September 13, 2013 (Copyright © 2013 by Penton. Used by permission):

A former long-time Massey Energy employee receives jail time for crimes he committed at Massey Energy's White Buck operations in Nicholas County, W.Va.

> Sandy Smith reported:
> David Hughart, a former Massey Energy official, was sentenced Sept. 10 to 42 months in jail after pleading guilty to two federal charges: Conspiracy to impede the Mine Safety and Health Administration (MSHA) and conspiracy to violate mine health and safety laws.
> Hughart is one of several Massey Energy employees have been sentenced to prison for violating federal mining safety and health standards and for warning mine operators when MSHA inspections were going to occur. These violations contributed to the April 5, 2010 fire and explosion at the Upper Big Branch coal mine that killed 29 miners.
> U.S. District Judge Irene Berger sentenced Hughart to a year longer than the 24- to 30-month sentence recommended by federal guidelines because of the safety risk to the miners created by his crimes and to send a message to other mine operators not to cut corners when the lives of miners are at stake. "This sentence will promote respect for the law," Berger said at sentencing.

The full article can be viewed at:

> http://ehstoday.com/safety/another-massey-energy-official-sentenced-federal-criminal-charges

---

Are Hairstylists Safe at Work?

Katie Moisse, for *ABC News'* "Good Morning America," reported on September 8, 2011, in "Brazilian Blowout Hair Treatment Takes Heat From FDA," that some hair products could be hazardous to stylists' health.

The full article and video can be viewed at:

> http://abcnews.go.com/Health/Wellness/brazilian-blowout-fda-warns-formaldehyde-false-labeling/story?id=14471900&page=2

DISCUSSION QUESTIONS

1. What is white-collar crime and what distinguishes such offenses from traditional crimes?

2. What is mail fraud? Is the act of mailing something so significant that it must be a central part of the fraud?

3. What is insider trading and why is it illegal? What effect does insider trading have on the perception of fairness in the stock market?

4. What is money laundering and what are the motives behind this crime? Is money laundering intimately connected with other crimes? Why or why not?

5. What is antitrust? How does it undermine market forces and capitalism?

6. What is identity fraud and why is it so damaging to an individual victim?

7. Provide an example of an environmental crime and consider why it can be so dangerous to public health.

8. Can occupational safety crimes be as dangerous as street crime? Can they result in death? If so, how?

WEB LINKS

1. The U.S. Department of Treasury can be visited at: http://www.treasury.gov/Pages/default.aspx

2. The Security and Exchange Commission can be visited at: http://www.sec.gov/

3. The Federal Trade Commission's Bureau of Consumer Protection can be visited at: http://www.ftc.gov/about-ftc/bureaus-offices/bureau-consumer-protection

4. The U.S. Environmental Protection Agency can be visited at: http://www.epa.gov/

5. The U.S. Department of Labor's Occupational Health and Safety Administration can be visited at: https://www.osha.gov/

6. The U.S. Department of Justice can be visited at: http://www.justice.gov/

CHAPTER XI

Gang Crime

What exactly is a 'gang?'

© anetapics/Shutterstock.com

A. WHAT IS A "GANG"? LEGAL DEFINITIONS

According to Jeffrey T. Wennar in *Ganging Up on Gangs: The Steps Necessary for Effectively Prosecuting Gang Violence*, 5 Crim. L. Brief 3, 3 (2010), **"There is no one uniform definition among the states as to what constitutes a criminal street gang."** Wennar explained that **states typically identify criminal street gangs as "constituting three or more persons who have a common name or identifying sign, symbol, tattoo or other physical marking, style of dress or use of a hand sign, and whose members individually or collectively engage in a pattern of criminal activity."** A selection of state definitions is provided on the following page

353

Alabama § 13A-6-26: Compelling Streetgang Membership

(a) For purposes of this section, the term "streetgang" means any combination, confederation, alliance, network, conspiracy, understanding, or other similar arrangement in law or in fact, of three or more persons that, through its membership or through the agency of any member, engages in a course or pattern of criminal activity.

Oklahoma § 856: Causing, Aiding, Abetting or Encouraging Minor to be Delinquent or Runaway Child, to Commit Felony or to Become Involved with Criminal Street Gang

. . . F. "Criminal street gang" means any ongoing organization, association, or group of five or more persons that specifically either promotes, sponsors, or assists in, or participates in, and requires as a condition of membership or continued membership, the commission of one or more of the following criminal acts:

1. Assault, battery, or assault and battery with a deadly weapon . . . ;
2. Aggravated assault and battery . . . ;
3. Robbery by force or fear . . . ;
4. Robbery or attempted robbery with a dangerous weapon or imitation firearm . . . ;
5. Unlawful homicide or manslaughter . . . :
6. The sale, possession for sale, transportation, manufacture, offer for sale, or offer to manufacture controlled dangerous substances . . . ;
7. Trafficking in illegal drugs . . . :
8. Arson . . . :
9. The influence or intimidation of witnesses and jurors . . . ;
10. Theft of any vehicle . . . :
11. Rape . . . ;
12. Extortion . . . ;
13. Transporting a loaded firearm in a motor vehicle . . . ;
14. Possession of a concealed weapon . . . ; or
15. Shooting or discharging a firearm . . .

VIDEO: The Newest Supreme Court Justice is Sworn In

U.S. Supreme Court Justice Neil Gorsuch is sworn in as the newest justice on the nation's highest court at:

https://www.youtube.com/watch?v=QjIn3kGxvDY

Wisconsin §939.22: Words and Phrases Defined

. . . (9) "Criminal gang" means an ongoing organization, association or group of 3 or more persons, whether formal or informal, that has as one of its primary activities the commission of one or more of the criminal acts, or acts that would be criminal if the actor were an adult, specified in . . . that has a common name or a common identifying sign or symbol; and whose members individually or collectively engage in or have engaged in a pattern of criminal gang activity.

The federal government provides the following definition in 18 U.S.C.A. Section 521 (2002):

"Criminal street gang" means an ongoing group, club, organization, or association of 5 or more persons
  (A) that has as 1 of its primary purposes the commission of 1 or more of the criminal offenses described in subsection (C);
  (B) the members of which engage, or have engaged within the past 5 years, in a continuing series of offenses described in subsection (C); and
  (C) the activities of which affect interstate or foreign commerce.

These U.S. Supreme Court justices act in concert and dress the same. Are they a gang?

© Everett Historical/Shutterstock.com

The National Gang Center

For the latest information on gangs and access to the *National Gang Center Quarterly Newsletter*, visit the National Gang Center at:

http://www.nationalgangcenter.gov/

Tips for Success for Future Law Students and Lawyers

As a Lawyer, Do Not Blame Your Staff

People make mistakes. The key is accountability. Suppose your staff misses a deadline or improperly performs some necessary legal procedure. No one will listen to you—not the judge, the opposing side, or your client—if you blame your staff for the error. As a lawyer, you are at the top of the pyramid and, therefore, are responsible for all those working below you. When something goes wrong, grit your teeth and own it.

B. GANG "MEMBERSHIP" DEFINED

Even if law enforcement can identify a group as a "criminal street gang," how do police identify a person as an official "member" of such a gang? According to Martin Baker, in *Stuck in the Thicket: Struggling with Interpretation and Application of California's Anti-Gang STEP Act*, 11 Berkeley J. Crim. L. 101, 110 (2006), the Stanislaus County Sheriff's Department in **California deems a person a gang member if they fulfill "two or more of the following criteria"**:

1. Admit to being a gang member.
2. Have been arrested on suspicion of offenses consistent with usual gang activity.
3. Have been identified as a gang member by an informant.
4. Have been seen affiliating with documented gang members.
5. Have been seen displaying gang symbols and-or hand signs.
6. Have been seen wearing gang dress or having gang paraphernalia.
7. Have gang tattoos.

C. CALIFORNIA STREET TERRORISM ENFORCEMENT AND PREVENTION (STEP) ACT

The California legislature understood the dramatic change it was making in passing the STEP Act, and therefore aimed to explain the reasons for implementing this new law by offering a series of "legislative findings" as noted below.

California Penal Code § 186.21: Legislative Findings and Declarations

The Legislature hereby finds and declares that it is the right of every person, regardless of race, color, creed, religion, national origin, gender, gender identity, gender expression, age, sexual orientation, or handicap, to be secure and protected from fear, intimidation, and physical harm caused by the activities of violent groups and individuals. It is not the intent of this chapter to interfere with the exercise of the constitutionally protected rights of freedom of expression and association. The Legislature hereby recognizes the constitutional right of every citizen to harbor and express beliefs on any lawful subject whatsoever, to lawfully associate with others who share similar beliefs, to petition lawfully constituted authority for a redress of perceived grievances, and to participate in the electoral process.

The Legislature, however, further finds that **the State of California is in a state of crisis which has been caused by violent street gangs whose members threaten, terrorize, and commit a multitude of crimes against the peaceful citizens of their neighborhoods**. These activities, both individually and collectively, present a clear and present danger to public order and safety and are not constitutionally protected. The Legislature finds that there are nearly 600 criminal street gangs operating in California, and that the number of gang-related murders is increasing. The Legislature also finds that in Los Angeles County alone there were 328 gang-related murders in 1986, and that gang homicides in 1987 have increased 80 percent over 1986. It is the intent of the Legislature in enacting this chapter to seek the eradication of criminal activity by street gangs by focusing upon patterns of criminal gang activity and upon the organized nature of street gangs, which together, are the chief source of terror created by street gangs. The Legislature further finds that an effective means of punishing and deterring the criminal activities of street gangs is through forfeiture of the profits, proceeds, and instrumentalities acquired, accumulated, or used by street gangs.

Biography—Judge

Justice Thurgood Marshall

- Born in Baltimore, Maryland, on July 2, 1908.
- After being denied admission, due to race prejudice, to Maryland School of Law, attended Howard University School of Law.
- Was an attorney for the National Association for the Advancement of Colored People, for which he risked his safety in litigating cases in the Deep South.
- Argued *Brown v. Board of Education* before the U.S. Supreme Court, causing the court to overturn its "separate but equal doctrine" in ordering the desegregation of public schools.
- Served as the U.S. Solicitor General and on the Court of Appeals.
- Was appointed Associate Justice to the Supreme Court by President Lyndon B. Johnson in 1967.
- Was the first African American to serve as a U.S. Supreme Court justice.
- Supposedly once quipped, "I have a lifetime appointment and I intend to serve it. I expect to die at 110, shot by a jealous husband." According to John Fox, in "The Biographies of the Robes" on PBS, http://www.pbs.org/wnet/supremecourt/rights/robes_marshall.html.
- Was a strong liberal voice on a court that shifted toward increasingly conservative rulings, often leaving him in the dissent.

A significant part of the STEP Act is Penal Code Section 186.22, as provided below.

California Penal Code § 186.22: Participation in Criminal Street Gang

(a) Any person who actively participates in any criminal street gang with knowledge that its members engage in or have engaged in a pattern of criminal gang activity, and who willfully promotes, furthers, or assists in any felonious criminal conduct by members of that gang, shall be punished by imprisonment in a county jail for a period not to exceed one year, or by imprisonment in the state prison for 16 months, or two or three years.

(b)

(1) Except as provided in paragraphs (4) and (5), any person who is convicted of a felony committed for the benefit of, at the direction of, or in association with any criminal street gang, with the specific intent to promote, further, or assist in any criminal conduct by gang members, shall, upon conviction of that felony, in addition and consecutive to the punishment prescribed for the felony or attempted felony of which he or she has been convicted, be punished as follows:

(A) Except as provided in subparagraphs (B) and (C), the person shall be punished by an additional term of two, three, or four years at the court's discretion.

(B) If the felony is a serious felony, as defined in subdivision (c) of Section 1192.7, the person shall be punished by an additional term of five years.

(C) If the felony is a violent felony, as defined in subdivision (c) of Section 667.5, the person shall be punished by an additional term of 10 years.

(2) If the underlying felony described in paragraph (1) is committed on the grounds of, or within 1,000 feet of, a public or private elementary, vocational, junior high, or high school, during hours in which the facility is open for classes or school-related programs or when minors are using the facility, that fact shall be a circumstance in aggravation of the crime in imposing a term under paragraph (1).

(3) The court shall select the sentence enhancement which, in the court's discretion, best serves the interests of justice and shall state the reasons for its choice on the record at the time of the sentencing . . .

(4) Any person who is convicted of a felony enumerated in this paragraph committed for the benefit of, at the direction of, or in association with any criminal street gang, with the specific intent to promote, further, or assist in any criminal conduct by gang members, shall, upon conviction of that felony, be sentenced to an indeterminate term of life imprisonment with a minimum term of the indeterminate sentence calculated as the greater of:

(A) The term determined by the court pursuant to Section 1170 for the underlying conviction, including any enhancement . . .

(B) Imprisonment in the state prison for 15 years, if the felony is a home invasion robbery, in violation of subparagraph (A) of paragraph (1) of subdivision (a) of Section 213; carjacking, as defined in Section 215; a felony violation of Section 246; or a violation of Section 12022.55.

(C) Imprisonment in the state prison for seven years, if the felony is extortion, as defined in Section 519; or threats to victims and witnesses, as defined in Section 136.1.

(5) Except as provided in paragraph (4), any person who violates this subdivision in the commission of a felony punishable by imprisonment in the state prison for life shall not be paroled until a minimum of 15 calendar years have been served . . .

(d) Any person who is convicted of a public offense punishable as a felony or a misdemeanor, which is committed for the benefit of, at the direction of, or in association with any criminal street gang, with the specific intent to promote, further, or assist in any criminal conduct by gang members, shall be punished by imprisonment in a county jail not to exceed one year, or by imprisonment in a state prison for one, two, or three years . . .

(e) As used in this chapter, "pattern of criminal gang activity" means the commission of, attempted commission of, conspiracy to commit, or solicitation of, sustained juvenile petition for, or conviction of two or more of the following offenses, provided at least one of these offenses occurred after the effective date of this chapter and the last of those offenses occurred within three years after a prior offense, and the offenses were committed on separate occasions, or by two or more persons:

(1) Assault with a deadly weapon or by means of force likely to produce great bodily injury, as defined in Section 245.

(2) Robbery . . . (. . . Section 211) . . .

(3) Unlawful homicide or manslaughter, (. . . Section 187) . . .

(4) The sale, possession for sale, transportation, manufacture, offer for sale, or offer to manufacture controlled substances as defined in Sections 11054, 11055, 11056, 11057, and 11058 of the Health and Safety Code.

(5) Shooting at an inhabited dwelling or occupied motor vehicle, (. . . in Section 246).

(6) Discharging or permitting the discharge of a firearm from a motor vehicle . . .

(7) Arson, . . . (. . . Section 450) . . .

(8) The intimidation of witnesses and victims, as defined in Section 136.1.

(9) Grand theft, as defined in subdivision (a) or (c) of Section 487.

(10) Grand theft of any firearm, vehicle, trailer, or vessel.

(11) Burglary, as defined in Section 459.

(12) Rape, as defined in Section 261.

(13) Looting, as defined in Section 463.

(14) Money laundering, as defined in Section 186.10.

(15) Kidnapping, as defined in Section 207.

(16) Mayhem, as defined in Section 203.

(17) Aggravated mayhem, as defined in Section 205.

(18) Torture, as defined in Section 206.

(19) Felony extortion, as defined in Sections 518 and 520.

(20) Felony vandalism, as defined in paragraph (1) of subdivision (b) of Section 594.

(21) Carjacking, as defined in Section 215.

(22) The sale, delivery, or transfer of a firearm . . .

(23) Possession of a pistol, revolver, or other firearm capable of being concealed upon the person . . .

(24) Threats to commit crimes resulting in death or great bodily injury, as defined in Section 422.

(25) Theft and unlawful taking or driving of a vehicle, as defined in Section 10851 of the Vehicle Code.

(26) Felony theft of an access card or account information, as defined in Section 484e.

(27) Counterfeiting, designing, using, or attempting to use an access card, as defined in Section 484f.

(28) Felony fraudulent use of an access card or account information, as defined in Section 484g.

(29) Unlawful use of personal identifying information to obtain credit, goods, services, or medical information, as defined in Section 530.5.

(30) Wrongfully obtaining Department of Motor Vehicles documentation . . .

(31) Prohibited possession of a firearm . . .

(32) Carrying a concealed firearm . . .

(33) Carrying a loaded firearm . . .

(f) As used in this chapter, "criminal street gang" means any ongoing organization, association, or group of three or more persons, whether formal or informal, having as one of its primary activities the commission of one or more of the criminal acts enumerated in paragraphs (1) to (25), inclusive, or (31) to (33), inclusive, of subdivision (e), having a common name or common identifying sign or symbol, and whose members individually or collectively engage in or have engaged in a pattern of criminal gang activity . . .

(i) In order to secure a conviction or sustain a juvenile petition, pursuant to subdivision (a) it is not necessary for the prosecution to prove that the person devotes all, or a substantial part, of his or her time or efforts to the criminal street gang, nor is it necessary to prove that the person is a member of the criminal street gang. Active participation in the criminal street gang is all that is required.

(j) A pattern of gang activity may be shown by the commission of one or more of the offenses enumerated in paragraphs (26) to (30), inclusive, of subdivision (e), and the commission of one or more of the offenses enumerated in paragraphs (1) to (25), inclusive, or (31) to (33), inclusive, of subdivision (e). A pattern of gang activity cannot be established solely by proof of commission of offenses enumerated in paragraphs (26) to (30), inclusive, of subdivision (e), alone . . . [112]

VIDEO: A Workday for an LAPD Gang Cop

A video following police pursuing gangs in Los Angeles can be viewed at:

https://www.youtube.com/watch?v=G5SWsL4IEPk

"Seamless Web" Connection

California Penal Code § 186.22 "Participation in Criminal Street Gang," given above, allows prosecution of any "person who actively participates" in a gang. The California legislature purposely limited criminal liability to only those who *actively participate* in gang activity rather than those who just happen to be members of a gang. This cautious crafting of the gang statute connects this law through the seamless web to the fundamental element of actus reus explored in Chapter 2. The actus reus requirement—that a person can only be convicted of a crime if he or she commits a criminal act—ensures that the law punishes people for what they do, not for who they are. Recall that in Chapter 2, *Robinson v. California* ruled that prosecuting a person for his or her "status" rather than his or her acts was unconstitutional.

Do's and Don'ts for Hearings, Trials, and Appeals

Cross Examination

Do use leading questions, such as, "Isn't it true that you could not see the stabbing because a street light was out?" or "Isn't it true that you hate my client because he is now dating your old girlfriend?" The opposing side called this witness and so he or she has a story that could potentially harm your case. It is fully proper to control the witness fully and expose his or her falsehoods. **Don't** lose your temper with a witness unless it is for dramatic effect in front of the jury.

The "two key provisions" in the STEP Act above are (1) the creation of "a new crime of 'active participation in a criminal gang,'" and (2) the creation of "enhanced penalties" for certain crimes found to be gang related. Martin Baker, in *Stuck in the Thicket: Struggling with Interpretation and Application of California's Anti-Gang STEP Act*, 11 Berkeley J. Crim. L. 101, 103 (2006), describes the "fundamental difference" between these two provisions as follows: **"(T)he active participation provision punishes participation in criminal activity from within a criminal street gang while the enhancement provision punishes facilitation of criminal street gang activity from within or without the gang itself."**

D.   PROSECUTING GANG CRIME UNDER THE STEP ACT

How can courts determine that a particular group of people is a "**criminal street gang**"? **What is a criminal street gang**? If a necessary ingredient for a criminal street gang is that its **primary activities** are the **commission of crimes listed in a statute**, how does one distinguish between "**primary activities**" and "**activities**" that are not considered primary? The following case considers such issues.

LEGAL ANALYSIS

People v. Sengpadychith
26 Cal. 4th 316 (2001).
Justice Kennard delivered the opinion of the California Supreme Court.

Facts

At 5:00 p.m. on May 9, 1996, Soeury "Eve" Pen was in the front yard of her home in San Jose with her friends Joel Dacanay, Pao Av, and Sal Vong, when defendant, who was her former boyfriend and a member of the Triple S gang, telephoned. Eve refused to talk to him. Dacanay, a member of Real Pinoy Brothers (RPB), Triple S's main rival, returned the call and issued a gang challenge, in which Av and Vong joined.

Around 6:45 p.m., defendant and some companions drove to Eve's house in a car and a truck. Standing outside were Av, Vong, and Dacanay. Also with them were Graylone Brown and Travis Cruz. Someone in the car yelled "Who's RPB?" Dacanay answered *he* was. Defendant then got out of the truck with a handgun and started firing, hitting Cruz in the chest. Defendant also shot through a window and a wall of a nearby house, and he and a companion both shot through the rear window of a van parked on the street.

Detective Marty Hogan of the San Jose Police Department's Violent Crime Unit, which investigates gang crimes, testified to a September 3, 1993, shooting committed by Triple S member Darius Augustin. That crime, like the shootings in this case, was in Detective Hogan's opinion committed to benefit the Triple S gang.

The trial court instructed the jury on the criminal street gang sentence enhancement but failed to explain that, to trigger that provision, the jury had to find that one of Triple S's primary activities was the commission of one or more statutorily enumerated felonies. (See § 186.22, subds. (e) & (f).)

The jury convicted defendant of four counts of attempted murder and of shooting at an unoccupied motor vehicle. But it acquitted him of shooting at an inhabited dwelling house, finding him guilty of the lesser included offense of grossly negligent discharge of a firearm (§ 246.3). The jury also found true each of the criminal street gang and other sentence-enhancement allegations.

Issue

May the jury consider the circumstances of the charged crimes on the issue of the group's primary activities? We hold that it can.

Rule and Analysis

Step by step, this court continues its struggle through the thicket of statutory construction issues presented by the California Street Terrorism Enforcement and Prevention Act, [also known as the STEP Act. This case involves PC 186.22(b), a sentence enhancement for felonies committed "for the benefit of, at the direction of, or in association with any *criminal street gang.*"]

The STEP Act [PC 186.22(f)] defines a criminal street gang as "any ongoing organization, association, or group of three or more persons, whether formal or informal, *having as one of its*

primary activities the commission of one or more of [certain enumerated] criminal acts *** **having a common name or common identifying sign or symbol, and whose members individually or collectively engage in or have engaged in a pattern of criminal gang activity."** *** Nothing in this statutory language prohibits the trier of fact from considering the circumstances of the *present* or charged offense in deciding whether the group has as one of its primary activities the commission of one or more of the statutorily listed crimes.

Evidence of past or present conduct by gang members involving the commission of one or more of the statutorily enumerated crimes is relevant in determining the group's primary activities. **Both past and present offenses [reasonably tend to show the group's primary activity and therefore fall within the general rule of admissibility.]**

[Evidence] of either past or present criminal acts listed in [PC 186.22(e)] is admissible to establish the statutorily required primary activities of the alleged criminal street gang. Would such evidence alone be sufficient to prove the group's primary activities? Not necessarily. **The phrase "primary activities," as used in the gang statute, implies that the commission of one or more of the statutorily enumerated crimes is one of the group's "chief" or "principal" occupations.** *** That definition would necessarily exclude the occasional commission of those crimes by the group's members. *** "Though members of the Los Angeles Police Department may commit an enumerated offense while on duty, the commission of crime is not a *primary activity* of the department. [PC 186.22] requires that one of the primary activities of the group or association itself be the commission of [specified crimes.] Similarly, environmental activists or any other group engaged in civil disobedience could not be considered a criminal street gang under the statutory definition unless one of the primary activities of the group was the commission of one of the [25] enumerated crimes found within the statute."

Sufficient proof of the gang's primary activities might consist of evidence that the group's members *consistently and repeatedly* have committed criminal activity listed in the gang statute. Also sufficient might be expert testimony. [In a past case, a police gang expert appropriately testified that a gang] was primarily engaged in the sale of narcotics and witness intimidation, both statutorily enumerated felonies. *** The gang expert based his opinion on [his conversations with gang members,] on "his personal investigations of hundreds of crimes committed by gang members," [and information from colleagues in his own department and other law enforcement agencies.]

Conclusion

Despite the Court's determination that a jury can properly consider the circumstances of the charged crimes on the issue of the group's *primary* activities, the Court reversed the conviction and remanded the case because of other issues.[113]

Gang Crime Intersects with Hate Crimes

Winnie Hu and Kate Pastor reported in the *New York Times* on February 20, 2014, in an article entitled, "14-Year Term for Leader in Bronx Antigay Attack," about the sentencing of a street gang leader.
The full article can be viewed at:

http://www.nytimes.com/2014/02/21/nyregion/14-year-term-for-leader-in-bronx-antigay-attack.html?_r=1

---

113. Reprinted with the permission of LexisNexis.

> ## Learn from My (and Others') Mistakes
>
> ### Do Not Threaten to Jail a Juror for Coming Back Late from Lunch
>
> Prosecutors want jurors to focus on the heinousness of the crime, not the cruelty of the punishment. So, a trial judge did me no favors when he embarrassed a juror returning late from lunch with a long harangue about all the county and state money the juror wasted by holding up the trial proceedings and then by announcing to the juror that if he was ever again late, that juror would be put in a jail cell. The juror now placed himself in the shoes of the defendant rather than with the victim.

E.   COMMISSION OF A CRIME IN FURTHERANCE OF GANG'S INTEREST

How can juries or judges tell if a criminal commits a crime "in furtherance" of a gang's interest? This inquiry, considered in the case below, often amounts to **looking at all the facts** surrounding a person's acts.

LEGAL ANALYSIS

Randolph v. State
334 Ga.App. 475 (2015).
Judge Branch wrote the opinion for the Court of Appeals of Georgia.

Facts

[A] jury found Davan Randolph guilty of distributing marijuana, conspiring to distribute marijuana, and violating the Georgia Street Gang Terrorism and Prevention Act. [We] reverse the gang activity conviction.

[Randolph admitted that he had met Foley, smoked marijuana with him,] and regularly bought small amounts of the drug from him for personal use. Randolph said that he had introduced other people—some of whom he knew and some of whom he did not know—to Foley as potential customers. Randolph *** had also helped Foley deliver marijuana: "[I]f I had friends that wanted some and I was already going to get some and me and a friend of mine were planning to get together or something I would . . . go ahead and get theirs and take it to them." [Randolph admitted] that Foley would bring his marijuana and scales to Randolph's girlfriend's house, where he and Foley "would weigh it up and we would put it in bags." *** Foley would repay him for this assistance with approximately $25 worth of marijuana.

Randolph testified that he used to belong to the Folk Nation gang and that he had introduced Foley to some fellow gang members, or "brothers," who then bought marijuana from him. Randolph said that these people—not him—were the ones who arranged to buy a large quantity of marijuana from Foley [and committed other crimes.] [Ultimately, Randolph was convicted of violating the Georgia Street Gang Terrorism and Prevention Act.]

Issue

Whether there was insufficient evidence to support his conviction for violating [OCGA 16-15-1] Georgia Street Gang Terrorism and Prevention Act because the state failed to present evidence that Randolph's marijuana distribution crimes were intended to further the interests of the gang.

Rule and Analysis

The Georgia Street Gang Terrorism and Prevention Act [OCGA 16-15-4(a)] prohibits a person associated with a criminal street gang from participating in criminal street gang activity through the commission of a number of listed offenses. [OCGA 16-15-3(2) defines "Criminal street gang"] as "any . . . group of three or more persons associated in fact, whether formal or informal, which engages in criminal gang activity." [OCGA 16-15-3(1)(A) defines "Criminal gang activity,"] as "the commission, attempted commission, conspiracy to commit, or solicitation, coercion, or intimidation of another person to commit" any of a number of offenses, including "racketeering activity." "Racketeering activity" includes violations of the Georgia Controlled Substances Act. *** **It is not enough, however, for the state simply to show that the defendant and other gang members committed a criminal act; rather, "there must be some nexus between the act and an intent to further street gang activity."** ***

*** Our case law has supplied no test, guidelines, or list of factors relevant to determining whether the commission of a predicate crime was meant to "further the interests of the [gang," Instead,] we have simply analyzed the evidence in each particular case and found it to be sufficient. And in each case, the state has shown something more than the mere commission of a crime by gang members.

[In *Zamudio v. State*, we rejected the gang-member defendant's argument that the state failed to prove that a] fight that formed the basis of the criminal charges against him was undertaken to further the gang's interest. [The] victim was a former member of a rival gang who had recently rejected the defendant's overture to "hang out" and that immediately before the fight broke out, the defendant "started arguing about gang-related stuff." [This] evidence authorized the jury to find a nexus between the defendant['s] actions in seeking out and beating up the victim and [his] intent to further gang activity by ensuring that the gang responded strongly to the victim's disrespect of a gang member's offer of association. ***

[In Alston v. State] we held that evidence that the defendant and two fellow gang members wore gang colors to "represent" and talked about their gang affiliation moments before committing an armed robbery was sufficient to demonstrate a nexus between the crime and an intent to further gang activity. In addition, the state presented evidence that after the crime, one defendant wrote a letter acknowledging that he had violated gang rules by implicating his fellow gang members in the crime, and there was expert testimony that "the gang's reputation is furthered by committing highly visible crimes in a manner which allows the witnesses and the victims to discern that a particular gang committed the crime." ***

Here, the [state] showed that Randolph, who was a member of Folk Nation, had introduced Foley, who was not affiliated with a gang, to a variety of other people—some gang-affiliated and some not—and had helped Foley distribute small amounts of marijuana to those people. Thus, while the state may have shown that Randolph intended, by distributing marijuana, to further the interests of individual gang members in obtaining small quantities of marijuana for personal use, the state did not show that Randolph meant to further the interests of Folk Nation as an entity. There was no evidence, for example, that Randolph wore gang colors or accessories, talked about his gang affiliation, or otherwise "represented" the gang while he was committing drug crimes. Nor was there any evidence that Randolph's distribution of personal-use amounts of marijuana to individual gang members benefitted the gang itself through monetary profit, enhanced reputation, or other means.

Conclusion

Because the state failed to present evidence of the necessary nexus between Randolph's drug crimes and an intent to further gang interests, his conviction under the Georgia Street Gang Terrorism and Prevention Act must be reversed.[114]

F.   THE CHALLENGE OF PROSECUTING GANGS WITHOUT VIOLATING THE CONSTITUTION

Those prosecuting gang members for gang activity can accidentally violate rights guaranteed by the United States Constitution. In the case below, the United States Supreme Court considered **whether a city ordinance, which prohibited "criminal street gang members" from "loitering" with one another or with other persons in any public place (with "no apparent purpose"), was unconstitutionally vague in violation of Fourteenth Amendment due process.**

The loitering case, below, considers the constitutionality of Chicago's Gang ordinance.

LEGAL ANALYSIS

City of Chicago v. Morales
527 U.S. 41 (1999).
Justice Stevens delivered the opinion for the United States Supreme Court.

Facts

In 1992, the Chicago City Council enacted the Gang Congregation Ordinance, which prohibits "criminal street gang members" from "loitering" with one another or with other persons in any public place. The question presented is whether the Supreme Court of Illinois correctly held that the ordinance violates the Due Process Clause of the Fourteenth Amendment to the Federal Constitution. ***

[After hearings, the city] council found that a continuing increase in criminal street gang activity was largely responsible for the city's [increasing rates of murder, violent crimes, and drug related crimes. "The] burgeoning presence of street gang members in public places has intimidated many law abiding citizens." [Gang] members "establish control over identifiable areas . . . by loitering in those areas and intimidating others from entering those areas; and . . . members of criminal street gangs avoid arrest by committing no offense punishable under existing laws when they know the police are present . . . ."

---

114. Reprinted from Westlaw, with permission of Thomson Reuters.

["Loitering] in public places by criminal street gang members creates a justifiable fear for the safety of persons and property in the area." ***

The ordinance creates a criminal offense [that] involves four predicates. First, the police officer must reasonably believe that at least one of the two or more persons present in a "public place" is a "criminal street gang member." Second, the persons must be "loitering," which the ordinance defines as "remaining in any one place with no apparent purpose." Third, the officer must then order "all" of the persons to disperse and remove themselves "from the area." Fourth, a person must disobey the officer's order. If any person, whether a gang member or not, disobeys the officer's order, that person is guilty of violating the ordinance. ***

[The ordinance states in pertinent part:

"(a) Whenever a police officer observes a person whom he reasonably believes to be a criminal street gang member loitering in any public place with one or more other persons, he shall order all such persons to disperse and remove themselves from the area. Any person who does not promptly obey such an order is in violation of this section.

"(b) It shall be an affirmative defense to an alleged violation of this section that no person who was observed loitering was in fact a member of a criminal street gang.

"(c) As used in this section:

"(1) 'Loiter' means to remain in any one place with no apparent purpose.

"(2) 'Criminal street gang' means any ongoing organization, association in fact or group of three or more persons, whether formal or informal, having as one of its substantial activities the commission of one or more of the criminal acts enumerated in paragraph (3), and whose members individually or collectively engage in or have engaged in a pattern of criminal gang activity . . .

"(5) 'Public place' means the public way and any other location open to the public, whether publicly or privately owned.***]

During [three years,] the police issued over 89,000 dispersal orders and arrested over 42,000 people for violating the ordinance. *** In respondent Youkhana's case, the trial judge held that the "ordinance fails to notify individuals what conduct is prohibited, and it encourages arbitrary and capricious enforcement by police." ***

The Illinois Supreme Court *** held "that the gang loitering ordinance violates due process of law in that it is impermissibly vague on its face and an arbitrary restriction on personal liberties." ***

In support of its vagueness holding, the court pointed out that the definition of "loitering" in the ordinance drew no distinction between innocent conduct and conduct calculated to cause harm. "Moreover, the definition of 'loiter' provided by the ordinance does not assist in clearly articulating the proscriptions of the ordinance." ***

["The ordinance defines 'loiter' to mean 'to remain in any one place with no apparent purpose.' *** People with entirely legitimate and lawful purposes will not always be able to make their purposes apparent to an observing police officer. For example, a person waiting to hail a taxi, resting on a corner during a job, or stepping into a doorway to evade a rain shower has a perfectly legitimate purpose in all these scenarios; however, that purpose will rarely be apparent to an observer." ***]

Issue

Whether Chicago's Gang Congregation ordinance, which prohibited "criminal street gang members" from "loitering" with one another or with other persons in any public place, was unconstitutionally vague.

Rule and Analysis

[Chicago's ordinance is unconstitutionally vague.]

["The] very presence of a large collection of obviously brazen, insistent, and lawless gang members and hangers-on on the public ways intimidates residents, who become afraid even to leave their homes and go about their business. That, in turn, imperils community residents' sense of safety and security, detracts from property values, and can ultimately destabilize entire neighborhoods." [A] law that directly prohibited such intimidating conduct would be constitutional, but this ordinance broadly covers a significant amount of additional activity. Uncertainty about the scope of that additional coverage provides the basis for respondents' claim that the ordinance is too vague. ***

[The] **freedom to loiter for innocent purposes is part of the "liberty" protected by the Due Process Clause of the Fourteenth Amendment**. [This "right to remove from one place to another according to inclination" is "an attribute of personal liberty" protected by the Constitution. An] individual's decision to remain in a public place of his choice is as much a part of his liberty as the freedom of movement inside frontiers that is "a part of our heritage" *** or the right to move "to whatsoever place one's own inclination may direct." ***

Vagueness may invalidate a criminal law for either of two independent reasons. First, it may fail to provide the kind of notice that will enable ordinary people to understand what conduct it prohibits; second, it may authorize and even encourage arbitrary and discriminatory enforcement. [We] first consider whether the ordinance provides fair notice to the citizen. ***

[A **law fails to meet the requirements of the Due Process Clause if it is so vague and standardless that it leaves the public uncertain as to the conduct it prohibits.** While] the term "loiter" may have a common and accepted meaning, *** the definition of that term in this ordinance—"to remain in any one place with no apparent purpose"—does not. It is difficult to imagine how any citizen of the city of Chicago standing in a public place with a group of people would know if he or she had an "apparent purpose." If she were talking to another person, would she have an apparent purpose? If she were frequently checking her watch and looking expectantly down the street, would she have an apparent purpose? ***

[The vagueness that dooms this ordinance is] about what loitering is covered by the ordinance and what is not. [State] courts have uniformly invalidated laws that do not join the term "loitering" with a second specific element of the crime. ***

The city's [response to the notice concern] is that loiterers are not subject to sanction until after they have failed to comply with an officer's order to disperse. [This response unpersuasive for two reasons.]

First, **the purpose of the fair notice requirement is to enable the ordinary citizen to conform his or her conduct to the law. "No one may be required at peril of life, liberty or property to speculate as to the meaning of penal statutes."** *** Although it is true that a loiterer is not subject to criminal sanctions unless he or she disobeys a dispersal order, the loitering is the conduct that the ordinance is designed to prohibit. If the loitering is in fact harmless and innocent, the dispersal order itself is an unjustified impairment of liberty. ***

Second, **the terms of the dispersal order compound the inadequacy of the notice.** *** It provides that the officer "shall order all such persons to disperse and remove themselves from the area." *** This vague phrasing raises a host of questions. After such an order issues, how long must the loiterers remain apart? How far must they move? If each loiterer walks around the block and they meet again at the same location, are they subject to arrest or merely to being ordered to disperse again? As we do here, we have found vagueness in a criminal statute exacerbated by the use of the standards of "neighborhood" and "locality." ***

*** The Constitution does not permit a legislature to "set a net large enough to catch all possible offenders, and leave it to the courts to step inside and say who could be rightfully detained, and who should be set at large." *** This ordinance is therefore vague " *** in the sense that no standard of conduct is specified at all." ***

The broad sweep of the ordinance also violates [the requirement that a legislature establish minimal guidelines to govern law enforcement.] There are no such guidelines in the ordinance. In any public place in the city of Chicago, persons who stand or sit in the company of a gang member may be ordered to disperse unless their purpose is apparent. The mandatory language in the enactment directs the police to issue an order without first making any inquiry about their possible purposes. It matters not whether the reason that a gang member and his father, for example, might loiter near Wrigley Field is to rob an unsuspecting fan or just to get a glimpse of Sammy Sosa leaving the ballpark; in either event, if their purpose is not apparent to a nearby police officer, she may—indeed, she "shall"—order them to disperse.

[Since the ordinance reaches a substantial amount of innocent conduct, we ask if it "necessarily entrusts lawmaking to the moment-to-moment judgment of the policeman on his beat." The] principal source of the vast discretion conferred on the police in this case is the definition of loitering as "to remain in any one place with no apparent purpose."

[The city argues] that the text of the ordinance limits the officer's discretion in three ways. First, it does not permit the officer to issue a dispersal order to anyone who is moving along or who has an apparent purpose. Second, it does not permit an arrest if individuals obey a dispersal order. Third, no order can issue unless the officer reasonably believes that one of the loiterers is a member of a criminal street gang.

[W]e find each of these limitations insufficient. That the ordinance does not apply to people who are moving—that is, to activity that would not constitute loitering under any possible definition of the term—does not even address the question of how much discretion the police enjoy in deciding which stationary persons to disperse under the ordinance. *** The "no apparent purpose" standard for making that decision is inherently subjective because its application depends on whether some purpose is "apparent" to the officer on the scene. ***

Presumably an officer would have discretion to treat some purposes—perhaps a purpose to engage in idle conversation or simply to enjoy a cool breeze on a warm evening—as too frivolous to be apparent if he suspected a different ulterior motive. ***

[The] requirement that the officer reasonably believe that a group of loiterers contains a gang member does place a limit on the authority to order dispersal. That limitation would no doubt be sufficient if the ordinance only applied to loitering that had an apparently harmful purpose or effect, or possibly if it only applied to loitering by persons reasonably believed to be criminal gang members. But this ordinance *** requires no harmful purpose and applies to non-gang members as well as suspected gang members. It applies to everyone in the city who may remain in one place with one suspected gang member as long as their purpose is not apparent to an officer observing them. Friends, relatives, teachers, counselors, or even total strangers might unwittingly engage in forbidden loitering if they happen to engage in idle conversation with a gang member. ***

[The] ordinance does not provide sufficiently specific limits on the enforcement discretion of the police "to meet constitutional standards for definiteness and clarity." [The ordinance affords too much discretion to the police and too little notice to citizens who wish to use the public streets.]

Conclusion

The ordinance was unconstitutionally vague. [The] judgment of the Supreme Court of Illinois is affirmed.

Legal Skills: How to "Green" a Witness

Witnesses have been known to change their stories. Some crime victims, still under the emotional sway of a crime, will contact police and name their attacker, only to recant the accusation later when on the witness stand. This dramatic shift is due in large measure to relationships. An individual in a gang or trapped in domestic violence might be responding to concerns having little to do with the initial charge. A common tactic witnesses take on the witness stand is to simply "fail to remember" the earlier statement rather than to outright contradict it. What can a prosecutor do when faced with a witness suffering such a selective memory loss?

The answer is provided in *People v. Green*, 3 Cal.3d 981 (1971), a case now so famous that its name has become a verb. As a result of this case, prosecutors now routinely "Green" an uncooperative witness. When a witness has a sudden and incredible memory loss about one of his or her prior statements, a deputy district attorney will go through the statement, line-by-line, to force the witness to deny each assertion on the record. In this fashion, the prosecutor can get the statement into evidence for the jury to hear and also expose the witness, by his or her continued refusal to remember any of the specified statement, as less than truthful.

Justice O'Connor, with whom Justice Breyer joins, concurring in part and concurring in the judgment.

I agree with the Court that Chicago's Gang Congregation Ordinance, Chicago Municipal Code § 8-4-015 (1992) (gang loitering ordinance or ordinance) is unconstitutionally vague. A penal law is void for vagueness if it fails to "define the criminal offense with sufficient definiteness that ordinary people can understand what conduct is prohibited" or fails to establish guidelines to prevent "arbitrary and discriminatory enforcement" of the law. *** Of these, "the more important aspect of vagueness doctrine 'is . . . the requirement that a legislature establish minimal guidelines to govern

"Legally, vagueness means, uh . . . whatever?"

law enforcement.'" *** I share Justice Thomas' concern about the consequences of gang violence, and I agree that some degree of police discretion is necessary to allow the police "to perform their peacekeeping responsibilities satisfactorily." *** A criminal law, however, must not permit policemen, prosecutors, and juries to conduct "'a standardless sweep . . . to pursue their personal predilections.'" ***

Accordingly, I join Parts I, II, and V of the Court's opinion and concur in the judgment. ***

"Seamless Web" Connection

In *City of Chicago v. Morales*, the case above, the court was concerned about the clarity of a gang statute. This "vagueness" issue connects this case with the constitutional concerns discussed in Chapter 1. *Morales'* vagueness discussion also connects this case to criminal law's focus on morality and blame, also discussed in Chapter 1.

What Is the Problem? True Motives Underlying Tensions between Courtroom Actors

Tension between Prosecutors and Victims

The prosecutor's client is not the individual victim, but all the people in the relevant jurisdiction. As a deputy D.A., I emphasized to juries that I represented "The People" (Defense counsel, as a proper advocate, would couch my role in Orwellian terms, telling jurors that I represented "The State" or "The Government"). Since D.A.'s are duty-bound to all the people, the interests they advocate do not always align with the victim's. A victim might truly believe that a crime occurred but a D.A. will refuse to file the case, bound by the ethical obligation to only file cases having a reasonable possibility of being proven beyond a reasonable doubt to an objective fact finder. Also, in certain situations, a prosecution must proceed even though the victim has had second thoughts and wishes the case to be thrown out. While I did all I could to help victims, I took care to not forget this bigger picture.

DISCUSSION QUESTIONS

1. What is the legal definition of a criminal street gang?

2. Could definitions of gangs be so vague as to violate the Constitution? How do legislatures avoid writing laws that can be voided for vagueness?

3. Why are gangs so dangerous?

4. How can law enforcement determine gang membership and identify who is and who is not in a gang?

5. What is the Street Terrorism Enforcement and Prevention (STEP) Act? How does it operate in California?

WEB LINKS

1. For analysis of the STEP Act bill, including the financial ramifications and lists of the STEP Act's supporters and opponents, see: http://www.leginfo.ca.gov/pub/13-14/bill/sen/sb_0451-0500/sb_473_cfa_20130528_224846_sen_floor.html

2. To review "Prosecuting Gang Cases: What Local Prosecutors Need to Know," from American Prosecutors Research Institute (APRI) Special Topics Series and the Bureau of Justice, U.S. Department of Justice, see: http://www.ndaa.org/pdf/gang_cases.pdf

3. For a different view of the STEP Act, see: Sara Lynn Van Hofwegen *Unjust and Ineffective: A Critical Look at California's STEP Act* 18 Southern California Interdisciplinary Law Journal 679 (2009), at: http://www.law.usc.edu/why/students/orgs/ilj/assets/docs/18-3%20Van%20Hofwegen.pdf

4. José Martinez for *On Central* of *Southern California Public Radio* suggested on March 6, 2012, that you "Know Your Graffiti: Art, vandalism or gang device?" at: http://www.oncentral.org/news/2012/03/06/know-your-graffiti-art-vandalism-or-gang-device/

CHAPTER XII

Controlled Substance Crimes

Should refined sugar, perhaps addictive and unhealthy, be labeled a controlled substance?

A. WHAT ARE "CONTROLLED SUBSTANCES" AND WHO CONTROLS THEM?

Not all drugs are created equal. **The U.S. Congress created lists of controlled substances (called "schedules") and placed the substances on these schedules according to the potential dangerousness of these drugs.** While **controlled substances ranked in Schedule I are the worst, Schedule V drugs are the least dangerous.**

21 USCS § 812: Schedules of Controlled Substances

(a) Establishment. There are established five schedules of controlled substances, to be known as schedules I, II, III, IV, and V. Such schedules shall initially consist of the substances listed in this section. The schedules established by this section shall be updated and republished on a semiannual basis during the two-year period beginning one year after the date of enactment of this title [enacted Oct. 27, 1970] and shall be updated and republished on an annual basis thereafter.

(b) Placement on schedules; findings required. Except where control is required by United States obligations under an international treaty, convention, or protocol, in effect on the effective date of this part, and except in the case of an immediate precursor, a drug or other substance may not be placed in any schedule unless the findings required for such schedule are made with respect to such drug or other substance. The findings required for each of the schedules are as follows:

(1) **SCHEDULE I.**

(A) The drug or other substance has a high potential for abuse.

(B) The drug or other substance has no currently accepted medical use in treatment in the United States.

(C) There is a lack of accepted safety for use of the drug or other substance under medical supervision.

(2) **SCHEDULE II.**

(A) The drug or other substance has a high potential for abuse.

(B) The drug or other substance has a currently accepted medical use in treatment in the United States or a currently accepted medical use with severe restrictions.

(C) Abuse of the drug or other substances may lead to severe psychological or physical dependence.

(3) **SCHEDULE III.**

(A) The drug or other substance has a potential for abuse less than the drugs or other substances in schedules I and II.

(B) The drug or other substance has a currently accepted medical use in treatment in the United States.

(C) Abuse of the drug or other substance may lead to moderate or low physical dependence or high psychological dependence.

(4) **SCHEDULE IV.**

(A) The drug or other substance has a low potential for abuse relative to the drugs or other substances in schedule III.

(B) The drug or other substance has a currently accepted medical use in treatment in the United States.

(C) Abuse of the drug or other substance may lead to limited physical dependence or psychological dependence relative to the drugs or other substances in schedule III.

(5) **SCHEDULE V.**

(A) The drug or other substance has a low potential for abuse relative to the drugs or other substances in schedule IV.

(B) The drug or other substance has a currently accepted medical use in treatment in the United States.

(C) Abuse of the drug or other substance may lead to limited physical dependence or psychological dependence relative to the drugs or other substances in schedule IV.

(c) Initial schedules of controlled substances [Caution: For amended schedules, see 21 CFR Part 1308.]. Schedules I, II, III, IV, and V shall, unless and until amended pursuant to section 201 [21 USCS § 811], consist of the following drugs or other substances, by whatever official name, common or usual name, chemical name, or brand name designated:

(The following is a severely edited version of a long list of substances listed in each schedule).

SCHEDULE I

(a) Unless specifically excepted or unless listed in another schedule, any of the following opiates, including their isomers, esters, ethers, salts, and salts of isomers, esters, and ethers, whenever the existence of such isomers, esters, ethers, and salts is possible within the specific chemical designation:

(b) . . .

(10) Heroin.

(c)

(1) 3, 4-methylenedioxy amphetamine . . .

(9) Lysergic acid diethylamide.

(10) Marihuana.

(11) Mescaline.

(12) Peyote . . .

(15) Psilocybin.

SCHEDULE II

(a) . . .

(1) Opium and opiate, and any salt, compound, derivative, or preparation of opium or opiate . . .

(3) Opium poppy and poppy straw.

(1) coca [Coca] leaves, except coca leaves and extracts of coca leaves from which cocaine . . .

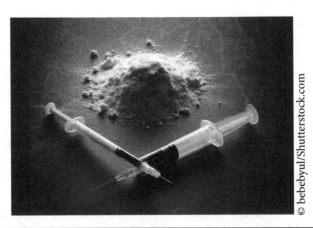

© bebebyul/Shutterstock.com

VIDEO: Does This Body Camera Show an Officer Planting Drugs?

A video about a state attorney dismissing cases due to their connection to an officer apparently caught planting drugs is at:

https://www.youtube.com/watch?v=3Q7qU6RwvP0

The lists in Schedules I through V have evolved and expanded over time to adapt to the advent of new drugs. **Since legislation in Congress takes time, however, it is difficult for the government to respond to urgent dangers.** Some drugs, known as "**designer drugs**" are created so quickly that Congress cannot react soon enough to address their harms. To speed up the process, **can Congress delegate part of its legislative authority to the executive branch by enabling the Attorney General to criminalize a particular drug, or does this violate the Constitution?** The following case considers a law that established a faster process to combat newly created designer drugs.

LEGAL ANALYSIS

Touby v. United States
500 U.S. 160 (1991).
Justice O'Connor delivered the opinion for the United States Supreme Court.

Facts

Petitioners were convicted of manufacturing and conspiring to manufacture "Euphoria," a drug temporarily designated as a schedule I controlled substance pursuant to § 201(h) of the Controlled Substances Act, 98 Stat. 2071, 21 U. S. C. § 811(h). We consider whether § 201(h) unconstitutionally delegates legislative power to the Attorney General and whether the Attorney General's subdelegation to the Drug Enforcement Administration (DEA) was authorized by statute. ***

In 1970, Congress enacted the Controlled Substances Act [Act.] The Act establishes five categories or "schedules" of controlled substances, the manufacture, possession, and distribution of which the Act regulates or prohibits. **Violations involving schedule I substances carry the most severe penalties, as these substances are believed to pose the most serious threat to public safety.** Relevant here, § 201(a) of the Act authorizes the Attorney General to add or remove substances, or to move a substance from one schedule to another. § 201(a), 21 U. S. C. § 811(a).

When adding a substance to a schedule, the Attorney General must follow specified procedures. First, the Attorney General must request a scientific and medical evaluation from the Secretary of Health and Human Services (HHS), together with a recommendation as to whether the substance should be controlled. A substance cannot be scheduled if the Secretary recommends against it. *** Second, the Attorney General must consider eight factors with respect to the substance, including its potential for abuse, scientific evidence of its pharmacological effect, its psychic or physiological dependence liability, and whether the substance is an immediate precursor of a substance already controlled. *** Third, the Attorney General must comply with the notice-and-hearing provisions *** which permit comment by interested parties. [The] Act permits any aggrieved person to challenge the scheduling of a substance by the Attorney General in a court of appeals. ***

It takes time to comply with these procedural requirements. From the time when law enforcement officials identify a dangerous new drug, it typically takes 6 to 12 months to add it to one of the schedules. *** **Drug traffickers were able to take advantage of this time gap by designing drugs that were similar in pharmacological effect to scheduled substances but differed slightly in chemical composition, so that existing schedules did not apply to them.** These "designer drugs" were developed and widely marketed long before the Government was able to schedule them and initiate prosecutions. ***

To combat the "designer drug" problem, Congress in 1984 amended the Act to create an expedited procedure by which the Attorney General can schedule a substance on a temporary basis when doing so is "necessary to avoid an imminent hazard to the public safety." [Temporary scheduling allows the

Attorney General to bypass several of the requirements for permanent scheduling.] The Attorney General need consider only three of the eight factors required for permanent scheduling. [The] Attorney General need provide only a 30-day notice of the proposed scheduling. [The HHS Secretary's] prior approval of a proposed scheduling order is not required. [An] order to schedule a substance temporarily "is not subject to judicial review."

Because it has fewer procedural requirements, temporary scheduling enables the Government to respond more quickly to the threat posed by dangerous new drugs. ***

The Attorney General promulgated regulations delegating to the DEA his powers under the Act, including the power to schedule controlled substances on a temporary basis. *** Pursuant to that delegation, the DEA Administrator issued an order scheduling temporarily 4-methylaminorex, known more commonly as "Euphoria," as a schedule I controlled substance. ***

While the temporary scheduling order was in effect, DEA agents, executing a valid search warrant, discovered a fully operational drug laboratory in Daniel and Lyrissa Touby's home. The Toubys were indicted for manufacturing and conspiring to manufacture Euphoria. They moved to dismiss the indictment on the grounds that § 201(h) unconstitutionally delegates legislative power to the Attorney General, and that the Attorney General improperly delegated his temporary scheduling authority to the DEA. [We affirm the lower court's refusal to dismiss the charges].

Issue

Whether, in delegating its power to determine new controlled substances on an emergency basis to the Attorney General, who in turn delegated these powers to the DEA, did Congress violate the Constitution by abdicating its law making power to the Executive branch.

Rule and Analysis

The Constitution provides that "all legislative Powers herein granted shall be vested in a Congress of the United States." U. S. Const., Art. I, § 1. From this language the Court has derived the **nondelegation doctrine**: that **Congress may not constitutionally delegate its legislative power to another branch of Government**. "The nondelegation doctrine is rooted in the principle of separation of powers that underlies our tripartite system of Government." ***

We have long recognized that the nondelegation doctrine does not prevent Congress from seeking assistance, within proper limits, from its coordinate Branches. *** **Thus, Congress does not violate the Constitution merely because it legislates in broad terms, leaving a certain degree of discretion to executive or judicial actors**. So long as Congress "lay[s] down by legislative act an intelligible principle to which the person or body authorized to [act] is directed to conform, such legislative action is not a forbidden delegation of legislative power." ***

It is clear that in §§ 201(h) and 202(b) Congress has placed multiple specific restrictions on the Attorney General's discretion to define criminal conduct. These restrictions satisfy the constitutional requirements of the nondelegation doctrine. ***

Having concluded that Congress did not unconstitutionally delegate legislative power to the Attorney General, we consider petitioners' claim that the Attorney General improperly delegated his temporary scheduling power to the DEA. Petitioners insist that delegation within the Executive Branch is permitted only to the extent authorized by Congress, and that Congress did not authorize the delegation of temporary scheduling power from the Attorney General to the DEA.

We disagree. Section 501(a) of the Act states plainly that "the Attorney General may delegate any of his functions under [the Controlled Substances Act] to any officer or employee of the Department of Justice." ***

Conclusion

Since there was no improper delegation from Congress to the Attorney General or from the Attorney General to the DEA, [the judgment is affirmed].

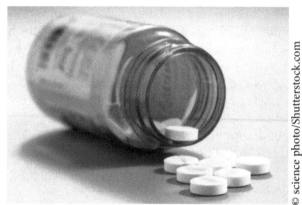

Are prescription pills driving drug crime?

Are Pharmaceuticals to Blame for Our Current Drug Crisis?

60 Minutes correspondent Bill Whitaker, for *CBS News*, reported on October 15, 2017, in *Ex-DEA Agent: Opioid Crisis Fueled by Drug Industry and Congress: Whistleblower Joe Rannazzisi says drug distributors pumped opioids into U.S. communities—knowing that people were dying—and says industry lobbyists and Congress derailed the DEA's efforts to stop it,* that our current drug problem might come from disturbingly surprising sources. The article can be viewed at:

https://www.cbsnews.com/news/ex-dea-agent-opioid-crisis-fueled-by-drug-industry-and-congress/

Tips for Success for Future Law Enforcement

As an Officer or Deputy, Appreciate the Fact That You Are Working with People

Being a public safety officer demands so much; it is important to constantly keep abreast of so many things, including the law, department policy, court procedures, and safety. However, perhaps the most important part of the job is working with people. You will meet all sorts of folks, often during their worst times. For the safety of yourself, other officers, and the case, it is important to rely not only on observation and judgment, but also empathy and active listening. People who feel they are being heard will be more forthcoming, so reflecting back what you have heard will encourage more communication and correct errors. Officers have been told to "come in low"—meaning with a calm demeanor, which they can intensify if the facts require. In contrast, an officer that routinely "comes in high"—meaning aggressive and loud, has nowhere to go to change tactics.

B.   POSSESSION OF A CONTROLLED SUBSTANCE

Elements of possession

As explained in *People v. Rushing* 209 Cal. App. 3d 618, 621(1989), "**The essential elements of the offense of unlawful possession of a controlled substance are actual or constructive possession in an amount sufficient to be used as a controlled substance with knowledge of its presence and its nature as a controlled substance.**" These elements seem at first glance to be relatively straightforward. Hidden within them, however, are a series of subtle questions that have to be analyzed in order for possession to be truly understood.

Possession can take several forms:

1.   **Actual**

     As you hold this criminal law book, you are in "actual possession" of it. **Actual possession involves the physical touching of an item**. If a person holds a drug in his or her hand, in the pocket of the coat he or she is wearing, or in a body orifice, the person has actual possession of the drug.

2.   **Constructive**

     Constructive possession is not as straightforward as actual possession, for the person is not physically touching the drug in question. Instead, **the person exerts "dominion or control" or has "care and management" of the drug**. Courts call this kind of possession "constructive" possession because courts will "construe" possession despite the lack of physical touching. Examples of constructive possession include having an item in one's home, car, or office. Even though the possessor is not in direct contact with the item, he or she controls the area where the item is found (home, car, office) by occupying the space, having a key to the area, storing personal items there, or excluding others. Constructive possession might be more difficult to prove to a jury because the person is not touching the drug. Further, there might exist problems in proving that the person actually knew the item was within the area under his or her control. As with so many mens rea issues, knowledge of a controlled substance's presence can be proven with circumstantial evidence.

3.   **Joint**

     Joint possession is shared possession. One need not exclude all others from possessing an item in order to be guilty of possessing it. If two people share possession of a controlled substance, both are guilty of possession of it.

California Health & Safety Code § 11350: Unlawful Possession

(a) Except as otherwise provided in this division, **every person who possesses (1) any controlled substance** specified in subdivision (b) or (c), or paragraph (1) of subdivision (f) of Section 11054, specified in paragraph (14), (15), or (20) of subdivision (d) of Section 11054, or specified in subdivision (b) or (c) of Section 11055, or specified in subdivision (h) of Section 11056, or (2) any controlled substance classified in Schedule III, IV, or V which is a narcotic drug, **unless upon the written prescription** of a physician, dentist, podiatrist, or veterinarian licensed to practice in this state, **shall be punished by imprisonment** . . .

(Note: The mention of code sections 11054, 11055, and 11056 all direct the reader to California's version of the five schedules Congress created in the Controlled Substances Act, as discussed in the beginning of the chapter.)

Biography—Prosecutor

Jackie Lacey

- Born on February 27, 1957, in Los Angeles, California, and grew up in the Crenshaw district.
- Earned a J.D. at University of Southern California School of Law.
- Became a deputy district attorney with the Los Angeles Office in 1986.
- She is "the first woman and first African-American to serve as Los Angeles County District Attorney since the office was established in 1850," according to the Los Angeles District Attorney's website at http://da.lacounty.gov/about/meet-the-da.
- The L.A.D.A website also notes, "**established the Conviction Review Unit to assess claims of actual innocence** based on newly discovered evidence."
- Has "dedicated one lunch hour a week to teaching fifth-graders at Lorena Street Elementary School in Boyle Heights about the criminal justice system," according to the L.A.D.A. website.
- Leads "a staff of roughly 1,000 lawyers, nearly 300 investigators and about 800 support staff employees" according to the Jack Webb Awards at http://2017jackwebbawards.laphs.org/about-jackie-lacey/.

The case below provides an example of how **constructive possession can be proven even though the person accused is not found actually touching the drugs**. To establish constructive possession, the courts typically look for facts that show the defendant **knew of the presence of the drug**, **had the power to exercise dominion and control** over the drug, and **intended to exercise dominion and control** over the drug. These cases often rely on **circumstantial evidence**.

LEGAL ANALYSIS

Ramirez v. United States
49 A.3d 1246 (2012).
Chief Justice Washington delivered the opinion for the District of Columbia Court of Appeals.

Facts

On April 23, 2010, Metropolitan Police Department officers executed a search warrant [on an apartment, finding] two men: Pascual Luna, who was seated at the dining room table in the kitchen; and Mr. Ramirez, who was walking out of the kitchen. [Ramirez resided on a bed in the living room of the apartment.]

Police found drugs and drug paraphernalia throughout the apartment. In the kitchen, police found, *** 43 ziplock bags containing a white powdery substance and assorted drug paraphernalia, including digital scales. Inside the kitchen sink was a plate with white powder residue. The kitchen sink's faucet was running, the plate was wet, and there was a large quantity of a white powdery substance underneath the plate.

In a closet directly next to the bed in the living room where Mr. Ramirez resided, police found a ziplock bag containing a white powdery substance in the pocket of a pair of jeans, a backpack which contained a digital scale, a jacket with $1,250 in one of its pockets, mail matter bearing Mr. Ramirez's name, and two photos of Mr. Ramirez. In the back bedroom where Mr. Luna resided, police recovered additional drugs and drug paraphernalia. Police searched Mr. Ramirez and Mr. Luna and found $102 on Mr. Ramirez, and ziplock bags containing a white powdery substance and $520 on Mr. Luna.

An expert in the distribution and use of narcotics in the District of Columbia testified that powdered cocaine is usually packaged in small ziplock bags and that digital scales are used to measure cocaine and to cut up small portions of pure cocaine before adding cutting agents. [The ziplock bag in Mr. Ramirez's closet contained 0.11 grams of cocaine.]

[The jury convicted Ramirez's of possession of cocaine and possession of drug paraphernalia. On appeal, Ramirez claims that the evidence was insufficient to support his convictions. We affirm.]

Issue

Whether the evidence was sufficient to establish that the defendant constructively possessed the contraband items.

Rule and Analysis

Possession of drugs, drug paraphernalia, or other contraband can be proven by showing either actual or constructive possession. *** To prove constructive possession, the government must show "that the defendant (1) knew of the presence of the contraband, (2) had the power to exercise dominion and control over it, and (3) intended to exercise dominion and control over it." *** "Constructive possession may be sole or joint and may be proven by direct or circumstantial evidence." ***

Constructive possession requires more than mere presence of the accused on the premises, or simply his proximity to the drugs. *** There must be "something more in the totality of the circumstances that . . . **establishes that the accused meant to exercise dominion or control** over the narcotics." *** In general, however, "a jury is entitled to infer that a person exercises constructive possession over items found in his home." ***

"Evidence suggesting that a defendant has regular access to the premises, such as possession of a key, may also be sufficient to establish constructive possession." *** "The inference that a person who occupies an apartment has dominion and control over its contents applies even when that person shares the premises with others, although it is plainly not as strong an inference in that circumstance." ***

[The] evidence was sufficient to show that Mr. Ramirez constructively possessed drugs and drug paraphernalia. When police ultimately forced their way into the apartment (after knocking and receiving no response), Mr. Ramirez was in the kitchen, along with 27.2 grams of cocaine and digital scales. The sink's faucet was running in what may have been an attempt to dispose of the drugs. Mr. Ramirez acknowledged that he resided in the apartment where the search warrant was executed and, when asked where in the apartment he resided, he pointed to the bed in the living room. Near the bed in the living room, in a closet, police recovered mail addressed to Mr. Ramirez, photos of Mr. Ramirez, and, inside a pair of pants, a ziplock bag of cocaine. Based on the foregoing, we are satisfied that the government met its obligation to show "something more in the totality of the circumstances" than Mr. Ramirez's mere presence, *** and we are satisfied that a reasonable juror could infer that Mr. Ramirez intended to exercise dominion and control over the drugs and drug paraphernalia found in his apartment. ***

Conclusion

There was enough evidence that the defendant constructively possessed the contraband. Accordingly, the judgment of the trial court is [affirmed].[115]

Note

The Statute Ramirez violated in the case above was:

D.C. Code § 48-904.01: Prohibited acts A; penalties . . .

. . . (d) (1) It is unlawful for any person knowingly or intentionally to possess a controlled substance unless the substance was obtained directly from, or pursuant to, a valid prescription or order of a practitioner while acting in the course of his or her professional practice . . . (A)ny person who violates this subsection is guilty of a misdemeanor and upon conviction may be imprisoned for not more than 180 days . . .

"Seamless Web" Connection

In *Ramirez v. United States*, discussed above, the court had to figure out whether the defendant "meant to exercise dominion or control over the narcotics." This analysis regarding proof of mens rea involved weighing all of the circumstances of the case in order to determine what was going on in the defendant's mind. Such reasoning involves using "circumstantial" or "indirect" evidence to prove mens rea, connecting this case through the seamless web to Chapter 1.

© Garsya/Shutterstock.com

The amount of time a person holds a drug is a relevant factor in using the 'momentary possession' defense.

---

115. Reprinted with the permission of LexisNexis.

What Is "Momentary Possession" or "Transitory Possession"?

The California Supreme Court explained the significance of "momentary possession" in *People v. Martin*, 25 Cal. 4th 1180 (2001). In this case, the defendant, Robert Louis Martin, was living with his girlfriend, Janelle Davis, when Janelle's nineteen-year-old son, Guy Davis, came visiting. When Janelle discovered a "small packet of white powder" in Guy's room, she handed it to the defendant, asking him to "[get] rid of it." Instead of immediately disposing of the methamphetamine, the defendant got into an argument with his visitors, which devolved into an ugly fight in which the defendant swung a metal pipe at various people. Police arrived and arrested the defendant. During a search at the station, police found the bindle in Martin's pants pocket, which contained ".12 grams of methamphetamine." When questioned about the methamphetamine, the defendant responded, "I don't know how I got it, and it's not mine. I don't know how it got there." [A jury convicted defendant of HS 11377(a) possession of methamphetamine.] *Martin* reasoned:

> The essential **elements of unlawful possession of a controlled substance are "dominion and control of the substance in a quantity usable for consumption or sale, with knowledge of its presence and of its restricted dangerous drug character**. Each of these elements may be established circumstantially." [Possession is illegal without regard to the specific intent in possessing the substance.] Although the possessor's knowledge of the presence of the controlled substance and its nature as a restricted dangerous drug must be shown, no further showing of a subjective mental state is required.

> [An earlier case, People v. Mijares,] held that, under limited circumstances, **facts showing only a "brief," "transitory" or "momentary" possession could constitute a complete defense to the crime**. [The *Mijares* theory has been alternately described as the "temporary possession defense," the "momentary possession defense," the "transitory possession defense," and the "disposal defense." [*Mijares* emphasized] that our decision in no way insulates from prosecution under the narcotics laws those individuals who, fearing they are about to be apprehended, remove contraband from their immediate possession. *** We leave intact the rule that from such conduct 'it could be inferred that defendant at one time exercised physical dominion' over the narcotic.]

> [The issue in *Mijares* was whether the act of momentarily handling a narcotic for the sole purpose of disposal constituted unlawful "possession." A bystander saw Mijares slap a passenger in a parked car, his friend,] across the face. [Mijares then removed an object from the car and threw it into a nearby field.] He then drove his friend, who was suffering from a heroin overdose, to a fire station. The friend, who was not breathing, was revived. [Authorities determined the object Mijares threw contained heroin and so arrested Mijares.] At trial Mijares claimed he believed his friend was overdosing and needed medical help. Suspecting the friend might still have narcotics on his person if he had recently taken drugs, Mijares looked inside the friend's pockets, found the narcotics outfit, and threw it out of the car before driving to the fire station for help. ***

> "**[In throwing the heroin out of the car,] Mijares maintained momentary possession for the sole purpose of putting an end to the unlawful possession of [his friend**."The] physical control inherent "during the brief moment involved in abandoning the narcotic" was not possession for purposes of the statute. **[If] such transitory control were to constitute possession, "manifest injustice to admittedly innocent individuals" could result**. *** As an example, we referred to the witness who saw the defendant throw the object. Had she "briefly picked up the package and identified the substance as heroin and then placed the outfit back on the ground, during the time after which she had realized

its narcotic character she, too, would have been guilty of possession under an unduly strict reading of [the statute], notwithstanding the fact that her transitory handling of the contraband might have been motivated solely by curiosity." [We refuse to read the possession statutes to allow convictions under such guileless circumstances.] **To 'possess' means to have actual control, care and management of, and not a passing control, fleeting and shadowy in its nature."** ***

[Mijares is supported by] a Prohibition era case, *Garland v. State*, in which the Mississippi Supreme Court declared that a wife who had been arrested for throwing out a jug of illegal alcohol had possessed it for the sole purpose of putting an end to the unlawful possession of the liquor by her husband. ***

"When a defendant relies on the *Mijares* defense, he or she essentially admits the commission of the offense of simple possession of narcotics: The defendant exercised control over the narcotics, he or she knew of its nature and presence, and possessed a usable amount. [The defendant, however, also asserts that he possessed the narcotics for the limited purpose of disposal, abandonment, or destruction. *Mijares*] offers a judicially created exception of lawful possession under certain specific circumstances as a matter of public policy, similar to the defenses of entrapment and necessity."

[**Recognizing**] a **"momentary possession" defense serves the salutary purpose and sound public policy of encouraging disposal and discouraging retention of dangerous items such as controlled substances**. [De minimis possession and reflexive response was not a criminal possession. *Mijares* repeatedly focused] on the fleeting and transitory nature of defendant's possession of his passenger's "narcotics outfit" during the instant he removed it from the latter's person and threw it into the nearby field. [Such momentary or transitory handling or possession, coupled with intent to dispose, could establish a defense to unlawful possession of narcotics.]

[**The defense of transitory possession devised in** *Mijares* **applies only to momentary or transitory possession of contraband for the purpose of disposal**.]

Returning to the facts of this case, even assuming arguendo the jury fully credited Janelle Davis's testimony that she found the methamphetamine bindle in her son Guy's room and handed it over to defendant with a request that he dispose of it, defendant was still not entitled to *** the *Mijares* transitory possession instruction. [As much as four hours had elapsed between the time Davis first gave the narcotics to defendant and the time police arrived. The relevant time of possession was "not a fleeting instantaneous possession. According] to the officers' testimony, an additional 30 minutes elapsed between the time they arrived and questioned defendant and others, and the time defendant was placed under arrest. At least another 10 minutes elapsed from the time defendant was arrested and transported to the police station until the point he was searched, leading to discovery of the narcotics in his pants pocket. There is no indication in the record that during these periods defendant made any attempt, or took any physical action, to dispose of the methamphetamine bindle, much less enlist the assistance of the officers in doing so. Indeed, there is nothing in the record from which to infer that defendant would have voluntarily relinquished possession of the drugs were it not for the search conducted incident to his arrest and booking that led to recovery of the methamphetamine bindle. [Defendant was not entitled to a *Mijares* instruction on transitory possession for the purpose of disposal.][116]

---

116. Reprinted with the permission of LexisNexis.

Legal Skills: How to Put on a Bench Trial

A "bench trial," also known as a "court trial," is a trial that is heard by a judge sitting as fact finder instead of impanelling a jury. Court trials are typically done with cases where the facts could inflame a jury, where there is a particularly subtle point of law, or where there is little factual dispute. Sometimes, a bench trial is done as a "slow plea," where evidence is presented with all courtroom actors hoping that the defendant will realize the hopelessness of his or her case and accept a plea for his own best interests.

Since only a judge hears bench trials, they are quicker, easier, and cheaper than a full-blown jury trial. Also, they lack any need for showmanship that attorneys, most of whom are natural hams, would employ when trying to woo a jury. Any dramatic flourish would not only fall on deaf ears, but would insult the judge's intelligence. At a court trial, keep it simple, brief, and clear.

When police find only a small amount of a drug in a person's possession, 'usable quantity' can become an issue.

© GraCon Design/Shutterstock.com

The "Usable Quantity" Requirement for Possession in Some States

Just about any dollar bill that has been in circulation, certainly those having the $20 denomination, will have trace amounts of cocaine on them. Cases exist where drug-detecting dogs have alerted to a person merely because the person was carrying a large roll of dollar bills. Does this mean that anyone who is carrying a $20 bill is guilty of possession of cocaine?

Not in Nevada, according to its Supreme Court in *Beutler v. State*, 504 P.2d 699 (1972). In *Beutler*, sheriffs entered Ernie Ray Beutler's apartment and seized the following: "candy, vitamin pills, debris from an ash tray, dust particles from a coffee table, a capsule from a waste basket, a match box, brown powder from a compact in the purse of a woman occupant, some 'green leafy substance' from a toilet bowl, several pipes and other items." The court noted:

> The bounty was delivered to Budd F. Rude, who testified that by chemical testing he determined that some of the items were not contraband but that he did identify (a) marijuana and its residue; that it had been smoked in the pipes at an unknown prior time; (b) LSD; (c) sodium seconal barbitol [sic] and (d) one gram of an undetermined mixture of methyl benzoylecgonine and lactose [cut cocaine].

> [There really was not enough marijuana to weigh or to roll even one cigarette, and] he made no quantitative analysis of the seized items. There is nothing in this record to indicate *** that the other items of identified contraband were of a sufficient quantity to be used in the customary manner to obtain a narcotic effect. The pharmacologic potency was not established and there are no statutory provisions to assist or guide the court in making that determination.

The court ruled, "the conviction cannot stand" because:

> **Contraband used as the basis for prosecution must be of such a quantity and quality as to be susceptible of use as a narcotic**. *** We cannot ascertain whether the contraband identified by the chemist meets this test. ***

> **[Possession] of minute quantities of a narcotic, useless for either sale or consumption, is an insufficient foundation upon which to sustain a conviction for possession.** . . . The charge of possession of a narcotic drug requires a union of act and intent. **The intent necessary to establish the crime of possession simply does not exist when the amount is so minute as to be incapable of being applied to any use, even though chemical analysis may identify a trace of narcotics."** ***[117]

The Supreme Court of Hawaii, in *State v. Vance*, 602 P.2d 933 (1979), reached a different conclusion. In this case, an officer arrested the defendant, John Ray Vance, when Vance knocked "a fellow policeman unconscious." Before placing Vance in a holding cell, police searched him for weapons and contraband, finding in his pants pocket "a small bottle containing a white powder with a silver spoon-like object attached to it and a glass vial containing a white powder residue." Later chemical testing revealed that the ".7584 gram of white powder" contained "approximately 17.5 percent cocaine or a total of .1327 gram of the narcotic drug."

The issue on appeal was "Whether the prosecution must prove that [possession of] a usable amount of the drugs or quantities capable of producing a narcotic effect to sustain a conviction." *Vance* refused to find a "usable quantity" requirement in Hawaii:

> [Defendant argues that a drug conviction] may not be sustained without proof of narcotic potential or an amount usable for sale or consumption and that the prosecution failed to proffer such evidence.

> [Defendant cites cases where] courts have inferred a usable quantity standard in laws making criminal the possession of "a" or "any" narcotic drug. These cases involved statutes that were silent as to quantity of drug necessary to constitute a violation. In *People v. Leal*, for example, **the Supreme Court of California held that possession of useless traces of a narcotic does not constitute a criminal act** within the meaning of Health and Safety Code § 11500. That provision *** did not expressly specify the amount necessary to be punishable under the statute.

> **We are also aware that courts in at least an equal number of jurisdictions have followed a different line of interpretation. These courts have interpreted similar statutory provisions to prohibit the possession of any identifiable quantity of the narcotic drug.** *** The rationale for these decisions is that statutes regulating possession of narcotic drugs are designed to prohibit the illegal possession of any amount of such drugs, and that, in the absence of a specific statutory provision, a usable quantity standard should not be implied. ***

> Unlike the statutes considered in the cases cited above, [**Hawaii's**] HRS § 712-1243 directly addresses the issue of the amount of a dangerous drug necessary to constitute an offense under the statute. HRS § 712-1243 states in full as follows:

> (1) **A person commits the offense of promoting a dangerous drug in the third degree if he knowingly possesses any dangerous drug *in any amount*.** ***

117. Reprinted with the permission of LexisNexis.

HRS § 712-1243 is part of a statutory scheme designed to provide more severe punishment for possession of greater quantities of drugs. [The Commentary states in pertinent part as follows: It is the purpose of the Code to hit hardest at the illegal trafficker in dangerous drugs, harmful drugs, and detrimental drugs. The scheme devised for so doing is to arrange the sanctions relating to each substance, either for possession or distributing, on the basis of the amounts involved. Such amounts are meant to reflect, i.e., provide an indicia of the position of the defendant in the illegal drug traffic.]

The statutory design indicates that the Legislature not only carefully considered the precise amount of a drug that need be possessed to constitute an offense under the relevant statute but that they devised their entire scheme of sanctions on the basis of the amounts involved. Thus, the direct and unambiguous language of our statute prohibits us from judicially amending the provision to include a usable quantity standard.

[Under] HRS § 712-1243 the State must prove only the knowing possession of a dangerous drug in any amount and that the conviction of John Vance for the possession of .1327 gram of cocaine [was] not in error.

*** We, therefore, affirm the convictions below.[118]

VIDEO: Police Shoot and Arrest Armed Suspect

WARNING: GRAPHIC VIDEO. Officers approach, shoot and handcuff an armed suspect at:

https://www.youtube.com/watch?v=yHK41COLq6Y

Do's and Don'ts for Hearings, Trials, and Appeals

Rebuttal

Don't "sandbag." During rebuttal, an attorney is supposed to limit his or her witnesses to "rebutting," or proving wrong, the opposing side's witness testimony. A prosecutor should not instead call a witness to prove the guilt of the defendant, for this was supposed to be done in the prosecution's "case-in-chief," where the D.A. provided all evidence to prove the defendant committed the crime charged. **Do** call witnesses to show the bias, inaccuracy, or confusion of opposing counsel's witnesses.

118. Reprinted with the permission of LexisNexis.

Can a Person Be Found Guilty of "Possession" if He Has Used Up the Evidence before Arrest?

The Supreme Court of California considered this issue in *People v. Palaschak,* 9 Cal. 4th 1236 (1995). In this case, the defendant, Douglas Andrew Palaschak, asked the receptionist of his law office, Jessica Jobin, to get him some lysergic acid diethylamide (LSD). Jobin then obtained fifty doses of LSD and gave defendant a birthday card containing two "hits" or doses of LSD. Both defendant and Jobin consumed LSD. Defendant told his secretary, Melissa S., that he was "frying on acid" and asked her "to join them." Instead, Melissa called the police, who:

> found defendant and Jobin experiencing symptoms of LSD ingestion, namely, hallucinations, confusion, dizziness, and lip-licking. Defendant volunteered that he had taken LSD and requested assistance from the officers. Jobin produced the 46 remaining hits of LSD from her purse at the officers' request. The officers then arrested Jobin and defendant.

> One month after his arrest, defendant admitted to two newspaper reporters that he had ingested LSD on the day of his arrest. He stated that the drug provided "a better social environment" in his office.

A jury convicted the defendant of (Health & Saf. Code, § 11377, subd. (a)). The Court of Appeal held that the defendant could not have committed possession of LSD because, "by the time of his arrest, he had ingested the LSD formerly in his possession and no longer had 'dominion and control' over the substance in his body." The Supreme Court overruled the Court of Appeal, explaining:

> [We] consider whether a person who possesses illegal drugs prior to ingesting them may be convicted of the offense of possessing those drugs. **[An offender may be convicted of drug possession] despite having ingested the drugs prior to arrest.** To rule otherwise would read into the drug possession statutes a "possession when arrested" requirement that would permit persons facing arrest for possession of illegal drugs to avoid possession charges merely by ingesting those drugs.

The Court of Appeal had been swayed by the following argument: "(If) proof of ingestion of illegal drugs were sufficient to sustain a possession charge, then every person under the influence of an illegal drug could be charged with possessing it because, logically, one who ingests a drug must have possessed it at least temporarily." The Supreme Court was not convinced, declaring, "it is arguable that not all occasions of drug use necessarily and inevitably involve criminal possession. For example, depending on the circumstances, mere ingestion of a drug owned or possessed by another might not involve sufficient control over the drug, or knowledge of its character, to sustain a drug possession charge." The Court of Appeal's argument:

> makes little sense when applied to a case, such as the present one, in which there exists sufficient direct or circumstantial evidence of past possession, over and above evidence of mere use or ingestion. Here, *** defendant was "charged with possession on May 9, 1991, not possession at the time of arrest." A simple hypothetical example may help to illustrate the primary problem with the Court of [Appeal's analysis. If the evidence showed that the defendant was in possession of an illegal drug that he *destroyed* by flushing it down the toilet, defendant nonetheless could be convicted of illegal possession based on evidence, whether direct or circumstantial, that the substance was in his possession immediately before he was arrested.]

The Supreme Court reversed the Court of Appeal, explaining:

[Loss or destruction of evidence *by ingestion* should not defeat a possession charge.]

[We see no reason why a drug possession charge could not be based on direct or circumstantial evidence of past possession. **[The narcotics possession statutes do not require proof of possession *at the very time of arrest*.]**

The essential elements of possession of a controlled substance are "dominion and control of the substance in a quantity usable for consumption or sale, with knowledge of its presence and of its restricted dangerous drug character. Each of these elements may be established circumstantially." [These] elements of possession were amply established by the evidence in this case, which included the testimony of a percipient witness, defendant's secretary, Jobin. Thus, the record shows that defendant requested and obtained from Jobin two doses or "hits" of LSD contained in a birthday card. Defendant kept the card for a day, then removed the LSD from the card and ingested one and one-half doses, giving the remaining half dose to Jobin. On being arrested, defendant readily admitted ingesting the drug. He confirmed this fact to news reporters. The arresting officers testified that defendant was under the influence of LSD, and lab technicians verified that the remaining doses of LSD in Jobin's possession were indeed LSD. [There is no question that Defendant possessed LSD prior to ingesting it.]

[If direct or circumstantial evidence establishes that the defendant possessed an illegal drug, no compelling reason appears why that evidence should not be sufficient to sustain a possession conviction. Judgment of the Court of Appeal is reversed.][119]

LEGAL ANALYSIS

State v. Gradt
192 Wash.App. 230 (2016).
Judge Maxa delivered the opinion for the Court of Appeals of Washington.

Facts

[Michael R. Gradt, convicted of possession of 40 grams or less of marijuana, challenges the district court's failure to dismiss his charges after voters passed Initiative 502 (I–502), which decriminalized the possession of small quantities of marijuana. *** Gradt argues that I–502 should be applied to marijuana possession charges pending at the time it became effective despite [a] general saving statute, which requires criminal charges to be prosecuted based on the law in effect at the time of the crime. We hold that the saving statute has no effect because I–502 expressed an intent to dismiss all pending prosecutions of marijuana possession. [We reverse and dismiss Gradt's conviction.]

On September 15, 2012, Gradt received a citation for possession of 40 grams or less of marijuana in violation of RCW 69.50.4014. At the time, Gradt was 61 years old.

119. Reprinted with the permission of LexisNexis.

On November 6, 2012, Washington voters passed I–502, which decriminalized possession of small amounts of marijuana for individuals over 21 years of age. Initiative 502, § 20(3), Laws of 2013, ch. 3. Under the Washington Constitution, I–502 became effective 30 days later, on December 6, 2012. CONST. art. II, § 1(d).

[Gradt] filed a motion to dismiss his pending prosecution in light of I–502. The district court denied his motion. [The district court subsequently found Gradt guilty of possessing 40 grams or less of marijuana.]

Issue

Whether Washington State should prosecute the defendant for marijuana possession that occurred prior to the decriminalization of marijuana possession in the state.

Rule and Analysis

Under the common law, all pending criminal charges must be prosecuted based on the law in effect at the time of trial. [The general saving statute, partially repealing the common law,] "saves" offenses already committed from the effects of amendment or repeal and requires that crimes be prosecuted under the law in effect at the time of the offense, unless an intent to affect pending litigation was expressed in the amending or repealing act. [The general saving statute provides in part:]

No offense committed . . . previous to the time when any statutory provision shall be repealed . . . shall be affected by such repeal, *unless a contrary intention is expressly declared in the repealing act.* ***

Gradt argues that [the general saving statute] is inapplicable because I–502 conveys an intention to apply its repeal of the crime of possession of small quantities of marijuana to pending charges for that crime. We agree.

Prior to the passage of I–502, former RCW 69.50.4014 (2012) criminalized the possession of 40 grams or less of marijuana as a misdemeanor. Section 20(3) of I–502 proposed an amendment to former RCW 69.50.4013 providing that "[t]he possession, by a person twenty-one years of age or older, of useable marijuana or marijuana-infused products in amounts that do not exceed those set forth in section 15(3) of this act is not a violation of this section, this chapter, or any other provision of Washington state law."

Section 1 of I–502, *** states:

The people intend to stop treating adult marijuana use as a crime and try a new approach that:

(1) Allows law enforcement resources to be focused on violent and property crimes;

(2) Generates new state and local tax revenue for education, health care, research, and substance abuse prevention; and

(3) Takes marijuana out of the hands of illegal drug organizations and brings it under a tightly regulated, state-licensed system similar to that for controlling hard alcohol.

Laws of 2013, ch. 3. ***

The people decided to decriminalize possession of small amounts of marijuana in part to allow "law enforcement resources to be focused on violent and property crimes." * However, if the State continued to prosecute possession of small amounts of marijuana occurring before I–502's effective date, law enforcement resources would continue to be diverted from violent and property crimes long after I–502's effective date.** For example, the State has continued to devote resources to this case more than three years after the initiative passed. ***

Because the intent language of I–502 can be reasonably interpreted as applying to charges pending when the initiative took effect, we hold that the language of section 1 of I–502 fairly conveys an intention to apply the initiative's decriminalization of marijuana possession to charges for possession of small amounts of marijuana that were pending on I–502's effective date. In addition, the stated purpose of refocusing law enforcement resources signals that any ambiguity should be resolved in this manner. Therefore, we hold that the general saving statute is inapplicable to I–502. ***

Conclusion

Gradt was charged with possession of a small amount of marijuana before enactment of I–502, but his conviction occurred after its effective date. [The State could not lawfully prosecute Gradt for possession of a small amount of marijuana after the initiative's effective date. We reverse and dismiss Gradt's conviction.][120]

VIDEO: Sheriffs in Arizona Arrest Drug Dealer

Maricopa County Sheriffs arrest a drug dealer and recover his tar heroin at:

https://www.youtube.com/watch?v=bit0mYbdnBk

Deaths Resulting from Government Policies during Prohibition, America's Prior War on Drugs

Deborah Blum, in her July/August article in *Mental_Floss*, "4 Toxic Moments in History," described a dangerous policy the United States government pursued to combat the drinking of alcohol during prohibition.

The entire article can be viewed at:

http://mentalfloss.com/article/51750/4-toxic-moments-history

Learn from My (and Others') Mistakes

Fully Pay Attention to Everything Happening in the Courtroom

During a preliminary hearing for arson, I focused intently on my witness, a donut shop owner who was explaining how the defendant had poured gasoline over the front of her store. I honed in on her testimony so much that I missed what else was happening in the courtroom. It turned out that the defendant had been repeatedly yelling "F--- Y--" to the judge. The judge had responded by ordering the defendant to stop and threatening to find him in contempt. I suddenly became aware of the problem when the judge shouted to have the defendant "gagged and shackled." When the defendant returned, he had a gag that covered his face up to his eyes and wore chains connecting his handcuffs and leg shackles. My inattention did not harm my case, but I did miss quite a show.

---

120. Reprinted from Westlaw, with permission of Thomson Reuters.

C. POSSESSION FOR SALE

While possession for sale or possession with the intent to distribute requires all the elements existing in simple possession, **these aggravated possession crimes also require that the prosecution prove the additional element of intent to commit future sale or distribution.** As with all criminal cases, although we cannot directly know what another person is thinking, **we can use circumstantial evidence to divine intent.** The case below provides such an example.

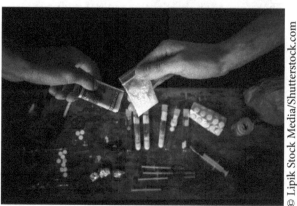

© Lipik Stock Media/Shutterstock.com

Possession for sale can be proven with less evidence than offered in this photo.

LEGAL ANALYSIS

Scott v. Commonwealth
684 S.E.2d 833 (2009).
Justice Powell wrote the opinion of the Court of Appeals of Virginia.

Facts

[During an investigation following a report of drug activity, police noticed that the defendant, William Lee Scott, was holding a hand-rolled cigar containing marijuana. When police began to handcuff Scott, he tried to flee, dropping a loaded 9-millimeter handgun. Officers then searched Scott's clothing] by shaking his pants. Three baggies fell to the ground: one containing marijuana, another containing a single "rock" of cocaine, and a third containing cocaine powder. The total weight of the cocaine was 0.733 gram: 0.443 gram of rock cocaine and 0.290 gram of cocaine powder. [Scott was also in possession of one tablet of 3,4-Methylenedioxyamphetamine [MDA], a Schedule I drug.] The officers did not find a smoking device or distribution paraphernalia such as scales, baggy corners, or razor blades on appellant. ***

At trial, Officer Watson testified as an expert in narcotics distribution. According to Officer Watson, a heavy drug user typically consumed two to three grams of cocaine per day. He testified that, based on the totality of the circumstances, Scott's possession of the drugs was inconsistent with personal use.

[The trial court found Scott guilty of possession of cocaine with intent to distribute.]

Issue

Whether the evidence was sufficient to convict Scott for possession of cocaine with intent to distribute.

Rule and Analysis

[The evidence was sufficient to convict Scott for possession of cocaine with intent to distribute.]

[Because direct proof of intent to distribute drugs is often impossible, it must be shown by circumstantial evidence.] "**Circumstantial evidence is as competent and is entitled to as much weight as direct evidence, provided it is sufficiently convincing to exclude every reasonable hypothesis except that of guilt.**" [The prosecution need only exclude reasonable hypotheses of innocence that flow from the evidence, not those that spring from the imagination of the defendant.]

Among the circumstances that tend to prove an intent to distribute are "the quantity of the drugs seized, the manner in which they are packaged, and the presence of . . . equipment related to drug distribution." *** Pagers and firearms are among the equipment that has been recognized as tools of the drug trade, the possession of which are probative of intent to distribute. **[The absence of paraphernalia suggestive of personal use is regularly recognized as a factor indicating an intent to distribute.]**

"While no single piece of evidence may be sufficient, the 'combined force of many concurrent and related circumstances, each insufficient in itself, may lead a reasonable mind irresistibly to a conclusion.'" *** Here, the only evidence indicating that the drugs were for personal use was the small quantity of drugs found in Scott's possession. [The quantity of narcotics possessed is only one factor to be considered.] **"Thus, a conviction for possession with the intent to distribute may be upheld even though the quantity of drugs seized is consistent with personal use."** ***

There is ample evidence indicating that Scott's possession of the drugs was inconsistent with personal use. Officer Watson, an expert in narcotics distribution, testified that, in light of the "totality of the circumstances," because Scott was carrying a firearm, his possession of drugs was inconsistent with personal use. Possession of a firearm, a recognized tool of the drug trade, is regularly recognized as a factor indicating an intent to distribute. [Officer Watson testified that defendant possessed] no paraphernalia consistent with personal use of cocaine. ***

Also of significance is the fact that Scott possessed multiple drugs. We have recognized that *** simultaneous possession of a combination of disparate drugs can be indicative of the possessor's intent to distribute. [The drugs were packaged individually in baggie corners, making them easier and more profitable to sell.] Finally, it is relevant that Scott compounded the incriminating nature of the circumstances by readily admitting that he smoked marijuana approximately once a week, but made no such admission regarding the cocaine which he possessed. Scott's assertion that he uses one type of drug, contrasted with his silence regarding the use of the other type "undermines [Scott]'s argument that personal use is the only reasonable hypothesis of possession." ***

Conclusion

[The] evidence, when considered as a whole, is sufficient to support the trial court's findings that Scott possessed cocaine with the intent to distribute. [Judgment affirmed.][121]

---

121. Reprinted with the permission of LexisNexis.

Strange Drug Trafficking

Sophia Soo of *Reuters* reported on September 12, 2013, in "Canadian Woman Hides Drugs in Fake Pregnant Belly," that, "Colombian authorities arrest a Canadian woman for trying to smuggle two kilograms of cocaine hidden under a fake pregnancy belly."

The video for this case can be viewed at:

http://www.reuters.com/video/2013/09/10/canadian-woman-hides-drugs-in-fake-pregn?videoId=273730451

D.   SALES, MANUFACTURE, DISTRIBUTION

Washington D.C. Code § 48-904.01: Prohibited Acts A; Penalties

(a) (1) . . . (I)t is unlawful for any person knowingly or intentionally to manufacture, distribute, or possess, with intent to manufacture or distribute, a controlled substance.

(2) Any person who violates this subsection with respect to:

(A) A controlled substance classified in Schedule I or II that is a narcotic or abusive drug shall be imprisoned for not more than 30 years or fined . . . , or both;

(B) Any other controlled substance classified in Schedule I, II, or III, except for a narcotic or abusive drug, is guilty of a crime and upon conviction may be imprisoned for not more than 5 years, fined . . . , or both; except that upon conviction of manufacturing, distributing or possessing with intent to distribute 1/2 pound or less of marijuana, a person who has not previously been convicted of manufacturing, distributing or possessing with intent to distribute a controlled substance or attempting to manufacture, distribute, or possess with intent to distribute a controlled substance may be imprisoned for not more than 180 days or fined . . . , or both;

(C) A substance classified in Schedule IV, is guilty of a crime and upon conviction may be imprisoned for not more than 3 years, fined . . . ; or

(D) A substance classified in Schedule V, is guilty of a crime and upon conviction may be imprisoned for not more than one year, fined . . . , or both.

Marijuana Legalization Comes with Taxation and Regulation

As seen in Colorado below, with legalization of marijuana comes taxation, regulation, and even in certain circumstances, refrigeration:

Colorado: C.R.S.A. 12-43.4-404: Retail marijuana products manufacturing license

(1)(a) A retail marijuana products manufacturing license may be issued to a person who manufactures retail marijuana products pursuant to the terms and conditions of this article.

(b) A retail marijuana products manufacturer may cultivate its own retail marijuana if it obtains a retail marijuana cultivation facility license, or it may purchase retail marijuana from a licensed retail marijuana cultivation facility. A retail marijuana products manufacturer shall track all of its retail marijuana from the point it is either transferred from its retail marijuana cultivation facility or the point when it is delivered to the retail marijuana products manufacturer from a licensed retail marijuana cultivation facility to the point of transfer to a licensed retail marijuana store.

. . .

(d) A retail marijuana products manufacturer shall not accept any retail marijuana purchased from a retail marijuana cultivation facility unless the retail marijuana products manufacturer is provided with evidence that any applicable excise tax due . . . was paid.

(e) A retail marijuana products manufacturer shall not:

(I) Add any marijuana to a food product where the manufacturer of the food product holds a trademark to the food product's name; except that a manufacturer may use a trademarked food product if the manufacturer uses the product as a component or as part of a recipe and where the marijuana product manufacturer does not state or advertise to the consumer that the final retail marijuana product contains a trademarked food product;

(II) Intentionally or knowingly label or package a retail marijuana product in a manner that would cause a reasonable consumer confusion as to whether the retail marijuana product was a trademarked food product; or

(III) Label or package a product in a manner that violates any federal trademark law or regulation.

. . .

(9) All retail marijuana products that require refrigeration to prevent spoilage must be stored and transported in a refrigerated environment.

. . .

"Counterfeit Drug," "Look-Alike Drug" or "In Lieu of" or "Bunk" Crimes

The law considers controlled substances to be so dangerous that even pretending to sell them can be prosecuted as a crime. The Supreme Court of Iowa, in *State v. Freeman*, 450 N.W.2d 826 (1990), offered insight into the criminalization of this activity. In this case, the defendant, Robert Eric Freeman:

agreed to sell a controlled substance, cocaine, to Keith Hatcher. Unfortunately for Freeman, Hatcher was cooperating with the government. Hatcher gave Freeman $200, and Freeman gave Hatcher approximately two grams of what was supposed to be cocaine. To everyone's surprise, the "cocaine" turned out to be acetaminophen. Acetaminophen is not a controlled substance.

A trial judge then convicted Freeman of delivering "a simulated controlled substance with respect to a substance represented to be cocaine, in violation of Iowa Code section 204.401(2)(a) (1987)." The Supreme Court affirmed, reasoning:

Reading sections 204.401(2) and 204.101(27) together shows that **the gist of this offense**

Macadamia nuts, similar to the ones pictured here, have been used in "Look-Alike" drug cases to pass for rock cocaine. Sellers have also used soap chips, pebbles, and hardened pieces of French fries.

© BW Folsom/Shutterstock.com

is *knowing representation* of a substance to be a controlled substance and delivery of a noncontrolled substance. [Statutes like section 204.401(2) are designed "to discourage anyone from engaging or appearing to engage in the narcotics traffic rather than to define the contractual rights of the pusher and his victim.]

Likewise, the Supreme Court of Illinois ruled in *People v. Upton*, 500 N.E.2d 943 (1986), that **"look-alike drug" or "misrepresentation narcotics" statutes were "reasonably related to the legitimate purpose of discouraging illicit traffic in narcotics."** California concurred in *People v. Hill* (1992) 6 Cal. App.4th 33, which noted:

[The "look-alike" statute, HS 11355, entitled "**in lieu of**,"] which in essence proscribes, first, the making of "a 'deal' to supply a controlled substance, and, second, some activity with respect to 'any other liquid, substance, or material' in apparent consummation," may superficially appear aimed at fraud or deceit. However, its true aim is to discourage anyone from engaging or appearing to engage in drug traffic. ***"The vice which the statute attacks is one aspect of the narcotics traffic, not fraud or breach of contract." *** Such transactions, in fact, are illegal *** and therefore *against* public policy to protect.

DISCUSSION QUESTIONS

1. What does the "controlled" in controlled substance crimes mean?

2. Are all controlled substances equally dangerous? What are the criteria used to classify controlled substances?

3. What is the difference between actual and constructive possession? Can a person really possess something they are not touching?

4. What is the difference between possession of a controlled substance and possession of a controlled substance for the purpose of sale?

5. Can a person be prosecuted for a crime for pretending to sell a controlled substance when the substance he or she is selling is actually a "noncontrolled" (lawful) substance? Why or why not?

WEB LINKS

1. The Office of National Drug Control Policy (ONDCP), run by what is informally known as the nation's "drug czar," has a website at: http://www.whitehouse.gov/ondcp

2. To view a summary of the Uniform Controlled Substances Act, visit the Uniform Law Commission at: http://www.uniformlaws.org/ActSummary.aspx?title=Controlled%20Substances%20Act

3. Michael Martinez of *CNN* offered on January 1, 2014, "10 things to know about nation's first recreational marijuana shops in Colorado" which can be seen at: http://www.cnn.com/2013/12/28/us/10-things-colorado-recreational-marijuana/

4. The website for the U.S. Drug Enforcement Administration (DEA) can be visited at: http://www.justice.gov/dea/index.shtml

CHAPTER XIII

Crimes against the State

A. TREASON

1. Common Law

Blackstone, in *Commentaries*, Vol. IV, at 76, **deemed treason to be "the highest civil crime**, which (considered as a member of the community) **any man can possibly commit."** He warned, "it ought therefore to be the most precisely ascertained. For if the crime of high treason be indeterminate, this alone *** is sufficient to make any government degenerate into arbitrary power." Despite this concern, in "the ancient common law, there was a great latitude left in the breast of the judges, to determine what was treason, or not." Blackstone himself offered the following vague definition of treason as involving "a betraying, treachery, or breach of faith."

2. Treason Law in the United States

When our founders crafted the United States Constitution, their abiding concern was to create an effective government while at the same time protect our citizens from official overreach. The Constitution, therefore, was meant to define and limit government power over individual freedom. Since our national charter did not cover wrongs committed by individual citizens, it had no need to

© Lightspring/Shutterstock.com

speak about crimes. The sole exception is treason, which is the only crime the Constitution mentions, as follows:

> **Treason against the United States, shall consist only in levying War against them, or in adhering to their Enemies, giving them Aid and Comfort. No Person shall be convicted of Treason unless on the Testimony of two Witnesses to the same overt Act, or on Confession in open Court.**

United States Constitution, Article III, Section 3.

Legal commentator Mary-Rose Papandrea, in her law review article, *Leaker Traitor Whistleblower Spy: National Security Leaks and the First Amendment* 94 B.U. L. Rev 449 (2014), explained the treason clause as follows:

> **Treason can take two forms**: (1) **levying war against the United States, or** (2) **adhering to the enemy**. No one has been charged with the first type of treason since the end of the Civil War, and while the second type "has achieved a considerably longer and more useful existence," only one person has been charged with treason since World War II.

In identifying the "one person" charged with treason, Papandrea referenced an October 12, 2006, *New York Times* article entitled, "American in Qaeda Tapes Accused of Treason" by Eric Lichtblau. The full article can be viewed at:

http://www.nytimes.com/2006/10/12/us/12treason.html?pagewanted=print&_r=0

Source: Boston University Law Review.

General George Washington was heartbroken by the betrayal of one of his favorite generals, Benedict Arnold, pictured here.

© Everett Historical/Shutterstock.com

VIDEO: U.S. Supreme Court Justice Sonia Sotomayor Discusses Whether the Constitution is a "Living" or "Dead" Document

In a *60 Minutes* interview, Justice Sonia Sotomayor explains why our Constitution is a living document at:

https://www.youtube.com/watch?v=kHvgiEWH6A4

The founders knew what they were about when discussing treason, for they arguably committed it in rebelling against the English crown. The founders' own awareness of their vulnerability to a charge of treason is illustrated by a small story offered by the Franklin biographer, Walter Isaacson in *Benjamin Franklin: An American Life* at 313 (Simon & Schuster 2003):

> At the official signing of the parchment copy [of the Declaration of Independence] John Hancock, the president of the Congress, penned his name with his famous flourish. "There must be no pulling different ways," he declared. "We must all hang together." According to the early American historian Jared Sparks, Franklin replied: "Yes, we must indeed, all hang together, or most assuredly we shall all hang separately." Their lives, as well as their sacred honor, had been put on the line.

The Founders also knew the agony of betrayal. When one of George Washington's favorite generals, Benedict Arnold, turned traitor to the British, Washington was horribly anguished. As noted by Willard Sterne Randall in *George Washington: A Life* at 381 (Henry Holt and Company, Inc. 1997), Washington, with his "head down, hand trembling with its load of treasonous papers," said, "Arnold has betrayed me. Who can I trust now?"

Justice Story, as noted in his 1833 *Commentaries on the Constitution of the United States: With a Preliminary Review of the Constitutional History of the Colonies and States, Before the Adoption of the Constitution*, 669–671 (1833), explained that treason caused so deep a public resentment that even "a charge of this nature . . . whether just or unjust [subjects a person] to suspicion and hatred." The Constitutional Convention therefore created an "impassable barrier against arbitrary constructions" of the law of treason in our country." First, **treason was limited to only two kinds: "the levying of war against the United States," and "adhering to their enemies, giving them aid and comfort."** These two phrases were taken directly from an English statute defining treason so that the words came with a "well-settled interpretation" of what constituted treason.

Justice Story also explained **the Constitutional requirement that conviction for treason could only be based "on the Testimony of two Witnesses to the same overt Act, or on Confession in open Court." These safeguards were meant to protect people "against false testimony, and unguarded confessions, to their utter ruin."**

Treason is so feared and dangerous because it is a crime not just against an individual or group of people, but our entire nation. The U.S. Supreme Court, in *Hanauer v. Doane*, 79 U.S. 342, 347 (1871), declared: **"No crime is greater than treason."** The Court decided *Hanauer* in the wake of the Civil War. The case involved a seller who supplied the confederates. The Court was not sympathetic to the seller's wish to obtain compensation under the contract, as explained below:

> We have already decided *** that a contract made in aid of the late rebellion, or in furtherance and support thereof, is void. *** Any contract, tinctured with the vice of giving aid and support to the rebellion, can receive no countenance or sanction from the courts of the country. ***

No crime is greater than treason. **He who, being bound by his allegiance to a government, sells goods to the agent of an armed combination to overthrow that government, knowing that the purchaser buys them for that treasonable purpose, is himself guilty of treason** *** He voluntarily aids the treason. He cannot be permitted to stand on the nice metaphysical distinction that, although he knows that the purchaser buys the goods for the purpose of aiding the rebellion, he does not sell them for that purpose. The consequences of his acts are too serious and enormous to admit of such a plea. He must be taken to intend the consequences of his own voluntary act.

"Seamless Web" Connection

The discussion above regarding the founders' personal experiences with the dangers of treason and their wise effort to avoid improperly broad definitions of this crime highlight the hazards that can potentially occur when emotion and politics threaten to infect the law. This danger of politics affecting law connects the treason discussion with *Cummings v. Missouri*, the case in Chapter 1 involving bills of attainder passed in the emotional aftermath of the civil war.

Tips for Success for Future Law Enforcement

Respect the Constitution as a Protector of Rights for Everyone Rather Than a Game Used by the Guilty

Some days it will seem as if you are on a crime treadmill, running as fast as you can yet never catching up with all the crimes being committed. Also, there will be certain criminals who are not only guilty but also plain obnoxious. There will be temptations to take shortcuts with the Constitution in order to save valuable time or to seize an opportunity to bring a criminal to justice that will otherwise be irretrievably lost. The criminal before you may hardly seem "worthy" of any Constitutional rights. In these times of stress, it is crucial to remember that the true importance of the Constitution is that it applies to everyone—rights only have meaning if they apply in every situation, no matter how difficult. Remember, we are a nation of laws not of men, so the police can only enforce the law by following the law. You do not want to be responsible for, "Rights declared in words" to "be lost in reality." *Olmstead v. United States*, **277 U.S. 438, 473 (1928)** (Brandeis, J., dissenting).

What exactly is "**adhering to the enemy**"? **This second kind of treason possesses two elements:** (1) "**adhering to the enemy,**" and (2) providing "**aid and comfort**" to the enemy. What **intent** is required to convict for such a crime? The following United States Supreme Court case considers these issues.

LEGAL ANALYSIS

Cramer v. United States
325 U.S. 1 (1945).
Justice Jackson delivered the opinion of the United States Supreme Court.

Facts

Anthony Cramer, the petitioner, stands convicted of violating Section 1 of the Criminal Code, which provides: **"Whoever, owing allegiance to the United States, levies war against them or adheres to their enemies, giving them aid and comfort within the United States or elsewhere, is guilty of treason."**

© Sascha Burkard/Shutterstock.com

Cramer owed allegiance to the United States. A German by birth, [he became naturalized in 1936. He associated with two German saboteurs who in June 1942 landed on our shores from enemy submarines to disrupt U.S. industry.] One of those, spared from execution, appeared as a government witness on the trial of Cramer. He testified that Werner Thiel and Edward Kerling were [saboteurs and explained their plot.]

[Cramer, drafted into the German Army, fought against the United States in 1918. After World War I, he came to this country, intending to remain permanently. Although Cramer had no foreknowledge that saboteurs were coming to this country, he had previously known one of the saboteurs, Werner Thiel, as a coworker and roommate.] Thiel early and frankly avowed adherence to the National Socialist movement in Germany. [He returned to Germany in 1941 to help Germany. Cramer stayed in Indiana, becoming a member and officer of the Friends of New Germany.]

Before the attack upon Pearl Harbor, Cramer openly opposed participation by this country in the war against Germany. He refused to work on war materials. He expressed concern about being drafted into our army and "misused" for purposes of "world conquest." ***

[Finding a note under his door, Cramer went to the Grand Central Station, where Thiel appeared.] Cramer had supposed that Thiel was in Germany. [They had some drinks in a public place.] Cramer denies that Thiel revealed his mission of sabotage. [Cramer suspected that Thiel arrived in America by submarine, but Thiel refused to confirm it.] Thiel asked about a girl who was a mutual acquaintance. [Cramer knew where she was, and wrote to her to come to New York. Thiel gave Cramer his money belt containing $3,600, without disclosing that the German Government provided it. Cramer held onto the money for Thiel.]

After the second of these meetings Thiel and Kerling, who was present briefly at one meeting, were arrested. Cramer's expectation of meeting Thiel later and of bringing him [their mutual acquaintance] was foiled. Shortly thereafter Cramer was arrested, tried, and found guilty. The trial judge [refused to impose death, stating:]

"It does not appear that this defendant Cramer was aware that Thiel and Kerling were in possession of explosives or other means for destroying factories and property in the United States or planned to do that.

"From the evidence it appears that Cramer had no more guilty knowledge of any subversive purposes on the part of Thiel or Kerling than a vague idea that they came here for the purpose of organizing pro-German propaganda and agitation. If there were any proof that they had confided in him what their real purposes were, or that he knew or believed what they really were, I should not hesitate to impose the death penalty."

Issue

Does treason require the overt act be committed with guilty intent?

Rule and Analysis

[Our forefathers were not reluctant to punish as treason any genuine breach of allegiance.] The betrayal of Washington by Arnold was fresh in mind. They were far more awake to powerful enemies with designs on this continent than some of the intervening generations have been. England was entrenched in Canada to the north and Spain had repossessed Florida to the south, and each had been the scene of invasion of the Colonies. [The] settlements were surrounded by Indians—not negligible as enemies themselves, and especially threatening when allied to European foes. The proposed national government could not for some years become firmly seated in the tradition or in the habits of the people. There is no evidence that the forefathers intended to withdraw the treason offense from use as an effective instrument of the new nation's security against treachery that would aid external enemies.

The forefathers also had suffered from disloyalty. Success of the Revolution had been threatened by the adherence of a considerable part of the population to the king. The Continental Congress adopted a resolution after a report by its "Committee on Spies" which in effect declared that all persons residing within any colony owed allegiance to it, and that if any such persons adhered to the King of Great Britain, giving him aid and comfort, they were guilty of treason.

[Their experience with treason accusations was many-sided. Many of them were descendants of those who had fled from measures against sedition and heresy.] **Now the treason offense was under revision by a Convention whose members almost to a man had themselves been guilty of treason under any interpretation of British law.** [The men who framed that instrument [for the most part] had been traitors themselves, and having risked their necks under the law they feared despotism and arbitrary power more than they feared treason.] "Every member of that Convention—every officer and soldier of the Revolution from Washington down to private, every man or woman who had given succor or supplies to a member of the patriot army, everybody who had advocated American independence . . . could have been prosecuted and might have been convicted as 'traitors' under the British law of constructive treason."] Every step in the great work of their lives from the first mild protests against kingly misrule to the final act of separation had been taken under the threat of treason charges. [This was doubtless the meaning of **Franklin's quip at the signing of the Declaration of Independence** that **if the signers did not hang together they should hang separately.** It was also the meaning of the cries of "Treason" which interrupted Patrick Henry in the speech in the Virginia House of Burgesses evoking the famous reply "If this be treason, make the most of it."] The Declaration of Independence [denounced George III "for transporting us beyond Seas to be tried for pretended offenses."]

[**The founders at the Convention looked back upon a long history of use and abuse of the treason charge. History taught them**] **to fear abuse of the treason charge almost as much as they feared treason itself.** The interplay in the Convention of their two fears accounts for the problem which faces us today. ***

[The Convention adopted every limitation upon treason prosecutions that governments had created.] The framers combined all of [the] known protections and added two of their own which had no precedent. They wrote into the organic act of the new government a prohibition of legislative or judicial creation of new treasons. And a venerable safeguard against false testimony was given a novel application by requiring two witnesses to the same overt act. ***

Distrust of treason prosecutions was not just a transient mood of the Revolutionists. In the century and a half of our national existence not one execution on a federal treason conviction has taken place. Never before has this Court had occasion to review a conviction. *** After constitutional requirements have been satisfied, and after juries have convicted and courts have sentenced, Presidents again and again have intervened to mitigate judicial severity or to pardon entirely. We have managed to do without treason prosecutions to a degree that probably would be impossible except while a people was singularly confident of external security and internal stability. ***

[The framers guarded against two dangers of treason prosecutions:] (1) perversion by established authority to repress peaceful political opposition; and (2) conviction of the innocent as a result of perjury, passion, or inadequate evidence. The first danger could be diminished by closely circumscribing the kind of conduct which should be treason—making the constitutional definition exclusive, making it clear, and making the offense one not susceptible of being inferred from all sorts of insubordinations. The second danger lay in the manner of trial and was one which would be diminished mainly by procedural requirements. ***

Treason of adherence to an enemy was old in the law. [The framers restricted treason by "adherence to an enemy" by requiring that there also be conduct which gave the enemy aid and comfort.]

[The] crime of treason consists of two elements: adherence to the enemy; and rendering him aid and comfort. A citizen intellectually or emotionally may favor the enemy and harbor sympathies or convictions disloyal to this country's policy or interest, but so long as he commits no act of aid and comfort to the enemy, there is no treason. On the other hand, a citizen may take actions which do aid and comfort the enemy—making a speech critical of the government or opposing its measures, profiteering, striking in defense plants or essential work, and the hundred other things which impair our cohesion and diminish our strength—but if there is no adherence to the enemy in this, if there is no intent to betray, there is no treason.

[To make treason the defendant not only must intend the act, but he must intend to betray his country by means of the act.]

The indictment charged Cramer with adhering to the enemies of the United States, giving them aid and comfort, and set forth [the following overt acts]:

"1. Anthony Cramer [met] with Werner Thiel and Edward John Kerling, enemies of the United States *** and did confer, treat, and counsel with said Werner Thiel and Edward John Kerling *** for the purpose of giving and with intent to give aid and comfort to said enemies, Werner Thiel and Edward John Kerling.

"2. Anthony Cramer *** did accompany, confer, treat, and counsel with Werner Thiel, an enemy of the United States, *** for the purpose of giving and with intent to give aid and comfort to said enemy, Werner Thiel." ***

[FBI agents testified that Cramer met Thiel and Kerling] and that they drank together and engaged long and earnestly in conversation. This is the sum of the overt acts as established by the testimony of two witnesses. There is no two-witness proof of what they said nor in what language they conversed. There is no showing that Cramer gave them any information whatever of value to their mission. *** No effort at secrecy is shown, for they met in public places. Cramer furnished them no shelter, nothing that can be called sustenance or supplies, and there is no evidence that he gave them encouragement or counsel, or even paid for their drinks.

[It] is difficult to perceive any advantage which this meeting afforded to Thiel and Kerling as enemies or how it strengthened Germany or weakened the United States in any way whatever. It may be true that the saboteurs were cultivating Cramer as a potential "source of information and an avenue for contact."

But there is no proof either by two witnesses or by even one witness or by any circumstance that Cramer gave them information or established any "contact" for them with any person other than an attempt to bring about a rendezvous between Thiel and a girl, or that being "seen in public with a citizen above suspicion" was of any assistance to the enemy. Meeting with Cramer in public drinking places to tipple and trifle [did not advance the saboteurs' mission.]

The shortcomings of the overt act submitted are emphasized by contrast with others which the indictment charged but which the prosecution withdrew [due to] insufficiency of proof. It appears that Cramer took from Thiel for safekeeping a money belt containing about $3,600, some $160 of which he held in his room concealed in books for Thiel's use as needed. [The] rest Cramer put in his safe-deposit box in a bank for safekeeping. All of this was at Thiel's request. That Thiel would be aided by having the security of a safe-deposit box for his funds, plus availability of smaller amounts, and by being relieved of the risks of carrying large sums on his person—without disclosing his presence or identity to a bank—seems obvious. The inference of intent from such act is also very different from the intent manifest by drinking and talking together. Taking what must have seemed a large sum of money for safekeeping is not a usual amenity of social intercourse. That such responsibilities are undertaken and such trust bestowed without the scratch of a pen to show it, implies some degree of mutuality and concert from which a jury could say that aid and comfort was given and was intended. If these acts had been submitted as overt acts of treason, *** we would have a quite different case. *** But this transaction was not proven ***. The overt acts based on it were expressly withdrawn from the jury, and Cramer has not been convicted of treason on account of such acts. We cannot sustain a conviction for the acts submitted on the theory that, even if insufficient, some unsubmitted ones may be resorted to as proof of treason. Evidence of the money transaction serves only to show how much went out of the case when it was withdrawn. ***

[The brief clause defining treason is packed with controversy and difficulty.]

"As there is no crime which can more excite and agitate the passions of men than treason, no charge demands more from the tribunal before which it is made, a deliberate and temperate inquiry. [None] can be more solemn, none more important to the citizen or to the government; none can more affect the safety of both. [It] is, therefore, more safe, as well as more consonant to the principles of our constitution, that the crime of treason should not be extended by construction to doubtful cases. ***

[The treason rule is severely restrictive.] The provision was adopted not merely in spite of the difficulties it put in the way of prosecution but because of them. And it was not by whim or by accident, but because one of the most venerated of that venerated group considered that "prosecutions for treason were generally virulent." Time has not made the accusation of treachery less poisonous, nor the task of judging one charged with betraying the country, including his triers, less susceptible to the influence of suspicion and rancor. The innovations made by the forefathers in the law of treason were conceived in a faith such as Paine put in the maxim that "He that would make his own liberty secure must guard even his enemy from oppression; for if he violates this duty he establishes a precedent that will reach himself." We still put trust in it. ***

Conclusion

We hold that overt acts 1 and 2 are insufficient as proved to support the judgment of conviction. [Reversed.]

Do's and Don'ts for Hearings, Trials, and Appeals

Opening Argument

Do respect the jury's attention span by limiting your argument to the necessary points. However, **don't** be so fearful of the time that you fail to establish all elements of your case beyond a reasonable doubt. **Don't** define the law for the jury, at least not without the trial judge's prior approval, because the judge on his or her own, will interrupt your argument to alert the jury that only the judge can instruct the jury on the law.

---

18 USCS § 2381: Treason

Whoever, owing allegiance to the United States, levies war against them or adheres to their enemies, giving them aid and comfort within the United States or elsewhere, is guilty of treason and shall suffer death, or shall be imprisoned not less than five years and fined under this title but not less than $10,000; and shall be incapable of holding any office under the United States.

In considering the above statute, Justice Scalia in his dissenting opinion in the United States Supreme Court case, *Hamdi v. Rumsfeld*, 542 U.S. 507 560–61 (2004) explained, **"The modern treason statute *** basically tracks the language of the constitutional provision."** He also listed related crimes against the state:

> Other provisions of Title 18 criminalize various acts of warmaking and adherence to the enemy. See, *e.g.*, [Section 32](destruction of aircraft or aircraft facilities), [Section 2332a](use of weapons of mass destruction), [Section 2332b](acts of terrorism transcending national boundaries), [Section 2339A](providing material support to terrorists), [Section 2339B] (providing material support to certain terrorist organizations), *** [Section 2383](rebellion or insurrection), [Section 2384](seditious conspiracy), [Section 2390](enlistment to serve in armed hostility against the United States). ***

Who Is an "Enemy" of the United States and What Constitutes "Aid and Comfort"?

Papandrea, in *Leaker Traitor Whistleblower Spy: National Security Leaks and the First Amendment* 94 B.U. L. Rev 449. 499 (2014), noted that our Constitution does not provide guidance for "defining 'enemy' within the Treason Clause" and "is also silent on whether a formal declaration of war is required." Papandrea explained:

> **[The] few decisions to address the matter limit the term "enemy" to "subjects or citizens of a foreign State at war with our own."** Thus, once war has been declared against the United States, a foreign power's subjects, military, agents, and spies are enemies of the United States until the cessation of hostilities. For example, the Rosenbergs, who famously gave nuclear secrets to the Soviet Union in the 1950s, were not charged with treason because the United States was not at war with Russia at that time. In the context

of the United States' struggle against terrorism, however, organizations such as Al Qaeda might qualify as "enemies" under the Treason Clause.

Assuming Al Qaeda is an enemy under the Treason Clause, the transmission of classified information directly to Al Qaeda would plainly satisfy the "aid and comfort" to the enemy requirement. It does not matter whether the information was useful to the enemy or its disclosure harmful to the United States; indeed, even entirely futile attempts to aid the enemy can be treason. It is less clear whether the government could bring treason charges against someone who disseminates classified information directly to the public (perhaps through a personal blog) or through some sort of media intermediary (such as WikiLeaks or the New York Times) with the asserted intent of informing the American public. [The] Treason Clause does not contain language indicating that aiding the enemy can happen "directly or indirectly." A defendant might argue that aiding the enemy under the Treason Clause requires the government to demonstrate that the individual disclosed the information to the public or through an intermediary with the intent that it would reach the enemy.

The government is likely to respond that the subjective intent of the defendant is irrelevant in determining whether the defendant provided aid and comfort to the enemy. Instead, it might argue, the defendant is assumed to be aware that the enemy can access anything revealed to the public at large. The Court's treason cases do not expressly require one to act with the enemy's consent of the enemy or have any sort of direct relationship with the enemy, although in all of the cases the defendants did, in fact, serve as agents of the enemy. Requiring some sort of direct relationship, agreement, or arrangement with the enemy would seem essential to avoid a dramatic expansion of the Treason Clause. Any number of actions can "aid" the enemy—from sabotaging a weapons plant to criticizing the United States—but unless this act is done at the behest or at least in cooperation with the enemy, it does not seem correct to call this act "treason."

Source: Boston University Law Review.

Learn from My (and Others') Mistakes

Only Use a Bench Warrant on Your Own Witness as a Last Resort

Being a witness is not a pleasant experience. Time in court means lost income from your job or business and disruption of your daily routine. Parking in downtown can be expensive, the waits to be called as a witness long and unpredictable, and the lawyers rude. Many witnesses are hesitant or uncooperative even without having a personal relationship with the defendant or fearing for their lives should they testify. So, many witnesses have to be persuaded to appear in court. Start with compassion and courtesy. Do not make the mistake several young D.A.'s do of quickly threatening to issue a bench warrant to bring the witness to court. Witnesses, when rudely threatened with arrest, will suddenly have memory problems or even testify in a fashion exactly opposite to earlier interviews. Only use a bench warrant when all other options have failed and the witness is absolutely crucial to the case. When I sensed that the phone conversation was going badly, I would confirm with the witness his or her address and biographical details so I would be able to warn about the bench warrant for arrest only as a last resort.

B.   CRIMES UNDER THE ESPIONAGE ACT

Does the "Espionage Act" only cover foreign spies actively committing espionage on the United States? Or does this law have sections that cover other activities, such as the **leaking of sensitive government information? What exactly makes information "sensitive" under the act?** The following case considers such concerns.

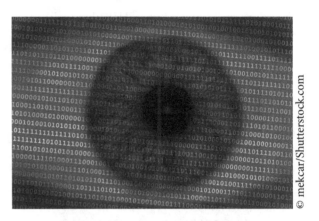

© mekcar/Shutterstock.com

LEGAL ANALYSIS

United States v. Hassan Abu-Jihaad
600 F. Supp. 2d 362 (2009).
Judge Mark R. Kravitz delivered the opinion of the United States District Court for the District of Connecticut.

Facts

[A jury convicted Defendant Hassan Abu-Jihaad for disclosing national defense information to those not entitled to receive it in violation of 18 U.S.C. § 793(d).] The Government alleged that in 2001, while Mr. Abu-Jihaad was serving as a U.S. Navy Signalman aboard the destroyer, the *U.S.S. Benfold*, he disclosed classified information regarding the movement of the Fifth Fleet Battle Group, which included the aircraft carrier, the *U.S.S. Constellation*, to individuals in London associated with Azzam Publications, an organization that the Government alleged supported violent Islamic jihad. According to the Government, Mr. Abu-Jihaad knew or intended that the information he disclosed would be used to kill United States nationals. [A new trial is not appropriate.]

Issue

[**Whether the evidence permits a rational jury to find Mr. Abu-Jihaad guilty of disclosing national defense information to those not entitled to receive it.**]

Rule and Analysis

[**The evidence was sufficient to support a verdict that Mr. Abu-Jihaad disclosed classified information.**]

    Azzam Publications. [The Department of Homeland Security began investigating Azzam Publications ("Azzam"), which operated several websites. Azzam websites contained information that promoted violent Islamic jihad, or "holy war."] Azzam advertised itself as a provider of breaking news about conflict areas like Afghanistan, Bosnia, and Chechnya. [Azzam glorified martyrdom in the name of jihad.]

[An Azzam] website sought cash donations for the Taliban and offered a copy of Osama bin Laden's "Declaration of War Against the Americans Occupying the Land of the Two Holy Places." That Declaration asked Muslims to rise up [against the U.S. and to kill U.S. military personnel in the Arabian Peninsula to rid the Peninsula of infidels.]

The Battlegroup Document. [British authorities, investigating Azzam, found a floppy disk containing a document protected with the password "lp."] The file contained a three-page unsigned document [about the deployment of U.S. Naval Forces from the west coast of the United States to the Persian Gulf in the spring of 2001.]

[This "Battlegroup Document" purported to predict ship movements, as follows:]

In the coming days the United States will be deploying a large naval/marine force to the Middle East.

This will be a two group force: the Battle Group (BG) and the Amphibious Readiness Group (ARG)—[which will replace] the already deployed groups in the gulf.

The BG mission is to hold up the sanctions against Iraq, e.g. patrolling the No-Fly Zone, carry out Maritime Interception Operations (MIO) or launch strikes.

There is a possibility that the ships and submarines that are capable will carry out a strike against Afghanistan. Main targets: Osama and the Mujahideen, Taliban etc.

*** They will meet up with the other ships that are part of the BG which are stationed in Hawaii. Their first port stop is Hawaii on March 20, 2001, where some ships will load Tomahawk D missiles. The same missiles used on Afghanistan and Sudan. ***

[The document included an assessment of the battlegroup's vulnerabilities:]

Weakness:

They have nothing to stop a small craft with RPG etc, except their Seals' stinger missiles. Deploy ops in Gulf 29 April–04 October. 29th APRIL is more likely the day through the Straits. For the whole of March is tax-free—a moral booster. Many sailors do not like the Gulf. *** Please destroy message. ***

Hassan Abu-Jihaad and His E-mail Communications With Azzam. [A U.S. agent located eleven e-mails between Azzam and Abu-Jihaad sent during the time when Abu-jihaad was assigned to the *Benfold*. The Defendant, born Paul Raphael Hall, had legally changed his name to "Hassan Abu-Jihaad" in 1997. Mujahideen often choose as a "nom de guerre" an Arabic "kunya," which begins with "Abu," meaning "father of." The term "jihad"] literally means "holy struggle," and in the context of mujahideen "exclusively refers to individuals on a battlefield, fighting in the cause of Allah."

[In his e-mails, Abu-Jihaad shared with Azzam] his identity and his status as an active member of the U.S. Navy stationed aboard a warship deployed to the Persian Gulf. The e-mails [showed that Abu-Jihaad read the Azzam websites, bought Azzam videos that supported violent Islamic jihad, and himself supported violent Islamic jihad.]

The jury heard testimony [that Abu-Jihaad praised the suicide boat bombing of the *Cole*—a U.S. Navy destroyer like the *Benfold*—as a "martyrdom operation."] Al-Qaida had taken public credit for the bombing, which killed seventeen U.S. sailors and caused millions of dollars of damage. ***

The Battlegroup Mission and Transit Plan. *** The final version of the Transit Plan dated February 24, 2001, contained a port call that had not appeared in the [earlier] revisions: a brief stop for the *Benfold* to load ammunition at the naval magazine in Lualualei, Pearl Harbor, Hawaii on March 20, 2001. *** The *Benfold* was the only ship in the battlegroup to pull into Pearl Harbor to load ammunition.

*** Commander Wylie testified that before the *Benfold's* deployment from San Diego on March 15, 2001, access to the Transit Plan would have been limited to the ship's officers, the operations specialists in the CIC, the quartermasters and signalmen, and the radio operators who processed the message. *** Commander Wylie testified that during this period, the signalmen worked alongside the quartermasters to finish last-minute preparations for the ship's charts. [As a signalman on the *Benfold*, Mr. Abu-Jihaad had access to the Transit Plan.]

Confidential Information. The Transit Plan was classified at the "confidential" level. [Information can be classified] ranging in increasing seriousness from "confidential," to "secret," to "top secret." "Confidential" information is defined as "information, the unauthorized disclosure of which reasonably could be expected to cause damage to the national security." ***

[To] be found guilty of disclosing national defense information to those not entitled to receive it in violation of 18 U.S.C. § 793(d), the Government was required to prove the following essential elements:

(1) [Abu-Jihaad] **lawfully had possession of, access to, control over, or was entrusted with information relating to the national defense.**
(2) [Abu-Jihaad] **had reason to believe that such information could be used to the injury of the United States or to the advantage of any foreign nation.**
(3) [Abu-Jihaad] **willfully communicated, delivered, transmitted or caused to be communicated, delivered, or transmitted such information.**
(4) [Abu-Jihaad] **did so to a person not entitled to receive it.**

[The Court declines to set aside the jury's conviction on the disclosure of classified information charge.]

[Abu-Jihaad makes two main challenges to the jury's verdict. First, he argues that the information in the Battlegroup Document did not relate to the national defense and was not "closely held."] Second, he argues that the evidence was insufficient [to show] he communicated national defense information to a person not entitled to receive it.

1. Closely Held National Defense Information. [Abu-Jihaad argued that much of the information in the Battlegroup Document is flat wrong and/or was commonly known and therefore could not] relate to our national defense. The Government rejoins that there are three specific pieces of information in the Battlegroup Document that *** do relate to national defense and were closely held as of the date the Battlegroup Document was apparently created:

▶ The fact that vessels would stop in Hawaii on March 20, 2001, to load ammunition;
▶ The fact that the battlegroup would deploy from San Diego on March 15 and the *Constellation* would be in Sydney, Australia, on April 6, 2001; and
▶ The fact that the battlegroup would transit the Strait of Hormuz *** on April 29, 2001.

[A rational jury could conclude that each of these pieces of information constituted closely held national defense information.]

["National] defense" is a "generic concept of broad connotations, referring to the military and naval establishments and the related activities of national preparedness." [**The phrase 'information relating to the national defense' has consistently been construed broadly to include information dealing with military matters.**] "**Congress intended 'national defense' to encompass a broad range of information and rejected attempts to narrow the reach of the statutory language.**"

Given the breadth of the phrase "information relating to the national defense," a rational jury could conclude *** that the particular information noted above qualifies as national defense information. [Advance disclosure of where the battlegroup would be at any point in time was of significant concern.] This was true even of the erroneous information regarding when the battlegroup would transit the Strait of Hormuz. The movement of vessels and the dates on which they will arrive in port or transit the Strait of Hormuz most certainly relates to U.S. Naval Forces and their preparedness. [While completely inaccurate information may well not relate to the national defense,] the date on which the *Benfold* would arrive in Hawaii to load ammunition was accurate, as was the date the battlegroup would deploy from

San Diego and the date on which the *Constellation* would be in Sydney. The Battlegroup Document was wrong about the date for transiting the Strait of Hormuz—it was not the evening of April 29 but rather was the evening of May 2 ***. Nonetheless, given the proximity of the dates, [there was still a concern] if enemies of the United States knew that information. [The] Strait of Hormuz is a choke point where U.S. Navy vessels are particularly vulnerable to attack. [Disclosure] of where the battlegroup would be at any particular time is of significant concern because disclosure eliminates "one of the key tactical elements that you like to have on your side, which is surprise." ***

["**Information relating to the national defense has two limits.**] First, the information must be "closely held."** In *United States v. Heine*, 151 F.2d 813 (2d Cir. 1945), the defendant was indicted for espionage because during the early stages of World War II he had provided a German automobile company with information about the U.S. aviation industries that he gathered from magazines, books, newspapers, and publicly available catalogs and journals. All of the information provided by the defendant "came from sources that were lawfully accessible to anyone who was willing to take the pains to find, sift and collate it." [Disseminating] information that the Government had never kept secret could not support a conviction for espionage. ***

[Abu-Jihaad argues that so much information about the battlegroup was publicly available] that the information in the Battlegroup Document was not closely held. [A] rational jury could find] that the above-noted three pieces of information were closely held by the Government. [The information in the Transit Plan] was classified confidential and was not to be shared with individuals who did not have authority to obtain that information. [The] classification of the information by the executive branch is highly probative of whether the information at issue is 'information relating to the national defense.'" *** Abu-Jihaad received training on the classification of documents and therefore knew that information in the Transit Plan was not to be shared with unauthorized individuals.

[While] there was ample public information available about the general movement of the battlegroup, [there was no public information about a] stop in Hawaii on March 20. [A jury could conclude that the information about the dates for the stop in Hawaii] and the transit of the Strait was closely held.

[**The second limit**] on the scope of national defense information is [**that the individual who discloses national defense information have "reason to believe the information**] could be used to the injury of the United States or to the advantage of any foreign [nation."**] Mr. Abu-Jihaad makes no argument based on this element, and for good reason. [Advance] disclosure of specific dates for ammunition loading, port calls, or transiting the Strait could be used to injure the United States. The *** Battlegroup Document, which focuses on vulnerabilities and weaknesses, only confirm that the information in the document is intended to injure the United States. [The jury could conclude] that Azzam was a conduit of information to violent Islamic jihadi groups. In view of what happened to the *Cole*, it is abundantly clear that advance knowledge of key battlegroup dates by Islamic jihadi groups would be injurious to U.S. interests.

2. Disclosure by Mr. Abu-Jihaad. [A jury could conclude that] Abu-Jihaad was the source of the national defense information [by finding that] Abu-Jihaad supplied the key national defense information in the Battlegroup Document. [Abu-Jihaad had a motive to disclose national defense information to Azzam.] From the Azzam websites, which *** Mr. Abu-Jihaad visited frequently, he knew that Azzam supported the Taliban, al-Qaida, and violent Islamic jihad. *** Azzam had sought support from its readership for the Taliban [and] extolled the virtues of martyrdom. [In his *Cole* e-mail] Abu-Jihaad praised the bombing of the *Cole* as a "martyrdom operation," and derided the United States as an "infidel" and "Kuffar nation." It is also fair to read his e-mail as giving thanks to the "mujahideen" as "american enemies" and as the "true champions and soldiers of Allah." ***

[**The jury could conclude that**] Abu-Jihaad had access to the information in the Battlegroup Document. [As a signalman,] Abu-Jihaad has access to the Transit Plan. He had a "secret" clearance, was a member of the navigational division that was working on the Transit Plan, and had access to the chart room where the Transit Plan was kept. [The] nature of the information contained in the Battlegroup Document is consistent with that which would come from a person, like Mr. Abu-Jihaad, who had access only to the Transit Plan, and not also to the SIPRnet, which contained significantly more classified information. ***

[Abu-Jihaad] had the opportunity to convey this information to Azzam. [He] was in frequent communication with Azzam. [He] is the only person with a military e-mail address that Azzam chose to save in its address book. ***

[Abu-Jihaad was] interested in secrecy, since he used coded words to discuss jihad and logistics. [**A jury could conclude**] **that Mr. Abu-Jihaad may well have provided intelligence information while in the Navy.** *** The information in the Battlegroup Document appears to come from an insider who has specific knowledge of some things and imperfect knowledge of other matters. [The document also ended with: "Please destroy message."] If the Battlegroup Document had been created from open-source information or from guesses about port dates based on a review of internet postings, there would be no reason to include such a plea. ***

Conclusion

A rational jury could find Mr. Abu-Jihaad guilty of disclosing national defense information to those not entitled to receive it.[122]

This Cuban postage stamp commemorates the 25th anniversary of the U.S. execution of Ethel and Julius Rosenberg for espionage.

Russians Hack Pentagon

In his December 15, 2016, *CBS News* article, "Russian hack almost brought the U.S. military to its knees," David Martin reported that Russian hackers attacked the Joint Chiefs of Staff email. The article can be viewed at:

https://www.cbsnews.com/news/russian-hack-almost-brought-the-u-s-military-to-its-knees/

---

122. Reprinted with the permission of LexisNexis.

Biography—Defense Counsel

Clarence Darrow

- Born on April 18, 1857, in Kinsman, Ohio.
- Attended the University of Michigan Law School.
- Once represented railroads, but resigned to defend Eugene Debs—who would later become the Socialist Party candidate for president of the U.S.—and who was currently the president of the American Railway Union fighting the railroads in the Pullman Strike.
- Represented convicted murderers Leopold and Loeb, saving them from the death penalty.
- Defended John T. Scopes, a Dayton, Ohio, high school teacher accused of violating state law by teaching Darwin's theory of evolution, in the famous "Monkey Trial."
- During the Scopes trial, **Darrow called William Jennings Bryan**, who was helping the prosecution, **to the witness stand and severely cross-examined him about his belief in the literal truth of the Bible. Days after the trial, Bryan died**, perhaps due to the strain of defending his religious views at trial.
- According to T.A. Frail, in a Smithsonian.com article, "Everything You Didn't Know About Clarence Darrow," at http://www.smithsonianmag.com/history/everything-you-didnt-know-about-clarence-darrow-14990899/#BelG2bXxvDRV0hPC.99, Darrow might have tried to bribe potential witnesses in one of his cases.
- Chose to defend underdogs, whether strikers, anarchists, or criminal defendants.

Is Julian Assange Guilty of Espionage?

Ellen Nakashima and Jerry Markon reported in their November 30, 2010, *Washington Post* article, "WikiLeaks founder could be charged under Espionage Act" that authorities were investigating the possibility of criminal law violations.

The full article can be viewed at:

http://www.washingtonpost.com/wp-dyn/content/article/2010/11/29/AR2010112905973.html

---

Bradley Manning and Edward Snowden: Traitors or Whistleblowers?

Charlie Savage, in his July 30, 2013, *New York Times* article, "Manning Is Acquitted of Aiding the Enemy," reported that a military judge found Pfc. Bradley Manning not guilty of the charges against him.

The full article can be viewed at:

http://www.nytimes.com/2013/07/31/us/bradley-manning-verdict.html

Charlie Savage and Emmarie Huetteman, in their August 21, 2013, *New York Times* article, "Manning Sentenced to 35 Years for a Pivotal Leak of U.S. Files" reported later that Pfc. Bradley Manning did get sentenced for leaking information.

The full article can be viewed at:

http://www.nytimes.com/2013/08/22/us/manning-sentenced-for-leaking-government-secrets.html?_r=0

Although, as noted above, Manning was accused of committing a "gigantic leak," apparently his is dwarfed by the repeated and continuing leaks by Edward Snowden. In an "NBC News Exclusive with Brian Williams," the *Nightly News* anchor interviewed Edward Snowden in Moscow. Brian Williams reported that "the 30 year old American . . . is responsible for the most staggering theft of American intelligence secrets in the modern era. He is wanted on espionage charges. He continues to live in exile in Russia." The interview includes a discussion of Snowden's role in United States intelligence.

Last year, when Snowden began leaking details of NSA spying programs and left the country, administration officials played down his work history, using descriptions such as "systems administrator" to describe his role at the agency. In June, President Barack Obama himself told reporters: "No, I'm not going to be scrambling jets to get a 29-year-old hacker."

Snowden told Williams that those terms were "misleading."

In the Defense Intelligence Agency job, Snowden said, he "developed sources and methods for keeping our information and people secure in the most hostile and dangerous environments around the world."

The full story and a video can be viewed at:

http://www.nbcnews.com/feature/edward-snowden-interview/exclusive-edward-snowden-tells-brian-williams-i-was-trained-spy-n115746

For a timeline starting at Snowden's birth and highlighting his career and leaks, see:

http://www.nbcnews.com/feature/edward-snowden-interview/edward-snowden-timeline-n114871

This timeline lists various exposures made by Snowden, including "the NSA's (National Security Agency) collection of domestic email and telephone metadata," and an NSA program called PRISM, "which forces biggest US internet companies to hand over data on domestic users," and "Boundless Informant" which shows NSA collected nearly 3 billion pieces of intelligence inside the U.S. in February 2013 alone.

The timeline also provided the government reaction to the revelations, noting that the Justice Department charged Snowden with "theft, 'unauthorized communication of national defense information' and 'willful communication of classified communications intelligence information to an unauthorized person'—the latter two charges violations of the 1917 Espionage Act."

The leaks exposed alarming and questionable activity, such as "NSA funding for British intelligence because U.K. can collect data that would be illegal for NSA to do," and "British cyber spies demonstrated a pilot program to their U.S. partners in 2012 in which they were able to monitor YouTube in real time and collect addresses from the billions of videos watched daily, as well as some user information, for analysis. At the time, they were also able to spy on Facebook and Twitter."

The NSA's collection of phone data prompted conflicting rulings from federal courts and congressional hearings. This is a continuing and evolving story. Papandrea, in *Leaker Traitor Whistleblower Spy: National Security Leaks and the First Amendment* 94 B.U. L. Rev 449 (2014), noted: "Leakers are commonly charged under § 793(d) of the Espionage Act, which applies to those with authorized possession of national security information. This provision prohibits the 'willful' communication of national security documents and information "to any person not entitled to receive it"—which most scholars have interpreted to include the press."

Source: Boston University Law Review.

VIDEO: Snowden Interview

Nightline interviewed Edward Snowden, who released U.S. intelligence secrets at:

https://www.youtube.com/watch?v=FIej-73VLW8

What Is the Problem? True Motives Underlying Tensions between Courtroom Actors

Tensions between Judges and Defense Attorneys

Judges aim to have justice that is not only fair and equal, but also swift. Constantly aware of the crushing volume of cases and the preciousness of time, judges push to move trials along. Defense attorneys also feel the pressure of huge caseloads. However, knowing that the prosecution's case is more like fish than wine, meaning that the State's evidence grows stale over time, defense attorneys might seek "continuances" (postponements) to gather more defense evidence. It does not hurt the defense case if prosecution witnesses become frustrated with continual delays or their memories fade. This institutional conflict between judge and defense attorney can play out in heated discussions over when a case should be brought to trial.

© Everett Historical/Shutterstock.com

C. TERRORISM

18 USCS § 2332a: Use of Weapons of Mass Destruction

(a) Offense against a national of the United States or within the United States. A person who, without lawful authority, uses, threatens, or attempts or conspires to use, a weapon of mass destruction--

(1) against a national of the United States while such national is outside of the United States;

(2) against any person or property within the United States, and

(A) the mail or any facility of interstate or foreign commerce is used in furtherance of the offense;

(B) such property is used in interstate or foreign commerce or in an activity that affects interstate or foreign commerce;

(C) any perpetrator travels in or causes another to travel in interstate or foreign commerce in furtherance of the offense; or

(D) the offense, or the results of the offense, affect interstate or foreign commerce, or, in the case of a threat, attempt, or conspiracy, would have affected interstate or foreign commerce;

(3) against any property that is owned, leased or used by the United States or by any department or agency of the United States, whether the property is within or outside of the United States; or

(4) against any property within the United States that is owned, leased, or used by a foreign government, shall be imprisoned for any term of years or for life, and if death results, shall be punished by death or imprisoned for any term of years or for life.

(b) Offense by national of the United States outside of the United States. Any national of the United States who, without lawful authority, uses, or threatens, attempts, or conspires to use, a weapon of mass destruction outside of the United States shall be imprisoned for any term of years or for life, and if death results, shall be punished by death, or by imprisonment for any term of years or for life.

(c) Definitions. For purposes of this section—

. . . (2) the term "weapon of mass destruction" means . . .

(B) any weapon that is designed or intended to cause death or serious bodily injury through the release, dissemination, or impact of toxic or poisonous chemicals, or their precursors;

(C) any weapon involving a biological agent, toxin, or vector . . . or

(D) any weapon that is designed to release radiation or radioactivity at a level dangerous to human life...

How is the statute, Section 2332a "Use of a weapon of mass destruction" proven, especially in the wake of a terrible tragedy in a highly visible case? The opinions below, involving the prosecution of Oklahoma City Bomber Tim McVeigh, offer insights into the court's handling of these issues. The facts presented come from one opinion while the ruling on the law comes from another opinion in this extensively litigated case.

LEGAL ANALYSIS

United States v. Timothy McVeigh
153 F.3d 1166 (1999).
[Presenting Facts. *Hooks v. Ward,* 184 F.3d 1206 (1999) disapproved of language in the opinion unrelated to this presentation of facts.)]

Circuit Judge Ebel delivered the opinion of the United States Court of Appeals for the Tenth Circuit.

Facts

Defendant-appellant Timothy J. McVeigh *** was tried, convicted, and sentenced to death on eleven counts stemming from the bombing of the Alfred P. Murrah Federal Building *** in Oklahoma City, Oklahoma, that resulted in the deaths of 168 people. ***

At 9:02 in the morning of April 19, 1995, a massive explosion tore apart the Murrah Building in Oklahoma City, Oklahoma, killing a total of 168 people and injuring hundreds more. [A federal grand jury indicted McVeigh and Terry Lynn Nichols] charging: one count of conspiracy to use a weapon of mass destruction in violation of 18 U.S.C. § 2332a and 18 U.S.C. § 2(a) & (b); one count of use of a weapon of mass destruction in violation of 18 U.S.C. § 2332a and 18 U.S.C. § 2(a) & [and other counts.]

*** The destruction of the Murrah Building killed 163 people in the building and five people outside. Fifteen children in the Murrah Building day care center, visible from the front of the building, and four children visiting the building were included among the victims. Eight federal law enforcement officials also lost their lives. The explosion, felt and heard six miles away, tore a gaping hole into the front of the Murrah Building and covered the streets with glass, debris, rocks, and chunks of concrete. [Emergency workers made heroic efforts to rescue people still trapped in the building.]

The Murrah Building was destroyed by a 3,000–6,000 pound bomb comprised of an ammonium nitrate-based explosive carried inside a rented Ryder truck. *** McVeigh and Nichols sought, bought, and stole all the materials needed to construct the bomb. ***

In a letter to Michael and Lori Fortier *** McVeigh disclosed that he and Terry Nichols had decided to take some type of positive offensive action against the federal government in response to the government's siege of the Branch Davidians in Waco, Texas in 1993. [McVeigh told the Fortiers that he planned to blow up a federal building to cause] a general uprising in America and that the bombing would occur on the anniversary of the end of the Waco siege. McVeigh rationalized the inevitable loss of life by concluding that anyone who worked in the federal building was guilty by association with those responsible for Waco.***

During the search of the blast site, the FBI located the rear axle of the Ryder truck used to carry the bomb. The vehicle identification number from the axle matched that of the Ryder truck rented to McVeigh *** and picked up by McVeigh two days prior to the blast. McVeigh rented the truck under the name "Robert Kling" using a phony South Dakota drivers license that Lori Fortier had helped McVeigh create.

McVeigh drove to Oklahoma City in the rented Ryder truck, which he had made into a bomb, parking the vehicle in front of the Murrah Building and running to the yellow Mercury that he and Nichols had stashed as a getaway car in a nearby alley. *** McVeigh deliberately parked the car so that a building would stand between the car and the blast, shielding McVeigh from the explosion. The bomb then exploded.

Just 77 minutes after the blast, Oklahoma State Trooper Charles Hanger [stopped McVeigh because his] car had no license tags. [Hanger arrested, booked, and incarcerated McVeigh for unlawfully carrying a weapon and transporting a loaded firearm.] Two days later *** the federal government filed a Complaint against McVeigh for unlawful destruction by explosives. Oklahoma then transferred McVeigh to federal custody on the federal bombing charges. An FBI test performed later found that McVeigh's clothing and the earplugs contained explosives residue, including PETN, EGDN, and nitroglycerine—chemicals associated with the materials used in the construction of the bomb.

A subsequent inventory search of the yellow Mercury uncovered a sealed envelope containing documents arguing that the federal government had commenced open warfare on the liberty of the American people and justifying the killing of government officials in the defense of liberty. ***

LEGAL ANALYSIS

United States v. Timothy McVeigh
940 F. Supp. 1571 (1996).
Chief Judge Matsch delivered the opinion for the United States District Court of Colorado
[Presenting Issue, Rule, Analysis, & Conclusion].

Issue

Whether an "intention to kill" is an essential element of 18 U.S.C. § 2332a "use of a weapon of mass destruction" or whether the prosecution instead need only prove that the deaths of the victims "resulted from the use of the described explosive device."

Rule and Analysis

[§ 2332a(a) defines] the criminal conduct as using, attempting to use or conspiring to use a weapon of mass destruction against (1) nationals of the United States while outside of the United States, (2) any person within the United States and (3) any property owned, leased or used by the United States. [The statute gives] alternative punishments depending upon **whether death results.** Structurally, there is little doubt that **the conditional phrase "if death results" operates to enhance the penalty when death is the consequence of the criminal conduct.** ***

[Congress] intended that resulting deaths enhance the penalty rather than define the crimes under both § 2332a.

Row of empty chairs at Oklahoma City Memorial.

© Mike McCarville/Shutterstock.com

Conclusion

[**An intention to kill is not required for conviction of the offenses charged.**] The required intent [is an intent to use that a weapon of mass destruction against the persons in the Murrah Building.]

18 USCS § 2332b: Acts of Terrorism Transcending National Boundaries

(a) Prohibited acts.

(1) Offenses. Whoever, involving conduct transcending national boundaries and in a circumstance described in subsection (b)—

(A) kills, kidnaps, maims, commits an assault resulting in serious bodily injury, or assaults with a dangerous weapon any person within the United States; or

(B) creates a substantial risk of serious bodily injury to any other person by destroying or damaging any structure, conveyance, or other real or personal property within the United States . . . ; in violation of the laws of any State, or the United States, shall be punished . . .

(2) Treatment of threats, attempts and conspiracies. Whoever threatens to commit an offense under paragraph (1), or attempts or conspires to do so, shall be punished . . .

(b) Jurisdictional bases.

(1) Circumstances. The circumstances referred to in subsection (a) are—

(A) the mail or any facility of interstate or foreign commerce is used in furtherance of the offense;

(B) the offense obstructs, delays, or affects interstate or foreign commerce . . . ;

(C) the victim, or intended victim, is the United States Government, a member of the uniformed services, or any official, officer, employee, or agent of the legislative, executive, or judicial branches, or of any department or agency, of the United States;

(D) the structure, conveyance, or other real or personal property is, in whole or in part, owned, possessed, or leased to the United States, . . . ;

(E) the offense is committed in the territorial sea . . . ; or

(F) the offense is committed within the special maritime and territorial jurisdiction of the United States...

(g) Definitions. As used in this section--

(1) the term "conduct transcending national boundaries" means conduct occurring outside of the United States in addition to the conduct occurring in the United States; ...

(5) the term "Federal crime of terrorism" means an offense that--

(A) is calculated to influence or affect the conduct of government by intimidation or coercion, or to retaliate against government conduct; and

(B) is a violation of—

(i) . . . destruction of aircraft or aircraft facilities . . . violence at international airports)...arson within special maritime and territorial jurisdiction . . . biological weapons . . . variola virus . . . chemical weapons . . . congressional, cabinet, and Supreme Court assassination and kidnapping . . . nuclear materials . . .

Legal Skills: How to Explain a Case Result to a Victim

Cases do not always go the prosecutor's way. When a district attorney loses a case, or takes a guilty plea to a lesser charge, such results might not meet a victim's expectations. The first task in explaining a result to a victim is to not wait until the bad result occurs. A prosecutor should alert the victim and family members to the possibility of a bad outcome. The presentation of evidence, witnesses' behavior on the witness stand, and juries' decisions are unpredictable. The fact that any trial has risks and that individual cases have particular problems should be fully and clearly explained to those involved, both at the outset and throughout the process in order to minimize surprise.

Candor is crucial. Bad news should not be minimized or hidden because victims need to understand the truth of their situation so that they can best cope with it. Finally, empathy, within the bounds of professionalism, should be part of any discussion. The prosecutor needs to appreciate the ordeal the victim is experiencing in order to provide sufficient help.

Terror by Poison

Ever wonder why so much packaging, seals, and glue surround our over-the-counter medications? The hassle of opening such containers can be traced directly back to the frightening and mysterious murders caused by the "Tylenol Killer" who slipped the poison, cyanide, into bottles of the pain reliever. The consequences of this act of terrorism were analyzed by Dr. Howard Markel in the September 29, 2014, *PBS News Hour* article, "How the Tylenol murders of 1982 changed the way we consume medication." This article can be viewed at:

https://www.pbs.org/newshour/health/tylenol-murders-1982

NPR reported on February 15, 2011, in "The Anthrax Investigation—Timeline: How the Anthrax Terror Unfolded," about a terror attack that occurred quite closely to the 9/11 attacks. One week after the terrorist attack on the World Trade Center and the Pentagon, letters containing anthrax bacteria were mailed to Congress and various media companies. One delivery ultimately killed Bob Stevens, who worked for American Media. This article can be visited at:

https://www.npr.org/2011/02/15/93170200/timeline-how-the-anthrax-terror-unfolded

David Johnston and Carl Hulse of *The New York Times* reported in the February 4, 2004, article, "Ricin on Capitol Hill: The Overview; Finding of Deadly Poison Ricin in Office Disrupts the Senate" that the Senate suffered from a poison scare when ricin was sent to Senator Bill Frist. The article can be visited at:

http://www.nytimes.com/2004/02/04/us/ricin-capitol-hill-overview-finding-deadly-poison-office-disrupts-senate.html

DISCUSSION QUESTIONS

1. Did Edward Snowden commit treason? Was he merely a whistleblower? Is there some crime between these two extremes he committed? What about Bradley Manning or Julian Assange or our nation's founders?

2. What exactly is treason? Does treason actually require that a person go to war against his or her own country, or do other actions fulfill treason?

3. What was treason at common law? Would common law treason pass constitutional muster if it were written in the United States today? Why or why not?

4. Does a person have to be a spy to be prosecuted under the espionage act? Why or why not?

5. What does the federal statute criminalizing use of a weapon of mass destruction require to be proven?

WEB LINKS

1. The United States Department of Justice offered a press release regarding a recent case alleging treason, "U.S. Citizen Indicted on Treason, Material Support Charges for Providing Aid and Comfort to al Qaeda" at: http://www.justice.gov/opa/pr/2006/October/06_nsd_695.html

2. Many of Snowden's revelations were reported by *The Guardian*, a newspaper in England. *The Guardian* can be viewed at: http://www.theguardian.com/us.

3. The Department of Homeland Security, created in the wake of the September 11, 2001, terrorist attacks, can be found at: http://www.dhs.gov/.

4. The Defense Advanced Research Projects Agency (DARPA) pursues scientific and technological research to protect the nation from attack, including terrorist acts at: http://www.darpa.mil/default.aspx. According to Dr. Tony Tether, the director of DARPA, who submitted a report to the *Subcommittee on Terrorism, Unconventional Threats and Capabilities House Armed Services Committee United States House of Representatives* on March 13, 2008: "DARPA was created out of the shock of Sputnik . . . [The] need for DARPA's mission—to prevent the technological surprise of the United States and create it for our adversaries by keeping our military on the technological cutting edge—remains."

CHAPTER XIV

Inchoate (Incomplete) Crimes and Parties to Crimes

© Everett Collection/Shutterstock.com

A. ATTEMPT

The North Carolina Court of Appeals, in *State v. Bumgarner*, 556 S.E.2d 324 (2001), has offered a simple **definition of the crime of attempt**: "**An attempt to commit a crime is an act done with intent to commit that crime, carried beyond mere preparation to commit it, but falling short of its actual commission.**" Although this definition seems obvious and straightforward, it contains several complexities that the courts have had to consider.

1.   Common Law

Suppose there was no law creating criminal liability for those who attempted to commit a crime. Police, seeing a person committing acts that suspiciously looked like he or she was about to commit a crime, could not intervene because there was technically no reason to stop a person who had not violated any law. Crime prevention, to say the least, would be impaired. This scenario is not completely fanciful, for, as Dressler and Michaels noted in *Understanding Criminal Law* by Joshua Dressler and Alan Michaels, Copyright © 2013 by Matthew Bender & Co, **"the general offense of attempt was not recognized until 1784,"** in *Rex v. Scofield*. The authors explained that until *Scofield*, "a miss was as good as a mile." **When the common law did create the crime of attempt, it amounted to only a misdemeanor, "regardless of the nature or seriousness"** of the crime the person was attempting to commit.

The common law compensated in the short term with crimes such as burglary and nightwalking. Burglary at common law could be viewed as a kind of attempt crime for it punished those who broke and entered "with the intent to commit a felony therein," and therefore were *attempting* to commit a crime inside the dwelling house. To understand that nightwalkers were likely committing attempt crimes, one must understand what nightwalking was. During the time of common law, before the advent of electricity, law-abiding citizens stayed indoors when darkness fell. Therefore, as Blackstone explained in his *Commenatries*, Vol. IV, at 289, **nightwalkers, presumably having no reason to lurk about except to commit crimes under cover of darkness, could be arrested and placed in "custody till the morning."**

"Seamless Web" Connection

As noted by the discussion above, "attempt" was not recognized as a crime until the late eighteenth century. Before this, common law had specific crimes, such as burglary, which punished certain attempt conduct rather than a general prohibition against attempt. Here the crime of attempt connects through the seamless web to the crime of burglary, discussed in Chapter 9.

---

2.   Current Law

Model Penal Code § 5.01: Criminal Attempt

(1) Definition of Attempt.

A person is guilty of an attempt to commit a crime if, acting with the kind of culpability otherwise required for commission of the crime, he:

(a) purposely engages in conduct that would constitute the crime if the attendant circumstances were as he believes them to be; or

(b) when causing a particular result is an element of the crime, does or omits to do anything with the purpose of causing or with the belief that it will cause such result without further conduct on his part; or

(c) purposely does or omits to do anything that, under the circumstances as he believes them to be, is an act or omission constituting a substantial step in a course of conduct planned to culminate in his commission of the crime.

(2) Conduct That May Be Held Substantial Step Under Subsection (1)(c). Conduct shall not be held to constitute a substantial step under Subsection (1)(c) of this Section unless it is strongly corroborative

of the actor's criminal purpose. Without negativing the sufficiency of other conduct, the following, if strongly corroborative of the actor's criminal purpose, shall not be held insufficient as a matter of law:

(a) lying in wait, searching for or following the contemplated victim of the crime;

(b) enticing or seeking to entice the contemplated victim of the crime to go to the place contemplated for its commission;

(c) reconnoitering the place contemplated for the commission of the crime;

(d) unlawful entry of a structure, vehicle or enclosure in which it is contemplated that the crime will be committed;

(e) possession of materials to be employed in the commission of the crime, that are specially designed for such unlawful use or that can serve no lawful purpose of the actor under the circumstances;

(f) possession, collection or fabrication of materials to be employed in the commission of the crime, at or near the place contemplated for its commission, if such possession, collection or fabrication serves no lawful purpose of the actor under the circumstances;

(g) soliciting an innocent agent to engage in conduct constituting an element of the crime.

(3) Conduct Designed to Aid Another in Commission of a Crime.

A person who engages in conduct designed to aid another to commit a crime that would establish his complicity under Section 2.06 if the crime were committed by such other person, is guilty of an attempt to commit the crime, although the crime is not committed or attempted by such other person . . . [123]

VIDEO: Suge Knight Charged with Murder and Attempted Murder

WARNING: GRAPHIC VIDEO. In this graphic security camera video, Suge Knight apparently ran over victims. This video can be viewed at:

https://www.youtube.com/watch?v=PwhYxEFqmbw

Tips for Success for Future Law Students and Lawyers

Always Listen to Your Client

While lawyers become deeply involved in their cases, doing their absolute best for their clients, at the end of the day, they do not have to live with the results. While the attorney moves on to the next case, it is the client who has to live with the consequences of the decisions made during negotiation or litigation. Lawyers are supposed to fully inform their clients of all reasonable options available and to specify the costs and benefits of each decision. But, so long as the client is acting legally and with full understanding after complete consultation, his or her judgment decides the goal of the case. (A lawyer, of course, is free to determine tactical decisions.) Therefore, it is important to communicate to the client that the choice is his or hers to make. Then a lawyer must actually listen to what the client decides. Finally, it is important to genuinely honor the client's choice even if you do not agree with it.

An attempt, by definition, is not a completed crime. Since an attempt is essentially a failure, it can be difficult to pinpoint exactly when it is completed. If a person has failed in committing a crime, how can one distinguish between, on the one hand, a "**completed attempt**"—one that can be identified as a criminal attempt worthy of prosecution—and on the other hand, activity which will not fulfill attempt because it was so preliminary as to be "**mere preparation**"? The following case considers various tests, such as "**last proximate act**" and "**overt act**" as possible tools to help answer this issue.

In the case below, Staples planned on burglarizing a bank vault.

LEGAL ANALYSIS

People v. Staples
6 Cal. App. 3d 61 (1970).
Justice Reppy wrote the opinion for the Court of Appeal of California.

Facts

[While his wife was away on a trip, defendant, Edmund Beauclerc Staples, a mathematician, under an assumed name, rented an office on the second floor of a building in Hollywood [knowing that the room was over the vault of the bank below.] Defendant paid rent for the period from October 23 to November 23. The landlord had 10 days before commencement of the rental period within which to finish some interior repairs. [During this prerental period, defendant brought into the office drilling tools, acetylene gas tanks,] a blow torch, a blanket, and a linoleum rug. The landlord observed these items when he [checked on the repair work. Learning that no one was in the building on Saturdays, defendant chose that day to drill two groups of holes into the floor of the office above the vault]. He stopped drilling before the holes went through the floor. He came back to the office several times thinking he might slowly drill down, covering the holes with the linoleum rug. [The] landlord notified the police and turned the tools and equipment over to them. Defendant did not pay any more rent. [Police arrested defendant, who voluntarily confessed in writing as follows:]

"... I drilled some small holes in the floor of the room. Because of tiredness, fear, and the implications of what I was doing, I stopped and went to sleep.

"[The] commencement of my plan made me begin to realize that even if I were to succeed a fugitive life of living off of stolen money would not give the enjoyment of the life of a mathematician however humble a job I might have.

"I still had not given up my plan however. I felt I had made a certain investment of time, money, effort and a certain [psychological] commitment to the concept.

"I came back several times thinking I might *** slowly drill down (covering the hole with a rug of linoleum square. [As time went on, my wife came back and my life as bank robber seemed more and more absurd."]

Defendant was [found guilty of PC 664/459 attempted burglary. He appealed, arguing there was insufficient evidence to] convict him of a criminal attempt.] Defendant claims that his actions were all preparatory in nature and never reached a stage of advancement in relation to the substantive crime which he concededly intended to commit [burglary of the bank vault] so that criminal responsibility might attach.

Issue

Whether there was sufficient evidence that the defendant had:

> **1) the specific intent to commit a burglary of the bank, and 2) that his acts toward that goal went beyond mere preparation.**

Rule and Analysis

[To prove that defendant committed an attempt to burglarize, the prosecution must show that he had the specific intent to commit a burglary of the bank and that his acts toward that goal went beyond mere preparation.]

The required specific intent was clearly established in the instant case. Defendant admitted in his written confession that he rented the office fully intending to burglarize the bank, that he brought in tools and equipment to accomplish this purpose, and that he began drilling into the floor with the intent of making an entry into the bank.

The question of whether defendant's conduct went beyond "mere preparation" [exposes the ambiguity and uncertainty that permeates the law of attempts.]

[The] confusion in this area is a result of the broad statutory language of **PC 664**, which reads in part: **"Any person who attempts to commit any crime, but fails, or is prevented or intercepted in the perpetration thereof, is punishable [for attempt.]"** This is a very general proscription against all attempts [which] does not differentiate between the various types of attempts which may be considered culpable. ***

[There are *at least two* general categories of attempts, both of which fall within the statute.]

In the first category are those situations where the actor does all acts necessary (including the last proximate act) to commit the substantive crime, but nonetheless he somehow is unsuccessful. This lack of success is either a "failure" or a "prevention" brought about because of some extraneous circumstances, e.g., a malfunction of equipment (or) a situation wherein circumstances were at variance with what the actor believe them to be. [The "classic" case occurs when the pickpocket thrusts his hand into an empty pocket.] Certain convictions for attempted murder illustrate the first category. Some turn on situations wherein the actor fires a weapon at a person but misses ***; takes aim at an intended victim and pulls the trigger, but the firing mechanism malfunctions ***; plants on an aircraft a homemade bomb which sputters but does not explode. ***

In the above situations [after] a defendant has done all acts necessary under normal conditions to commit crime, he is culpable for an attempt if he is unsuccessful *because* of an extraneous or fortuitous circumstance. ***

[Under] **California law overt act, which, when added to the requisite intent, is sufficient to bring about a criminal attempt, need not be the last proximate or ultimate step towards commission of the substantive crime.** "It is not necessary that the overt act proved should have been the ultimate step toward the consummation of the design. It is sufficient if it was 'the first or some subsequent step in a direct movement towards the commission of the offense after the preparations are made.' *** **Police officers need not wait until a suspect, who aims a gun at his intended victim, actually pulls the trigger before they arrest him**; nor do these officers need to wait until a suspect, who is forcing the lock of a bank door, actually breaks in before they arrest him for attempted burglary.

This rule makes for a second category of "attempts." *** Applying criminal culpability to acts directly moving toward commission of crime [but short of the last proximate act necessary to consummate the criminal design] under section 664 is an obvious safeguard to society because it makes it unnecessary for police to wait before intervening until the actor has done the substantive evil sought to be prevented. It allows such criminal conduct to be stopped or intercepted when it becomes clear what the actor's intention is and when the acts done show that the perpetrator is actually putting his plan into action. *Discovering precisely what conduct falls within this latter category, however, often becomes a difficult problem.* Because of the lack of specificity of section 664, police, trial judges, jurors, and in the last analysis, appellate courts, face the dilemma of trying to identify that point beyond which conduct passes from innocent to criminal absent a specific event such as the commission of a prohibited substantive crime.

Our courts have come up with a variety of "tests" which try to distinguish acts of preparation from completed attempts. "The preparation consists in devising or arranging the means or measures necessary for the commission of the offense; the attempt is the direct movement toward the commission after the preparations are made." ***

None of the above statements of the law applicable to this category of attempts provide a litmus-like test, and perhaps no such test is achievable. Such precision is not required in this case, however. There was definitely substantial evidence entitling the trial judge to find that defendant's acts had gone beyond the preparation stage. Without specifically deciding where defendant's preparations left off and where his activities became a completed criminal attempt, we can say that his "drilling" activity clearly was an unequivocal and direct step toward the completion of the burglary. *** It was a fragment of the substantive crime contemplated *** i.e., the beginning of the "breaking" element. Further, defendant himself characterized his activity as the *actual commencement of his plan.* The drilling by defendant was obviously one of a series of acts which logic and ordinary experience indicate would result in the proscribed act of burglary. ***

[Bernard Witkin points out the difficulty of pinpointing in any given case the dividing line between acts of preparation and those acts which constitute the completed attempt. He suggests that courts review the entire factual pattern in what might be termed a "common sense approach" rather than trying to extrapolate from precisely drawn lines.]

The instant case provides an out-of-the-ordinary factual situation within the second category. Usually the actors in cases falling within that category of attempts are intercepted or caught in the act ***. Here, there was no direct proof of any actual interception. But it was clearly inferable by the trial judge that defendant became aware that the landlord had resumed control over the office and had turned defendant's equipment and tools over to the police. This was the equivalent of interception. ***

Conclusion

Since the evidence establishes both the defendant's specific intent to complete the attempted crime and that his actions moved beyond mere preparation into an actual attempt, the conviction is affirmed.[124]

Note

The California Supreme Court has echoed *Staples'* analysis in *People v. Kipp* 18 Cal. 4th 349 (1998). In *Kipp*, the court explained:

> **An attempt to commit a crime requires a specific intent to commit the crime and a direct but ineffectual act done toward its commission. *** The act must go beyond mere preparation, and it must show that the perpetrator is putting his or her plan into action, but the act need not be the last proximate or ultimate step toward commission of the substantive crime. *****

A Driver of a Porsche Allegedly Attempts to Murder a Homeless Man

Samantha Schmidt reported on September 13, 2017, for the *Washington Post* in, "Homeless man asked woman to move Porsche so he could sleep. Then she shot him police say," that Katie Quackenbush allegedly responded to a homeless man's complaint about her car's exhaust by exiting her car to shoot him. The article can be visited at:

> https://www.washingtonpost.com/news/morning-mix/wp/2017/09/13/
> homeless-man-asked-woman-to-move-porsche-so-he-could-sleep-then-
> she-shot-him-police-say/?utm_term=.96a49dbc6d82

California Penal Code § 21a: Elements of Attempt

An attempt to commit a crime consists of two elements: a specific intent to commit the crime, and a direct but ineffectual act done toward its commission.[125]

When Do Attempts Start? Distinguishing between "Mere Preparation" and "Actual Attempt"

As explained by the California Supreme Court in *People v. Johnson, People v. Dixon,* and *People v. Lee* (2013) 57 Cal. 4th 250,

> **Criminal activity exists along a continuum**. At its conclusion is the commission of a completed crime, like murder. **The principle of attempt recognizes that some measure**

---

124. Reprinted with the permission of LexisNexis.
125. From *Deering's California Codes Annotated.* Copyright © 2014 by Matthew Bender & Company, Inc., a member of the LexisNexis Group. Reprinted with the permission of LexisNexis.

of criminal culpability may attach before a defendant actually completes the intended crime. Thus, a person who tries to commit a crime but who fails, or is foiled, may still be convicted of an attempt to commit that crime. Yet, attempt still involves both mens rea and actus reus. "An attempt to commit a crime consists of … a specific intent to commit the crime, and a direct but ineffectual act done toward its commission." (§ 21a.) To ensure that attempt principles do not punish a guilty mental state alone, an act toward the completion of the crime is required before an attempt will be recognized. [When a defendant acts with the requisite specific intent, that is, with the intent to engage in the conduct and/or bring about the consequences forbidden by the attempted crime, and performs an act that goes beyond mere preparation and shows that the perpetrator is putting his or her plan into action, the defendant may be convicted of criminal attempt.] For example, if a person decides to commit murder but does nothing more, he has committed no crime. If he buys a gun and plans the shooting, but does no more, he will not be guilty of attempt. But if he goes beyond preparation and planning and does an act sufficiently close to completing the crime, like rushing up to his intended victim with the gun drawn, that act may constitute an attempt to commit murder.[126]

[For example, in *People v. Anderson*,] ("Defendant's conduct in concealing the gun on his person and going to the general vicinity of the Curran theater with intent to commit robbery may . . . be classified as mere acts of preparation but when he 'walked in there [Curran Theater entrance] about two feet from the grill' and 'pulled out the gun' and 'was just going to put it up in the cage when it went off', we are satisfied that his conduct passed far beyond the preparatory stage and constituted direct and positive overt acts that would have reasonably tended toward the perpetration of the robbery . . . .") [In *People v. Morales*, there was] substantial evidence of attempted murder where the defendant "loaded his gun, drove to his victim's neighborhood, and finally hid in a position that would give him a clear shot at [the victim if the victim left by the front door".]

Is "Impossibility" a Defense to Attempt Crimes?

In *State v. Moretti and Schmidt*, 244 A.2d 499 (1968), a man in New Jersey tried to commit an illegal abortion on a woman who was not pregnant. In *People v. Jaffe*, 78 N.E. 169 (1906) a man in New York accepted twenty yards of cloth, believing the cloth to be stolen, only learning later that it was not stolen. In the Missouri case, *State v. Taylor*, 133 S.W.2d 336 (1939), a man offered a bribe to a person he believed was a juror, but who was not actually a juror. In the New York case, *People v. Moran*, 25 N.E. 412 (1890), a would-be thief picked an empty pocket. In *State v. Guffey*, 262 S.W.2d 152 (1953), a hunter in Missouri shot a stuffed deer believing he was shooting a live deer out of season. The person in each case certainly had the blameworthy mens rea to commit a crime. **Yet, each defendant not only did not complete the crime attempted, he or she could not have completed it, because the crime aimed for was impossible to commit under the circumstances. What should the law do with these people?**

The answer the law gives is that "it depends." The traditional approach, discussed by LaFave in *Criminal Law*, at 631, bases the assignment of guilt on the *kind* of impossibility that prevents completion of the crime. According to LaFave, **the kinds of impossibility include (1) Factual impossibility, (2) Legal impossibility, and even (3) Inherent impossibility**.

---

126. Reprinted with the permission of LexisNexis.

a)   Factual Impossibility

LaFave, in *Criminal Law,* at 633, notes that **factual impossibility is not a defense because, "if what the defendant intends to accomplish is proscribed by the criminal law**, but he is unable to bring about that result because of some circumstances unknown to him when he engaged in the attempt, then he may be convicted." Examples LaFave offered include attempting to steal from an empty pocket, trying to kill with an unloaded gun, attempting to commit rape by an impotent man, trying to perform an abortion on an unpregnant woman, and "attempted sexual exploitation of a minor by communicating via the Internet with a person he mistakenly believed was under age." Each of these acts, even if ineffective, is still blameworthy and committed by an individual who could pose a danger if the facts were otherwise.

It would be factually impossible to murder the dead person lying beneath this tombstone.

b)   Legal Impossibility

What if you intended to speed down a highway in a state you have just visited by driving in excess of 65 miles per hour, yet the actual speed limit on that particular highway is 75 miles per hour? You purposely, even with evil intent, planned to violate the law by going 70, but were safely five miles below the limit—did you commit a crime? No, due to the **"legal impossibility"** of committing speeding by going 70 in a 75 miles per hour zone. (This example of course assumes no extra facts such as rain, hazardous road conditions, or presence of road workers or ambulances). LaFave considers a better analysis for such situations to be the fundamental **"principle of legality,"** where **"the defendant did not intend to do anything which had been made criminal, and what is not criminal may not be turned into a crime after the fact by characterizing his acts as an attempt."**

c)   Inherent Impossibility

What if someone threatened to cast a spell of death upon you? Chances are, although you might feel uncomfortable about antagonizing someone so much as to wish for your death, you would not feel that your life was in imminent danger. This is because of the **"inherent impossibility"** of killing someone with a curse. LaFave offered an example presented by Justice Maxey in his dissenting opinion in *Commonwealth v. Johnson*, 312 Pa. 140, 152–53 (1933). In this case, a county prosecutor visited the defendant, a physician, to investigate his curious claims of miraculous cures. The prosecutor falsely told the defendant that he had a sister who was ill.

Defendant told the prosecutor to write her name on a piece of paper. The prosecutor accordingly wrote the fictitious name. Defendant placed this paper on the knob of what was apparently an electrical instrument (which was never plugged to an electrical source) and rubbed it. Having done so he informed the prosecutor that he found his sister had been suffering from sarcoma. He rubbed again several times and then informed his visitors that the sister had a blood clot on the brain, that she had beef worms, that she was anemic and that her gall duct was in good condition. The prosecutor then stated that he would bring his sister in to see defendant, who replied that he did not think it necessary, that he had patients he had never seen who were taking his treatment and being cured, that he had just received a telegram from Europe informing him that his treatments had helped a woman to give birth to a child and that he had patients in England, France, South America, India and Africa, and practically all over the United States. Defendant asked from his visitors for treating their supposititious sister a fee of $65 a month for a period of from nine to twelve months. [The prosecutor paid the defendant] $25 in marked bills, promising the remainder later. They then left defendant's office and shortly thereafter two other county detectives entered and arrested him, finding the marked bills in his possession.

While the Supreme Court of Pennsylvania reinstated the defendant's conviction for attempted theft by false pretenses, Justice Maxey disagreed, offering the following hypothetical example:

Even though a "voodoo doctor" just arrived here from Haiti actually believed that his malediction would surely bring death to the person on whom he was invoking it, I cannot conceive of an American court upholding a conviction of such a maledicting "doctor" for attempted murder or even attempted assault and battery. Murderous maledictions might have to be punished by the law as disorderly conduct but they could not be classed as attempted crimes unless the courts so far departed from the law of criminal attempts as to engage in legislation. A malediction arising out of a murderous intent is not such a substantial overt act that it would support a charge of attempted murder.[127]

LaFave noted this hypothetical example has been the subject of frequent discussion regarding the concept of inherent impossibility.

The Supreme Court of New Jersey in *State v. Moretti and Schmidt,* 244 A.2d 499, 503 (1968), considered the effort to compartmentalize impossibility as an exercise in futility, stating:

Many courts hold that where there is a "legal impossibility" of completing the substantive crime the defendant cannot be guilty of an attempt, but where there is "factual impossibility" the accused may be convicted. We think **the effort to compartmentalize factual patterns into these categories of factual or legal impossibility is but an illusory test leading to contradictory, and sometimes absurd, results.**

The court concluded that the "defense of impossibility in a prosecution for an attempted crime has resulted in a confused mass of law throughout the country."

The Model Penal Code, in Section 5.01(a), aimed to avoid the impossibility conundrum by providing, A person is guilty of an attempt to commit a crime if, acting with the kind of culpability otherwise required for commission of the crime, he:

(a) purposely engages in conduct that would constitute the crime if the attendant circumstances were as he believes them to be.

---

127. Reprinted with the permission of LexisNexis.

3.   Abandonment or Withdrawal

Remember the "humble" mathematician in *People v. Staples* 6 Cal. App. 3d 61 (1970)? In that case, Staples rented a room above a bank in order to burglarize it. He even began drilling down into the floor to enter the bank below. Staples never finished the task for one of two reasons: (1) when his wife returned home, his "life as bank robber seemed more and more absurd," or (2) the landlord stopped him by notifying the police and handing over the burglary tools to them. These facts present the issue of abandonment or withdrawal. If Staples chose on his own to abandon his attempt due to his return to moral reasoning with the return of his wife, then his withdrawal would be voluntary. If instead he only stopped because he was compelled to do so by the landlord and police, then his withdrawal was involuntary. *Staples* explained the legal significance of the defendant's abandonment or withdrawal in California as follows:

> The inference of this nonvoluntary character of defendant's abandonment was a proper one for the trial judge to draw. *** However, it would seem that the character of the abandonment in situations of this type, whether it be voluntary (prompted by pangs of conscience or a change of heart) or nonvoluntary (established by inference in the instant case), is not controlling. **The relevant factor is the determination of whether the acts of the perpetrator have reached such a *** stage of advancement that they can be classified as an attempt. Once that attempt is found there can be no exculpatory abandonment.** *** One of the purposes of the criminal law is to protect society from those who intend to injure it. When it is established that the defendant intended to commit a specific crime and that in carrying out this intention he committed an act that caused harm or sufficient danger of harm, it is immaterial that for some collateral reason he could not complete the intended crime." [In the instant case defendant's drilling was done without permission and did cause property damage.]

Unlike California, the Model Penal Code allows abandonment or withdrawal to be a valid defense to a charge of attempt.

Model Penal Code § 5.01: Attempt, Renunciation

(4) Renunciation of Criminal Purpose.

When the actor's conduct would otherwise constitute an attempt under Subsection (1)(b) or (1)(c) of this Section, **it is an affirmative defense that he abandoned his effort to commit the crime** or otherwise prevented its commission, **under circumstances manifesting a complete and voluntary renunciation of his criminal purpose**. The establishment of such defense does not, however, affect the liability of an accomplice who did not join in such abandonment or prevention.

Within the meaning of this Article, renunciation of criminal purpose is not voluntary if it is motivated, in whole or in part, by circumstances, not present or apparent at the inception of the actor's course of conduct, that increase the probability of detection or apprehension or that make more difficult the accomplishment of the criminal purpose.

Renunciation is not complete if it is motivated by a decision to postpone the criminal conduct until a more advantageous time or to transfer the criminal effort to another but similar objective or victim.[128]

---

128. From *The Model Penal Code* by the American Law Institute. Copyright © 1962 by the American Law Institute. Used by permission.

VIDEO: Guilty Pleas to Attempted Capital Murder

Two defendants pleaded guilty to attempted murder of a police officer at:

https://www.youtube.com/watch?v=DgGljj0mmJ8

Teens Attempt Murder to Please "Slender Man"

KTLA 5 News/CNN Wire reported on October 7, 2017, in "Wisconsin Teen Who Repeatedly Stabbed Classmate to Impress 'Slenderman' Will Go to Mental Institution Under Plea Deal," that fifteen-year-old Morgan Geyser pleaded guilty to attempted murder for stabbing a fellow student in order to satisfy "Slenderman," a character on the Internet. The article can be viewed at:

http://ktla.com/2017/10/07/wisconsin-teen-who-repeatedly-stabbed-classmate-to-impress-slenderman-will-go-to-mental-institution-under-plea-deal/

Rachel Chason of the *Washington Post* reported on September 29, 2017, in "They stabbed their friend to impress Slender Man. Now the teens are going to mental hospitals," that the attempt involved two persons, Morgan Geyser and Annissa Weier, who were both twelve years old at the time they stabbed the victim, Payton Leutner, acting as "servants" of Slender Man. This article can be visited at:

https://www.washingtonpost.com/news/true-crime/wp/2017/09/29/they-stabbed-their-friend-to-impress-slender-man-now-the-teens-are-going-to-mental-hospitals/?utm_term=.29ecd0c1c2c9

B.   CONSPIRACY

1.   Common Law

Blackstone, in his *Commentaries*, Vol. IV, at 136, had little to say on conspiracy, writing only about conspiracy to falsely indict an innocent man of a felony. LaFave, in *Criminal Law*, at 649, explained, **"The crime of conspiracy, unknown to the early common law, emerged from the enactment of three statutes during the reign of Edward I."** LaFave noted that, originally, conspiracy was so narrow that it included "Combinations only to procure false indictments or to bring false appeals or to maintain vexatious suits." Over time, however, conspiracy greatly expanded.

A conspiracy requires at least two people to agree.

© VojtechVlk/Shutterstock.com

2.   Current Law

The government does not take conspiracies lightly. **People who form conspiracies to commit a crime can be charged, tried, and punished for both the crimes committed and the conspiracies formed to commit those crimes.** Thus, if Ann and Bud agree to commit a robbery of Cathy and follow through by robbing Cathy, the defendants Ann and Bud can be prosecuted for both the conspiracy to rob and the robbery itself. These conspirators might serve sentences where the punishments for robbery and conspiracy to rob are served consecutively. Ann and Bud might serve 5 years for robbery and then 3 more for the conspiracy to rob. Moreover, as seen in *People v. Tatman* below, **while committing a particular crime alone might constitute only a misdemeanor, conspiring to commit the misdemeanor might itself expose the conspirators to felony liability**.

What is so frightening and dangerous about conspiracy to merit such harsh treatment? The United States Supreme Court, in *Callanan v. United States*, 364 U.S. 587 (1961), provided an explanation when drawing a distinction between a substantive offense (for example, robbery) and a conspiracy to commit that offense (for instance, conspiracy to commit robbery). *Callanan* noted:

> [The commission of the substantive offense and a conspiracy to commit it are separate and distinct offenses. The Court once] upheld a two-year sentence for conspiracy over the objection that the crime which was the object of the unlawful agreement could only be punished by a $ 100 fine. ***
>
> [**This principle recognizes that collective criminal agreement—partnership in crime—presents a greater potential threat to the public than individual wrongful acts.**] Concerted action both increases the likelihood that the criminal object will be successfully attained and decreases the probability that the individuals involved will depart from their path of criminality. **Group association for criminal purposes often, if not normally, makes possible the attainment of ends more complex than those which one criminal could accomplish.** Nor is the danger of a conspiratorial group limited to the particular end toward which it has embarked. Combination in crime makes more likely the commission of crimes unrelated to the original purpose for which the group was formed. In sum, the danger which a conspiracy generates is not confined to the substantive offense which is the immediate aim of the enterprise.

People v. Tatman, 20 Cal. App.4th 1 (1993) saw the greater dangers posed by conspiracy as justifying punishing a conspiracy to violate the Fish and Game Code as a felony even though commission of the offense alone was merely a misdemeanor. In *Tatman*, the defendant and his co-conspirator, Brady, "were found with abalone in a hidden compartment aboard the fishing vessel 'Hell Raisers' and . . . they transported approximately 196 abalone into Noyo Harbor." The defendant, Tatman, argued, "the general conspiracy statute in the Penal Code cannot be used to elevate misdemeanor offenses in the Fish and Game Code to a felony." The court disagreed, explaining:

> A violation of any provision of the Fish and Game Code or any regulation adopted pursuant thereto is a misdemeanor. *** **A conspiracy to commit a misdemeanor may be punished as a felony** (Pen. Code, § 182, subd. (a)), and if the illegal object of a conspiracy is accomplished, **a defendant may be separately liable for both the conspiracy and the substantive offense.** *** A conspiracy to commit a misdemeanor does not elevate the misdemeanor to a felony. It is the unlawful agreement to commit a criminal offense that constitutes a felony. **The theory behind these principles is that collaborative criminal activities pose a greater potential threat to the public than individual acts.**"

Tatman found three reasons to explain the "group danger" of conspiracy: 1) **groups of criminals can divide the labor**, enabling them to choose "more elaborate and ambitious goals" and to increase the likelihood' of success, 2) **a group's "moral support" strengthens the "perseverance of each member of the conspiracy**," and 3) "even if a single conspirator" considers "stopping the wheels" of the conspiracy, **"a return to the status quo will be much more difficult since it will entail persuasion of the other conspirators."**[129]

Biography—Criminal

Charles Manson—Head of the "Manson Family" Murderers

- Born on November 12, 1934, in Cincinnati Ohio.
- The case, *People v. Manson*, 61 Cal.App.3d 102 (1976), reported the following:
- A jury convicted Manson, along with codefendants Patricia Krenwinkel, Susan Atkins, and Leslie Van Houten, guilty of first degree murder.
- In Los Angeles on August 9, 1969, the Manson family committed "The Tate Murders." Sharon Tate (wife of movie director Roman Polanski), Wojiciech Frykowski, Abigail Folger, Steve Parent, and Jay Sebring were murdered.
- On the front door, the word, "Pig" had been written in blood.
- The murders were particularly brutal: "Tate suffered 16 stab wounds." Folger had been "stabbed 28 times." Sebring had "seven penetrating stab wounds and one fatal gunshot wound." Frykowski had "51 stab wounds and his scalp had 13 lacerations," along with two gunshot wounds. Parent was shot five times.
- On August 10, 1969, members of Manson's group committed "The La Bianca Murders." Sixteen-year-old Frank Struthers found his mother, Rosemary La Bianca, and his step-father, Leno, dead.
- Mr. La Bianca's "face covered with a blood-soaked pillow case. His hands were tied behind his back with a leather thong. A carving fork was stuck in his stomach, the two tines inserted down to the place where they divide. On Mr. La Bianca's stomach was scratched the word 'War.' An electric cord was knotted around his neck. The coroner's examination revealed 13 stab wounds, in addition to the scratches, and 14 puncture wounds apparently made by the tines of the carving fork. A knife was found protruding from his neck."
- Mrs. La Bianca's "hands were tied with an electric cord. A pillow case was over her head and an electric cord was wound about her neck. Her body revealed 41 separate stab wounds."
- **"'Death to the Pigs' was written in blood on a wall in the living room; over a door, 'Rise'; and on a refrigerator door, 'Healter (sic) Skelter.'"**
- Although originally given the death penalty, Manson saw his sentence changed to life in prison after the U.S. Supreme Court deemed the death penalty, as carried out at that time, unconstitutional as cruel and unusual punishment in *Furman v. Georgia*, 408 U.S. 238 (1972). [Since the sentence of "life without the possibility of parole" did not then exist, Manson's sentence changed to life.]
- Died November 19, 2017, at age eighty-three. The November 20, 2017, *Washington Post* article, "Charles Manson, cult leader and murder-rampage mastermind who terrified nation, dies at 83," by Paul Valentine, can be viewed at: https://www.washingtonpost.com/local/obituaries/charles-manson-cult-leader-and-serial-killer-who-terrified-nation-dies-at-83/2017/11/20/152b1630-ca75-11e7-b0cf-7689a9f2d84e_story.html?undefined=&utm_term=.8d5b5b660e00&wpisrc=nl_most&wpmm=1

---

129. Reprinted with the permission of LexisNexis.

Model Penal Code § 5.03: Criminal Conspiracy

(1) Definition of Conspiracy. A person is guilty of conspiracy with another person or persons to commit a crime if with the purpose of promoting or facilitating its commission he:

(a) agrees with such other person or persons that they or one or more of them will engage in conduct that constitutes such crime or an attempt or solicitation to commit such crime; or

(b) agrees to aid such other person or persons in the planning or commission of such crime or of an attempt or solicitation to commit such crime.

(2) Scope of Conspiratorial Relationship.

If a person guilty of conspiracy, as defined by Subsection (1) of this Section, knows that a person with whom he conspires to commit a crime has conspired with another person or persons to commit the same crime, he is guilty of conspiring with such other person or persons, whether or not he knows their identity, to commit such crime.

(3) Conspiracy with Multiple Criminal Objectives. If a person conspires to commit a number of crimes, he is guilty of only one conspiracy so long as such multiple crimes are the object of the same agreement or continuous conspiratorial relationship.

(4) Joinder and Venue in Conspiracy Prosecutions.

(a) Subject to the provisions of paragraph (b) of this Subsection, two or more persons charged with criminal conspiracy may be prosecuted jointly if:

(i) they are charged with conspiring with one another; or

(ii) the conspiracies alleged, whether they have the same or different parties, are so related that they constitute different aspects of a scheme of organized criminal conduct.

(b) In any joint prosecution under paragraph (a) of this Subsection: *Selected Sections* of the Model Penal Code Page 36.

(i) no defendant shall be charged with a conspiracy in any county [parish or district] other than one in which he entered into such conspiracy or in which an overt act pursuant to such conspiracy was done by him or by a person with whom he conspired; and

(ii) neither the liability of any defendant nor the admissibility against him of evidence of acts or declarations of another shall be enlarged by such joinder; and

(iii) the Court shall order a severance or take a special verdict as to any defendant who so requests, if it deems it necessary or appropriate to promote the fair determination of his guilt or innocence, and shall take any other proper measures to protect the fairness of the trial . . .[130]

a)   Agreement between Two or More Persons: What Is an "Agreement" and Who Precisely Has to Agree?

Conspiracy requires as its first element an "agreement" between two or more persons. What exactly is required for an agreement? If one person, intending to commit a crime, seeks agreement with another and the other person says, "Yes, I agree," is this enough to satisfy conspiracy law? What if the second person **never intends to genuinely agree** to commit a crime, but is simply **pretending, joking, or humoring** the person who sought the agreement? In the following case, the court explores this issue by exploring "**unilateral**" and "**bilateral**" agreements.

---

130. From *The Model Penal Code* by the American Law Institute. Copyright © 1962 by the American Law Institute. Used by permission.

It is commonly known that people make untruthful statements in bars.

LEGAL ANALYSIS

People v. Foster
457 N.E.2d 405 (1983).
Justice Underwood delivered the opinion for the Supreme Court of Illinois.

Facts

[Defendant, James Foster, initiated his plan to commit a robbery when he approached John Ragsdale in a bar and asked] if he was "interested in making some money." Defendant told Ragsdale of an elderly man, A. O. Hedrick, who kept many valuables in his possession. Although Ragsdale stated that he was interested in making money he did not believe defendant was serious until defendant returned to the bar the next day and discussed in detail his plan to rob Hedrick. In an effort to gather additional information, Ragsdale decided to feign agreement to defendant's plan but did not contact the police.

[Later, defendant went to Ragsdale's home to find out if he] was "ready to go." Since Ragsdale had not yet contacted the police he told defendant that he would not be ready until he found someone else to help them. Ragsdale [then informed the police of the planned robbery.] Defendant and Ragsdale were met at Hedrick's residence the following day and arrested.

[A jury convicted defendant of conspiracy to commit robbery. The appellate court reversed the conviction, reasoning that the conspiracy statute] required actual agreement between at least two persons to support a conspiracy conviction. [The court determined that Ragsdale never intended to agree to defendant's plan but merely feigned agreement.]

[The State argues on appeal that conspiracy needs only one of the participants to the conspiracy to actually intend to agree to commit an offense.]

Issue

Whether the Illinois legislature, in amending the conspiracy, intended to adopt the unilateral theory of conspiracy. Does conspiracy require the actual agreement between at least two persons or is it enough that one person intend to agree even though the other does not?

Rule and Analysis

[**For a conspiracy conviction under the unilateral theory, only one of the conspirators need intend to agree to the commission of an offense.**] Prior to the 1961 amendment the statute clearly encompassed the traditional, bilateral theory, requiring the actual agreement of at least two participants. [The former statute provided:]

> "If any *two or more persons* conspire or *agree together* * * * to do any illegal act * * * they shall be deemed guilty of a conspiracy." ***

The amended version of the statute provides:

> "*A person* commits conspiracy when, with intent that an offense be committed, *he agrees* with another to the commission of that offense." ***

Since the statute is [now] worded in terms of "a person" rather than "two or more persons" [the State urges] that only one person need intend to agree to the commission of an offense. [For support,] the State compares the Illinois statute with the **Model Penal Code [MPC] conspiracy** provision, [which] is also worded in terms of "a person":

"*A person* is guilty of conspiracy with another person or persons to commit a crime if with the purpose of promoting or facilitating its commission *he*:

(a) *agrees* **with such other person or persons that they or one or more of them will engage in conduct which constitutes such crime or an attempt or solicitation to commit such crime ***[131]**

The [MPC commentary] expressly indicates the drafters' intent to adopt the unilateral theory of conspiracy, [giving the MPC drafters' reason] for abandoning the traditional language "two or more persons":

"The definition of the Draft departs from the traditional view of conspiracy as an entirely bilateral or multilateral relationship, the view inherent in the standard formulation cast in terms of 'two or more persons' ***

[The] State reasons that the drafters would not have deleted the words "two or more persons" if they had intended to retain the bilateral theory. ***

[We are troubled by the Illinois' Conspiracy Statute Committee's failure to explain the reason for deleting the words "two or more persons" from the statute.] The comments simply do not address the unilateral/bilateral issue. [We doubt] that the drafters could have intended what represents a rather profound change in the law of conspiracy without mentioning it in the comments. ***

***Illinois does have a solicitation statute which embraces virtually every situation in which one could be convicted of conspiracy under the unilateral theory.** Moreover, the penalties for solicitation and conspiracy are substantially similar. There would appear to have been little need for the legislature to adopt the unilateral theory of conspiracy in light of the existence of the solicitation statute. ***

Conclusion

[**The conspiracy statute of Illinois] encompasses the bilateral theory of conspiracy. [The appellate court is therefore affirmed.**][132]

---

131. From *The Model Penal Code* by the American Law Institute. Copyright © 1962 by the American Law Institute. Used by permission.

132. Reprinted with the permission of LexisNexis.

Note

Not all courts agree with *Foster's* ruling. In *People v Vecellio*, 292 P.3d 1004 (2012), **the Colorado Court of Appeals adopted the "unilateral" definition of agreement for a conspiracy** when a jury convicted Todd George Vecellio of "conspiracy to commit sexual assault on a child by one in a position of trust."

Conspiracies need not be formed in smoke-filled rooms.

[Defendant contacted "Karina" in an Internet chat room that allowed users to contact other users about sexual interests.] According to her profile, Karina was a thirty-one-year-old single mother with a thirteen-year-old daughter, "Shayla." In actuality, Karina was an undercover police officer [with] the Internet Crimes Against Children (ICAC) task force. Shayla did not exist.

[Defendant learned from Karina that she and her] daughter were engaged in an incestuous relationship and that she was looking for a male to "teach" her daughter about sex by having three-way intercourse with them. Defendant responded that he was interested in having sex with both Karina and Shayla, [asked Karina questions about her and Shayla's sexual experiences together, and remarked that Karina's answers made him sexually excited. Defendant] expressed concerns that Karina was a "cop" and sought assurances from her that she was not.

Defendant [wanted to meet] them in person.] Karina sent defendant [fake photos of herself and Shayla.] Defendant sent Karina a photo of his erect penis. [The police learned that defendant was Vecellio,] a police officer for the University of Colorado at Colorado Springs (UCCS).

[Defendant and Karina planned to meet at a convenience store.] They agreed that once they [got "comfortable" with each other, they would] have three-way sex with Shayla. They also agreed that defendant would purchase condoms before making the trip. [Upon arrest, police found condoms on defendant.]

Defendant [argued] that he was conducting his own secret undercover investigation into Karina and the possible abuse of her daughter [in order to obtain a promotion. Defendant stated that he did not drive to the convenience store to have sex with Karina and Shayla, but only to] gather information about Karina so he could notify the authorities, save Shayla, and "be a hero." [Defendant had never previously conducted an ICAC investigation, did not save Karina's instant messages, did not record Karina's phone calls, and did not obtain authorization from his supervisor for his undercover operation.] The jury convicted defendant on all counts.

Defendant urged on appeal that, "in Colorado, the crime of conspiracy requires a real agreement between two true co-conspirators." Since "Karina was in actuality an undercover police officer who never intended to engage in any criminal activity, defendant contends that he never entered into an agreement with a true co-conspirator, and so the evidence was insufficient to convict him of conspiracy." The Court disagreed:

> **[Colorado follows] the "unilateral" approach to conspiracy, under which a defendant may be convicted of conspiracy by agreeing with another party to commit a crime, regardless of whether the other party is an undercover police officer who feigns agreement.** [The] fact that defendant agreed to commit a crime with an undercover police officer does not preclude his conviction. ***
>
> [Defendant] asks us to adopt the "bilateral" approach to conspiracy applied in the federal courts. [Conspiracy under the bilateral approach requires that at least two true co-conspirators agree. Under] the bilateral approach, a defendant cannot be convicted of conspiracy when the other party feigns agreement, such as in cases involving undercover government agents, because two true co-conspirators have not agreed to commit a crime.
>
> **[The modern trend in state courts is to rule that conspiracy is viable even when one of the participants is a government agent or is feigning agreement.]** Under the unilateral approach, the crime of conspiracy is committed when the defendant agrees with another person to act in a prohibited manner; the second party can feign agreement. [Because] the unilateral approach requires only that the defendant agree to proceed in a prohibited manner, the fact that the other party is an undercover police officer is irrelevant.[133]

In *State v. Rambousek*, 479 N.W.2d 832 (1992), the Supreme Court of North Dakota affirmed the conspiracy conviction of Raymond Rambousek by ruling that the state's conspiracy statute required only a "unilateral" agreement. The defendant had met with two undercover State Crime Bureau agents posing as "hit men." Rambousek discussed murdering a witness who could testify in a criminal case against him and even "signed certificate of title to a 1977 Cadillac to one of the undercover agents as partial payment for the contemplated murder." Upon conviction of conspiracy to commit murder, the defendant appealed, arguing he could not form a bilateral agreement with agents who never intended to kill anyone. The Court disagreed, reasoning:

> NDCC § 12.1-06-04(1) says:
>
> **"A person commits conspiracy if he agrees with one or more persons to engage in or cause conduct which, in fact, constitutes an offense or offenses, and any one or more of such persons does an overt act to effect an objective of the conspiracy.** The agreement need not be explicit, but may be implicit in the fact of collaboration or existence of other circumstances."
>
> *** "Under a unilateral formulation, the crime "of conspiracy is committed *when a person agrees* to proceed in a prohibited manner; under a bilateral formulation, the crime of conspiracy is committed *when two or more persons agree* to proceed in such manner. [The unilateral approach assesses the subjective individual behavior of a defendant, making irrelevant the conviction, acquittal, irresponsibility, or immunity of other co-conspirators.] Under the [bilateral approach, there must be at least two 'guilty' persons, two persons who have agreed."]

---

133. Reprinted with the permission of LexisNexis.

The language of North Dakota's statute clearly pointed to only requiring a unilateral agreement for conspiracy. The court adhered to a unilateral interpretation despite the following policy argument posed by Rambousek:

> Rambousek *** says that conspiracy statutes are aimed at the increased danger to society presented by secretive criminal behavior, but that a person "conspiring" with a governmental agent causes no public danger. [He argues:]
>
> "Such dangers, however, are non-existent when a person conspires' only with a government agent. There is no continuing criminal enterprise and ordinarily no inculcation of criminal knowledge and practices. Preventive intervention by law enforcement officers also is not a significant problem in such circumstances. The agent, as part of the 'conspiracy' is quite capable of monitoring the situation in order to prevent the completion of the contemplated criminal plan; in short, no cloak of secrecy surrounds any agreement to commit the criminal acts.
>
> It may be less dangerous to society to conspire with a person who merely feigns agreement to the conspiracy than with a person who actually agrees and intends to commit the offense. But the enterprise of weighing the danger is for the legislature, the policy-making branch of government. Rambousek's arguments are better directed to it.[134]

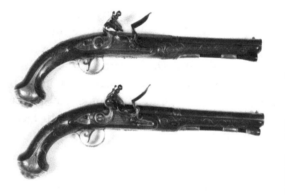

The crime of dueling was the kind of crime to which Wharton's Rule was meant to apply.

© Nik Keevil/Shutterstock.com

Wharton's Rule

Suppose Ann walks up to Bud, slaps his face with her gloves, and challenges Bud to a duel at dawn. His honor offended, Bud agrees, and the two parties meet on the dueling ground the next day. Both Ann and Bud are such poor marksmen that neither winds up harming the other in the duel. The police, however, arrest Ann and Bud and the State charges them with: Count 1: The crime of dueling, and

---

134. Reprinted with the permission of LexisNexis.

Count 2: Conspiracy to commit the crime of dueling. There seems to be a problem of fairness here. Since one cannot "duel" by herself, dueling by its very definition requires two people for its commission. Therefore, charging a dueler with both dueling and conspiracy to duel seems to be punishing a person twice for one criminal action. This concern prompted Wharton's Rule.

According to *People v. Johnson, People v. Dixon, and People v. Lee,* 57 Cal. 4th 250 (2013), Wharton's Rule "owes its name to Francis Wharton, whose treatise on criminal law identified the doctrine and its fundamental rationale." *Johnson* explained that Wharton's Rule applies to crimes that an individual could not commit acting alone. The Supreme Court of Rhode Island, in *State v. Mendoza,* 889 A.2d 153 (2005), described Wharton's Rule as: "a logical limitation to the prosecution of conspiracy." **Wharton's rule provides that "an agreement between two persons to commit an offense does not constitute conspiracy when the target offense is so defined that it can be committed only by the participation of two persons."** *Mendoza* noted that **traditionally, Wharton's rule applied to "dueling, bigamy, adultery, and incest."**

The Supreme Court of Washington, in *State v. Langworthy*, 594 P.2d 908, 910 (1979), described Wharton's Rule as the "widely recognized rule of construction" that states "when a substantive offense necessarily requires the participation of two persons, and where no more than two persons are alleged to have been involved in the agreement to commit the offense, the charge of conspiracy will not lie." *Langworthy* explained that this rule "was originally intended to preserve the distinction between the crime of conspiracy and the substantive offense, and to avoid double jeopardy problems." Today, however, Wharton's Rule is only a "rule of construction which creates a presumption that, in the absence of an expression of legislative intent to the contrary, the potential charge of conspiracy is merged into the substantive offense." *Mendoza* **expanded Wharton's Rule to cover "the buying and selling of contraband goods,"** because **"when the sale of some commodity, such as illegal drugs, is the substantive crime, the sale agreement itself cannot be the conspiracy, for it has no separate criminal object."** *Langworthy* agreed, reasoning:

> A delivery is an "actual, constructive, or attempted transfer *from one person to another* of a controlled substance". *** The substantive offense of delivery thus necessarily requires the participation of two persons—the deliverer and the intended recipient. If there is no intended recipient, there can be no delivery under this statute.[135]

Now suppose that in the dueling hypothetical scenario above, Ann and Bud invited a third person, Carl, along to the duel in order to have an unbiased person present to officiate over the rules of dueling. Carl, however helpful, is not absolutely necessary for the commission of the crime of dueling. Wharton's Rule, with the addition of Carl, would allow the prosecution to add a conspiracy count.

Mendoza explained that **if more than two people are involved in the agreement to commit a crime requiring two persons for its commission (such as dueling, delivering drugs), a prosecution for conspiracy can occur.** This is because "The presence of a third conspirator to a crime requiring only two participants for its commission . . . transforms the conspiratorial agreement into an offense distinct from any agreement implicit in the target crime, thereby rendering Wharton's Rule inapplicable."

---

135. Reprinted with the permission of LexisNexis.

b)   To Commit a Crime: What Constitutes a "Crime" for Purposes of Conspiracy?

Since conspiracy can be committed by agreeing to commit "any crime," can a conspiracy be based on an agreement to "actively participate in a criminal street gang"? What exactly would be **needed to establish such a conspiracy**? The following case considers these issues.

LEGAL ANALYSIS

People v. Johnson, People v. Dixon, and People v. Lee
57 Cal. 4th 250 (2013).
Corrigan delivered the opinion of a unanimous Supreme Court of California.

Facts

***Defendants Corey Ray Johnson, Joseph Kevin Dixon, and David Lee, Jr., were part of [the Bakersfield gang,] Country Boy Crips (CBC). CBC's rival gangs included the Eastside Crips and the Bloods. Dupree Jackson, a CBC member, testified for the prosecution under a grant of immunity. [He explained the different roles gang members filled.] Some sold drugs. Some patrolled the boundaries of the gang's territory, [while others] were "pretty boys" who brought women into the gang. Others would "ride with the guns" to seek out and kill enemies. Defendant Johnson sold drugs and was also a shooter for the gang with the moniker "Little Rifleman." Defendant Dixon was considered a gang leader. [Defendant Lee sold drugs and drove cars.]

[All three defendants were involved in a retaliatory shooting in which] Vanessa Alcala and James Wallace, neither of whom was a gang member, were killed. Alcala was pregnant.]

The jury convicted all defendants of three counts of first degree murder with multiple-murder and gang-murder special circumstances, *** active gang participation, and conspiracy. *** Conspiracy was charged as a single count against each defendant, [alleging] each had engaged in conspiracy to commit *** murder, and gang participation. The jury found each defendant guilty of conspiracy. ***

Issue

Whether one may conspire to actively participate in a criminal street gang.

Rule and Analysis

One can. **When an active gang participant possessing the required knowledge and intent agrees with fellow gang members to commit a felony, he has also agreed to commit the gang participation offense. That agreement constitutes conspiracy to commit the offense of active gang participation, and may be separately charged once a conspirator has committed an overt act.**

[PC 182 prohibits a conspiracy by two or more people to "commit any crime."] **"A conviction of conspiracy requires proof that the defendant and another person had the specific intent to agree or conspire to commit an offense, as well as the specific intent to commit the elements of that offense, together with proof of the commission of an overt act 'by one or more of the parties to such agreement' in furtherance of the conspiracy."** "[The] law of attempt and conspiracy covers inchoate crimes and allows intervention before" the underlying crime has been completed. ***

Criminal activity exists along a continuum. At its conclusion is the commission of a completed crime, like murder. ***

Conspiracy law attaches culpability at an earlier point along the continuum than attempt. "Conspiracy is an inchoate offense, the essence of which is an agreement to commit an unlawful act." *** Conspiracy separately punishes not the completed crime, or even its attempt. **The crime of conspiracy punishes the agreement itself and "does not require the commission of the substantive offense that is the object of the conspiracy."** [Conspiracy and the completed substantive offense to be separate crimes.]

[An] agreement to commit a crime, by itself, does not complete the crime of conspiracy. The commission of an overt act in furtherance of the agreement is also required. [PC 184 provides, "No agreement amounts to a conspiracy, unless some act, beside such agreement, be done within this state to effect the object thereof, by one or more of the parties to such agreement."] '[An] **overt act is an outward act done in pursuance of the crime and in manifestation of an intent or design, looking toward the accomplishment of the crime.'"** *** One purpose of the overt act requirement "is 'to show that an indictable conspiracy exists' because 'evil thoughts alone cannot constitute a criminal offense.' *** The overt act requirement also "provide[s] a *locus penitentiae*—an opportunity for the conspirators to reconsider, terminate the agreement, and thereby avoid punishment for the conspiracy." *** Once one of the conspirators has performed an overt act in furtherance of the agreement, "the association becomes an active force, it is the agreement, not the overt act, which is punishable. Hence the overt act need not amount to a criminal attempt and it need not be criminal in itself." ***

"**The elements of the gang participation offense in section 186.22(a) are: First, active participation in a criminal street gang, [which] is more than nominal or passive; second, knowledge that the gang's members engage in or have engaged in a pattern of criminal gang activity; and third, the willful promotion, furtherance, or assistance in *** any felonious criminal conduct by members of that gang.** ***A person who is not a member of a gang, but who actively participates in the gang, can be guilty of violating section 186.22(a). " *** A criminal street gang is defined as "any ongoing organization, association, or group of three or more persons, whether formal or informal, having as one of its primary activities the commission of [enumerated offenses], having a common name or common identifying sign or symbol, and whose members individually or collectively engage in or have engaged in a pattern of criminal gang activity." *** A pattern of criminal gang activity is "the commission of, attempted commission of, conspiracy to commit, or solicitation of, sustained juvenile petition for, or conviction of two or more [enumerated offenses."]

The offense of conspiracy to "commit any crime" was included in the original 1872 Penal Code. When the Legislature added section 186.22 in 1989 ***, it expressed no intention to preclude a conviction for a conspiracy to commit the crime of active gang participation. Entering its 15th decade since enactment, section 182 continues to prohibit a conspiracy to commit "any crime." ***

Concluding that one can conspire to actively participate in a gang is fully consistent with the underlying purposes of section 186.22(a). That provision is part of the California Street Terrorism Enforcement and Prevention Act [STEP Act]. "Underlying the STEP Act was the Legislature's recognition that 'California is in a state of crisis which has been caused by violent street gangs whose members threaten, terrorize, and commit a multitude of crimes ***.' The act's express purpose was 'to seek the eradication of criminal activity by street gangs.' ***" "Gang members tend to protect and avenge their associates. Crimes committed by gang members, whether or not they are gang related or committed for the benefit of the gang, thus pose dangers to the public *** not generally present when a crime is committed by someone with no gang affiliation. 'These activities, both individually and collectively, present a clear and present danger to public order and safety . . . .' *** Recognizing conspiracy to commit active gang participation as a valid offense furthers these purposes.

[Under] traditional conspiracy principles, when two or more defendants conspire to commit a substantive offense, they need not have previously known each other, have any ongoing association, or plan to associate in any way beyond the commission of the substantive offense. Traditional conspiracy, then, encompasses a stand-alone agreement by former strangers to commit a single crime. ***

[Conspirators] need not *expressly* agree at all: "To prove an agreement, it is not necessary to establish the parties met and expressly agreed; rather, '**a criminal conspiracy may be shown by direct or circumstantial evidence that the parties positively or tacitly came to a mutual understanding to accomplish** *the act* **and unlawful design.**' [Defendants' agreement to commit the various gang shootings here exhibited their intent not only to commit those particular shootings, but also to actively participate in their gang.]

[A] conspiracy requires an intentional agreement to commit the offense, a specific intent that one or more conspirators will commit the elements of that offense, and an overt act in furtherance of the conspiracy.*** The gang participation offense requires (1) participation in a gang that is more than nominal or passive, (2) knowledge of the gang's pattern of criminal gang activity, and (3) the willful promotion, furtherance, or assistance in felonious conduct by gang members. ***

A conspiracy to commit the gang participation offense may be committed, as here, by already-active gang participants. "The gist of the crime of conspiracy . . . is the agreement or confederation of the conspirators to commit one or more unlawful acts." [A single agreement to commit several crimes constitutes one conspiracy.]

The evidence established that defendants were active participants in CBC. Dixon was a gang leader. Johnson, "Little Rifleman," was a shooter and drug dealer for the gang. Lee sold drugs, obtained cars, and participated in gang shootings. There was also little question from defendants' conduct that they had the requisite knowledge of CBC's pattern of criminal gang activity, having committed much of it themselves. In this context, defendants agreed to commit various retaliatory shootings against rival gang members. Under these circumstances, once defendants agreed to commit a specific crime, for example, shooting a rival in retaliation, the agreement constituted a conspiracy to commit murder and assault. The agreement could also constitute a conspiracy to commit the conduct required to complete the gang participation offense. The agreement exhibited defendants' intent to commit all of the elements of substantive gang participation. Their agreement, coupled with their manifest participation in, and knowledge of, the gang's activities, constituted an agreement to further, promote or assist the felonious act of shooting rival gang members. Their agreement promoted commission of the shootings, making them more likely. Thus, just as a single agreement to kill someone with a firearm would encompass a conspiracy to commit both murder and assault with a firearm, a single agreement among active gang participants to commit a shooting with other gang members would additionally encompass a conspiracy to commit the gang participation offense. The conspiracy was completed once one of them committed an overt act toward the shooting.

Conclusion

*** **Defendants were active gang members, well aware of each other's active status and the gang's pattern of criminal gang activity. Their agreement to commit the various shootings here constituted an agreement to commit the gang participation offense and, once an overt act was performed, all the elements of conspiracy to violate section 186.22(a) were satisfied.** ***

California Penal Code § 182: Criminal Conspiracy; Acts Constituting; Punishment; Venue

(a) If two or more persons conspire:
(1) To commit any crime.

(2) Falsely and maliciously to indict another for any crime, or to procure another to be charged or arrested for any crime.

(3) Falsely to move or maintain any suit, action, or proceeding.

(4) To cheat and defraud any person of any property, by any means which are in themselves criminal, or to obtain money or property by false pretenses or by false promises with fraudulent intent not to perform those promises.

(5) To commit any act injurious to the public health, to public morals, or to pervert or obstruct justice, or the due administration of the laws.

(6) To commit any crime against the person of the President or Vice President of the United States, the Governor of any state or territory, any United States justice or judge, or the secretary of any of the executive departments of the United States . . .

(b) Upon a trial for conspiracy, in a case where an overt act is necessary to constitute the offense, the defendant cannot be convicted unless one or more overt acts are expressly alleged in the indictment or information, nor unless one of the acts alleged is proved; but other overt acts not alleged may be given in evidence.[136]

Do's and Don'ts for Hearings, Trials, and Appeals

Closing Argument

As a prosecutor, **do** save some of your biggest rocks to throw during your closing argument. The defense counsel, having only a closing argument, will not be able to make another argument after yours, so your argument will be the last words from an attorney the jury hears before going into the deliberation room. Further, the defense counsel will hesitate to object during your closing because to do so is quite bad form, on par with wiping your mouth with the back of your hand at a fancy dinner. **Don't** interrupt opposing counsel's argument so you can avoid such bad form on your own behalf.

---

c)   Overt Act: What Is Needed to Perform an Overt Act?

Model Penal Code § 5.03: Conspiracy, Overt Act, Renunciation

(5) Overt Act.

No person may be convicted of conspiracy to commit a crime, other than a felony of the first or second degree, unless an overt act in pursuance of such conspiracy is alleged and proved to have been done by him or by a person with whom he conspired.

Renunciation of Criminal Purpose.

It is an affirmative defense that the actor, after conspiring to commit a crime, thwarted the success of the conspiracy, under circumstances manifesting a complete and voluntary renunciation of his criminal purpose.[137]

---

136. From *Deering's California Codes Annotated.* Copyright © 2014 by Matthew Bender & Company, Inc., a member of the LexisNexis Group. Reprinted with the permission of LexisNexis.

137. From *The Model Penal Code* by the American Law Institute. Copyright © 1962 by the American Law Institute. Used by permission.

California Penal Code § 184: Overt Act Necessary

No agreement amounts to a conspiracy, unless some act, beside such agreement, be done within this state to effect the object thereof, by one or more of the parties to such agreement and the trial of cases of conspiracy may be had in any county in which any such act be done.

C. VICARIOUS LIABILITY: WHEN IS A CONSPIRATOR CRIMINALLY LIABLE FOR THE ACTS OF HIS OR HER COCONSPIRATORS?

The following case is controversial, having been criticized and questioned by courts and cited nearly 300 times in law review articles. The dissenting opinion is included below. **To fully understand this case, one must know the difference between a charge of conspiracy and additional charges for the substantive crimes committed to carry out the conspiracy.** Suppose Al and Beth agree (forming a conspiracy) to rob banks in a certain city. To carry out this conspiracy to rob banks, Al steals a new car for each robbery, so the car cannot be traced back to the robbers, Al and Beth. Since Al steals the cars in order to successfully commit the robberies, it can be said that the car thefts are "**substantive offenses**" committed "**in furtherance of**" **the conspiracy.** Since both Al and Beth agreed to commit the robberies, and since both benefit from the car thefts, **both are criminally liable not only for the original conspiracy to rob banks, but also for every substantive offense (such as car theft) committed as part of the conspiracy.**

Suppose Beth gets arrested but Al continues with the conspiracy by stealing cars and robbing banks. **While she sits in jail, is Beth criminally liable for each new car Al continues to steal (substantive offense) while continuing to carry out the conspiracy on his own?**

LEGAL ANALYSIS

Pinkerton v. United States
328 U.S. 640 (1946).
Justice Douglas delivered the opinion of the United States Supreme Court.

Facts

Walter and Daniel Pinkerton are brothers who live a short distance from each other on Daniel's farm. They were indicted for violations of the Internal Revenue Code. The indictment contained ten substantive counts and one conspiracy count. The jury found Walter guilty on nine of the substantive counts and on the conspiracy count. It found Daniel guilty on six of the substantive counts and on the conspiracy count.

"For two or more to confederate and combine together to commit or cause to be committed a breach of the criminal laws, is an offense of the gravest character, sometimes quite outweighing, in injury to the public, the mere commission of the contemplated crime. It involves deliberate plotting to subvert the laws, educating and preparing the conspirators for further and habitual criminal practices. And it is characterized by secrecy, rendering it difficult of detection, requiring more time for its discovery, and adding to the importance of punishing it when discovered." ***

[Although evidence existed to implicate Daniel in the conspiracy, there was no evidence to show that Daniel participated directly in the commission of the substantive offenses. There was evidence to show that Walter committed these substantive offenses in furtherance of the unlawful conspiracy existing between the brothers.]

Issue

Whether each defendant can be found guilty of the substantive offenses, if it was found at the time those offenses were committed defendants were parties to an unlawful conspiracy and the substantive offenses charged were in fact committed in furtherance of it.

Rule and Analysis

*** We have here a continuous conspiracy. **There is here no evidence of the affirmative action on the part of Daniel which is necessary to establish his withdrawal from it.** *** "Having joined in an unlawful scheme, having constituted agents for its performance, scheme and agency to be continuous until full fruition be secured, until he does some act to disavow or defeat the purpose he is in no situation to claim the delay of the law. **As the offense has not been terminated or accomplished he is still offending.** And we think, consciously offending, offending as certainly, as we have said, as at the first moment of his confederation, and consciously through every moment of its existence." **[So] long as the partnership in crime continues, the partners act for each other in carrying it forward. It is settled that "an overt act of one partner may be the act of all without any new agreement specifically directed to that act."** *** Motive or intent may be proved by the acts or declarations of some of the conspirators in furtherance of the common objective. *** A scheme to use the mails to defraud, which is joined in by more than one person, is a conspiracy. *** Yet all members are responsible, though only one did the mailing. *** The governing principle is the same when the substantive offense is committed by one of the conspirators in furtherance of the unlawful project. *** The criminal intent to do the act is established by the formation of the conspiracy. Each conspirator instigated the commission of the crime. The unlawful agreement contemplated precisely what was done. It was formed for the purpose. The act done was in execution of the enterprise. The rule which holds responsible one who counsels, procures, or commands another to commit a crime is founded on the same principle. That principle is recognized in the law of conspiracy when the overt act of one partner in crime is attributable to all. An overt act is an essential ingredient of the crime of conspiracy. *** If that can be supplied by the act of one conspirator, we fail to see why the same or other acts in furtherance of the conspiracy are likewise not attributable to the others for the purpose of holding them responsible for the substantive offense.

Conclusion

A different case would arise if the substantive offense committed by one of the conspirators was not in fact done in furtherance of the conspiracy, did not fall within the scope of the unlawful project, or was merely a part of the ramifications of the plan which could not be reasonably foreseen as a necessary or natural consequence of the unlawful agreement. But as we read this record, that is not this case. Affirmed.

Justice Rutledge, dissenting in part.

The judgment concerning Daniel Pinkerton should be reversed. In my opinion it is without precedent here and is a dangerous precedent to establish.

Daniel and Walter, who were brothers living near each other, were charged in several counts with substantive offenses, and then a conspiracy count was added naming those offenses as overt acts. The proof showed that **Walter alone committed the substantive crimes**. There was none to establish that

Daniel participated in them, aided and abetted Walter in committing them, or knew that he had done so. **Daniel in fact was in the penitentiary, under sentence for other crimes, when some of Walter's crimes were done.**

[The evidence showed that over several years Daniel and Walter had confederated to commit] unlawful possession, transportation, and dealing in whiskey, in fraud of the federal revenues. On this evidence both were convicted of conspiracy. Walter also was convicted on the substantive counts on the proof of his committing the crimes charged. [On] that evidence without more than the proof of Daniel's criminal agreement with Walter and the latter's overt acts, which were also the substantive offenses charged, the jury found Daniel guilty of those substantive offenses.]

[This ruling violates] the letter and the spirit of what Congress did when it separately defined the three classes of crime: (1) completed substantive offenses; (2) aiding, abetting [another to commit them; and (3) conspiracy to commit them.]

The three types of offense are not identical. *** The gist of conspiracy is the agreement; that of aiding, abetting or counseling is in consciously advising or assisting another to commit particular offenses, and thus becoming a party to them; that of substantive crime, going a step beyond mere aiding, abetting, counseling to completion of the offense.

[When] conspiracy has ripened into completed crime, or has advanced to the stage of aiding and abetting, it becomes easy to disregard their differences and loosely to treat one as identical with the other, that is, for every purpose except the most vital one of imposing sentence. And thus the substance, if not the technical effect, of double jeopardy or multiple punishment may be accomplished. Thus also may one be convicted of an offense not charged or proved against him, on evidence showing he committed another.

[There are dangers for abuse in applying the law of conspiracy.] The looseness with which the charge may be proved, the almost unlimited scope of vicarious responsibility for others' acts which follows once agreement is shown, the psychological advantages of such trials for securing convictions by attributing to one proof against another, these and other inducements require that the broad [discretion given prosecutors in relation to such charges be not expanded into new, wider and more dubious areas.]

*** Daniel has been held guilty of the substantive crimes committed only by Walter on proof that he did no more than conspire with him to commit offenses of the same general character. There was no evidence that he counseled, advised or had knowledge of those particular acts or offenses. There was, therefore, none that he aided, abetted or took part in them. There was only evidence sufficient to show that he had agreed with Walter at some past time to engage in such transactions generally. As to Daniel this was only evidence of conspiracy, not of substantive crime. ***

The Court's theory seems to be that Daniel and Walter became general partners in crime by virtue of their agreement and because of that agreement without more on his part Daniel became criminally responsible as a principal for everything Walter did thereafter in the nature of a criminal offense of the general sort the agreement contemplated, so long as there was not clear evidence that Daniel had withdrawn from or revoked the agreement. [The] result is a vicarious criminal responsibility as broad as, or broader than, the vicarious civil liability of a partner for acts done by a copartner in the course of the firm's business.

*** The effect of Daniel's conviction in this case *** is either to attribute to him Walter's guilt or to punish him twice for the same offense, namely, agreeing with Walter to engage in crime. Without the agreement Daniel was guilty of no crime on this record. With it and no more, so far as his own conduct is concerned, he was guilty of two.

[Daniel's] sentence for conspiracy should be annulled. So also should Daniel's sentence on all counts.

Note

It could be said that Justice Rutledge had the last word, for the Model Penal Code, in the provisions below, sought to limit vicarious liability to those who involved themselves more fully in the criminal activity.

Model Penal Code § 2.06: Liability for Conduct of Another; Complicity

(1) A person is guilty of an offense if it is committed by his own conduct or by the conduct of another person for which he is legally accountable, or both.

(2) A person is legally accountable for the conduct of another person when:

(a) acting with the kind of culpability that is sufficient for the commission of the offense, he causes an innocent or irresponsible person to engage in such conduct; or

(b) he is made accountable for the conduct of such other person by the Code or by the law defining the offense; or

(c) he is an accomplice of such other person in the commission of the offense.

(3) A person is an accomplice of another person in the commission of an offense if:

(a) with the purpose of promoting or facilitating the commission of the offense, he

(i) solicits such other person to commit it, or

(ii) aids or agrees or attempts to aid such other person in planning or committing it, or

(iii) having a legal duty to prevent the commission of the offense, fails to make proper effort so to do; or

(b) his conduct is expressly declared by law to establish his complicity . . .

Model Penal Code § 5.03: Conspiracy, Duration

. . .

(7) Duration of Conspiracy. For purposes of Section 1.06(4):

(a) conspiracy is a continuing course of conduct that terminates when the crime or crimes that are its object are committed or the agreement that they be committed is abandoned by the defendant and by those with whom he conspired; and

(b) such abandonment is presumed if neither the defendant nor anyone with whom he conspired does any overt act in pursuance of the conspiracy during the applicable period of limitation; and

(c) if an individual abandons the agreement, the conspiracy is terminated as to him only if and when he advises those with whom he conspired of his abandonment or he informs the law enforcement authorities of the existence of the conspiracy and of his participation therein.[138]

D.   SOLICITATION

There is an old philosophical question that asks, "If a tree falls in a forest and no one is there to hear it, did it make a sound?" Likewise, if a person sends a message and the would-be recipient does not receive it, can you say that the person really sent a message? In the following case, this question is considered in terms of **solicitation: whether there can be a solicitation even though the communication was never delivered to its intended recipient.** The following case presents the law for solicitation for both California and the Model Penal Code.

---

138. From *The Model Penal Code* by the American Law Institute. Copyright © 1962 by the American Law Institute. Used by permission.

LEGAL ANALYSIS

People v. Saephanh
80 Cal. App. 4th 451 (2000).
Justice Harris delivered the opinion for the California Court of Appeal.

Facts

[Appellant] had consensual sexual intercourse with Cassandra Y. Cassandra became pregnant and [she informed appellant of her pregnancy while he] was in prison. Appellant first asked if the baby was his and, when told it was, exclaimed, " 'Oh, I've been wanting a baby for a long time.' " Cassandra and appellant spoke about the baby every week and appellant was excited.

[While still incarcerated, appellant wrote a letter] to his friend and fellow gang member Cheng Saechao, also known as O. Dee. [It] stated, "By the way loc, could you & the homies do me a big favor & take care that white bitch, Cassie for me. ha, ha, ha!! Cuzz, it's too late to have abortion so I think a miss carrage would do just fine. I aint fista pay child sport for this bull-shit loc. You think you can get the homies or home girls do that for me before she have the baby on Aug. '98" (*Sic.*) At the time he wrote the letter, appellant was upset. He did not want to pay child support.

Vicki Lawrence, a correctional officer at Corcoran State Prison working for the investigative service unit, [as part of her normal duties,] read the letter appellant had written. [The institution's internal investigative unit intercepted the letter and so it] never reached the addressee.

[When interviewed by the Kings County District Attorney's Office, appellant admitted writing the letter, being serious when he wrote it, and thinking] that if Cassandra did not let him be a part of the baby's life, he wanted to "get rid of the baby." Appellant did not want to pay child support. Appellant was angry because Cassandra did not seem to love him, and there was an argument in which Cassandra told appellant he could not see the baby. Appellant expected Saechao and other gang members to punch Cassandra in the stomach during a fight or have her fall, thereby causing a miscarriage. ***

Issue

Whether there was sufficient evidence for a solicitation conviction even though the communication was never delivered to its intended recipient.

Rule and Analysis

Appellant contends there is insufficient evidence to support his conviction for solicitation of murder because the *** the soliciting communication was not received by the intended recipient and [so] no one was solicited. He asserts that California's solicitation statute, section 653f, requires proof of a completed communication. He suggests a "completed communication" occurs only when the intended recipient of the communication receives it. [**Section 653f, subdivision (b) provides: "Every person who, with the intent that the crime be committed, solicits another to commit or join in the commission of murder shall be punished** by imprisonment in the state prison for three, six, or nine years."]

In *State v. Cotton* (1990) 109 N.M. 769, *** the defendant was convicted of two counts of criminal solicitation. While he was incarcerated in New Mexico, he wrote two letters to his wife in Indiana suggesting that she warn their daughter not to testify against defendant on molestation charges and that she persuade their daughter to leave New Mexico and go to Indiana. Neither letter ever reached defendant's wife, both having landed in the hands of law enforcement. On appeal, the defendant claimed insufficient evidence to support the solicitation convictions because the letters never reached the intended recipient, the defendant's wife. ***

The New Mexico Court of Appeal agreed, [noting] that New Mexico's criminal solicitation statute "adopts in part, language defining the crime of solicitation as set out in the Model Penal Code." *** The court distinguished New Mexico's statute from the Model Penal Code, noting that New Mexico's solicitation statute "specifically omits that portion of the Model Penal Code subsection declaring that an uncommunicated solicitation to commit a crime may constitute the offense of criminal solicitation. The latter omission, we conclude, indicates an implicit legislative intent that the offense of solicitation requires some form of actual communication from the defendant to either an intermediary or the person intended to be solicited, indicating the subject matter of the solicitation." **[By] adopting in part the Model Penal Code section defining solicitation but omitting language from that section criminalizing uncommunicated solicitations, the New Mexico Legislature intended that the New Mexico statute not criminalize uncommunicated solicitations.** [One scholar even suggested uncommunicated solicitations may have to be prosecuted as *attempted* solicitation.]

[No] California authority has directly addressed the issue of whether one may be found guilty of solicitation where the intended recipient of the soliciting communication never received the message. ***

Does California's section 653f include in its ambit solicitations not received by the intended recipient? Section 653f, enacted in 1929, is not based on the Model Penal Code. [Thus, we need not follow *Cotton*. *Cotton* is] unpersuasive on the issue of whether section 653f criminalizes the making of soliciting communications not received by the intended recipient. ***

*** In interpreting a statute we ascertain legislative intent to effectuate the purpose of the law. To determine intent, we look first to the language of the statute, giving effect to its plain meaning. *** As noted, section 653f, subdivision (b) provides: "Every person who, with the intent that the crime be committed, solicits another to commit or join in the commission of murder shall be punished by imprisonment . . . ." **The plain language of section 653f, in particular the phrase "solicits another," demonstrates that proof the defendant's soliciting message was received by an intended recipient is required for liability to attach.** The facts of this case are illustrative of the plain meaning of the statute. Here, appellant intended to ask Saechao and the "homies or home girls" to kill Cassandra's fetus. However, neither Saechao nor the "homies or home girls" ever received the soliciting message. Thus, appellant did not solicit Saechao or the specifically designated others. *** **The crime of solicitation defined by section 653f requires that two or more persons must be involved, at least one being necessarily a solicitor and the other necessarily being the person solicited. We agree with appellant that solicitation requires a completed communication.**

Respondent insists that even if solicitation requires a completed communication, Vicki Lawrence, the correctional officer, received the letter. In our view, this argument evades the issue of whether appellant "solicited another." Appellant did not ask Vicki Lawrence to kill anyone, or do anything for that matter. She was not a person solicited.

Section 653f has the twofold purpose of protecting the inhabitants of California from being exposed to inducement to commit or join in the commission of crimes and preventing solicitations from resulting in the commission of the crimes solicited.*** Uncommunicated soliciting messages do not expose others to inducements to commit crimes. Nor is there a likelihood that an uncommunicated message would result in the commission of crimes. Thus, letters posted but not delivered do not give rise to the dangers from which section 653f seeks to protect society.

[Appellant then argued that he did not commit attempted solicitation because "attempted solicitation" is not a crime in California.] We disagree. "Every person who attempts to commit *any* *crime*, but fails, or is prevented or intercepted in its perpetration, shall be punished where no provision is made by law for the punishment of those attempts, . . ." (§ 664, italics added.)

Solicitation is a crime, and thus falls within section 664, which applies to the attempted commission of any crime. The plain language of section 664 makes clear the Legislature is aware of specific provisions regarding attempt in the context of some crimes, and it expressly applies to those crimes which do not address attempt. **Attempted solicitation of murder is a crime in California.*****

It does not necessarily follow that every solicitation is an attempted conspiracy. [Solicitation] is complete when the solicitation is made, i.e., when the soliciting message is received by its intended recipient. It is immaterial that the object of the solicitation is never consummated, or that no steps are taken towards its completion. ***

[Section 653f] was enacted *after* section 664. The Legislature presumably was aware of section 664, criminalizing an attempt to commit *any crime*, when it enacted section 653f. We conclude the absence of language expressly *exempting* section 653f from the ambit of section 664, in effect at the time section 653f was enacted, suggests the Legislature did not intend to foreclose convictions for attempted solicitation.

Pursuant to the plain language of sections 653f and 664, attempted solicitation of murder is a crime. We will direct that appellant's conviction be modified to a conviction of attempted solicitation of murder. ***

Conclusion

The judgment of conviction for solicitation of murder is vacated. The matter is remanded to the trial court [to convict on] attempted solicitation of murder. ***[139]

E. PARTIES TO CRIME

LaFave offers explanations for each kind of party to a crime.

1. Common Law

a) Principal in the First Degree

According to LaFave, in *Criminal Law*, at 701, **"A principal in the first degree may simply be defined as the criminal actor."** The person who actually commits the criminal act, while possessing the criminal intent, causing the forbidden harm to occur, is a principal in the first degree. Therefore, the person who, holding a gun and bag, says, "This is a robbery!" is a principal in the first degree. **Today, under California Penal Code 31, such a person would simply be called a "principal" for directly committing the act constituting the offense.**

Helping someone commit a crime could expose the helper to criminal liability as an accomplice.

© Igor Normann/Shutterstock.com

---

139. Reprinted with the permission of LexisNexis.

b)   Principal in the Second Degree

LaFave noted, "**To be a principal in the second degree, one must be present at the commission of a criminal offense and aid, counsel, command, or encourage the principal in the first degree in the commission of the offense.**" Instead of personally committing the crime, the principal in the second degree aids and abets the primary actor. In a robbery, the person who acts as a lookout or is driving the getaway car is a principal in the second degree. **Today, such aiders and abettors are simply "principals" under California Penal Code 31.**

c)   Accessory before the Fact

As LaFave explained, "**An accessory before the fact is one who orders, counsels, encourages, or otherwise aids and abets another to commit a felony and who is not present at the commission of the offense.**" Today, under California Penal Code 31, such aiders and abettors are again simply "principals."

d)   Accessory after the Fact

An accessory after the fact helps or harbors a principal, knowing that the principal committed a felony. The accessory helps in order to hinder or prevent the arrest, prosecution, and punishment of the principal. Today such persons can simply be called "accessories," as in the following statute:

Penal Code 32: Accessories Defined

Every person who, after a felony has been committed, harbors, conceals, or aids a principal in such a felony, with the intent that said principal may avoid or escape from arrest, trial, conviction or punishment, having knowledge that said principal has committed such felony or has been charged with such felony or convicted thereof, is an accessory to such felony.

Arcane procedural problems caused the various distinctions between the differing principals and accessories to lead to complexities that confused courts and undermined justice. Modern jurisdictions largely abolished the various distinctions, making direct actors and aider and abettors both face liability as principals.

2.   Modern Analysis of Accomplice Liability

Aiding and Abetting
California Penal Code § 31: Who Are Principals

All persons concerned in the commission of a crime, whether it be felony or misdemeanor, and **whether they directly commit the act constituting the offense, or aid and abet in its commission, or, not being present, have advised and encouraged its commission,** and all persons counseling, advising, or encouraging children under the age of fourteen years, or persons who are mentally incapacitated, to commit any crime, or who, by fraud, contrivance, or force, occasion the drunkenness of another for the purpose of causing him to commit any crime, or who, by threats, menaces, command, or coercion, compel another to commit any crime, **are principals** in any crime so committed.[140]

---

140. From *Deering's California Codes Annotated.* Copyright © 2014 by Matthew Bender & Company, Inc., a member of the LexisNexis Group. Reprinted with the permission of LexisNexis.

The Actus Reus: Just What Acts Amount to Aiding and Abetting a Crime?

If a person is present at a crime, what are the minimal actions a person must commit in order to be found guilty of aiding and abetting the crime? The following case considers this important issue.

LEGAL ANALYSIS

People v. Phan
14 Cal. App. 4th 1453 (1993).
Justice Woods delivered the opinion of the California Court of Appeal.

Facts

[At about 7:30 p.m. on March 17, 1991, four men entered a locked family residence, committing robbery and assault. Appellants Tra Van Nguyen and Ky Huynh Phan were two of the four men. When the home invasion began, only 19-year-old Patricia Tran, her 18-year-old sister Minh Tran, and their 3-year-old nephew were at home. Other family members, including their parents, Duc Tran, and his wife, Kimqui Do, were out at a banquet.]

[When inside, the four men, armed with guns, entered the sisters' bedroom, demanding that Patricia and Minh tell them where their mother had hidden money. The robbers removed a diamond ring and necklace from Minh. The sisters could hear the robbers ransacking the house and saying such things as 'Watch out for the door. See if somebody is coming. Check—you go check that room.' When the parents, Tran and Do, returned home with three of their children, the armed robbers forced the three children to lie face-down on the floor. They tied up, kicked, and beat Tran, demanding money. The robbers took Tran's wallet.]

Appellant Phan confronted Kimqui Do and ordered her to lie down but she did not. She stood next to him, "looked at his face straight up." He put a gun to her head and said "Lay down. Where's the money?" She removed a wallet from under her blouse and gave it to him. It contained $800 in rent money.

[Phan then] grabbed her hair, pointed his gun at her and demanded more money. In Vietnamese he said, "Where are the money? Give it to me. If not, I will cut your children's arm or hands." [Nguyen obtain a butcher knife from the kitchen and put it by the hand of the eight-year-old son. Phan said] "if she doesn't give the money, just cut off her child." Kimqui Do begged him not to cut off her child's hand and said "Whatever is in the house you can take it but I don't have any more money." [Phan, grabbing Do by her hair, dragged her from room to room, banging her head against the wall, saying, "Give me the money."]

[About 9 p.m. another of the Tran children, Paul Tran, returned home to find a stranger who told him to "come back." Paul "took off," hearing the stranger say "We got discovered." Paul called 911. About the same time, Minh Tran escaped through an outside passageway in her bedroom closet. She called the police. Patricia Tran saw one of the robbers holding her nephew.] She sprayed him with perfume and he fled.

[A jury convicted appellants of all charges. Appellant Nguyen contends there is insufficient evidence he aided and abetted the robbery of Minh Tran. His contentions are without merit and affirm the judgments.]

Issue

Whether there was sufficient evidence that the defendant aided and abetted robbery under these facts.

Rule and Analysis

Appellant does not assert there is insufficient evidence Minh Tran was robbed. Nor does he claim there is insufficient evidence he was one of the four intruders who committed the instant offenses. Rather, he contends there is insufficient evidence--notwithstanding his presence—he aided and abetted in the particular robbery of Minh Tran. His argument amounts to this: since there was no evidence he encouraged an associate to rob Minh Tran or assisted in the taking of her ring or necklace, he was not an aider or abettor in her robbery. *** Appellant is mistaken.

[**All persons concerned in the commission of a crime, whether they directly commit the act constituting the offense, or aid and abet in its commission, are principals in any crime so committed.** *People v. Durham*] applied this rule. Durham was convicted of the first degree murder of a police officer fatally shot not by Durham but by his companion, Edgar Robinson. When Robinson shot the officer Durham "was crouched on one knee with his hands half raised and his palms spread at about shoulder level." *** There was no evidence that immediately before the fatal shot Durham said or did anything to encourage Robinson to shoot. Despite this superficial absence of aiding and abetting evidence the Supreme Court affirmed the conviction. It stated: "[**He was a party to a compact of criminal conduct which included within its scope the forcible resistance of arrest** *and that he was also* 'present for the purposes of assisting in its commission**"**].

Similarly, when four men, in turn, each forcibly raped a victim, each man was convicted of *four* counts of forcible rape [in *People v. Mummert.*] In affirming the convictions the court explained how each had aided and abetted the offenses: "They aided and abetted by their actual presence, and by their acts they rendered actual assistance to the perpetrator. *** **At the time of the rape by each of the men the other three stood near by and abetted the perpetrator by presenting a show of force and by keeping watch against intrusion.** As each without resentment toward his acting confederate and without concern for the girl permitted the outrage, **they exemplified a united and single purpose which would brook no interference.** Each thus encouraged and aided his several companions and was therefore a principal in each of the crimes." ***

In *People* v. *Moore,* appellant argued he could not be convicted of robbery because he was four or five feet from the other two defendants and neither did nor said anything during the robbery. The Court of Appeal affirmed the robbery conviction stating: "Appellant was not a mere bystander or onlooker. **He may have committed no overt act during the robbery but none was required. His presence could have given encouragement to his companions and acted as a deterrent to any continued resistance on the part of [the victim].**" [One person fatally stabs victim. Three defendants, present at the stabbing and each armed with a knife, convicted of murder.]

As in *Durham,* it is accurate to say appellant "was a party to a compact of criminal conduct," a compact which embraced the looting of the Tran residence and all its occupants. The evidence is overwhelming that appellant was a principal in the robbery of Minh Tran. ***

Conclusion

Sufficient evidence existed that the appellant aided and abetted the robbery of Minh Tran. The judgments are affirmed.[141]

---

141. Reprinted with the permission of LexisNexis.

Mens Rea: What Must a Person Who Aids and Abets Be Thinking?

In *People v. Beeman*, 35 Cal. 3d 547 (1984), the California Supreme Court ruled **conviction of an aider and abettor "requires proof that an aider and abettor rendered aid with an intent or purpose of either committing, or of encouraging or facilitating commission of, the target offense."** In *Beeman*, robbers James Gray and Michael Burk robbed the defendant Beeman's sister-in-law, Marjorie Beeman "of valuable jewelry, including a 3.5 carat diamond ring."

> Burk knocked at the door of the victim's house, presented himself as a poll taker, and asked to be let in. When Mrs. Beeman asked for identification, he forced her into the hallway and entered. Gray, disguised in a ski mask, followed. The two subdued the victim, placed tape over her mouth and eyes and tied her to a bathroom fixture. Then they ransacked the house, taking numerous pieces of jewelry and a set of silverware. The jewelry included a 3.5 carat, heart-shaped diamond ring and a blue sapphire ring. The total value of these two rings was over $100,000. ***

Beeman, Burk and Gray were all arrested for the robbery. At the trial of Beeman, Burk testified that Beeman:

> had talked to him about rich relatives in Redding and had described a diamond ring worth $50,000. *** Appellant gave Burk the address and discussed the ruse of posing as a poll taker. It was decided that Gray and Burk would go to Redding because appellant wanted nothing to do with the actual robbery and because he feared being recognized. On the night before the offense appellant drew a floor plan of the victim's house and told Burk where the diamond ring was likely to be found. *** After the robbery was completed, Burk telephoned appellant to report success. Appellant said that he would call the friend who might buy the jewelry. Burk and Gray drove to appellant's house and showed him the "loot." Appellant was angry that the others had taken so much jewelry, and demanded that his cut be increased from 20 percent to one-third.

Beeman contradicted Burk and Gray, testifying that:

> [H]e did not participate in the robbery or its planning. He confirmed that Burk had lived with him on several occasions, and that he had told Burk about Mrs. Beeman's jewelry, the valuable diamond ring, and the Beeman ranch, in the course of day-to-day conversations. He claimed that he had sketched a floor plan of the house some nine months prior to the robbery, only for the purpose of comparing it with the layout of a house belonging to another brother. He at first denied and then admitted describing the Beeman family cars, but insisted this never occurred in the context of planning a robbery.

Beeman claimed Burk was the one who had thought of the robbery, and when he did so, Beeman "told Burk that his friends could do what they wanted but that he wanted no part of such a scheme." He did admit, however, that:

> Burk had told him of the poll taker ruse within a week before the robbery, and that Burk told him they had bought a cap gun and handcuffs. He further admitted that he had allowed Burk to take some old clothes left at the apartment by a former roommate. At that time Beeman told Burk: "If you're going to do a robbery, you can't look like a bum." Nevertheless, appellant explained that he did not know Burk was then planning to commit this robbery.

The *Beeman* Court offered the following analysis of the intent necessary for aiding and abetting:

[An] aider and abettor must have criminal intent in order to be convicted of a criminal offense. *** The act of encouraging or counseling itself implies a purpose or goal of furthering the encouraged result. "An aider and abettor's fundamental purpose, motive and intent is to aid and assist the perpetrator in the latter's commission of the crime." ***

Direct evidence of the mental state of the accused is rarely available except through his or her testimony. The trier of fact is and must be free to disbelieve the testimony and to infer that the truth is otherwise when such an inference is supported by circumstantial evidence. [An] act which has the effect of giving aid and encouragement, and which is done with knowledge of the criminal purpose of the person aided, may indicate that the actor intended to assist in fulfillment of the known criminal purpose. However, as illustrated [in the example of a feigned accomplice not guilty because lacks common intent with the perpetrator to unite in the commission of the crime], the act may be done with some other purpose which precludes criminal liability.

If the jury were instructed that the law conclusively presumes the intention of the accused solely from his or her voluntary acts, it would "'effectively eliminate intent as an ingredient of the offense'" and would "'conflict with the [presumption of innocence which extends to every element of the crime.'"]

[We conclude that the law requires] proof that an aider and abettor act with knowledge of the criminal purpose of the perpetrator *and* with an intent or purpose either of committing, or of encouraging or facilitating commission of, the offense. *

When the definition of the offense includes the intent to do some act or achieve some consequence beyond the *actus reus* of the crime *** the aider and abettor must share the specific intent of the perpetrator. *** The liability of an aider and abettor extends also to the natural and reasonable consequences of the acts he knowingly and intentionally aids and encourages. ***

[The] word "abet," *** encompasses the intent required by law, the word is arcane and its full import unlikely to be recognized by modern jurors. **"[Abet]" means to encourage or facilitate, and implicitly to harbor an intent to further the crime encouraged. ***

[An] appropriate instruction should inform the jury that a person aids and abets the commission of a crime when he or she, acting with (1) knowledge of the unlawful purpose of the perpetrator; and (2) the intent or purpose of committing, encouraging, or facilitating the commission of the offense, (3) by act or advice aids, promotes, encourages or instigates, the commission of the crime. *

Under these circumstances, where the defense centered on the very element as to which the jury was inadequately [instructed, we find error. It] is reasonably probable that the jury would have reached a result more favorable to appellant had it been correctly instructed upon the mental element of aiding and abetting. ***

The Court thus reversed Beeman's conviction.[142]

---

142. Reprinted with the permission of LexisNexis.

Learn from My (and Others') Mistakes

Do Not Prosecute Someone for Stealing a Single Battery on Christmas Eve

As a brand new deputy D.A. in misdemeanors, I prosecuted a man for stealing a battery from a toy store on Christmas Eve. Before you jump to any conclusion that a jury trial over a battery theft is a bit of overkill, please know that the battery was one of the bigger ones—"Size D." What the jury was not allowed to know was that this particular theft was only one of many this defendant had committed (the jury would not hear such evidence because it was deemed prejudicial and inflammatory). To make the case worse, he had a $20 bill in his pocket when arrested. At the trial, which took place a year later (just before Christmas), the defendant argued that he had rushed to the store to buy a battery for a toy he was wrapping for his son and in his haste forgot to pay for it. Unhappy with our Office's priorities, the jury acquitted the defendant.

The Controversial Case of Jeremy Strohmeyer and David Cash

60 Minutes, in "Bad Samaritan," reported on David Cash, who reportedly failed to intervene when his friend, Jeremy Strohmeyer, sexually assaulted and killed a seven-year-old girl in a bathroom. Even though he admitted to personally seeing his friend restrain and threaten the girl in a bathroom stall, the video records him saying that he walked out rather than speak to his friend or stop him from attacking the girl. Cash was not prosecuted for aiding and abetting or for any crime for his failure to act. The prosecutor who spoke to *60 Minutes* explained that, although Cash's behavior was "morally reprehensible," "moral reprehensibility is not a crime." She further explained, "watching and failing to report, regrettably, is not a crime." The prosecutor also noted that his "morally bankrupt" behavior has not come without cost, for he will be judged in "the court of public opinion."

The videos can be viewed on YouTube at:

http://www.youtube.com/watch?v=KqTdXOQmXrc

and

http://www.youtube.com/watch?v=xJeAOcC7c6M

Time Magazine's report on David Cash, "The Bad Samaritan" by Cathy Booth/Berkeley on Sunday, June 24, 2001, can be viewed at:

http://content.time.com/time/magazine/article/0,9171,139892,00.html

In her July 19, 1998, report, Nora Zamichow of *The Los Angeles Times* reviewed Jeremy Strohmeyer's life in "The Fractured Life of Jeremy Strohmeyer:

Once a promising honor student, he began to slide into a darker world. Now, he stands accused of killing a little girl in a Nevada casino."

This article can be viewed at:

http://articles.latimes.com/1998/jul/19/news/mn-5552

F. VICARIOUS LIABILITY

Can a person be **vicariously liable**—in other words, can he or she **be guilty of a crime that someone else commits**—based on his or her **status or relationship** to the guilty actor? **Can parents face criminal liability simply because they are the mother or father of a minor child who committed a criminal act?** Or does **due process require that any criminal liability be based on a person voluntarily committing some kind of act or omission?** The case below considers this issue of vicarious liability.

LEGAL ANALYSIS

State v. Akers
119 N.H. 161 (1979).
Justice Grimes delivered the opinion for the Supreme Court of New Hampshire.

Facts

*** The defendants are fathers whose minor sons were found guilty of driving snowmobiles in violation of RSA 269-C:6-a II *** (operating on public way) and III *** (reasonable speed).

RSA 269-C:24 IV, which pertains to the operation and licensing of Off Highway Recreational Vehicles (OHRV), provides that "[the] parents or guardians or persons assuming responsibility will be responsible for any damage incurred or for any violations of this chapter by any person under the age of 18." Following a verdict of guilty for violating RSA 269-C:24 IV, the two defendants *** argue that (1) RSA 269-C:24 IV, the statute under which they were convicted, was not intended by the legislature to impose criminal responsibility, and (2) if in fact the legislative intention was to impose criminal responsibility, then the statute would violate N.H. Const. pt. I, art. 15 and U.S. Const. amend. XIV, § 1.

Issue

[Whether,] under New Hampshire's Constitution and Criminal Code, parents of minors can be held criminally responsible for their children's offenses solely on the basis of their parental status.

Rule and Analysis

[We hold that parents cannot be held criminally responsible vicariously for the offenses of the child.]
We first address the defendants' claim that the legislature's intention in enacting RSA 269-C:24 IV did not encompass the imposition of criminal sanctions on parents whose minor children have committed violations. [The legislature requires] that in interpreting its enactments, we must construe "[words and phrases] according to the common and approved usage of the language."[We construe the criminal code provisions according to the fair import of their terms and to promote justice."]

The language of RSA 269-C:24 IV, "parents . . . will be responsible . . . for any violations of this chapter by any person under the age of 18," clearly indicates the legislature's intention to hold the parents criminally responsible for the OHRV violations of their minor children.

It is a general principle [that a person is not guilty of an offense unless his criminal liability is based on conduct that includes a voluntary *act* or the voluntary omission to perform an act of which he is physically capable.] RSA 269-C:24 IV seeks to impose criminal liability on parents for the acts of their children without basing liability on any voluntary act or omission on the part of the parents.

Because the statute makes no reference at all to parental conduct or acts, it seeks to impose criminal responsibility solely because of their parental status.

The legislature has not specified any voluntary acts or omissions for which parents are sought to be made criminally responsible and it is not a judicial function to supply them. It is fundamental to the rule of law and due process that acts or omissions which are to be the basis of criminal liability must be specified in advance and not *ex post facto*. N.H. Const. pt. I, art. 23. ***

It is argued that liability may be imposed on parents under the provisions of RSA 626:8 II(b), which authorizes imposing criminal liability for conduct of another when "he is made accountable for the conduct of such other person by the law defining the offense." This provision comes from the Model Penal Code § 2.04(2)(b). The illustrations of this type of liability in the comments to the Code all relate to situations involving employees and agents, and no suggestion is made that it was intended to authorize imposing vicarious criminal liability on one merely because of his status as a parent. ***

Without passing upon the validity of statutes that might seek to impose vicarious criminal liability on the part of an employer for acts of his employees, [**we hold**] **that any attempt to impose such liability on parents simply because they occupy the status of parents, without more offends the due process clause of our State constitution.** ***

Parenthood lies at the very foundation of our civilization. The continuance of the human race is entirely dependent upon it. It was firmly entrenched in the Judeo-Christian ethic when "in the beginning" man was commanded to "be fruitful and multiply." *Genesis* I. **Considering the nature of parenthood, we are convinced that the status of parenthood cannot be made a crime. This, however, is the effect of RSA 269-C:24 IV.** Even if the parent has been as careful as anyone could be, even if the parent has forbidden the conduct, and even if the parent is justifiably unaware of the activities of the child, criminal liability is still imposed under the wording of the present statute. There is no other basis for criminal responsibility other than the fact that a person is the parent of one who violates the law.

Conclusion

Because the net effect of the statute is to punish parenthood, the result is forbidden by substantive due process requirements of N.H. Const. pt. I, art. 15.

Exceptions sustained.[143]

How powerful a doctrine is **vicarious liability**? Just how far will the law stretch **to find a person guilty of a crime due to someone else's acts**? Suppose Ann, Bud, and Cathy together rob Doug. During the robbery, Bud committed a "**provocative act**" by shooting at the robbery victim, Doug, thus "provoking" Doug to shoot back. Doug missed Bud, however, instead killing his co-felon, Cathy. **Can Ann be found vicariously liable for the homicide of her co-felon, Cathy, due to the "provocative act" of one of her other co-felons, Bud?**

When can you be blamed for someone else's actions?

© BonNontawat/Shutterstock.com

---

143. Reprinted with the permission of LexisNexis.

LEGAL ANALYSIS

People v. Concha
47 Cal.4th 653 (2009).
Justice Chin delivered the opinion of the Supreme Court of California.

Facts

On July 14, 2005, Reyas Concha, Julio Hernandez, Max Sanchez, and a fourth unidentified man threatened to kill Jimmy Lee Harris during an apparent attempted robbery. Harris fled from the assailants and ran down the middle of a street in Los Angeles. The four men pursued Harris for over a quarter of a mile before cornering him against a fence. Harris attempted to scale the fence and one or more of the assailants began stabbing him. The stabbing continued for several seconds. Harris, realizing that his life was in danger [from the attempted murder,] turned around and attempted to fight the four men off. Harris pulled a pocket knife from his pocket and "began to stab as many of them as [he] could." Harris then fled and found someone who called the police. Harris suffered severe injuries, but he survived. Sanchez died from the stab wounds that Harris inflicted during the attack.

The jury convicted defendants of [PC 664/187] attempted first degree murder of Harris. Relying on the provocative act murder doctrine, the jury also convicted defendants of [PC187(a) first degree murder of Sanchez.] The jury specifically found true allegations that the attempted murder of Harris was committed willfully, deliberately, and with premeditation. [The] jury was not asked to find, and did not specifically find, that each defendant personally acted willfully, deliberately, and with premeditation during the attempt. ***

Issue

Whether a defendant may be liable for first degree murder when his accomplice is killed by the intended victim in the course of an attempted murder.

Rule and Analysis

Defendants contend the provocative act murder doctrine limits a defendant's liability to second degree murder when the defendant's accomplice is killed by the victim during a willful, deliberate, and premeditated attempt to commit murder. We disagree.

Murder is the unlawful killing of a person with malice aforethought. *** To satisfy the actus reus element of murder, an act of either the defendant *or an accomplice* must be the proximate cause of death. [To satisfy murder's mens rea element, the defendant must personally act with malice aforethought.]

A defendant can be liable for the unlawful killings of both the intended victims and any unintended victims. "'[There] is no requirement of an unlawful intent to kill *an intended victim*. The law speaks in terms of an unlawful intent to kill *a* person, not *the* person *intended to be killed*.'"

For example, a defendant is liable for both murder and attempted murder if he or an accomplice attempts to kill a specific person and instead kills a bystander. [Also,] a defendant is liable for two murders if, in the course of killing his intended victim, he or an accomplice also kills a bystander. [A] defendant may be liable for murder when he possesses the appropriate mens rea and either the defendant or an accomplice causes an unlawful death. [A *mens rea* . . . is an elastic thing of unlimited supply . . . It may combine with a single actus reus to make a single crime. It may as readily combine with a hundred *acti rei*, intended and unintended, to make a hundred crimes.]

In the present case, although it is apparent that defendants Concha and Hernandez did not intend to kill their accomplice, they had the intent to kill *a* person when they attacked their intended victim, and therefore are guilty of murder as to any killing either of them proximately caused while acting together pursuant to their intent to kill.

Once liability for murder "is otherwise established, [PC189 may be invoked to determine its degree." PC 189 states that if an unlawful killing is "willful, deliberate, and premeditated," it is murder of the first degree.] If the intent is premeditated, the murder or murders are first degree." *** While joint participants involved in proximately causing a murder "are tied to a "single and common *actus reus*," "the individual *mentes reae* or levels of guilt of the joint participants are permitted to float free and are not tied to each other in any way. If their *mentes reae* are different, their independent levels of guilt . . . will necessarily be different as well."

[If a defendant in some manner proximately caused a death, and the defendant did so with a premeditated intent to kill, then the defendant is guilty of *first degree* murder."]

Defendants contend provocative act murder is limited to second degree murder.] However, that is not the case. [When] malice is *express* because the defendant possessed a specific intent to kill, first degree murder liability may be proper if the charged defendant personally acted willfully, deliberately, and with premeditation. ***

["Provocative act murder" is merely shorthand for a killing where, during commission of a crime, the intermediary (i.e., a police officer or crime victim) is provoked by the defendant's conduct into a response that results] in someone's death." [The] provocative act murder doctrine does not limit a defendant's liability to second degree murder where a defendant's accomplice is killed by the victim or a police officer in the course of an attempted murder. ***

[A defendant is liable for murder when the defendant or an accomplice proximately causes an unlawful death, and the defendant personally acts with malice.] Once liability for murder is established in a provocative act murder case *, the degree of murder liability is determined by examining the defendant's personal mens rea. *** Where the individual defendant personally intends to kill and acts with that intent willfully, deliberately, and with premeditation, the defendant may be liable for first degree murder for each unlawful killing proximately caused by his or her acts, including a provocative act murder. *****

We next address the need for the jury to consider whether a defendant *personally* acted willfully, deliberately, and with premeditation during an attempted murder that proximately caused the death of an unintended person (a provocative act murder) when two or more defendants are charged with joint participation in the attempted murder.

[For] the mens rea required for a first degree murder conviction, the jury must find that the individual defendant *personally* acted willfully, and with deliberation and premeditation during the attempted murder.

[The trial court erred when instructing on first degree murder by not providing an instruction that explained that for a defendant to be found guilty of *first degree murder,* he *personally* has to have acted willfully, deliberately, and with premeditation when he committed the attempted murder.

Conclusion

[First degree murder liability can be established in a provocative act murder case. A] defendant may be convicted of first degree murder under these circumstances if the defendant personally acted willfully, deliberately, and with premeditation during the attempted murder.

However, we reverse because the instructions on first degree murder for the death of Sanchez failed to require the jury to find whether each defendant personally acted willfully, deliberately, and with premeditation during the course of the attempted murder of Harris.[144]

The case below applies the vicarious liability of provocative act murder to the situation where **the person committing the provocative act becomes one of the deceased persons**.

LEGAL ANALYSIS

People v. Garcia
69 Cal. App. 4th 1324 (1999).
Justice Vartabedian delivered the opinion for the California Court of Appeal.

Facts

Custodio Garcia, defendant, was one of four perpetrators involved in a home invasion. Two of his accomplices were shot and killed by the victim of the home invasion. *** The trial court found defendant guilty of conspiracy to commit robbery, burglary, and murder. *** Defendant appeals, claiming he was improperly convicted of the provocative act murder of his accomplice because: (1) there was no provocative act, (2) his guilt cannot be based on the provocative act of a deceased accomplice, even though that accomplice is not the one alleged in the information as the murder victim, and (3) the murder victim himself committed a provocative act which was the sole cause of his death, thus absolving defendant of legal culpability. *** We affirm.

Defendant, Adrian Alvarez, Nemecio Quezada, and one other individual went to the apartment of Narcisio Pena at approximately 4:00 a.m. Pena was asleep in one of the two upstairs bedrooms with his girlfriend when the four men broke down the front door with a sledgehammer. All four men went upstairs. Pena heard a loud noise and heard footsteps running up the stairs. He grabbed his .38-caliber pistol. Pena opened the bedroom door slightly to see what was going on, and he saw three or four men in the upstairs hallway of his apartment. Pena tried to close the bedroom door; the men rushed the door and tried to push it open. While Pena was attempting to close the door, someone fired a round into the bedroom. Pena saw the muzzle flash and heard the shot. Pena fired several rounds back and managed to shut the door. ***

Police arrived. The body of Quezada was outside of Pena's apartment. A .40-caliber Smith & Wesson gun was found next to his body. *** The body of Alvarez was found at the foot of the stairs. A nine-millimeter handgun was next to his body. The gun was loaded with a live round in the chamber. ***

Quezada and Alvarez were each killed by a single gunshot wound. The bullets retrieved from their bodies were .38-caliber bullets. ***

Issues

1. **Was there a provocative act?**
2. **Can defendant's conviction be based on the provocative act of a deceased accomplice who is not the alleged murder victim?**

---

144. Reprinted from Westlaw, with permission of Thomson Reuters.

Rule and Analysis

Was there a provocative act?

[The] provocative act theory of murder is invoked when a victim or police officer has killed a felon. [Liability is not based on a felony-murder theory because "[w]hen a killing is not committed by a robber [felon] or by his accomplice but by his victim, malice aforethought is not attributable to the robber, for the killing is not committed by him in the perpetration or attempt to perpetrate robbery."] **To qualify as a provocative act under the provocative act theory of murder, the conduct of the felon must be sufficiently provocative of lethal response to support a finding of implied malice.** "[Mere] participation in an armed robbery is not sufficient to invoke murder liability, direct or vicarious, when the victim resists and kills." ***

Defendant claims that Quezada's [discharge of a handgun into the ceiling was not life threatening and so there was no provocative act to support provocative act murder.]

["A] person who initiates a gun battle in the course of committing a felony intentionally and with a conscious disregard for life commits an act that is likely to cause death." [A gun battle can be initiated by acts of provocation falling short of firing the first shot.] Circumstances "'fraught with grave and inherent danger to human life'" are sufficient to raise an inference of malice. [Quezada] fired a gun into an occupied bedroom. Although the bullet ended up in the ceiling, this does not diminish the gravity of the act. First, the fact that the bullet wound up in the ceiling does not necessarily prove that this was where the gun was intentionally aimed. During the struggle at the door the gun may have been jostled, causing it to be fired in a direction other than where it was intended. *** Furthermore, Pena probably was not aware that the bullet was headed toward the ceiling and merely knew that the room he was occupying with his girlfriend had been fired upon. The gun battle was initiated when Quezada fired his .40-caliber gun into the room occupied by Pena and his girlfriend. This act *** was an act done with a conscious disregard for life. There was substantial evidence of a provocative act.

Can defendant's conviction be based on the provocative act of a deceased accomplice who is not the alleged murder victim?

Defendant cites the general rule that the provocative conduct of a criminal actor who is killed by the victim cannot form the basis for a murder for which his accomplices can be held responsible. [Defendant] asserts that if Quezada's act was a provocative act, any provocative act he committed is irrelevant because he died.

In *People v. Antick*, the defendant and his accomplice, Bose, burglarized a home. Later, officers approached a car suspected to have been used in the burglary. Bose was seated in the driver's seat. The defendant was not in the car [but was nearby. The officer ordered Bose out of the car and drew his gun. The] defendant approached the car. Bose pulled a [gun and shot] at the officer. The officer fired at Bose. Bose ran. Another officer ordered Bose to stop. When he did not, the second officer fired, killing Bose. The defendant was convicted of the murder of Bose.

The Supreme Court reversed the defendant's murder conviction. Although Bose's conduct in initiating the gun battle may have established the requisite malice, Bose's conduct (provocative act) did not result in the unlawful killing of another human being, but resulted in Bose's death. **Because Bose could not be guilty of murder in connection with his own death,". . . it is impossible to base defendant's liability for this offense upon his vicarious responsibility for the crime of his accomplice."** *** The defendant was not guilty of murder because he "was convicted of murder based upon his vicarious liability for the acts of an accomplice who could not himself have been found guilty of that offense." ***

[*Antick* has caused courts to state] that to prove the provocative act theory it must be shown that the defendant or a surviving accomplice committed a life-threatening act beyond that necessary to commit the robbery. *** Although this component refers to a surviving accomplice, this reference is meant to exclude liability when the deceased provocateur accomplice is the sole cause of his death and is the accomplice whom defendant is charged with murdering.

Here, although Quezada is deceased, defendant is not charged with Quezada's death; he is charged with Alvarez's death. Quezada's act resulted in the unlawful killing of another human being, Alvarez. Because Quezada, if he had survived, could have been found guilty of the murder of another human being, Alvarez, defendant's liability is based upon defendant's vicarious responsibility for the crime of his accomplice, Quezada. The circumstance that Quezada also died should not reduce defendant's criminal responsibility. Thus, **the surviving accomplice phrase, so often repeated, is meant to exclude a defendant from being charged with the murder of a sole provocateur; it was not formulated to preclude liability when a provocateur-accomplice does an act that results in the unlawful killing of *another* human being.** "It is only in cases like *Antick*, where the defendant's responsibility for murder is based on his vicarious liability for the acts of an accomplice *who could not himself have been guilty of the offense* that liability will not lie." ***

Conclusion

Defendant was properly convicted of [Alvarez's death. Affirmed.][145]

DISCUSSION QUESTIONS

1. How can a person's "mere preparation" be distinguished from an actual crime of attempt?

2. What is the difference between "factual impossibility" and "legal impossibility" for purposes of attempt?

3. Once a person commits an attempt crime, can he or she avoid criminal liability by withdrawing from or abandoning the attempt?

4. Why are conspiracies so dangerous? How does the law respond to this danger?

5. What is the difference between conspiracy and solicitation?

6. What are the different "parties to crime" at common law?

7. What are the differences between common law accomplice liability and accomplice liability today?

8. What does "vicarious liability" mean and how does it relate to conspiracy law?

---

145. Reprinted with the permission of LexisNexis.

WEB LINKS

1. Federal law handles "attempt" crimes in its own way, as noted in "Attempt: An Overview of Federal Criminal Law," September 13, 2011, by Charles Doyle, at: http://www.law.umaryland.edu/marshall/crsreports/crsdocuments/R42001_09132011.pdf. Doyle explains: "It is not a crime to attempt to commit most federal offenses. Unlike state law, federal law has no generally applicable crime of attempt. Congress, however, has outlawed the attempt to commit a substantial number of federal crimes on an individual basis."

2. For further consideration of how to "get out" of a conspiracy, see R. Michael Cassidy and Gregory I. Massing, *The Model Penal Code's Wrong Turn: Renunciation as a Defense to Criminal Conspiracy* 64 Florida L. Rev. 353 (2012) at: http://www.floridalawreview.com/wp-content/uploads/Cassidy_BOOK.pdf. The authors note, "While the Model Penal Code was certainly one of the most influential developments in criminal law in the past century, the American Law Institute (ALI) took a seriously wrong turn by recognizing "renunciation" as a defense to the crime of conspiracy."

3. The New York jury instructions for solicitation can be viewed at: http://www.nycourts.gov/judges/cji/2-PenalLaw/100/art100hp.shtml and http://www.nycourts.gov/judges/cji/2-PenalLaw/100/100-10.pdf.

CHAPTER
XV

Defenses: Justification

"Justification" versus "Excuse"

This book has divided defenses into two chapters: (1) "Justification" and (2) "Excuse." Legal commentator Claire O. Finklestein noted in *Duress: A Philosophical Account of the Defense in Law* 37 Ariz. L. Rev. 251, 251 (1995):

> J.L. Austin expresses the common understanding of **the distinction between justifications and excuses**, respectively, when he says: **"In the one defense . . . we accept responsibility but deny that it was bad: in the other, we admit that it was bad but don't accept full, or even any, responsibility."**

Self-defense is a legal justification.

In applying this distinction, **justifications include self-defense, necessity, and consent,** where the defendants urge that although they committed the prohibited acts, there was a good, indeed defensible, reason for doing so. In contrast, **examples of excuses include insanity and duress, where defendants accept that their conduct was wrong, but claim they should not receive the law's punishment because they were not blameworthy for the harmful result.**

A. SELF-DEFENSE

Nothing is more reasonable than the idea that if someone tries to wrongfully hurt you, you should be able to properly defend yourself against such an attack. Perhaps the intuitive reasonableness of self-defense enables this criminal defense to strike a chord with juries. When assessing the issues in self-defense, one should hew closely to this concept of reasonableness.

VIDEO: Chief Justice Discusses Oral Argument for Nation's Highest Court

U.S. Supreme Court Chief Justice John Roberts speaks about the importance of answering questions in oral argument at:

https://www.youtube.com/watch?v=UJQ7Ds4nAmA

Self-Defense at Common Law

Blackstone, in *Commentaries*, Vol. III, at 3–4, recognized not only the practical need to defend oneself against attack, but also the human emotions motivating such a natural reaction. He explained:

> The defence of one's self, or the mutual and reciprocal defence of such as stand in the relations of husband and wife, parent and child, master and servant. In these cases, **if the party himself, or any of these his relations, be forcibly attacked in his person or property, it is lawful for him to repel force by force**; and the breach of the peace, which happens, is chargeable upon him only who began the affray. For the law, in this case, respects the passions of the human mind; and (when external violence is offered to a man himself, or those to whom he bears a near connection) makes it lawful in him to do himself that immediate justice, to which he is prompted by nature, and which no prudential motives are strong enough to restrain. It considers that the future process of law is by no means an adequate remedy for injuries accompanied with force; since it is impossible to say, to what wanton lengths of reapine or cruelty outrages of this sort might be carried, unless it were permitted a man immediately to oppose one violence with another. **Self-defence therefore as it is justly called the primary law of nature, so it is not, neither can it be in fact, taken away be the law of society**. In the English law particularly it is held an excuse for breaches of the peace, nay even for homicide itself: but care must be taken that the resistance does not exceed the bounds of mere defence and prevention; for then the defender would himself become an aggressor.

Many of the concepts that Blackstone mentions, such as the immediacy of the threat, the necessity for the use of force, and the reasonableness or proportionality of force in responding to the attack, are still relevant today. These concepts are explored in the cases below.

VIDEO: Being a Vigilante Is Not the Same as Using Self Defense or Defense of Others

This graphic video shows a group of persons brutally attacking a victim they mistakenly believe committed a crime. This video can be seen at:

https://www.youtube.com/watch?v=4oS9IwQKwh4

Model Penal Code § 3.04: Use of Force in Self-Protection

(1) Use of Force Justifiable for Protection of the Person.

Subject to the provisions of this Section and of Section 3.09, the use of force upon or toward another person is justifiable when the actor believes that such force is immediately necessary for the purpose of protecting himself against the use of unlawful force by such other person on the present occasion . . .[146]

Four elements traditionally exist **for most formulations of self-defense: (1) Apparent necessity in the need to defend (actual and reasonable belief in the need to defend), (2) Imminence of threat, (3) Use of reasonable force in defending oneself (this is roughly matching force with that of the attack), (4) To counter an unlawful harm.**

1. Actual and Reasonable Belief in Need to Defend

Traditionally, **a person can commit violence in self-defense only if he or she both actually (subjectively) and reasonably (objectively) believes in the need to defend.** New York's statute allowed self-defense for a person if: "**He reasonably believes**" in the need to defend. The following case considered whether this statute's language meant that the person had to both actually and reasonably believe in the need to defend (the traditional standard), or whether this language instead meant that the person only needed to actually believe in the need to defend (a rather curious interpretation). The case below is particularly **noteworthy** because it involved a **notorious shooting** that caused the nation to consider self-defense in the context of **race** and **vigilantism**.

The Goetz case, on the following page, occurred on the New York City subway.

© Benoit Daoust/Shutterstock.com

---

146. From *The Model Penal Code* by the American Law Institute. Copyright © 1962 by the American Law Institute. Used by permission.

People v. Goetz
497 N.E.2d 41 (1986).
Justice Wachtler delivered the opinion of the Court of Appeals of New York.

Facts

[At the time of this opinion, no jury had heard the facts in this case. The matter reached New York's highest court before trial.] A Grand Jury has indicted defendant on attempted murder, assault, and other charges for having shot and wounded four youths on a New York City subway train after one or two of the youths approached him and asked for $5. The lower courts *** dismissed the attempted murder, assault and weapons possession charges. We now reverse and reinstate all counts of the indictment.

[A trial jury will ultimately determine what occurred in this case. We have summarized the facts from the evidence before the Grand Jury.]

[Troy Canty, Darryl Cabey, James Ramseur, and Barry Allen road a subway in the rear portion of a train car.] Two of the four, Ramseur and Cabey, had screwdrivers inside their coats, [used to break into video machine coin boxes. Defendant Bernhard Goetz sat down in the same car occupied by the four youths. Goetz was carrying an unlicensed and loaded .38 caliber pistol in a waistband holster.]

[Without displaying a weapon, Canty approached Goetz, possibly with Allen beside him, and stated "give me five dollars." Goetz stood up, pulled out his handgun and fired] four shots in rapid succession. The first shot hit Canty in the chest; the second struck Allen in the back; the third went through Ramseur's arm and into his left side; the fourth was fired at Cabey [but missed.] After Goetz briefly surveyed the scene around him, he fired another shot at Cabey, who then was sitting on the end bench of the car. The bullet entered the rear of Cabey's side and severed his spinal cord.

[The conductor, who heard the shots, arrived to find Goetz sitting on a bench and the injured youths lying on the floor or slumped against a seat.] Goetz told the conductor that the four youths had tried to rob him.

While the conductor was aiding the youths, Goetz *** jumped onto the tracks and fled. *** Ramseur and Canty, initially listed in critical condition, have fully recovered. Cabey remains paralyzed, and has suffered some degree of brain damage. [Goetz later surrendered to police, making taped and *Mirandized* statements. Goetz admitted that he illegally possessed a handgun that he had purchased after being mugged.]

[Goetz fully described the shooting in his statements. Canty, followed by one of the other youths, stood to the defendant's left, while the other two youths remained to his right.] Canty then said "give me five dollars". Goetz stated that he knew from the smile on Canty's face that they wanted to "play with me". Although he was certain that none of the youths had a gun, [feared, based on prior experiences, being "maimed."]

Goetz then established "a pattern of fire," deciding specifically to fire from left to right. His stated intention at that point was to "murder [the four youths], to hurt them, to make them suffer as much as possible". [Goetz aimed] for the center of the body of each of the four. Goetz recalled that the first two he shot "tried to run through the crowd [but] they had nowhere to run". Goetz then turned to his right to "go after the other two". One of these two "tried to run through the wall of the train, but * * * he had nowhere to go". The other youth (Cabey) "tried pretending that he wasn't with [the others]" by standing still, holding on to one of the subway hand straps, and not looking at Goetz. Goetz nonetheless fired his fourth shot at him. He then ran back to the first two youths to make sure they had been "taken care of". [Goetz told the police, "I said [to Cabey, 'you] seem to be all right, here's another'", and he then fired the shot which severed Cabey's spinal cord. Goetz added that "if I was a little more under self-control * * * I would have put the barrel against his forehead and fired." He also admitted that "if I had had more [bullets], I would have shot them again, and again, and again."

[The lower court dismissed all counts of the indictment other than the reckless endangerment charge. The court found that the prosecutor, in explaining] the justification defense, had erroneously introduced an objective element into this defense by instructing the grand jurors to consider whether Goetz's conduct was that of a "reasonable man in situation". The court *** concluded that the statutory test for whether the use of deadly force is justified to protect a person should be wholly subjective, focusing entirely on the defendant's state of mind when he used such force. ***

Issue

Whether New York's requirement for self defense that an actor can only use deadly force when "he reasonably believes" in the need to use such force has both actual [subjective] and reasonable [objective] requirements.

Rule and Analysis

Penal Law article 35 recognizes the defense of justification, which permits the use of force [for] self-defense and defense of a third person (Penal Law § 35.15). Penal Law § 35.15 (1) [provides: **"a person may] use physical force upon another person when and to the extent he *reasonably believes* such to be necessary to defend himself or a third person from what he *reasonably believes* to be the use or imminent use of unlawful physical force by such other person."** ***

Section 35.15 (2) sets forth further limitations on *** the use of "deadly physical force": "A person may not use deadly physical force upon another person [unless] (a) He *reasonably believes* that such other person is using or about to use deadly physical force * * * or (b) He *reasonably believes* that such other person is committing or attempting to commit a kidnapping, forcible rape, forcible sodomy or robbery." ***

Because the evidence before the second Grand Jury included statements by Goetz that he acted to protect himself from being maimed or to avert a robbery, the prosecutor correctly chose to [instruct on the justification defense.] The prosecutor properly instructed the grand jurors to consider whether the use of deadly physical force was justified to prevent either serious physical injury or a robbery. ***

[One] of the grand jurors asked for clarification of the term "reasonably believes". The prosecutor [instructed the grand jurors to consider the circumstances] and determine "whether the defendant's conduct was that of a reasonable man in the defendant's situation". [The lower court dismissed the charges because the prosecutor specifically used "a reasonable man" as the standard. Since] section 35.15 uses the term *"he* reasonably believes", [the lower court ruled that the appropriate test] is whether a defendant's beliefs and reactions were "reasonable *to him*". Under that reading of the statute, a jury which believed a defendant's testimony that he felt that his own actions were warranted and were reasonable would have to acquit him, regardless of what anyone else in defendant's situation might have concluded. Such an interpretation defies the ordinary meaning and significance of the term "reasonably" in a statute, and misconstrues the clear intent of the Legislature *** to retain an objective element as part of any provision authorizing the use of deadly physical force.

[New York Penal statutes codified the common law right to use deadly physical force, under appropriate circumstances, in self-defense.] These provisions have never required that an actor's belief as to the intention of another person to inflict serious injury be correct in order for the use of deadly force to be justified, but they have uniformly required that the belief comport with an objective notion of reasonableness. ***

[Under] Model Penal Code § 3.04 (2) (b), a defendant charged with murder (or attempted murder) need only show that he *"[believed]* that [the use of deadly force] was necessary to protect himself against death, serious bodily injury, kidnapping or [forcible] sexual intercourse" to prevail on a self-defense claim. [The] Model Penal Code recognized that the wholly subjective test set forth in section 3.04 differed from the existing law in most States by its omission of any requirement of reasonableness. ***

New York did not follow the Model Penal Code's equation of a mistake as to the need to use deadly force with a mistake negating an element of a crime. *** The drafters of the new Penal Law adopted in large part the structure and content of Model Penal Code § 3.04, but, crucially, inserted the word "reasonably" before "believes".

Statutes or rules of law requiring a person to act "reasonably" or to have a "reasonable belief" uniformly prescribe conduct meeting an objective standard measured with reference to how "a reasonable person" could have acted. ***

The prosecutor's instruction to the second Grand Jury that it had to determine whether, under the circumstances, Goetz's conduct was that of a reasonable man in his situation was thus essentially an accurate charge.

Conclusion

[New York retains the objective reasonableness standard for self defense. The dismissed counts of the indictment are reinstated.][147]

What Ever Happened to Bernard Goetz?

Bernard Goetz rescues squirrels. Stephen Rex Brown of the *New York Daily News* reported on June 29, 2015, in, "Subway vigilante Bernard Goetz fighting the possible eviction of his pet squirrel," that Goetz is in litigation with his landlord about the living arrangements of a three-legged squirrel. The article can be viewed at:

http://www.nydailynews.com/new-york/bernie-goetz-fighting-eviction-pet-squirrel-article-1.2274624

In the YouTube video, "Subway Gunman, veggie Bernie Goetz plays with his squirrel," a squirrel can be seen running around Goetz's office and on his person. The video can be viewed at:

https://www.youtube.com/watch?v=FjF5cclrP8Q

---

147. Reprinted with the permission of LexisNexis.

"Imperfect" Self-Defense

The California Supreme Court in, *In Re Christian S.* 7 Cal. 4th 768 (1994), considered the imperfect self-defense argument of Christian S., a minor accused of murdering his bully, Robert Elliot. In this case,

> [The victim, Elliott, was a skinhead] and a possible gang member. After being physically and verbally harassed and threatened by Elliott's friends for about a year, [defendant Christian] began to carry a handgun. Elliott, who blamed defendant for damaging Elliott's truck, chased defendant down the beach one day, repeatedly threatening "to get him" and challenging him to fire his weapon. Elliott halted his advance each time defendant pointed his gun at Elliott. Finally, after some additional taunting by Elliott, defendant shot and killed Elliott from a range of at least 20 feet.

The defendant claimed the trial court wrongfully found that he committed murder by rejecting the his imperfect self defense contention. *Christian S.* noted:

> We explained imperfect self-defense in [the *People v. Flannel* case.] We concluded that **"An honest but unreasonable belief that it is necessary to defend oneself from imminent peril to life or great bodily injury negates malice aforethought, the mental element necessary for murder, so that the chargeable offense is reduced to manslaughter."**

> [The Legislature has not] eliminated the doctrine of imperfect self-defense. When the trier of fact finds that a defendant killed another person because the defendant actually but unreasonably believed he was in imminent danger of death or great bodily injury, the defendant is deemed to have acted without malice and cannot be convicted of murder.

The court remanded the case so that it could be determined whether the defendant held such an actual belief in the need to defend at the time he killed the victim.

"Seamless Web" Connection

The examination of "honest" and "reasonable" beliefs in the *People v. Goetz* and *In Re Christian S.* cases above explore whether the defendant actually held a belief and whether a reasonable person in the defendant's shoes would hold such a belief. The exploration of honest/actual/subjective beliefs and reasonable/objective beliefs also occurs in cases involving the mistake of fact defense. *Goetz* and *In Re Christian S.* therefore connect to the honest v. reasonable belief analysis in the excuse defense, mistake of fact, in Chapter 16.

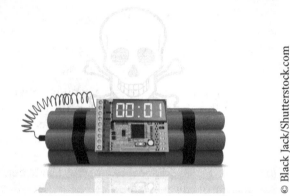

© Black Jack/Shutterstock.com

To use self-defense, a person must be faced with a threat that is imminent, meaning in the present.

2. Imminence of Threat

Self-defense can only be validly used when the threat to the person employing it is "imminent." Just **how immediate** must a threat be to satisfy this "imminence" standard? How is "imminence" measured in the context of a **domestic violence relationship**, where **danger** might seem **ever-present**? The case below demonstrates the difficulty of applying a **common law defense**, created centuries ago, to domestic violence cases today.

LEGAL ANALYSIS

State v. Stewart
763 P.2d 572 (1988).
Justice Lockett delivered the opinion for the Supreme Court of Kansas.

Facts

[Mike Stewart abused his wife, Peggy, and her two daughters, Carla and Laura, from a prior marriage. Mike hit and kicked Peggy and once woke her from a sound sleep by beating her with a baseball bat. He shot one of Peggy's pet cats, and then held the gun against her head and threatened to pull the trigger. Once, when Peggy was working at a cafe, Mike came in and ran all the customers off with a gun because he wanted Peggy to go home and have sex with him right that minute. Mike also forced Peggy to take more than her prescribed dosage of medication for paranoid schizophrenia.

Social workers told Peggy that Mike was taking "indecent liberties" with her daughters. Mike taunted Peggy by stating that Carla, her 12-year-old daughter, was "more of a wife" to him than Peggy. When Peggy demanded that Mike stop abusing Carla, Mike held a shotgun to Peggy's head and threatened to kill her. When Mike ordered Peggy to kill and bury Carla, she filed for divorce.

Peggy left Mike, running away to live with her daughter, Laura, who had moved to Oklahoma. Laura hospitalized Peggy because she was suicidal. Peggy was diagnosed as having toxic psychosis as a result of a medication overdose. Mike came to the hospital to return Peggy to Kansas and she agreed. Mike told the hospital staff that he "needed his housekeeper."

Mike threatened to kill Peggy if she ever ran away again. As soon as they arrived at the house, Mike forced Peggy to have oral sex. Peggy discovered a loaded .357 magnum that she hid under the mattress. As she cleaned house, Mike kept making remarks that she should not bother because she would not be there long. Mike and Peggy went to bed at 8:00 p.m. As Mike slept, Peggy heard voices in her head repeating, "kill or be killed." At 10:00 p.m., Peggy retrieved the gun and killed her husband while he slept. At this time, there were vehicles in the driveway and Peggy had access to the car keys.

Peggy told police she shot Mike to "get this over with, this misery and this torment." Peggy was not sure why she got the gun out. She stated, "My head started playing games with me" and "I didn't want to be by myself again. I got the gun out because there had been remarks made about me being out there alone."

One expert witness at trial diagnosed Peggy as suffering from "battered woman syndrome," or post-traumatic stress syndrome. Another doctor testified that Mike was preparing to escalate the violence in retaliation for Peggy's running away. Loaded guns, veiled threats, and increased sexual demands indicate escalation of the cycle. Thus, Peggy had a repressed knowledge that she was in a "really grave lethal situation."]

The State's expert [rejected battered woman syndrome and learned helplessness as explanations for why women do not leave an abusive relationship. The] trial judge gave an instruction on self-defense to the jury. The jury found Peggy not guilty.

[In Kansas, although] the State may not appeal an acquittal, it may reserve questions for appeal. [The prosecution's appeal] must raise a question of statewide interest, the answer to which is essential to the just administration of criminal law.

Issue

Whether the use of deadly force in self-defense provided by K.S.A. 21-3211 excuses a homicide committed by a battered wife where there is no evidence of a deadly threat or imminent danger contemporaneous with the killing.

Rule and Analysis

[The State argues] that the trial court erred in giving a self-defense instruction since Peggy Stewart was in no imminent danger when she shot her sleeping husband. We agree. *** We further hold that the trial judge's self-defense instruction improperly allowed the jury to determine the reasonableness of defendant's belief that she was in imminent danger from her individual subjective viewpoint rather than the viewpoint of a reasonable person in her circumstances. ***

Under the common law, the excuse for killing in self-defense is founded upon necessity, be it real or apparent. **[Before] a person can take the life of another, it must reasonably appear that his own life must have been in imminent danger**, or that he was in imminent danger of some great bodily injury from the hands of the person killed. **No one can attack and kill another because he may fear injury at some future time." [The perceived imminent danger had to occur in the present time, at the time in which the defendant and the deceased were engaged in their final conflict.]**

These common-law principles [are in K.S.A. 21-3211:] "A person is justified in the use of force against an aggressor when and to the extent it appears to him and he reasonably believes that such conduct is necessary to defend himself or another against such aggressor's imminent use of unlawful force."

The traditional concept of self-defense has posited one-time conflicts between persons of somewhat equal size and strength. When the defendant claiming self-defense is a victim of long-term domestic violence, such as a battered spouse, such traditional concepts may not apply. Because of the prior history of abuse, and the difference in strength and size between the abused and the abuser, the accused in such cases may choose to defend during a momentary lull in the abuse, rather than during a conflict. [**A self-defense instruction requires facts that**] **show that the spouse was in imminent danger close to the time of the killing.**

A person is justified in using force against an aggressor when it appears to that person and he or she reasonably believes such force to be necessary. A reasonable belief implies both an honest belief and the existence of [facts that would persuade a reasonable person to that belief.]

Where self-defense is asserted, evidence of the deceased's long-term cruelty and violence towards the defendant is admissible. [Expert] evidence of the battered woman syndrome is relevant to a determination of the reasonableness of the defendant's perception of danger. [However, the existence of the battered woman syndrome in and of itself does not operate as a defense to murder.]

[**To instruct a jury on self-defense, there must be some showing of an imminent threat.**] **There is no exception to this requirement where the defendant has suffered long-term domestic abuse and the victim is the abuser.** [The issue is not whether the defendant believes homicide is the solution to past or future problems with the batterer, but rather whether circumstances surrounding the killing were sufficient to create a reasonable belief in the defendant that the use of deadly force was necessary.]

[*State v. Hundley* offers a contrast to the present case. *Hundley*] involved a severely abused wife, Betty Hundley, who shot her husband, Carl, when he threatened her and reached for a beer bottle. Several weeks prior to the shooting, Betty had moved to a motel. Carl continued to harass her and threaten her life. On the day of the shooting, Carl threatened to kill her. That night he forcibly broke into Betty's motel room, beat and choked her, painfully shaved her pubic hair, and forced her to have intercourse with him. Thereafter, he pounded a beer bottle on the night stand and demanded that Betty get him some cigarettes. Betty testified that he had attacked her with beer bottles before. She pulled a gun from her purse and demanded that Carl leave. When Carl saw the gun he stated: "You are dead, bitch, now." Betty fired the gun and killed Carl.

[*Hundley*] involved a threat of death to the wife and a violent confrontation between husband and wife, contemporaneous with the shooting. [In the present case], however, there is an absence of imminent danger to defendant: Peggy told a nurse at the Oklahoma hospital of her desire to kill Mike. She later voluntarily agreed to return home with Mike. *** Peggy showed no inclination to leave. In fact, immediately after the shooting, Peggy told the police that she was upset because she thought Mike would leave her. Prior to the shooting, Peggy hid the loaded gun. The cars were in the driveway and Peggy had access to the car keys. After being abused, Peggy went to bed with Mike at 8 p.m. Peggy lay there for two hours, then retrieved the gun from where she had hidden it and shot Mike while he slept. Under these facts, the giving of the self-defense instruction was erroneous. [Here], a battered woman cannot reasonably fear imminent life-threatening danger from her sleeping spouse. ***

"To permit capital punishment to be imposed upon the subjective conclusion of the [abused] individual that prior acts and conduct of the deceased justified the killing would amount to a leap into the abyss of anarchy." ***

Conclusion

[When] a battered woman kills her sleeping spouse when there is no imminent danger, the killing is not reasonably necessary and a self-defense instruction may not be given. To hold otherwise in this case would in effect allow the execution of the abuser for past or future acts and conduct.[148]

---

148. Reprinted with the permission of LexisNexis.

Many lay people would not be surprised by *Stewart's* outcome, figuring that the real factor deciding the case was the "He had it coming" defense, which is not formally recognized by law.

© BlueSkyImage/Shutterstock.com

3.   Use of Reasonable Force

The following case provides insight into the **self-defense** requirement that the defendant defend himself with only "**reasonable force**." Can **shooting a gun** ever be considered "reasonable force" against a **thrown rock**? As noted by the case below, it depends on "**the totality of the circumstances**"—looking at all of the facts in the case. *Williams* also provides insight into the debate between the defendant having to **retreat before using deadly force** or being able to "**stand his ground**."

LEGAL ANALYSIS

People v. Williams
205 N.E.2d 749 (1965).
Justice Lyons delivered the opinion for the Appellate Court of Illinois.

Facts

On April 12, 1963, at about eight o'clock in the evening, defendant, while driving a Yellow Cab south on Princeton Avenue [in Chicago, stopped for a traffic light. He observed a group of young men] beating an old man, later identified as one Joseph Bell. The victim of the assault, while lying on the sidewalk, called to defendant for help. When defendant shouted to the boys to leave the victim alone, the boys shouted back insults. [A rock or brick struck defendant's cab. Defendant stopped his cab near the boys.] He fired two shots in their direction. The boys ran. Defendant drove away. One of the boys, Kenneth Boatner, age 16, was killed, the result of a bullet wound in the brain.

[Defendant first told the police he knew nothing of the shooting, but later agreed to tell the truth.] He also gave the police his .380 Beretta revolver, which he admitted firing at the boys. In a signed statement, admitted into evidence, he stated:

[I noticed the boys who were beating the man up. One] of them threw a rock at my cab. I then stopped the cab about twenty feet, opened the cab door on my side and took the gun from my belt *** and stepped out of the cab with one leg in the cab and the other out. I then held my hand with the gun in it and fired two shots over the roof of the cab in the direction of the boys on the corner. [After waiving jury trial, defendant was convicted of involuntary manslaughter.]

Issue

Whether the defendant used "reasonable force" in proportion to the threat for purposes of self defense when he fired a gun at a gang that had thrown a brick at his car.

Rule and Analysis

[The elements which justify the use of force in the defense of a person are:] (1) that force is threatened against a person; (2) that the person threatened is not the aggressor; (3) that the danger of harm is imminent; (4) that the force threatened is unlawful; (5) that the person threatened must actually believe: (a) that a danger exists, (b) that the use of force is necessary to avert the danger, (c) that the kind and amount of force which he uses is necessary; and (6) that the above beliefs are reasonable. [Deadly force can only be used in] those situations in which (a) the threatened force will cause death or great bodily harm or (b) the force threatened is a forcible felony.

It is uncontroverted that a brick was thrown at defendant. Thus, **(1)** the use of force was threatened against defendant. [The State does not contend that defendant was the aggressor **(2)**.]

The State contends that the **(3)** danger to defendant was not imminent [because] the deceased did not have the present ability of carrying out the alleged threat. This contention is invalid. There were several boys in the gang and they had just thrown a cement block and a brick at defendant's cab, the latter causing substantial damage to the right door (a picture of the damage to the cab was introduced in evidence). The gang was a short distance from defendant. They had the present ability to carry out the threatened use of force. The deceased, identified as part of the gang that damaged the cab, also had the present ability to carry out the threatened harm.

The evidence that the gang threw a brick against the cab of defendant was sufficient to show that the threatened force was unlawful **(4)**. Thus, we can proceed to the fifth and sixth elements.

To satisfy the fifth and sixth elements it must be determined whether or not defendant **(5)** actually believed that **(a)** a danger existed; that the **(b)** use of force was necessary to avert the danger; that **(c)** the kind and amount of force used was necessary; and that **(6)** such belief was reasonable. A belief is reasonable even if the defendant is mistaken. Defendant had just seen an elderly man beaten up. Furthermore, we again emphasize the fact that the gang, consisting of a number of young men, had just thrown a cement block and a brick at defendant's cab and that they caused substantial damage to the cab. Defendant testified that when he stopped his cab, the gang started to move toward him. There is only one conclusion that can be reached—defendant actually believed that a danger existed. ***

Next we must determine the difficult question of whether or not defendant reasonably believed that the kind and amount of force which he used was necessary. Again we stress the principle that belief is reasonable even if the defendant is mistaken. In reviewing the facts we must sustain defendant's contention that he believed the use of a gun was necessary. Defendant had been robbed several weeks before the incident. He was a cab driver approaching a vicious gang of youths. It was night time. Defendant had just observed Bell being beaten up and stomped on. The gang told him to mind his own business. [His] cab was hit by a brick. The gang of young men were obviously hostile to him because of his intrusion. He had no other weapon. Furthermore, what is really important is defendant's state of mind at the time of the incident. He testified that he was afraid that he would be beat up like Bell. He knew that the gang was aware that, as a cab driver, he had money on his person. Defendant in using the gun reasonably believed that the kind of force used was necessary. [Defendant] testified, [and the trial judge believed,] that he shot up in the air to scare the boys off.] We can only conclude that defendant reasonably believed that both the kind and amount of force used was necessary under the circumstances.

Finally, we must determine if the use of deadly force by defendant was justified. **[Deadly force] is justified if the threatened force would cause death or great bodily harm or is a forcible felony.** It is apparent that the throwing of bricks at defendant could have caused death or great bodily harm if defendant was struck by one of them. Defendant was justified in using deadly force to protect his person.

In this case we only hold that when a person comes to the aid of another who has been the victim of a battery, said person has the right to use deadly force, if the parties who were the assailants attack him and if the other requirements of self-defense are met. **The circumstances of this case present a situation in which we approach the minimum borderline of self-defense.** The circumstances are such, however, that the judgment must be reversed.

Conclusion

There was sufficient evidence for all of the elements of self defense, including the element that the defendant use reasonable force in defending himself.

Judgment reversed.[149]

Model Penal Code § 3.04: Use of Force in Self-Protection

(2)(b) The use of deadly force is not justifiable under this Section unless the actor believes that such force is necessary to protect himself against death, serious bodily injury, kidnapping or sexual intercourse compelled by force or threat . . .[150]

4.   To Counter an Unlawful Harm

If a person starts a fight (is the "aggressor,") can he or she ever regain the right to self-defense? In order for an aggressor to gain such a right, he or she must (1) **withdraw from the conflict**, and (2) **communicate that withdrawal** to "remove any just apprehension or fear the original victim may be experiencing." The following case considers the facts of a robbery to see if such a withdrawal occurred.

LEGAL ANALYSIS

Bellcourt v. State
390 N.W.2d 269 (1986).
Justice Amdahl delivered the opinion of the Minnesota Supreme Court.

Facts

[Defendant John Clinton Bellcourt appealed from a conviction for first-degree felony murder, arguing the trial court erred in refusing to instruct the jury on the revival of an aggressor's right to self-defense.] We affirm.

[Having run out of beer and money, defendant and his friend Norris decided to rob the Minnehaha Liquor Store.] Since defendant was a regular customer at the store and knew he would be recognized, he covered his fingerless left hand with a mitten and his face with a ski mask. [Defendant had a .357 revolver when he and Norris entered the store.] On duty at the store were the checkout clerk, Eileen Riddle; the owner, James Nordin; his son, Paul; and Dave Ceason, the store's delivery driver. ***

Defendant ordered James Nordin to open the safe. [James Nordin shot defendant with his .38 revolver.] The bullet hit defendant in the chest at an angle, about 4 inches below his left nipple, went through part of his stomach, and broke a rib on the right side of his back. ***

Defendant testified that the shot knocked the wind out of him and he began losing control of his body. He took a couple of sidesteps and fell on the floor; the ski mask had turned on his face, partially obstructing his vision. Through one eyehole, he saw a gun coming toward his face, with the hand holding the gun becoming white and tightening. He testified that he tried to readjust the mask with his bad hand, but he just made the problem worse and his gun "went off." He finally got the mask off, yelled "I think I'm hit," got up and ran out of the store.

Paul Nordin [saw his father James Nordin] leaning on a garbage can, about 3 feet in front of the safe, and defendant lying on his right side on the floor. Defendant's mask had come off. Paul stated that his father said something like "No, John, don't" and defendant began to fire again. Paul saw the bullets come out James' back, then James pivoted and fell on his face. ***

*** James Nordin died at the scene from massive internal hemorrhaging caused by gunshot wounds. [A jury convicted Defendant of first-degree murder.]

Issue

Whether defendant was entitled to a jury instruction on self-defense even though he, as a robber, was the initial aggressor.

Rule and Analysis

In Minnesota, three conditions must exist in order to excuse or justify the use of deadly force under Minn. Stat. §§ 609.06,.065 (1984):

(1) **The killing must have been done in the belief that it was necessary to avert death or grievous bodily harm.**

(2) **The judgment of the defendant as to the gravity of the peril to which he was exposed must have been reasonable under the circumstances.**

(3) **The defendant's election to kill must have been such as a reasonable man would have made in light of the danger to be apprehended.** ***

An aggressor in an incident has no right to a claim of self-defense. However, **where the defendant is the original aggressor** in an incident giving rise to his self-defense claim, an instruction on **self-defense will be available to him only if he actually and in good faith withdraws from the conflict and communicates that withdrawal, expressly or impliedly, to his intended victim**. [Other jurisdictions make] clear that an aggressor has the duty to employ all means in his power to avert the necessity of killing, and before his right to self-defense may be revived, he must clearly manifest a good-faith intention to withdraw from the affray and must remove any just apprehension or fear the original victim may be experiencing. *** If the circumstances are such that it is impossible for defendant to communicate the withdrawal, "'it is attributable to his own fault and he must abide by the consequences.'"*** In the present case, a self-defense instruction would be justified only if a reasonable juror could find that defendant had withdrawn from the confrontation. Clearly, **there was no withdrawal here**. At the time defendant was shot, he was holding five people at gunpoint. After being hit, he fell to the floor but held on to his gun. Had he truly intended to withdraw from the robbery and communicate that withdrawal to his victim, he would have either released the gun, said something to the effect of "I give up," or both. Instead, he lifted his gun in James Nordin's direction and pulled the trigger 5 times. Defendant then rose, ran out of the store, and was seen by a disinterested witness carrying a bag that we can assume contained the robbery loot. In other words, after the shooting, defendant completed the robbery by his asportation of the money. ***

Conclusion

Defendant clearly did not withdraw from the crime and an instruction on self-defense would have been improper. *** Affirmed.[151]

"Seamless Web" Connection

The *Bellcourt v. State* case above noted that being labeled an aggressor could cause a defendant to no longer be eligible for self-defense. Similarly, in *People v. Newton* in Chapter 2, being deemed an aggressor could cause a defendant to lose the opportunity to use the unconsciousness defense. Here, a seamless web connection can be made between self-defense and unconsciousness because both employ an analysis condemning the original aggressor.

---

5.   Retreat Requirement

Model Penal Code § 3.04: Use of Force in Self-Protection

(2)(b) The use of deadly force is not justifiable under this Section . . . if:

(ii) the actor knows that he can avoid the necessity of using such force with complete safety by retreating or by surrendering possession of a thing to a person asserting a claim of right thereto or by complying with a demand that he abstain from any action that he has no duty to take, except that:

(A) the actor is not obliged to retreat from his dwelling or place of work, unless he was the initial aggressor or is assailed in his place of work by another person whose place of work the actor knows it to be.[152]

Suppose a person throws a punch at you. You can defend yourself by blocking that punch. In so doing, you are roughly matching a nondeadly threat with nondeadly force. If instead a person threatens you with a gun or knife, or is committing a crime threatening serious bodily injury (such as robbery), you can match this deadly threat with deadly force. **Before using deadly force, however, must you first attempt to retreat, or can you stand your ground?** The following case explores this issue.

---

151. Reprinted with the permission of LexisNexis.

152. From *The Model Penal Code* by the American Law Institute. Copyright © 1962 by the American Law Institute. Used by permission.

LEGAL ANALYSIS

People v. Williams
205 N.E.2d 749 (1965).
[For the full facts of this case regarding a cab driver shooting and killing a juvenile after a gang threw a brick at his car, see "3. Use of Reasonable Force" above.]

Issue

Whether the defendant had to retreat before using deadly force in self defense or whether he could "stand his ground" while still relying on the defense.

Rule and Analysis

The State contends that defendant could have driven away from the scene of the incident with his cab and thus the use of force was unnecessary. We disagree. *** **When a defendant is where he has a lawful right to be, he has a right to stand his ground, and if reasonably apprehensive of injury is justified in taking his assailant's life.** *** Defendant was under no duty to flee. Furthermore, defendant testified that he had not left the area, because of his desire to help the victim of the assault, Joseph Bell. We will take judicial notice of the fact, that recently there have been a number of publicized assaults and homicides, in which the victims called upon their fellow citizens to render aid. In many instances these fellow citizens refused to get involved. Here [is] a man who took it upon himself to get involved, when a victim called for help. [Public] policy forbids us to say a person must leave the victim of a brutal beating lie on the street when called upon to render aid. **A citizen must feel free to help the victim of an assault**. The State alleges that there was no danger to the victim Bell, as the gang of young men had already walked away from Bell and apparently had terminated the beating. They conclude that defendant should have left the scene of the incident. This allegation does not take into consideration the fact that the gang could have returned and further assaulted the victim after defendant left. We must also consider the language in the stipulation that if Bell testified, he would say of defendant, "the only thing I know, *he saved my life.*" ***

George Zimmerman after his "Stand Your Ground" Case in Florida

Writing for *Salon.com*, Katie McDonough reported on November 22, 2013, in her article, "George Zimmerman could still get his guns back," that:

A judge ordered Zimmerman to surrender his firearms, but that's only for the time being.

Less than three months after his estranged wife called the police to report him for allegedly threatening her with a firearm during a domestic dispute, George Zimmerman is in the news for allegedly threatening his current girlfriend, Samantha Scheibe, with a firearm during a domestic dispute. But this time, charges were filed.

As a result, a Florida judge on Tuesday ordered Zimmerman to surrender his firearms—weapons he was allowed to keep and conceal despite a history of the use of deadly force.

But being required to give them up doesn't mean he won't get them back. In fact, it doesn't even mean he will have to give them up.[153]

This article can be viewed at:

http://www.salon.com/2013/11/22/george_zimmerman_could_still_get_his_guns_back/

In the "*Perspective*" portion of the *Los Angeles Times*, Robin Abcarian wrote about Zimmerman's domestic troubles in "Will George Zimmerman's dueling 911 calls cancel each other out?" Abcarian declared that Zimmerman would get in trouble sooner or later.
This article and video can be viewed at:

http://www.latimes.com/local/lanow/la-me-ln-will-george-zimmermans-dueling-911-calls-cancel-each-other-out-20131119,0,6302563.story#axzz2lCkifAnL

B.   DEFENSE OF OTHERS

Model Penal Code § 3.05: Use of Force for the Protection of Other Persons

(1) Subject to the provisions of this Section and of Section 3.09, the use of force upon or toward the person of another is justifiable to protect a third person when:

(a) the actor would be justified under Section 3.04 in using such force to protect himself against the injury he believes to be threatened to the person whom he seeks to protect; and

(b) under the circumstances as the actor believes them to be, the person whom he seeks to protect would be justified in using such protective force; and

(c) the actor believes that his intervention is necessary for the protection of such other person.

(2) Notwithstanding Subsection (1) of this Section:

(a) when the actor would be obliged under Section 3.04 to retreat, to surrender the possession of a thing or to comply with a demand before using force in self-protection, he is not obliged to do so before using force for the protection of another person, unless he knows that he can thereby secure the complete safety of such other person; and

(b) when the person whom the actor seeks to protect would be obliged under Section 3.04 to retreat, to surrender the possession of a thing or to comply with a demand if he knew that he could obtain complete safety by so doing, the actor is obliged to try to cause him to do so before using force in his protection if the actor knows that he can obtain complete safety in that way; and

(c) neither the actor nor the person whom he seeks to protect is obliged to retreat when in the other's dwelling or place of work to any greater extent than in his own.[154]

---

153. From "George Zimmerman could still get his guns back" by Katie McDonough, Salon.com, November 22, 2013. Copyright © 2014 Salon Media Group, Inc. Used by permission.
154. From *The Model Penal Code* by the American Law Institute. Copyright © 1962 by the American Law Institute. Used by permission.

In Ruling on the Defense of Others, Should the Law Promote Heroism or Caution?

Suppose, while walking down the street, you glance down an alley only to see an old friend being beaten to death by two assailants. Your first impulse is to run away to safety, but your better nature causes you to rush to your friend's aid. You run up and punch the attackers, each of whom fall back and stop fighting. Suddenly, you hear, "Cut!" You now, for the first time, see a handheld camera and various other persons in the background. It turned out that your friend was in no danger; instead he was acting in a small scene of an action movie. The men you hit were not attackers but stuntmen, the blood not real but makeup. You are then charged with two counts of assault.

How should the law assess a person committing violence in order to defend another person? Further, what should the law do about a person who acts violently to save another when the supposed victim was actually in no danger and the would-be defender was mistaken about the need to defend in the first place? Some jurisdictions promote heroism, allowing the person acting on the mistaken belief to use the "defense of others" defense so long as he or she reasonably believed in the need to defend. Others do not allow the defense for mistaken defenders, even if their belief was reasonable. In these jurisdictions, known as "alter ego" jurisdictions, the would-be defender becomes the "alter ego" of the person he or she seeks to defend, and therefore only possesses the right to defend that the supposed victim had. The "alter ego" jurisdictions favor caution over misguided heroism.

Reasonable Belief

The Supreme Court of Wyoming adopted this form of "the defense of others" defense in *Duckett v. State*, 966 P.2d 941 (1998). In *Duckett*, Steven Wayne Duckett and his wife were visiting the home of Mary Carlson and her boyfriend, Mylo Hetler. After drinking and playing music, which was tape-recorded on a karoake machine, Carlson and Duckett argued over "their respective talents." Carlson demanded the Ducketts leave the premises, which ultimately resulted in Carlson and Duckett's wife physically fighting while Hetler and Duckett struggled on the floor. Duckett stabbed Hetler eight times. The *Duckett* court noted:

> Duckett testified that when his wife reached for the musical tape, Carlson pushed her away. Duckett then reached for the musical tape, but stopped when he heard his wife scream, "Help. She's killing me." Duckett turned, and saw Carlson on top of his wife, slamming her head against the concrete floor. When he moved to help her, Hetler jumped off the couch and tackled him. *** Hetler was on top of Duckett as they struggled. Duckett told Hetler to free him because Carlson was killing his wife and he needed to help her. Duckett asked Hetler to help him stop Carlson. As the two men fought, Duckett could hear his wife begging for help while he continued to hear her head hitting the floor. [He told Hetler he "was going to have to hurt him."] Duckett pulled his knife and stabbed Hetler, but it only made Hetler angrier. Duckett continued to stab until he was able to push Hetler off of him. As Duckett tried to get to his wife, "somebody [swung him] towards the garage door." He again moved toward his wife, and "somebody had the baseball bat [and chased him] out the door."

> Realizing there was nothing more he could do to reach his wife, Duckett fled [down the street knocking on doors, finally getting someone to call 911 by explaining that] his wife was assaulted and he had stabbed someone. [Duckett spoke with the operator. When he got back to the area, he saw his wife leaving the house next door to Carlson's. Duckett grabbed her and ran away.]

At Duckett's aggravated assault trial, the judge instructed the jury, "For the 'defense of others,' ***
the Defendant must have used necessary force *against the person perceived to be threatening someone
else.*" Duckett argued the court erred in denying him the defense of others defense. *Duckett* explained:

> **[Defense of another takes its] content from defense of self. The defender is not
> justified in using force unless he or she reasonably believes the person defended is
> in immediate danger of unlawful bodily harm, and that the force is reasonable and
> necessary to prevent that threat.**

> [Duckett] testified that he never believed *he* was in imminent danger, but stabbed Hetler
> because he believed his wife was in imminent danger and that Hetler would not allow him
> to go to her rescue.

> **[The] specific issue in this case is whether the justification for inflicting harm on a
> person in "defense of others" applies to situations in which the person harmed did
> not actually threaten the person defended, but actively prevented the rescuer from
> reaching the assailant. ***

> *** However, we see no reasoned distinction between the justification to use force against
> an individual approaching the fray and the use of force against one knowingly standing
> guard to prevent rescue. In either case, the assailant's purpose, and the danger to the
> victim, is furthered by the actions of the assailant's confederate, and the danger to the
> victim may be alleviated only by the use of force against those acting in concert with the
> actual assailant. ***

> **We therefore hold that a person raising the "defense of others" in justification for
> injury to a person other than the victim's actual assailant must show a reasonable
> belief that the person defended is in imminent danger of unlawful bodily harm, and a
> reasonable belief that another person is associated and participating with the actual
> assailant, and the force used against any aggressor is reasonable and necessary to
> prevent the harm.**

> [We] find the evidence sufficient to warrant an instruction on the defense of others. Carlson
> initiated the fight when she grabbed Mrs. Duckett and threw her to the floor. Carlson was
> intoxicated, and was much larger than her victim. Hetler attacked Duckett to prevent
> Duckett from interfering with the assault on Mrs. Duckett. Duckett, and presumably
> Hetler, saw Carlson beating Mrs. Duckett's head against a concrete floor. Mrs. Duckett
> was screaming as Duckett and Hetler struggled, and both participants continued to hear
> Mrs. Duckett's head hitting the cement. Despite Duckett's frantic pleas for help in rescuing
> his wife, Hetler deliberately held Duckett back while Carlson continued her assault. It was
> only then that Duckett used his knife to break free. Even then, Duckett was again prevented
> from assisting his wife. Left with no other choice, he fled for help.

> We, therefore, reverse and remand for a new trial.[155]

Alter Ego

The Supreme Court of Rhode Island adopted this form of "the defense of others" in *State v. Gelinas*,
417 A.2d 1381 (1980). A jury convicted Terrence Gelinas "of assault on a uniformed police officer
engaged in the performance of his duties." In *Gelinas*, two Woonsocket police officers, Magnan and
LeDuc, confiscated liquor from four juveniles and ordered them into their patrol car. One of the four,

---

155. Reprinted with the permission of LexisNexis.

defendant's younger brother Billy Gelinas, refused, causing Officer Magnan to placed his hand on him. Billy struggled, causing Magnan to try to subdue him while Officer LeDuc fended off the crowd with his nightstick. Billy's older brothers, Eddy Gelinas and defendant, Terrence Gelinas, got involved. The defendant shoved Officer LeDuc, threatening, "Leave my brother alone, LeDuc, or I'm going to get you." When the crowd began pressing in, LeDuc ran to his cruiser to radio for help. Officer LeDuc then saw "his partner struggling on the ground with both Billy and Eddy Gelinas, the latter striking the officer with a piece of tar about the back and head." Officer LeDuc then struck Eddy Gelinas with his club. LeDuc turned around "to defend against an anticipated attack from defendant whom he knew to have followed close behind." Defendant struck Officer LeDuc in the face. When LeDuc fell on the ground, defendant "sat on him and began striking him." The defendant picked up a piece of concrete and stuck LeDuc "in the face with it as he lay on the ground." Thereafter, LeDuc "could not see." The *Gelinas* court chose the "alter ego" form of defense of others, explaining:

> [Two contrasting principles can control the defense of another. Some] jurisdictions adhere to the somewhat antiquated view that a person may only defend others to whom he is somehow related, either by consanguinity, employment, marriage, or acquaintance. [These] states believe that the relationship between the protector and his charge not only compels action but also minimizes the likelihood that the actor will misinterpret the situation, [interceding on behalf of the wrongdoer. We believe that restricting the privilege only to family members ignores the important social goal of crime prevention, a duty of every citizen. **Some states take] the position that a third-party intervenor stands in the shoes of a person whom he is aiding. Under this view it is immaterial whether the intervenor defendant acted as a reasonable person ***; the right attaches to the defendant only when the person being defended would have had the right of self-defense.** ***. In contrast, other jurisdictions focus on the conduct of the intervenor without regard to the self-defense claim of the arrestee and hold that an intervenor may aid another if it appears to be necessary, though he acts on a mistaken belief, even in a situation in which the person who is aided would not have had the right to claim self-defense. ***

> [We] hereby adopt the rule that one who comes to the aid of an arrestee must do so at his own peril and should be excused only when the individual would himself be justified in defending himself from the use of excessive force by the arresting officer. *** **A third party intervenor stands in the shoes of the person whom he is aiding. The defendant may use such force to prevent injury to the person he aids as defendant would use in self-defense.** ***

> The defendant [was entitled to an instruction that he] was justified in interfering with the arrest of his brother if the arrestee was himself justified in resisting arrest. [The trial judge] adequately charged the jury as to the rights of a person who defends another against the use of excessive force. He told the jury in clear language that unless they found that Officer LeDuc has used excessive force against defendant's brother, they could not find that defendant had acted justifiably. This instruction is consistent with the rule we adopt today since if Officer LeDuc had not used excessive force, Edward could have had no right to resist the arrest, and, accordingly, defendant could not have been privileged to come to Edward's defense. The jury therefore resolved this factual issue [with a proper instruction. The conviction is affirmed.][156]

---

156. Reprinted with the permission of LexisNexis.

Biography—Police

Jeri Williams

- Spent over twenty years "rising through the ranks" at the Phoenix Police Department, becoming Assistant Chief in 2009, according to Megan Cassidy and Garrett Mitchell of *The Arizona Republic*, in "'I. Am. Your. Chief.': Jeri Williams, Phoenix's first female police chief, now on duty," at http://www.azcentral.com/story/news/local/phoenix/2016/10/28/phoenix-police-chief-jeri-williams-sworn-today/92890036/.
- Williams then went to California to lead the Oxnard Police Department.
- In Oxnard, Williams **also served as an ordained minister**, according to Wendy Lueng of the *Ventura County Star*, in "Police Chief Jeri Williams wraps up tenure in Oxnard," September 14, 2016, http://www.vcstar.com/story/news/local/communities/oxnard/2016/09/14/police-chief-jeri-williams-wraps-up-tenure-oxnard/90345382/.
- The *Ventura County Star* reported, Williams "is charismatic and always showed empathy, the opposite of a robotic police officer."
- In 2016, Williams returned to Arizona to become Chief of the Phoenix Police Department, which, according to *The Arizona Republic*, has "nearly 4,000 employees on its payroll, covers 500 square miles and operates a $475 million budget."

C.   DEFENSE OF PROPERTY

Texas Penal Code § 9.41: Protection of One's Own Property

(a) A person in lawful possession of land or tangible, movable property is justified in using force against another when and to the degree the actor reasonably believes the force is immediately necessary to prevent or terminate the other's trespass on the land or unlawful interference with the property.

(b) A person unlawfully dispossessed of land or tangible, movable property by another is justified in using force against the other when and to the degree the actor reasonably believes the force is immediately necessary to reenter the land or recover the property if the actor uses the force immediately or in fresh pursuit after the dispossession and:

(1) the actor reasonably believes the other had no claim of right when he dispossessed the actor; or

(2) the other accomplished the dispossession by using force, threat, or fraud against the actor.

Texas Penal Code § 9.42: Deadly Force to Protect Property

A person is justified in using deadly force against another to protect land or tangible, movable property:

(1) if he would be justified in using force against the other under Section 9.41; and

(2) when and to the degree he reasonably believes the deadly force is immediately necessary:

(A) to prevent the other's imminent commission of arson, burglary, robbery, aggravated robbery, theft during the nighttime, or criminal mischief during the nighttime; or

(B) to prevent the other who is fleeing immediately after committing burglary, robbery, aggravated robbery, or theft during the nighttime from escaping with the property; and

(3) he reasonably believes that:

(A) the land or property cannot be protected or recovered by any other means; or

(B) the use of force other than deadly force to protect or recover the land or property would expose the actor or another to a substantial risk of death or serious bodily injury.

What evidence must a person offer in order to make a defense-of-property claim for use of deadly force? The following case considers evidence that the defendant was faced with a **felony threatening death or serious bodily injury** (aggravated robbery in Texas). Note that **if the defendant presents such evidence**, an appellate court **will require the trial judge to allow the defendant to make his defense of property defense** to the jury. The appellate court only rules on the law, leaving issues of credibility or believability of evidence to the trial jury to judge.

LEGAL ANALYSIS

Sparks v. State
177 S.W.3d 127 (2005).
Justice Alcala delivered the opinion for the Court of Appeals of Texas.

Facts

[A jury convicted Appellant, Donald Sparks, of murder of Deborah Lauren Alexander (Lauren), and aggravated assault of Samuel Keith Thompson (Sammy). The trial court improperly instructed the jury on self-defense and defense of property.]

[Appellant, a 70 year-old retired widower, had been friends with Lauren for three years. After both appellant and Lauren smoked crack cocaine,] Lauren introduced appellant to Sammy. Sammy and Lauren then went to appellant's trailer where they] slept on appellant's couch while appellant lay on his bed.]

Sammy testified as follows. Appellant lay on his bed with a .22 rifle next to him as Sammy and Lauren slept on the sofa. When they all rose at about 9:00 a.m., appellant and Lauren started arguing. [Appellant shot Lauren in the face with his .22 rifle and then pointed the rifle at Sammy. Sammy rushed at appellant and grabbed the end of the .22 rifle's barrel,] causing the gun to discharge a bullet that struck Sammy's left thumb. Sammy took possession of the .22 rifle. As Sammy tried to unlock the door to leave the trailer, appellant, now armed with a .410 shotgun, shot at Sammy, but missed him. Sammy opened the door and ran outside. Appellant [again shot at and missed Sammy.] Sammy then heard another muffled gunshot that sounded as if it came from inside the trailer house. Sammy ran [away and called for police and an ambulance.]

Appellant testified as follows. At around 3 a.m., [Lauren became "out of control" causing appellant to fear that Lauren and Sammy would rob him. At 9:00 a.m., when appellant refused to loan Lauren money, she stabbed appellant three times in the arm with a pair of scissors, but appellant "really didn't think Lauren would hurt him."] Sammy, who had hidden appellant's .410 shotgun inside his jacket, pulled out the .410 shotgun, pointed it at appellant and said, "I have to have my money cause [sic] my wife will kill me if I don't get it," which caused appellant to fear for his life. In a sudden reverse of emotion, Lauren switched the focus of her aggression to Sammy and attacked him in an attempt to protect appellant.

[Appellant pointed his .22 rifle] at Sammy, who was on top of Lauren, beating her with his hands and with the sawed-off .410 shotgun. [Sammy] "brought up the shotgun . . . and then grabbed appellant's .22 rifle, which discharged, shooting Lauren. Sammy grabbed appellant, slung him around like a "rag doll," and tried to shoot him with the .22 rifle, but it would not fire. When Sammy pointed the .410 shotgun under appellant's chin, appellant used all of his strength to push the .410 shotgun off, which caused it to fire, shooting Lauren a second time. Sammy threw down the .410 shotgun, picked up the .22 rifle, and ran out the door. [Appellant picked up the .410 shotgun, went outside, shot at Sammy, and missed him. As he ran, Sammy fired the .22 rifle towards appellant's trailer. Appellant then called police.]

Issue

Whether the appellant had a valid "defense of property" defense for his killing of Lauren and his harming of Sammy.

Rule and Analysis

[Texas law provides] that a person may use non-deadly force to defend property under certain circumstances. Section 9.41 of the Penal Code states the following: (a) **A person in lawful possession of land or tangible, movable property is justified in using force against another when and to the degree the actor reasonably believes the force is immediately necessary to prevent or terminate the other's trespass on the land or unlawful interference with the property**. (b) A person unlawfully dispossessed of land or tangible, movable property by another is justified in using force against the other when and to the degree the actor reasonably believes the force is immediately necessary to reenter the land or recover the property if the actor uses the force immediately or in fresh pursuit after the dispossession and; (1) the actor reasonably believes the other had no claim of right when he dispossessed the actor; or (2) the other accomplished the dispossession by using force, threat, or fraud against the actor.

[Texas Penal Code Section 9.42] provides that a person is justified in using deadly force to defend property under certain circumstances, as follows:

> **A person is justified in using deadly force against another to protect land or tangible, movable property**: (1) if he would be justified in using force against the other under Section 9.41; and (2) when and to the degree he reasonably believes the force is immediately necessary: (A) **to prevent the other's imminent commission of arson, burglary, robbery, aggravated robbery**, theft during the nighttime, or criminal mischief during the nighttime; or (B) **to prevent the other who is fleeing immediately after committing burglary, robbery**, aggravated robbery, or theft during the nighttime from escaping with the property; and (3) he reasonably believes that: (A) the land or property cannot be protected or recovered by any other means; or (B) the use of force other than deadly force to protect or recover the land or property would expose the actor or another to a substantial risk of death or serious bodily injury. ***
>
> According to appellant, Sammy pointed the .410 shotgun at him and demanded his money, which caused him to fear for his life. Appellant testified that, in response to this aggravated robbery, he armed himself with the .22 rifle and struggled with Sammy, who used the sawed-off .410 shotgun to beat Lauren. Appellant further testified that his .22 rifle discharged, when Sammy grabbed it, and shot Lauren. **Without regard to its credibility, appellant's testimony was sufficient to raise the issue of his right to use deadly force to defend his property.** [The trial court mistakenly denied] a defense-of-property instruction concerning appellant's right to use deadly force to defend his property from Sammy for both the murder and aggravated assault offenses. ***
>
> Although, according to appellant's testimony, Lauren had previously stabbed appellant after he refused to give her more money, appellant clearly stated that, when he armed himself

with the .22 rifle that morning when Lauren was shot, Lauren was in the course of defending appellant from Sammy's threats with the .410 shotgun, and he "really didn't think Lauren would hurt [appellant.]" The trial court did not err, therefore, by denying the defense-of-property instruction concerning Lauren, who, by appellant's own testimony was assisting him and not attacking or robbing him when appellant acted to defend his property. ***

Conclusion

The trial court erred by denying a defense-of-property instruction concerning appellant's right to use deadly force to defend his property from Sammy. [The judgment is reversed.][157]

Note

The Court of Appeal was careful to explain that it was not finding that Sparks's version of events were true, but only that his testimony raised a conflict in the facts that allowed him a right to the "defense of property" jury instruction. The court remanded the case to the lower court to have a jury hash out the facts.

The following case involved a trap gun.

Suppose a burglar repeatedly breaks into your home when you are away. **What force can you use to defend your property from the burglar**? Do you have to stay at home all the time in order to protect it from intruders or can you set up a **"trap gun"** which will automatically fire on any prowler? What about the fact that **not all burglaries are equally dangerous** to victims? Perhaps **homicide** can only be **"justified"** when it is against burglars who intend to commit **"forcible or atrocious felonies"** within the home. The case following considers these issues.

---

157. Reprinted with the permission of LexisNexis.

LEGAL ANALYSIS

People v. Ceballos
12 Cal. 3d 470 (1974).
Justice Burke delivered the opinion of the Supreme Court of California.

Facts

[Defendant, living alone, sometimes slept in the garage. He had about $2,500 worth of property there.]

[The defendant noticed that some of his tools were stolen, the lock on his garage doors was bent, and the doors had pry marks. He] mounted a loaded .22 caliber pistol in the garage. The pistol was aimed at the center of the garage doors and was [rigged to] discharge if the door was opened several inches.

The damage to defendant's lock had been done by a 16-year-old boy named Stephen and a 15-year-old boy named Robert. [The] boys returned to defendant's house while he was away. Neither boy was armed with a gun or knife. After looking in the windows and seeing no one, Stephen [removed the garage door lock] with a crowbar, and, as he pulled the door outward, he was hit in the face with a bullet from the pistol.

Stephen testified: He intended to go into the garage "[for] musical equipment" because he had a debt to pay to a friend. [He claimed he was not sure if he was going to steal. He was there "to look around," and [didn't know] "if I would have actually stolen."

Defendant [testified that after noticing the pry marks on his garage door, he felt he should set up a trap to keep the burglar out of his home because] "somebody was trying to steal my property . . . and I don't want to come home some night and have the thief in there . . . usually a thief is pretty desperate . . . and . . . they just pick up a weapon . . . if they don't have one . . . and do the best they can." ***

[The jury convicted defendant of assault with a deadly weapon.] Defendant contends that had he been present he would have been justified in shooting Stephen since Stephen was attempting to commit burglary [and] defendant had a right to do indirectly what he could have done directly, and that therefore any attempt by him to commit a violent injury upon Stephen was not "unlawful" and hence not an assault. The People argue [that use of] a trap gun constitutes excessive force, and that in any event the circumstances were not in fact such as to warrant the use of deadly force. ***

Issues

1. **Whether it is lawful to defend the home with a trap gun that will automatically fire when a door is opened.**
2. **Whether the defendant used reasonable force to defend his home.**

Rule and Analysis

At common law in England it was held that a trespasser, having knowledge that there are spring guns in a wood, cannot maintain an action for an injury received [due to] his accidentally stepping on the wire of such gun. [That case aroused such a protest] that it was abrogated seven years later by a statute, which made it a misdemeanor to set spring guns with intent to inflict grievous bodily injury but excluded from its operation a spring gun set between sunset and sunrise in a dwelling house for the protection thereof. ***

In the United States, courts have concluded that **a person may be held criminally liable [for setting up on his premises a deadly mechanical device which kills or injures another.]** Allowing persons, at their own risk, to employ deadly mechanical devices imperils the lives of children, firemen and policemen acting within the scope of their employment, and others. Where the actor is present, there is always the possibility he will realize that deadly force is not necessary, but deadly mechanical devices are without mercy or discretion. Such devices "are silent instrumentalities of death. They deal death and destruction to the innocent as well as the criminal intruder without the slightest warning. The taking of human life [or infliction of great bodily injury by such means is brutally savage and inhuman."]

[Even if the defendant were present, he would not be] justified in shooting Stephen. [PC 197 provides:] **"Homicide is . . . justifiable . . . 1. When resisting any attempt to murder any person, or to commit a felony, or to do some great bodily injury upon any person; or, 2. When committed in defense of habitation, property, or person, against one who manifestly intends or endeavors, by violence or surprise, to commit a felony."** ***

[PC 197 (1)] appears to permit killing to prevent any "felony," but in view of the large number of felonies today and the inclusion of many that do not involve a danger of serious bodily harm, a literal reading of the section is undesirable. [Therefore **PC 197 should be read with] the limitation that the felony be some atrocious crime attempted to be committed by force.**] We must look . . . into the character of the crime, and the manner of its perpetration. *** *When these do not reasonably create a fear of great bodily harm*, as they could not if defendant apprehended only a misdemeanor assault, *there is no cause for the exaction of a human life."* ***

[PC 197 (2) is also so limited. At common law, a killing or use of deadly force to prevent a felony was justified only if the offense was a forcible and atrocious crime.]

Examples of forcible and atrocious crimes are murder, mayhem, rape and robbery. [Although burglary has been included in the list of such crimes,] in view of the wide scope of [PC 459 burglary, compared with the common law definition of that offense, it cannot be said that under all circumstances PC 459 burglary constitutes a forcible and atrocious crime.]

Where the character and manner of the burglary do not reasonably create a fear of great bodily harm, there is no cause [for the use of deadly force.] The character and manner of the burglary could not reasonably create such a fear unless the burglary threatened, or was reasonably believed to threaten, death or serious bodily harm.

In the instant case the asserted burglary did not threaten death or serious bodily harm, since no one but Stephen and Robert was then on the premises. ***

[Defendant was not justified under PC 197 (1) or (2) in shooting Stephen to prevent him from committing burglary.]

[According to the older interpretation of the common law, extreme force may be used to prevent dispossession of the dwelling house. Also, if another attempted to burn a dwelling, the owner could use deadly force to defend his "castle" against the threatened harm. Here we are not concerned with dispossession or burning of a dwelling.]

Conclusion

[As a matter of law the exception to the rule of liability for injuries inflicted by a deadly mechanical device does not apply under these circumstances.] The judgment is affirmed.[158]

---

158. Reprinted with the permission of LexisNexis.

Do's and Don'ts for Hearings, Trials, and Appeals

Oral Argument before Any Appellate Court

Don't interrupt the justice while he or she is speaking, arguing, or asking you a question. **Don't** go over your time limits. **Do** directly address the question the Justice is asking because dodging it will not make it go away and this is your one opportunity in argument to address a particular issue important to that justice.

D. NECESSITY

Suppose you are in prison quietly paying your debt to society when a fire breaks out. Must you stay put, turning your punishment into a death sentence? As recognized by the New Jersey Supreme Court in *State v. Burford*, 163 N.J. 16 (2000), courts, even from the time of common law, acknowledged the necessity of escape in these circumstances, because, "when a prisoner flees a fire, 'he is not to be hanged because he would not stay to be burnt.'"

As noted by Markus D. Dubber in *Criminal Law Model Penal Code* at 194, Foundation Press (2002), **necessity has been called "the mother of all justifications."** The Model Penal Code, in Section 3.02(1) provides in part:

> **Conduct which the actor believes to be necessary to avoid harm or evil to himself or to another is justifiable, provided that . . . the harm or evil sought to be avoided by such conduct is greater than that sought to be prevented by the law defining the offense charged.**[159]

In its Commentaries explaining the Model Penal Code, the American Law Institute offered as examples of necessity such instances as destroying property to prevent the spread of a fire, tossing cargo overboard to save the ship, violating curfew in order to safely reach an air raid shelter, and a pharmacist dispensing medicine without prescription in a medical emergency.

Being Your Own Legislature

Can a person become a legislature of one, "passing" laws that control his or her own behavior regardless of the laws of the state? This "necessity" question arises in cases of political protest or civil disobedience. Defendants have tried to create their own law in a variety of contexts, such as burning Selective Service offices "in an effort to move the United States toward terminating the conflict in Southeast Asia" in *United States v. Simpson*, 460 F.2d 515 (1972), vandalizing component parts of nuclear missiles and pouring blood on blueprints of warheads in order to avert the threat of nuclear war in *Commonwealth v. Schuchardt*, 557 N.E.2d 1380, 1381 (1990), and operating a needle exchange program in violation of state law in an effort to combat the spread of AIDS in *Commonwealth v. Leno*, 616 N.E.2d 453 (1993). As noted in the case below, necessity is not a viable defense in these cases.

---

159. From *The Model Penal Code* by the American Law Institute. Copyright © 1962 by the American Law Institute. Used by permission.

The case below involved the attempted use of the necessity defense to defend protests against military involvement in El Salvador.

Suppose your government is doing something you find morally reprehensible. You, as a lone citizen, cannot employ lobbyists or make big campaign contributions. So, you choose what you see as a common symbol of federal government oppression, the local IRS office, and obstruct its daily work as a means of protesting against the government's activity. You understand that you are committing a wrong, but you see it as **the lesser of two evils**, because doing nothing while the government is currently causing bloodshed (**imminent harm**) in another country is an even greater evil. Is the **necessity defense** available to you? **What if everyone attacked** a federal office whenever the government did something of which they did not approve?

LEGAL ANALYSIS

United States v. Schoon
971 F.2d 193 (1991).
Justice Boochever delivered the opinion for the United States Court of Appeals for the Ninth Circuit.

Facts

Gregory Schoon, Raymond Kennon, Jr., and Patricia Manning appeal their convictions for obstructing activities of the Internal Revenue Service Office in Tucson, Arizona. [The charges stem from their protests] of United States involvement in El Salvador. They claim the district court improperly denied them a necessity defense. Because we hold the necessity defense inapplicable in cases like this, we affirm.

On December 4, 1989, thirty people, including appellants, gained admittance to the IRS office in Tucson, where they chanted "keep America's tax dollars out of El Salvador," splashed simulated blood on the counters, walls, and carpeting, and generally obstructed the office's operation. ***

[At trial, appellants offered] testimony about conditions in El Salvador as the motivation for their conduct. They attempted to assert a necessity defense, essentially contending that their acts in protest of American involvement in El Salvador were necessary to avoid further bloodshed in that country. While finding appellants motivated solely by humanitarian concerns, the court [barred the defense as a matter of law.]

Issue

Whether the necessity defense is available to defendants obstructing activities at IRS offices in an effort to protest the United States involvement in El Salvador.

Rule and Analysis

[**To invoke the necessity defense**, the defendants must show:] (1) **they were faced with a choice of evils and chose the lesser evil**; (2) **they acted to prevent imminent harm**; (3) **they reasonably anticipated a direct causal relationship between their conduct and the harm to be averted**; and (4) **they had no legal alternatives to violating the law**. ***

[There is a deep and systemic reason for the absence of federal case law allowing a necessity defense in an indirect civil disobedience case. "Civil disobedience" is the willful violation of a law, undertaken for the purpose of social or political protest.] Indirect civil disobedience involves violating a law or interfering with a government policy that is not, itself, the object of protest. Direct civil disobedience, on the other hand, involves protesting the existence of a law by breaking that law or by preventing the execution of that law in a specific instance in which a particularized harm would otherwise follow. *** This case involves indirect civil disobedience because these protestors were not challenging the laws under which they were charged. In contrast, the civil rights lunch counter sit-ins, for example, constituted direct civil disobedience because the protestors were challenging the rule that prevented them from sitting at lunch counters. ***

[**The necessity defense is inapplicable to indirect civil disobedience cases. Necessity is a utilitarian defense, justifying**] **criminal acts taken to avert a greater harm, maximizing social welfare by allowing a crime to be committed where the social benefits of the crime outweigh the social costs of failing to commit the crime.** *** Pursuant to the defense, prisoners could escape a burning prison, *** a person lost in the woods could steal food from a cabin to survive, *** an embargo could be violated because adverse weather conditions necessitated sale of the cargo at a foreign port, *** a crew could mutiny where their ship was thought to be unseaworthy*** and property could be destroyed to prevent the spread of fire. ***

What all the traditional necessity cases have in common is that the commission of the "crime" averted the occurrence of an even greater "harm." [**The] necessity defense allows us to act as individual legislatures, amending a particular criminal provision or crafting a one-time exception to it**, subject to court review, when a real legislature would formally do the same under those circumstances. For example, by allowing prisoners who escape a burning jail to claim the justification of necessity, we assume the lawmaker, confronting this problem, would have allowed for an exception to the law proscribing prison escapes.

Because the necessity doctrine is utilitarian, however, strict requirements contain its exercise so as to prevent nonbeneficial criminal conduct. For example, "'if the criminal act cannot abate the threatened harm, society receives no benefit from the criminal conduct.'" *** Similarly, to forgive a crime taken to avert a lesser harm would fail to maximize social utility. The cost of the crime would outweigh the harm averted by its commission. Likewise, criminal acts cannot be condoned to thwart threats, yet to be imminent, or those for which there are legal alternatives to abate the harm.

Analysis of three of the necessity defense's four elements leads us to the conclusion that necessity can never be proved in a case of indirect civil disobedience. ***

1. Balance of Harms

[If] the thing to be averted is not a harm at all, the balance of harms necessarily would disfavor any criminal action. Indirect civil disobedience seeks [to repeal a law or change governmental policy by mobilizing public opinion through symbolic action.] These protestors violate a law, not because it is unconstitutional or otherwise improper, but because doing so calls public attention to their objectives. Thus, the most immediate "harm" this form of protest targets is the *existence* of the law or policy. However, the mere existence of a constitutional law or governmental policy cannot constitute a legally cognizable harm. *** "In a society based on democratic decision making, this is how values are ranked—a protester cannot simply assert that her view of what is best should trump the decision of the majority of elected representatives." ***

[Any general harm that results from the targeted law or policy is too insubstantial an injury to be legally recognized.] The law could not function were people allowed to rely on their *subjective* beliefs and value judgments in determining which harms justified the taking of criminal action. [Toleration of such conduct would be inevitably anarchic.]

The protest in this case was in the form of indirect civil disobedience, aimed at reversal of the government's El Salvador policy. That policy does not violate the Constitution, [the procedure adopting the policy was proper, and appellants were not prevented from participating in the democratic processes choosing the policy.] The most immediate harm the appellants sought to avert was the existence of the government's El Salvador policy, which is not in itself a legally cognizable harm. Moreover, any harms resulting from the operation of this policy are insufficiently concrete to be legally cognizable as harms for purposes of the necessity defense.

[The mere existence of a policy or validly enacted law] cannot constitute a cognizable harm. If there is no cognizable harm to prevent, the harm resulting from criminal action taken for the purpose of securing the repeal of the law or policy necessarily outweighs any benefit of the action.

2. Causal Relationship between Criminal Conduct and Harm to be Averted

[A court must judge the likelihood that a harm will be avoided] by the taking of illegal action. [There] will never be such likelihood in cases of indirect political protest. In the traditional cases, a prisoner flees a burning cell and averts death, or someone demolishes a home to create a firebreak and prevents the conflagration of an entire community. The nexus between the act undertaken and the result sought is a close one. Ordinarily it is the volitional illegal act alone which, once taken, abates the evil.

In political necessity cases involving indirect civil disobedience against congressional acts, however, the act alone is unlikely to abate the evil precisely because the action is indirect. Here, the IRS obstruction [is] unlikely to abate the killings in El Salvador, or immediately change Congress's policy; instead, it takes another *volitional* actor not controlled by the protestor to take a further step; Congress must change its mind.

3. Legal Alternatives

[Necessity does not apply to these indirect civil disobedience cases because] legal alternatives will never be deemed exhausted when the harm can be mitigated by congressional action. [The] harm indirect civil disobedience aims to prevent is the continued existence of a law or policy. Because congressional action can *always* mitigate this "harm," lawful political activity to spur such action will always be a legal alternative. [We] cannot say that this legal alternative will always exist in cases of direct civil disobedience, where protestors act to avert a concrete harm flowing from the operation of the targeted law or policy. [Necessity requires the absence of any legal alternative to the illegal conduct which could reasonably be expected to stop an imminent evil.] A prisoner fleeing a burning jail [need not wait in his cell because someone might conceivably save him. Such a legal alternative is ill-suited to avoiding death in a fire.]

[In *Dorrell*], an indirect civil disobedience case involving a trespass on Vandenburg Air Force Base to protest the MX missile program, we rejected Dorrell's claims that legal alternatives, like lobbying Congress, were unavailable because they were futile. [The] "possibility" that Congress will change its mind is sufficient in the context of the democratic process to make lawful political action a reasonable alternative to indirect civil disobedience. [Petitioning] Congress to change a policy is *always* a legal alternative in such cases, regardless of the likelihood of the plea's success. Thus, indirect civil disobedience can never meet the necessity defense requirement that there be a lack of legal alternatives.

***The real problem here is that litigants are trying to distort to their purposes an age-old common law doctrine meant for a very different set of circumstances. What these cases are really about is gaining notoriety for a cause—the defense allows protestors to get their political grievances discussed in a courtroom. *** It is precisely this political motive that has left [courts uneasy.] Because these attempts to invoke the necessity defense [force the courts to choose among causes and because the criminal acts] do not maximize social good, they should be subject to a *per se* rule of exclusion.

[The failure of the defense of necessity in a case like ours not as coincidental, but rather] the natural consequence of the historic limitation of the doctrine. Indirect protests of congressional policies can never meet all the requirements of the necessity doctrine. [The] necessity defense is not available in such cases.

Conclusion

Because the necessity defense was not intended as justification for illegal acts taken in indirect political protest, we affirm the district court's refusal to admit evidence of necessity. Affirmed.

Is Marijuana a Medical Necessity?

Several states have created "medical marijuana" laws while others have enacted laws decriminalizing marijuana. In *United States v. Oakland Cannabis Buyers' Cooperative*, 532 U.S. 483 (2001), the U.S. Supreme Court refused to recognize a "medical necessity" defense for marijuana. Justice Thomas, writing for the court, ruled that there was no medical necessity exception to the Controlled Substances Act for the the manufacture and distribution of marijuana. The *Oakland Cannabis* court noted that the Controlled Substances Act has made it unlawful for anyone to knowingly or intentionally "manufacture, distribute, or dispense, or possess with intent to manufacture, distribute, or dispense, a controlled substance." Marijuana is listed in this statute as a "schedule I" controlled substance—

The U.S. Supreme Court has rejected a medical necessity defense for marijuana distribution.

the most dangerous level. As for necessity, the Court found that this defense "traditionally covered the situation where physical forces beyond the actor's control rendered illegal conduct the lesser of two evils." Applying necessity "under our constitutional system, in which federal crimes are defined by statute rather than by common law," would be "especially" controversial.

Oakland Cannabis ruled that a medical necessity defense for marijuana was "at odds" with the Controlled Substances Act because the legislature itself had determined that "marijuana has no medical benefits worthy of an exception (outside the confines of a Government-approved research project)." The Act found that marijuana had "no currently accepted medical use" at all. The court thus held that" medical necessity is not a defense to manufacturing and distributing marijuana."

Those supporting the legalization of marijuana cannot look for help from another branch of government because the U.S. Attorney General has signaled that federal law enforcement will pursue marijuana prosecutions regardless of decriminalization on the state level.

What Are the Differences between "Necessity" and "Duress"?

The U.S. Court of Appeals for the Ninth Circuit has distinguished between the defenses of duress and necessity in *United States v. Contento-Pachon*, 723 F.2d 691 (1983). In this case, a man named Jorge coerced Juan Manuel Contento-Pachon, a taxicab driver in Bogota, Columbia, during the height of the cocaine cartels, to swallow 129 cocaine-filled balloons for transportation to the United States. Contento-Pachon only agreed to transport the cocaine because Jorge had threatened to kill his wife and three-year-old if he refused. U.S. Customs caught the defendant in Los Angeles when an x-ray revealed the cocaine.

The Court of Appeals considered three differences between the two defenses that defendant had offered: (1) **duress**, **and** (2) **necessity**.

1.   Source of Threat

Necessity, known as the "choice of evils" defense because it places a person in a situation where he or she "is **faced with a choice of two evils and must then decide whether to commit a crime or an alternative act that constitutes a greater evil**," traditionally had as a **source of coercion "the physical forces of nature."** In contrast, **duress** applied when the **threat of harm had a human source.**

A tornado could be the kind of natural threat justifying a necessity defense.

2.   Existence of Free Will

The court also pointed to another traditional difference between the two defenses. **Necessity** is based on the theory that "**the defendant's free will was properly exercised** to achieve the greater good." In contrast, with **duress**, the person is **not acting pursuant to his or her own free will** because an outside force overcame or broke any free will.

3.   For the Greater Good

Finally, the defense of **necessity** "is usually invoked when the **defendant acted in the interest of the general welfare.**" The *Contento-Pachon* court offered as examples for use of necessity as a defense the following: (1) bringing laetrile into the United States for the treatment of cancer patients, (2) unlawfully entering a naval base to protest the Trident missile system, (3) burning Selective Service System records to protest United States military action. In contrast, while **duress** involves a choice of a good over an evil, it is usually in the personal context of **protecting loved ones rather than for the promotion of the general welfare**.

Having established these three differences, the Court in *Contento-Pachon* also acknowledged the changing nature of the law by declaring, "**modern courts have tended to blur the distinction between duress and necessity.**" Other courts, such as the Supreme Court of Montana in *State v. Ottwell*, 784 P.2d 402, 404 (1989), have flatly stated, "Modern cases and statutes tend to abandon all distinctions characterizing necessity, duress, and other similar defenses . . . Montana's compulsion statute follows this trend."

Learn from My (and Others') Mistakes

Do Not Block in a Juror's Car (Or, Maybe Do So)

Parking in downtown Los Angeles is a mess. In a rush to get to court for trial one day, I forgot to leave my key with the attendant in stacked parking. At the end of the day, I came out to see the parking lot virtually empty save for one woman who was furious that I had trapped her car. Terribly ashamed, I told her repeatedly I was genuinely sorry for wasting her valuable time. The next day, this same woman's name was called during voir dire, causing her to come up from the crowded seats in the back of the courtroom and sit in the jury box. I approached the bench and explained to the judge and counsel that I had had contact with this juror outside of court. At first the defense counsel was enraged, yet when he heard about me blocking her in, he happily removed his objection to her presence on the jury. She seemed to be a fair person, so I did not kick her from the jury either. The case ultimately hung 11-1 in favor of acquittal. The lone juror who stuck by me was the juror whose car I had trapped in the parking lot. I have always thought that our encounter must have shown her that I was an honest person and so she believed my case. Either that or she gave me a pity vote!

E.   CONSENT

Generally, a victim's consent to the commission of a crime is not a defense. In *State v. West*, 57 S.W. 1071 (1900), the Court ruled, "Private persons can not license crime and it is no excuse that the evil-doer has any one's consent thereto." **Since a crime is a public offense that harms all of society, a single person, even the targeted victim of a crime, cannot relieve the wrongdoer of criminal responsibility.** If Al consents to Beth shooting him, the rest of society still faces the problems associated with the shooting, whether they be a misdirected bullet hitting an innocent bystander or just the cost in resources of Al's resulting visit to the emergency room. Therefore, as noted in *State v Brown*, 364 A.2d 27, 32 (1976), "as a matter of public policy, a person cannot avoid criminal responsibility for an assault that causes injury or carries a risk of serious harm, even if the victim asked for or consented to the act" because **the State has an interest in protecting those persons who invite, consent to and permit others to assault and batter them**. Not to enforce these laws which are geared to protect such people would seriously threaten the dignity, peace, health and security of our society."

Further, **courts have questioned the mental health of those who consent to harmful attacks on their person**. In *People v. Samuels*, 250 Cal. App.2d 501 (1967), in which the defendant was depicted in a sadomasochistic film whipping another person, the Court declared, "It is a matter of common knowledge that a normal person in full possession of his mental faculties does not freely consent to the use, upon himself, of force likely to produce great bodily injury."

There are exceptions to the general rule that a victim's consent cannot be a defense. Firstly, consent of the victim is a valid defense if the crime charged has as one of its elements the *lack* of consent. The prime example here is rape, which involves intercourse committed "*without* the consent" of, or against the will of, the victim. In a rape case, if the defendant can prove that the victim consented to the bodily intrusion involved in intercourse, then he will be able to negate the "without consent" element, thus establishing a defense to the charge. Thus, rape, which *Khalil H.* (discussed below) described as "expressly" requiring a lack of consent, is open to the consent defense.

Secondly, certain occupations, particularly organized sports, are only possible if the participants have the defense of consent available. *Samuels* explained, "consent of the victim is not generally a defense to assault or battery, except in a situation involving ordinary physical contact or blows incident to sports such as football, boxing or wrestling." If consent were not recognized as a defense to violence in certain occupations, then professional sports, such as football or hockey, would lose their very identity.

Consent to Cannibalism

Luke Harding of *The Guardian* newspaper in his December 3, 2003, article, *"Victim of cannibal agreed to be eaten,"* reported that the cannibal had fulfilled his fantasy.

The full article can be viewed at:

http://www.theguardian.com/world/2003/dec/04/germany.lukeharding

---

Consent to Needed Surgeries—What Surgeries Are "Needed"?

Courts such as *Khalil H.* (as discussed below) couch their rejection of the consent defense in careful language, limiting it to activity that is "against public policy." So, while a person cannot consent to being carved up with a knife by his neighbor, he or she can consent to even deeper incisions performed by a surgeon during a needed operation. Much, of course, can turn on what is meant by a "needed operation."

In the article, "Bridging Society, Culture, and Law: The Issue of Female Circumcision: Bridges and Barricades: Rethinking Polemics and Intransigence in the Campaign Against Female Circumcision," 47 Case W. Res. 275 (1997), author L. Amede Obiora considered the concept of consent in the context of the controversial medical procedure, female circumcision. Female circumcision is such a polarizing issue that people even disagree on a definition for it. Obiora described it variously as "genital scarification and reconstruction," and "the ritualized marking of female genitalia." The author noted that, with the mildest form of the procedure, "the clitoris is barely nicked or pricked to shed a few drops of blood" while a more radical form involved "clitoridectomy" or even "infibulation."

In the context of female circumcision, Obiora discussed the defense of consent as follows:

> The basic right to bodily integrity, inherent in the notion of self-determination, considers unlawful interference an assault or battery. By implication, therefore, an act undertaken with appropriate consent, such as an authorized surgical procedure, does not constitute an offense. Consent is ineffective for malicious wounding or serious injuries. Consent is not a defense in a criminal prosecution because a criminal offense is theoretically a wrong affecting the general public and cannot be licensed by the individual directly harmed. Also, consent may be vitiated where it is given without a sincere appreciation of the relevant procedure's entire ramifications for the right of self-determination.

Ultimately, Obiora urged a "middle course" in regulating rather than prohibiting female circumcision in an effort to reconcile "the need to protect women with a respect for embodied socio-cultural identities."

For a YouTube video regarding an individual case of female circumcision, see "'The Cut' Documentary—Female Genital Mutilation/Cutting" at

http://www.youtube.com/watch?v=rMCQk-TBHPA.

Hazing and Consent

Who would ever consent to any act of violence? The problem of a victim willfully submitting to physical harm, particularly in the hopes of joining a group, unfortunately has long been common, as noted by the case, *In the Matter of Khalil H.*, 910 N.Y.S.2d 553 (2010). In this case, a juvenile, Khalil H., began the school year by recruiting the victim for the "Lost Boys" gang, "a group of teenage boys who banded together to provide each other with protection." Khalil explained that entry into membership required that the victim submit to a "jumping in," where the other gang members would repeatedly strike him. The victim "agreed to participate in this initiation ritual because

Hazing can have criminal consequences.

© Raihana Asrai/Shutterstock.com

he wanted to become a member of the "Lost Boys." Although the victim was beaten and kicked during the jumping in, he was not held down and did not attempt to leave. Authorities pursued a hazing case upon discovery of a recording the gang made of the jumping in. The Supreme Court of New York, which decided *Khalil H.*, refused to accept the victim's consent to the acts of violence as a valid defense.

Khalil H. noted the sad reality that, "Often, those who are victims of hazing are, to some degree, willing to accept humiliation and physical abuse from others in order to gain social acceptance." Victims therefore "willingly subject themselves to these acts to be accepted. Many times they have no idea of how bad the hazing will be until they are put in the situation. By then, it is too late and they accept the consequences rather than 'lose face' by backing out."

Khalil H. **defined hazing** as involving **"an initiation process which humiliates, degrades, abuses, or physically endangers persons who desire membership in an organization."** The Court traced hazing "back to the Middle Ages at European universities" and possibly back to "ancient Greek civilization." The Court wryly noted, "organizations and affiliations which engage in hazing 'have never suffered for ideas in contriving new forms of hazing.'" *Khalil H.* offered a particularly dangerous example which occurred at Cornell University's annual banquet in 1894: "While the banquet was in progress, students from the sophomore class released chlorine gas into the banquet hall, resulting in injuries to some of the freshmen and the death of a cook."

One of New York's most important cases involving hazing was *People v. Lenti*, 260 N.Y.S.2d 284 (1965). In *Lenti*, the defendants, Robert Lenti, Robert Pellegrino, Gaetano Aliseo, and Frank Gannon were put on trial for the crime of "hazing" in violation of section 1030 of New York law. While attending an "institution of learning," the defendants acted "in concert" to haze Omega Gamma Delta fraternity pledges during an initiation ritual known as "Hell Night." The hazing included assaulting pledges "Michael Kalogris, Daniel William Alexander, John Thomas Brennan, David Dennis and Richard Stewart" by "striking them about the body and face with clenched fists, open hands, forearms and feet." The state also charged defendants with assault.

The County Court of New York, Special Term, Nassau County determined that **the hazing statute, Section 1030, was unenforceable due to vagueness and ambiguity. Due to the statute's flaws, the Court reluctantly dismissed the hazing and assault counts**. In hopes of focusing "legislative attention on the unenforceable aspects of the statute," the Court explained that, "a new statute should be sufficiently informative" that "all men subject to its penalties may know what acts it is their duty to avoid." The court suggested the legislature, when amending the law, precisely define relevant terms. For example, **it offered the following definition to clarify what was meant by hazing: "Hazing should be defined as any act or series of acts which cause, or is likely to cause bodily danger or physical harm; or to mistreat by playing stunts or practice abusive or ridiculous tricks, that subject an individual to personal indignity or ridicule."** Also in an effort to aid in enforceability, the Court warned the legislature, "Mere membership in a fraternity should not constitute aiding and abetting in hazing practices, unless it is established that a member actively participated in the planning of the practices."

The Court did not wish to ruffle the feathers of the legislature, a co-equal branch. So, it included some diplomatic language explaining its suggestions: "These recommendations are being made with a proper perspective of the fine and sensitive balance that exists between the function of the judiciary and that of the legislative." Still, the Court warned, "Unless and until the Legislature so acts, courts will be seriously handicapped in an attempt to enforce penal statutes that contain the vagueness and indefiniteness of section 1030."

The *Lenti* **Court then recognized the legal problem central to hazing cases—victims actively participate in the process of hazing.** The Court noted that the statute referred to "participants, which of necessity must include the pledges, the individuals for whom this statute was enacted to protect. Are pledges who participate equally guilty of hazing under the terms of this statute?"

Active participation brought up the question of consent, prompting the Court to ask a whole host of questions: "When does the hazing treatment administered exceed the consent given? If the consent is given intelligently, voluntarily and free of deceit or fraud, is this a complete bar and a defense to the acts prohibited by the section? Do the participants have a legal obligation to abandon the activities, or resort to acts of self-defense in order to dissolve the consent as a defense to make it no longer binding?"

The Court answered these questions with one statement: **"Consent of the pledges certainly should not be a bar to prosecution; intelligent consent cannot be a defense when the public conscience and morals are shocked . . . nor participation by pledges deem them accomplices."**

The Court explained its rule against consent being a defense by condemning hazing. It declared, "The acts committed by the defendants and fellow members of this fraternity are not being condoned by this court. In fact, this court will pontificate to the extent whereby it will reveal its conscience is clearly shocked by the conduct these defendants and the members of this fraternity have exhibited; their conduct in the treatment of their contemporaries can only be characterized as sadistic, barbaric and immoral. The dangers inherent in hazing procedures and practices cannot be eliminated unless society, in close co-operation with school administrators, develop policies and attitudes that exhibit an awareness of the wrong and conscientious desire to eliminate it."

The Court labeled "Hell Night" as shameful, degrading, and despicable. It recommend the following policy: "The duly elected officers of a fraternity should be directed by law to incorporate a copy of this statute into the by-laws of the fraternity, and to read to prospective pledges a copy of this statute before each and every duly constituted pledge meeting. Failure to do so should constitute a violation of this section by the officer of the fraternity officially conducting the meeting."[160]

---

160. Reprinted with the permission of LexisNexis.

Florida A&M University found itself in a lethal hazing case where a band member, Robert Champion, died after running a gauntlet where fellow band members attacked him with blows from hands and instruments. For specifics on the case, see the article "Defendant pleads in FAMU case" by the *Associated Press*, August 2, 2013, at

http://espn.go.com/college-football/story/_/id/9532629/famu-band-hazing-female-defendant-pleads-no-contest.

Justin Carissimo of *CBS News* reported on November 13, 2017 in, "Tim Piazza Death Investigation: Prosecutor announces new charges," that fraternity brothers of Beta Theta Pi at Pennsylvania State University face charges in the death of Tim Piazza after he was served 18 drinks in less than a half-hour. The article can be viewed at:

https://www.cbsnews.com/news/tim-piazza-death-investigation-beta-theta-pi-latest/

McKinney's Penal Law § 120.17: Hazing in the Second Degree

A person is guilty of hazing in the second degree when, in the course of another person's initiation or affiliation with any organization, he intentionally or recklessly engages in conduct which creates a substantial risk of physical injury to such other person or a third person.

Hazing in the second degree is a violation.

6 New York Prac., Criminal Law § 5:20 (4th ed.) Hazing

Hazing in the second degree, a violation under N.Y. Penal Law 120.17, is committed when (1) "in the course of another person's initiation into or affiliation with any organization," someone (2) "engages in conduct which creates a substantial risk of physical injury to such other person or a third person" (3) either intentionally or recklessly. No actual injury need occur; intentionally or recklessly engaging in the risk-creating conduct is sufficient.

Hazing in the first degree, a class A misdemeanor under N.Y. Penal Law 120.17, is identical to second degree hazing except that it requires that the defendant's conduct actually cause physical injury.

Although these offenses apply to the initiation or affiliation rites of "any organization," their enactment was the product of public concern over the sometimes life-threatening initiation rites of college fraternities. The Legislature recognized the need to protect youths who can all too easily be bullied or humiliated into engaging in risky or life-threatening conduct in return for social acceptance. ***

DISCUSSION QUESTIONS

1. What is the difference between a defense of "justification" and a defense of "excuse"?

2. How is the defense of self-defense limited by the law so that people do not use it for vigilantism or revenge?

3. What is "reasonable force" for self-defense and how is it measured?

4. Do all states have a "retreat" requirement before deadly force can be used? Why should or should not such a requirement exist?

5. What are the two basic approaches or versions of "defense of others"?

6. What is the necessity defense? Is it available whenever a person feels a criminal act is necessary to promote a greater good?

7. Can a person consent to physical assault? Why or why not?

WEB LINKS

1. Texas' jury charges on the defense of using deadly force to protect property (Section 9.42) can be downloaded from: www.tdcaa.com/content/section-942-deadly-force-protect-property.

2. New York's "Criminal Jury Instructions" for "Justification: Use of Deadly Physical Force in Defense of a Person Penal Law 35.15" can be found at: http://www.nycourts.gov/judges/cji/1-General/Defenses/CJI2d.Justification.Person.Deadly_Force.pdf

3. New York's "Criminal Jury Instructions" for Necessity, or "Justification: Defense of Necessity as an Emergency Measure Penal Law 35.05 (2)" is at: http://www.nycourts.gov/judges/cji/1-General/Defenses/CJI2d.Justification.Emergency.35.05%282%29.pdf

4. The Oklahoma State Courts Network's "Jury Instructions—Criminal OUJI 8-59" provides a definition for the consent defense in any case involving a charge of kidnapping at: http://www.oscn.net/applications/oscn/DeliverDocument.asp?CiteID=471942

CHAPTER XVI

Defenses: Excuse

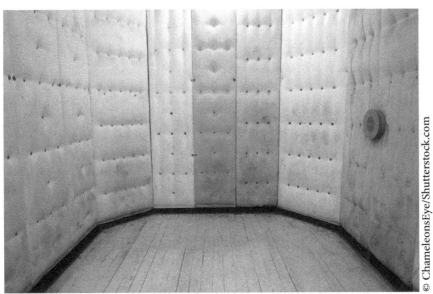

This is a 'padded cell in Old Melbourne Gaol' (Jail).

© ChameleonsEye/Shutterstock.com

A.   INSANITY

Insanity as a Legal Concept

How can anyone who commits a brutal killing or any other heinous act not be insane in some way? It is certainly reasonable to view a person who can kill without remorse or who enjoys harming others as somehow suffering from some kind of mental illness.

Mental illness, however, is not the same as insanity. The term, "mental illness," describes a medical conclusion reached by psychologists and psychiatrists. In this context, a doctor will diagnose and treat a patient, often with reference to the *Diagnostic and Statistical Manual of Mental Disorders*. Here, medical professionals will reach diagnoses such as "schizophrenic," "bipolar," or "obsessive compulsive disorder." In this context, the aim is to identify an underlying condition so that it can be successfully addressed.

Insanity, in contrast, is not a medical diagnosis, but a legal determination. Doctors may offer opinions about insanity, but it is judges or jurors who decide who is and who is not insane. Insanity is therefore a legal determination about who should be held responsible for bad or harmful acts.

Imagine living the waking nightmare that is insanity. Consider just one example: you suffer a delusion that everyone is intent on killing you. Even your friends and loved ones cannot be trusted. Your fight-or-flight hormones are constantly rushing through your system, disrupting sleep, eating, or even a moment's reflection. The fear, helplessness, and loneliness are overwhelming. You cannot put together a coherent thought and the ability to distinguish what is real and what is not eludes you. A violent act is committed and someone is hurt or dies. You are blamed for the harm. You either do not even remember being involved in the act with which you are charged or think you acted in the only way you could to survive. Have you committed a crime?

Insanity requires a return to one of the most fundamental elements of crime—mens rea. Since most crimes can only be committed when the criminal act "concurs" with the criminal intent—one must be thinking guilty while he or she is acting guilty, a person who is suffering such severe mental illness that he or she cannot form an evil intent is not responsible for his or her acts, no matter how bad those acts are. This crucial concept that the criminal law only punishes the blameworthy, and the only persons that can be blamed are those who intended to do their acts, provides the foundation for the insanity defense.

"Seamless Web" Connection

With the exploration of insanity in the last chapter of this book, criminal law has come full circle. Since the insanity defense is based on the theory that persons suffering from severe mental illness cannot form the mens rea or criminal intent needed for crime, insanity is connected through the seamless web to one of the most important requirements of criminal law—that most crimes require that a person be thinking guilty while they are doing guilty. Mens rea, the fundamental element explored in Chapter 3, is crucial to understanding the insanity defense.

1. Common Law—M'Naghten, Queen Victoria, and the Founder of England's Bobbies, Sir Robert Peel

A federal court in *United States v. Ewing*, 494 F.3d 607, 618, n. 5 (2007), quoting Richard Moran, *Knowing Right from Wrong* (1981), explained that the **M'Naghten test for insanity** requires:

> **[T]o establish a defense on the ground of insanity, it must be clearly proved that, at the time of committing the act, the party accused was labouring under such a defect of reason, from disease of the mind, as not to know the nature and quality of the act he was doing, or, if he did know it, that he did not know he was doing what was wrong.**

M'Naghten's definition of insanity is the starting point for understanding the insanity defense in every jurisdiction in the United States. Later courts and legislatures either adopted M'Naghten or created alternative definitions of insanity in reaction to the deficits they believed existed in this famous standard.

As explained in, *United States v. Ewing*,

> *M'Naghten's Case*, 8 Eng. Rep. 718 (1843), concerned a [British trial.] In 1843, acting under a delusion that the Tory political party was persecuting him, Daniel M'Naghten shot and killed Edward Drummond, private secretary to Prime Minister Sir Robert Peel. [M'Naghten based his insanity defense on the theory that a defendant could not be convicted of any act committed while he was under a delusion, regardless of whether the act was a direct product of that delusion.] The jury found M'Naghten not guilty by reason of insanity. In response to public and royal outrage following the verdict, the House of Lords asked the judges of the Queen's Bench to answer five questions regarding the proper formulation of the insanity defense. *** Their responses served as the basis for the development of American law on the insanity defense over the next 150 years.

Edward Drummond, the shooting casualty, was the victim of mistaken identity, for "M'Naghten apparently shot Drummond under the mistaken belief that he was Prime Minister Peel." As explained in *United States v. Freeman*, 357 F.2d 606 (1966), Drummond died and Peel lived because Drummond happened to be riding in the carriage normally reserved for Peel, the chief of the Queen's government.

Freeman noted that M'Naghten delusionally claimed:

> "The tories in my native city have compelled me to do this. They follow and persecute me wherever I go, and have entirely destroyed my peace of mind * * *. I cannot sleep at night in consequence of the course they pursue towards me. * * * They have accused me of crimes of which I am not guilty, they do everything in their power to harass and persecute me; in fact they wish to murder me."

M'Naghten's acquittal raised "the Queen's ire." In language that might not have been used to describe the actions of a king, *Freeman* described the Queen's intervention after M'Naghten escaped conviction:

> Mid-19th Century England was in a state of social upheaval and there had been three attempts on the life of the Queen and one on the Prince Consort. Indeed, Queen Victoria was so concerned about M'Naghten's acquittal that she summoned the House of Lords to

"take the opinion of the Judges on the law governing such cases." Consequently, the fifteen judges of the common law courts were called in a somewhat extraordinary session under a not too subtle atmosphere of pressure to answer five prolix and obtuse questions on the status of criminal responsibility in England. Significantly, it was Lord Chief Justice Tindal who responded for fourteen of the fifteen judges, and thus articulated what has come to be known as the M'Naghten Rules or M'Naghten test. Rather than relying on Dr. Ray's monumental work which had apparently impressed him at M'Naghten's trial, Tindal, with the Queen's breath upon him, reaffirmed the old restricted right-wrong test despite its 16th Century roots and the fact that it, in effect, echoed such uninformed concepts as phrenology and monomania.

Freeman described an atmosphere in the wake of the M'Naghten acquittal that still occurs after high-profile acquittals today:

> A good example of the establishment's reaction to M'Naghten's acquittal is the address of the Lord Chancellor to the House of Lords: "A gentleman in the prime of life, of a most amiable character, incapable of giving offence or of injuring any individual, was murdered in the streets of this metropolis in open day. The assassin was secure; he was committed for trial; that trial has taken place, and he has escaped with impunity. Your Lordships will not be surprised that these circumstances have created a deep feeling in the public mind, and that many persons should, upon the first impression, be disposed to think that there is some great defect in the laws of the country with reference to this subject which calls for a revision of those laws in order that a repetition of such outrage may be prevented."

The *Freeman* Court thus carefully reviewed the history of M'Naughten as a means of explaining what it saw as the test's "critical infirmities."

For Insanity, What Is in a Name?

The M'Naghten Rule is so controversial that even its spelling is the subject of dispute. As noted in *Freeman*, Justice Frankfurter of the United States Supreme Court once criticized a newspaper for misspelling M'Naghten's name, as follows:

Justice Frankfurter advised *The Times* (London) that it had misspelled this inglorious individual's name who had "occasioned considerable conflict between law and medicine" and that referring to him in an article as "M'Naughten" instead of "M'Naghten" would make "inroads on his fame." When *The Times* replied that its spelling was based on "a letter signed by the man itself," the Justice displayed that pixy humor which delighted so many of his intimates by writing the Editor, "To what extent is a lunatic's spelling even of his own name to be deemed an authority?" *Of Law and Life and Other Things that Matter: Papers and Addresses of Felix Frankfurter,* 1956–1963, 1–4 (Kurland ed. 1964).

2.   The Modern M'Naghten Rule: California's Insanity Test Under Penal Code 25(b)

West's Ann. Cal. Penal Code § 25: Insanity Defense

(b) In any criminal proceeding, including any juvenile court proceeding, in which a plea of not guilty by reason of insanity is entered, this defense shall be found by the trier of fact only when the accused person proves by a preponderance of the evidence that he or she was incapable of knowing or understanding the nature and quality of his or her act and of distinguishing right from wrong at the time of the commission of the offense.

Suppose a person is suffering from such a **severe mental illness** that he or she cannot understand the **wrongfulness of his or her act**, even though he or she understands the **nature and quality of the act**. For instance, what if Ann shoots her boss, fully aware that she is killing him, because she genuinely believes he is the devil who will destroy humankind? Is Ann legally insane because she does not know the wrongfulness of killing her boss, or must she also not understand the nature and quality of her act? The following case considers this important question, along with issues of **constitutional law** and **statutory interpretation**.

Bust of Zeus. In *People v. Skinner,* the defendant thought he had a God-given right to kill his wife.

LEGAL ANALYSIS

People v. Skinner
39 Cal. 3d 765 (1985).
Justice Grodin delivered the opinion of the Supreme Court of California.

Facts

Defendant, Jesse Skinner, strangled his wife while he was on a day pass from the Camarillo State Hospital at which he was a patient. [At the trial] on his plea of not guilty by reason of insanity, a clinical and forensic psychologist [testified] that defendant suffered from either classical paranoic schizophrenia, or schizoaffective illness with significant paranoid features. A delusional product of this illness was a belief held by defendant that the marriage vow "till death do us part" bestows on a marital partner a God-given right to kill the other partner who has violated or was inclined to violate the marital vows, and that because the vows reflect the direct wishes of God, the killing is with complete moral and criminal impunity. The act is not wrongful because it is sanctified by the will and desire of God. ***

[California followed the M'Naghten test of insanity for over a century until the California Supreme Court rejected M'Naghten in *People v. Drew*. California then passed Proposition 8 in an effort to return California to the M'Naghten standard. **Proposition 8's insanity test differed from the traditional M'Naghten rule by stating that anyone attempting to prove insanity must establish that he or she is *both* incapable of understanding the nature and quality of his or her act "*and*" the wrongfulness of the act, where the original test required proof only of one prong *or* the other.**]

[Since the defendant, Skinner, could not meet both prongs of the M'Naghten test, the trial judge found that defendant did not prove he was insane at the time he killed his wife.] Defendant knew the nature and quality of his act. He knew that his act was homicidal. He was unable to distinguish right and wrong, however, in that he did not know that this particular killing was wrongful or criminal. ***

[Defendant appeals from his conviction of second degree murder due to the trial court's finding that he was sane at the time of the offense. The] judge acknowledged that it was more likely than not that defendant suffered from a mental disease, paranoid schizophrenia, which played a significant part in the killing. The judge stated that under the *Drew* test of legal insanity defendant would qualify as insane, and also found that "under the right-wrong prong of section 25(b), the defendant would qualify as legally insane; but under the other prong, he clearly does not." Concluding that by the use of the conjunctive "and" in section 25(b), the electorate demonstrated an intent to establish a stricter test of legal insanity than the M'Naghten test, *** the judge found that defendant had not established that he was legally insane.

Issue

Whether the trial court's conclusion that section 25(b) requires that a defendant meet both prongs of the M'Naghten test to prove insanity was correct, and if not, whether the court's finding that defendant met the "right-wrong" aspect of the test requires reversal.

Rule and Analysis

For over a century prior to the decision in *People v. Drew* (1978) 22 Cal. 3d 333, California courts [defined the insanity defense using] the two-pronged test adopted by the House of Lords in **M'Naghten's Case** (1843) 10 Clark & Fin. 200, 210 [8 Eng. Rep. 718, 722]: "**[To establish a defense] of insanity, it must be clearly proved that, at the time of the committing the act, the party accused was labouring under such a defect of reason, from disease of the mind, as not to know the nature and quality of the act he was doing;** *or,* **if he did know it, that he did not know he was doing what was wrong.**" ***

[Some jurisdictions criticized or rejected M'Naghten. *Drew* followed suit, adopting the **MPC test for mental incapacity**]: "**A person is not responsible for criminal conduct if at the time of such conduct as a result of mental disease or defect he lacks substantial capacity either to appreciate the criminality [wrongfulness] of his conduct or to conform his conduct to the requirements of law.**"

In June 1982 the California electorate adopted an [initiative, Proposition 8, which established a statutory definition of insanity under **PC 25(b):**] "**In any criminal proceeding . . . in which a plea of not guilty by reason of insanity is entered, this defense shall be found by the trier of fact only when the accused person proves by a preponderance of the evidence that he or she was incapable of knowing or understanding the nature and quality of his or her act** *and* **of distinguishing right from wrong at the time of the commission of the offense.**" ***

[PC 25(b) was designed to eliminate the *Drew* test and to reinstate the M'Naghten test.] However, the section uses the conjunctive "and" instead of the disjunctive "or" to connect the two prongs. Read literally, therefore, section 25(b) would do more than reinstate the M'Naghten test. It would strip the insanity defense from an accused who, by reason of mental disease, is incapable of knowing that the act he was doing was wrong. That is, in fact, the interpretation adopted by the trial court in this case. ***

Mindful [of our obligation wherever possible both to carry out the intent of the electorate and to construe statutes so as to preserve their constitutionality, we] conclude that section 25(b) restores the M'Naghten test as it existed in this state before *Drew*.]

[It is fundamental to our jurisprudence that a person cannot be convicted for acts performed while insane. This is because wrongful intent is an essential element of crime.]

[When the legislature adopted the Penal Code in 1872, the two-prong M'Naghten test defined legal insanity. M'Naghten has been the insanity test for over a century.]

[Since wrongful intent is a fundamental aspect of criminal law, a statute exposing a defendant, whose mental illness causes inability to appreciate the wrongfulness of his act, to death or imprisonment raises serious questions under the Constitution's due process and cruel and unusual punishment provisions. These difficult constitutional questions can be avoided if section 25(b) does no more than return to the pre-*Drew* California version of the M'Naghten test.]

If the use of the conjunctive "and" in section 25(b) is not a draftsman's error, a defendant must now establish both that he "was incapable of knowing or understanding the nature and quality of his or her act *and* of distinguishing right from wrong." [Statutory and constitutional construction mandates that courts, in construing a measure, not undertake to rewrite its unambiguous language.] That rule is not applied, however, when it appears clear that a word has been erroneously used, and a judicial correction will best carry out the intent of the adopting body. [The inadvertent use of "and" where the intent of a statute seems clearly to require "or" is a familiar example of a drafting error which may properly be rectified by judicial construction.]

[Since 1850 the disjunctive M'Naghten test has been the insanity rule. Had the drafters of Proposition 8 intended both to reject the MPC-*Drew* test and M'Naghten, we would anticipate that this intent would be expressed in some more obvious manner than the substitution of a single conjunctive in a lengthy initiative provision.]

Applying section 25(b) as a conjunctive test of insanity would erase that fundamental principle. It would return the law to that which preceded M'Naghten, a test known variously as **the "wild beast test"** and as the "good and evil test" under which **an accused could be found insane only if he was "totally deprived of his understanding and memory, and doth not know what he is doing, no more than an infant, than a brute, or a wild beast. . . ."** [Nothing in Proposition 8's language indicates that such a fundamental change in the law of insanity as that was intended. PC 25(b) reinstated M'Naghten as it was applied in California prior to *Drew* as the test of legal insanity.]

[The] defendant was aware of the nature and quality of his homicidal act. He knew that he was committing an act of strangulation that would, and was intended to, kill a human being. He was not able to comprehend that the act was wrong because his mental illness caused him to believe that the act was not only morally justified but was expected of him. He believed that the homicide was "right." ***

[The court then considered whether the California M'Naghten test of insanity required that the defendant know the act is "morally wrong" or "legally wrong."] [A defendant who is incapable of understanding that his act is morally wrong is not criminally liable merely because he knows the act is unlawful. For example:] A mother kills her infant child to whom she has been devotedly attached. She knows the nature and quality of the act; she knows that the law condemns it; but she is inspired by an insane delusion that God has appeared to her and ordained the sacrifice. *It seems a mockery to say that, within the meaning of the statute, she knows that the act is wrong.* If the definition propounded by the trial judge is right, it would be the duty of a jury to hold her responsible for the crime. [Knowledge that an act is forbidden by law will usually permit the inference of knowledge that it is also condemned as an offense against good morals.] Obedience to the law is itself a moral duty. If, however, there is an insane delusion that God has appeared to the defendant and ordained the commission of a crime, we think it cannot be said of the offender that he knows the act to be wrong. ***

Conclusion

The trial court found, on clearly sufficient evidence, that defendant could not distinguish right and wrong with regard to his act. *** The judgment is reversed and the superior court is directed to enter a judgment of not guilty by reason of insanity. *** [161]

What If the Defendant Who Argues That He or She Cannot Understand the Wrongfulness of His or Her Act Does Not Suffer from Any Mental Illness?

In *Skinner's* exploration of what it means to be incapable of understanding the "wrongfulness" of an act, the court considered the distinction between "moral" wrongs and "legal" wrongs. *Skinner* considered the example of a mother who kills her beloved child following what she perceives to be a command from God. She kills knowing that she is ending a life and knowing that such an act violates the state's law against murder. Still, since the mother is acting on the word of God, she cannot know it is morally wrong.

This hypothetical led to an exploration once carried out by Justice Cardozo, one of the most famous jurists in New York. Justice Cardozo considered the situation where a person was incapable of understanding the wrongfulness of his or her act despite being legally sane. Suppose, for instance, that a person operates under a set of moral standards so different from society's that, although he or she suffers no mental illness, the person simply does not see the wrongfulness of his or her act. In theory, the terrorists who carried out the 9/11 attacks could have argued that they believed their killings of thousands of innocents were not morally wrong because they were carrying out the will of God. Justice Cardozo offered the following answer to such a contention:

> "It is not enough, to relieve from criminal liability, that the prisoner is morally depraved ***. It is not enough that he has views of right and wrong at variance with those that find expression in the law. The variance must have its origin in some disease of the mind ***. The anarchist is not at liberty to break the law because he reasons that all government is wrong. The devotee of a religious cult that enjoins polygamy or human sacrifice as a duty is not thereby relieved from responsibility before the law. [In such cases the belief is not the product of disease.] Cases will doubtless arise where criminals will take shelter behind a professed belief that their crime was ordained by God. *** We can safely leave such fabrications to the common sense of juries." [*People v. Schmidt*, 216 N.Y. 324, 340 (1915).]

---

3. The Different Definitions of "Insanity"

Since insanity is a legal concept, it can vary among jurisdictions. Suppose Al, who suffers mental illness, goes on a seeming crime spree road trip starting in Maine and heading down the eastern seaboard to Florida. Although Al commits the same actus reus in each state he enters (say, shooting a person to death), he might not face the same criminal liability in each jurisdiction, because each state provides its own definition of "insanity." A law which offers a broad definition of insanity, or which has lower burdens of proof for establishing the defense, might find Al "insane" and therefore not criminally responsible for his bad act. Conversely, a state with a restrictive definition or high burdens of proof could find that Al failed to establish insanity, and therefore is guilty of a crime.

---

161. Reprinted with the permission of LexisNexis.

a)   The "Irresistible Impulse" Test and "Volition"

We are not merely thinking machines, determining every act by cold calculation. Despite our best efforts, our willpower is overcome and we succumb to a compulsion and break a diet or scratch an itch. Under the sway of emotion, we say something rash, make a big purchase, or fall in love. The M'Naghten standard, which judges a person's sanity merely by inquiring about what one *knows* or does not *know* (**cognition**), fails to account for these other mental states of will (**volition**) or feelings (**emotion**). Courts have tried to fix M'Naghten's narrowness by including volition, emotion, or both into an insanity test. The Irresistible Impulse test was an early attempt to cure M'Naghten's shortcomings by adding a volition element to insanity.

The irresistible impulse rule preserves M'Naghten's two ways to establish insanity. Therefore, if a defendant can prove that, while committing the act, he or she, due to a mental disease or defect, (1) **was incapable of knowing the nature and quality of his or her act**, or (2) **was incapable of knowing the wrongfulness of his or her act**, then the accused can still be deemed insane. In addition to these two "cognition" (to "know") prongs, the irresistible impulse test then adds a third route to acquittal: the accused, even if he or she understood either the nature and quality or the wrongfulness of the act, he or she (3) **was incapable of resisting the impulse or urge to do the act** anyway. The mental disease effectively robs the defendant of the ability to choose not do the act, or stop him or herself from committing it.

Irresistible impulse was adopted as early as 1887 by the Alabama Supreme Court in *Parsons v. State*, 2 So. 854 (1887). In *Parsons,* a mother (Nancy) and daughter (Joe) were convicted of murder for shooting Bennet Parsons. Nancy claimed she was insane at the time of the shooting.

Parsons lamented that the law of insanity, influenced by "ancient theories," caused the insane to be "executed as criminals." Long ago, "lunatics were not regarded as 'unfortunate sufferers from disease,' but rather as subjects of demoniacal possession." Aiming to correct such errors, *Parsons* declared, "There cannot be, and there is not, in any locality or age, a law punishing men for what they cannot avoid."

> [Since insanity can subvert the freedom of the will, destroying the power of the sufferer] *to choose* between the right and wrong, although he perceive it,—by which we mean the power of volition to adhere in action to the right and abstain from the wrong,—is such a one criminally responsible for an act done under the influence of such controlling disease? We clearly think not.

Parsons offered these questions for the jury in considering the insanity defense:

> *First.* Was the defendant at the time of the commission of the alleged crime, as matter of fact, afflicted with a *disease of the mind*, so as to be . . . insane? *Second,* If such be the case, did he know right from wrong, as applied to the particular act in question? If he did not have such knowledge, be is not legally responsible. *Third,* If he did have such knowledge, he may nevertheless not be legally responsible if the two following conditions concur: (1) If, by reason of the duress of such mental disease, he had so far lost the *power to choose* between the right and wrong, and to avoid doing the act in question; as that his free agency was at the time destroyed; (2) and if, at the same time, the alleged crime was so connected with such mental disease, in the relation of cause and effect, as to have been the product of it *solely.*

The irresistible impulse test always had its skeptics. The most significant concern was the question of whether there was any scientific evidence of such a thing as an impulse that could not be resisted. The biggest threat to the irresistible impulse test came not from psychologists or lawyers, but from a would-be assassin. What doomed the test for many jurisdictions was its greatest success—President Reagan's attacker, John Hinckley, successfully used the irresistible impulse test to gain an acquittal, outraging the nation.

The Man Who Undermined Support for the Irresistible Impulse Test

In 1981, John Hinckley attempted to assassinate Ronald Reagan, severely wounding the president and others, including press secretary James Brady, as explained in Kimberly Collins, Gabe Hinkebein, and Staci Schorgl, *The John Hinckley Trial: Key Figures*, University of Missouri at Kansas City Law School, at http://law2.umkc.edu/faculty/projects/ftrials/hinckley/hinckleykeyfigures.htm. **After a jury acquitted Hinckley due to insanity, Congress passed the Insanity Defense Reform Act of 1984 (IDRA). IDRA abolished the "irresistible impulse" basis of insanity that Hinckley had successfully used as a means for proving insanity.** In removing the volition element of insanity, Congress limited the insanity defense to focus only on cognition. Further, Congress increased the burden of persuasion that the defendant had to meet in order to establish the insanity defense. Prior to Hinckley and the IDRA, defendants had to prove they were insane at the time of the act by a "preponderance of evidence," which essentially involved causing the jury to reach a level of certainty exceeding 50 percent. **The IDRA increased the defendant's burden of proving insanity from the preponderance of evidence to "clear and convincing evidence."** Although not as high as the prosecution's traditional standard of beyond a reasonable doubt, clear and convincing evidence mandates the jury be even more certain than before when deciding a defendant was insane at the time of the wrongful act.

For a discussion of John Hinckley and his case, the UMKC Law School offers the following website:

http://famous-trials.com/johnhinckley

According to an article in the *Los Angeles Times*, "John Hinckley Jr. Behaving Normally, Secret Service Says," by Wes Venteicher in the paper's Washington Bureau, "The man who shot President Reagan and three others in 1981 is raising no alarm when he leaves his mental hospital for visits, the documents say." This article is available at:

http://articles.latimes.com/2013/apr/12/nation/la-na-hinckley-20130413.

VIDEO: Attempted Assassination of President Reagan

WARNING: GRAPHIC VIDEO. John Hinckley attempted to assassinate President Ronald Reagan at:

https://www.youtube.com/watch?v=7X5Xjbnches

b)   The Federal Test

The Insanity Defense Reform Act of 1984, in 18 USCS Section 17, provides:

§ 17. Insanity Defense:

(a) Affirmative defense. **It is an affirmative defense to a prosecution under any Federal statute that, at the time of the commission of the acts constituting the offense, the defendant, as a result of a severe mental disease or defect, was unable to appreciate the nature and quality or the wrongfulness of his acts.** Mental disease or defect does not otherwise constitute a defense.

(b) Burden of proof. **The defendant has the burden of proving the defense of insanity by clear and convincing evidence**.

United States v. Ewing, 494 F.3d 607 (2007) interpreted the Insanity Defense Reform Act of 1984 (IDRA). John E. Ewing, suffering from paranoid schizophrenia, attacked a judge with a Molotov cocktail. The courtroom was engulfed in flames, causing jurors and litigants in the trial being heard at the time to escape in panic.

In reviewing Ewing's conviction, the United States Court of Appeals for the Seventh Circuit reasoned that since IDRA adopted the elements of the M'Naghten test, it would interpret IDRA by reference to the common law that developed around M'Naghten. The court explained, "Where Congress uses terms that have accumulated settled meaning" under common law, a court must infer "that Congress means to incorporate the established meaning of these terms." By adhering to the common law, *Ewing* was able to reject the defendant's call for applying a new interpretation for the "wrongfulness" that hinged on the defendant's own subjective view of what is right and wrong. *Ewing* instead judged "wrongfulness" by the "objective societal standards of morality." Ewing could thank John Hinckley for straddling him with a harsher federal insanity standard.

c)   The Model Penal Code Test

Model Penal Code § 4.01: Mental Incapacity

(1) **A person is not responsible for criminal conduct if at the time of such conduct as a result of mental disease or defect he lacks substantial capacity either to appreciate the criminality of his conduct or to conform his conduct to the requirements of the law.**

(2) The terms "mental disease or defect" do not include an abnormality manifested only by repeated criminal or otherwise antisocial conduct.

Under the provisions of the Model Code, a defendant is entitled to acquittal nu reason of insanity if the evidence shows that, because of a mental disease or defect, he

(a) lacked substantial capacity to appreciate the criminality of his conduct; or
(b) lacked substantial capacity to conform his conduct to the requirements of the law.[162]

Suppose you went car shopping on a tight budget. You uniformly answered "No!" to every upgrade the salesperson suggested you add to your purchase. You left the lot driving a car that did not even come with floor mats. In contrast, your neighbor, Al, sought every feature for his new car. Al agreed to seat-warmers, the latest upgrades in technology, a fancy paint job and special rims for his wheels.

---

162. From *The Model Penal Code* by the American Law Institute. Copyright © 1962 by the American Law Institute. Used by permission.

Now suppose that instead of purchasing vehicles, you and Al were using insanity defenses. You have the M'Naghten test, which only looks at cognition. Your insanity defense, being the simple M'Naghten test, would be like the stripped-down car you had earlier purchased. In contrast, Al has the Model Penal Code (MPC) defense. The MPC not only looks at possible impairment of cognition, but with its broader language, "appreciate," also considers impairment of emotion. Not only that, but MPC also has an irresistible impulse element ("lacked substantial capacity to conform his conduct to the requirements of the law") which assesses impairment of volition. With all these and still other extra bells and whistles, Al's MPC test would have everything, just like the car Al had purchased. Were they given the choice, defendants would prefer the extra opportunities to demonstrate their lack of responsibility for the wrongful acts they committed. Unfortunately for them, the defendants do not get to choose whether they can use M'Naghten, MPC, or some other insanity test. Instead, such rules are decided by the legal authorities of the jurisdictions wherein the crime was committed.

What Should Be Done with a Mentally Ill Mother Who Drowns Her Children? Texas Answered with Both Imposition of the Death Penalty and an Acquittal

Andea Yates, while suffering from postpartum depression, drowned her five children in Clear Lake, Texas, on June 20, 2001. During her first trial, the prosecution, attempting to establish premeditation, called psychiatrist Park Dietz, who testified that Yates thought of the idea about drowning her children by watching an episode of *Law & Order*. It was later learned that no such episode ever aired. Dietz tried to correct his mistake, as explained by *CNN* at: "Andrea Yates Case: Witness at Heart of Appeal Explains Error," December 31, 2007, at:

> http://www.cnn.com/2007/US/law/12/11/court.archive.yates2/index.html?_s=PM:US.

Yates explained her behavior as guided by Satan, who "destroys and then leaves." For details about the trial, see *Time* Magazine's "Andrea Yates: More to the Story," by Timothy Roche, March 18, 2002, at:

> http://www.time.com/time/nation/article/0,8599,218445,00.html

In 2005, a Texas appellate court overturned Yates' conviction and ordered a new trial. At the second trial, in 2006, Yates was found not guilty by reason of insanity. *CNN's* timeline about Yates' life and case is available in the article, "Andrea Yates Fast Facts," in *CNN Library*, March 25, 2013, at:

> http://www.cnn.com/2013/03/25/us/andrea-yates-fast-facts

As to Yates' current situation, see *How Andrea Yates Lives, and Lives with Herself, a Decade Later: Ten years after being convicted of murdering her five children, her attorney says she is "doing well" and contributing to the postpartum depression awareness effort her trial instigated*, by Andrew Cohen, March 12, 2012, at:

> http://www.theatlantic.com/national/archive/2012/03/how-andrea-yates-lives-and-lives-with-herself-a-decade-later/254302/.

4. Present Sanity

We are all presumed competent to be prosecuted. **The inquiry of mental competence is triggered when someone (defense counsel, prosecutor, or judge) "declares a doubt" about a defendant's competence.** This typically can happen if the defendant is behaving erratically in the courtroom. Then, inquiries are made to determine if the defendant is "presently sane" or "mentally competent" to go through criminal justice proceedings. The defendant's mental competence is particularly important in our system of justice since it is adversarial in nature. An adversarial system of justice, as opposed to the inquisitorial system of justice used in some parts of Europe, can only work if both adversaries (the prosecution and the defense) are able to fight for their side in the case. If a person is so mentally ill that he or she cannot understand the proceedings or take part in his or her own defense, then the entire scheme of pursuing truth through the battle of two equally-matched adversaries cannot function.

The United States Supreme Court provided the test for present sanity or mental competence to stand trial in *Dusky v. United States*, 362 U.S. 402 (1960). *Dusky* ruled:

> [The record in this case does not sufficiently support the findings of competency to stand trial. It] is not enough for the district judge to find that "the defendant [is] oriented to time and place and [has] some recollection of events," but that the "test must be whether he has sufficient present ability to consult with his lawyer with a reasonable degree of rational understanding—and whether he has a rational as well as factual understanding of the proceedings against him."

As a result of *Dusky* and other cases, **mental competence can be tested** by a three-part rule:

1. **Whether the defendant knows and understands the nature of the proceedings against him or her,** and
2. **Whether the defendant knows and understands his or her role in the proceedings,** and
3. **Whether the defendant can assist counsel in his or her own defense.**

5. Post-Judgment Insanity or Mental Competence for Punishment

Stephen B. Bright, in *The Death Penalty as the Answer to Crime: Costly, Counterproductive and Corrupting* 36 Santa Clara L. Rev. 1069 (1996), described "the execution of a brain damaged man" in Arkansas while then-Governor Bill Clinton was running for the presidency, as follows:

> Clinton flew back to Arkansas to make a show of denying clemency for Ricky Ray Rector, an African-American sentenced to death by an all-white jury for the murder of a white police officer. After shooting the officer, Rector had put the gun up to his own head and shot out the front part of his brain.

© Lesya Dolyuk/Shutterstock.com

In the following case, an inmate saved his pecan pie to eat after his execution.

By the time of his execution, Rector had grown to some 300 pounds. In the days before his execution, Rector barked at the moon, laughed inappropriately, and said he was going to vote for Clinton for President. Rector had the habit of saving his dessert after dinner every night and eating it later. Bill Clinton came back to Arkansas, and with much fanfare presided over the execution of Ricky Rector. It was discovered later that night that Ricky Rector had put aside his pecan pie. He had so little appreciation of what death meant that he thought he was going to come back that evening after the execution and finish off his dessert.

Rector's saving dessert to enjoy after he was executed casts doubt on his ability to understand the true nature of the penalty that was imposed upon him. Such concerns were addressed in *Walton v. Johnson*, 440 F.3d 160 (2005). In this case, Percy Levar Walton,

murdered three people, an elderly couple and a younger man, in their homes in two separate incidents during November 1996. Although the physical evidence alone overwhelmingly established Walton's guilt, Walton also admitted to several other jail inmates that he committed the murders, and he described the graphic details of the murders to his cellmate.

The defense raised a question whether the defendant was mentally competent to be executed. The court noted:

Walton's retained experts, Drs. Anand Pandurangi and Reuben Gur, testified that Walton is suffering from schizophrenia and has borderline delusional ideas about his ability to come back to life after his execution. [Walton told Dr. Pandurangi] that, despite his impending death sentence, he wanted a motorcycle, a telephone, and to look good at the mall. [Walton told the doctor that "people who die go to the graveyard . . . but everybody comes back."] Despite Walton's responses acknowledging that death does occur, Dr. Pandurangi [believed that Walton did not comprehend that he was going to die] for murdering three people.

Walton still found the defendant competent for punishment, ruling:
[There] is substantial evidence supporting the district court's finding that Walton is not mentally incompetent.
Judge Wilkinson, concurring, offered the following reasoning:

"The Eighth Amendment forbids the execution only of those who are unaware of the punishment they are about to suffer and why they are to suffer it." *Ford v. Wainwright*, 477 U.S. 399 (1986) (Powell, J., concurring in part and concurring in the judgment). ***
The Powell test [named after Justice Powell, who concurred in *Ford*] appreciates that the Constitution does not [allow] judicial forays into inherently philosophical arenas. Nowhere does the Eighth Amendment mandate that a defendant understand the end of life in a particular way before he may be executed. The amendment provides no definition of death, and it certainly does not license judges to discover one. That task is well beyond our competence and authority, and is best left to religious leaders, scientists, philosophers, and the private recesses of individual belief. The multiplicity of views on this most sensitive and intimate of subjects all but guarantees that any definition of death—even one as seemingly generic as "the end of physical life"—will fail to respect the views of many who may not see death in this way.
At the same time, Justice Powell's test recognizes that the Eighth Amendment must provide a meaningful independent check on the coercive exercise of state power. This cannot

occur if competency is simply a rote formality devoid of any actual insight into a defendant's mental capacity. ***

The question is how to avoid a subjective and non-inclusive definition of death, without allowing competency to become a meaningless concept. Justice Powell sought to resolve this tension by requiring under the Eighth Amendment an objective, individualized inquiry into a particular defendant's mental competence. That is precisely what took place here. [The] district court was in the best position to evaluate Walton's mental state, and it applied the Powell test in an exceedingly careful and thorough fashion. It conducted two evidentiary hearings, heard testimony from Walton himself as well as multiple witnesses for each side who had interviewed him, and took the additional step of commissioning a psychiatric examination of its own. [The] majority opinion reflects in its own conscientious fashion the care taken in this weighty matter by the trial court. ***

Chief Judge Wilkins, dissenting, did not share the rest of the Court's certainty, declaring:

I would not at this point hold that Walton is actually incompetent under *Ford*. My concern, rather, is with the narrowness of the inquiry made by the district court and the substantial possibility that Walton does not know that his execution will mean the end of his physical life. I respectfully dissent.

As an example of the problems presented in the case, the Chief Judge offered the testimony of Dr. Ruben Gur, who had examined Walton as follows:

I told (Walton) "(Y)ou were sentenced to death."...I asked him if he could repeat after me, and he said, "Yes." And I asked him to do that, and he said, "I'm going to be executed."
And I said, "That's right. And do you understand what happens when you get executed?"
And he said, "I don't know."
I said, "Well, you die."
He says, "Yes, I die."
"Do you understand what it means that you die?"
And he says, "Yes."
And I said, "Well, what does it mean?"
He says, "It means you're dead."
I said, "That's right. . . . What's going to happen then?" . . .
And he said, **"After execution, I'm going to get a Burger King."**

B. DIMINISHED CAPACITY

United States v. Freeman, 357 F.2d 606, 618 (1966), criticized insanity's M'Naghten rule as failing to recognize "degrees of incapacity." *Freeman* complained that under M'Naghten, "Either the defendant knows right from wrong or he does not and that is the only choice the jury is given." The court found such an "on" or "off" option to be "grossly unrealistic," because "The law must recognize that when there is no black and white it must content itself with different shades of gray."

In other words, assume that a person is suffering from mental illness, head trauma, or impairment from a substance that affects his or her mental capacity. Although the person does not have the *full* capacity to understand the nature of his or her acts or the wrongfulness of those acts, this person does have *some* ability to do so. The capacity to understand the nature or wrongfulness of the act is shrunken, limited, or diminished. Courts accepted a person's "diminished capacity" to understand his or her own acts as a defense that filled a gap between the sane, who are fully aware of their actions, and the insane, who lack all capacity to understand the nature or wrongfulness of their actions. In particular, *People v. Wells* 33 Cal. 2d 330 (1949), the case establishing diminished capacity in California, held "evidence of diminished mental capacity, whether caused by intoxication, trauma, or disease, can be used to show that a defendant did not have a specific mental state essential to an offense." One way defendants employed the diminished capacity defense was to negate or block the specific intent the prosecution needed to prove for establishing the commission of a specific intent crime. For example, suppose Ann became intoxicated by drinking too much alcohol at a party. Police then arrested Ann for burglary when they found her climbing into the window of a neighbor's home after she left the party. Ann could theoretically argue that she was so inebriated she was unaware that she was breaking into someone else's home and so could not form the specific intent needed for burglary. Here, diminished capacity due to alcohol consumption could be used to negate burglary's specific intent to commit a theft or felony within the home.

Dan White's Controversial Use of Diminished Capacity

The diminished capacity defense became quite controversial, particularly after a jury found Dan White, a member of San Francisco's Board of Supervisors, guilty of voluntary manslaughter, rather than first-degree murder, for the killings of Supervisor Harvey Milk and Mayor George Moscone. As reported by Robert Lindsey in the *New York Times* article, "Dan White, Killer of San Francisco Mayor, a Suicide," "Mr. White's lawyer argued that his client was mentally unstable and had a 'diminished capacity' at the time of the shooting, in part, he argued, because Mr. White had an addiction for sugary junk foods. Although critics deplored what they called **the 'Twinkie defense,'** it succeeded with jurors." *People v. White*, 117 Cal. App. 3d 270, 172 Cal. Rptr. 612 (1981), provided the following facts of the case:

> [Defendant resigned from his position as a supervisor for San Francisco. He asked to be reinstated. Mayor George Moscone chose not to reappoint him.] Supervisor Harvey Milk opposed defendant's reappointment.
>
> The mayor scheduled a press conference on Monday, November 27, at 11:30 a.m., to announce the new supervisor. On Sunday, November 26, [a reporter told defendant] that he was not going to be reinstated. At approximately 10 a.m. on the following morning, defendant [asked his aide for a ride to city hall. The aide delivered defendant] to the front entrance to city hall on Polk Street. Instead of entering the building at the regular entrance, where he would be required to pass through a metal detector, defendant went to the McAllister Street side of city hall and entered the building through a basement window. Defendant went up to the mayor's office on the second floor and asked the appointment secretary if he could see the mayor. Defendant was admitted to the mayor's office at 10:40 a.m. [The] secretary heard defendant's raised voice in the mayor's office and a series of dull thuds. The mayor's deputy then saw defendant running down the corridor, outside of the mayor's office. The deputy entered the mayor's private sitting room and found the mayor's body. An autopsy revealed that the mayor had been shot four times: twice in the body and twice in the head. The wounds to the head were delivered after the mayor was lying on the floor, incapacitated by the body wounds, and were fired from a distance of one foot from the head. The slugs were from semijacketed .38 caliber bullets.
>
> Shortly before 11 a.m., defendant [used his key to enter a door leading to the supervisors' offices.] Defendant entered Supervisor Harvey Milk's office and, in a normal tone of voice,

asked to speak with Supervisor Milk. Defendant and Milk went across the hall to defendant's office. Approximately 15 seconds later, shots were heard in defendant's office. Defendant left his office and rushed down the corridor. Supervisor Milk's body was found in defendant's office. An autopsy revealed that Supervisor Milk had been shot five times: three times in the body and twice in the back of the head. The head wounds were delivered while Supervisor Milk was on the floor, incapacitated by the body wounds. The slugs were from semijacketed .38 caliber bullets.

[Later, defendant met his wife at a cathedral.] After meeting, they walked together to a police station where defendant surrendered himself to the police. The police removed a .38 caliber Smith and Wesson Chief Special revolver from a holster on defendant's right hip. The shots that killed Mayor Moscone and Supervisor Milk were fired from defendant's gun.

[Defendant gave a statement to police after *Miranda* warnings.] He stated that he had been under pressure financially, politically, and at home. He had resigned from the board of supervisors to relieve some of the pressure. However, because of family support, he changed his mind and asked to be reappointed. Initially, he was assured by the mayor that he would be reappointed. Later, he discovered that Supervisor Milk was working against his reappointment and that he was being used as a political "scapegoat."

Defendant stated that, since he never heard from the mayor personally, he went to city hall on November 27 to ask the mayor about the reappointment. Before leaving home, he armed himself with a revolver. When he met the mayor and was told that he would not be reappointed, he got "fuzzy" and there was "a roaring in his ears." He thought about the effect his not being reappointed would have on his family and about how the mayor was going to lie to everybody about him not being a good supervisor, so he "just shot him." "[Out] of instinct" he then reloaded his gun with extra shells from his pocket before leaving the mayor's office. Defendant stated that he then left the mayor's office and saw Supervisor Milk's aide in the corridor. He thought how Supervisor Milk had worked against him and decided he would "go talk to him." When they met, Supervisor Milk "smirked" at him. He "got all flushed" and shot Milk.

At the trial, defendant presented a diminished capacity defense. [He called psychiatrists to the witness stand, all of which determined that White was suffering from depression. The doctors believed such depression caused the lack of capacity to form such mental states premeditation or intention to kill, or to deliberate. One psychiatrist testified that the defendant "was in a disassociated state of mind and blocked out all awareness of his duty not to kill." The prosecution's psychiatrist testified that White was only "moderately depressed" was "had the capacity to deliberate and premeditate."]

The jury found defendant guilty of two counts of voluntary manslaughter, a lesser included offense of the crime of murder. The jury also found, as true, charges that, in the commission of the two offenses, defendant was armed with and used a firearm. Given the seemingly strong evidence of premeditation and intent to kill, the jury's acquittal of White on the more serious charges was so controversial that it cast doubt on the ability of the criminal justice system to render justice.[163]

As noted in the *New York Times*, Dan White ultimately committed suicide at age 39. For a discussion of the circumstances of this event, see "Dan White, Killer of San Francisco Mayor, a Suicide," October 22, 1985, by Robert Lindsey, at:

http://www.nytimes.com/1985/10/22/us/dan-white-killer-of-san-francisco-mayor-a-suicide.html

---

163. Reprinted with the permission of LexisNexis.

As a result of such controversies, the unpopular defense of diminished capacity was abolished by legislation in California.

California Penal Code § 25: Diminished Capacity; Insanity

(a) **The defense of diminished capacity is hereby abolished.** In a criminal action, as well as any juvenile court proceeding, **evidence concerning an accused person's intoxication, trauma, mental illness, disease, or defect shall not be admissible to show or negate capacity to form the particular purpose, intent**, motive, malice aforethought, knowledge, or other mental state required for the [crime] charged.

(b) . . .

(c) Notwithstanding the foregoing, **evidence of diminished capacity or of a mental disorder may be considered by the court only at the time of sentencing** or other disposition or commitment . . .[164]

In the constant tug-of-war between the branches of government, the courts did not passively accept the abolishment of diminished capacity. Recognizing that juries could no longer ask if a defendant lacked the *capacity* to form a mental state (as done with "diminished capacity"), courts shifted their focus to whether a defendant had *actually* formed a mental state (now called **"diminished actuality"**). As noted by the Supreme Court in *People v. Williams* 16 Cal. 4th 635 (1997):

> [When **our Legislature eliminated the defense of diminished capacity**] it precluded jury consideration of mental disease, defect, or disorder as evidence of a defendant's *capacity* to form a requisite criminal intent, **but it did not preclude jury consideration of mental condition in deciding whether a defendant *actually* formed the requisite criminal intent.**
> ***

Biography—Judge

Justice Scalia

- Born on March 11, 1936, in Trenton, New Jersey, earned his LL.B. (roughly equivalent to today's J.D.) from Harvard Law School, and was a law professor, government lawyer, and U.S. Court of Appeals Judge.
- Colorful and controversial U.S. Supreme Court Associate Justice appointed to the court by Ronald Reagan.
- Turned the U.S. Supreme Court into a "hot bench," where it is now the norm to have the justices pepper the lawyers with many questions during oral argument.
- In *King v. Burwell*, 135 S.Ct. 2480, 2500, 2501 (2015) (Scalia J., dissenting), he called the Court's ruling on the Affordable Care Act (aka "Obama Care") to be a "bit of interpretive **jiggery-pokery**" and "**Pure applesauce**."
- Close friend of Justice Elena Kagan, with whom he went deer hunting. Tracy Mueller, in the September 2, 2016 article for the University of Arizona James E. Rogers College of Law entitled, "Supreme Court Justice Kagan on Remembering Justice Scalia, Political Pressures, and Texting (or Not) Among the Justices" at https://law.arizona.edu/supreme-court-kagan-scalia-university-arizona-law-lecture discussed the justices' bond.
- Known as an "originalist" or "textualist."

---

164. From *Deering's California Codes Annotated.* Copyright © 2014 by Matthew Bender & Company, Inc., a member of the LexisNexis Group. Reprinted with the permission of LexisNexis.

C. DURESS

1.   Common Law

Blackstone, in *Commentaries*, Vol. IV, at 27, described **duress** as **"a defect of will"** in which **"a man is urged to do that which his judgment disapproves."** He declared, "As punishments are . . . only inflicted for the abuse of that free-will, which God has given to man, it is highly just and equitable that a man should be excused for those acts, which are done through unavoidable force and compulsion."

For specific **elements of the duress defense,** Blackstone required **"threats or menaces, which induce a fear of death or other bodily harm,** and which take away for that reason the guilt of many crimes . . . at least before the human tribunal." The "fear, which compels a man to do an unwarrantable action, ought to be just and well grounded." **Duress,** no matter how compelling, **was not available as a defense for murder.** Instead, since murder was a crime against the natural law of God, the person under duress "ought rather die himself, than escape by the murder of an innocent."

© Instudio 68/Shutterstock.com

2.   Current Law

The Supreme Judicial Court of Massachusetts, in *Commonwealth v. Vasquez*, 971 N.E.2d 783 (2012), defined duress as:

> **[A] present, immediate, and pending threat of such a nature as to induce a well-founded and reasonable fear of death or serious bodily injury if the criminal act is not done, with no reasonable and available chance of escape, and where no person of reasonable firmness could have acted otherwise in the circumstances.** [However, duress] is not available to a person who recklessly puts himself in a position where coercion probably will be applied.

Vasquez explained the duress defense as follows:

> "The rationale of the defense [of duress] is not that the defendant, faced with the unnerving threat of harm unless he does an act which violates the literal language of the criminal law, somehow loses his mental capacity to commit the crime in question. Nor is it that the defendant has not engaged in a voluntary act. Rather it is that, even though he has done the act the crime requires and has the mental state which the crime requires, his conduct which violates the literal language of the criminal law is justified because he has thereby avoided a harm of greater magnitude."

Claire O. Finkelstein offered the following elements for duress in *Duress: A Philosophical Account of the Defense in Law*, 37 Ariz. L. Rev. 251, 253 (1995):

The core requirements for claiming the defense are generally accepted as the following:

(1) The defendant must have no reasonable opportunity to escape from the coercive situation.

(2) The defendant must be threatened with significant harm—death or serious bodily injury.

(3) The threatened harm must be illegal.

(4) The threat must be of imminent harm.

(5) The defendant must not have placed herself voluntarily in a situation in which she could expect to be subject to coercion, as is the case when a person joins a violent criminal organization.

The two [marginal requirements are:]

(6) Duress must not be pleaded as a defense to murder.

(7) The defendant must have been acting on a specific command from the coercer.

How does duress work in domestic violence situations? Can **"battered woman syndrome"** [BWS] testimony be used to explain why a battered woman **stayed with her tormentor**, or **the sincerity of a defendant's perception that she is being threatened with imminent danger**, or the **reasonableness of a defendant's conduct?** All of these issues are explored in the following case.

LEGAL ANALYSIS

State v. B.H.
870 A.2d 273 (2005).
Justice LaVecchia wrote the opinion of a unanimous New Jersey Supreme Court.

Facts

[B.H. left her husband, S.H., taking their two daughters to a women's shelter. She told a counselor that her husband had forced her to have sexual intercourse with L.H., her seven-year-old stepson. B.H. reported the incident to the Division of Youth and Family Services (DYFS). She reunited with her husband when she left the shelter. Later, in a taped statement at police headquarters, B.H. voluntarily admitted to having engaged in sexual intercourse with her stepson while her husband watched. B.H. stated] S.H., had physically and sexually assaulted her on other occasions but she denied that he had threatened her with any violence on the day that the incident with her stepson took place.

Q. Did he threaten you in any way?
A. At one point when I said that I didn't think it was a good idea, he said that he would leave me if I didn't. ***
Q. When this happened, when you had sex with [L.H.] . . . were you, at that point, ever afraid of [S.H.] and what he might do to you if you didn't have sex with [L.H.]?
A. Like I said, he threatened to leave me and I, I love him and I, I don't (inaudible).
Q. Did *** he ever threaten you physically to do physical harm at that point?
A. No.

At trial it was brought out that [L.H. accidentally discovered S.H. and B.H. having sexual intercourse. S.H. told L.H. to lower his pants and placed the child on top of B.H. Following S.H.'s directions, L.H. engaged in sexual intercourse with B.H. B.H. testified that she did not protest or attempt to leave. However, at trial, B.H. for the first time claimed that S.H. had threatened her.]

"He had his hand at my throat. He wouldn't let me off the bed. And I told him that I didn't want to do this ***. And he said that if I didn't go through with this, that he would make me pay and that I would never see my daughter again."

B.H. said that she lied in her earlier statement about S.H. because "at that point [S.H.] had already gotten into [her] head again," and he had instructed her not to reveal his role in the incident.

[B.H. testified about S.H.'s earlier incidents of physical, sexual, and emotional abuse. S.H. once held an ax to B.H.'s throat and repeatedly raped her. The abuse continued virtually] throughout their relationship.

[B.H. called Dr. Roger Raftery, a psychologist, who testified that battered woman syndrome (BWS) could explain why a woman stays in an abusive relationship. He found B.H. met the criteria for BWS. The State's psychiatrist, Dr. Timothy J. Michals,] stated that in his thirty years of practice he was unaware of any circumstance in which a battered woman had assaulted a third party at the direction of her batterer and that the syndrome was not useful in situations in which the woman harms a third person. ***

[The trial told the jury to consider:] 1) the immediacy of the threat, specifically whether the force or threat of force posed a danger of present, imminent, and impending harm to the defendant or her daughter; 2) the gravity of the harm; 3) the seriousness of the crime that was committed; 4) the age, health, size, and mental and physical condition of both the defendant and the person alleged to have coerced her; 5) the possibility for escape or resistance; and 6) the opportunity for seeking assistance from officials. The dispute in this matter focuses on the following limitation that the court placed on the jury's consideration of the expert testimony on battered woman syndrome:

> [Duress is unavailable to a defendant who recklessly placed herself in a situation where it was probable that she would be subjected to duress. BWS evidence is only offered to explain why the defendant hadn't left her husband. It may be considered on the issue of recklessness.]
>
> *The experts' testimony, then regarding battered woman syndrome was not offered to establish that a person of reasonable firmness in the defendant's situation would have been unable to resist, but, rather, to clear up any misconceptions that you may have concerning the activities of battered women, and to understand a battered woman's state of mind.*

[B.H. objected to the limitation on the BWS evidence. The jury convicted B.H. of first-degree aggravated sexual assault.]

Issue

Whether "battered woman syndrome" evidence is relevant for a duress defense in proving the reasonableness of the defendant's fear of the threat she was facing.

Rule and Analysis

["Battered] woman syndrome" describes a collection of common behavioral and psychological characteristics exhibited in women who repeatedly are physically and emotionally abused over a prolonged length of time by [a dominant male figure.]

[BWS explains] why a woman remains in an abusive relationship despite being subjected to repeated acts of abuse. [There is a "cycle of violence" that starts with a tension-building phase, followed by an acute battering incident, and then a loving-contrition phase.] After the cycle of violence repeats itself several times, learned helplessness may set in [where the victim becomes] conditioned into believing that she is powerless to escape from the abuse. ***

Learned helplessness, often [with social isolation and economic deprivation,] results in preventing the battered woman from leaving her abuser. [A battered woman's state of mind can only be understood by knowing the unique pressures she is facing. We have allowed BWS for self defense because this testimony clarifies and refutes myths about battered women, and assists juries in determining the honesty of a defendant's belief that deadly force was necessary to protect herself against her abuser.]

[We now consider BWS with respect to duress. The] Legislature codified duress as an affirmative defense. *** *N.J.S.A.* 2C:2-9 provides:

a. **[It is an affirmative defense that the actor engaged in the conduct charged] because he was coerced to do so by the use of, or a threat to use, unlawful force against his person or the person of another, which a person of reasonable firmness in his situation would have been unable to resist.**

b. **[This defense] is unavailable if the actor recklessly placed himself in a situation in which it was probable that he would be subjected to duress.** [For murder,] the defense is only available to reduce the degree of the crime to manslaughter.

c. **It is not a defense that a woman acted on the command of her husband, unless she acted under such coercion as would establish a defense under this section.** ***

The [duress statute states explicitly:] a defendant is not excused for committing a criminal act affecting an innocent person unless the threat of coercion is sufficient that "a person of reasonable firmness in his situation would have been unable to resist." [**The accused must be judged against an objective standard, regardless of her own capacities or weaknesses. A**] defendant's idiosyncratic, subjective, or psychological] incapacity to resist a coercive threat does not set the bar. [The threat must be sufficiently grave to coerce a non-heroic, but reasonably firm, person into crime.]

[Duress must satisfy two distinct components. First, the defendant actually must believe in and be frightened by the likelihood of the threatened harm. Second,] a defendant's level of resistance to the particular threat must meet community standards of reasonableness. The jury must evaluate a defendant's response to the threat by applying the standard of the "person of reasonable firmness." [This objective standard presupposes an ordinary person without "serious mental and emotional defects." The objective standard of duress upholds society's duty to protect innocent third parties from harm.]

In making this assessment, the jury must consider objectively such factors as the gravity of the threat, the proximity of the impending harm being threatened, opportunities for escape, likely execution of the threat, and the seriousness of the crime defendant committed. *** A defendant's personal timidity or lack of firmness in the face of intimidation does not serve as the measure for his or her conduct. Community expectations prevail in judging a defendant's response to a threat. ***

[We turn to two components of duress: 1) the sincerity of a defendant's perception that she is being threatened—that she honestly believes that there is an imminent threat of danger, and 2) the reasonableness of a defendant's conduct—that the defendant experienced a coercion that a person of reasonable firmness in that situation would have been unable to withstand. For the first component, battered woman syndrome testimony is relevant.] It was found helpful for a similar state-of-mind purpose in respect of self-defense and has been used repeatedly in self-defense contexts when a jury must assess the credibility of a defendant claiming fear of perceived imminent danger from her abuser. [BWS evidence goes to the heart of the subjective state-of-mind assessment.] The jury must decide whether a defendant actually believed that she was under a threat of coercion.

[BWS evidence is relevant to the subjective component of a battered woman's coercion defense. It aids the woman in bolstering] her credibility before the fact-finder. It supports the honesty of her fear [and her belief that committing a crime was the only way to avert harm, even in the absence of an objectively imminent and explicit threat.]

[For the first component of duress, **BWS evidence] is relevant and admissible on the question of the sincerity of defendant's claim that she perceived a threat of harm** from S.H. when she engaged in sexual intercourse with her seven-year-old stepson. It was error not to have permitted the jury to hear evidence about battered woman syndrome in connection with that subjective state-of-mind component of defendant's claim of duress. ***

[**BWS evidence is not relevant in assessing duress' second component, the objective reasonableness of the defendant's conduct in response to a threat by another**.] The jury must evaluate objectively the defendant's criminal conduct toward a third person, and whether a person of ordinary strength and willpower would refuse to do the criminal act even in the face of the harm threatened. The idiosyncratic fact that the defendant may be susceptible to the demands of her abuser because she suffers from battered woman syndrome becomes irrelevant in that assessment. [The trial court correctly instructed the jury that BWS evidence was not to be used when determining whether "a person of reasonable firmness" in the defendant's situation would have been unable to resist.]

Conclusion

[BWS evidence is not relevant for assessing duress's standard of a "person of reasonable firmness." BWS evidence is relevant to a defendant's subjective perception of a threat from her abuser and so can be relevant to her credibility. BWS evidence also explains why a defendant would remain with her abuser and, therefore, why such a defendant ought not to be perceived as acting recklessly. BWS expert testimony was improperly restricted by limiting its use only to evaluating defendant's recklessness. Conviction reversed.][165]

What if you are threatened with death unless you kill an innocent person? Should you be able to defend your killing by arguing that you only killed because you were coerced to do so?

Suppose someone threatens to kill you unless you kill some innocent third person. Can you murder the innocent person and claim that you only killed under duress? **What are your options** in such a setting? The following case considers **whether the duress defense is valid for murder.**

LEGAL ANALYSIS

People v. Anderson
28 Cal. 4th 767 (2002).
Justice Chin delivered the opinion of the Supreme Court of California.

Facts

Defendant was charged with kidnapping and murdering Margaret Armstrong in a camp area near Eureka. [Defendant and others suspected] the victim of molesting two girls who resided in the camp. Ron Kiern, the father of one of the girls, pleaded guilty to Armstrong's second degree murder and testified at defendant's trial.

---

165. Reprinted with the permission of LexisNexis.

[A] group of people, including defendant and Kiern, confronted Armstrong at the camp. Members of the group dragged Armstrong to a nearby field, beat her, put duct tape over her mouth, tied her naked to a bush, and abandoned her. [Later, defendant and Kiern saw Armstrong going naked down the street. They grabbed Armstrong, forced her into a sleeping bag, duct taped the bag, and placed her, screaming, into the trunk of Kiern's car.]

[Defendant picked up a large rock and handed it to Kiern.] Kiern appeared to hit Armstrong with the rock, silencing her. Kiern testified that defendant said Armstrong had to die. [Defendant dropped a small boulder onto Armstrong's head and then picked up the rock and handed it to Kiern, telling him to drop it on Armstrong or something would happen to his family. Kiern dropped the rock. Kiern and defendant told others that Armstrong was dead.]

The evidence indicated that defendant and Kiern disposed of Armstrong's body by rolling it down a ravine. One witness testified that Kiern stated he had stepped on her neck until it crunched to ensure she was dead before putting her in the ravine. The body was never found.

Defendant testified [that] he had tried to convince Kiern to take Armstrong to the hospital after she had been beaten. When he and Kiern saw her going down the road beaten and naked, Kiern grabbed her and put her in the backseat of the car. Back at camp, Kiern put Armstrong in the sleeping bag and bound it with duct tape. At Kiern's instruction, defendant opened the trunk and Kiern put Armstrong inside. Kiern told defendant to retrieve a certain rock the size of a cantaloupe. Defendant said, "Man, you are out of your mind for something like that." Kiern responded, "Give me the rock or I'll beat the shit out of you." Defendant gave him the rock because Kiern was bigger than he and he was "not in shape" to fight. When asked what he thought Kiern would have done if he had said no, defendant replied: "Punch me out, break my back, break my neck. Who knows." Kiern hit Armstrong over the head with the rock two or three times. Kiern's wife was standing there yelling, "Kill the bitch."

Defendant testified that later they left in Kiern's car. They pulled over and Kiern opened the trunk. Armstrong was still moaning and moving around. Defendant tried to convince Kiern to take her to a hospital, but Kiern refused. Defendant got back into the car. A few minutes later, Kiern closed the trunk, got in the car, and said, "She's dead now. I stomped on her neck and broke it."

A jury convicted defendant of first degree murder and kidnapping. Based primarily on his testimony that Kiern threatened to "beat the shit out of" him, defendant contended on appeal that the trial court erred in refusing to instruct the jury on duress as a defense to the murder charge. ***

Issue

Whether Duress Is a Defense to Murder.

Rule and Analysis

Over two centuries ago, William **Blackstone, the great commentator on the common law, said that duress is no excuse for killing an innocent person**: "[Though] a man be violently assaulted, and hath no other possible means of escaping death, but by killing an innocent person, this fear and force shall not acquit him of murder; for he ought rather to die himself than escape by the murder of an innocent." ***

We granted review to decide whether these words apply in California. We conclude that, as in Blackstone's England, so today in California: **fear for one's own life does not justify killing an innocent person. Duress is not a defense to murder. [Duress] cannot reduce murder to manslaughter**. Although one may debate whether a killing under duress should be manslaughter rather than murder, if a new form of manslaughter is to be created, the Legislature, not this court, should do it. ***

At common law, the general rule was, and still is today, what Blackstone stated: duress is no defense to killing an innocent person. [By "innocent," we mean merely that the person did not cause the duress, not that the person has never committed a crime.] "Stemming from antiquity, the nearly 'unbroken tradition' of Anglo-American common law is that duress never excuses murder, that the person threatened with his own demise 'ought rather to die himself, than escape by the murder of an innocent.'" ***

[The rationale for allowing the defense of duress for other crimes "is that] it is better that the defendant, faced with a choice of evils, choose to do the lesser evil (violate the criminal law) in order to avoid the greater evil threatened by the other person. *** This rationale, however, "is strained when a defendant is confronted with taking the life of an innocent third person in the face of a threat on his own life. . . . **When the defendant commits murder under duress, the resulting harm—i.e. the death of an innocent person—is at least as great as the threatened harm—i.e. the death of the defendant.**" [When] confronted with an apparent kill-an-innocent-person-or-be-killed situation, a person can always choose to resist. As a practical matter, death will rarely, if ever, inevitably result from a choice not to kill. The law should require people to choose to resist rather than kill an innocent person.

A state may, of course, modify the common law rule by statute. **The Model Penal Code, for example, does not exclude murder from the duress defense.** ***

Since its adoption in 1872, Penal Code section 26 3 has provided: "All persons are capable of committing crimes except those belonging to the following classes: [Persons unless the crime be punishable with death] who committed the act or made the omission charged under threats of menaces sufficient to show that they had reasonable cause to and did believe their lives would be endangered if they refused." ***

A person can always choose to resist rather than kill an innocent person. The law must encourage, even require, everyone to seek an alternative to killing. Crimes are often committed by more than one person; the criminal law must also, perhaps especially, deter those crimes. California today is tormented by gang violence. If duress is recognized as a defense to the killing of innocents, then a street or prison gang need only create an internal reign of terror and murder can be justified, at least by the actual killer. Persons who know they can claim duress will be more likely to follow a gang order to kill instead of resisting than would those who know they must face the consequences of their acts. Accepting the duress defense for any form of murder would thus encourage killing. Absent a stronger indication than the language of section 26, we do not believe the Legislature intended to remove the sanctions of the criminal law from the killing of an innocent even under duress. ***

Conclusion

[Duress is not a defense to any form of murder.] We affirm the judgment.[166]

Note

In *Commonwealth v. Vasquesz*, 971 N.E.2d 783 (2012), the Supreme Judicial Court of Massachusetts declared, "**Every State appellate court, except one, that has decided whether duress may be a defense to murder under the State's common law has held that it is no defense to intentional murder.** The *Vasquez* court noted that **the lone holdout, Pennsylvania, has made "duress a defense to all crimes."**

---

166. Reprinted with the permission of LexisNexis.

D. INTOXICATION

1. Voluntary Intoxication

Voluntary intoxication compels a consideration of the underlying purpose of criminal law. Do we define crimes in criminal statutes and prosecute persons for violating those laws in order to single out the blameworthy for punishment, or for the harms such individuals cause to society? If criminal law's aim were to pinpoint those wrongdoers who are the most evil, then punishing those who are too intoxicated to appreciate the nature of their acts would serve little purpose. If instead the focus is on the harm to society rather than the mental state of the actor, then punishment could not only deter this individual from risking such harm by staying

sober, but also alert others that their actions, whatever their sobriety, have consequences. Mitchell Keiter, in "Criminal Law: Just Say No Excuse: The Rise and Fall of the Intoxication Defense," 87 J. Crim. L. & Criminology 482 (1997), presented the issue as follows:

> On perhaps no other legal issue have courts so widely differed, or so often changed their views, as that of the legal responsibility of intoxicated offenders. The question contrasts the individual's right to avoid punishment for the unintended consequences of his acts with what then-New Hampshire Supreme Court Justice David Souter described as the individual's "responsibility . . . to stay sober if his intoxication will jeopardize the lives and safety of others." The issue presents the choice of whether the magnitude of an offense should be measured from the objective perspective of the community or the subjective perspective of the offender.

VIDEO: Discussions about the Death Penalty

Panels and speakers discussing the death penalty can be viewed at:

https://www.youtube.com/watch?v=UNxPZ2PrE_U

https://www.youtube.com/watch?v=RlyhG4NzCwI

https://www.youtube.com/watch?v=LBEVJvm0Lsw

https://www.youtube.com/watch?v=GXTXsVZS4hM

The history of the court's struggles with voluntary intoxication is presented in the following case, *Montana v. Egelhoff*. People experiencing intoxication have lessened inhibitions and therefore are more likely to do things they would not do while sober. Since a person who has **voluntarily become intoxicated** is in **less control** of himself or herself, should this drunken condition act as a **defense** excusing bad acts such a **murder**? Or, since the person **voluntarily ingested the intoxicant, knowing that it would cause a lessening of self-control**, should he or she still be guilty for any resulting harm?

LEGAL ANALYSIS

Montana v. Egelhoff
518 U.S. 37 (1996).
Justice Scalia delivered the opinion of the United States Supreme Court.

Facts

[While picking mushrooms in Montana, respondent, James Allen Egelhoff] made friends with Roberta Pavola and John Christenson, who were doing the same. [The] three sold the mushrooms they had collected and spent the rest of the day and evening drinking. [Around midnight, Lincoln County sheriff deputies, responding to reports of a possible drunk driver, discovered Christenson's station wagon stuck in a ditch.] In the front seat were Pavola and Christenson, each dead from a single gunshot to the head. In the rear of the car lay respondent, alive and yelling obscenities. His blood-alcohol content measured .36 percent. [Near] the brake pedal, lay respondent's .38 caliber handgun, with four loaded rounds and two empty casings; respondent had gunshot residue on his hands.

Respondent was charged with two counts of deliberate homicide [for] "purposely" or "knowingly" causing the death of another human being. Mont. Code Ann. § 45-5-102 (1995). [The jury charge] instructed that "[a] person acts purposely when it is his conscious object to engage in conduct of that nature or to cause such a result," and that "[a] person acts knowingly when he is aware of his conduct or when he is aware under the circumstances his conduct constitutes a crime; or, when he is aware there exists the high probability that his conduct will cause a specific result." [Respondent argued at trial that an unidentified fourth person must have committed the murders; his own extreme intoxication, he claimed, had rendered him physically incapable of committing the murders.] Although respondent was allowed to make this use of the evidence that he was intoxicated, the jury was instructed, *** that it could not consider respondent's "intoxicated condition . . . in determining the existence of a mental state which is an element of the offense." [The jury convicted respondent of both counts.]

Issue

Whether refusing to let the jury consider voluntary intoxication in deciding whether the respondent possessed the requisite mental state violated Fourteenth Amendment Due Process.

Rule and Analysis

[Historical practice is our primary guide in determining whether the principle in question is fundamental.] Here that gives respondent little support. *** Blackstone, citing Coke, explained that the law viewed intoxication "as an aggravation of the offence, rather than as an excuse for any criminal misbehaviour." *** This stern rejection of inebriation as a defense became a fixture of early American law as well. [American legal editors wrote that drunkenness can never be received as a ground to excuse an offence.]

[In response to an argument for a voluntary intoxication defense, Justice Story declared:] "This is the first time, that I ever remember it to have been contended, that the commission of one crime was an excuse for another. Drunkenness is a gross vice, and in the contemplation of some of our laws is a crime; [rather than being an excuse for murder, it is an aggravation of its malignity."]

***"If a person that is drunk kills another, this shall be Felony, and he shall be hanged for it, and yet he did it through Ignorance, for when he was drunk he had *no Understanding* nor Memory; but inasmuch as that Ignorance was occasioned by his own Act and Folly, and he might have avoided it, he shall not be privileged thereby." ***

Over the course of the 19th century, courts carved out an exception to the common law's traditional across-the-board condemnation of the drunken offender, allowing a jury to consider a defendant's intoxication when assessing whether he possessed the mental state needed to commit the crime charged, where the crime was one requiring a "specific intent." The emergence of this new rule is often traced to an 1819 English case, in which Justice Holroyd is reported to have held that "though voluntary drunkenness cannot excuse from the commission of crime, yet where, as on a charge of murder, the material question is, whether an act was premeditated or done only with sudden heat and impulse, the fact of the party being intoxicated [is] a circumstance proper to be taken into consideration." [By the end of the 19th century, most American jurisdictions allowed the consideration of intoxication in determining whether a defendant was capable of forming the specific intent necessary to commit a crime.]

[Instead of the uniform acceptance one would expect for a rule that enjoys "fundamental principle" status, we find that fully one-fifth of the States either never adopted the "new common-law" rule at issue here or have recently abandoned it.]

It is not surprising that many States have held fast to or resurrected the common-law rule prohibiting consideration of voluntary intoxication in the determination of *mens rea*. [That] rule has considerable justification—which alone casts doubt upon the proposition that the opposite rule is a "fundamental principle." A large number of crimes, especially violent crimes, are committed by intoxicated offenders; modern studies put the numbers as high as half of all homicides, for example. *** Disallowing consideration of voluntary intoxication has the effect of increasing the punishment for all unlawful acts committed in that state, and thereby deters drunkenness or irresponsible behavior while drunk. The rule also serves as a specific deterrent, ensuring that those who prove incapable of controlling violent impulses while voluntarily intoxicated go to prison. And finally, the rule comports with and implements society's moral perception that one who has voluntarily impaired his own faculties should be responsible for the consequences.***

*** Some recent studies suggest that the connection between drunkenness and crime is as much cultural as pharmacological—that is, that drunks are violent not simply because alcohol makes them that way, but because they are behaving in accord with their learned belief that drunks are violent. *** This not only adds additional support to the traditional view that an intoxicated criminal is not deserving of exoneration, but it suggests that juries—who possess the same learned belief as the intoxicated offender—will be too quick to accept the claim that the defendant was biologically incapable of forming the requisite *mens rea*. Treating the matter as one of excluding misleading evidence therefore makes some sense. ***

In sum, not every widespread experiment with a procedural rule favorable to criminal defendants establishes a fundamental principle of justice. **Although the rule allowing a jury to consider evidence of a defendant's voluntary intoxication where relevant to *mens rea* has gained considerable acceptance, it is of too recent vintage, and has not received sufficiently uniform and permanent allegiance, to**

qualify as fundamental, especially since it displaces a lengthy common law tradition which remains supported by valid justifications today.***

Conclusion

[Montana has] decided to resurrect the rule of an earlier era, disallowing consideration of voluntary intoxication when a defendant's state of mind is at issue.

Nothing in the Due Process Clause prevents them from doing so, and the judgment of the Supreme Court of Montana to the contrary must be reversed.

It is so ordered.

2.   Involuntary Intoxication

In contrast to voluntary intoxication, courts have had little trouble deeming involuntary intoxication a valid defense. This might be due in large part to the fact that the defendant him or herself is victimized by being intoxicated through no fault of his or her own. The battleground for involuntary intoxication cases thus moves to what precisely amounts to "involuntary" ingestion of impairing substances.

LaFave, in *Criminal Law* at 506–07, identified **three ways to become involuntarily intoxicated** (1) **under "duress,"** (2) due to **"pathological intoxication,"** where, even though "the defendant knew what substance he was taking," but the resulting intoxication he or she experienced was "grossly excessive in degree, given the amount of the intoxicant," and, (3) **by "innocent mistake** by the defendant as to the character of the substance taken. A person cannot establish involuntary intoxication due to duress simply due to social pressure, as noted in *Borland v. State*, 158 Ark. 37; 249 S.W. 591 (1923). In *Borland*, the defendant was convicted of first-degree murder for killing the victim, Frank Heath. The defendant appealed, contending he was not guilty because he committed the killing while being involuntarily intoxicated. The court rejected the defense, explaining that the defendant:

> contends that he drank whiskey, which intoxicated him, at the suggestion of Seth W. Poston, and not of his own volition. **Drinking whiskey at the request of another does not make the drinking, or the drunkenness therefrom, involuntary.** One must be coerced to drink before his act or the effect can be classified as involuntary. One necessarily wills to drink who drinks at the invitation or mere suggestion of another. [Poston did not force appellant to drink, so the voluntary drunkenness instructions were proper.]

A court considered **pathological intoxication**, where a person's reaction to a substance causes an unexpected intoxicating effect, in *Brancaccio v. State*, 698 So.2d 597 (1997). In *Brancaccio*, sixteen-year-old Victor Brancaccio was convicted of first-degree murder and kidnapping for killing a woman he had encountered on a walk. The defendant had told police that the victim had "asked him to stop cursing and called him low class." He then "punched her repeatedly, led her to a vacant lot, and continued to punch her and kick her" until a passing car frightened him away. The defendant later returned and attempted to set the victim's body on fire. The defendant "then left and returned with spray paint, painting her body red in order to cover up his fingerprints." A medical examiner concluded the victim "had suffered at least four severe and potentially fatal blows to her head, as well as massive trauma to her chest."

The defendant contended, "the medication he was taking (Zoloft), which was prescribed to him during his recent confinement in a mental hospital, had caused him to lose control." The defendant had been previously committed to a mental health center for threatening to kill his parents and himself. Doctors placed the defendant on the antidepressant, Zoloft. **The defendant suffered a rare reaction** to Zoloft, becoming more irritable, loud, and subject to angry outbursts. He even attempted suicide by holding his breath.

The Court of Appeal of Florida noted:

> The defense of involuntary intoxication has been explained: ***
>
> Generally speaking, an accused may be completely relieved of criminal responsibility if, because of involuntary intoxication, he was temporarily rendered legally insane at the time he committed the offense. And again speaking generally, the courts have considered one to be involuntarily intoxicated when he has become intoxicated through the fault of another, by accident, inadvertence, or mistake on his own part, or because of a physiological or psychological condition beyond his control.
>
> The practice of relieving one of criminal responsibility for offenses committed while in a state of involuntary intoxication extends back to the earliest days of the common law. Involuntary intoxication, it appears, was first recognized as that caused by the unskillfulness of a physician or by the contrivance of one's enemies. Today, where the intoxication is induced through the fault of another and without any fault on the part of the accused, it is generally treated as involuntary. Intoxication caused by the force, duress, fraud, or contrivance of another, for whatever purpose, without any fault on the part of the accused, is uniformly recognized as involuntary intoxication.

Brancaccio reversed, concluding, "the court erred in refusing to instruct the jury on appellant's primary defense, which was that he was involuntarily intoxicated as a result of the medication he was taking pursuant to a prescription."[167]

The final way to become involuntarily intoxicated, by **mistakenly** (and therefore **unknowingly**) **ingesting** an impairing substance, is the subject of the following case. When reading this case, consider whether a person can suffer such severe **involuntary intoxication** that he or she suffers a **mistake of fact** that a criminal act has to be committed in order to achieve a greater good (**necessity**).

In *People v. Scott,* following, the defendant feared he was being pursued by the CIA.

---

167. Reprinted with the permission of LexisNexis.

LEGAL ANALYSIS

People v. Scott
146 Cal. App. 3d 823 (1983).
Justice Kaufman delivered the opinion of the California Court of Appeal.

Facts

Defendant Walter Stephen Scott appeals from a judgment of conviction of two counts of [PC 664/ VC 10851 attempted unlawful driving or taking of a vehicle. Defendant,] accompanied by his brother Charles Scott, attended a family reunion-type party. [The defendant drank from a large punch bowl filled with red punch.]

The defendant's brother left the party to get more ice. Upon returning, the brother] noticed that the behavior of the party guests had changed dramatically. [A number of guests holding cups of punch were] behaving strangely and in some cases bizarrely. One man, pointing to the floor, stated there was a dog in the room. Several people holding glasses of punch in their hands were vomiting. When the brother finally located defendant, he noticed that defendant's eyes were unusually large and dilated, and that defendant appeared uncoordinated. Defendant also appeared not to recognize his brother. Feeling that something was wrong, the brother took defendant by the hand and led him out of the house and into his car.

On the way home defendant told his brother he could see a big fireball in the sky and that he could see the brother and his in-laws in the flames. Defendant described it as "Hell" and he stated either that they were trying to pull him in there or he was trying to pull them out. [Defendant] stuck his head out of the car window and stated that he felt "good enough to fly home." The brother [believed defendant might be on PCP (phencyclidine).]

[The next morning, the defendant seemed to be back to normal. Defendant did not recall what he had done the evening before.]

[Defendant] stated that at some point during the party he began to see intense colors and heard helicopters and loud sirens. He stated that his body was clumsy, he was sweating, had difficulty talking, and felt as if his heart was beating rapidly. [Defendant remembered his attempt to jump out of the car window on the ride home.]

[When he awakened the next morning, defendant felt queasy and decided not to go to work. He] took his mother-in-law, Frances Nichols, with him to purchase some glass to replace broken windows at his house.

[On] the return glass-purchase trip [Ms. Nichols] observed defendant looking over his shoulder frequently, driving fast and making rapid lane changes. While on the freeway defendant stated to Ms. Nichols the CIA was after him and was following him in an airplane because he was a secret agent. He said he had to get to the police for help. He started calling Ms. Nichols "Baby," an affectionate term that he usually addressed to his wife. Defendant was sweating profusely and repeatedly stated that he was thirsty. [Defendant's eyes were "glassy and weird" and] he was talking fast and that he did not seem to be making sense. [When the car overheated and stopped running, defendant jumped out of the car and ran up the offramp.] Ms. Nichols eventually lost sight of him.

About this time, 13-year-old Robert Briggs was sitting on his motor bike in the driveway of a gas station in Riverside County. Defendant approached him, stated he was a secret agent and demanded the boy give him the motor bike. When Robert refused, defendant hit him on the helmet, knocking him off the bike, and then proceeded to mount the bike. Defendant attempted to kick-start the cycle, but was unsuccessful.

Douglas Bushlen was driving his pickup truck [when he saw a man knock a kid off a motor bike.] He then observed other people trying to get the man off the bike and decided to drive into the service station and offer assistance. The man, defendant, then ran toward Bushlen's stopped truck and jumped on the back of it. Defendant told Bushlen to drive on, that he was from the FBI and the CIA. Bushlen then drove to and parked at the Magnolia Lumber Yard; a few minutes later defendant got off the truck.

Bushlen testified that defendant seemed "kind of crazy" and appeared restless and hyperactive. He also appeared frightened and stated in a loud voice that the President of the United States and he had fallen out of an airplane. He appeared to be under the influence of something and did not seem to know who or where he was.

Christopher Bell was operating a forklift at the Magnolia Lumber Yard when defendant arrived in the back of Bushlen's pickup truck. Bell observed defendant banging on the side of the truck stating that he was with the secret police and that he wanted to get inside the truck. [Defendant then] walked toward Bell and pointed toward the freeway, stating that the President was going by. Bell stopped the forklift and got off. Defendant then jumped on top of the forklift and tried to start it, declaring that he needed the forklift for police business. Bell removed the key from the ignition and told defendant he could use the telephone inside the store to call the police. [Defendant] was speaking in a loud voice and was perspiring profusely.

Once inside the building, defendant called Information in an attempt to get in touch with Washington, D.C., stating *** he was from the CIA. When the call failed to go through, defendant [then called the police] and stated that "they" were trying to "kill the President." He stated either that he or the President had fallen out of an airplane.

Defendant then hung up the phone, ran out of the building, jumped into a nearby truck and tried to start it. The truck's owner, Cecil Endeman, followed close behind. Endeman's stepson was sitting in the passenger seat when defendant jumped inside, closed the door and asked, "How do you start this vehicle?" Defendant then announced in a loud voice, "I'm with the CIA and I need to use the car." Endeman demanded that defendant get out of the car, at which point defendant ran back inside the building.

Defendant then telephoned his mother, stating: "I don't know where I'm at but tell somebody to come get me." He then asked the owner of the lumber yard to call the police. [Police arrested defendant.] While in the squad car, defendant screamed that he was innocent, that he was a CIA agent and had credentials. At some point defendant began thrusting his feet against the car door. Wensel eventually placed additional restraints on him. Defendant repeatedly demanded that he be released immediately. ***

Issue

Whether the evidence supports the court's finding that defendant had the requisite mens rea—the specific intent to temporarily deprive the owners of their vehicles, even though he was involuntary intoxicated and therefore in a delusional state at the time he committed the acts leading to his conviction.

Rule and Analysis

[Defendant asserted an involuntary intoxication defense to negate the specific intent requirement of section 10851. His witnesses testified] that at the time of the commission of the alleged offenses defendant was acting irrationally and in a bizarre manner and appeared to be under the influence of something. [Three defense psychiatrists testified that at the time of the incident defendant did not have the mental capacity to form the specific intent to deprive the owners of their vehicles.]

[Defendant] unknowingly and therefore involuntarily ingested some kind of hallucinogen which caused him to act in a bizarre and irrational manner and that, acting under the delusion that he was a secret agent and that he was acting to save his own life or possibly that of the President, defendant attempted to "take" vehicles belonging to others without their consent. The only question is whether or not a crime has been committed. Under the circumstances we believe not.

[PC 26 Three] includes among persons incapable of committing a crime, "Persons who committed the act or made the omission charged under an ignorance or mistake of fact, which disproves any criminal intent." [In] attempting to commandeer the vehicles **defendant acted under a mistake of fact: he thought he was a secret government agent acting to protect his own life or possibly that of the President.** When a person commits an act based on a mistake of fact, his guilt or innocence is determined as if the facts were as he perceived them. *** If in fact defendant were a government agent and either his life or the life of the President were in danger and defendant attempted to commandeer the vehicles for the purpose of saving his own life or that of the President, his actions would have been legally justified under the doctrine of necessity. ***

Conclusion

[Defendant's conduct falls within subdivision Three of Penal Code section 26, the conviction] is reversed with directions to the trial court to enter a judgment of not guilty.[168]

Note

Involuntary intoxication set up a cascade of defenses here. To properly assess the defendant's guilt in *People v. Scott*, one must first apply the rule of involuntary intoxication, which then placed the defendant in a setting where he suffered a "mistake of fact," which led him to act according to the doctrine of "necessity."

When Voluntary Intoxication Causes Unconsciousness

Unconsciousness is a defense to a crime. Voluntary intoxication is not. What happens if a person becomes unconscious due to voluntary intoxication and then commits some wrongful action? Does the person have a valid unconsciousness defense or an invalid intoxication defense?

The answer is provided in *People v. Velez*, 175 Cal. App.3d 785(1985). In *Velez*, "defendant Alfredo Eddie Velez voluntarily smoked" marijuana "furnished by others at a social gathering." The cigarette contained phencyclidine (PCP), rendering defendant legally unconscious. "While thus unconscious, defendant brutally assaulted the victim and was ultimately convicted by a jury of [PC 245(a)(1) assault with a deadly weapon,] with the special finding that his victim was over 60 years old at the time of the crime."

The defendant kicked in the locked door of an elderly couple who were watching television. Velez "attacked the victim with a screwdriver, stabbing him all over his body, including his eyes. Defendant also stomped on him." As a result of the defendant's attack, "the victim is partially blind, his hearing is impaired, his legs are stiff, and he has no feeling in his left palm."

The California Court of Appeal explained, "Defendant contends the trial court erred in instructing the jury to the effect that unconsciousness caused by voluntary intoxication is not a defense to a

---

168. Reprinted with the permission of LexisNexis.

charge of assault with a deadly weapon. Defendant asserts that unconsciousness, however caused, is a complete defense even to a general intent crime. We must disagree."

The Court reasoned as follows:

Section 26 provides in pertinent part: **"All persons are capable of committing crimes except those belonging to the following classes:**

"Four—Persons who committed the act charged without being conscious thereof."

This statute obviously suggests that one who is unconscious for any reason is incapable of committing a crime.

However, section 22 provides in pertinent part: "(a) **No act committed by a person while in a state of voluntary intoxication is less criminal by reason of his having been in such condition**. Evidence of voluntary intoxication shall not be admitted to negate the capacity to form any mental states for the crimes charged, including, but not limited to, purpose, intent, knowledge, premeditation, deliberation or malice aforethought, with which the accused committed the act.

"(b) Evidence of voluntary intoxication is admissible solely on the issue of whether or not the defendant actually formed a required specific intent, premeditated, deliberated, or harbored malice aforethought, when a specific intent crime is charged."

Section 22 says no act committed by a person who is voluntarily intoxicated is less criminal but the statute does not mention unconsciousness. But **what if unconsciousness is precisely the condition caused by voluntary intoxication? Which statute controls, section 22 or section 26?** ***

The answer [is:] **"Unconsciousness is ordinarily a complete defense to a criminal charge. *** If the state of unconsciousness is caused by voluntary intoxication, however, it is not a complete defense**. Intoxication can so diminish a person's mental capacity that he is unable to achieve a specific state of mind requisite to a crime, but, even if it is sufficient to destroy volition, it cannot excuse homicide. *** *Unconsciousness caused by voluntary intoxication is governed by Penal Code section 22, rather than section 26*, and it is not a defense when a crime requires only a general intent. *** The union or joint operation of act and intent or criminal negligence must exist in every crime . . . (Pen. Code, § 20), and is deemed to exist irrespective of unconsciousness arising from voluntary intoxication. An instruction that does not distinguish unconsciousness caused by voluntary intoxication from that induced by other causes is erroneous."***

Section 22 provides that unconsciousness caused by voluntary intoxication is available only as a partial defense to an offense requiring a specific intent; it is not a defense to a general intent crime such as assault with a deadly weapon. ***

[Defendant's] defense was that he smoked marijuana given to him at a social gathering by others, but he did not in fact know it contained PCP, which produced an unexpected intoxicating effect. This defense depends on the validity of defendant's assumptions that the cigarette did not contain PCP and would produce a predictable intoxicating effect. [These] assumptions are tested not by defendant's subjective belief but rather by the standard of a reasonable person. In this regard, it is common knowledge that unlawful street drugs do not come with warranties of purity or quality associated with lawfully acquired drugs such as alcohol. [Unlike] alcohol, unlawful street drugs are frequently not the substance they purport to be or are contaminated with other substances not apparent to the naked eye. *** In particular, marijuana is frequently contaminated with PCP or other psychoactive drugs. ***

*** Marijuana cigarettes laced with PCP were sufficiently common among defendant's acquaintances that they were given a nickname: "K.J.'s." Indeed, one of defendant's own experts, psychologist Dr. Steven Edwin Lerner, testified that PCP was commonly concealed in hand-rolled cigarettes containing various leaf materials including marijuana, and that the most common method of PCP intoxication involved smoking "joints."

Putting aside the question whether a defendant may be precluded in all circumstances from invoking the absolute defense of involuntary intoxication where he has consumed an unlawful drug, we hold **a reasonable person has no right to assume that a marijuana cigarette furnished to him by others at a social gathering will not contain PCP**; nor may such a person assume such a marijuana cigarette will produce any predictable intoxicating effect. Absent these assumptions, defendant cannot contend he was involuntarily intoxicated, because he had no right to expect the substance he consumed was other than it was nor that it would produce an intoxicating effect different from the one it did. We therefore conclude defendant was voluntarily intoxicated as a matter of law within the meaning of section 22.

Reason supports the *Velez* court's conclusion. If one voluntarily ingested a controlled substance, then the law can conclude that the person became voluntarily intoxicated. Since the intoxication was voluntary, the person did not become unconscious involuntarily, because he or she was at fault for taking the action that caused the condition of unconsciousness. Being at fault, the person is *voluntarily* unconscious, which itself does not provide a valid defense.[169]

E.   INFANCY

The case following provides a cogent explanation of both the **common law approach toward the "infancy" defense** and the **modern view of a criminal defense based on age of the perpetrator**. Note that the court: (1) explains the **history of the juvenile courts** and the **infancy defense**, and (2) **borrows M'Naghten's "knowledge of the difference between right and wrong" test** for use in determining capacity based on age/infancy.

© Geipi/Shutterstock.com

The 'infancy' defense applies to persons older than babies.

---

169. Reprinted with the permission of LexisNexis.

LEGAL ANALYSIS

In Re Devon T.
584 A.2d 1287 (1991).
Justice Moylan wrote the opinion of the Court of Special Appeals of Maryland.

Facts

The juvenile appellant, Devon T., [who was 13 years, 10 months, and 2 weeks of age at the time of the offense], was charged with committing an act which, if committed by an adult, would have constituted the crime of possession of heroin with intent to distribute. In the Circuit Court for Baltimore City, Judge Roger W. Brown found that Devon was delinquent. The heart of the case against Devon was that when on May 25, 1989, Devon was directed to empty his pockets by the security guard at the Booker T. Washington Middle School, under the watchful eye of the Assistant Principal, the search produced a brown bag containing twenty zip-lock pink plastic bags which, in turn, contained heroin.

Issue

Whether the State met its burden in offering legally sufficient evidence to rebut the presumptive incapacity of the defendant due to his "infancy."

Rule and Analysis

[The Court summarized the common law rule regarding the defense of infancy as follows: The] infancy defense [is] an instance of the broader phenomenon of a defense based upon lack of moral responsibility or capacity. The criminal law generally will only impose its retributive or deterrent sanctions upon those who are morally blameworthy—those who know they are doing wrong but nonetheless persist in their wrongdoing. ***

[The mental quality that is the indispensible condition] of criminal responsibility is the capacity to distinguish right from wrong:

Children Under the Age of Seven Years.—Children under the age of seven years are, by an arbitrary rule of the common law, conclusively presumed to be *doli incapax*, or incapable of entertaining a criminal intent, and no evidence can be received to show capacity in fact.

Children Between the Ages of 7 and 14.—Children between the ages of 7 and 14 are presumed to be incapable of entertaining a criminal intent, but the presumption is not conclusive, as in the case of children under the age of 7. It may be rebutted by showing in the particular case that the accused was of sufficient intelligence to distinguish between right and wrong, and to understand the nature and illegality of the particular act, or, as it is sometimes said, that he was possessed of 'a mischievous discretion.'" ***

A child is not criminally responsible unless he is old enough, and intelligent enough, to be capable of entertaining a criminal intent; and to be capable of entertaining a criminal intent he must be capable of distinguishing between right and wrong as to the particular act.

With the creation shortly after the turn of the present century of juvenile courts in America, *** the question arose as to whether the infancy defense had any pertinence to a juvenile delinquency adjudication. Under the initially prevailing philosophy that the State was acting in delinquency cases as *parens patriae* (sovereign parent of the country), the State was perceived to be not the retributive punisher of the child for its misdeeds but the paternalistic guardian of the child for its own best interests.

Under such a regime, the moral responsibility or blameworthiness of the child was of no consequence. Morally responsible or not, the child was in apparent need of the State's rehabilitative intervention and the delinquency adjudication was but the avenue for such intervention. ***

It being clear that the finding in a juvenile proceeding that a child is delinquent is not the equivalent of a determination arrived at in a criminal proceeding that he has committed a crime, it follows that it is not a prerequisite to a finding that a person is a delinquent child that the State show under the common law rule that the child had such maturity in fact as to have a guilty knowledge that he was doing wrong, that is the capacity to commit crime. . . . The child is delinquent, not because he committed a crime, but . . . because he requires supervision, treatment or rehabilitation. . . . He is not to be punished but afforded supervision and treatment to be made aware of what is right and what is wrong so as to be amenable to the criminal laws.

Over the course of the century, however, buffeted by unanticipated urban deterioration and staggering case loads, the reforming vision *** of the movement faded. Although continuing to stress rehabilitation over retribution more heavily than did the adult criminal courts, delinquency adjudications nonetheless took on, in practice if not in theory, many of the attributes of junior varsity criminal trials. The Supreme Court, *** acknowledged this slow but inexorable transformation of the juvenile court apparatus into one with increasingly penal overtones. It ultimately guaranteed, therefore, a juvenile charged with delinquency most of the due process protections afforded an adult charged with crime. [Included in those guarantees is the requirement that the prosecution prove beyond a reasonable doubt every fact and element necessary to constitute the charged crime. Since a crime usually consists of a guilty mind as well as a guilty act, the State is required to prove beyond a reasonable doubt the existence of a criminally responsible *mens rea* when proceeding in a quasi-penal fashion against a juvenile, just as it would in a criminal proceeding against an adult.]

*** A finding of delinquency, unlike other proceedings in a juvenile court, [connotes some degree of blameworthiness and exposes the delinquent to the possibility of unpleasant sanctions.] Clearly, the juvenile would have as an available defense to the delinquency charge 1) the fact that he was too criminally insane to have known that what he did was wrong, 2) that he was too mentally retarded to have known that what he did was wrong, or 3) that he was too involuntarily intoxicated through no fault of his own to have known that what he did was wrong. It would be inconceivable that he could be found blameworthy and suffer sanctions, notwithstanding precisely the same lack of understanding and absence of moral accountability, simply because the cognitive defect was caused by infancy rather than by one of the other incapacitating mechanisms.

The Supreme Court of California in the case of *In re Gladys R.*, 1 Cal.3d 855, 83 Cal.Rptr. 671, 464 P.2d 127 (1970), pioneered the application of the infancy defense to delinquency proceedings. [The Maryland Court of Appeals joined] the modern trend, [by noting]: "A principal reason supporting the applicability of the defense is that juvenile statutes typically require, for a delinquency adjudication, that the child commit an act which constitutes a crime if committed by an adult, and if the child lacks capacity to have the requisite *mens rea* for a particular crime, he has not committed an act amounting to a crime."

*** Careful review of the recent history of the juvenile court reveals that the juvenile justice system has turned from rehabilitation to principles of accountability in dealing with youthful offenders. In light of this, continued reliance on the rehabilitative ideal to undercut key protections against sanctioning the innocent in the justice process, such as the infancy defense, is intellectually and institutionally problematic."

In a juvenile delinquency adjudication, however, the defense of infancy is now indisputably available in precisely the same manner as it is available in a criminal trial. *** Once the question of criminal incapacity because of infancy is legitimately in the case, *** the due process clause [demands] that the burdens of proof *** are allocated to the State.***

Our attention, rather, turns to the two remaining questions: 1) what precisely is that quality of mind that constitutes criminal capacity in an infant? and 2) was the State's evidence in this case legally sufficient to satisfy its burden of production that the infant here possessed such mental capacity?

[Devon alerted the court as to his age, properly triggering the infancy defense requiring the state to prove his mental capacity to commit a crime]. [W]hat precisely was that quality of Devon's mind as to which the State was required to produce legally sufficient evidence? It was required to produce evidence permitting the reasonable inference that Devon—the Ghost of M'Naghten speaks:—"at the time of doing the act knew the difference between right and wrong." [The Court analogized the inability to form an evil intent due to infancy to mental incapacity caused by insanity.]

The analogy between incapacity due to infancy and incapacity due to insanity, *** has lost some of its original symmetry to the extent that [insanity has] been broadened (directly or indirectly) to include a volitional as well as a cognitive component. The infancy defense retains its exclusive concern with the cognitive element.

[For the infancy defense under Maryland law], the pivotal mental quality being examined was M'Naghten's classic cognitive appreciation of the difference between right and wrong:

"[The State had to show] that the individual 'had discretion to judge between good and evil;' 'knew right from wrong;' had 'a guilty knowledge of wrong-doing.' *** Perhaps the most modern definition of the test is simply that the surrounding circumstances must demonstrate, beyond a reasonable doubt, that the individual knew what he was doing and that it was wrong." ***

In short, when Devon walked around the Booker T. Washington Middle School with twenty zip-lock bags of heroin, apparently for sale or other distribution, could Devon pass the M'Naghten test? [Could the trial judge] infer that Devon knew the difference between right and wrong and knew *** that what he was doing was wrong?

[The] only mental quality we are probing is the cognitive capacity to distinguish right from wrong. Other aspects of Devon's mental and psychological make-up, such as his scholastic attainments, his I.Q., his social maturity, his societal adjustment, his basic personality, etc., might well require evidentiary input from psychologists, from parents, from [or] teachers. [Knowledge of the difference between right and wrong, however,] may sometimes permissibly be inferred from the very circumstances of the criminal or delinquent act itself.

[Also], "It is generally held that the presumption of incapacity due to youth is 'extremely strong at the age of seven and diminishes gradually until it disappears entirely at the age of fourteen . . . .' Since the strength of the presumption of incapacity decreases with the increase in the years of the accused, the quantum of proof necessary to overcome the presumption would diminish in substantially the same ratio." ***

Some analysis may be helpful as to how a presumption "diminishes gradually until it disappears entirely," as to how "incapacity decreases" as age increases, and as to how "the quantum of proof . . . diminish[es] in substantially the same ratio."

On the issue of Devon's knowledge of the difference between right and wrong, *** [the evidence was] that Devon, at the time of the allegedly delinquent act, was 13 years, 10 months, and 2 weeks of age. [This is] substantial, although not quite sufficient, proof of his cognitive capacity.

The applicable common law . . . with relation to the infancy defense establishes that on the day before their seventh birthday, no persons possess cognitive capacity. (0 per cent). It also establishes that on the day of their fourteenth birthday, all persons (at least as far as age is concerned) possess cognitive capacity. (100 per cent). [Between] the day of the seventh birthday and the day before the fourteenth birthday, the percentage of persons possessing such capacity steadily increases. *** Assuming a steady rate of climb, the mid-point where fifty per cent of persons will lack cognitive capacity and fifty per cent will possess it would be at 10 years and 6 months of age. That is the scale on which we must place Devon. ***

We stress that the burden in that regard, notwithstanding the probabilities, was nonetheless on the State. The fact that the quantum of proof necessary to overcome presumptive incapacity diminishes in substantially the same ratio as the infant's age increases only serves to lessen the State's burden, not to eliminate it. [We hold the State successfully carried its burden. A minor factor . . . was that Devon was essentially at or near grade level in middle school, which included grades 6, 7, and 8.]

[During the hearing before the juvenile master, Devon was fully able to understand legal advice and exercise his rights regarding the right to remain silent and to testify. The exchange with respect to the risk of and the privilege against self-incrimination enables an observer to] infer some knowledge on Devon's part of the significance of incrimination. ***

[The trial judge noted that Devon was "stonewalling" to protect others. The judge told Devon and another juvenile,] "Neither one of you want to tell me. Right? Which shows that you are hanging around with the wrong people and protecting them. Right?"

This inferable allegiance to the Underworld's "Code of Silence" suggests that Devon [was no mere baby] caught up in a web they did not comprehend. The permitted inference, rather, was that they were fully conscious of the ongoing war between lawful authority and those who flout it and had deliberately chosen to adhere to the latter camp.

We turn, most significantly, to the circumstances of the criminal act itself. *** The prosecution, in brief, cannot obtain the conviction of such a person without showing that he had such maturity in fact as to have a guilty knowledge that he was doing wrong. Conduct of the defendant such as concealing himself or the evidence of his misdeed may be such under all the circumstances as to authorize a finding of such maturity." [The defendant's conduct] relating to the acts charged may be most relevant in overcoming the presumption. Thus hiding the body, inquiry as to the detection of poison, bribery of a witness, or false accusation of others have all been relied upon in finding capacity." ***

[U]se of a secluded location or concealment was present in this case. The case broke when a grandmother . . . complained to the authorities at Booker T. Washington Middle School that several of her grandson's classmates were being truant on a regular basis and were using her home, while she was out working, as the "hide out" from which to sell drugs. *** Children who are unaware that what they are doing is wrong have no need to hide out or to conceal their activities.

The most significant circumstance was the very nature of the criminal activity in which Devon engaged. It was not mere possession of heroin. It was possession of twenty packets of heroin with the intent to distribute. *** There were no needle marks or other indications of personal use on Devon's body. Nothing in the information developed by the Juvenile Services Agency on Devon and his family gave any indication that this sixth grader, directly or indirectly, had the affluence to purchase drugs for himself in that amount. Indeed, [Devon] acknowledged that he had been selling drugs for two days when the current offense occurred. His motivation was "that he just wanted something to do."

Conclusion

The evidence in this case [indicated that Devon] and several other students had been regularly using the absent grandmother's home as a base from which to sell drugs. The circumstances clearly indicated that Devon and his companions were not innocent children unaware of the difference between games and crimes but "street wise" young delinquents knowingly involved in illicit activities. Realistically, one cannot engage in the business of selling drugs without some knowledge as to sources of supply, some pattern for receiving and passing on the money, some

network of potential customers, and some *modus operandi* to avoid the eye of the police and of school authorities. It is almost inconceivable that such a crime could be engaged in without the drug pusher's being aware that it was against the law. That is, by definition, criminal capacity.

We hold that the surrounding circumstances here were legally sufficient to overcome the slight residual weight of the presumption of incapacity due to infancy.

*** **Judgment Affirmed.**[170]

What Should Be Done with the Violent Juvenile Offender?

The question of what options to pursue with a juvenile can be particularly troubling when the offender is especially violent or near adulthood, as seen in the case, *In the Matter of the Welfare of: D.F.B., Child,* 433 N.W.2d 79 (1988). In *D.F.B.,* the Supreme Court of Minnesota had to decide whether an offender should be treated within the juvenile system or referred to the adult system. The case involved the following facts:

> D.F.B., age 16, used an ax to kill his parents and a younger brother and younger sister. Experts agree that D.F.B.] was experiencing severe depression at the time he committed the murders, and that his feeling that he was trapped in a family situation not to his liking somehow led him to the conclusion that the only remedy was to kill the parents. [D.F.B. has said that he killed the younger siblings not because he was angry with them but to spare them further pain.] The experts, however, disagree over the ultimate issue of whether D.F.B. is unamenable to treatment in the juvenile court system consistent with the public safety. Dr. Carl Malmquist, the [court psychiatrist, reported] that he has "serious reservations" as to whether D.F.B. can be treated appropriately and effectively in the juvenile court system before he reaches age 19. He recommended "long term" treatment with the aim of "a whole reconstruction of how [D.F.B.] deals with aggression." James Gilbertson, Ph.D., opined that D.F.B. can be treated successfully in 2-1/2 years, and probably in considerably less time. However, he acknowledged that many such depressed people fail in treatment and/or have recurrences after treatment. It appears that [Minnesota's treatment programs for depression] generally provide security only as an initial component of the program.

The trial court had denied the state's motion to prosecute D.F.B. as an adult because it felt it had no other choice since the juvenile had "produced substantial evidence of amenability to treatment in the juvenile court system consistent with the public safety." The trial court made this decision with misgivings because it was otherwise "inclined to grant" the state's petition.

The court of appeals reversed the trial court, concluding that keeping D.F.B. in the juvenile court system was inconsistent with the intent of the legislature. Prior to the ruling in *D.F.B.,* the state legislature had amended the law, which once considered the purpose of the juvenile court to be to "secure for each minor . . . the care and guidance, preferably in his own home, as will serve the spiritual, emotional, mental, and physical welfare of the minor and the best interests of the state." While retaining this purpose "for neglected and dependent children," the legislature changed the purpose of the law for "those charged with delinquent acts" to "promote the public safety and reduce juvenile delinquency by maintaining the integrity of the substantive law prohibiting certain behavior and by developing individual responsibility for lawful behavior."

The Minnesota Supreme Court ruled that all factors surrounding a case had to be considered in deciding whether to have a minor kept in juvenile proceedings or sent to adult court. "[The] fact that the juvenile is already 18 at the time the delinquency petition is filed and the fact that the offense he is

---

170. Reprinted with the permission of LexisNexis.

charged with is a serious offense such as first-degree pre-meditated murder alone are insufficient bases for certification" as an adult.

[D.F.B.] offered evidence bearing both on "amenability to treatment and on public safety." One defense expert testified that D.F.B. could not only be treated successfully, but could be treated in the juvenile court system consistent with the public safety. This showing thus required the state to meet the burden of proof, looking at all of the facts of the case, that "the juvenile is unamenable to treatment in the juvenile court system consistent with the public safety." The Supreme Court concluded that the evidence justified referring the juvenile to adult court. The court's conclusion did not rest only on the fact that D.F.B. committed a heinous offense. Instead, all the factors, "including the offense with which D.F.B. is charged, the manner in which he committed the offense, the interests of society in the outcome of this case, the testimony of Dr. Malmquist suggesting that treatment of D.F.B. might be unsuccessful, and the weakness of [the defense doctor's testimony] show that the state met its burden of proving that D.F.B. is unamenable to treatment in the juvenile court system consistent with the public safety."[171]

The youth of the offender also raises a question about whether a sentence of life without parole is appropriate, as was explored in *Graham v. Florida*, 560 U.S. 48 (2010). In this case, Terrance Jamar Graham, born of crack-addicted parents and diagnosed with attention deficit hyperactivity disorder, began drinking as early as age nine. At sixteen, the defendant participated in an attempted robbery of a restaurant where the manager was beaten in the head with a metal bar. Less than six months later, thirty-four days short of his eighteenth birthday, Graham took part in a home invasion robbery where victims were held at gunpoint and barricaded in a closet. Later that same night, Graham attempted a second robbery, during which one of his co-felons was shot.

At sentencing, the judge told Graham, "Mr. Graham, as I look back on your case, yours is really candidly a sad situation." The judge gave Graham the maximum, which was essentially a life sentence without parole (LWOP), explaining:

> And I don't understand why you would be given such a great opportunity to do something with your life and why you would throw it away. The only thing that I can rationalize is that you decided that this is how you were going to lead your life and that there is nothing that we can do for you. [This] is an escalating pattern of criminal conduct on your part and *** we can't help you any further. We can't do anything to deter you. This is the way you are going to lead your life ***. You've made that decision. ***

> So then it becomes a focus, if I can't do anything to help you, if I can't do anything to get you back on the right path, then I have to start focusing on the community and trying to protect the community from your actions. [That is where we are today.]

> I have reviewed the statute. I don't see where any further juvenile sanctions would be appropriate. I don't see where any youthful offender sanctions would be appropriate. Given your escalating pattern of criminal conduct, it is apparent to the Court that you have decided that this is the way you are going to live your life and that the only thing I can do now is to try and protect the community from your actions.

The United States Supreme Court in *Graham* had to decide whether the Eighth Amendment's Cruel and Unusual Punishment Clause prohibits a juvenile offender from being sentenced to life in prison without parole for a nonhomicide crime. The court noted, "The Eighth Amendment states: 'Excessive bail shall not be required, nor excessive fines imposed, nor cruel and unusual punishments inflicted.'" To determine whether a punishment is cruel and unusual, courts must look beyond historical conceptions to "the evolving standards of decency that mark the progress of a maturing society."

171. Reprinted with the permission of LexisNexis.

The court, searching for a national consensus on LWOP sentencing of juvenile nonhomicide offenders, found that while several states had laws on the books allowing for such sentences, actual LWOP sentences were "exceedingly rare." "[It] is fair to say that a national consensus has developed against it." Next, the court considered "the culpability of the offenders at issue in light of their crimes and characteristics, along with the severity of the punishment in question." The juvenile status of Graham here was relevant because "juveniles have lessened culpability they are less deserving of the most severe punishments." The court noted,

> As compared to adults, juveniles have a 'lack of maturity and an underdeveloped sense of responsibility'; they 'are more vulnerable or susceptible to negative influences and outside pressures, including peer pressure'; and their characters are 'not as well formed.' These salient characteristics mean that '[i]t is difficult even for expert psychologists to differentiate between the juvenile offender whose crime reflects unfortunate yet transient immaturity, and the rare juvenile offender whose crime reflects irreparable corruption.' Accordingly, 'juvenile offenders cannot with reliability be classified among the worst offenders.' A juvenile is not absolved of responsibility for his actions, but his transgression' is not as morally reprehensible as that of an adult.'

Further, "defendants who do not kill, intend to kill, or foresee that life will be taken are categorically less deserving of the most serious forms of punishment than are murderers." Therefore, "when compared to an adult murderer, a juvenile offender who did not kill or intend to kill has a twice diminished moral culpability. The age of the offender and the nature of the crime each bear on the analysis."

The court deemed LWOP as "the second most severe penalty permitted by law," which shares "some characteristics with death sentences that are shared by no other sentences." In both death and LWOP cases, "the sentence alters the offender's life by a forfeiture that is irrevocable. It deprives the convict of the most basic liberties without giving hope of restoration." LWOP for a juvenile "means denial of hope; it means that good behavior and character improvement are immaterial; it means that whatever the future might hold in store for the mind and spirit of [the convict], he will remain in prison for the rest of his days." LWOP was especially harsh for juveniles because they would "serve more years and a greater percentage of [their lives] in prison than an adult offender."

The court also concluded that none of the legitimate goals—retribution, deterrence, incapacitation, or rehabilitation—justified LWOP for the juvenile nonhomicide offender. Retribution could not support LWOP in the case because "the case for retribution is not as strong with a minor as with an adult." Further, "Deterrence does not suffice to justify the sentence" because "the same characteristics that render juveniles less culpable than adults" (immaturity and impetuosity) suggest that juvenile offenders "will be less susceptible to deterrence." Incapacitation is unavailing as support for LWOP because it would have to be based on the assumption that the juvenile is "incorrigible" and thus "forever will be a danger to society." The problem here is that, "The characteristics of juveniles make that judgment questionable." "It is difficult even for expert psychologists to differentiate between the juvenile offender whose crime reflects unfortunate yet transient immaturity, and the rare juvenile offender whose crime reflects irreparable corruption." Finally, rehabilitation cannot justify LWOP because this penalty "forswears altogether the rehabilitative ideal." Especially in light of the juvenile's potential for change and his or her limited moral culpability, LWOP is inappropriate for juveniles.

The court therefore held that "for a juvenile offender who did not commit homicide the Eighth Amendment forbids the sentence of life without parole." While a "State is not required to guarantee eventual freedom to a juvenile offender convicted of a nonhomicide crime," it must "give defendants like Graham some meaningful opportunity to obtain release based on demonstrated maturity and rehabilitation." The court declared, "The Eighth Amendment does not foreclose the possibility that persons convicted of nonhomicide crimes committed before adulthood will remain behind bars for life. It does forbid states from making the judgment at the outset that those offenders never will be fit to reenter society."

F.   MISTAKE

Since the common law, a person acting while suffering from ignorance or mistake had a valid defense even though the actor committed some forbidden act. As Blackstone noted in his *Commentaries*, Vol. IV, at 27:

> (I)gnorance or mistake is another defect of will; when a man, intending to do a lawful act, does that which is unlawful. For here the deed (meaning criminal act) and the will (roughly meaning criminal intent) acting separately, there is not that conjunction between them (meaning concurrence), which is necessary to form a criminal act.

Ignorance or mistake, however, has been treated quite differently depending on whether the source of confusion was a mistake of fact or a mistake of law. Blackstone explained this difference by offering an example:

> [The defense] must be an ignorance or mistake of fact, and not an error in point of law. As if a man, intending to kill a thief or housebreaker in his own house, by mistake kills one of his own family, this is no criminal action: but if a man thinks he has a right to kill a person excommunicated or outlawed, wherever he meets him, and does so; this is willful murder.

Mistake of law could not be tolerated as a defense, for it would undermine the power of the law itself. Otherwise, a person aiming to free himself from the limits and punishments of the law would actively avoid learning it. Those most ignorant of the law would be the most free to flout it. Blackstone therefore offered the following famous statement of law:

> For mistake in point of law . . . is in criminal cases no sort of defence. *Ignorantia juris, quod quisque tenetur scire, neminem excusat*, is as well the maxim of our own law.

Black's Law Dictionary, Fifth Edition, at 673, translates the above Latin phrase as "Ignorance of the law, which everyone is bound to know, excuses no man."

1.   Mistake of Fact

a)   Common Law

The common law handled the mistake of fact defense differently depending on whether the defendant was charged with a general intent crime or a specific intent crime.

For a *general intent* crime, the defendant had to prove all of the following:

a.   The defendant possessed an actual and genuine (subjective) belief in his or her own mistake that negated criminal intent, and

b.   The defendant possessed a reasonable (objective) belief in his or her own mistake that negated criminal intent, and

c.   If the facts were as the defendant mistakenly believed, his or her act would not be criminal.

In contrast, for a *specific intent* crime, the only things the defendant had to prove was:

a. The defendant possessed an actual and genuine (subjective) belief in his or her own mistake that negated criminal intent.
b. If the facts were as the defendant mistakenly believed, his or her act would not be criminal.

The mistake of fact for a specific intent crime had only two elements—an actual belief in the mistake which then negated criminal intent. These elements were all that were needed because a genuine belief in the mistake would negate the specific intent, thus making proof of the specific intent crime impossible.

(1) General Intent Crimes

Suppose a man, Al, has sexual intercourse with a female under **age 18**, Beth, reasonably believing she is over 18, the age of majority. Should Al's **actual and reasonable mistake of fact as to the female's age be a valid defense** to a charge of statutory rape? What if, instead, Al has sexual intercourse with a female he **knows to be under age 18** (and who is actually 13), but whom he **reasonably believes is over the age of 14**? Would the same defense and reasoning apply in both cases? The following case considers the law and policy issues about mistake of fact with victims of differing ages.

LEGAL ANALYSIS

People v. Olsen
36 Cal. 3d 638 (1984).
Chief Justice Bird delivered the opinion for the Supreme Court of California.

Facts

In early June 1981, Shawn M. was 13 years and 10 months old. At that time, her parents were entertaining out-of-town guests. Since one of the visitors was using Shawn's bedroom, Shawn suggested that she sleep in her family's camper trailer which was parked in the driveway in front of the house. Shawn's parents agreed to this arrangement on the condition that she keep the windows shut and the door locked.

On the night of June 3rd, Shawn's father, who is partially blind, was awakened by the barking of the family's three dogs. He went out the front door and heard male voices coming from the trailer. Mr. M. opened the door of the trailer ***. He then heard a male voice say, "Let's get the hell out of here."

Mr. M. could see three persons on the bed. One of the males, appellant Edward Olsen, jumped off the bed and tried to get out the door. Mr. M. wrestled with him and held him around the throat. *** The other male, James Garcia, stabbed Mr. M. in the right shoulder. Both appellant and Garcia then ran away.

[Shawn testified that both Olsen and Garcia had asked to be let in. Shawn said nothing to them and each man left. Later, Shawn awoke with Garcia holding a knife by her side and his hand over her mouth.] Although Shawn testified she locked the trailer door, she failed to explain how Garcia entered the trailer. [The trailer revealed no signs of a forced entry. Olsen then had sexual intercourse with Shawn while Garcia threatened her with a knife. During this intercourse, Shawn's father entered the trailer.]

Shawn testified that she [had known Garcia for about one year. She] was very good friends "off and on" with appellant and that during one three-month period she spent almost every day at appellant's house. At the time of the incident, however, Shawn considered Garcia her boyfriend.

[Shawn admitted that she had engaged in intercourse before the night of June 3rd, but denied having any such prior experience with either Garcia or appellant. She did admit having had sexual relations, short of intercourse, with both of them in the past. Shawn admitted that she told both Garcia and appellant that she was over 16 years old and conceded that she looked as if she were over 16. Patricia Alvarez, a police officer, testified that appellant told her that he thought Shawn was 17.]

Garcia testified [that he] first met Shawn in the summer of 1980 when she introduced herself to him. [On the day before the offense,] Shawn invited him to spend the night in the trailer with her so that they could have sex. He and Shawn engaged in sexual intercourse about four times that evening. Shawn invited Garcia to come back the following night at midnight.

The next night, after two unsuccessful attempts to enter the trailer, Garcia and appellant were told by Shawn to return at midnight. Garcia knocked on the trailer door. Shawn [opened the door, invited them in, and told them she wanted to "take both of them on."] When Mr. M. entered the trailer, appellant was on top of Shawn. Garcia denied threatening Shawn with a knife, taking her nightgown off, breaking into the trailer or forcing her to have sex with them.

[Appellant's] sister corroborated Shawn's testimony that Shawn made daily visits to the Olsen home during a three-month period. [She indicated that there was circumstantial evidence that the two had intercourse in Appellant's bedroom.]

[The] court found Garcia and appellant guilty of violating section 288, subdivision (a). [Appellant appealed,] contending that a good faith, reasonable mistake of age is a defense to a section 288 charge.

Issue

Is a reasonable mistake as to the victim's age a defense to lewd or lascivious conduct with a child under the age of 14 years Pen. Code, § 288, subd. (a)?

Rule and Analysis

*** Section 288, subdivision (a) provides in relevant part: "Any person who shall willfully and lewdly commit any lewd or lascivious act . . . upon or with the body, or any part or member thereof, of a child under the age of 14 years, with the intent of arousing, appealing to, or gratifying the lust or passions or sexual desires of such person or of such child, shall be guilty of a felony and shall be imprisoned in the state prison for a term of three, six, or eight years." ***

The language of section 288 is silent as to whether a good faith, reasonable mistake as to the victim's age constitutes a defense to a charge under that statute. Resort is thus made to judicial decisions discussing the defense. Although this court has not considered the question, it has recognized a mistake of age defense in other contexts.

Twenty years ago, this court in *People v. Hernandez* (1964) 61 Cal. 2d 529, overruled established precedent, and held that an accused's good faith, reasonable belief that a victim was 18 years or more of age was a defense to a charge of statutory rape. [*Hernandez* marked a clear break from the "universally accepted view of the courts in this country." The view that mistake of age is not a defense to a charge of statutory rape still prevails in the overwhelming majority of jurisdictions.]

In *Hernandez*, the accused was charged with statutory rape of a girl who was 17 years and 9 months old, and who had voluntarily engaged in an act of sexual intercourse. [When *Hernandez* was decided, statutory rape was defined in section 261, subdivision 1. A 1970 amendment recodified subdivision 1 as section 261.5 (unlawful sexual intercourse).] The trial court refused to allow the accused to present evidence of his good faith, reasonable belief that the prosecutrix was 18 or over. *** On appeal, this court held it reversible error to exclude such evidence. ***

The *Hernandez* court acknowledged that an accused possesses criminal intent when he acts without a belief that his victim is 18 or over. However, the court determined that if one engages in sexual intercourse with a female and reasonably believes she is 18 or over, then the essential element of criminal intent is missing. ***

[*People v. Vogel* (1956) 46 Cal.2d 798 held] that a good faith belief that a previous marriage had been terminated was a valid defense to a charge of bigamy. *** [*Hernandez*] stated, "the reluctance to accord to a charge of statutory rape the defense of a lack of criminal intent has no greater justification than in the case of other statutory crimes [such as bigamy], where the Legislature has made identical provision with respect to intent." *** Thus, "it cannot be a greater wrong to entertain a bona fide but erroneous belief that a valid consent to an act of sexual intercourse has been obtained." ***

The *Hernandez* court, however, cautioned that its holding was not "indicative of a withdrawal from the sound policy that it is in the public interest to protect the sexually naive female from exploitation. No responsible person would hesitate to condemn as untenable a claimed good faith belief in the age of consent of an 'infant' female whose obviously tender years preclude the existence of reasonable grounds for that belief." ***

***There exists a strong public policy to protect children of tender years. ***Section 288 was enacted for that very purpose. *** Furthermore, even the *Hernandez* court recognized this important policy when it made clear that it did not contemplate applying the mistake of age defense in cases where the victim is of "tender years." ***

Moreover, other language in *Hernandez* strongly suggests that a reasonable mistake as to age would not be a defense to a section 288 charge. (*Hernandez* referred to young females under the age of 14 as "infants.") The *Hernandez* court's use of that term, therefore, evidenced a belief that a mistake of age defense would be untenable when the offense involved a child that young. ***

This conclusion is supported by the Legislature's enactment of section 1203.066. [which] renders certain individuals convicted of lewd or lascivious conduct who "honestly and reasonably believed the victim was 14 years old or older" eligible for probation. The Legislature's enactment of section 1203.066, subdivision (a)(3), in the face of a corresponding failure to amend section 288 to provide for a reasonable mistake of age defense, strongly indicates that the Legislature did not intend such a defense to a section 288 charge. *** To recognize such a defense would render section 1203.066, subdivision (a)(3) a nullity, since the question of probation for individuals who had entertained an honest and reasonable belief in the victim's age would never arise. It is well established that courts are "exceedingly reluctant to attach an interpretation to a particular statute which renders other existing provisions unnecessary." ***

Other legislative provisions also support the holding that a reasonable mistake of age is not a defense to a section 288 charge. [The] Legislature has recognized that persons under 14 years of age are in need of special protection. [Section 26 provides in relevant part: "All persons are capable of committing crimes except those belonging to the following classes: *** One—Children under the age of 14, in the absence of clear proof that at the time of committing the act charged against them, they knew its wrongfulness."] That statute creates a rebuttable presumption that children under the age of 14 are incapable of knowing the wrongfulness of their actions and, therefore, are incapable of committing a crime. 20 [When] the child is a victim, rather than an accused, similar "special protection," not given to older teenagers, should be afforded. By its very terms, section 288 furthers that goal.

The Legislature has also determined that persons who commit sexual offenses on children under the age of 14 should be punished more severely than those who commit such offenses on children under the age of 18. [The] differences in punishment support the view that children under the age of 14 are given special protection.]

It is significant that a violation of section 288 carries a much harsher penalty than does unlawful sexual intercourse (§ 261.5), the crime involved in *Hernandez*. *** The different penalties for these two

offenses further supports the view that there exists a strong public policy to protect children under 14.
***

It is true that at common law "an honest and reasonable belief in the existence of circumstances, which, if true, would make the act for which the person is indicted an innocent act, has always been held to be a good defense."*** However, it is evident that the public policy considerations in protecting children under the age of 14 from lewd or lascivious conduct are substantial—far more so than those associated with unlawful sexual intercourse. These strong public policies are reflected in several Penal Code statutes, and they compel a different rule as to section 288.

The legislative purpose of section 288 would not be served by recognizing a defense of reasonable mistake of age. Thus, one who commits lewd or lascivious acts with a child, even with a good faith belief that the child is 14 years of age or older, does so at his or her peril.

Conclusion

The trial court properly rejected appellant's claim that his good faith, reasonable mistake as to the victim's age was a defense to a lewd or lascivious conduct charge with a child under 14 years of age. Accordingly, the judgment of conviction is affirmed.[172]

(2) Specific Intent Crimes

In *People v. Lawson* 215 Cal. App. 4th 108 (2013), the court discussed the mistake of fact defense when applied to specific intent crimes. The *Lawson* court considered this defense by reviewing an earlier case, *People v. Russell* (2006) 144 Cal. App. 4th 1415. The Court explained:

> (T)he particular "defense" of mistake of fact requires, at a minimum, an actual belief "in the existence of circumstances, which, if true, would make the act with which the person is charged an innocent act . . ." *** For general intent crimes, the defendant's mistaken belief must be both actual and reasonable, but if the mental state of the crime is a specific intent or knowledge, then the mistaken belief must only be actual. *** In all cases, however, the defendant's mistaken belief must relate to a set of circumstances which, if existent or true, would make the act charged an innocent act.
>
> *Russell* illustrates the proper application of the mistake-of-fact defense. In *Russell*, a person's motorcycle broke down while he was riding it, and he pushed it to a nearby repair shop. *** Because the shop was closed, he left the motorcycle next to a fenced area near the shop [close to several trash bins]. The police later found the motorcycle near a tent in a nearby homeless encampment. *** The defendant lived in the tent and when questioned, told the police he was the owner of the motorcycle. [He had] found the motorcycle in a commercial parking lot, and the area he described was the same place the motorcycle had been left after it broke down. *** At trial, the defendant testified he "saw the motorcycle sitting next to the large trash receptacles behind [the motorcycle shop] and thought it was abandoned." *** The defendant was convicted of receiving stolen property, and on appeal claimed the trial court had a duty to instruct the jury sua sponte on mistake of fact. *** The *Russell* court agreed.

---

172. Reprinted with the permission of LexisNexis.

Lawson, however, abrogated *Russell* on procedural grounds (ruling that trial courts need *not* instruct juries *sua sponte* [on their own motion] about the mistake of fact defense). Otherwise, *Lawson* adhered to *Russell's* ruling on the mistake of fact defense for specific intent crimes.[173]

b) Model Penal Code

Model Penal Code § 2.04: Ignorance or Mistake (Fact)

(1) Ignorance or mistake as to a matter of fact or law is a defense if:

(a) the ignorance or mistake negatives the purpose, knowledge, belief, recklessness or negligence required to establish a material element of the offense; or

(b) the law provides that the state of mind established by such ignorance or mistake constitutes a defense.

(2) Although ignorance or mistake would otherwise afford a defense to the offense charged, the defense is not available if the defendant would be guilty of another offense had the situation been as he supposed. In such case, however, the ignorance or mistake of the defendant shall reduce the grade and degree of the offense of which he may be convicted to those of the offense of which he would be guilty had the situation been as he supposed . . .[174]

2. Mistake of Law

Dressler opened his discussion of mistake of law by offering a legal maxim quite similar to Blackstone's (stated above). Dressler's version is more concise, providing: *"ignorantia legis neminem excusat,"* which roughly translates to "Ignorance of the law is no excuse." Like many ancient rules, this one has some exceptions, which we will explore. This maxim is, however, as Dressler describes, "deeply imbedded in Anglo-American jurisprudence" for valid reasons.

One way to consider the importance of this rule is to consider its absence; what would happen if ignorance of the law *were* a valid defense? Those most free to do what they wish, and therefore the most powerful, would be persons who were the most ignorant of the law. There would be an incentive to put your head in the sand whenever someone raised the topic of law.

Model Penal Code § 2.04: Ignorance or Mistake (Law)

. . .

(3) A belief that conduct does not legally constitute an offense is a defense to a prosecution for that offense based upon such conduct when:

(a) the statute or other enactment defining the offense is not known to the actor and has not been published or otherwise reasonably made available prior to the conduct alleged; or

(b) he acts in reasonable reliance upon an official statement of the law, afterward determined to be invalid or erroneous, contained in (i) a statute or other enactment; (ii) a judicial decision, opinion or judgment; (iii) an administrative order or grant of permission; or (iv) an official interpretation of the public officer or body charged by law with responsibility for the interpretation, administration or enforcement of the law defining the offense.

(4) The defendant must prove a defense arising under Subsection (3) of this Section by a preponderance of evidence.[175]

---

173. Reprinted with the permission of LexisNexis.

174. and 175. From *The Model Penal Code* by the American Law Institute. Copyright © 1962 by the American Law Institute. Used by permission.

G. ACCIDENT

1. Common Law

Blackstone, in *Commentaries*, Vol. IV, at 26, recognized that, sometimes, bad things occur simply by accident or misfortune rather than by fault. In this context, Blackstone noted that a person could commit "an unlawful act by *misfortune* or *chance*, and not by design." He declared that, "if any accidental mischief happens to follow from the performance of a *lawful* act, the party stands excused from all guilt." Therefore the accident of fate acted as a defense to a criminal charge.

© Gino Santa Maria/Shutterstock.com

2. Current Law

California Penal Code § 26: Persons Capable of Committing Crimes; Exceptions

All persons are capable of committing crimes except those belonging to the following classes:

> ...
>
> Five—Persons who committed the act or made the omission charged through misfortune or by accident, when it appears that there was no evil design, intention, or culpable negligence.[176]

Is "Accident or Misfortune" Even a Defense Separate from the Requirement that the Prosecution Prove Intent?

The California Supreme Court, in *People v. Anderson*, 51 Cal.4th 989 (2011), a robbery case (discussed in the robbery section above), considered the defense of "accident" as follows:

> We turn now to the question of whether trial courts generally have a duty to instruct on accident, (even if not asked to by the defendant), when the issue is raised by the evidence. We conclude they do not.

> Penal Code section 26 states the statutory defense: "All persons are capable of committing crimes except those belonging to the following classes: *** Five—Persons who committed the act or made the omission charged through misfortune or by accident, when it appears that there was no evil design, intention, or culpable negligence." [CALCRIM No. 3404] explains a defendant is not guilty of a charged crime if he or she acted "without the intent required for that crime, but acted instead accidentally." [The law recognizes a defense of accident.]

---

176. From *Deering's California Codes Annotated*. Copyright © 2014 by Matthew Bender & Company, Inc., a member of the LexisNexis Group. Reprinted with the permission of LexisNexis.

One commentator opines that statutory provisions codifying "a defense for an actor who commits the act or omission constituting an offense 'through misfortune or by accident, when it appears that there was no evil design, intention, or culpable negligence.' *** have historical significance, [but] are now unnecessary restatements, in a defense format, of the requirements of the definitional elements of an offense. To say that it is a defense that the criminal conduct or omission was committed by a non-negligent accident, is simply to say that all result element offenses [i.e., offenses that require an intent to produce a particular result] require at least proof of negligence as to causing the prohibited result. This is already made clear by the culpability requirements of specific offense definitions." *** A trial court's responsibility to instruct on accident [extends no further than to provide,] *upon request*, a pinpoint instruction relating the evidence to the mental element required for the charged crime.

H. ENTRAPMENT

There is so much crime that police can hardly handle all those who violate the law. There have been situations, however, where officers lure people into committing crimes so that they can then arrest and prosecute them. If the government is involved in instigating crime, is it fair for it to then punish the people it lured into committing criminal offenses?

1. The Subjective Approach

The **defense of entrapment** involves the government ensnaring or entrapping a person in criminal activity rather than legitimately pursuing those who happily commit crimes all by themselves. Entrapment comes in **two different forms**, depending on what the jurisdiction employing the entrapment defense wishes to accomplish. If the courts' only concern is ensuring that the person they are judging is a criminal bent on committing crime, then they adopt a "**subjective**" standard which simply asks **if the defendant was "predisposed to commit the crime."** If instead the courts view entrapment as part **of a broader mission to prevent government illegality in general** (such as stopping searches in violation of the Fourth Amendment and confessions obtained in violation of the Fifth Amendment), then the jurisdiction will adopt an "**objective**" standard

One form of entrapment focuses on the government luring persons into committing a crime much as the Venus Flytrap lures in its prey.

which inquires **whether the government's actions would cause a "normally law-abiding citizen" to commit a crime.** The two approaches are explored in the two cases below. In the first case, the United States Supreme Court weighs in on the subjective form of entrapment, and in the second case, the California Supreme Court considers the objective form of entrapment.

LEGAL ANALYSIS

Jacobson v. United States
503 U.S. 540 (1992).
Justice White delivered the opinion of the United States Supreme Court.

Facts

In February 1984, petitioner, a 56-year-old veteran-turned-farmer who supported his elderly father in Nebraska, ordered two magazines and a brochure from a California adult bookstore. The magazines, entitled *Bare Boys I* and *Bare Boys II*, contained photographs of nude preteen and teenage boys. The contents of the magazines startled petitioner, who testified that he had expected to receive photographs of "young men 18 years or older." ***

The young men depicted in the magazines were not engaged in sexual activity, and petitioner's receipt of the magazines was legal under both federal and Nebraska law. Within three months, the law with respect to child pornography changed; Congress passed the Act illegalizing the receipt through the mails of sexually explicit depictions of children. In the very month that the new provision became law, postal inspectors found petitioner's name on the mailing list of the California bookstore that had mailed him *Bare Boys I* and *II*. There followed over the next 2 1/2 years repeated efforts by two Government agencies, through five fictitious organizations and a bogus pen pal, to explore petitioner's willingness to break the new law by ordering sexually explicit photographs of children through the mail.

The Government began its efforts in January 1985 when a postal inspector sent petitioner a letter supposedly from the American Hedonist Society, which in fact was a fictitious organization. The letter [stated] that members had the "right to read what we desire, the right to discuss similar interests with those who share our philosophy ***" Petitioner enrolled in the organization. ***

[In] May 1986, petitioner received a solicitation from a second fictitious consumer research company, "Midlands Data Research." ***

Petitioner then heard from yet another Government creation, "Heartland Institute for a New Tomorrow" (HINT), which proclaimed that it was "an organization founded to protect and promote sexual freedom and freedom of choice. We believe that arbitrarily imposed legislative sanctions restricting *your* sexual freedom should be rescinded through the legislative process." [Petitioner] wrote: "Not only sexual expression but freedom of the press is under attack. We must be ever vigilant to counter attack right wing fundamentalists who are determined to curtail our freedoms." ***

HINT [portrayed] itself as a lobbying organization seeking to repeal "all statutes which regulate sexual activities, except those laws which deal with violent behavior, such as rape. ***'" [Lobbying] efforts were to be funded by sales from a catalog. *** "

[The Government wrote] to petitioner, using the pseudonym "Carl Long," [and employing] a tactic known as "mirroring," [which "reflects] whatever the interests are of the person we are writing to." *** Petitioner responded: "As far as my likes are concerned, I like good looking young guys (in their late teens and early 20's) doing their thing together." *** Petitioner's letters to "Long" made no reference to child pornography. After writing two letters, petitioner discontinued the correspondence.

***By March 1987, *** 26 months had passed since the Postal Service had commenced its mailings to petitioner. Although petitioner had responded to surveys and letters, the Government had no evidence that petitioner had ever intentionally possessed or been exposed to child pornography. ***

[A] second Government agency, the Customs Service, included petitioner in its own child pornography sting. ***

The Postal Service also continued its efforts in the Jacobson case, writing to petitioner as the "Far Eastern Trading Company Ltd.," [claiming:] "We have devised a method of getting these to you without prying eyes of U. S. Customs seizing your mail *** once we have posted our material through your system, it cannot be opened for any inspection without authorization of a judge." ***

The letter *** asked petitioner to sign an affirmation that he was "not a law enforcement officer or agent of the U. S. Government acting in an undercover capacity for the purpose of entrapping Far Eastern Trading Company." [Petitioner ordered] *Boys Who Love Boys*, *** a pornographic magazine depicting young boys engaged in various sexual activities. Petitioner was arrested after a controlled delivery of a photocopy of the magazine.

When petitioner was asked at trial why he placed such an order, he explained that the Government had succeeded in piquing his curiosity:

"Well, the statement was made of all the trouble and the hysteria over pornography and I wanted to see what the material was. *** I didn't know for sure what kind of sexual action they were referring to. ***"

In petitioner's home, the Government found the *Bare Boys* magazines and materials that the Government had sent to him in the course of its protracted investigation, but no other materials that would indicate that petitioner collected, or was actively interested in, child pornography.

On September 24, 1987, petitioner Keith Jacobson was indicted for violating a provision of the Child Protection Act of 1984 (Act), *** which criminalizes the knowing receipt through the mails of a "visual depiction [that] involves the use of a minor engaging in sexually explicit conduct . . . ." 18 U. S. C. § 2252(a)(2)(A). Petitioner defended on the ground that the Government entrapped him into committing the crime through a series of communications from undercover agents that spanned the 26 months preceding his arrest. Petitioner was found guilty after a jury trial. ***

Issue

Whether the government committed entrapment in its investigation of the defendant by targeting him for 26 months with repeated mailings and communications from Government agents and fictitious organizations.

Rule and Analysis

Because the Government overstepped the line between setting a trap for the "unwary innocent" and the "unwary criminal," *** and as a matter of law failed to establish that petitioner was independently predisposed to commit the crime for which he was arrested, we reverse *** his conviction. ***

There can be no dispute about the evils of child pornography or the difficulties that laws and law enforcement have encountered in eliminating it. [The] Government may use undercover agents to enforce the law. "It is well settled that the fact that officers or employees of the Government merely afford opportunities or facilities for the commission of the offense does not defeat the prosecution. Artifice and stratagem may be employed to catch those engaged in criminal enterprises." ***

In their zeal to enforce the law, however, Government agents may not originate a criminal design, implant in an innocent person's mind the disposition to commit a criminal act, and then induce commission of the crime so that the Government may prosecute. *** Where the Government has induced an individual to break the law and the defense of entrapment is at issue, as it was in this case, the prosecution must prove beyond reasonable doubt that the defendant was disposed to commit the criminal act prior to first being approached by Government agents. ***

Thus, an agent deployed to stop the traffic in illegal drugs may offer the opportunity to buy or sell drugs and, if the offer is accepted, make an arrest on the spot or later. In such a typical case, or in a more elaborate "sting" operation involving government-sponsored fencing where the defendant is simply provided with the opportunity to commit a crime, the entrapment defense is of little use because the ready commission of the criminal act amply demonstrates the defendant's predisposition. ***Had the agents in this case simply offered petitioner the opportunity to order child pornography through the mails, and petitioner—who must be presumed to know the law—had promptly availed himself of this criminal opportunity, it is unlikely that his entrapment defense would have warranted a jury instruction. *** But that is not what happened here. By the time petitioner finally placed his order, he had already been the target of 26 months of repeated mailings and communications from Government agents and fictitious organizations. Therefore, although he had become predisposed to break the law by May 1987, it is our view that the Government did not prove that this predisposition was independent and not the product of the attention that the Government had directed at petitioner since January 1985. ***

The prosecution's evidence of predisposition falls into two categories: evidence developed prior to the Postal Service's mail campaign, and that developed during the course of the investigation. The sole piece of preinvestigation evidence is petitioner's 1984 order and receipt of the *Bare Boys* magazines. But this is scant if any proof of petitioner's predisposition to commit an illegal act. *** It may indicate a predisposition to view sexually oriented photographs that are responsive to his sexual tastes; but evidence that merely indicates a generic inclination to act within a broad range, not all of which is criminal, is of little probative value in establishing predisposition.

Furthermore, petitioner was acting within the law at the time he received these magazines. Receipt through the mails of sexually explicit depictions of children for noncommercial use did not become illegal under federal law until May 1984, and Nebraska had no law that forbade petitioner's possession of such material until 1988. *** Evidence of predisposition to do what once was lawful is not, by itself, sufficient to show predisposition to do what is now illegal, for there is a common understanding that most people obey the law even when they disapprove of it. *** Hence, the fact that petitioner legally ordered and received the *Bare Boys* magazines does little to further the Government's burden of proving that petitioner was predisposed to commit a criminal act. This is particularly true given petitioner's unchallenged testimony that he did not know until they arrived that the magazines would depict minors.

The prosecution's evidence gathered during the investigation also fails to carry the Government's burden. Petitioner's responses to the many communications prior to the ultimate criminal act were at most indicative of certain personal inclinations, including a predisposition to view photographs of preteen sex and a willingness to promote a given agenda by supporting lobbying organizations. Even so, petitioner's responses hardly support an inference that he would commit the crime of receiving child pornography through the mails. Furthermore, a person's inclinations and "fantasies . . . are his own and beyond the reach of government . . ." ***

[By] waving the banner of individual rights and disparaging the legitimacy and constitutionality of efforts to restrict the availability of sexually explicit materials, the Government not only excited petitioner's interest in sexually explicit materials banned by law but also exerted substantial pressure on petitioner to obtain and read such material as part of a fight against censorship and the infringement of individual rights. For instance, HINT described itself as "an organization founded to protect and promote sexual freedom and freedom of choice" and stated that "the most appropriate means to accomplish [its] objectives is to promote honest dialogue among concerned individuals and to continue its lobbying efforts with State Legislators." *** These lobbying efforts were to be financed through catalog sales. *** Mailings from the equally fictitious American Hedonist Society, ***, and the correspondence from the nonexistent Carl Long, *** endorsed these themes.

Similarly, the two solicitations in the spring of 1987 raised the spectre of censorship while suggesting that petitioner ought to be allowed to do what he had been solicited to do. [The] Government solicitations suggested that receiving this material was something that petitioner ought to be allowed to do.

Petitioner's ready response to these solicitations cannot be enough to establish beyond reasonable doubt that he was predisposed, prior to the Government acts intended to create predisposition, to commit the crime of receiving child pornography through the mails. *** The evidence that petitioner was ready and willing to commit the offense came only after the Government had devoted 2½ years to convincing him that he had or should have the right to engage in the very behavior proscribed by law. Rational jurors could not say beyond a reasonable doubt that petitioner possessed the requisite predisposition prior to the Government's investigation and that it existed independent of the Government's many and varied approaches to petitioner. "[The Government may not] play on the weaknesses of an innocent party and beguile him into committing crimes which he otherwise would not have attempted." ***

Law enforcement officials go too far when they "implant in the mind of an innocent person the *disposition* to commit the alleged offense and induce its commission in order that they may prosecute. [We] are "unable to conclude that it was the intention of the Congress in enacting this statute that its processes of detection and enforcement should be abused by the instigation by government officials of an act on the part of persons otherwise innocent in order to lure them to its commission and to punish them." *** When the Government's quest for convictions leads to the apprehension of an otherwise law-abiding citizen who, if left to his own devices, likely would have never run afoul of the law, the courts should intervene.

Conclusion

[The] prosecution failed, as a matter of law, to adduce evidence to support the jury verdict that petitioner was predisposed, independent of the Government's acts and beyond a reasonable doubt, to violate the law by receiving child pornography through the mails. [We reverse the conviction.] *It is so ordered.*

Note

This Supreme Court case is so significant that it has been cited in over 200 law review articles.

2.   The Objective Approach

LEGAL ANALYSIS

People v. Watson
22 Cal. 4th 220 (2000).
Justice Chin delivered the opinion for the Supreme Court of California.

Facts

One March evening in 1997, Bakersfield police officers conducted a vehicle theft "sting" operation. They staged an arrest of a plainclothes police officer driving a black 1980 Chevrolet Monte Carlo that belonged to the police department. The arresting officers activated the emergency lights and siren of their marked patrol car and stopped the Monte Carlo. The Monte Carlo's driver drove into a parking lot and parked. While a group of spectators watched, a uniformed police officer approached the Monte Carlo, ordered the driver out, patted him down, handcuffed him, placed him in the backseat of the patrol car, and drove away, leaving the Monte Carlo behind. The police left the Monte Carlo unlocked with the keys in the ignition to make it easier to take. They wanted to "give the impression [the driver] was arrested and the vehicle was left there."

A couple of hours later, police arrested defendant after he drove the Monte Carlo from the parking lot. He told the arresting officer that his niece had informed him of the earlier apparent arrest and told him to "come and take" the car. He did just that, intending to use it to "roll," i.e., to drive it.

Defendant was charged with taking a vehicle. (Veh. Code, § 10851, subd. (a).) At the first trial, the court instructed the jury on entrapment. The jury was unable to reach a verdict, and the court declared a mistrial. At the second trial, the court refused to instruct on entrapment, finding insufficient evidence to support the defense. The jury found defendant guilty. ***

Issue

Whether police committed entrapment of the defendant in the motor vehicle theft case.

Rule and Analysis

The trial court was required to instruct the second jury on the defense of entrapment if, but only if, substantial evidence supported the defense. *** In California, the test for entrapment focuses on the police conduct and is objective. Entrapment is established if the law enforcement conduct is likely to induce a *normally law-abiding person* to commit the offense. *** "[Such] a person would normally resist the temptation to commit a crime presented by the simple opportunity to act unlawfully. Official conduct that does no more than offer that opportunity to the suspect—for example, a decoy program—is therefore permissible; but it is impermissible for the police or their agents to pressure the suspect by overbearing conduct such as badgering, cajoling, importuning, or other affirmative acts likely to induce a normally law-abiding person to commit the crime." ***

The [court offered] two guiding principles. "First, if the actions of the law enforcement agent would generate in a normally law-abiding person a motive for the crime other than ordinary criminal intent, entrapment will be established." *** Defendant does not rely on this principle. He does not claim his motive in taking the car was other than ordinary criminal intent. Instead, he relies on the second principle: "Second, affirmative police conduct that would make commission of the crime unusually attractive to a normally law-abiding person will likewise constitute entrapment. Such conduct would include, for example, a guarantee that the act is not illegal or the offense will go undetected, an offer of exorbitant consideration, or any similar enticement."***

Citing this second principle, the Court of Appeal concluded this case warranted an entrapment instruction because the jury might have found that "the police made taking the car unusually attractive" by sending the message, "'You can take this car and get away with it.'" Such a message, the Court of Appeal concluded, might constitute "any similar enticement." *** We disagree. *** Normally, police conduct must be directed at a specific person or persons to constitute entrapment. The police must "pressure the suspect by overbearing conduct . . ." *** Except perhaps in extreme circumstances, the second *** principle is limited to instances of individual, personal enticement, excluding communications made to the world at large. Merely providing people in general an opportunity to commit a crime is not an improper enticement or otherwise entrapment. "[The] rule is clear that 'ruses, stings, and decoys are permissible stratagems in the enforcement of criminal law, and they become invalid only when badgering or importuning takes place to an extent and degree that is likely to induce an otherwise law-abiding person to commit a crime.'" *** The sting operation in this case presents no evidence of entrapment, both because the police did not specifically intend it as a communication to defendant personally, and because it did not actually *guarantee* anything, but merely conveyed the idea detection was unlikely. The police did nothing more than present to the general community a tempting opportunity to take the Monte Carlo. Some persons, obviously including defendant, might have found the temptation hard to resist. But a person who steals when given the opportunity is an opportunistic thief, not a normally law-abiding person. Specifically, normally law-abiding persons do not take a car not belonging to them merely because it is unlocked with the keys in the ignition and it appears they will not be caught. Defendant presented no evidence of any personal contact whatever between police and himself; certainly he could not show that the police cajoled him, gave him any enticement or guarantee, or even knew or cared who he was. ***

Justice Mosk argues that "next we may anticipate arranging for a homeowner to leave his front door open all night to attract a burglar. Or a bank to leave a signed check on the counter to attract a forger. Or leaving a loaded gun on a park bench to attract a potential robber." *** A big difference exists, however, between the police risking their own property in tightly controlled circumstances and asking the public to do the same (or, in the loaded gun hypothetical, to invite violence) in uncontrolled circumstances. Moreover, the police might reasonably believe that sting operations like this *deter*, not encourage, crime. For example, once word of this case circulated in the community, future would-be car thieves might hesitate before taking advantage of what appears to be an easy target.

Conclusion

The trial court correctly refused to instruct the second jury on entrapment. [We] remand the matter for further proceedings consistent with our opinion.[177]

DISCUSSION QUESTIONS

1. Why does the law choose to not punish as criminal bad actions committed by insane persons? What is the rationale behind this government inaction?

2. Is insanity the same as being mentally ill?

3. Is the "insanity defense" the same thing as "present insanity" or" mental incompetence" to proceed to trial? Explain each of these concepts.

4. How can there be different definitions of insanity? How can "insanity" be tested differently by different states?

5. What is the difference between insanity and diminished capacity?

6. What is duress? Is this defense available to those who murder a person?

7. If a person is intoxicated when they commit a criminal act, does the fact that the person is intoxicated lessen his or her guilt? Why or why not? Does it matter how the person became intoxicated?

8. What is the relationship between the infancy defense and mens rea or criminal intent?

9. How can a mistake of fact negate criminal intent?

10. What are the differences between the subjective and objective approaches to entrapment?

177. Reprinted with the permission of LexisNexis.

WEB LINKS

1. Massachusetts's Court System has "Jury Instruction 9.220 Mental Impairment Short of Insanity" at: http://www.mass.gov/courts/docs/courts-and-judges/courts/district-court/jury-instructions-criminal/6000-9999/9220-defenses-mental-impairment-short-of-insanity.pdf

2. *CBS News'* Farhan Bokhari reported in an April 12, 2014, article entitled, "Attempted-murder charge against 9-month old dismissed in Pakistan," that exposed the deficiencies of the country's judicial system and police. The full article can be viewed at: http://www.cbsnews.com/news/attempted-murder-charge-against-9-month-old-dismissed-in-pakistan/

3. Texas' jury charges on the defense of mistake of law (Section 8.03) can be downloaded from: http://www.tdcaa.com/content/section-803-mistake-law.

4. Texas' jury charges on the defense of Entrapment (Section 8.06) can be downloaded from: www.tdcaa.com/content/section-806-entrapment

APPENDIX
I

The United States Constitution

© David Smart/Shutterstock.com

PREAMBLE

We the People of the United States, in Order to form a more perfect Union, establish Justice, insure domestic Tranquility, provide for the common defence, promote the general Welfare, and secure the Blessings of Liberty to ourselves and our Posterity, do ordain and establish this Constitution for the United States of America.

ARTICLE. I.

Section. 1.

All legislative Powers herein granted shall be vested in a Congress of the United States, which shall consist of a Senate and House of Representatives.

Section. 2.

The House of Representatives shall be composed of Members chosen every second Year by the People of the several States, and the Electors in each State shall have the Qualifications requisite for Electors of the most numerous Branch of the State Legislature.

No Person shall be a Representative who shall not have attained to the Age of twenty five Years, and been seven Years a Citizen of the United States, and who shall not, when elected, be an Inhabitant of that State in which he shall be chosen.

Representatives and direct Taxes shall be apportioned among the several States which may be included within this Union, according to their respective Numbers, which shall be determined by adding to the whole Number of free Persons, including those bound to Service for a Term of Years, and excluding Indians not taxed, three fifths of all other Persons. The actual Enumeration shall be made within three Years after the first Meeting of the Congress of the United States, and within every subsequent Term of ten Years, in such Manner as they shall by Law direct. The Number of Representatives shall not exceed one for every thirty Thousand, but each State shall have at Least one Representative; and until such enumeration shall be made, the State of New Hampshire shall be entitled to chuse three, Massachusetts eight, Rhode-Island and Providence Plantations one, Connecticut five, New-York six, New Jersey four, Pennsylvania eight, Delaware one, Maryland six, Virginia ten, North Carolina five, South Carolina five, and Georgia three.

When vacancies happen in the Representation from any State, the Executive Authority thereof shall issue Writs of Election to fill such Vacancies.

The House of Representatives shall chuse their Speaker and other Officers; and shall have the sole Power of Impeachment.

Section. 3.

The Senate of the United States shall be composed of two Senators from each State, chosen by the Legislature thereof for six Years; and each Senator shall have one Vote.

Immediately after they shall be assembled in Consequence of the first Election, they shall be divided as equally as may be into three Classes. The Seats of the Senators of the first Class shall be vacated at the Expiration of the second Year, of the second Class at the Expiration of the fourth Year, and of the third Class at the Expiration of the sixth Year, so that one third may be chosen every second Year; and if Vacancies happen by Resignation, or otherwise, during the Recess of the Legislature of any State, the Executive thereof may make temporary Appointments until the next Meeting of the Legislature, which shall then fill such Vacancies.

No Person shall be a Senator who shall not have attained to the Age of thirty Years, and been nine Years a Citizen of the United States, and who shall not, when elected, be an Inhabitant of that State for which he shall be chosen.

The Vice President of the United States shall be President of the Senate, but shall have no Vote, unless they be equally divided.

The Senate shall chuse their other Officers, and also a President pro tempore, in the Absence of the Vice President, or when he shall exercise the Office of President of the United States.

The Senate shall have the sole Power to try all Impeachments. When sitting for that Purpose, they shall be on Oath or Affirmation. When the President of the United States is tried, the Chief Justice shall preside: And no Person shall be convicted without the Concurrence of two thirds of the Members present.

Judgment in Cases of Impeachment shall not extend further than to removal from Office, and disqualification to hold and enjoy any Office of honor, Trust or Profit under the United States: but the Party convicted shall nevertheless be liable and subject to Indictment, Trial, Judgment and Punishment, according to Law.

Section. 4.

The Times, Places and Manner of holding Elections for Senators and Representatives, shall be prescribed in each State by the Legislature thereof; but the Congress may at any time by Law make or alter such Regulations, except as to the Places of chusing Senators.

The Congress shall assemble at least once in every Year, and such Meeting shall be on the first Monday in December, unless they shall by Law appoint a different Day.

Section. 5.

Each House shall be the Judge of the Elections, Returns and Qualifications of its own Members, and a Majority of each shall constitute a Quorum to do Business; but a smaller Number may adjourn from day to day, and may be authorized to compel the Attendance of absent Members, in such Manner, and under such Penalties as each House may provide.

Each House may determine the Rules of its Proceedings, punish its Members for disorderly Behaviour, and, with the Concurrence of two thirds, expel a Member.

Each House shall keep a Journal of its Proceedings, and from time to time publish the same, excepting such Parts as may in their Judgment require Secrecy; and the Yeas and Nays of the Members of either House on any question shall, at the Desire of one fifth of those Present, be entered on the Journal.

Neither House, during the Session of Congress, shall, without the Consent of the other, adjourn for more than three days, nor to any other Place than that in which the two Houses shall be sitting.

Section. 6.

The Senators and Representatives shall receive a Compensation for their Services, to be ascertained by Law, and paid out of the Treasury of the United States. They shall in all Cases, except Treason, Felony and

Breach of the Peace, be privileged from Arrest during their Attendance at the Session of their respective Houses, and in going to and returning from the same; and for any Speech or Debate in either House, they shall not be questioned in any other Place.

No Senator or Representative shall, during the Time for which he was elected, be appointed to any civil Office under the Authority of the United States, which shall have been created, or the Emoluments whereof shall have been encreased during such time; and no Person holding any Office under the United States, shall be a Member of either House during his Continuance in Office.

Section. 7.

All Bills for raising Revenue shall originate in the House of Representatives; but the Senate may propose or concur with Amendments as on other Bills.

Every Bill which shall have passed the House of Representatives and the Senate, shall, before it become a Law, be presented to the President of the United States: If he approve he shall sign it, but if not he shall return it, with his Objections to that House in which it shall have originated, who shall enter the Objections at large on their Journal, and proceed to reconsider it. If after such Reconsideration two thirds of that House shall agree to pass the Bill, it shall be sent, together with the Objections, to the other House, by which it shall likewise be reconsidered, and if approved by two thirds of that House, it shall become a Law. But in all such Cases the Votes of both Houses shall be determined by yeas and Nays, and the Names of the Persons voting for and against the Bill shall be entered on the Journal of each House respectively. If any Bill shall not be returned by the President within ten Days (Sundays excepted) after it shall have been presented to him, the Same shall be a Law, in like Manner as if he had signed it, unless the Congress by their Adjournment prevent its Return, in which Case it shall not be a Law.

Every Order, Resolution, or Vote to which the Concurrence of the Senate and House of Representatives may be necessary (except on a question of Adjournment) shall be presented to the President of the United States; and before the Same shall take Effect, shall be approved by him, or being disapproved by him, shall be repassed by two thirds of the Senate and House of Representatives, according to the Rules and Limitations prescribed in the Case of a Bill.

Section. 8.

The Congress shall have Power To lay and collect Taxes, Duties, Imposts and Excises, to pay the Debts and provide for the common Defence and general Welfare of the United States; but all Duties, Imposts and Excises shall be uniform throughout the United States;

To borrow Money on the credit of the United States;

To regulate Commerce with foreign Nations, and among the several States, and with the Indian Tribes;

To establish an uniform Rule of Naturalization, and uniform Laws on the subject of Bankruptcies throughout the United States;

To coin Money, regulate the Value thereof, and of foreign Coin, and fix the Standard of Weights and Measures;

To provide for the Punishment of counterfeiting the Securities and current Coin of the United States;

To establish Post Offices and post Roads;

To promote the Progress of Science and useful Arts, by securing for limited Times to Authors and Inventors the exclusive Right to their respective Writings and Discoveries;

To constitute Tribunals inferior to the supreme Court;

To define and punish Piracies and Felonies committed on the high Seas, and Offences against the Law of Nations;

To declare War, grant Letters of Marque and Reprisal, and make Rules concerning Captures on Land and Water;

To raise and support Armies, but no Appropriation of Money to that Use shall be for a longer Term than two Years;

To provide and maintain a Navy;

To make Rules for the Government and Regulation of the land and naval Forces;

To provide for calling forth the Militia to execute the Laws of the Union, suppress Insurrections and repel Invasions;

To provide for organizing, arming, and disciplining, the Militia, and for governing such Part of them as may be employed in the Service of the United States, reserving to the States respectively, the Appointment of the Officers, and the Authority of training the Militia according to the discipline prescribed by Congress;

To exercise exclusive Legislation in all Cases whatsoever, over such District (not exceeding ten Miles square) as may, by Cession of particular States, and the Acceptance of Congress, become the Seat of the Government of the United States, and to exercise like Authority over all Places purchased by the Consent of the Legislature of the State in which the Same shall be, for the Erection of Forts, Magazines, Arsenals, dock-Yards, and other needful Buildings;—And

To make all Laws which shall be necessary and proper for carrying into Execution the foregoing Powers, and all other Powers vested by this Constitution in the Government of the United States, or in any Department or Officer thereof.

Section. 9.

The Migration or Importation of such Persons as any of the States now existing shall think proper to admit, shall not be prohibited by the Congress prior to the Year one thousand eight hundred and eight, but a Tax or duty may be imposed on such Importation, not exceeding ten dollars for each Person.

The Privilege of the Writ of Habeas Corpus shall not be suspended, unless when in Cases of Rebellion or Invasion the public Safety may require it.

No Bill of Attainder or ex post facto Law shall be passed.

No Capitation, or other direct, Tax shall be laid, unless in Proportion to the Census or enumeration herein before directed to be taken.

No Tax or Duty shall be laid on Articles exported from any State.

No Preference shall be given by any Regulation of Commerce or Revenue to the Ports of one State over those of another; nor shall Vessels bound to, or from, one State, be obliged to enter, clear, or pay Duties in another.

No Money shall be drawn from the Treasury, but in Consequence of Appropriations made by Law; and a regular Statement and Account of the Receipts and Expenditures of all public Money shall be published from time to time.

No Title of Nobility shall be granted by the United States: And no Person holding any Office of Profit or Trust under them, shall, without the Consent of the Congress, accept of any present, Emolument, Office, or Title, of any kind whatever, from any King, Prince, or foreign State.

Section. 10.

No State shall enter into any Treaty, Alliance, or Confederation; grant Letters of Marque and Reprisal; coin Money; emit Bills of Credit; make any Thing but gold and silver Coin a Tender in Payment of Debts; pass any Bill of Attainder, ex post facto Law, or Law impairing the Obligation of Contracts, or grant any Title of Nobility.

No State shall, without the Consent of the Congress, lay any Imposts or Duties on Imports or Exports, except what may be absolutely necessary for executing it's inspection Laws: and the net Produce of all Duties and Imposts, laid by any State on Imports or Exports, shall be for the Use of the Treasury of the United States; and all such Laws shall be subject to the Revision and Controul of the Congress.

No State shall, without the Consent of Congress, lay any Duty of Tonnage, keep Troops, or Ships of War in time of Peace, enter into any Agreement or Compact with another State, or with a foreign Power, or engage in War, unless actually invaded, or in such imminent Danger as will not admit of delay.

ARTICLE. II.

Section. 1.

The executive Power shall be vested in a President of the United States of America. He shall hold his Office during the Term of four Years, and, together with the Vice President, chosen for the same Term, be elected, as follows:

Each State shall appoint, in such Manner as the Legislature thereof may direct, a Number of Electors, equal to the whole Number of Senators and Representatives to which the State may be entitled in the Congress: but no Senator or Representative, or Person holding an Office of Trust or Profit under the United States, shall be appointed an Elector.

The Electors shall meet in their respective States, and vote by Ballot for two Persons, of whom one at least shall not be an Inhabitant of the same State with themselves. And they shall make a List of all the Persons voted for, and of the Number of Votes for each; which List they shall sign and certify, and transmit sealed to the Seat of the Government of the United States, directed to the President of the Senate. The President of the Senate shall, in the Presence of the Senate and House of Representatives, open all the Certificates, and the Votes shall then be counted. The Person having the greatest Number of Votes shall be the President, if such Number be a Majority of the whole Number of Electors appointed; and if there be more than one who have such Majority, and have an equal Number of Votes, then the House of Representatives shall immediately chuse by Ballot one of them for President; and if no Person have a Majority, then from the five highest on the List the said House shall in like Manner chuse the President. But in chusing the President, the Votes shall be taken by States, the Representation from each State having one Vote; A quorum for this purpose shall consist of a Member or Members from two thirds of the States, and a Majority of all the States shall be necessary to a Choice. In every Case, after the Choice of the President, the Person having the greatest Number of Votes of the Electors shall be the Vice President. But if there should remain two or more who have equal Votes, the Senate shall chuse from them by Ballot the Vice President.

The Congress may determine the Time of chusing the Electors, and the Day on which they shall give their Votes; which Day shall be the same throughout the United States.

No Person except a natural born Citizen, or a Citizen of the United States, at the time of the Adoption of this Constitution, shall be eligible to the Office of President; neither shall any Person be eligible to that Office who shall not have attained to the Age of thirty five Years, and been fourteen Years a Resident within the United States.

In Case of the Removal of the President from Office, or of his Death, Resignation, or Inability to discharge the Powers and Duties of the said Office, the Same shall devolve on the Vice President, and the Congress may by Law provide for the Case of Removal, Death, Resignation or Inability, both of the President and Vice President, declaring what Officer shall then act as President, and such Officer shall act accordingly, until the Disability be removed, or a President shall be elected.

The President shall, at stated Times, receive for his Services, a Compensation, which shall neither be increased nor diminished during the Period for which he shall have been elected, and he shall not receive within that Period any other Emolument from the United States, or any of them.

Before he enter on the Execution of his Office, he shall take the following Oath or Affirmation:—"I do solemnly swear (or affirm) that I will faithfully execute the Office of President of the United States, and will to the best of my Ability, preserve, protect and defend the Constitution of the United States."

Section. 2.

The President shall be Commander in Chief of the Army and Navy of the United States, and of the Militia of the several States, when called into the actual Service of the United States; he may require the Opinion, in writing, of the principal Officer in each of the executive Departments, upon any Subject relating to the Duties of their respective Offices, and he shall have Power to grant Reprieves and Pardons for Offences against the United States, except in Cases of Impeachment.

He shall have Power, by and with the Advice and Consent of the Senate, to make Treaties, provided two thirds of the Senators present concur; and he shall nominate, and by and with the Advice and Consent of the Senate, shall appoint Ambassadors, other public Ministers and Consuls, Judges of the supreme Court, and all other Officers of the United States, whose Appointments are not herein otherwise provided for, and which shall be established by Law: but the Congress may by Law vest the Appointment of such inferior Officers, as they think proper, in the President alone, in the Courts of Law, or in the Heads of Departments.

The President shall have Power to fill up all Vacancies that may happen during the Recess of the Senate, by granting Commissions which shall expire at the End of their next Session.

Section. 3.

He shall from time to time give to the Congress Information of the State of the Union, and recommend to their Consideration such Measures as he shall judge necessary and expedient; he may, on extraordinary Occasions, convene both Houses, or either of them, and in Case of Disagreement between them, with Respect to the Time of Adjournment, he may adjourn them to such Time as he shall think proper; he shall receive Ambassadors and other public Ministers; he shall take Care that the Laws be faithfully executed, and shall Commission all the Officers of the United States.

Section. 4.

The President, Vice President and all civil Officers of the United States, shall be removed from Office on Impeachment for, and Conviction of, Treason, Bribery, or other high Crimes and Misdemeanors.

ARTICLE III.

Section. 1.

The judicial Power of the United States shall be vested in one supreme Court, and in such inferior Courts as the Congress may from time to time ordain and establish. The Judges, both of the supreme and inferior Courts, shall hold their Offices during good Behaviour, and shall, at stated Times, receive for their Services a Compensation, which shall not be diminished during their Continuance in Office.

Section. 2.

The judicial Power shall extend to all Cases, in Law and Equity, arising under this Constitution, the Laws of the United States, and Treaties made, or which shall be made, under their Authority;—to all Cases affecting Ambassadors, other public Ministers and Consuls;—to all Cases of admiralty and maritime Jurisdiction;—to Controversies to which the United States shall be a Party;—to Controversies between two or more States;—between a State and Citizens of another State,—between Citizens of different States,--between Citizens of the same State claiming Lands under Grants of different States, and between a State, or the Citizens thereof, and foreign States, Citizens or Subjects.

In all Cases affecting Ambassadors, other public Ministers and Consuls, and those in which a State shall be Party, the supreme Court shall have original Jurisdiction. In all the other Cases before mentioned, the supreme Court shall have appellate Jurisdiction, both as to Law and Fact, with such Exceptions, and under such Regulations as the Congress shall make.

The Trial of all Crimes, except in Cases of Impeachment, shall be by Jury; and such Trial shall be held in the State where the said Crimes shall have been committed; but when not committed within any State, the Trial shall be at such Place or Places as the Congress may by Law have directed.

Section. 3.

Treason against the United States, shall consist only in levying War against them, or in adhering to their Enemies, giving them Aid and Comfort. No Person shall be convicted of Treason unless on the Testimony of two Witnesses to the same overt Act, or on Confession in open Court.

The Congress shall have Power to declare the Punishment of Treason, but no Attainder of Treason shall work Corruption of Blood, or Forfeiture except during the Life of the Person attainted.

ARTICLE. IV.

Section. 1.

Full Faith and Credit shall be given in each State to the public Acts, Records, and judicial Proceedings of every other State. And the Congress may by general Laws prescribe the Manner in which such Acts, Records and Proceedings shall be proved, and the Effect thereof.

Section. 2.

The Citizens of each State shall be entitled to all Privileges and Immunities of Citizens in the several States.

A Person charged in any State with Treason, Felony, or other Crime, who shall flee from Justice, and be found in another State, shall on Demand of the executive Authority of the State from which he fled, be delivered up, to be removed to the State having Jurisdiction of the Crime.

No Person held to Service or Labour in one State, under the Laws thereof, escaping into another, shall, in Consequence of any Law or Regulation therein, be discharged from such Service or Labour, but shall be delivered up on Claim of the Party to whom such Service or Labour may be due.

Section. 3.

New States may be admitted by the Congress into this Union; but no new State shall be formed or erected within the Jurisdiction of any other State; nor any State be formed by the Junction of two or more States, or Parts of States, without the Consent of the Legislatures of the States concerned as well as of the Congress.

The Congress shall have Power to dispose of and make all needful Rules and Regulations respecting the Territory or other Property belonging to the United States; and nothing in this Constitution shall be so construed as to Prejudice any Claims of the United States, or of any particular State.

Section. 4.

The United States shall guarantee to every State in this Union a Republican Form of Government, and shall protect each of them against Invasion; and on Application of the Legislature, or of the Executive (when the Legislature cannot be convened), against domestic Violence.

ARTICLE. V.

The Congress, whenever two thirds of both Houses shall deem it necessary, shall propose Amendments to this Constitution, or, on the Application of the Legislatures of two thirds of the several States, shall call a Convention for proposing Amendments, which, in either Case, shall be valid to all Intents and Purposes, as Part of this Constitution, when ratified by the Legislatures of three fourths of the several States, or by Conventions in three fourths thereof, as the one or the other Mode of Ratification may be proposed by the Congress; Provided that no Amendment which may be made prior to the Year One thousand eight hundred and eight shall in any Manner affect the first and fourth Clauses in the Ninth Section of the first Article; and that no State, without its Consent, shall be deprived of its equal Suffrage in the Senate.

ARTICLE. VI.

All Debts contracted and Engagements entered into, before the Adoption of this Constitution, shall be as valid against the United States under this Constitution, as under the Confederation.

This Constitution, and the Laws of the United States which shall be made in Pursuance thereof; and all Treaties made, or which shall be made, under the Authority of the United States, shall be the supreme Law of the Land; and the Judges in every State shall be bound thereby, any Thing in the Constitution or Laws of any State to the Contrary notwithstanding.

The Senators and Representatives before mentioned, and the Members of the several State Legislatures, and all executive and judicial Officers, both of the United States and of the several States, shall be bound by Oath or Affirmation, to support this Constitution; but no religious Test shall ever be required as a Qualification to any Office or public Trust under the United States.

ARTICLE. VII.

The Ratification of the Conventions of nine States, shall be sufficient for the Establishment of this Constitution between the States so ratifying the Same.

Done in Convention, by the unanimous consent of the States present, the seventeenth day September, in the year of our Lord one thousand seven hundred and eighty-seven, and of the independence of the United States of America the twelfth. In witness whereof we have hereunto subscribed our names.

Amendment I

Congress shall make no law respecting an establishment of religion, or prohibiting the free exercise thereof; or abridging the freedom of speech, or of the press; or the right of the people peaceably to assemble, and to petition the government for a redress of grievances.

Amendment II

A well regulated militia, being necessary to the security of a free state, the right of the people to keep and bear arms, shall not be infringed.

Amendment III

No soldier shall, in time of peace be quartered in any house, without the consent of the owner, nor in time of war, but in a manner to be prescribed by law.

Amendment IV

The right of the people to be secure in their persons, houses, papers, and effects, against unreasonable searches and seizures, shall not be violated, and no warrants shall issue, but upon probable cause, supported by oath or affirmation, and particularly describing the place to be searched, and the persons or things to be seized.

Amendment V

No person shall be held to answer for a capital, or otherwise infamous crime, unless on a presentment or indictment of a grand jury, except in cases arising in the land or naval forces, or in the militia, when in actual service in time of war or public danger; nor shall any person be subject for the same offense to be twice put in jeopardy of life or limb; nor shall be compelled in any criminal case to be a witness against himself, nor be deprived of life, liberty, or property, without due process of law; nor shall private property be taken for public use, without just compensation.

Amendment VI

In all criminal prosecutions, the accused shall enjoy the right to a speedy and public trial, by an impartial jury of the state and district wherein the crime shall have been committed, which district shall have been previously ascertained by law, and to be informed of the nature and cause of the accusation; to be confronted with the witnesses against him; to have compulsory process for obtaining witnesses in his favor, and to have the assistance of counsel for his defense.

Amendment VII

In suits at common law, where the value in controversy shall exceed twenty dollars, the right of trial by jury shall be preserved, and no fact tried by a jury, shall be otherwise reexamined in any court of the United States, than according to the rules of the common law.

Amendment VIII

Excessive bail shall not be required, nor excessive fines imposed, nor cruel and unusual punishments inflicted.

Amendment IX

The enumeration in the Constitution, of certain rights, shall not be construed to deny or disparage others retained by the people.

Amendment X

The powers not delegated to the United States by the Constitution, nor prohibited by it to the states, are reserved to the states respectively, or to the people.

Amendment XI

The judicial power of the United States shall not be construed to extend to any suit in law or equity, commenced or prosecuted against one of the United States by citizens of another State, or by citizens or subjects of any foreign state.

Amendment XII

1. The Electors shall meet in their respective States and vote by ballot for President and Vice-President, one of whom, at least, shall not be an inhabitant of the same State with themselves; they shall name in their ballots the person voted for as President, and in distinct ballots the person voted for as Vice-President, and of the number of votes for each, which lists they shall sign and certify, and transmit sealed to the seat of the Government of the United States, directed to the President of the Senate; the President of the Senate shall, in the presence of the Senate and House of Representatives, open all the certificates and the votes shall then be counted;—The person having the greatest number of votes for President, shall be the President, if such number be a majority of the whole number of Electors appointed; and if no person have such majority, then from the persons having the highest numbers not exceeding three on the list of those voted for as President, the House of Representatives shall choose immediately, by ballot, the President. But in choosing the President, the votes shall be taken by States, the representation from each State having one vote; a quorum for this purpose shall consist of a member or members from two-thirds of the States, and a majority of all the States shall be necessary to a choice. And if the House of Representatives shall not choose a President whenever the right of choice shall devolve upon them, before the fourth day of March next following, then the Vice-President shall act as President, as in case of the death or other constitutional disability of the President.
3. The person having the greatest number of votes as Vice-President, shall be the Vice-President, if such numbers be a majority of the whole number of electors appointed, and if no person have a majority, then from the two highest numbers on the list, the Senate shall choose the Vice-President; a quorum for the purpose shall consist of two-thirds of the whole number of Senators, and a majority of the whole number shall be necessary to a choice. But no person constitutionally ineligible to the office of President shall be eligible to that of Vice-President of the United States.

Amendment XIII

1. Neither slavery nor involuntary servitude, except as a punishment for crime whereof the party shall have been duly convicted, shall exist within the United States, or any place subject to their jurisdiction.

2. Congress shall have power to enforce this article by appropriate legislation.

Amendment XIV

1. All persons born or naturalized in the United States, and subject to the jurisdiction thereof, are citizens of the United States and of the State wherein they reside. No State shall make or enforce any law which shall abridge the privileges or immunities of citizens of the United States; nor shall any State deprive any person of life, liberty, or property, without due process of law; nor to deny to any person within its jurisdiction the equal protection of the laws.
2. Representatives shall be apportioned among the several States according to their respective numbers, counting the whole number of persons in each State, excluding Indians not taxed. But when the right to vote at any election for the choice of Electors for President and Vice-President of the United States, Representatives in Congress, the executive and judicial officers of a State, or the members of the legislature thereof, is denied to any of the male inhabitants of such State, being twenty-one years of age, and citizens of the United States, or in any way abridged, except for participation in rebellion, or other crime, the basis of representation therein shall be reduced in the proportion which the number of such male citizens shall bear to the whole number of male citizens twenty-one years of age in such State.
3. No person shall be a Senator or Representative in Congress, or Elector of President and Vice-President, or hold any office, civil or military, under the United States, or under any State, who, having previously taken an oath, as a member of Congress, or as an officer of the United States, or as a member of any State Legislature, or as an executive or judicial officer of any State, to support the Constitution of the United States, shall have engaged in insurrection or rebellion against the same, or given aid or comfort to the enemies thereof. But Congress may by a vote of two-thirds of each House, remove such disability.
4. The validity of the public debt of the United States, authorized by law, including debts incurred for payment of pensions and bounties for services in suppressing insurrection or rebellion, shall not be questioned. But neither the United States nor any State shall assume or pay any debt or obligation incurred in aid of insurrection or rebellion against the United States, or any claim for the loss or emancipation of any slave; but all such debts, obligations and claims shall be held illegal and void.
5. The Congress shall have the power to enforce, by appropriate legislation, the provisions of this article.

Amendment XV

1. The right of citizens of the United States to vote shall not be denied or abridged by the United States or by any State on account of race, color, or previous condition of servitude.
2. The Congress shall have the power to enforce this article by appropriate legislation.

Amendment XVI

The Congress shall have power to lay and collect taxes on incomes, from whatever sources derived, without apportionment among the several States, and without regard to any census or enumeration.

Amendment XVII

1. The Senate of the United States shall be composed of two Senators from each State, elected by the people thereof, for six years; and each Senator shall have one vote. The electors in each State shall have the qualifications requisite for electors of the most numerous branch of the State Legislatures.
2. When vacancies happen in the representation of any State in the Senate, the executive authority of such State shall issue writs of election to fill such vacancies: Provided, That the Legislature of any State may empower the Executive thereof to make temporary appointments until the people fill the vacancies by election as the Legislature may direct.
3. This amendment shall not be so construed as to affect the election or term of any Senator chosen before it becomes valid as part of the Constitution.

Amendment XVIII

1. After one year from the ratification of this article the manufacture, sale, or transportation of intoxicating liquors within, the importation thereof into, or the exportation thereof from the United States and all territory subject to the jurisdiction thereof for beverage purposes is hereby prohibited.
2. The Congress and the several States shall have concurrent power to enforce this article by appropriate legislation.
3. This article shall be inoperative unless it shall have been ratified as an amendment to the Constitution by the Legislatures of the several States, as provided in the Constitution, within seven years from the date of the submission hereof to the States by the Congress.

Amendment XIX

1. The right of citizens of the United States to vote shall not be denied or abridged by the United States or by any State on account of sex.
2. Congress shall have power to enforce this article by appropriate legislation.

Amendment XX

1. The terms of the President and the Vice-President shall end at noon on the 20th day of January, and the terms of Senators and Representatives at noon on the 3rd day of January, of the years in which such terms would have ended if this article had not been ratified; and the terms of their successors shall then begin.
2. The Congress shall assemble at least once in every year, and such meeting shall begin at noon on the 3rd day of January, unless they shall by law appoint a different day.
3. If, at the time fixed for the beginning of the term of the President, the President elect shall have died, the Vice-President elect shall become President. If a President shall not have been chosen before the time fixed for the beginning of his term, or if the President elect shall have failed to qualify, then the Vice-President elect shall act as President until a President shall have qualified; and the Congress may by law provide for the case wherein neither a President elect nor a Vice-President shall have qualified, declaring who shall then act as President, or the manner in which one who is to act shall be selected, and such person shall act accordingly until a President or Vice-President shall have qualified.

4. The Congress may by law provide for the case of the death of any of the persons from whom the House of representatives may choose a President whenever the right of choice shall have devolved upon them, and for the case of the death of any of the persons from whom the Senate may choose a Vice-President whenever the right of choice shall have devolved upon them.

5. Sections 1 and 2 shall take effect on the 15th day of October following the ratification of this article (October 1933).

6. This article shall be inoperative unless it shall have been ratified as an amendment to the Constitution by the Legislatures of three-fourths of the several States within seven years from the date of its submission.

Amendment XXI

1. The Eighteenth article of amendment to the Constitution of the United States is hereby repealed.

2. The transportation or importation into any State, Territory, or Possession of the United States for delivery or use therein of intoxicating liquors, in violation of the laws thereof, is hereby prohibited.

3. This article shall be inoperative unless it shall have been ratified as an amendment to the Constitution by conventions in the several States, as provided in the Constitution, within seven years from the date of the submission hereof to the States by the Congress.

Amendment XXII

1. No person shall be elected to the office of the President more than twice, and no person who has held the office of President, or acted as President, for more that two years of a term to which some other person was elected President shall be elected to the office of President more than once.

2. But this Article shall not apply to any person holding the office of President when this Article was proposed by Congress, and shall not prevent any person who may be holding the office of President, or acting as President, during the term the term within which this Article becomes operative from holding the office of President or acting as President during the remainder of such term.

3. This article shall be inoperative unless it shall have been ratified as an amendment to the Constitution by the Legislatures of three-fourths of the several States within seven years from the date of its submission to the States by the Congress.

Amendment XXIII

1. The District constituting the seat of Government of the United States shall appoint in such manner as Congress may direct:

2. A number of electors of President and Vice President equal to the whole number of Senators and Representatives in Congress to which the District would be entitled if it were a State, but in no event more than the least populous State; they shall be in addition to those appointed by the States, but they shall be considered, for the purposes of the election of President and Vice President, to be electors appointed by a State; and they shall meet in the District and perform such duties as provided by the twelfth article of amendment.

3. The Congress shall have power to enforce this article by appropriate legislation.

Amendment XXIV

1. The right of citizens of the United States to vote in any primary or other election for President or Vice President, for electors for President or Vice President, or for Senator or Representative in Congress, shall not be denied or abridged by the United States or any State by reason of failure to pay poll tax or any other tax.
2. Congress shall have power to enforce this article by appropriate legislation.

Amendment XXV—Presidential disability and succession

1. In case of the removal of the President from office or of his death or resignation, the Vice President shall become President.
2. Whenever there is a vacancy in the office of the Vice President, the President shall nominate a Vice President who shall take the office upon confirmation by a majority vote of both houses of Congress
3. Whenever the President transmits to the President Pro tempore of the Senate and the Speaker of the House of Representatives his written declaration that he is unable to discharge the powers and duties of his office, and until he transmits to them a written declaration to the contrary, such powers and duties shall be discharged by the Vice President as Acting President.
4. Whenever the Vice President and a majority of either the principal officers of the executive departments or of such other body as Congress may by law provide, transmits to the President Pro tempore of the Senate and the Speaker of the House of Representatives their written declaration that the President is unable to discharge the powers and duties of his office, the Vice President shall immediately assume the powers and duties of the office as Acting President.
5. Thereafter, when the President transmits to the President Pro tempore of the Senate and the Speaker of the House of Representatives his written declaration that no inability exists, he shall resume the powers and duties of his office unless the Vice President and a majority of either the principal officers of the executive departments or of such other body as Congress may by law provide, transmits within four days to the President Pro tempore of the Senate and the Speaker of the House of Representatives their written declaration that the President is unable to discharge the powers and duties of his office. Thereupon Congress shall decide the issue, assembling within forty-eight hours for that purpose if not in session. If the Congress, within twenty-one days after receipt of the latter written declaration, or, if Congress is not in session within twenty-one days after Congress is required to assemble, determines by two-thirds vote of both houses that the President is unable to discharge the powers and duties of his office, the Vice President shall continue to discharge the same as Acting President; otherwise, the President shall resume the powers and duties of his office.

Amendment XXVI

The right of citizens of the United States, who are 18 years of age or older, to vote shall not be denied or abridged by the United States or any state on account of age.

The Congress shall have power to enforce this article by appropriate legislation.

Amendment XXVII

No law, varying the compensation for services of the Senators and Representatives, shall take effect, until an election of Representatives shall have intervened.

APPENDIX

II

How to Brief a Case

© Gunnar Pippel/Shutterstock.com

Cases can be so long and confusing that they require some tool enabling the reader to capture what is truly important. Also, when a professor calls on a student in class or a judge questions a lawyer's argument in court, the stress of the moment can cause the mind to go blank. Law students and lawyers therefore use the **"case brief"** to make sense of what they read and to aid memory when they are on the hot seat. Case briefs follow the structure provided in **legal analysis**.

Recall that in Chapter 1, we learned that **legal analysis follows the structure of "IRAC."** "F" (typically left out of the acronym, IRAC) stands for **Facts**, "I" for **Issue**, "R" for **Rule**, "A" for **Analysis**, and "C" for **Conclusion**. The parts of legal analysis make up most of a case brief.

Name and Citation

The first part of a brief provides the case name and citation. For example, the citation for the case, *People v. Martinez*, listed on page 157 in Chapter 6, is (1970) 3 Cal. App. 3d 886. This will allow any law student, lawyer, or judge to locate this case on any legal search engine or in any law library in the country. "(1970)" is the year the court decided the case. "Cal. App." tells the reader that the case was published, or "reported," in the official reports of the California Court of Appeal. "3d" is the third series of the reporter (a new series is added whenever the publisher runs out of manageable numbers in the current reporter). "3" is the volume of the reporter while "886" is the page number. With this citation, a lawyer can walk up to the shelves holding the California Court of Appeal reporter, grab volume 3 of the third series, and turn to page 886 to find the case.

Facts

The Facts for a case brief are nothing more than a short version of the story that occurred in the case. The key to writing facts is to remember that you are making a case *brief*—not a case long. A short statement of only the relevant facts is all that is needed.

(Procedural Posture)

This is the one part of a case brief that is required for law school and practice but typically not for university courses. It is a short description of where the case is and how it got there. For example, the case you are briefing could be before the U.S. Supreme Court. It could have come to this highest court in the country through a variety of routes: writ of certiorari, habeas corpus, or appeal. Unless your professor instructs otherwise, this part of the case brief is usually dispensed with for college classes.

Issue

The issue is the legal question which the parties are fighting over and which the court has to answer in order to decide the case. Look for hints to identify the issue. For example, seek out the word "whether" as in "We are here to determine whether there is sufficient evidence of malice aforethought to establish murder in this case." The best judges make the issue clear by writing, "The issue is . . ." or "The question presented is . . ."

Rule

The rule is the legal tool that judges and lawyers use to answer the issue of a case. A rule is a general statement of law that the court will then apply to the particular facts of an individual case. Look for rules to come from statutes, other cases, administrative regulations (such as those created by the IRS or the FDA), and constitutions of states and the federal government. When briefing criminal law cases, the most common sources of rules are statutes and case law.

Analysis

Analysis involves applying a general rule to the particular facts of the case.

Conclusion

The conclusion is the decision reached in a particular case. Instead of saying that they "conclude" that enough evidence exists to support a conviction, courts will often say that they "hold" that there is enough evidence. A court's conclusion is therefore called its "holding." A conclusion should ideally be a single short sentence.

EXAMPLE

The following is an example of a brief for the case of *People v. Martinez* (1970) 3 Cal. App.3d 886, on page 159 in Chapter 6.

Name and Citation

People v. Martinez (1970) 3 Cal. App.3d 886

Facts

While uniformed Police Officer Polson was helping a fellow officer make an arrest at a loud party, the defendant approached him and repeatedly shouted at him. The defendant then kicked the officer in the shin with his bare foot. Since he was wearing motorcycle boots, the officer suffered no injury although the kick "smarted" a bit.

Issue

Whether kicking a person wearing motorcycle boots with a bare foot amounts to "use of force or violence" for a battery?

Rule

California's PC 242 defines battery as "any willful and unlawful use of force or violence upon person of another." Any harmful or offensive touching is enough for "unlawful use of force or violence."

Analysis

Since the defendant caused his foot to touch the officer's booted leg, and since the court will *not* say that it is "*un*offensive," this touching is enough to fulfill the "willful and unlawful use of force or violence" portion of battery, even though it caused no injury to the victim.

Conclusion

Since the defendant's kick without injury fulfilled "willful and unlawful use of force or violence," he is guilty of fulfilling the elements of battery.

APPENDIX
III

Selective List of State Law Enforcement Agencies

© Schmidt_Alex/Shutterstock.com

POLICE DEPARTMENTS

The States are listed in alphabetical order. The Police Departments listed in order of city population.

ALABAMA
Birmingham Police Department

Website = http://police.birminghamal.gov/,

Careers = http://police.birminghamal.gov/join-the-team/

Montgomery Police Department

Website = http://www.montgomeryal.gov/city-government/city-departments/police,

Careers = http://www.montgomeryal.gov/city-government/city-departments/police/careers

Mobile Police Department

Website = https://www.mobilepd.org/

Careers = https://www.mobilepd.org/join-us/

Huntsville Police Department

Website = https://www.huntsvilleal.gov/residents/public-safety/huntsville-police/

Careers = https://www.huntsvilleal.gov/residents/public-safety/huntsville-police/join-police-force/

Tuscaloosa Police Department

Website = http://www.tuscaloosa.com/pd

Careers = http://www.tuscaloosa.com/Government/Departments/Human-Resources/human-resources

ALASKA
Anchorage Police Department

Website = https://www.muni.org/Departments/police/Pages/default.aspx

Careers = https://www.muni.org/Departments/employee_relations/Pages/jol.aspx

Juneau Police Department

Website = http://www.juneaupolice.com/

Careers = http://www.juneau.org/jpd/recruitment.php

Fairbanks Police Department

Website = http://www.fairbanksalaska.us/police-department/

Careers = http://www.fairbanksalaska.us/police-department/fpd-recruitment/

ARIZONA

Phoenix Police Department

Website = https://www.phoenix.gov/police

Careers = https://www.phoenix.gov/police/joinphxpd

Tucson Police Department

Website = https://www.tucsonaz.gov/police

Careers = https://www.tucsonaz.gov/police/jobs

Mesa Police Department

Website = http://www.mesaaz.gov/residents/police

Careers = http://www.mpdjobs.com/

Chandler Police Department

Website = https://www.chandlerpd.com/

Careers = https://www.chandlerpd.com/careers/

Glendale Police Department

Website = https://www.glendaleaz.com/police/

Careers = https://www.glendaleaz.com/policejobs/recruit.cfm

ARKANSAS

Little Rock Police Department

Website = https://www.littlerock.gov/for-residents/police-department/

Careers = https://www.littlerock.gov/for-job-seekers/become-a-police-officer/

Fort Smith Police Department

Website = http://www.fortsmithpd.org/

Careers = http://www.fortsmithpd.org/EmploymentOpps.asp

Fayetteville Police Department

Website = http://www.fayetteville-ar.gov/167/Police-Department

Careers = http://www.fayetteville-ar.gov/1127/Police-Careers

Springdale Police Department

Website = http://www.springdalear.gov/200/Police-Department

Careers = http://www.springdalear.gov/218/Careers

Jonesboro Police Department

Website = http://www.jonesboropolice.com/

Careers = http://www.jonesboropolice.com/joinjpd

CALIFORNIA

Los Angeles Police Department

Website = http://www.lapdonline.org/

Careers = http://www.lapdonline.org/join_the_team/content_basic_view/23954

San Diego Police Department

Website = https://www.sandiego.gov/police

Careers = https://www.sandiego.gov/police/recruiting

San Jose Police Department

Website = http://www.sjpdyou.com/police.html?utm_campaign=sjpd&utm_source=Adwords&utm_medium=ppc

Careers = http://www.sjpd.org/JoinSJPDBlue/

San Francisco Police Department

Website = http://sanfranciscopolice.org

Careers = http://sanfranciscopolice.org/career-opportunities

Fresno Police Department

Website = https://www.fresno.gov/police/

Careers = https://www.fresno.gov/police/employment-volunteer-services/

Long Beach Police Department

Website = http://www.longbeach.gov/police/

Careers = http://www.longbeach.gov/police/about-the-lbpd/employment/join-lbpd/

Sacramento Police Department

Website = https://www.cityofsacramento.org/Police

Careers = https://www.cityofsacramento.org/Police/Join-SPD

Oakland Police Department

Website = http://www2.oaklandnet.com/government/o/OPD/index.htm

Careers = http://www2.oaklandnet.com/government/o/OPD/s/career/index.htm

Santa Ana Police Department

Website = http://www.ci.santa-ana.ca.us/pd/

Careers = http://joinsantaanapd.org/

Anaheim Police Department

Website = http://www.anaheim.net/171/Police-Department

Careers = http://agency.governmentjobs.com/anaheim/default.cfm

Fullerton Police Department

Website = http://www.fullertonpd.org/

Careers = https://www.governmentjobs.com/careers/fullerton

COLORADO

Denver Police Department

Website = https://www.denvergov.org/content/denvergov/en/police-department.html

Careers = https://www.denvergov.org/content/denvergov/en/police-department/jobs.html

Colorado Springs Police Department

Website = https://cspd.coloradosprings.gov

Careers = https://cspd.coloradosprings.gov/content/police-employment-0

Aurora Police Department

Website = https://www.auroragov.org/residents/public_safety/police

Careers = https://www.auroragov.org/residents/public_safety/police/JoinTheAPD/

Fort Collins Police Department

Website = https://www.fcgov.com/police/

Careers = https://www.fcgov.com/policejobs/

CONNECTICUT

Bridgeport Police Department

Website = http://www.bridgeportct.gov/police

Careers = https://www.policeapp.com/Entry-Level-Brookfield-CT-Police-Officer-Jobs/130/

New Haven Police Department

Website = http://www.cityofnewhaven.com/police/

Careers = http://www.cityofnewhaven.com/Police/Recruitment.asp

Hartford Police Department

Website = http://www.hartford.gov/police

Careers = http://www.hartford.gov/police/recruitment

Waterbury Police Department

Website = http://www.wtbypd.org

Careers = http://www.wtbypd.org/AboutUs/Careers/tabid/94/Default.aspx

DELAWARE

Wilmington Police Department

Website = https://www.wilmingtonde.gov/government/city-departments/department-of-police

Careers = https://www.wilmingtonde.gov/government/city-departments/human-resources/facts-about-city-employment/recruitment

Dover Police Department

Website = https://doverpolice.org

Careers = https://doverpolice.org/careers-2/

Newark Police Department

Website = http://www.cityofnewarkde.us/17/Police

Careers = http://www.cityofnewarkde.us/898/Career-Opportunities-as-a-Police-Officer

Middletown Police Department

Website = http://www.middletownde.org/Middletown-Police-/

Careers = http://www.middletownde.org/index.cfm?fuseaction=hr.hrList

FLORIDA
Miami Police Department

Website = http://www.miamidade.gov/police/

Careers = http://www.miamigov.com/employeerel/pages/PORecruitment/PO_Requirements.asp

Tampa Police Department

Website = https://www.tampagov.net/police

Careers = https://www.tampagov.net/police/join-tpd

St. Petersburg Police Department

Website = http://police.stpete.org

Careers = http://police.stpete.org/employment/

Orlando Police Department

Website = http://www.cityoforlando.net/police/

Careers = http://www.cityoforlando.net/police/recruiting/

GEORGIA
Atlanta Police Department

Website = http://www.atlantapd.org

Careers = https://www.joinatlantapd.org

Columbus Police Department

Website = http://www.columbusga.org/police/

Careers = http://www.protectcolumbus.com/#

Macon Police Department

Website = http://www.cityofmacon.org/html/cityhall/pd.html

Careers = http://www.policejobsinfo.com/find-a-police-job/see-who-is-hiring/ga/macon-police-officer/

Savannah Police Department

Website = http://scmpd.org

Careers = http://scmpd.org/joinscmpd/

HAWAII

Honolulu Police Department

Website = http://www.honolulupd.org/department/index.php

Careers = http://www.joinhonolulupd.org

Hilo Police Department

Website = http://www.hawaiicounty.gov/police/

Careers = https://www.how-to-become-a-police-officer.com/states/hawaii/

IDAHO

Boise Police Department

Website = http://police.cityofboise.org

Careers = http://police.cityofboise.org/home/join-bpd/

Nampa Police Department

Website = http://nampapolice.org/588/Police

Careers = http://nampapolice.org/697/Employment

Meridian Police Department

Website = http://www.meridiancity.org/police.aspx

Careers = http://www.meridiancity.org/police.aspx?id=247

Idaho Falls Police Department

Website = https://www.idahofallsidaho.gov/153/Police-Department

Careers = https://www.idahofallsidaho.gov/819/Police-Officer-Recruiting

ILLINOIS

Chicago Police Department

Website = https://www.cityofchicago.org/city/en/depts/cpd.html

Careers = http://home.chicagopolice.org/inside-the-cpd/bethechange/chicago-police-officer-recruitment/

Aurora Police Department

Website = https://www.aurora-il.org/apd/

Careers = https://www.aurora-il.org/apd/recruiting/test_location.php

Joliet Police Department

Website = https://jolietpolice.org

Careers = https://jolietpolice.org/get-involved/recruiting/

Springfield Police Department

Website = http://spd.springfield.il.us

Careers = http://www.springfield.il.us/Default.aspx

Peoria Police Department

Website = http://www.peoriagov.org/peoria-police-department/

Careers = http://www.peoriagov.org/peoria-police-department/police-career-opportunities/

INDIANA

Indianapolis Police Department

Website = https://nextdoor.com/agency-post/in/indianapolis/indianapolis-metropolitan-police-department/non-emergency-contact-17286899/

Careers = http://www.cops.com/indianapolis_recruiting/

Fort Wayne Police Department

Website = http://www.fwpd.org

Careers = http://www.fwpd.org/careers/career-opportunities/

Evansville Police Department

Website = http://www.evansvillepolice.com

Careers = http://www.evansvillepolice.com/sites/default/files/files/NEW%20EPD%20Application%20Instructions%20V2.pdf

South Bend Police Department

Website = https://police.southbendin.gov

Careers = https://police.southbendin.gov/get-involved/start-career-sbpd

Bloomington Police Department

Website = https://bloomington.in.gov/police

Careers = https://bloomington.in.gov/sections/viewSection.php?section_id=210

IOWA

Des Moines Police Department

Website = https://www.dmgov.org/departments/police/Pages/default.aspx

Careers = https://www.dmgov.org/Departments/Police/Pages/PoliceRecruitment.aspx

Cedar Rapids Police Department

Website = http://www.cedar-rapids.org/local_government/departments_g_-_v/police/index.php

Careers = http://www.cedar-rapids.org/local_government/departments_g_-_v/police/employment.php

Davenport Police Department

Website = http://www.cityofdavenportiowa.com/department/index.php?structureid=22

Careers = http://www.cityofdavenportiowa.com/department/division.php?structureid=186

KANSAS

Wichita Police Department

Website = http://www.wichita.gov/Government/Departments/WPD/Pages/default.aspx

Careers = http://www.wichita.gov/Government/Departments/WPD/Pages/Recruitment.aspx

Overland Park Police Department

Website = http://www.opkansas.org/city-government/police-department/

Careers = https://www.opkansas.org/about-overland-park/career-opportunities/public-safety-qualifications/police-officer-qualifications/

Kansas City Police Department

Website = http://www.kckpd.org

Careers = http://www.kckpd.org/careers.html

Topeka Police Department

Website = https://www.topeka.org/tpd

Careers = https://www.topeka.org/hr/Pages/Police-Recruitment-Process.aspx

Olathe Police Department

Website = http://www.olatheks.org/government/police

Careers = http://www.olatheks.org/government/police/police-careers

Lawrence Police Department

Website = http://police.lawrenceks.org

Careers = http://police.lawrenceks.org/content/recruiting-information

KENTUCKY

Louisville Police Department

Website = http://www.lmpd.com

Careers = https://louisvilleky.gov/government/police/police-recruit-application-and-selection-process

Lexington Police Department

Website = https://www.lexingtonky.gov/departments/police

Careers = https://www.lexingtonky.gov/browse/jobs-and-contracts/careers-with-the-lexington-police-department

Bowling Green Police Department

Website = https://www.bgky.org/police

Careers = http://www.bgky.org/police/job-opportunities

LOUISIANA

New Orleans Police Department

Website = http://www.nola.gov/nopd/

Careers = http://joinnopd.org

Baton Rouge Police Department

Website = http://www.brgov.com/dept/brpd/

Careers = http://www.brgov.com/dept/brpd/recruit.htm

Shreveport Police Department

Website = https://www.shreveportla.gov/index.aspx?nid=422

Careers = https://www.shreveportla.gov/index.aspx?NID=447

Lafayette Police Department

Website = http://www.lafayettela.gov/policedepartment/pages/default.aspx

Careers = http://www.lafayettela.gov/PoliceDepartment/Recruiting/Pages/Police-Officer.aspx

MAINE

Portland Police Department

Website = http://portlandmaine.gov/202/Police

Careers = http://portlandmaine.gov/1024/CareersJoin-Us

Bangor Police Department

Website = http://www.bangormaine.gov/content/318/354/default.aspx

Careers = http://www.bangormaine.gov/filestorage/318/354/PoliceOfficerApplication.pdf

MARYLAND

Baltimore Police Department

Website = http://www.baltimorepolice.org

Careers = http://www.baltimorepolice.org/recruitment

Howard County Police Department

Website = https://www.howardcountymd.gov/Departments/Police

Careers = https://www.howardcountymd.gov/Departments/Police/Careers

Montgomery County Police Department

Website = https://www.montgomerycountymd.gov/POL/districts/5d/index.html

Careers = https://www.montgomerycountymd.gov/pol/career/index.html

MASSACHUSETTS

Boston Police Department

Website = https://www.boston.gov/departments/police

Careers = http://www.mass.gov/veterans/employment-and-training/civil-service/join-the-boston-police-department.html

Worcester Police Department

Website = http://www.worcesterma.gov/e-services/faqs/police

Careers = http://www.worcesterma.gov/e-services/employment-opportunities

Springfield Police Department

Website = https://www.springfield-ma.gov/police/

Careers = https://www.springfield-ma.gov/police/index.php?id=potp

Cambridge Police Department

Website = http://www.cambridgema.gov/cpd

Careers = http://www.cambridgema.gov/cpd/communityresources/recruitmentandemployment

MICHIGAN

Detroit Police Department

Website = http://www.detroitmi.gov/police

Careers = http://www.detroitmi.gov/How-Do-I/Find/DPD-Jobs

Grand Rapids Police Department

Website = http://grcity.us/police-department/Pages/default.aspx

Careers = http://grcity.us/police-department/Pages/Recruiting.aspx

Sterling Heights Police Department

Website = https://www.sterling-heights.net/466/Police-Department

Careers = https://www.sterling-heights.net/487/Apply-for-a-City-Job

Lansing Police Department

Website = https://www.lansingmi.gov/398/Police-Department

Careers = https://www.lansingmi.gov/420/Recruiting-Hiring

MINNESOTA

Minneapolis Police Department

Website = http://www.ci.minneapolis.mn.us/police/index.htm

Careers = http://www.ci.minneapolis.mn.us/police/recruiting/police_recruiting_recruit

St. Paul Police Department

Website = https://www.stpaul.gov/departments/police

Careers = https://www.stpaul.gov/departments/police/administration-office-chief/become-saint-paul-police-officer

Rochester Police Department

Website = http://www.rochestermn.gov/departments/police

Careers = http://www.rochestermn.gov/departments/police/about-us/careers-recruitment

Bloomington Police Department

Website = https://www.bloomingtonmn.gov/pd/bloomington-police-department-bloomington-minnesota

Careers = https://www.bloomingtonmn.gov/pd/bloomington-police-department-bloomington-minnesota

Duluth Police Department

Website = http://www.duluthmn.gov/police/

Careers = http://www.duluthmn.gov/police/hiring-an-officer/

MISSISSIPPI

Jackson Police Department

Website = http://www.jacksonms.gov/index.aspx?nid=196

Careers = http://www.jacksonms.gov/index.aspx?NID=205

Gulfport Police Department

Website = http://www.gulfport-ms.gov/police/

Careers = http://www.gulfport-ms.gov/police/employment.html

Hattiesburg Police Department

Website = http://www.hattiesburgms.com/government/departments/police-department/

Careers = http://www.hattiesburgms.com/government/departments/police-department/training-academy/

South Haven Police Department

Website = https://www.southaven.org/212/Police

Careers = https://www.southaven.org/659/Recruitment

Biloxi Police Department

Website = https://www.biloxi.ms.us/departments/police-department/

Careers = https://www.biloxi.ms.us/departments/human-resources/

MISSOURI

Kansas City Police Department

Website = http://kcmo.gov/police/#.WP55AlKZNXE

Careers = http://kcmo.gov/police/careers-employment-section/careers-civilian/careers-job-opportunities/#.WP55LVKZNXE

St. Louis Police Department

Website = http://www.slmpd.org/index.shtml

Careers = http://www.slmpd.org/careers.shtml

Springfield Police Department

Website = https://www.springfieldmo.gov/171/Police

Careers = https://www.springfieldmo.gov/2597/Become-a-Police-Officer

Independence Police Department

Website = https://www.ci.independence.mo.us/ipd/

Careers = http://www.ci.independence.mo.us/ipd/employment

Columbia Police Department

Website = http://www.como.gov/police/

Careers = http://www.como.gov/police/join-our-team/

MONTANA

Billings Police Department

Website = http://ci.billings.mt.us/101/Police

Careers = http://ci.billings.mt.us/jobs.aspx

Missoula Police Department

Website = http://www.ci.missoula.mt.us/332/Police-Department

Careers = http://www.ci.missoula.mt.us/364/Employment

Great Falls Police Department

Website = https://greatfallsmt.net/police

Careers = https://greatfallsmt.net/police/gfpd-employment

NEBRASKA

Omaha Police Department

Website = https://police.cityofomaha.org

Careers = https://police.cityofomaha.org/employment

Lincoln Police Department

Website = http://www.lincoln.ne.gov/city/police/

Careers = http://www.lincoln.ne.gov/city/police/rebenefitsofc.htm

NEVADA

Las Vegas Police Department

Website = http://www.lvmpd.com

Careers = http://www.lvmpd.com/Employment.aspx

Henderson Police Department

Website = http://www.cityofhenderson.com/police/home

Careers = http://www.cityofhenderson.com/police/join-hpd

NEW HAMPSHIRE

Manchester Police Department

Website = https://www.manchesternh.gov/Departments/Police

Careers = https://www.manchesternh.gov/Departments/Police/Recruitment-and-Training/Recruitment-and-Selection

Nashua Police Department

Website = http://www.nashuapd.com

Careers = http://www.nashuapd.com/?A=careers

Concord Police Department

Website = http://www.concordnh.gov/index.aspx?NID=807

Careers = http://www.concordnh.gov/index.aspx?NID=836

NEW JERSEY

Newark Police Department

Website = http://newarkpdonline.org

Careers = https://www.newarknj.gov/departments/public-safety

Jersey City Police Department

Website = http://www.njjcpd.org

Careers = http://www.njjcpd.org/node/4

Paterson Police Department

Website = http://patersonpd.com/home.html

Careers = http://patersonpd.com/recruitment.html

NEW MEXICO

Albuquerque Police Department

Website = https://www.cabq.gov/police/

Careers = http://apdonline.com

Las Cruces Police Department

Website = http://www.las-cruces.org/departments/police-department

Careers = http://www.las-cruces.org/en/departments/police-department/recruiting-and-training-academy

Rio Rancho Police Department

Website = http://www.ci.rio-rancho.nm.us/index.aspx?NID=17

Careers = http://www.ci.rio-rancho.nm.us/index.aspx?NID=200

Santa Fe Police Department

Website = https://www.santafenm.gov/police

Careers = http://www.santafenm.gov/police_recruiting

NEW YORK
New York Police Department

Website = http://www.nyc.gov/html/nypd/html/home/home.shtml

Careers = http://www.nyc.gov/html/nypd/html/careers/careers.shtml

Buffalo Police Department

Website = http://www.bpdny.org/

Careers = http://www.bpdny.org/home/about/employment

Rochester Police Department

Website = http://www.cityofrochester.gov/police/

Careers = http://www.cityofrochester.gov/joinrpd/

Yonkers Police Department

Website = http://www.yonkersny.gov/live/public-safety/police-department

Careers = http://www.yonkersny.gov/work/jobs-civil-service-exams

NORTH CAROLINA
Charlotte Police Department

Website = http://charlottenc.gov/CMPD/Pages/default.aspx

Careers = http://charlottenc.gov/CMPD/Organization/Pages/OfcoftheChief/TrainingAcademy.aspx

Raleigh Police Department

Website = https://www.raleighnc.gov/safety/content/Departments/Articles/Police.html

Careers = https://www.raleighnc.gov/safety/content/Police/Articles/PoliceRecruitment.html

Greensboro Police Department

Website = http://www.greensboro-nc.gov/index.aspx?page=1045

Careers = http://www.greensboro-nc.gov/index.aspx?page=1886

Durham Police Department

Website = https://durhamnc.gov/149/Police-Department

Careers = https://durhamnc.gov/157/Recruiting-Employment

Winston-Salem Police Department

Website = http://www.cityofws.org/police

Careers = http://www.cityofws.org/departments/police/employment/become-a-police-officer

NORTH DAKOTA
Fargo Police Department

Website = http://www.cityoffargo.com/CityInfo/Departments/Police/

Careers = http://www.cityoffargo.com/CityInfo/Departments/Police/CareerOpportunities/

Bismarck Police Department

Website = http://www.bismarcknd.gov/94/Police

Careers = http://www.bismarcknd.gov/377/Employment

Grand Forks Police Department

Website = http://www.grandforksgov.com/government/police

Careers = http://www.grandforksgov.com/government/city-departments/police-department/job-openings

OHIO
Columbus Police Department

Website = https://www.columbus.gov/police/

Careers = https://www.columbus.gov/police-recruitment/

Cleveland Police Department

Website = http://www.city.cleveland.oh.us/CityofCleveland/Home/Government/CityAgencies/PublicSafety/Police

Careers = http://www.city.cleveland.oh.us/CityofCleveland/Home/Government/CityAgencies/PublicSafety/SafetyRecruitment

Cincinnati Police Department

Website = http://www.cincinnati-oh.gov/police/

Careers = http://www.cincinnati-oh.gov/police/recruiting/

Toledo Police Department

Website = https://toledopolice.com/

Careers = https://toledopolice.com/inside-tpd/careers.html

Akron Police Department

Website = http://www.akronohio.gov/cms/site/10c5e96e7db5b10f/

Careers = http://www.akronohio.gov/cms/site/b5af3517d18ead74/

OKLAHOMA

Oklahoma City Police Department

Website = https://www.okc.gov/departments/police

Careers = https://www.okc.gov/departments/police/recruiting

Tulsa Police Department

Website = https://www.tulsapolice.org/

Careers = https://www.tulsapolice.org/join-tpd/recruiting.aspx

Norman Police Department

Website = http://normanpd.normanok.gov/

Careers = http://normanpd.normanok.gov/pd/recruiting

Broken Arrow Police Department

Website = http://www.brokenarrowok.gov/90/Police-Department

Careers = http://www.brokenarrowok.gov/237/Recruitment

Lawton Police Department

Website = https://www.lawtonpd.com/

Careers = https://www.lawtonpd.com/Training/jobapply.html

OREGON
Portland Police Department

Website = https://www.portlandoregon.gov/police/

Careers = https://www.joinportlandpolice.com/

Eugene Police Department

Website = https://www.eugene-or.gov/162/Police

Careers = https://www.eugene-or.gov/913/Police-Hiring-Process

Hillsboro Police Department

Website = https://www.hillsboro-oregon.gov/departments/police

Careers = https://www.hillsboro-oregon.gov/departments/police/career-volunteer-opportunities

Beaverton Police Department

Website = http://www.beavertonpolice.org/

Careers = http://www.beavertonpolice.org/189/Officer-Qualifications

PENNSYLVANIA
Philadelphia Police Department

Website = https://joinphillypd.com/index.php

Careers = https://joinphillypd.com/

Pittsburgh Police Department

Website = http://pittsburghpa.gov/police/

Careers = http://pittsburghpa.gov/personnel/police

Allentown Police Department

Website = http://www.allentownpa.gov/Police

Careers = http://www.allentownpa.gov/Police/Police-Academy

Erie Police Department

Website = http://www.erie.pa.us/police/Home.aspx

Careers = http://www.erie.pa.us/police/Recruitment/Recruitment.aspx

Reading Police Department

Website = https://www.readingpa.gov/content/police-department

Careers = https://www.readingpa.gov/content/police-department-recruitment

RHODE ISLAND

Providence Police Department

Website = https://www.providenceri.com/police

Careers = https://www.providenceri.com/police/recruitment

Warwick Police Department

Website = http://www.warwickpd.org/

Careers = http://www.warwickpd.org/index.php/recruitment-drive

Cranston Police Department

Website = http://www.cranstonpoliceri.com/

Careers = http://www.cranstonpoliceri.com/Training/index.php

Pawtucket Police Department

Website = http://www.pawtucketpolice.com/

Careers = http://www.pawtucketpolice.com/employment/

SOUTH CAROLINA

Columbia Police Department

Website = https://columbiapd.net/

Careers = https://columbiapd.net/recruiting/

Charleston Police Department

Website = http://www.charleston-sc.gov/police

Careers = http://www.charleston-sc.gov/jobs.aspx

Mt. Pleasant Police Department

Website = http://www.tompsc.com/index.aspx?NID=166

Careers = http://www.tompsc.com/index.aspx?NID=189

Rock Hill Police Department

Website = http://www.cityofrockhill.com/departments/police/more/police-department

Careers = http://www.rhpdrecruit.com/

SOUTH DAKOTA
Sioux Falls Police Department

Website = http://www.siouxfalls.org/police

Careers = http://www.siouxfalls.org/human-resources/police-employment

Rapid City Police Department

Website = http://www.rcgov.org/departments/police-department.html

Careers = http://www.rcgov.org/departments/police-department/careers-police-dept.html

Aberdeen Police Department

Website = http://www.aberdeen.sd.us/21/Police

Careers = http://www.aberdeen.sd.us/166/Recruitment

TENNESSEE
Memphis Police Department

Website = http://www.memphispolice.org/

Careers = http://www.joinmpd.com/

Nashville Police Department

Website = http://www.nashville.gov/Police-Department.aspx

Careers = http://www.nashville.gov/Police-Department/Get-Involved/Become-a-Police-Officer.aspx

Knoxville Police Department

Website = http://knoxvilletn.gov/government/city_departments_offices/police_department/

Careers = http://www.knoxvilletn.gov/government/city_departments_offices/police_department/management_services_division/recruitment_employment_opportunities/

Chattanooga Police Department

Website = http://www.chattanooga.gov/police-department

Careers = http://www.chattanooga.gov/police-department/employmentrecruitment

Clarksville Police Department

Website = http://www.cityofclarksville.com/index.aspx?page=177

Careers = http://www.cityofclarksville.com/index.aspx?page=395

TEXAS

Houston Police Department

Website = http://www.houstontx.gov/police/

Careers = http://www.houstontx.gov/hr/careers.html

San Antonio Police Department

Website = http://www.sanantonio.gov/SAPD

Careers = http://www.sanantonio.gov/SAPD/SAPD-Recruiting

Dallas Police Department

Website = http://www.dallaspolice.net/

Careers = http://www.dallaspolice.net/join-dpd

Austin Police Department

Website = https://www.sanantonio.gov/sapd

Careers = http://www.sanantonio.gov/SAPD/SAPD-Recruiting

Fort Worth Police Department

Website = https://www.fortworthpd.com/

Careers = https://www.fortworthpd.com/Recruiting/

UTAH

Salt Lake City Police Department

Website = http://www.slcpd.com/

Careers = http://www.slcpd.com/careers/

West Valley City Police Department

Website = http://www.wvc-ut.gov/24/Police-Department

Careers = http://www.wvc-ut.gov/1075/Recruiting-Hiring

Provo Police Department

Website = http://www.provo.org/city-services/new-provo-police

Careers = http://www.provo.org/departments/human-resources/employment-opportunities

West Jordan Police Department

Website = https://www.westjordan.utah.gov/police

Careers = https://www.westjordan.utah.gov/human-resources

VERMONT

Burlington Police Department

Website = https://www.burlingtonvt.gov/Police

Careers = https://www.burlingtonvt.gov/Police/Careers/Apply

South Burlington Police Department

Website = http://www.sburl.com/index.asp?Type=B_BASIC&SEC=%7B134E920B-87B0-41D9-8E35-8B6E4431340D%7D

Careers = http://www.sburl.com/index.asp?Type=B_JOB&SEC={7A11F34A-2A41-4A34-A8FF-65090C21C783

Colchester Police Department

Website = http://colchestervt.gov/261/Police-Department

Careers = http://colchestervt.gov/270/Employment

Rutland Police Department

Website = http://www.rutlandcity.org/index.asp?SEC=3F786BB0-2D1B-4ED9-BE84-5AFF727586DE&Type=B_BASIC

Careers = http://www.rutlandcity.org/index.asp?SEC=3F786BB0-2D1B-4ED9-BE84-5AFF727586DE&DE=18820F4F-CEED-44BD-B530-C5BA8384216C&Type=B_BASIC

VIRGINIA

Virginia Beach Police Department

Website = https://www.vbgov.com/government/departments/police/Pages/default.aspx

Careers = https://www.vbgov.com/government/departments/police/profstanddiv/Pages/employment.aspx

Norfolk Police Department

Website = http://www.norfolk.gov/police

Careers = http://www.norfolk.gov/index.aspx?NID=308

Chesapeake Police Department

Website = http://www.cityofchesapeake.net/government/City-Departments/Departments/Police-Department.htm

Careers = http://www.cityofchesapeake.net/government/City-Departments/Departments/Police-Department/pdemployment.htm

Arlington Police Department

Website = https://police.arlingtonva.us/

Careers = https://police.arlingtonva.us/jobs/

Richmond Police Department

Website = http://www.richmondgov.com/Police/

Careers = http://www.richmondgov.com/Police/RecruitTestingSchedule.aspx

WASHINGTON

Seattle Police Department

Website = https://www.seattle.gov/police

Careers = http://www.seattle.gov/police/police-jobs

Spokane Police Department

Website = https://my.spokanecity.org/police/

Careers = https://my.spokanecity.org/police/

Tacoma Police Department

Website = https://www.cityoftacoma.org/government/city_departments/police/

Careers = https://www.cityoftacoma.org/government/city_departments/police/Hiring_Process

Vancouver Police Department

Website = http://www.cityofvancouver.us/police

Careers = http://www.cityofvancouver.us/police/page/careers

Bellevue Police Department

Website = http://www.ci.bellevue.wa.us/police.htm

Careers = https://www.governmentjobs.com/careers/bellevuewa

WEST VIRGINIA
Charleston Police Department

Website = http://charlestonwvpolice.org/

Careers = http://charlestonwvpolice.org/employment.html

Huntington Police Department

Website = http://www.hpdwv.com/

Careers = http://www.hpdwv.com/recruit/

Parkersburg Police Department

Website = http://pkbpolice.com/wp/home/

Careers = http://pkbpolice.com/wp/recruitment/

Morgantown Police Department

Website = http://www.morgantownwv.gov/quick-links/police-department/

Careers = http://www.morgantownwv.gov/quick-links/jobs/

WISCONSIN
Milwaukee Police Department

Website = http://city.milwaukee.gov/police#.WP_3PbcUUdU

Careers = http://city.milwaukee.gov/fpc/Jobs/Police-Officer.htm#.WP_3IbcUUdU

Madison Police Department

Website = http://www.cityofmadison.com/police/

Careers = http://www.cityofmadison.com/police/jointeam/

Green Bay Police Department

Website = http://www.gbpolice.org/

Careers = http://www.gbpolice.org/?page_id=791

Kenosha Police Department

Website = http://kenoshapolice.com/home

Careers = http://www.kenoshapolice.com/police-jobs

Racine Police Department

Website = http://cityofracine.org/Police/

Careers = https://www.governmentjobs.com/careers/racinewi?keywords=police

WYOMING

Cheyenne Police Department

Website = http://www.cheyennepd.org/

Careers = http://www.cheyennepd.org/index.aspx?NID=31

Casper Police Department

Website = http://www.casperwy.gov/government/departments/police/

Careers = http://casperwy.gov/government/departments/police/police_recruitment/

Gillette Police Department

Website = http://www.gillettewy.gov/city-government/departments/police

Careers = http://www.gillettewy.gov/city-government/departments/human-resources/police-employment-information

Laramie Police Department

Website = https://www.cityoflaramie.org/index.aspx?nid=97

Careers = https://www.cityoflaramie.org/index.aspx?NID=265

SHERIFF DEPARTMENTS OR STATE TROOPERS

The States are listed in alphabetical order. The Sheriff Departments or State Troopers are listed in order of county population.

ALABAMA
Jefferson

Website = https://jeffcosheriff.net/

Careers = https://jeffcosheriff.net/careers/

Mobile

Website = http://www.mobileso.com

Careers = http://www.mobileso.com/join-the-team/

Madison

Website = http://www.madisoncountysheriffal.org

Careers = http://www.madisoncountysheriffal.org/employment.php

ALASKA
State Police

Website = http://www.dps.state.ak.us

Careers = http://www.dps.state.ak.us/ast/recruit/hiring.aspx

ARIZONA
Maricopa

Website = https://www.mcso.org

Careers = https://www.mcso.org/Employment/DeputySheriff

Pinal

Website = http://www.pinalcountyaz.gov/Sheriff/Pages/home.aspx

Careers = http://www.pinalcountyaz.gov/Sheriff/Pages/Recruitment.aspx

CALIFORNIA

Los Angeles

Website = http://sheriff.lacounty.gov/wps/portal/lasd

Careers = http://lasdcareers.org

San Diego

Website = http://www.sdsheriff.net

Careers = http://www.sdsheriff.net/recruitment.html

Orange

Website = http://www.ocsd.org

Careers = http://www.ocsd.org/join

Riverside

Website = http://www.riversidesheriff.org

Careers = http://www.joinrsd.org

Santa Clara

Website = https://www.sccgov.org/sites/gosheriff/Pages/gosheriff.aspx

Careers = https://www.sccgov.org/sites/gosheriff/career-opportunities/Pages/home.aspx

Alameda

Website = https://www.alamedacountysheriff.org

Careers = https://www.alamedacountysheriff.org/careers.php

COLORADO

Denver

Website = https://www.denvergov.org/content/denvergov/en/sheriff-department.html

Careers = https://www.denvergov.org/content/denvergov/en/sheriff-department/jobs.html

El Paso

Website = https://www.epcsheriffsoffice.com

Careers = https://www.epcsheriffsoffice.com/employment-opportunities

Arapahoe

Website = http://www.arapahoegov.com/sheriff

Careers = http://www.arapahoegov.com/index.aspx?nid=911

CONNECTICUT

State Department of Emergencey Services and Public Protection

Website = http://www.ct.gov/despp/cwp/view.asp?a=4201&q=494678&desppNAV_GID=2077

Careers = http://www.ct.gov/despp/cwp/view.asp?a=4215&q=494752

Hartford

Website = https://harfordsheriff.org

Careers = https://harfordsheriff.org/employment/

DELAWARE

New Castle

Website = http://www.nccde.org/167/Sheriffs-Office

Careers = http://nccde.org/132/Employment

Sussex

Website = https://www.sussexcountyde.gov/sheriffs-office

Careers = https://www.sussexcountyde.gov/current-job-openings

Kent

Website = http://www.co.kent.de.us/sheriffs-office.aspx

Careers = http://www.co.kent.de.us/personnel/employment.aspx

FLORIDA
Jacksonville

Website = http://www.coj.net/departments/sheriffs-office.aspx

Careers = http://www.joinjso.com

Broward

Website = http://www.sheriff.org

Careers = https://www.governmentjobs.com/careers/browardsheriff

Palm Beach

Website = http://www.pbso.org

Careers = http://www.pbso.org/inside-pbso/administration/human-resources/

GEORGIA
Fulton

Website = http://www.fultonsheriff.net

Careers = http://www.fultonsheriff.net/Employment_Opportunity.html

Gwinnett

Website = http://www.gwinnettcountysheriff.com

Careers = https://www.gwinnettcounty.com/portal/gwinnett/Departments/Sheriff/
SheriffEmployment

Cobb

Website = http://www.cobbsheriff.org

Careers = http://www.cobbsheriff.org/recruitment/

DeKalb

Website = http://www.dekalbsheriff.org/web/home_message.php

Careers = http://www.dekalbsheriff.org/web/employment/indexV2.php

Augusta

Website = http://www.augustaga.gov/294/Sheriff

Careers = http://www.richmondcountysheriffsoffice.com/employment.cfm

Bibb

Website = http://bibbsheriff.us

Careers = http://bibbsheriff.us/bso-training/

HAWAII
State Department of Public Safety

Website = http://dps.hawaii.gov/about/divisions/law-enforcement-division/sheriff-division/

Careers = http://agency.governmentjobs.com/hawaii/job_bulletin.cfm?JobID=446686

IDAHO
Ada

Website = https://www.adasheriff.org

Careers = https://www.adasheriff.org/Careers

Canyon

Website = https://www.canyonco.org/elected-officials/sheriff/

Careers = https://www.canyonco.org/job/deputy/

ILLINOIS
Cook

Website = http://www.cookcountysheriff.com/index.html

Careers = http://www.cookcountysheriff.com/employment/EmploymentOpportunities.html

Dupage

Website = http://www.dupagesheriff.org/Default.aspx

Careers = http://www.dupagesheriff.org/AboutUs/103/

Lake

Website = http://www.lakecountyil.gov/209/Sheriffs-Office

Careers = http://www.lakecountyil.gov/2193/Career-Opportunities

INDIANA
Marion

Website = http://www.marionso.com

Careers = http://www.marionso.com/careers/

Lake

Website = http://www.lakecountysheriff.com

Careers = http://www.lakecountysheriff.com/page.php?id=93

Allen

Website = http://www.allencountysheriff.org

Careers = http://www.allencountysheriff.org/department/human-resources/

Hamilton

Website = http://www.hamiltoncounty.in.gov/166/Sheriffs-Office

Careers = http://www.hamiltoncounty.in.gov/595/Recruitment

IOWA
Polk

Website = https://www.polkcountyiowa.gov/sheriff/

Careers = https://www.polkcountyiowa.gov/hr/job-opportunities/

Linn

Website = http://www.linncounty.org/151/Sheriffs-Office

Careers = http://linncounty.org/274/Employment-Opportunities

KANSAS
Johnson

Website = http://www.jocogov.org/dept/sheriff/home

Careers = http://www.jocogov.org/dept/human-resources/career-opportunities

Sedgwick

Website = http://www.sedgwickcounty.org/sheriff/

Careers = http://www.sedgwickcounty.org/sheriff/employment.asp

KENTUCKY
Jefferson

Website = http://www.jcsoky.org

Careers = http://www.jcsoky.org/employment.htm

Fayette

Website = http://fayettesheriff.com

Careers = http://fayettesheriff.com/?page_id=7

Kenton

Website = http://www.kentoncountysheriff.org

Careers = http://www.kentoncountysheriff.org/jobs/index.php

LOUISIANA
East Baton Rouge Parish

Website = http://www.ebrso.org

Careers = http://www.ebrso.org/Careers.aspx

Jefferson Parish

Website = https://www.jpso.com

Careers = https://www.jpso.com/jobs.aspx

Orleans Parish

Website = http://www.opcso.org

Careers = http://www.opcso.org/index.php?option=com_content&view=article&id=550&Itemid=811

MAINE
Cumberland

Website = http://www.cumberlandso.org

Careers = http://www.cumberlandso.org/227/Employment

York

Website = http://www.yorkcountyso.com

Careers = http://www.yorkcountyso.com/employment/Default.aspx

Penobscot

Website = http://www.penobscot-sheriff.net

Careers = http://www.penobscot-sheriff.net/job-descriptions/

MARYLAND
Montgomery

Website = http://www.montgomerycountymd.gov/sheriff/

Careers = http://www.montgomerycountymd.gov/sheriff/category/applicant-testing-dates.html/

Prince George's

Website = http://www.princegeorgescountymd.gov/622/Sheriff

Careers = http://www.princegeorgescountymd.gov/662/Join-The-Agency

Baltimore

Website = http://www.baltimorecountymd.gov/agencies/sheriff

Careers = http://www.baltimorecountymd.gov/Agencies/humanresources/jobs/index.html

MASSACHUSETTS
Middlesex

Website = http://www.middlesexsheriff.org

Careers = http://www.middlesexsheriff.org/hr

Worcester

Website = http://worcestercountysheriff.com

Careers = http://worcestercountysheriff.com/employment/

Essex

Website = http://www.mass.gov/essexsheriff/

Careers = http://www.mass.gov/essexsheriff/careers/

MICHIGAN
Wayne

Website = http://www.waynecounty.com/sheriff/index.htm

Careers = http://www.waynecounty.com/sheriff/employment.htm

Oakland

Website = https://www.oakgov.com/sheriff

Careers = https://www.oakgov.com/sheriff/Pages/jobs/---Apply-for-a-Job.aspx

Macomb

Website = http://sheriff.macombgov.org/Sheriff-Home

Careers = http://clerk.accessmacomb.com/Clerk-Services-CivilService

MINNESOTA
Hennepin

Website = http://www.hennepinsheriff.org

Careers = http://www.hennepinsheriff.org/careers-internship

Ramsey

Website = https://www.ramseycounty.us/your-government/leadership/sheriffs-office

Careers = https://www.ramseycounty.us/jobs

MISSISSIPPI
Hinds

Website = http://www.hindscountyms.com/elected-offices/sheriff

Careers = http://www.hindscountyms.com/departments/personnel

Harrison

Website = http://harrisoncountysheriff.com/events/category/community-relations/

Careers = http://harrisoncountysheriff.com/careers/

Desoto

Website = http://www.desotocountyms.gov/223/Sheriffs-Department

Careers = http://www.desotocountyms.gov/341/Employment-Application

MISSOURI
St. Louis

Website = http://www.stlouisco.com/LawandPublicSafety/CircuitCourt/SheriffsOffice

Careers = http://www.stlouisco.com/YourGovernment/CountyDepartments/Personnel

Jackson

Website = http://www.jacksoncountysheriff.org

Careers = http://www.jacksoncountysheriff.org/154/Careers

St. Charles

Website = http://www.sccmo.org/1421/Sheriff

Careers = http://www.sccmo.org/172/Job-Seeker-Services

MONTANA
Yellowstone

Website = http://www.co.yellowstone.mt.gov/Sheriff/

Careers = http://www.co.yellowstone.mt.gov/human_resources/

Missoula

Website = https://www.missoulacounty.us/government/public-safety/sheriff-s-office

Careers = http://www.ci.missoula.mt.us/364/Employment

Gallatin

Website = http://gallatincomt.virtualtownhall.net/Public_Documents/gallatincomt_sheriff/sheriffdept

Careers = http://gallatincomt.virtualtownhall.net/Public_Documents/gallatincomt_sheriff/LEEO_Ver2

NEBRASKA
Douglas

Website = https://www.omahasheriff.org/

Careers = https://www.omahasheriff.org/employment

Lancaster

Website = http://lancaster.ne.gov/SHERIFF/index.htm

Careers = http://lancaster.ne.gov/SHERIFF/recruit.htm

Sarpy

Website = http://www.sarpy.com/sheriff/

Careers = http://www.sarpy.com/sheriff/careers.html

NEVADA
Clark

Website = http://www.clarkcountynv.gov/election/Pages/Sheriff.aspx

Careers = http://www.clarkcountynv.gov/human-resources/Pages/EmploymentOpportunities.aspx

Washoe

Website = https://www.washoecounty.us/humanresources/Careers/sheriffs_office.php

Careers = https://www.washoecounty.us/humanresources/Careers/index.php

Carson City

Website = http://www.carson.org/government/departments-g-z/sheriff-s-office#ad-image-0

Careers = http://www.carson.org/government/departments-g-z/sheriff-s-office/about-us/join-the-team-be-a-deputy-sheriff

NEW HAMPSHIRE
Hillsborough

Website = http://www.hcsonh.us/

Careers = http://www.hillsboroughcountynh.org/hr/jobpostings.html

Rockingham

Website = http://www.rockso.org/

Careers = http://www.rockso.org/employment/default.html

NEW JERSEY
Bergen

Website = http://www.bcsd.us/Default.aspx

Careers = http://www.bcsd.us/SitePages/JoinBCSO.aspx

Middlesex

Website = http://www.middlesexcountynj.gov/Government/Departments/PSH/Pages/Office_Sheriff.aspx

Careers = http://www.middlesexcountynj.gov/Government/Departments/PSH/Pages/Career-Opportunities.aspx

Essex

Website = http://www.essexsheriff.com/

Careers = http://www.essexsheriff.com/employment/

NEW MEXICO
Bernalillo

Website = http://www.bernalillocountysheriff.com/index.html

Careers = http://www.bernalillocountysheriff.com/recruiting.html

Dona Ana

Website = https://donaanacounty.org/sheriff

Careers = https://donaanacounty.org/sheriff

Santa Fe

Website = https://www.santafecountynm.gov/sheriff

Careers = https://www.santafecountynm.gov/sheriff/recruitment

NEW YORK
State Police

Website = https://www.troopers.ny.gov/

Careers = http://www.nytrooper.com/qualifications

NORTH CAROLINA
Mecklenburg

Website = http://www.mecksheriff.com/

Careers = http://www.mecksheriff.com/careers/

Wake

Website = http://www.wakegov.com/sheriff/Pages/default.aspx

Careers = http://www.wakegov.com/sheriff/Pages/employment.aspx

Guilford

Website = http://www.gcsonc.com/

Careers = http://www.gcsonc.com/detention-officer

NORTH DAKOTA
Cass

Website = https://www.casscountynd.gov/county/depts/sheriff/Pages/default.aspx

Careers = https://www.casscountynd.gov/county/depts/sheriff/recruitment/Pages/default.aspx

Burleigh

Website = http://www.burleighco.com/departments/sheriff/

Careers = https://burleighco.com/departments/sheriff/employment/

Grand Forks

Website = http://gfcounty.nd.gov/sheriffs-department

Careers = http://gfcounty.nd.gov/Jobs

OHIO

Franklin

Website = https://sheriff.franklincountyohio.gov/

Careers = https://sheriff.franklincountyohio.gov/employment/

Cuyahoga

Website = http://sheriff.cuyahogacounty.us/

Careers = http://sheriff.cuyahogacounty.us/en-US/Employment.aspx

Hamilton

Website = https://www.hcso.org/

Careers = http://www.hcso.org/employment/

OKLAHOMA

Oklahoma

Website = https://www.oklahomacounty.org/sheriff/

Careers = https://www.oklahomacounty.org/sheriff/careers/

Tulsa

Website = http://www.tcso.org/

Careers = http://www.tcso.org/Administration.html#employment

Cleveland

Website = http://www.ccso-ok.us/

Careers = http://www.ccso-ok.us/Jobs.aspx

OREGON

Multnomah

Website = http://www.mcso.us/profiles/

Careers = https://multco.us/jobs

Washington

Website = http://www.co.washington.or.us/sheriff/

Careers = http://www.co.washington.or.us/Sheriff/GetInvolved/employment.cfm

Clackamas

Website = http://www.clackamas.us/sheriff/

Careers = http://www.clackamas.us/sheriff/recruiting/

PENNSYLVANIA
Philadelphia

Website = http://www.officeofphiladelphiasheriff.com/en

Careers = http://www.officeofphiladelphiasheriff.com/en/blog-general/104-job-opportunities-as-a-deputy-sheriff

Allegheny

Website = http://www.sheriffalleghenycounty.com/

Careers = http://www.alleghenycounty.us/Human-Services/Careers.aspx

Montgomery

Website = http://www.montcopa.org/397/Sheriffs-Office

Careers = http://www.montcopa.org/jobs.aspx

RHODE ISLAND
Providence

Website = http://sheriffs.ri.gov/

Careers = http://sheriffs.ri.gov/recruitment/generalrequirements.php

SOUTH CAROLINA
Greenville

Website = http://www.gcso.org/

Careers = https://www.greenvillecounty.org/HumanResources/HiringProcedure.aspx

Richland

Website = http://www.rcsd.net/

Careers = http://www.rcsd.net/gen/employ.htm

Charleston

Website = https://www.charlestoncounty.org/departments/sheriff/

Careers = http://sheriff.charlestoncounty.org/admin-services.php#human-resources

SOUTH DAKOTA

Minnehaha

Website = http://www.minnehahacounty.org/dept/so/so.php

Careers = http://www.minnehahacounty.org/dept/so/jobOpportunities/jobOpportunities.php

Pennington

Website = http://www.pennco.org/sheriff/

Careers = http://www.pennco.org/HR

Lincoln

Website = http://lincolncountysd.org/Page.cfm/Departments/14/Sheriff

Careers = https://www.governmentjobs.com/careers/lincolncountysd

TENNESSEE

Shelby

Website = http://www.shelby-sheriff.org/

Careers = http://www.shelby-sheriff.org/admin/hr.html

Davidson

Website = http://www.nashville.gov/Sheriffs-Office.aspx

Careers = http://www.nashville.gov/Sheriffs-Office/Employment.aspx

Knox

Website = http://www.knoxsheriff.org/

Careers = http://www.knoxsheriff.org/employment/pdfs/employment_app.pdf

TEXAS

Harris

Website = http://www.harriscountyso.org/

Careers = http://www.sheriff.hctx.net/Recruitment/RecruitDefault.aspx

Dallas

Website = http://www.dallascounty.org/department/sheriff/sheriff_index.php

Careers = http://www.dallascounty.org/department/sheriff/recruitment_intro.php

Tarrant

Website = http://access.tarrantcounty.com/en/sheriff.html

Careers = http://access.tarrantcounty.com/en/sheriff.html

UTAH

Salt Lake

Website = https://slsheriff.org/

Careers = https://slsheriff.org/page_employment.php

Utah

Website = http://www.co.utah.ut.us/dept/sheriff/

Careers = http://www.utahcounty.gov/Dept/Pers/JobDescriptionDetails.asp?ID=12442

Davis

Website = http://www.daviscountyutah.gov/sheriff

Careers = http://www.daviscountyutah.gov/human-resources/

VERMONT

Chittenden

Website = http://www.chittendencountysheriff.com/

Careers = http://www.chittendencountysheriff.com/employment_page.html

Rutland

Website = https://www.rutlandsheriff.net/

Careers = https://www.rutlandsheriff.net/employment.php

VIRGINIA

Fairfax

Website = http://www.fairfaxcounty.gov/sheriff/

Careers = http://www.fairfaxcounty.gov/sheriff/jobs/

Prince William

Website = http://www.pwcgov.org/government/dept/sheriff/pages/default.aspx

Careers = https://www.governmentjobs.com/careers/pwcgov

Loudoun

Website = https://sheriff.loudoun.gov/

Careers = https://sheriff.loudoun.gov/index.aspx?NID=197

WASHINGTON

King

Website = http://www.kingcounty.gov/depts/sheriff.aspx

Careers = http://www.kingcounty.gov/depts/sheriff/careers/Careers.aspx

Pierce

Website = http://www.co.pierce.wa.us/121/Sheriff

Careers = http://www.co.pierce.wa.us/130/Jobs---Join-Our-Team

Snohomish

Website = http://snohomishcountywa.gov/1949/Sheriffs-Office

Careers = https://snohomishcountywa.gov/238/Careers

WEST VIRGINIA

Kanawha

Website = http://www.kanawhasheriff.us/

Careers = http://www.kanawhasheriff.us/employment-opportunities/

Berkeley

Website = http://countyclerk.berkeleywv.org/countyclerk/site-page/deputy-sheriff

Careers = http://countyclerk.berkeleywv.org/countyclerk/site-page/berkeley-county-deputy-sheriff-application-process

Monongalia

Website = http://www.monsheriff.com/

Careers = http://www.policejobsinfo.com/career-descriptions/agency-links/wv/

WISCONSIN
Milwaukee

Website = http://county.milwaukee.gov/OfficeoftheSheriff7719.htm

Careers = http://county.milwaukee.gov/Careers

Dane

Website = https://www.danesheriff.com/

Careers = https://www.danesheriff.com/Divisions/ExecutiveServices/hiring_supp_deputies.aspx

Waukesha

Website = https://www.waukeshacounty.gov/sheriff/

Careers = https://www.waukeshacounty.gov/defaultwc.aspx?id=38262

WYOMING
Laramie

Website = http://laramiecounty.com/_officials/Sheriff/index.aspx

Careers = http://laramiecounty.com/_officials/Sheriff/Opportunity.aspx

Natrona

Website = http://www.natrona.net/118/Sheriff

Careers = http://www.natrona.net/123/Employment

Campbell

Website = https://www.ccgov.net/186/Sheriffs-Office

Careers = https://www.ccgov.net/jobs.aspx

APPENDIX
IV

Selective List of Federal Law Enforcement and Intelligence Agencies

FEDERAL LAW ENFORCEMENT AGENCIES

Air Force Office of Special Investigations (Defense Department)

Website = http://www.osi.af.mil/

Careers = http://www.osi.af.mil/VACANCY/

Army Criminal Investigation Command (Defense Department)

Website = http://www.cid.army.mil/

Careers = http://www.cid.army.mil/militaryagents2.html

Bureau of Alcohol, Tobacco, Firearms, and Explosives (Justice Department)

Website = https://www.atf.gov/

Careers = https://www.atf.gov/careers

Bureau of Diplomatic Security (State Department)

Website = https://www.state.gov/m/ds/

Careers = https://careers.state.gov/ds/

Customs and Border Protection (Department of Homeland Security)

Website = https://www.cbp.gov/

Careers = https://www.cbp.gov/careers

Defense Criminal Investigative Service (Defense Department)

Website = http://www.dodig.mil/INV_DCIS/index.cfm

Careers = http://www.dodig.mil/Careers/index.html

Drug Enforcement Administration (Justice Department)

Website = https://www.dea.gov/index.shtml

Careers = https://www.dea.gov/careers/occupations.shtml

Federal Air Marshal Service (Transportation Safety Administration)

Website = https://www.tsa.gov/news/testimony/2015/09/17/testimony-federal-air-marshal-service

Careers = https://www.tsa.gov/news/testimony/2015/09/17/testimony-federal-air-marshal-service

Federal Bureau of Investigation (Justice Department)

Website = https://www.fbi.gov/

Careers = https://www.fbijobs.gov/

Federal Protective Service (Department of Homeland Security)

Website = https://www.dhs.gov/topic/federal-protective-service

Careers = https://www.dhs.gov/topic/homeland-security-jobs

Immigration and Customs Enforcement (Department of Homeland Security)

Website = https://www.ice.gov/

Careers = https://www.ice.gov/careers

Inspector General (Department of Homeland Security)

Website = https://www.oig.dhs.gov/

Careers = https://www.oig.dhs.gov/index.php?option=com_content&view=article&id=41&Itemid=17

Inspector General (Justice Department)

Website = https://oig.justice.gov/

Careers = https://oig.justice.gov/about/careers.htm

Inspector General (Nuclear Regulatory Commission)

Website = https://www.nrc.gov/about-nrc/organization/oigfuncdesc.html

Careers = https://www.nrc.gov/about-nrc/employment/apply.html

Investigative Services, National Park Services (Interior Department)

Website = https://www.nps.gov/orgs/1563/index.htm

Careers = https://www.nps.gov/orgs/1563/isb-career.htm

IRS Criminal Investigations Division (Treasury Department)

Website = https://www.irs.gov/uac/criminal-enforcement-1

Careers = https://jobs.irs.gov/resources/job-descriptions/irs-criminal-investigation-special-agent

Law Enforcement and Investigations (Agriculture Department, Forest Service)

Website = https://www.fs.fed.us/working-with-us/jobs

Careers = https://www.fs.usda.gov/detail/r10/recreation/safety-ethics/?cid=stelprdb5390819

Marine Corps Criminal Investigation Division (Defense Department)

Website = http://www.lejeune.marines.mil/Offices-Staff/Marine-Corps-Police/Criminal-Investigation/

Careers = https://rmi.marines.com/request-information

National Nuclear Security Administration (Energy Department)

Website = https://nnsa.energy.gov/

Careers = https://nnsa.energy.gov/federalemployment

Naval Criminal Investigative Service (Defense Department)

Website = http://www.ncis.navy.mil/Pages/publicdefault.aspx

Careers = http://www.ncis.navy.mil/Careers/Pages/default.aspx

Office for Law Enforcement—National Oceanic and Atmospheric Administration (Commerce Department)

Website = http://www.nmfs.noaa.gov/ole/

Careers = http://www.careers.noaa.gov/

Pentagon Force Protection Agency

Website = http://www.pfpa.mil/

Careers = http://www.pfpa.mil/apply.html

Postal Inspection Service

Website = https://postalinspectors.uspis.gov/

Careers = https://postalinspectors.uspis.gov/employment/positions.aspx

Secret Service

Website = https://www.secretservice.gov/

Careers = https://www.secretservice.gov/join/careers/

United State Capitol Police

Website = https://www.uscp.gov/

Careers = https://www.uscp.gov/careers

United States Marshal Service

Website = https://www.usmarshals.gov/

Careers = https://www.usmarshals.gov/careers/index.html

United States Mint Police (Treasury Department)

Website = https://www.usmint.gov/about/mint-police

Careers = https://www.usmint.gov/about/careers

INTELLIGENCE AGENCIES

Air Force Intelligence, Surveillance, and Reconnaissance

Website = http://www.af.mil/ISR.aspx

Careers = https://www.airforce.com/careers/detail/airborne-intelligence-surveillance-and-reconnaissance-isr-operator

Army Military Intelligence

Website = http://www.goarmy.com/

Careers = http://www.goarmy.com/careers-and-jobs/browse-career-and-job-categories/intelligence-and-combat-support/military-intelligence-officer.html

Bureau of Intelligence and Research (State Department)

Website = https://www.state.gov/s/inr/

Careers = https://careers.state.gov/

Central Intelligence Agency

Website = https://www.cia.gov/index.html

Careers = https://www.cia.gov/careers

Coast Guard Investigative Service

Website = https://www.uscg.mil/hq/cg2/cgis/history.asp

Careers = https://www.uscg.mil/top/careers.asp

Defense Intelligence Agency

Website = http://www.dia.mil/

Careers = http://www.dia.mil/Careers/

Department of Homeland Security

Website = https://www.dhs.gov/

Careers = https://www.dhs.gov/topic/homeland-security-jobs

Federal Bureau of Investigation Intelligence Branch

Website = https://www.fbi.gov/about/leadership-and-structure/intelligence-branch

Careers = https://www.fbi.gov/video-repository/fbi-careers-intelligence-analyst-1.mp4/view

Marine Corps Intelligence Department

Website = http://www.hqmc.marines.mil/intelligence

Careers = http://www.hqmc.marines.mil/intelligence/Civilian-Career/

National Geospatial-Intelligence Agency

Website = https://www.nga.mil/Pages/Default.aspx

Careers = https://www.nga.mil/Careers/Pages/default.aspx

National Reconnaissance Agency

Website = http://www.nro.gov/

Careers = http://www.nro.gov/careers/index.html

National Security Agency

Website = https://www.nsa.gov/

Careers = https://www.nsa.gov/careers/

Office of the Director of National Intelligence

Website = https://www.dni.gov/index.php

Careers = https://www.dni.gov/index.php/careers/career-opportunities

Office of Intelligence and Analysis (Treasury Department)

Website = https://www.treasury.gov/about/organizational-structure/offices/Pages/Office-of-Intelligence-Analysis.aspx

Careers = https://www.treasury.gov/careers/Pages/default.aspx

Office of Intelligence and Counterintelligence (Department of Energy)

Website = https://energy.gov/office-intelligence-and-counterintelligence

Careers = https://energy.gov/jobs/search?keyword=intelligence

Office of National Security Intelligence (Drug Enforcement Administration)

Website = https://www.dea.gov/ops/intel.shtml

Careers = https://www.dea.gov/careers/how-to-apply.shtml

Office of Naval Intelligence

Website = http://www.oni.navy.mil/

Careers = http://www.oni.navy.mil/Join-Us/Civilian-Careers/ONI-Police-Force/

Office of Terrorism and Financial Intelligence (Treasury Department)

Website = https://www.treasury.gov/about/organizational-structure/offices/Pages/Office-of-Terrorism-and-Financial-Intelligence.aspx

Careers = https://www.treasury.gov/careers/Pages/default.aspx

Index

M

Magness v. Superior Court, 292–294
Mail fraud, 325–328
    frauds and swindles, 325–326
    Schmuck v. United States, 326–327
Maim, 173, 176, 177. *See also* Mayhem
Majority opinion, 14
Malice aforethought, 121–133
    express malice, intent to kill, 122–124
    felony murder rule, 132–133
    implied malice, 124–131
    intent to commit serious bodily injury, 124
Malice afterthought, 119
Malum in se felony, 133
Malum prohibitum felony, 133
Manning, Bradley, 410–411
Manslaughter, 144–155
    California Supreme Court description of voluntary, 146–149
    involuntary, 150–154
    provocation and, 145
    by text, 145
    vehicular, 154–155
    voluntary, 145–150
Manson, Charles, 432
Marbury v. Madison, 262
Marijuana, 392–393, 495. *See also* Controlled substance; Controlled substance crime
Marshall, John, 262
Marshall, Thurgood, 357
Mayhem, 173–177
    common law, 173–174
    current law, 174
    People v. Newble, 174–176
May v. State, 54–55
McVeigh, Timothy J., 413–415
Medical condition, involuntariness and, 38–40
Medical marijuana, 495
Mens rea, 10, 65–85
    concurrence with actus reus, 67–70
    defined, 65–66
    distinguishing from motive, 71

    general intent and, 74–77
    proving with direct or indirect evidence, 77–79
    specific intent and, 74–77
    strict liability crimes, 80–85
    transferred intent and, 71–74
Mental state, concurrence and, 67
"Me too" movement, 227
Michaels, Alan, 420
Microsoft, 339, 341–342
Migratory Bird Treaty Act (MBTA), 81–82
Milner v. Apfel, 2
Miranda rights, 36
Mistake, 545–550
    of fact, 545–546
    general intent crimes, 546
    Model Penal Code (MPC), 550
    People v. Olsen, 546–549
    specific intent crimes, 549–550
Model Penal Code (MPC), 14, 15
    act definition, 34
    arson, 312
    assault, 171
    assisted suicide, 116
    attempt, renunciation, 429
    attempt to commit crime, 428
    burglary, 291
    causal relationship between conduct and result, 92
    conspiracy, duration, 447
    criminal conspiracy, 433
    ignorance or mistake of fact, 550
    kidnapping, 184
    liability for conduct of another, complicity, 447
    mental incapacity, 513–514
    mistake of law, 550
    omission, 35, 49
    overt act, 443
    possession, 58
    protection of others, 481
    rape, 215

Case Index